EXETER MEDIEVAL TEXTS AND STUDIES
General Editors: Marion Glasscoe, M.J. Swanton and Vincent Gillespie

Ælfric's Lives of the Virgin Spouses

This scholarly parallel-text edition is the first to bring together the stories of the little-known virgin spouses: Julian and Basilissa, Cecilia and Valerian, and Chrysanthus and Daria, all drawn from the *Lives of Saints* written by the Anglo-Saxon monk Ælfric.

Alongside Ælfric's original Old English texts, Robert Upchurch provides the reader with modern English parallel-text translations, and, as a useful comparison, the closest Latin source texts—again with parallel-text translations.

The introduction places the *Lives of the Virgin Spouses* in literary-historical and social contexts and explores Ælfric's interest in the hagiographical genre of chaste marriage. As a leading churchman writing at the time of the Viking raids at the end of the first millennium, Ælfric wrote his *Lives* to bolster the faith of English Christians. These three stories of couples who marry but do not consummate their unions point to the ideal of marital celibacy in Ælfric's programme of pastoral care. Taken together, the group provides an opportunity to emphasise different but related points about the literal and figurative types of chastity and purity appropriate to the laity in the closing decade of the tenth century.

Robert K. Upchurch is Assistant Professor in the Department of English, University of North Texas, Denton.

Ælfric's Lives of the Virgin Spouses

with modern English parallel-text translations

Julian and Basilissa
Cecilia and Valerian
and
Chrysanthus and Daria

edited by
Robert K. Upchurch

UNIVERSITY
of
EXETER
PRESS

Cover image: A portion of an illuminated miniature found on f. 73^r of a lavishly illustrated troper (Paris, Bibliothèque nationale, Ms. Lat. 9448) executed *c.* 1000 at Prüm, a monastery in western Germany whose collection of relics included the entire bodies of both Chrysanthus and Daria. In the image, the couple 'are seated and he gestures towards her, probably teaching her his Christian faith while devising their sham marriage' (J. Marquardt-Cherry, 'Ottonian Imperial Saints in the Prüm Troper', *Manuscripta* 33 [1989], 129–36, at 132). Used by permission of the Bibliothèque nationale de France.

First published in 2007 by
University of Exeter Press
Reed Hall, Streatham Drive
Exeter EX4 4QR
UK
www.exeterpress.co.uk

British Library Cataloguing in Publication Data
A catalogue record for this book is available from the British Library.

Hardback ISBN 978 0 85989 779 2
Paperback ISBN 978 0 85989 780 8

Typeset in TimesTen
by XL Publishing Services, Tiverton

Printed and bound by CPI Group (UK) Ltd, Croydon, CR0 4YY

For Karen

For Karen

CONTENTS

CONTENTS

ACKNOWLEDGEMENTS

For grant support that funded the research, writing and publication of this volume, I am grateful to the University of North Texas. Fellowships from the Vatican Film Library in St Louis, Missouri, and the Hill Monastic Manuscript Library at St John's University in Collegeville, Minnesota, likewise furthered my research, and I am grateful to Gregory Pass and Susan L'Engle, and Matthew Heintzelman and Theresa Vann for making my time at these institutions fruitful and enjoyable. Closer to home, I am indebted to the staff of the UNT Interlibrary Loan and Document Delivery Department for their marvellous work tracking down and securing loans of countless items, while Gayla Byerly, Mary Durio and Edward Hoyenski put many of those materials on the shelves.

In the early stages of the project Guy Philippart made available his unpublished lists of manuscripts for each legend studied here, while more recently Kevin Kiernan and Jonathan Wilcox provided me with forthcoming work. For particular points of advice I am grateful to Rosalind Love, Janet Marquardt, Jim Mulkin, Richard Pfaff, Rebecca Rushforth, Mary Swan and Teresa Webber. Scott Westrem, Suzanne Paul and Damian Fleming read and improved the Latin editions and translations. To Damian also goes credit for scrutinizing the Old English editions and translations as well. I owe a special debt of gratitude to Drew Jones whose careful reading of much of the manuscript late in the process resulted in suggestions and corrections that improved it markedly. Of course, any mistakes that remain are solely mine. For comments and criticisms on the Introduction, I am grateful to Jenny Adams, my most faithful critic, and Nicole Smith, a newfound one. Molly Dollar and Tyler Utt, student research assistants, helped, respectively, by checking transcriptions and by preparing a preliminary draft of the glossary entries for *Julian and Basilissa*. Among all those who have contributed to this project, Gordon Whatley deserves special mention for his unflagging generosity with his knowledge, time and good cheer. In addition to fielding a host of questions, he both proofread the transcription of *Chrysanthus and Daria* and provided me with his own translation of the *passio* of Cecilia and Valerian, which I frequently consulted as a guide.

At University of Exeter Press, I would like to thank Michael Swanton for his helpful suggestions for revision, and Anna Henderson for shepherding this book to its completion. I am also grateful for the expert and invaluable assistance of Jane Olorenshaw, who did the copy-editing, and Grant Shipcott, who did the typesetting.

Finally, my deepest debt of gratitude is to my family, my daughters Gabriela and Olivia, and especially my wife Karen, not only for her trusted eye but for her utter steadfastness. This book is for her.

ABBREVIATIONS

The lives of the virgin spouses appear as *Julian and Basilissa*, *Cecilia and Valerian*, and *Chrysanthus and Daria* throughout much of the editorial apparatus. The simple two-name format has been used for clarity, since the original Old English and Latin titles (and hence their translations into modern English) follow different formats. The original title of *Cecilia and Valerian* in both Old English and Latin also varies from the format adopted here in containing only Cecilia's name.

AS	*Acta Sanctorum*, ed. J. Bollandus et al., 68 vols (Brussels, 1643–1940)
ASE	*Anglo-Saxon England*
BHL	*Bibliotheca Hagiographica Latina Antiquiae et Mediae Aetatis*, ed. Socii Bollandiani, 2 vols (Brussels, 1893–1901); *Novum Supplementum*, ed. H. Fros (Brussels, 1986)
BHLms	*Bibliotheca Hagiographica Latina Manuscripta* (<http://bhlms.fltr.ucl.ac.be>)
CH I	*Ælfric's Catholic Homilies: The First Series*, ed. P. Clemoes, EETS SS 17 (Oxford, 1997)
CH II	*Ælfric's Catholic Homilies: The Second Series*, ed. M. Godden, EETS SS 5 (Oxford, 1979)
EETS	Early English Text Society
	OS Original Series
	SS Supplementary Series
HBS	Henry Bradshaw Society
LS	*Ælfric's Lives of Saints*, ed. and trans. W.W. Skeat, 2 vols in 4 parts, EETS OS 76, 82, 94, 114 (London, 1881–1900; repr. as 2 vols, London, 1966)
SH	*Homilies of Ælfric: A Supplementary Collection*, ed. J.C. Pope, EETS OS, 259–60 (London, 1967–68)

Manuscripts

Old English

J	London, British Library, Cotton MS Julius E. vii (s.xi^{in})

O   London, British Library, Cotton Otho B. x. (s.xi[1])
V   London, British Library, Cotton Vitellius D. xvii (s.xi[med])

Latin
B   Brussels, Bibliothèque Royale, MS 206 (s.xiii)
C   Cambridge, Corpus Christi College 9 (s.xi[q.2]/xi[med])
D   Dublin, Trinity College, MS 174 (s.xii[in])
H   Hereford, Cathedral Library, P.VII.6 (s.xii[2])
N   London, British Library, Cotton Nero E. i, pt i (s.xi[3/4])
P   Paris, Bibliothèque Nationale, Latin MS 13764 (s.x)
R   Rouen, Bibliothèque Municipale, MS U 026 (s.xi[ex]/xii[in])
S   Salisbury, Cathedral Library, MS 221 (s.xi[ex])
V   Rome, Vatican City, Biblioteca Apostolica Vaticana, MS Latini
             5771 (s.ix/x)

INTRODUCTION

Among the works of the Anglo-Saxon monk Ælfric (*c.*950–*c.*1010), arguably the finest writer of vernacular prose prior to the Norman Conquest, is the *Lives of Saints*, an Old English collection of saints' legends, sermons, biblical narratives and religious treatises.[1] By using the *Lives* to disseminate Christian doctrine and practice in English, he continues the tradition of King Alfred's educational programme, but Ælfric's audience is all Anglo-Saxon Christians, his goals are almost exclusively religious and his use of saints as didactic tools unparalleled in Old English literature.[2] In fact, he is the first medieval writer anywhere to render full-length versions of the stories of Julian and Basilissa, Cecilia and Valerian, and Chrysanthus and Daria into the vernacular and to direct them to the laity.

By the time Ælfric turned his attention to the *Lives of Saints* in the 990s, he was about forty years old and had established himself as a distinguished homilist, translator, grammarian and moralist.[3] His advice and writings were sought by some of the most powerful churchmen and landed warlords of his day, and he composed the *Lives* at the request of a father and son of one of England's preeminent families.[4] Ealdorman Æthelweard (fl. *c.*975–98) was the great-great grandson of King Æthelred I, a local ruler in Wessex of a territory that today encompasses Somerset, Dorset and Devon, and an adviser to Æthelred II (978–1016). Æthelweard's son Æthelmær (fl. 983–1005), served as Æthelred's steward and later succeeded to his father's ealdormanry. In or around 987, Æthelmær and his father founded the monastery of Cerne Abbas in Dorset, where Ælfric was transferred from Winchester, and in 1005 Æthelmær later re-founded a monastery at Eynsham with Ælfric as its abbot and himself (temporarily) as a monk.[5]

Yet while Ælfric's writings and pastoral career were bolstered by his personal relationship with Æthelweard and Æthelmær, the *Lives of Saints* also reflects the public educative work that he had begun previously in the *Catholic Homilies*. These two sets of forty sermons that Ælfric wrote between 990 and 995 were designed to be preached to the laity and to be read privately by clerics and laymen alike.[6] If indeed the sermons were responsible for attracting Æthelweard and Æthelmær as Ælfric's patrons, father and son would have benefited spiritually from their pointed instruction on various doctrines, sacraments and practices, their broad sweep of salvation history and their saints' lives illustrating the working out of Christ's salvation in history.[7] Ælfric sustains these points of focus in the *Lives* by providing Æthelweard and Æthelmær with five sermons and three tracts concentrated on Christian practice and doctrine, two Old Testament reading pieces and twenty-six saints' legends depicting God's work in and throughout history.[8]

Despite the similar educational thrusts of the two collections, Ælfric assembles the *Lives* to reinvigorate the 'listless faith' of English Christians and thereby gives the legends a collective purpose not evident in the lives in the *Catholic Homilies*.[9] To that end, he handpicks saints whose feast days are observed by monks rather than those celebrated by the general populace, as had been the case in the *Catholic Homilies*.[10] With his patrons and pious aristocratic households like theirs in mind, he features more male saints than female ones, more lay saints than clerical ones, and he repeats important types.[11] Among the twenty-six legends in the collection, five types are represented more than once—churchmen (6), soldiers (4), female virgin martyrs (4), kings (3) and virgin spouses (3)—and Ælfric's attention to these categories lends them a collective prominence that a single example would not otherwise acquire.[12] Modern readers may readily see the relevance of portraits of idealized churchmen, soldiers and kings to Ælfric's patrons. After all, aristocratic warlords had close contact with their sovereign and his thegns, as well as their own spiritual leaders, and legends depicting such figures provide prototypes for Anglo-Saxon counterparts. But what relevance would stories of virginal couples, not to mention female virgin martyrs, have had for men like Æthelweard and Æthelmær, who had families?[13] As I will argue below, stories of virgin spouses are key to Ælfric's project of rekindling the Christian faith among the English at the turn of the tenth century. Unlike churchmen, warriors and kings, who served as more straightforward models of behaviour, Julian and Basilissa, Cecilia and Valerian, and Chrysanthus and Daria captivated Ælfric's imagination because they provide him with models who embody the ascetic behaviour and orthodox belief central to his ideas of what it means for a layman to be a Christian.

To understand fully how Ælfric rewrites the stories to inculcate his audience with the saints' spiritual fervour, it is helpful to be familiar with the structure and themes of the Latin legends, and the ways in which their combinations of novel spiritual marriages and conventional martyrdoms piqued his interest. Moreover, a comparison of Ælfric's versions with treatments by other Anglo-Saxon authors reveals how English religious communities read the legends as relevant to their own lives and helps to explain why Ælfric highlights specific features when he redirects the stories to the laity. Finally, reading his versions in the light of his own programme of pastoral care allows us to map the way he rewrites the legends in relation to his own sermons on marital celibacy, spiritual purity and even clerical marriage. Not only will this homiletic background help to account for his many editorial decisions (which might otherwise perplex those comparing the Latin and Old English versions edited and translated below), but it also emphasizes the care Ælfric takes to achieve thematic unity within the individual legends and between the *Lives* and *Catholic Homilies* as well.

The Latin Legends of the Virgin Spouses

Attempting to classify the Latin legends of the virgin spouses illustrates their oddity as a subgenre of hagiography. As writings about the saints, the legends are, in the most general sense of the term, *vitae* or 'lives'. More useful for defining their origins and functions are Tom Hill's distinctions between 'primary' and 'secondary' *vitae*, and between 'legendary' and 'art' *vitae*. Following this first distinction, *Julian and Basilissa, Cecilia and Valerian*, and *Chrysanthus and Daria* are secondary rather than primary *vitae* because none represents 'a primary written witness to the life and deeds' of the saints.[14] Rather, the accounts are 'lives of men and women whose sanctity could simply be taken for granted by the author' and thus are 'characteristically unhistorical'.[15] Cecilia and Valerian, and Chrysanthus and Daria purportedly lived in the third century, but their legends were composed about three hundred years later. *Julian and Basilissa*, which was originally written in Greek before being translated into Latin, is set in the fourth century, yet it is difficult to date their legend earlier than the sixth century.[16] And while there is evidence, for example, that a Chrysanthus and Daria were buried in sand pits outside the gates of Rome and that the crypt of a Cecilia was discovered adjacent to papal catacombs in the same city, the narratives themselves have no historical validity.[17]

That these secondary *vitae* are also 'art *vitae*' as opposed to 'legendary *vitae*' stems from the fact that they were not primarly intended to be read in the context of a worship service.[18] Legendary *vitae* were to be read during the services of 'regular' or monastic clergy and their 'secular' counterparts, who led more public lives while performing services at local churches or cathedrals and attending to the daily needs of those who worshipped there. Both sets of clergy organized their day around eight worship services or 'offices' (the cycle known as the 'Divine Office' or the 'Canonical Hours'). Though different in form for the monastic and secular clergy, the Night Office (later Matins) would have incorporated a series of readings ('legenda') from the saint's life (and perhaps chants drawn from the readings).[19] Constraints of time and a need for comprehensibility dictate that these legendary *vitae*, which are often abbreviations of longer texts, be concise, rhetorically spare and plot-driven. Art *vitae*, by contrast, were read privately as devotional material or publicly when monks took their meals, and they are lengthy, elaborately constructed and rhetorically sophisticated literary creations.[20] Indeed, Hippolyte Delehaye, a scholar of church history and hagiography, described *Cecilia and Valerian* as a 'romance' written by 'a pious storyteller', a description that also fits *Julian and Basilissa* and *Chrysanthus and Daria*.[21]

Further classifying these secondary art *vitae* according to content reveals that they are actually hybrids of two principal hagiographical genres, the *vita* and *passio*. As noted above, the word *vita* refers generally to writing about the saints, but it is also used specifically for an account of the life of a confessor, a man of religious vocation who acknowledges or confesses that he is a Christian but is not killed for doing so. The *vita* follows this formula:

> the saint is born of noble stock; his birth is accompanied by miraculous portents; as a youth he excels at learning and reveals that he is destined for saintly activity; he turns from secular to holy life (often forsaking his family) and so proceeds through the various ecclesiastical grades; he reveals his sanctity while still on earth by performing various miracles; eventually he sees his death approaching and, after instructing his disciples or followers, dies calmly; after his death many miracles occur at his tomb.[22]

By contrast, the *passio*, a Latin word for 'suffering', shifts the narrative focus to the saint's martyrdom and is structured according to these conventions:

> the saint, usually of noble birth, adopts Christianity in days when the state government is pagan; the saint is brought before a local magistrate or governor and asked to recant his/her Christianity by sacrificing to the gods; the saint refuses to do so, even on the pain of innumerable tortures (normally described in excruciating detail), and is eventually killed, usually by beheading.[23]

While the Latin *incipits*, the opening words, that precede Ælfric's Old English legends of the virgin spouses designate each text as a *passio*, the original authors grafted elements of the *vita* onto a standard *passio* narrative to create an uncommon hybrid. Before initiating the saints' inexorable march towards martyrdom, each author dwells at length on their exemplary manner of life much as a *vita* would. So important is the *vita* portion of the legends studied here that it occupies one quarter of *Julian and Basilissa* (lines 1–231 [pp. 114–28]), one half of *Cecilia and*

Valerian (lines 1–342 [pp. 172–94]) and three-fifths of *Chrysanthus and Daria* (lines 1–291 [pp. 218–36]).

Without a doubt, the most novel elements of these unusual *vita* sections are their spiritual marriages. These unions, wherein married couples remain virgins, represent the authors' surprisingly unorthodox attempts to provide the laity with models of sanctity in the early Middle Ages when 'clerical asceticism [had come] to dominate the hagiographical discourse'.[24] Unconsummated wedlock is unorthodox because it contravenes the procreative purpose of marriage established by biblical command ('Be fruitful and multiply' [Genesis 1.22]) and supported by patristic authority.[25] Nevertheless, depictions of virgin spouses constitute the hagiographers' understandable responses to a brand of Christianity that had taken on increasingly ascetic overtones in the early Middle Ages. *Julian and Basilissa, Cecilia and Valerian*, and *Chrysanthus and Daria* were written between the late fifth and seventh centuries, by which time the perpetual virginity of the religious elite had been enshrined as the Christian virtue *par excellence*. Even when married couples fulfilled their biblical obligations to procreate, they were considered to have less merit and were entitled to fewer heavenly rewards than those clerics who lived out their lives in chastity. Spiritual marriage thus became a way for hagiographers to respond to either real or perceived ascetic impulses among the laity with a model that avoids undermining marriage and that figuratively redefines its procreative activity as spiritual childbearing.[26] Despite this novel, even odd solution, the authors 'struck a responsive chord', a fact borne out by the several hundred copies of the legends that survive.[27]

Julian and Basilissa best dramatizes the tensions between the biblically sanctioned, procreative imperatives of Christian marriage and the ascetic impulses of early medieval Christianity, and it provides clear examples of the strategies hagiographers use to legitimize spiritual marriage at a time when the monastery was the preferred locus for the pursuit of the virginal life.[28] Its author clearly felt the need to address why the couple pursues perpetual virginity in marriage rather than a monastery. To that end, he builds in parental compulsion, divine approbation, secrecy and monastic vocations to explain and sanction the arrangement. On the one hand, Julian's Christian parents want him to marry and produce an heir because they understand the Bible to encourage such behaviour.[29] On the other hand, Julian's 'grace of holiness' (line 13 [p. 114]) manifests itself in a vow of chastity. To resolve this tension, the hagiographer has Christ appear to Julian in a vision, order him to take a wife and promise that she too will want to remain a virgin. Only then is Julian able to sidestep his parents' demand and the biblical directive to marry. With Christ's subsequent assurance that the couple will convert many others to chastity, the hagiographer begins to transform the procreative aim of marriage from a physical into a figurative one.

Still, the contravention of biblical and patristic ideals prompts the author to sanction the union with extraordinary fanfare, even though it will remain shrouded in secrecy and will ultimately find expression in a more conventional setting. Once Basilissa agrees to live chastely with Julian, a 'great spiritual spectacle' (line 85 [p. 118]) occurs during which Christ, the Virgin Mary, and hosts of male and female virgins shout their approbation in turns. Four angels appear with vials from which the fragrance of the couple's moral perfection ascends to God, two others bring them the Book of Life so they may read their names in it, and yet another pair brings the saints floral crowns, a gesture that simultaneously evokes a marriage ceremony, the awarding of the victor's wreath and the bestowal of the heavenly diadem of lilies and roses on virgin martyrs for their purity and sacrifice. Despite these validations, the couple's decision to keep their arrangement secret acknowledges the challenge that even divinely sanctioned chaste marriage poses to patrilineal succession and explains why the author subsequently lavishes attention on Julian and Basilissa's founding and supervision of monasteries where their spiritual offspring are produced.

The authors of *Cecilia and Valerian* and *Chrysanthus and Daria* contrive similar ways to sanctify chaste wedlock, and all three hagiographers use spiritual fruitfulness in the *vita* sections as backdrops against which workaday scenes from the *passiones* are transformed into dynamic proofs of the saints' holiness. Divine affirmation of celibate marriage in *Cecilia and Valerian* takes the form of Cecilia's angel, who threatens to kill Valerian should he want to consummate the union and who brings them crowns from paradise once Valerian has been baptized. Chrysanthus is miraculously saved from the diversions of five young virgins and, not without some verbal fireworks of his own, converts Daria to Christianity and chastity through his apologetics. After committing to marital celibacy, each couple then produces spiritual offspring prior to the onset of martyrdom. Julian and Basilissa, as mentioned above, oversee huge monastic communities, Cecilia and Valerian convert his brother Tiburtius, and so many men and women take vows of chastity in imitation of Chrysanthus and Daria that they spark a public outcry from their abandoned spouses and fiancées. In each case, the saints and their progeny draw the ire of the authorities, which provides catalysts for propelling the protagonists towards death.

Once the hagiographers change genres from *vita* to *passio*, the stock interrogations, tortures, miraculous interventions and conversions common to these 'epic passions' take on a larger significance when seen as part of a trajectory that leads from spiritual marriage to martyrdom.[30] Each time the saints refuse an offer of safety or friendship in exchange for sacrificing to the gods, they confirm that guarding their fleshly virginity has prepared them to preserve the purity of their faith. Each well-turned phrase and well-developed argument used to lecture magistrates, torturers or bystanders on the fallacies of pagan belief and the truth of Christianity further proves that these virgin husbands and wives are, in fact, 'not joined . . . by the heat of the body but . . . united . . . in the passion of the Holy Spirit' (lines 288–89 [p. 236]). Divine visions, celestial voices, heavenly succour, and an imperviousness to torture—in these legends alone saints are burned, scalped, blinded, stripped, boiled, beaten, chained, sewn up naked in an ox hide, thrown into a brothel and fed to wild animals—establish that the virginity of the married virgin is as valuable to God as that of any unmarried virgin martyr or accomplished ecclesiastic. Finally, in a mirror of the spiritual childbearing that brings the *vita* portion of the legends to a close, the saints' actions under torment lead to conversions of soldiers, torturers, a pagan governor's wife and son, a would-be seducer and crowds of onlookers. Even in the midst of martyrdom, they give birth to new offspring.

These hybrid stories of spiritual marriage and martyrdom had enduring appeal, and textual, iconographic and architectural evidence demonstrates the widespread popularity of the cults of these saints.[31] The earliest recognition in the West of the cult of the Egyptian saints Julian and Basilissa is an entry for their feast day (most commonly 6 or 9 January) in a fifth-century martyrology, a calendrical list of saints' names and feast days, that was drawn up in Italy.[32] The Latin *passio* is cited as early as the sixth century in a monastic rule composed southeast of Rome.[33] In Rome itself, frescoes, one dated to the eighth century (but now destroyed) and another to the ninth, signal the importance of the cult in that city, where as late as the eighteenth century the saints are honoured in another fresco.[34] In what is now southeastern France, as many as eighteen churches were dedicated to the pair between the fifth and eleventh centuries.[35] Farther north, the Frankish Queen Brunhild (567–613) may have sponsored the 'translation', or transfer, of the saints' relics from the East to the convent she established in Morigny (modern Morigny-Champigny).[36] Purportedly she also sent a piece of Julian's skull to the secular canons living in the church of St Basilissa in Paris, a city where the couple was later honoured in the ninth century with an altar at the monastery of Clermont, with special prayers at the monastery of St Denis and with various church dedications.[37] One of the earliest copies of the Latin legend survives in a late seventh- or early eighth-century legendary written at Luxeuil for use in Langres, a manuscript whose ancestors may have had connections with Morigny.[38] More relics arrived during the sixth and seventh centuries in Spain, where their feast day was commemorated in mass books used from the seventh to the eleventh century.[39] Monasteries in present-day Switzerland celebrated a yearly mass in honour of the pair in the late eighth or early ninth century, and the translation of their relics to the cathedral in Halberstadt in the tenth century signals the presence of a public cult in Germany.[40] No evidence of such popular veneration survives from medieval England, but the legend was known there as early as the seventh century, as Aldhelm of Malmesbury's epitome of *Julian and Basilissa* in his treatise on virginity attests.[41] Ælfric's treatment of the legend is the only other by an Anglo-Saxon author, and no Middle English version appears ever to have been composed. Despite the fact that the Latin legend seems not to have been widely known in England, at least 133 copies survive in libraries throughout Western Europe.[42]

Cecilia and Valerian are unique among the saints studied here in that their *passio*, which was almost certainly written in Rome between 495 and 500, provides early evidence of the cult, though a late eighth- or early ninth-century copy is the earliest to survive.[43] Because the hagiographer borrows the names of saints already venerated in different Roman cemeteries (Cecilia in one, and Valerian, Tiburtius and Maximus in another), Cecilia's feast day (22 November) is celebrated independently of the others (14 April).[44] Cecilia was venerated in the papal crypts of the cemetery of St Callistus just outside the gates of Rome from the late fifth century onwards, and two mosaics in Ravenna, a late fifth-century roundel in the Archbishop's Chapel and the celebrated Procession of Virgins (*c*.560) in the cathedral, attest to the rapid growth and spread of her cult in Italy.[45] Sometime between the late fifth and seventh centuries, she was included among a list of female saints in one of the intercessory prayers of the Canon of the Mass, the hallowed set of prayers recited to consecrate the Eucharist, a fact which helps explain why her feast day is preeminent. Moreover, after Cecilia and Valerian's relics were purportedly translated from a (different) cemetery to a Roman basilica in the ninth century, St Cecilia in Trastevere became an important 'station' church, where each year the pope would celebrate mass during Lent. Consequently, the prayers, biblical readings and choral texts used to celebrate her feast day and station day circulated throughout western Christendom in copies of Roman mass books, thereby making certain that Cecilia and Valerian would be widely venerated and their story well known.[46] Nearly 180 copies of the *passio* are extant.[47]

Surprisingly, there is little evidence until the later Middle Ages that public cults of Cecilia flourish outside of Italy. Twelfth-century German wall paintings of scenes from the *passio* once adorned the wall of a church in Cologne, and two thirteenth-century representations survive in French cathedrals: a stained glass window in Bourges depicting scenes from the legend and a relief of Cecilia and Valerian in Strasbourg.[48] Interest in Cecilia among artists explodes after the fourteenth century and culminates in Raphael's celebrated sixteenth-century painting, 'The Ecstasy of St Cecilia'.[49] In England, the only early evidence that suggests Cecilia and Valerian may have been venerated among the laity are entries in eleventh-century lists of relics that King Æthelstan (924/5–39) had given to the monks at Exeter in the tenth.[50] Anglo-Saxon monks were primarily responsible for honouring the memories of Cecilia and Valerian, which they did from at least the early seventh century onwards (thanks again in part to Aldhelm). Ælfric's version represents the first full translation of the legend into the English vernacular, but so popular would the story become that it exists in seven different Middle English versions, of which 'The Second Nun's Tale' in Chaucer's *Canterbury Tales* is the most well known to students of English literature.[51]

Like Cecilia and Valerian, Chrysanthus and Daria are Roman martyrs whose relics were venerated outside of Rome before being translated inside the city. Gregory of Tours, the Church historian, reports in the sixth century that he had visited the sand pits along the New Salarian Way where Chrysanthus and Daria were buried alive in the mid-third century. There he saw into the crypt through a latticed window that Pope Damasus I (366–88) had installed so that pilgrims could see the skeletons and communion vessels of the worshippers who, as the *passio* reports, were walled in and buried alive while honouring Chrysanthus and Daria.[52] Also in the sixth century, Daria appears with Cecilia in the Ravenna Procession of Virgins.[53] As was true for Cecilia and Valerian, Chrysanthus and Daria's feast day (usually 29 November) receives special commemoration in the early Roman mass books, whose revered status and frequent copying guaranteed the saints would be remembered in churches and monasteries throughout Western Europe.[54] Accordingly, just over 100 manuscripts preserve their legend.[55]

In the eighth and ninth centuries, respectively, the translation of Chrysanthus and Daria's relics, and those of the worshippers martyred at their tomb, from the New Salarian Way to various Roman churches commences the rapid diffusion of the cult.[56] In the ninth century alone, popes sent their relics to a church dedicated to them in Oria, Italy, to the monastery of Prüm (near Trier) in Germany and to the episcopal cathedral in Salzburg.[57] In the tenth century, relics went to Reggio, Italy, where another church was dedicated to them, and to England to King Æthelstan who later gave them to the monks at Exeter.[58] Once again, the earliest knowledge of their *passio* in England dates to Aldhelm, while vernacular versions later than Ælfric's survive in three Middle English collections.[59]

Treatments of the Latin Legends by Anglo-Saxon Authors other than Ælfric

Looking at the Anglo-Saxon treatments of *Julian and Basilissa*, *Cecilia and Valerian*, and *Chrysanthus and Daria* throws into relief the ways Ælfric has laicized the narratives. The earliest use of the saints as models for English religious communities is found in the Latin treatise on virginity by Aldhelm (*c*.640–709/710), abbot of Malmesbury and bishop of Sherborne, who addressed the *De virginitate* to the nuns at Barking, a double monastery in Essex (where presumably the monks living under the abbess's rule would have read the work as well).[60] Bede (672/3–735) wrote his Latin martyrology for the monasteries of Monkwearmouth and Jarrow, and a clerical audience is most probable for the anonymous ninth-century *Old English Martyrology*. Finally, evidence of when and how the lives of the married saints were commemorated in late Anglo-Saxon England survives in calendars, litanies and liturgical books used exclusively by the clergy. Their prayers and benedictions form abbreviated 'readings' of the legends that zero in on the saints' apposite virtues despite the fact that marriage provides the initial context for their expression. Ultimately, the clerical treatments remind us that Ælfric's decision to redirect the stories from the cloister to the hall returns them to their earlier status as works for the laity.

Aldhelm's *De virginitate*

The epitomes of *Julian and Basilissa*, *Chrysanthus and Daria*, and *Cecilia and Valerian* in the prose and verse versions of the *De virginitate* suggest that the stories symbolize for Aldhelm the special relationships of monks and nuns jointly pursuing the religious life in double monasteries in seventh-century Anglo-Saxon England. The prose version of the treatise, which Aldhelm completed first, includes five sets of virgin spouses (the three above, along with Amos [i.e. Ammon] and Malchus).[61] He gives prominence to the three pairs studied here: the contiguous epitomes of *Julian and Basilissa* and *Chrysanthus and Daria* are the longest in the *De virginitate* and occur, along with *Amos*, near its centre at a pivotal transitional point between catalogues of male and female virgins; Cecilia, moreover, holds pride of place among female virgins as first after Mary. The grouping of married saints near the middle of the *De virginitate* does not seem accidental, especially when considered in light of Stephanie Hollis's observation that

> Aldhelm's weaving together of the portraits of male and female
> saints . . . offers an image of the transcendental reality of the
> Barking double monastery. . . . Within the walls, like a garden
> 'enclosed about,' the double monastery, containing male and
> female religious united in chaste union, is implicitly a site for the
> recovery of paradisal innocence.[62]

Aldhelm's use of the metaphor of spiritual marriage in the *De virginitate* confirms Hollis's point, and his treatment of *Chrysanthus and Daria* demonstrates his comfort with depicting chaste husbands and wives learning, teaching and evangelizing together. In his opening remarks on virginity, he moulds his addressees in the images of the learned, celibate, fecund saints they will encounter later in the treatise. Using a well-established patristic allegory, Aldhelm first personifies the nuns of Barking as offspring of the chaste marriage between Christ and the Church, children 'brought forth from the fecund womb of ecclesiastical conception through the seed of the spiritual Word', and he praises them for 'growing learned in divine doctrine through maternal care' (though whether that of abbess Hildelith or mother Church, or both, he does not specify).[63] With characteristic amplification, Aldhelm compares the nuns' mental exertions with the physical exercise of wrestlers, archers, runners, horsemen and rowers, before settling on bees as the best metaphor for styling them as wise celibates who bear spiritual children when they teach what they know.[64]

Aldhelm likens a nun's accumulation of knowledge and wisdom to the bee's gathering of pollen and its asexual reproduction to their ability to bring forth spiritual children by instructing others in the faith.[65] In the longest extended simile in the *De virginitate*, he personifies the 'bees' of Barking buzzing to and fro among the 'flowers' of the Old and New Testaments, histories and chronicles, and books on grammar, spelling and metre, before returning to the hive. There the procreative process by which the bee makes honey and produces offspring symbolizes the nuns' ability to amass knowledge and impart it to other Christians:

> robbing the flowering fields of pastureland of an ineffable booty [the bee] produces her sweet family and children, innocent of the lascivious coupling of marriage, by means of a certain generative condensation of a very sweet juice; and in truth, the Church, striking vitally into the hearts of men with the double-keen sword-edge of the (two) Testaments, fertilizes through the chaste seed of the Word the offspring who are lawful heirs of eternity.[66]

Here the erstwhile daughters of Christ and the Church are transformed into virgin mothers. Because Aldhelm believed that bees reproduced asexually, it is not unusual that the image of the female bee nurturing her family gives way to a masculine depiction of mother Church, and by extension the nuns, penetrating and fertilizing souls through the teaching of Scripture. Given that nuns in double monasteries would likely have joined their fellow monks in the pastoral work of teaching and baptizing, it is no wonder that stories of learned couples like Chrysanthus and Daria, who were 'united . . . in the passion of the Holy Spirit' (line 289 [p. 236]), and like Julian and Basilissa, who were fruitful in spirit not flesh (lines 117–18 [p. 120]), caught Aldhelm's attention.[67]

Aldhelm's epitome of *Chrysanthus and Daria* most clearly recalls his descriptions of the nuns as children of the Church and as virgin mothers to other believers, and it prompts us to read the other accounts in a similar light.[68] His emphases on the nuns' learning and teaching in the introductory material explains why, even in the midst of reducing a nearly 4,800-word *passio* to 800, he dwells on Chrysanthus's intelligence and vast learning, which prepares him to grasp the 'doctrine of celestial philosophy' when he reads and studies the Gospels.[69] In a single sentence, which has no parallel in the *passio*, Aldhelm's description of Chrysanthus's transformation from educated 'neophyte' to 'outstanding teacher' encapsulates the process by which the bee turns its pollen into honey and more bees:

> And when, having been conceived in the womb of regenerating grace and having been brought forth by the fertile delivery of baptism, he was nourished in the reverend cradle of the Church, straightaway the young neophyte, after receiving the rudiments of the faith, becomes an outstanding teacher and fearing in no way the dangers of perfidious (enemies), he preaches Christ the son of God openly to all people.[70]

Echoes of the language Aldhelm used to describe the nuns' 'ecclesiastical conception' and spiritual generation are unmistakable in this description of Chrysanthus being born again, nurtured and made ready to teach. Aldhelm, furthermore, wastes no time in setting the generative cycle in motion. He compresses the long debates in the *passio* into a few sentences and nearly straightaway Chrysanthus converts Daria, who then takes up 'canonical writings and exegetical commentaries' in the manner of the nuns reading her story.[71] Like bees that generate more bees, the learned virgin spouses begin to make converts, yet those whom they win over do not come to their faith because of the saints' exemplary lives, as is the case in the *passio*, but 'as a result of their instruction'.[72]

As in the *passio*, Chrysanthus and Daria are martyred together, and Aldhelm's consoling final image of the saints prefigures the everlasting bond of Anglo-Saxon monks and nuns united in their preservation of virginity and bearing of spiritual fruit. He concludes by projecting Chrysanthus and Daria's spiritual marriage into eternity rather than recounting the inglorious deaths of those who came to venerate them. Understandably, he passes over the *passio*'s analogy between the couple's marriage bed and their burial pit, but he drives home the legend's point that their relationship will survive into the next life:

> . . . they died as martyrs, put to rest *together* in one crypt in the company of saints, ready to receive *together* the rewards for their merits, just as they had shared *together* in their torments (my italics).[73]

Aldhelm continues to emphasize their joint burial and resurrection in the verse epitome, where it is most clear that the saints symbolize a religious community like that at Barking. There he imagines on the Last Day the resurrection not only of Chrysanthus and Daria but also of all those like them who are 'rightly gathered in blessed *throngs*', a word used in the *De virginitate* to indicate virgins in general, the monks and nuns at Barking in particular, and the train of virgins who sing praises to the Lamb of God in Paradise.[74] Understood in this light, the chaste couple represents monks and nuns in English double houses joined in the pursuit of chastity while learning and teaching on earth so as to be made part of the 'virginal throng in close companies surround[ing] the Lamb in the ethereal heights of heaven'.[75]

The Martyrologies of Bede and the Old English Martyrologist

While prior to Ælfric there are no fuller Anglo-Saxon treatments of the legends of virgin spouses than Aldhelm's, entries from two early martyrologies attest to the different receptions the stories had in the eighth and ninth centuries. In his Latin martyrology, Bede omits the stories of Julian and Basilissa and Chrysanthus and Daria, and remains silent about Cecilia's virginity, editorial choices that may signal his resistance to their model of sanctity. By contrast, the Old English martyrologist includes long entries for all three pairs. Unfortunately, because we know neither who wrote the ninth-century *Old English Martyrology* nor for whom it was written, it is impossible to infer why the martyrologist chose to include the virgin spouses in his work. Nevertheless, the fact that he does not ignore the couples' celibate marriages suggests that he takes a cue from Aldhelm that Bede did not care to notice.

Bede's handling of Æthelthryth (23 June) and Cecilia (22 November) suggests that he is hesitant to embrace stories that, when read in a monastic context, could be understood to endorse an intimate camaraderie between the sexes. Æthelthryth and Cecilia are the only two virgin wives included among his highly selective 115 entries, which mention by name some 200 male and thirty-nine female saints.[76] Not only is Æthelthryth the martyrology's only female non-martyr and sole female English saint, but she is also the same woman Bede extols in the *Ecclesiastical History* in a chapter dedicated to her life and in a poem on virginity he composed in her honour.[77] Prior to her entry into religious life, she had remained a virgin despite being married twice, the second time for twelve years to King Ecgfrith of Northumbria (670–85). She died in 679, as the abbess of the double monastery of Ely, and for this reason Bede styles her 'virgin' and 'queen' in the martyrology.[78] His entry includes only one other detail from her life—'her body was found uncorrupted after it had been buried for sixteen years'—because Æthelthryth's translation from the graveyard into the church at Ely furnishes positive proof of her exceptional status as virgin wife.[79]

In contrast with Bede's approval of Æthelthryth's path from marriage to monastery, his decision to mention Cecilia's marriage to Valerian while keeping silent about her virginal status hints that he found their spiritual marriage to be an inappropriate model for an Anglo-Saxon religious community like his own. The entry for Cecilia begins by reporting that she 'thoroughly instructed her spouse Valerian and his brother Tiburtius both for belief in Christ and for martyrdom' and ends by noting that she survived Almachius's attempt to boil her and was beheaded.[80] Without an epithet such as 'virgin' or a reference to her chastity, Cecilia becomes indistinguishable from the other wives in the martyrology who were executed for their faith.[81] Bede's omission may stem from Cecilia's preeminent status as a saint in the Canon of the Mass whose story he could assume the monks would have known well; perhaps the fact that Cecilia was a martyr while Æthelthryth was not meant that Bede possessed enough information to complete his standard entry (name, date and manner of death) and felt the spiritual marriage to be extraneous. Yet when seen in the light of his distrust of the double monasteries of his day and of his idealization of the enclosure of women in single-sex houses, Bede's reticence seems purposeful.[82] Cecilia and Valerian's companionship was not a fitting model for the monastery, and virgin spouses apparently give him none of the comfort that he would have noticed Aldhelm took from them in the *De virginitate*.[83] This uneasiness may also explain why he does not include entries for Malchus, Amos, Julian and Basilissa, and Chrysanthus and Daria, all of whom were included in the prose *De virginitate* and all of whom except for Amos are found in the martyrology that served as Bede's model.[84]

The virgin spouses seem not to have troubled the Old English martyrologist in the same way they seem to have bothered Bede, although the martyrologist's reasons for including them among his 238 entries may have been no more than an 'interest in "the spectacularly miraculous"'.[85] This predilection for the dramatic explains, for example, his focus on the 'great spiritual spectacle' in *Julian and Basilissa* with its 'miraculous fragrance', 'heavenly light' and 'Christ himself . . . with a host of angels'.[86] It also accounts for his decision to conclude not with Julian's martyrdom but with his raising of a dead man who tells 'a sad story of his experience in hell'.[87] Similarly, the martyrologist spends nearly half of the entry for Cecilia concentrating on her revelation to Valerian that she has a guardian angel and on the crowns he later brings from paradise.[88] Nor does he fail to mark the miraculous sleep that overcomes the girls sent to seduce Chrysanthus.[89] Because he mentions that all these saints are married and yet have remained virgins, it is possible that the very idea of chaste marriage struck him as spectacular. Whatever his reasons for including them, the martyrologist's demonstrable interest in their stories aligns him less closely with Bede than with Aldhelm, one of his sources, and with other Anglo-Saxon authors like Ælfric who found these saints, their stories and their sanctity compelling.[90]

Calendar Entries, Litanies, Prayers and Benedictions

Liturgical evidence from late Anglo-Saxon England confirms that the lives of the virgin spouses continued to be honoured in later centuries. Twenty-seven calendars (lists of festivals and feast days by month and day) and calendar fragments serve as guides to the saints honoured in Anglo-Saxon monastic communities.[91] Likewise, litanies comprise formulaic prayers of petition whose supplications are punctuated by sets of invocations, among which are those appealing to martyrs, confessors and virgins for their help. When the virgin spouses appear among the fifty-nine surviving Anglo-Saxon litanies, Julian, Valerian and Chrysanthus appear in the lists of martyrs while Basilissa, Cecilia and Daria are among those for virgins.[92] Caution is advisable, however, when drawing conclusions about the popularity of the saints' cults from these sources. Calendars are not prescriptive, so it is impossible to assume, for example, that the five communities whose calendars commemorate Julian and Basilissa's feast day actually observed it.[93] And, monks who would have recited their names during a litany (only two of which mention both saints) need not have known anything about them.[94]

Traces of an active cult may be evident from references to the saints in a calendar and litany that belong to an eleventh-century psalter written at Croyland in Lincolnshire. The January calendar reads like the *incipits* of some copies of the *passio*[95]:

> v Id[us] [Natale] Sancti Iuliani martiris. Et Sanctę Basilissę sponse eius.
> (9 January. [The feast day] of Saint Julian the martyr and Saint Basilissa his wife.)[96]

It is the only entry in an Anglo-Saxon calendar to identify the pair as a married couple and may reflect the compiler's familiarity with the story. If the calendar functioned as a guide for worship in the Croyland community at large, and if the abbey possessed a copy of the legend, then the long *passio* would have been divided into readings and transformed into a legendary *vita* for the Night Office beginning on 8 January. Alternatively, should the calendar have aided the monks' private devotion, then they may have read the entire text on the vigil or feast day itself. Private devotion was certainly the occasion on which a monk would have recited the

Croyland litany, which is preserved in a psalter rather than a service book. Had the Croyland monks honoured Julian and Basilissa annually, as the calendar suggests, then a knowledge of their story would have lent greater specificity, even significance, to their litanic prayer, which invokes 'St Julian together with his companions'.[97]

Chrysanthus and Daria were more widely venerated and figured more significantly in Anglo-Saxon monastic devotions than Julian and Basilissa, so more evidence survives of the relevance English religious communities found in their legend. Ten calendars commemorate their festival, and one shows that the clergy at Canterbury held Chrysanthus and Daria in particular esteem in the tenth century.[98] That calendar distinguishes three ranks of saints and designates the festival of Chrysanthus and Daria (29 November) a feast of the second rank, that is less important than an apostle but more important than the majority of saints in the calendar.[99] Additionally, this is the only 'graded' calendar among three to single out the feast day for special attention.[100]

The Canterbury calendar was written between 979 and 987 during the episcopate of Archbishop Dunstan (959–88), one of the principal architects of the tenth-century monastic reform, and it prefaces Dunstan's sacramentary, the book he used to celebrate masses throughout the year and to perform various other services and rites.[101] The mass book was written on the Continent between 860 and 920, but it is worthy of note that it does not contain a separate mass for Chrysanthus and Daria, nor does either of its litanies mention them.[102] If Dunstan were responsible for the special attention paid to the saints in the calendar, then perhaps he meant to continue the veneration he observed at the monastery of St Peter's in Ghent, where he lived in exile from 956 to 958. More intriguing, though incapable of proof, is the possibility that he considered Chrysanthus and Daria to be fitting models for the secular clergy who continued to staff his cathedral despite the fact that some almost certainly would have had wives.[103] Whatever the reason for Dunstan's interest in these saints in the tenth century, the celibate cathedral canons at Exeter who recopied and amplified his sacramentary for their bishop in the eleventh century would have endorsed and observed the calendar's special designation for Chrysanthus and Daria, for the list of relics they inserted before the calendar includes both saints.[104]

Like Canterbury, Winchester was another key site of tenth-century monastic reform, and three eleventh-century Winchester texts illustrate the importance of Chrysanthus and Daria to the religious community where Ælfric had earlier been trained. A calendar and a litany were written around 1030 by Ælfwine, a monk of the New Minster, who included them in a private handbook.[105] The calendar, an aid to Ælfwine's private devotions, includes an entry for Chrysanthus and Daria (1 December), whom he implores to 'pray for me' in one of only two litanies that mention the pair together.[106] Should Ælfwine's personal favourites have reflected or influenced the observances of the New Minster monks he oversaw when he became abbot in 1031 or 1032, then his veneration of Chrysanthus and Daria would appear to continue a Winchester tradition that had an impact on Ælfric when he was a monk there some fifty years earlier.[107]

A mass book known as *The Missal of the New Minster* is the third source that demonstrates the continuing importance of Chrysanthus and Daria at Winchester, and one of its prayers furnishes a good example of how a particular community read the legend as pertinent to its members. Written around 1075, the missal contains a set of four prayers to be said during the mass celebrated in honour of their feast day.[108] Of the four prayers—the collect, secret, preface and post-communion—all but the first resemble prayers belonging to mass sets in two other Anglo-Saxon sacramentaries in that they do not directly engage the *passio* and thus contribute little to the reception history of the legend.[109] The collect, by contrast, picks up on the saints' decision to undertake chaste marriage 'as if there had been one will between [them]' (lines 282–83 [p. 236]) and their unified passion for martyrdom when they are buried alive 'enduring to the end in one desire, in one pit, as if in one bed' (lines 466–67 [p. 248]). As a result, the prayer constitutes an appeal for single-mindedness based on a singular example of it:

> Oh God, who converted the blessed virgin Daria through the eloquence of the holy Chrysanthus, grant that the goodness, which was in those who were of one mind to live chastely and to die for you, remains to intercede on our behalf with your majesty, through [Jesus Christ our Lord].[110]

As the prayer makes clear, the 'one mind' of Chrysanthus and Daria, which brought about acts of chastity and martyrdom, entitle them to intercede (with one mind) for the monks of Winchester. This appeal to the saints' unity is most noteworthy, not only because the prayer is original but also because it was composed early in the tenure of the Frenchman Riwallon who replaced the deposed Anglo-Saxon abbot Wulfric.[111] As was true for Aldhelm, chaste marriage here functions as a symbol of monastic solidarity within the confines of the cloister. This time, however, the bond imagined is not between nuns and monks in a double monastery but between French and English religious clergy pursuing common vocations in the midst of settling differences and, one imagines, in need of more than a little *eloquentia* to insure their success.

The feast days of Cecilia and Valerian are commemorated in a greater number and wider variety of liturgical books than either Julian and Basilissa or Chrysanthus and Daria, and prayers to Cecilia provide the

fullest picture of how English religious communities saw her life as rele-
vant to their own.[112] In addition to appearances in all the calendars and
nearly all the litanies, Cecilia boasts at least seven mass sets, eleven sets
of benedictions, two collects said at the conclusion of monastic offices on
her feast day, two private prayers and one office.[113] Many of these prayers
never refer to or borrow from the legend, but among those that do is a
group that emphasizes Cecilia's *constantia* or steadfastness, a theme
important to Ælfric as well. When, for example, Bishop Leofric used his
sacramentary and benedictional to celebrate Cecilia's feast day mass at
Exeter Cathedral in the third quarter of the eleventh century, the cathe-
dral's secular clergy, a chapter of canons living a quasi-monastic life
according to a common rule, would have been reminded of Cecilia's
exemplary steadfastness twice in a short space of time. First, those within
earshot of Leofric would have heard him recite a preface praising a
Cecilia who is 'not moved from her purpose by worldly seduction, not
allured by fleshly charms, not hindered by the frailty of her sex, not over-
come by the cruelty of torment' but who 'by preserving the purity of her
body and mind . . . is worthy to attain eternal blessedness'.[114] Before
distributing the elements just consecrated with this prayer, the bishop
would have then recited a three-part blessing in which he prayed for God
to strengthen the congregation's resolve to remain physically chaste and
spiritually pure.[115] More specifically, the benediction's request that God
'strengthen [the congregants] with the steadfastness of angelic chastity
and faith' and sanctify them by means of 'the gospel of His Christ and
divine discourse', recalls the *passio*'s description of Cecilia as one who
'carried the gospel of Christ always hidden in her heart and did not cease
day or night from divine discourse and prayer' (lines 45–47 [p. 174]).[116]
Thus the Exeter clergyman who penned this prayer celebrates Cecilia not
simply as a celestial benefactress but as a believer, like those in his
community, who sought to overcome the struggles of the *vita angelica*
here on earth and to earn a place in heaven for doing so.[117]

The need for Cecilia's help in meeting the challenges of the religious
life is most evident in an original private prayer found in a psalter written
in the first half of the eleventh century at the cathedral of Christ Church
in Canterbury.[118] This free-form devotional prayer, which is less
constrained by liturgical formula than the mass prayers examined above,
begins with generalized pleas for Cecilia's intercession on behalf of the
supplicant and concludes with petitions for the supplicant's bishop and
family. Its middle portion contains details from the *passio* and positions
Cecilia as an ideal intercessor and ascetic. Recalling her declaration that
Tiburtius is her 'kinsman' (line 180 [p. 182]), the petitioner prays for
Cecilia to intercede on his behalf and to make him a member of God's
family, and he recounts three episodes from the legend that show the effi-
cacy of her words. The remainder of the prayer's middle portion focuses

on the supplicant's identification with the saint as a cleric when he asks to become a new Cecilia—physically disciplined, devout, contemplative and divinely protected:

> O blessed Cecilia, virgin and martyr blessed by the Lord, by the grace of the love and fear of the Holy Spirit, give me, a sinner, a share in God's friendship and your spiritual love, just as you once won over your God with sighs and overpowered Almachius by the merits of your prayers. You incited Tiburtius and also Valerian, who were your partners in virginity, to martyrs' crowns. O holy and celebrated virgin Cecilia, I ask by your pious prayers and by the example of your chastity and your model that you cause me to mortify my body in this present life, and let me continually hold the gospel of Christ in my heart. Also, O pious mother Cecilia, by the power of God let me never cease from divine discourses and prayer by day or night. And help me, God's wretched one, to have as my friend an angel of God as the guardian and companion of my inner being who with the great zeal of God may watch over me in body and soul, and who inspires me in the commandments of God.[119]

As in the preface and benediction mentioned earlier, Cecilia's chief value as a model rests on those aspects of her behaviour most appropriate to a monk or cleric: mortification of the body, edification of the soul and contemplation of the divine, all of which the clergy pursued as part of a life of obedience lived out under the watchful care of God, his angels and St Cecilia. Unlike any other prayer to Cecilia that survives in Anglo-Saxon mass books, this one explicitly recognizes her role as spiritual mother, and the apostrophe to 'pious mother Cecilia' is the third of four maternal epithets in the prayer.[120] Cecilia's progeny, however, are not products of her chaste marriage with Valerian but rather of her spiritual union with Christ, whom the author refers to twice as Cecilia's 'bride-groom'.[121] Like Aldhelm before him, this writer styles her as *sponsa Christi* more in the mould of an unmarried virgin martyr than that of a celibate spouse. For the spiritual implications of Cecilia's earthly chaste marriage, we must look to Ælfric, and it is to him that we now turn.

Ælfric's Treatment of the Latin Legends in the *Lives of Saints*

Like other Anglo-Saxon authors, Ælfric understands these saints to be emblems of steadfastness and single-mindedness, but in redirecting their stories to the laity, he strives to make the lessons of the legends applicable to a wider audience.[122] For him, the saints' physical struggles against their adversaries symbolize every Christian's spiritual warfare against the devil, and their inviolable bodily and spiritual purity signifies the constancy all believers must possess if they are to merit eternal life. Ælfric never explicitly states that the legends are to be understood in this way; they are devotional texts, not exegetical sermons that explain how to interpret and apply a text to one's life. Nevertheless, his discussions of steadfastness, celibacy, and spiritual purity and productivity in other homilies help to explain why he used the saints' lives to promote asceticism and orthodoxy among the laity, and they clarify his intention to use such stories as inspiration for believers to keep their faith by steadfastly keeping pure their bodies and belief.

One sermon in particular drives home his point about the need for constancy in the Christian life: the *Memory of the Saints*, a sermon that almost certainly introduced the *Lives* when Ælfric originally issued it.[123] Here he makes clear that he expects his audience to take examples of virtuous behaviour from the collection's narratives so that they will remain faithful to Christian ideals and be found worthy of everlasting life.[124] The sermon begins with an overview of God's work in the lives of Old and New Testament figures, and of post-apostolic martyrs and confessors, all of whom Ælfric praises for their exemplary traits (David for meekness and mercy, Christ for humility and the martyrs for true belief). Having said at the sermon's outset that his audience 'may take good examples of how [patriarchs and saints] pleased God with their lives', he spends the remainder of the sermon enumerating the vices Christians should avoid and virtues they ought to practice should they hope to share in the everlasting life with Job, 'the steadfast thegn' who 'never desired to turn away from God's love', with Daniel, whom Ælfric lauds for his 'steadfast belief', and with John the Baptist, 'so steadfast a man of God' that Jesus declared him the greatest man born of a woman.[125]

In the sermon, Ælfric casts contemporary believers in the role of the saints of old and imagines them fending off the onslaughts of the devil, who ceaselessly considers 'how he may seduce Christians with vices and turn their minds to various sins'.[126] To emerge victorious from this spiritual warfare, believers must fix on virtue, obey Christ's commands and earn salvation by hard work. In return, God promises heavenly rest for those who remain 'steadfast until the everlasting life'.[127] This exhortation to constancy and the promise of eternal reward prompts the audience to associate their own struggles to be virtuous with the saints mentioned in the sermon and with the holy men and women included in the collection. Just as readers and listeners will have heard of Job, Daniel and John the Baptist, so too will they meet with the steadfastness of Agnes, Agatha, the Macabees, Edmund, Cecilia, and Chrysanthus and Daria.[128] Ælfric thus frames the legends as 'emblematic narratives', in which 'inner experience, either psychological or spiritual, is reflected by external events of the narrative'.[129] As such, the stories teach believers how to cleave to the eight virtues—moderation, chastity, generosity, patience, spiritual joy, steadfastness in a good work, true love for God and humility—in order to achieve the constancy that will win them an everlasting reward.[130]

Of the eight virtues listed above, the virgin spouses best personify chastity, and the wealth of associations the word *clænnyss* had for Ælfric indicates the range of lessons he could draw from the legends. The word can be defined as both 'chastity' and 'moral purity' (that is, 'freedom from sin'), and for Ælfric *clænnyss* is bodily and spiritual, individual and corporate, and as appropriate to the laity as to the clergy.[131] In the *Memory of the Saints*, his definition of the virtue of *clænnyss* —'that a layman keep himself free from adultery in proper marriage with rationality'—represents his shorthand for a couple's observance of periods of abstinence from sexual intercourse.[132] Obedient couples adopted celibacy temporarily during Lent, during fasts in Advent, Pentecost and mid September, and on festival Sundays and feast days celebrated by the Church at large. Since only procreative sex was lawful, couples were also expected to abstain during menstruation and from a woman's third month of pregnancy until forty days post partum. Uniquely, Ælfric requires couples to refrain permanently from intercourse once a woman reaches menopause. In the *Lives* he even idealizes a scenario in which a husband retires to the monastery after having fathered three sons with his wife and having lived chastely with her for thirty years.[133] Nor does he oppose marriages that begin and end in celibacy like those in the legends.[134] So whether in a mirror image or one imperfectly reflected, an audience of devout married laymen could identify their own virtuous behaviour with that of the celibate saints.

Ælfric recognized in the saints' chaste marriages the potential to offer his audience 'good examples' of their own celibate wedlock, which pious couples would have achieved when they obeyed the teaching that regulated intercourse within marriage. Reading the *Memory of the Saints* against *Julian and Basilissa* demonstrates how the legends provide a hagiographic context for these Ælfrician homiletics.[135] As mentioned earlier, Julian and Basilissa's virginal union ends the impasse between Julian's Christian parents, who want him to marry and have a son, and his own desire to remain a virgin for Christ. Christ's appearance to Julian with the command to marry and remain a virgin, and the divine spectacle in praise of the couple's chaste marriage override the biblical injunction to be fruitful and multiply. In narrating this episode, Ælfric, by contrast, ignores the parents' biblical challenge and does not mention their desire for a grandchild; his father and kinsmen merely ask him to marry.[136] By omitting the biblical challenge, the chaste marriage in Ælfric's account does not represent a solution to conflicting Christian beliefs but rather an extension of Christ's own teachings. Since Julian is asked only to marry, Ælfric makes him innocent of deceptiveness, a charge to which he is open in the *passio* when he agrees to fulfil his parents' wish despite his intention to remain celibate. By omitting the secrecy that shrouds the marriage, Ælfric also strips away any hint of heterodoxy or divisiveness from a union that runs counter to biblical precedents and medieval mores. He thus imagines in the hagiography a scenario he does not recommend in a homily: chaste marriage is holy and need not be secretly undertaken due to fear of parental disapproval or reprisal.

At the same time as Ælfric takes into consideration more literal applications of the saintly model, he also taps into the figurative connotations of *clænnyss*, equating 'moral purity' with orthodox belief and associating it with spiritual productivity. In the homilies he normally discusses the layman's spiritual virginity in terms of the patristic allegory by which Christ, the chaste bridegroom, weds an ever-virginal Church (composed of all believers) that continually engenders new Christians.[137] In the *Nativity of Mary*, for example, the Church 'always remains steadfast in God's belief and does not wish to turn away from the Saviour's belief to any paganism, from her bridegroom to shameful idol-worship or witchcraft or sorcery, (not away) from her Lord to any heresy whatsoever' and subsequently 'gives birth' when new members believe and are baptized into the faith.[138]

In the legends of the virgin spouses, the need for constancy explains why Ælfric uses verbs of turning, enticing, inclining and alluring to link episodes otherwise unconnected in the Latin texts and thereby to draw attention to the moral purity of the saints. A good example of such verbal concatenation is found in Ælfric's *Chrysanthus and Daria*.[139] Early on Chrysanthus decides 'to turn' (*cyrran*, line 13 [p. 86]) from darkness to light and to cleave to the Scriptures he has just read. His conversion prompts his father to imprison him, but when this punishment fails to persuade his son to renounce Christianity, Polemius hears from friends how 'to entice' (*geweman*, line 29) his son from Christ. He settles on five beautiful virgins whom he orders 'to turn' (*awendan*, line 37) Chrysanthus's thoughts from Christ and threatens to kill them should they not 'turn' (*bigan*, line 38) the young man's mind. When they fail to do so, Daria is sent 'to entice' (*geweman*, line 60) Chrysanthus from Christ but after hearing his arguments 'turns' (*gewendan*, line 85) instead to God.

Like the Church, the couple at once become 'steadfast' (*anræd*, line 86) in bodily and spiritual purity, and encourage others to follow suit. On account of their good example, many people soon 'turned' (*gebigan*, line 90) from devil worship 'to faith in Christ and to a chaste (or morally pure) life' (line 91). Later, a group of soldiers commanded by a tribune who had urged Chrysanthus 'to turn' (*awende*, line 125) from God all go 'steadfastly' (*anrædlice*, line 161) to their deaths having been led to faith by the saint. Repetition of this sort transforms otherwise routine refusals to yield to temptation, to sacrifice to the gods or to abjure Christianity into dramatic testimonials of believers' abilities to withstand pressure to disobey or disregard the tenets of their faith. Yet again the virgin spouses represent the Church that Ælfric describes in his sermons as a Christian body united in a 'virginity of belief, which honours one true God and does not wish adulterously to turn to false idolatry'.[140]

As is true for the Church, the constancy of the believer is not to be found exclusively in a virginity of belief but also in the engendering of spiritual offspring, and Ælfric adds references to the saints' teaching and exhortation that suggest he sees their conversionary activity as an expression of the Church's fecundity. Whereas the Church gives birth when new members are baptized into her fellowship of belief, individual Christians, in Ælfric's thinking, bear spiritual fruit when they instruct others in the faith. This instruction might take the form of teaching one's child or godchild the Lord's Prayer or Creed, which he says all believers must know, or the doctrines of the Trinity and bodily resurrection, which godparents would affirm at the baptism.[141] Teaching another adult, a clerical role that Ælfric unexpectedly assigns to lay folk, entails exhorting others to good deeds by one's own exemplary life and explaining to others the spiritual truths that God has revealed to oneself.[142]

In *Cecilia and Valerian*, for example, Ælfric forges links between teaching and spiritual procreation.[143] Whereas Pope Urban is responsible for teaching Valerian the rudiments of Christianity in the *passio*, in Ælfric's account it is Cecilia who 'instructed the young man for a long time until he believed in the living God and went to the pope', who then also 'taught him his faith' (lines 34–35 [p. 72] and 49 [p. 74], respectively). The significance of this addition becomes clear when Ælfric replaces a monetary metaphor with one of childbearing when Valerian begs Cecilia's guardian angel that his brother Tiburtius be saved too. In the Latin text, the angel promises Valerian that 'just as the Lord *redeemed* you through his servant Cecilia, so will he *redeem* your brother through you, and you will attain the palm of martyrdom together with him' (lines 136–38 [p. 180]). Ælfric prefers instead a metaphor of procreation and makes teaching a central element in the process of spiritual generation. His angel tells Valerian, 'your brother Tiburtius will be *born to everlasting life* through you, just as you believed in God *through Cecilia's instruction*, and you two, both you and your brother, shall be martyred together' (lines 67–69 [p. 74], my italics). Ælfric's reformulation thus recasts Cecilia's earlier conversion of Valerian as spiritual childbearing. It also provides a filter for reading in the same light subsequent moments when the saints' teaching and exhortation result in conversion: as Cecilia begot Valerian, so the two together beget Tiburtius; Tiburtius and Valerian beget Maximus, their torturer; Maximus begets the onlookers who convert when he testifies that he saw the martyred brothers' souls ascend to heaven; and the cycle returns to Cecilia, who converts another 400 pagans and continues to instruct the faithful in the three days between her botched beheading and death. Such is the process by which the virgin spouses and their spiritual offspring symbolize the ever-expanding Church at work in the world.

While the laity played a crucial role in the expansion of the universal Church for Ælfric, the bulk of the work fell to priests whom he charges with 'begett[ing] to God the children which laymen have begotten to this world', since the clergy is responsible for disseminating the orthodox doctrines English Christians would promote among their families and friends.[144] Just as ideal priests 'through their teaching and Christianity may acquire lay folk for God', so too do laymen who put into practice what their priests have taught 'acquire for God another person or more' if they too 'teach properly'.[145] Given this interdependency, Ælfric is particularly concerned about the fitness of the clergy who minister to the laity. They must not be unlearned, lazy or otherwise employed. They cannot be drunkards, flashy dressers, strife mongers, warriors or hunters. Above all, they must be chaste, married or not.[146]

Much to Ælfric's chagrin, marriage among the secular clergy was common in England in his day, as it had been since the late ninth century and would be until the turn of the twelfth, and a great number of Christians in the tenth century regularly witnessed married priests preaching, baptising, absolving, administering Communion, collecting tithes, visiting their sick and burying their dead.[147] However familiar clerical marriage might have been, Ælfric detested the practice. He found it offensive that a sexually active man would conduct mass and, at his most strident, insists that married priests divorce their wives.[148] Nor did he like it that they trained up their biological sons as future priests to inherit their fathers' endowments.[149] Yet the fact of the matter was that many believers had and would continue to receive their pastoral care from priestly husbands and fathers rather than reformed monks of Ælfric's ilk.

Because the tenth century in England was, as one scholar observes, 'a time of competing pastoral models', Ælfric uses the legends of the virgin spouses as part of his strategy to gain a competitive advantage for his brand of pastoral care.[150] Thus his decision to include in the *Lives* stories that promote his trademark asceticism and orthodoxy may represent an effort to solidify the support of his patrons (and that of their like-minded relatives and friends) for a monastic clergy at the expense of local, married or otherwise non-Reform priests.[151] The competition must have been stiff. Not fifteen miles away from his newly founded abbey, unre-formed secular clergymen staffed the episcopal cathedral at Sherborne until 998, nine years after Ælfric arrived at Cerne Abbas. Closer by were at least three, maybe as many as five, minsters and perhaps two smaller local churches served by priests who more likely than not would have been married. It could not have seemed encouraging to a man educated by bishop Æthelwold, the one principal reformer who ousted the unreformed clergy from his cathedral, to have found himself transferred from a monastic minster in urban Winchester to rural Dorset where, among nine possible local ecclesiastical establishments responsible for delivering pastoral care to the laity, only the abbey itself was certain to have been free of married priests.[152]

If we are to judge by Ælfric's repeated condemnations of clerical marriage, he remained undaunted in the face of these poor odds and seldom lost an opportunity to promote a reformed, monastic, celibate priesthood.[153] The stakes were material—whether dues, tithes, donations or bequests—but they also included people's ideological loyalties and, most crucially for Ælfric, their spiritual welfare.[154] If, as he says in a sermon in the *Lives*, Christ 'chose the pure for his pure service' and 'desires to have those that serve him in chastity' administer Communion, then loyalty to those who lived with a woman, the 'perverse' as Ælfric calls them, would have been ill-advised.[155]

When seen in the light of Ælfric's animus for unchaste, unreformed clergy, the legends of the virgin spouses advance a model of sanctity that tacitly undermines the familiar figure of the married clergyman and creates points of contact with a new type of priest whose customs would have been less widespread. On the one hand, the stories make available to the laity an asceticism and orthodoxy that would have rendered married priests undistinguishable from pious laymen in their manner of life (the priests would have been no more chaste than the observant layman), their priorities (they too had families to feed) and in one of their primary pastoral responsibilities (acquiring others for God).[156] If the old saw about familiarity and contempt held true in Anglo-Saxon England, this levelling between pious laymen and their spiritual advisers would have undercut the married priests' authority much in the same way Ælfric's link between a priest's chastity and an efficacious Communion does. On the other hand, by promoting celibacy and constancy, he inflects the legends with a monkishness that allows laymen to see themselves joined in the common pursuit of *clænnyss* with their monastic counterparts. Stories featuring spiritual fruitfulness call attention to the shared vision of a Church held by faithful Christians and their learned, virginal priests, who are able to instruct and care for their spiritual children rather than be distracted by their own biological ones.

Overemphasis on the personal and political desires that shaped Ælfric's vision of a unified clergy and laity may unduly minimize his genuine pastoral concerns for his flock, which would have included repentant (and thus chaste) married priests. He did not merely set his sights on the success of Cerne Abbas where he was a monk, or Eynsham, where he was abbot, or even on the Reform per se. Rather, by means of the

Reform's ideals and reformed clergymen like himself, he believed that England could stave off the depredations of the Vikings and that the English church could survive the devil's onslaughts.[157] Any chance of success, however, rested on observant laymen and conscientious clerics preserving their constancy in *clænnyss*, just as Julian and Basilissa, Cecilia and Valerian, and Chrysanthus and Daria had.[158]

At times, Ælfric can appear pessimistic about the prospect of winning either war. In a sermon in the *Lives*, he compares the security of bygone days 'when this island remained at peace, the monasteries were held in honour and the ordinary people were watchful against their enemies' to the uncertainty of his own age, asking 'What was to happen then afterwards when one destroyed the monasteries and had scorn for the worshippers of God but that pestilence and hunger came to us and afterward the heathen army had scorn for us?'[159] Seen in the light of the *Memory of the Saints* and his treatments of the virgin spouses, his remedy does not come as a surprise: having reminded his audience of God's promise of prosperity and peace for the obedient, and of hunger and devastation for the disobedient, Ælfric declares that 'we ought to worship God with true steadfastness'.[160]

Ælfric found comfort in his own unwavering belief in the unchanging nature of God and the unshakable victory of Christ over the devil in the Resurrection, and these certainties enable him in the *Memory of the Saints* to urge Christians living 'now in our days, in the end of the world' into spiritual battle with the promise of victory given to saints of old.[161] This confidence also explains why in the lines from *Chrysanthus and Daria* that were originally to have been the last of the collection he comforts his flock with the same guarantee of triumph for those Christians who will be alive at the very end of the world.[162] Even as he contemplates those dark days when Antichrist arrives and the saints cannot best the devil's deceptions with miracles of their own, his optimism breaks through. Yet again, the saints of God 'will be preserved through the Saviour's power if they preserve their faith until the end' (lines 247–48 [p. 98]). In this way, believers in Ælfric's day who lived out their faith steadfast in purity of body and belief could be certain that like the virgin saints before them and the saints of the tribulation after, they too would 'depart in *clænnyss* from this world to glory to live with Christ' (lines 226–27 [p. 96]).

The Language of the Old English Texts

To a great degree, the three Old English texts edited from London, British Library, Cotton MS Julius E. vii (J), an early eleventh-century copy of the *Lives of Saints* (plus some non-Ælfrician material), exhibit standard features of Late West Saxon, 'the carefully regularized form of written Old English that was adopted as standard in the later tenth century and cultivated throughout England until the end of the Anglo-Saxon period and beyond'.[163] Some of the non-standard forms mentioned below (and allowed to stand in the editions) reflect the practice of a scribe working in southern England 'who clearly had not been trained by someone thoroughly imbued with Ælfric's ideas of writing correct English, and who is noted for quite a number of orthographic peculiarities'.[164] Other idiosyncratic forms, occurring in *Julian and Basilissa*, represent corrections entered in the manuscript during 'an attempt to bring it up to date' after 1032, when a new church Cnut ordered to be built at Bury St Edmunds, where the manuscript may have originated, was finished.[165] Exceptions to the standard features are pointed out below, though the account is not intended to be exhaustive, and all examples can be located in the texts by consulting the Glossary, where a key to the abbreviations used below is also found.

Non-standard features in the inflexions of nouns include:

1. for the standard dative plural ending ~*um* for strong and weak nouns, ~*an* and ~*on* infrequently occur: *e.g.*, *digelan* (d.p.nt.), *fyþerhaman* (d.p.m.), and *maþon* (d.p.m.).
2. for the standard nominative plural ending ~*as* for strong masculine nouns, ~*es* infrequently occurs: *e.g.*, *beames* and *godes*;
3. for the standard nominative or accusative plural ending ~*u* for strong neuter nouns, ~*a* and ~*e* occasionally occur: *e.g.*, *deofla* (n.p.), *heafda* (a.p.), *mædena* (a.p.), *wita* (n./a.p.), and *mædene* (n./a.p.);
4. in one instance, the accusative plural form of a strong neuter noun, which would normally not have an ending, exhibits a 'parasite' *e*: *tacne*[166];
5. for the standard ending ~*e* in the singular accusative and dative cases of strong feminine nouns, ~*a* occasionally occurs: *e.g.*, *mildsunga* (a.), *heofunga* (d.), *leafa* (d.), *leasunga* (d.), *smyltinga* (d.) and *tida* (d.).

Non-standard features in the inflexions of adjectives include:

1. for the standard genitive plural ending ~*ra* for strong adjectives, ~*re* occurs infrequently: *e.g.*, *þinre* (f.) and *hyre* (m.). Similarly, there is confusion in the genitive plural of the demonstrative pronoun *se*: *e.g.*, *þære* (m.);
2. for the standard nominative plural ending ~*e* for a strong masculine adjective, ~*a* occurs occasionally: *e.g.*, *cristena*, *sylfa* and *unmildheorta*;
3. in one instance, the standard dative singular ending ~*re* for a strong feminine adjective is written ~*ra*: *liþra*;

4. for the standard dative plural ending ~*um* for weak adjectives, ~*an* appears occasionally: *e.g.*, *deadan* (m.), *dædan* (f.), *leofan* (m.) and *leofstan* (m.);
5. in one instance, the standard nominative singular ending ~*a* for a masculine adjective declined weak appears as ~*e*: *edcudode*;
6. the substitution of ~*a* for ~*e* also occurs once in the nominative singular of a feminine adjective declined weak: *beorhta*;
7. the ending ~*en* appears once for ~*an* in the accusative singular of a masculine adjective declined weak: *Christensen*; and
8. for the standard *agenne* (a.s.m. of *agen* 'own'), *agenre*, a form attested in the *Lives* and other Old English texts (see the entry for *agen* in the *Dictionary of Old English* [cited in n. 131]), appears once.

Non-standard features in the inflexions of verbs include:

1. for the standard ending ~*an* for infinitives, ~*on* appears at least three times: *beaton*, *forlæton*, and *setton*.
2. for the standard preterite indicative plural ending ~*on*, ~*an* occurs frequently: *e.g.*, *andweardan*, *arærdan*, *gebrohtan*, *coman*, *lyfedan*, *gelyfdan*, *næran*, *oncneowan*, *gesettan*, *stodan*, *wæran*, *woldan* and *gewytan*;
3. ~*en* for the preterite indicative plural occurs infrequently: *begeaten* and *eoden*;
4. the standard present subjunctive singular ending ~*e* occurs throughout with one exception: *forleosa*;
5. the standard preterite subjunctive plural ending ~*en* appears uniformly as ~*on* with two exceptions: *gehælan* and *healdan*;
6. occasionally, the standard present and preterite subjunctive plural ending ~*en* appears as ~*e* because 'when a pronoun of the 1st or 2nd person follows, the plural endings ~*aþ*, ~*on*, ~*en* can be reduced to ~*e*'[167]: *e.g. cume*, *mage*, *mihte*, *sceole*, *þurfe* and *wille*;
7. declensions of class 2 weak verbs follow the standard paradigm with few exceptions: *e.g. geopenade* (pret.ind.3s.) for the standard *geopenode*; and
8. present participles and inflected infinitives of class 2 weak verbs more often than not exhibit a ~*g*~ (respectively, ~*igende* and ~*igenne*), which is not typical of Late West Saxon usage[168]: *e.g.*, *arwurþigende*, *clipigende*, *wuldrigende* and *wunigende*, but *glitiende* and *þanciende*; *bedydrigenne*, *bodigenne*, *dweligenne*, *edcucigenne* and *wunigenne*, but *axienne*, *fullienne* and *þrowienne*.

Non-inflectional orthographical-phonological features include:

1. the frequent appearance of *æ* for *e*: *e.g.*, *astræhtum*, *awræccan*,

æhtnysse, ænde, ængel, ænglas, cwællere, cwæþ, cwæþende, dædan, dræhton, fæla, fæþera, gæra, mærcode, ræadaþ, slæge, gespræcan, spræce, gespræce, spræcst, geswæncte, þæs and *wæarþ*[169];

2. the substitution of ~*æ* for the inflexional ending ~*a* in one instance: *masspreostæ* (d.s.m.)[170];

3. the occasional appearance of *e* for *æ*: *e.g., adwesce, clennysse, efter, femnan, forbernan, gefretwod, screfe* and *welhreow*[171];

4. the sporadic appearance of *a* for *æ*: *e.g., baþe, maran, slape* and *swarum*[172];

5. two examples wherein an initial *h* is dropped: *raþe* for *hraþe* and *reppan* for *hreppan*[173]; and

6. the frequent but not exclusive use of *wur~* for the earlier *weor~* and *wyr~*.[174]

Ælfric's Latin Sources

Julian and Basilissa

The Latin text of the *Passio Sanctorum Martyrum Iuliani et Basilissae* that Ælfric used represents a distinct recension of the most common version of the legend, which is numbered 4529 in the *Biblioteca Hagiographica Latina (BHL)*, a comprehensive alphabetical list of some 9,000 saints whose lives are written in Latin.[175] Rather, he worked from a version of the *passio* numbered *BHL* 4532, an abridgement of *BHL* 4529 of almost 2,100 words. A text of the shorter version, edited here for the first time, survives in a well-known late eleventh-century English manuscript, London, British Library, Cotton Nero E. i, pt i, ff. 75ᵛ–85ʳ (s.xi³/⁴) [N].[176] Cotton Nero E. i, pts i and ii, and Cambridge, Corpus Christi College 9 (s.xiq.2/xiᵐᵉᵈ) preserve a copy of the so-called 'Cotton-Corpus Legendary' ('Cotton-Corpus'), a *hypothetical*, ninth-century Frankish collection of approximately 160 saints' lives that, in certain cases, preserves the particular form of Ælfric's immediate source.[177]

Patrick Zettel, who first identified the importance of 'Cotton-Corpus' to students of Ælfric, observed that the Cotton Nero text of *Julian and Basilissa* was very like that from which Ælfric worked, even though the *passio* was not an exact match.[178] My study of thirty-two English and Continental manuscripts of *BHL* 4532 confirms Zettel's observation.[179] The existence of at least four other copies (one English, three Continental) that provide equally valuable witnesses to the tradition Ælfric knew, however, argues against claims of distinctiveness for N.[180] No manuscript that I have seen accounts fully for the six instances Zettel identifies when Ælfric's version diverges from N.[181] Because each of the divergences are represented in the most common version of the *passio*, it seems likely that Ælfric worked from a hybrid of *BHL* 4529 and 4532 that has yet to be identified.[182]

Cecilia and Valerian

Nearly 180 copies of the *Passio Sanctae Caeciliae* (*BHL* 1495) have been identified, and this large number seems to have discouraged anyone from grouping the manuscripts into families and dividing them further into branches.[183] There are three 'Cotton-Corpus' copies: (1) CCCC 9, pp. 323–36 [C]; (2) Oxford, Bodleian Library, Bodley 354, ff. 108^r–16^v (s.xii^2); and (3) Hereford, Cathedral Library, P.VII.6, ff. 73^v–80^r (s.xii^2) [H]. The Bodley manuscript and H 'represent the "Cotton-Corpus" collection at a more advanced stage of development' than the eleventh-century C, and Zettel 'regards the Hereford manuscript . . . as textually the closest witness to Ælfric's sources'.[184] He observes that the Cecilia legend in H contains 'a few more precise parallels' than C.[185] A comparison of H with C and over 100 Continental manuscripts suggests, however, that H may actually belong to a textual tradition distinct from C. In fact, Ælfric seems to have worked from a version of *BHL* 1495 that was known in Italy in the late ninth or early tenth century, in Flanders in the eleventh century, and in France and England (at Hereford) in the twelfth, but not at Worcester where 'Cotton-Corpus' was copied in the third quarter of the eleventh century.[186]

One reading from H noted by Zettel proves especially useful for identifying manuscripts that belong to the recension of the legend Ælfric used.[187] When Ælfric reports Cecilia's botched beheading, he notes that the executioner leaves Cecilia for dead after striking her three times 'because the senators had said that no executioner ought to strike four times when he struck a guilty person' [lines 256–57 (p. 84)]). C has no parallel for this comment. H, by contrast, has 'And as it was then legally established that one could not receive a fourth stroke when being beheaded, the savage butcher left her half-dead' [lines 657–59, (p. 214)]). Zettel does not explain why C does not have this significant variant, but presumably he would attribute its absence to inaccurate copying of the hypothetical 'Cotton-Corpus'. That at least forty other copies of the *passio* in Continental manuscripts preserve this reading, however, raises the possibility that 'Cotton-Corpus' copies in H and C preserve distinct textual traditions.

Continental copies of the *passio* that resemble H can, in fact, account for all the readings Zettel finds in H but not in C, and in C but not in H.[188] Even though H imperfectly preserves the textual tradition that underlies Ælfric's immediate source, this branch of that tradition (though not one single exemplar) can account fully for the type of text Ælfric must have used. Because correspondences between H and other manuscripts of this family indicate that H belongs to a Continental tradition related to 'Cotton-Corpus' but unknown at Worcester, again the possibility remains open that Ælfric's exact source may yet be discovered.[189]

Chrysanthus and Daria

Several manuscripts of the *Passio Sanctorum Chrysanthi et Dariae* (*BHL* 1787) that I have examined correspond slightly more closely to Ælfric's immediate source than 'Cotton-Corpus' copies in CCCC9, pp. 379–89 [C]; Bodley 354, ff. 136ʳ–43ʳ; and Hereford P.VII.6, ff. 119ʳ–24ᵛ [H], which differs only slightly from C and the Bodley copy. None, however, is identical to Ælfric's text. The earliest of these three copies survives in a tenth-century manuscript from the monastery of St Rémy, Reims (Paris, Bibliothèque Nationale, Latin MS 13764, ff. 118ᵛ–37ʳ [P]), an area with strong ties to Anglo-Saxon England.[190] P is edited and translated because not only is it contemporary with Ælfric, but it also preserves a set of texts that suggest an exemplar from a site with a special interests in Chrysanthus and Daria.[191]

The following three examples demonstrate that P contains readings closer to Ælfric's immediate source than either C or H. First, in Ælfric's version, a friend of Chrysanthus's father opines that the boy has learned sorcery from the Christians 'and ofercom *mid þam* þa bylewitan mædene' ('and had *at that* overcome the simple-minded virgins' [line 54 (p. 88)]). Both C and H lack the adverb that would correspond to Ælfric's *mid þæm*. In P, by contrast, the friend explains, 'et *ideo* ... præualuit' ('and *for that reason* . . . he prevailed' [line 139 (p. 226)]). Second, only P has the reflexive pronoun *ipse* that accounts for Ælfric's *sylf* when he writes about Claudius that 'he *sylf* com þærto' ('he himself came to that place' [lines 119–20 (p. 92)]) to see the miraculous light suffusing Chrysanthus's prison cell. C and H have only 'veniens ad locum' ('he came to the place', whereas P reports that 'ipse ueniens ad locum' ('he himself came to the place' [line 326 (p. 240)]). And third, towards the end of the legend, Ælfric reports that the emperor ordered 'læden *buta* þa halgan *togædere* to anum sandpytte' ('*both* the saints to be led *together* to a sandpit' [lines 223–24 (p. 96)]), phrasing that reflects Numerian's command in P that they be buried 'utrosque simul' ('both together' [line 463 (p. 248)]) rather than simply *simul* ('together'), as C and H report. Though minute, the distinctions remind us that Ælfric's immediate source belonged to a wider European textual tradition rather than to a particularly English one.

At other times, P accounts for readings found in H but not in C, or one found in C but not in H. In this way, P furnishes a more complete idea of the tradition available to Ælfric than either 'Cotton-Corpus' text can. In the following example, P agrees with H but not C. In C, Claudius tells Chrysanthus that 'Deus tuus uerus est' ('Your God is true'). In P and H, however, Claudius confesses to Chrysanthus that 'Deus tuus Deus uerus est' ('Your God is the true God' [line 364 (p. 242)]), phrasing that corresponds precisely to Ælfric's 'þin God is soð God' (line 142 [p. 92]).[192] In a second example, P agrees with C against H: in the same episode of the legend, Claudius desires to worship the God, 'þe his *biggengan* macaþ swa mihtige on gewinne' ('who makes his *worshippers* so powerful in a conflict' [line 140 (p. 92)]). Ælfric's *biggengan* translates *cultores*, the reading found in C and P (line 359 [p. 242]) but not in H, which reports Claudius's desire to worship the God, 'who makes his *victors* (*uictores*) victorious in every battle.'

This second example cautions against too great a reliance on P. While *cultores* corresponds with *biggengan*, P and C's subjunctive verbs in the relative clause modifying God, 'qui cultores suos in omni *faciat* pugna uincentes' ('who *may make* his worshippers victorious in every battle'), do not match Ælfric's indicative one 'þe his biggengan *macaþ* swa mihtige on gewinne' ('who *makes* his worshippers so powerful in a conflict'). Despite reading *uictores*, H has the indicative *facit*, which corresponds exactly to Ælfric's chosen tense. Ælfric is certainly justified in translating the Latin subjunctive with an indicative Old English verb, but he may, in fact, have worked from a text that read 'qui *cultores* suos *facit* in omni pugna uincentes'.[193] These discrepancies raise important questions about Ælfric's preferences as a translator and his immediate source. The answers are beyond the scope of the present study, but the queries themselves alert us to the pertinence of seemingly small distinctions when working with copies of a legend whose textual tradition is so relatively stable.

Notes

1 *Ælfric's Lives of Saints* (cited as *LS*), ed. and trans. W.W. Skeat, 2 vols in 4 parts, EETS OS 76, 82, 94, 114 (London, 1881–1900; repr. as 2 vols, London, 1966). For a list of Ælfric's works see A. Kleist, 'Ælfric's Corpus: A Conspectus', *Florilegium* 18 (2001), 113–61, and 'The Ælfric Canon' in *Homilies of Ælfric: A Supplementary Collection* (cited as *SH*), ed. J.C. Pope, EETS OS, 259–60 (London, 1967–68), 1:136–45. An introduction to Ælfric's life and work is J. Hurt, *Ælfric* (New York, 1972). For convenience, secondary references occurring more than ten notes after a previous mention direct readers to initial citations.

2 For an overview of Ælfric's works in the context of late Anglo-Saxon literature, see S. Greenfield and D. Calder, *A New Critical History of Old English Literature* (New York, 1986), pp. 68–106, at p. 76.

3 On the dating of Ælfric's works, see P. Clemoes, 'The Chronology of Ælfric's Works' in *The Anglo-Saxons*, ed. P. Clemoes (London, 1959), pp. 212–47.

4 For Æthelweard and Æthelmær see S. Keynes, *The Diplomas of King Æthelred 'The Unready', 978–1016* (Cambridge, 1980), pp. 191–92; B. Yorke, 'Æthelmær, the Foundation of the Abbey at Cerne and the Politics of the Tenth Century' in *Cerne Abbey Millennium Lectures*, ed. K. Barker (Cerne Abbey, 1988), pp. 15–26, at pp. 15–20; *Prosopography of Anglo-Saxon England* at <http://eagle.cch.kcl.ac.uk:8080/pase/index.jsp>, accessed January 2006; and Patrick Wormald, 'Æthelweard (d. 998?)', *Oxford Dictionary of National Biography* (Oxford, 2004) at <http://www.oxforddnb.com/view/article/8918>, accessed August 2006.

5 See, Yorke, 'Æthelmær', pp. 19–20, and C. Jones, *Ælfric's Letter to the Monks of Eynsham* (Cambridge, 1998), pp. 13–15.

6 Editions of the two sets are: *Ælfric's Catholic Homilies: The First Series* [cited as *CH* I], ed. P. Clemoes, EETS SS 17 (Oxford, 1997) and *Ælfric's Catholic Homilies: The Second Series* [cited as *CH* II], ed. M. Godden, EETS SS 5 (Oxford, 1979). The sermons are translated in *The*

Homilies of the Anglo-Saxon Church, ed. and trans. B. Thorpe, 2 vols (London, 1844–46). On the audiences and dating of the *Catholic Homilies*, see *Ælfric's Catholic Homilies. Introduction, Commentary, and Glossary* [cited as *Commentary*], ed. M. Godden, EETS SS 18 (Oxford, 2000), pp. xxi–xxxvi.

7 Æthelweard appears to have received his own copy of the First Series of homilies prior to the set being circulated more widely (*Commentary*, p. 7, note on line 134 of *CH* I.OE Preface [p. 177]).

8 The most complete surviving copy of the *Lives of Saints*, and that which Skeat edits, is found in London, British Library, Cotton Julius E. vii. Julius E. vii does not represent the collection as Ælfric originally issued it, for it contains four non-Ælfrician lives (*LS* I.23 [pp. 488–541] and II.23 [pp. 2–53], 30 [pp. 190–219] and 33 [pp. 334–55]). Skeat's edition makes it difficult to grasp the didactic scope of the collection as a whole because he chose not to print three texts Ælfric appears to have appended to the *Lives* when he first issued it: *Interrogationes Sigeuulfi in Genesin* (Sigewulf's Questions about Genesis), *De falsis diis* (On False Gods) and *De duodecim abusiuis* (On Twelve Vices). Cotton Julius E. vii, however, contains a complete copy of the *Interrogationes*, part of *De falsis diis*, and none of *De duodecim abusiuis*. To understand Ælfric's didactic aims most fully, it is crucial to read the saints' lives and homilies alongside these texts. Editions of the three texts are, respectively: (1) *Interrogationes Sigeuulfi* = 'A Critical Edition of Ælfric's Translation of Alcuin's *Interrogationes Sigwulfi Presbiteri* and of the Related Texts *De Creatore et Creatura* and *De Sex Etatibus Huius Seculi*', ed. W. Stoneman (unpublished doctoral dissertation, University of Toronto, 1982), pp. 78–288; more accessible is G. Maclean, 'Ælfric's Version of *Alcuini Interrogationes Sigeuulfi in Genesin*', *Anglia* 6 (1883), 425–73 and *Anglia* 7 (1884), 1–59; (2) *De falsis diis* = *SH* II.21 [pp. 667–724]; (3) and *De duodecim abusiuis* = in *Old English Homilies, First Series*, ed. and trans. R. Morris, EETS OS 29 and 34 (London, 1867–68; repr. as 1 vol. Woodbridge, 1998), pp. 107 [line 22]- 119 [line 20]. On the contents of the *Lives* as Ælfric originally issued it, see J. Hill, 'The Dissemination of Ælfric's *Lives of Saints*' in *Holy Men and Holy Women: Old English Prose Saints' Lives and Their Contexts*, ed. P. Szarmach (Albany, 1996), pp. 235–59, at p. 237.

9 *LS* I.Latin Preface, lines 16–17 (p. 2). On the lack of any organizing principle of the saints' legends in the *Catholic Homilies*, see Godden, *Commentary*, pp. xxviii–xxix.

10 *LS* I.Latin Preface, lines 5–9 (p. 2). An exception in the *Catholic Homilies* is the feast day of SS Alexander, Eventius and Theodolus (*CH* II.18b) whose festival only monks would have celebrated (Godden, *Commentary*, p. xxvi).

11 On the possible audiences for the *Lives of Saints*, lay and clerical alike, see J. Wilcox, 'The Audience of Ælfric's *Lives of Saints* and the Face of Cotton Caligula A. xiv, fols. 93–130' in *Beatus vir: Studies in Anglo-Saxon and Old Norse Manuscripts in Memory of Phillip Pulsiano*, eds K. Wolf and A.N. Doane (Tempe, AZ: Arizona Center for Medieval and Renaissance Studies, 2006), pp. 228–63. Only five legends feature a female saint as the sole protagonist (Eugenia, Agnes, Agatha, Lucy and Æthelthryth); legends of lay saints outnumber those of ecclesiastical figures sixteen to ten.

12 Of the six churchmen, five are bishops (Basil, Swithun, Apollinaris, Denis, and Martin), and one is an abbot (Maurus). The four legends of soldier saints are Sebastian, the Forty Soldiers, George and St Maurice and his Companions (The Theban Legion), and the four female virgin martyrs are Eugenia, Agnes, Agatha and Lucy. The Persian kings, Abdon and Sennes, are treated in a single legend while two others feature the English kings, Oswald and Edmund. Single examples include the apostle Thomas, Mark the Evangelist, Britain's first martyr Alban, England's own virgin spouse, Æthelthryth, whose husbands were not, however, considered saints, and legends commemorating the feasts of the Exaltation of the Cross (a commemoration of the return of the Holy Cross to Jerusalem from Persia) and of the Chair of Peter (a celebration of the day the apostle assumed the office of bishop in Rome).

13 Æthelweard had at least one son, Æthelmær, who also had at least one son (Æthelweard) and one daughter (who is unnamed in the sources) (Yorke, 'Æthelmær', pp. 20 and 26, where there is a family tree). On the place of the female virgin martyrs in Ælfric's canon, see C. Cubitt, 'Virginity and Misogyny in Tenth- and Eleventh-Century England', *Gender and History* 12 (2000), 1–32. P. Thompson is completing a study of these saints.

14 T. Hill, '*Imago Dei*: Genre, Symbolism, and Anglo-Saxon Hagiography' in *Holy Men and Holy Women*, ed. Szarmach, pp. 35–50, at p. 36. Because Cecilia and Valerian are commemorated on separate feast days and because Cecilia is the preeminent saint, the story of the couple's marriage and martyrdoms circulates throughout the Middle Ages as *The Passio of Saint Cecilia the Virgin*, as is seen in the titles of the texts edited and translated below. However, to draw attention to the fact that the legend belongs to the subgenre of hagiography of chaste marriage and as a reminder why Ælfric prefers stories of virgin spouses, I refer to the legend throughout the Introduction as *Cecilia and Valerian*.

15 *Ibid.*, pp. 36–37 and 39, respectively.

16 The Latin *passio* is cited twice in *The Rule of the Master*, 'a veritable rule of life encompassing the entire existence, material and spiritual, of the monastic community and the individuals within it' that was written in the first quarter of the sixth century somewhere southeast of Rome by an anonymous author (*The Rule of the Master* [ed. by A. de Vogüé as *La Règle du Maître* (Paris, 1964)] and trans. L. Eberle and C. Philippi [Kalamazoo, 1977], pp. 7 [quotation] and 78–79 [dating and origin]). The citations occur, respectively, in ch. 90, verse 47 (p. 263) and ch. 91, verse 4 (p. 267). For information on the composition and dating of each of the legends and the relevant literature, see E.G. Whatley's entries for the saints in 'Acta Sanctorum' in *Sources of Anglo-Saxon Literary Culture*, vol. 1, ed. F. Biggs, et al. (Kalamazoo, 2001), 22–486.

17 On the historical evidence for Chrysanthus and Daria, see P. Allard, 'Chrysanthe et Daria (Saints)' in *Dictionnaire d'archéologie chrétienne et de liturgie*, eds F. Cabrol and H. Leclercq, 15 vols (Paris, 1907–53) 3, part 1: cols 1560–68. T. Connolly makes this point about Cecilia in *Mourning into Joy: Music, Raphael, and Saint Cecilia* (New Haven, 1994), pp. 23–38, at p. 25.

18 Hill, '*Imago Dei*', p. 37.

19 The readings and chants (responsories) of the Night Office would have continued the observance of the 'vigil' of a saint's feast day, during which the liturgical offices proper to the feast were substituted for the ordinary office in anticipation of the celebration the following day. (*N.B.*, the term 'Vigil' is also applied to the Night Office). The number of readings in the Night Office differed according to the type of community. The maximum number of readings is nine for secular use and twelve for monastic use, with variations according to the importance or 'rank' of the feast (see p. 16 and n. 99). On the readings for the Night Office as stipulated in the Benedictine Rule, see chapters 8–11, *The Rule of St Benedict in English*, ed. T. Fry (Collegeville, MN, 1982), pp. 38–41. Teresa Webber, who provided references to the reading practices mentioned in this and the next note in a lecture on 'Saints and Manuscripts' delivered at the Parker Library in Cambridge in July 2006, points out that at least one and perhaps all three sets of four readings could have been drawn from the saint's life on the feast day. For evidence of this practice in Anglo-Saxon England, see Ælfric's comments on the reading of saints' lives in the Night Office (Jones, *Ælfric's Letter to the Monks of Eynsham* [cited in n. 5], pp. 146–47 [§73]).

20 As Hill explains, the term 'art *vita*' recalls the 'art song' ('*Imago Dei*', p. 37), which refers to a technically difficult, melodically sophisticated and thematically complex song written for its own sake rather than as part of a larger musical composition. The *lieder* of Robert Schumann are a good example. For an example of a legendary *vita*, see that for Cecilia in the late medieval Salisbury breviary, a book containing the texts used to celebrate the Canonical Hours (*Breviarium ad usum insignis ecclesiae Sarum*, eds F. Procter and C. Wordsworth, 3 vols [Cambridge, 1879–86; repr. Farnborough, 1970], 3: cols 1079–92). The full version of the *passio* edited below runs to nearly 6,500 words, but the legendary *vita* in the Salisbury breviary, which consists of nine readings, totals just 1,800 words. On the practice of reading at mealtime and of private devotional reading in the Benedictine Rule, see, respectively, chapters 38 and 48 (*Rule of St Benedict*, ed. Fry, pp. 60–61 and 69–70). Part of the practice of private devotional reading included each monk being given a book during Lent, but while Benedict meant a book of the

Bible, Webber notes that communities from the ninth century onwards interpreted this as a book from the library, which could have been a collection of saints' lives.

21 Respectively, *Les passion des martyrs et les genres littéraires* (Brussels, 1966), p. 229, and *Étude sur le légendier romain: Les saints de novembre et de décembre* (Brussels, 1936), p. 80.

22 M. Lapidge, 'The Saintly Life in Anglo-Saxon England' in *The Cambridge Companion to Old English Literature*, eds M. Godden and M. Lapidge (Cambridge, 1991), pp. 243–63 at p. 253.

23 *Ibid.*, pp. 252–53.

24 D. Elliott, *Spiritual Marriage: Sexual Abstinence in Medieval Wedlock* (Princeton, 1993), p. 65. I depend on Elliott for much of the discussion of the hagiographers' handling of the issue of spiritual marriage, especially pp. 51–73. For the wider historical and cultural contexts for spiritual marriage, see P. Brown, *The Body and Society: Men, Women, and Sexual Renunciation in Early Christianity* (New York, 1988). On the hagiographical contexts for different models of chaste marriage, see B. de Gaiffier, '*Intactam sponsam relinquens* à propos de la vie de S. Alexis', *Analecta Bollandiana* 65 (1947), 157–95. For a general introduction to the subject and a bibliography, see M. McGlynn and R. Moll, 'Chaste Marriage in the Middle Ages' in *Handbook of Medieval Sexuality*, eds V. Bullough and J. Brundage (New York, 1996), pp. 103–21.

25 Delehaye remarks that 'as for the theme of virginity, it is exaggerated in a great many *passiones* probably written by monks whose orthodoxy is less than reassuring' (*Étude sur le légendier romain*, p. 80). Regarding the Church Fathers' definitions of marriage, see Elliott, *Spiritual Marriage*, pp. 37–50 and 55–63.

26 One such audience might have been the *continentes*, married couples who adopt chastity, who are mentioned in the prologue of *Cecilia and Valerian* (line 42 [p. 174]).

27 Elliott, *Spiritual Marriage*, p. 65.

28 The general points about strategy are Elliott's (*Spiritual Marriage*, pp. 65–66). Even the brief accounts of chaste marriage that contain the gist of the more elaborate, fanciful stories represented here register the model's chief difficulty. See, for example, the story of Maxima and Martinianus's chaste marriage in Victor of Vita's fifth-century *History of the Vandal Persecution*, the putative source of *Cecilia and Valerian* (*Victoris episcopi vitensis Historia persecutionis africanae provinciae*, ed. M. Petschenig [Vienna, 1881], pp. 13–17); and, for a translation, *Victor of Vita: History of the Vandal Persecution*, trans. J. Moorhead [Liverpool, 1992], p. 15 [Book I, §31–32]). See too the story of Ammon as adapted from a late fourth-century Greek text by Rufinus in his early fifth-century *A History of the Monks in Egypt* (*Tyrannius Rufinus, Historia monachorum, sive, De vita sanctorum patrum*, ed. E. Schulz-Flügel [Berlin, 1990], pp. 375–78). The striking similarities of fundamental details in Rufinus's account of Ammon and *Julian and Basilissa* raise the possibility that the author of the original Greek version of *Julian and Basilissa* may have been aware of Rufinus's Latin text, which is tellingly different than his Greek source (for a translation of which, see *The Lives of the Desert Fathers*, trans. N. Russell [London, 1980], pp. 111–12).

29 See the Commentary, notes on lines 17–18 (pp. 250–51).

30 The term is Delehaye's (*Les passions des martyrs*, p. 170), who describes in detail the fixed 'programme' (p. 172) of the epic *passio* in pp. 170–226, on which this paragraph draws.

31 I have deliberately focused on the early evidence for the dissemination of the cults.

32 *Martyrologium Hieronymianum*, eds J. Rossi and L. Duchesne (Brussels, 1894), p. 6, cited in Whatley, 'Acta Sanctorum' [cited in n. 16], p. 280.

33 See n. 16.

34 References to the early frescoes are from the full account of the iconographic traditions of these saints in *Lexikon der christlichen Ikonographie*, eds E. Kirschbaum and W. Braunfels, 8 vols (Rome, 1968–76), 7: cols 239–41. M. Rochelle mentions the eighteenth-century fresco in her entry for Julian and Basilissa in her *Post-biblical Saints Art Index* (Jefferson, NC, 1994).

35 P. Salmon, 'Le lectionnaire de Luxeuil: ses origines et l'église de Langres', *Revue Bénédictine* 63 (1941), 89–107, at 95.

36 A. Alwis, "The Luxeuil Connection: The Transmission of the *Vita* of Julian and Basilissa' in *Porphyrogenita: Essays on the History and Literature of Byzantium and the Latin East in honour of Julian Chrysostomides*, ed. C. Dendrinos, et al. (Aldershot, 2003), pp. 131–36, at p. 134.

37 *Ibid.*, pp. 134–35, for information on the translation, and Salmon, ed., 'Le lectionnaire de Luxeuil: ses origines', 95–96.

38 *Le lectionnaire de Luxeuil (Paris, ms. lat. 9427)*, ed. P. Salmon, 2 vols (Rome, 1944), 2 (*Édition et étude comparative*): 27–57. On the possible connections of the Luxeuil lectionary with Morigny, see Alwis, 'The Luxeuil Connection', p. 135.

39 Salmon, 'Le lectionnaire de Luxeuil: ses origines', 93–94. See also, A. Fábrega Grau, ed., *Pasionario Hispanico*, 2 vols (Madrid-Barcelona, 1953–55, 1: 202–03, who is less certain than Salmon about the early evidence for the relics (at p. 202).

40 For the prayer from a mass for Julian and Basilissa in the mass book written at the monastery of Chur and later used at St Gall, see item 2452 in *Corpus Orationum*, ed. E. Moeller, et al. (Turnhout, 1992-), a collection of critical editions of over 6,000 mass prayers. Salmon mentions the translation of the saints' relics to Halberstadt ('Le lectionnaire de Luxeuil: ses origines', p. 95).

41 See n. 61.

42 A list of most of these manuscripts can be found on the *Bibliotheca Hagiographica Latina Manuscripta* website [cited as *BHLms*] maintained by the Société des Bollandists in Belgium (<http://bhlms.fltr.ucl.ac.be>). Manuscripts can be accessed by *BHL* number or by the Latin names of the saints, in this case *BHL* 4529–4532 or 'Iulianus, Basilissa'; they may be viewed according to the location of the manuscripts (*fonds*) or their dates (*siècle*) from earliest to latest.

43 On the dating of the *passio* and the history of the cult, see Connolly, *Mourning into Joy* [cited in n. 17], pp. 23–59. Unless noted otherwise, information regarding the cult relies on Connolly's account. For the earliest manuscripts, one of which is a ninth-century copy made at Canterbury, see *BHLms*. Delehaye collates the Canterbury text with a tenth-century copy of the legend from Chartres (now destroyed) in his eclectic edition of the *passio* (*Étude sur le légendier romain* [cited in n. 21], pp. 194–220).

44 See Whatley's entry for 'Valerianus et Tiburtius' ('Acta Sanctorum' [cited in n. 16], pp. 461–62, at p. 461).

45 Connolly discusses and reproduces the images in *Mourning into Joy*, pp. 197–99. For full accounts of the iconographical tradition, see the entries for 'Caecilia von Rom' in *Lexikon der Christlichen Ikonographie*, 5: cols 455–63 and, with discussions of the *passio*, translation and cult as well, 'Cecilia, santa, martire di Roma' in *Bibliotheca Sanctorum*, 13 vols (Rome, 1961–70), 3: cols 1064–86, at cols 1081–86.

46 See, for example, the mass prayers for Cecilia's feast day in the so-called Gelasian Sacramentary, a seventh- or eighth-century mass book (*Liber sacramentorum Romanae aecclesiae ordinis anni circuli . . . [Sacramentarium Gelasianum]*, eds L.C. Mohlberg, L. Eizenhofer, and P. Siffrin, 3rd ed. (Rome, 1968), pp. 162–63. Cecilia appears in the Canon of the Mass on p. 186. See also the prayers in the eighth-century *Hadrianum* version of the Gregorian Sacramentary, which were amplified in a ninth-century supplement (*Le sacramentaire grégorien: Ses principales formes d'après les plus anciens manuscrits*, ed. J. Deshusses, 3rd rev. ed. [Fribourg, 1992], pp. 287, 558 and 666). On the origins and dates of these sacramentaries, see C. Vogel, *Medieval Liturgy: An Introduction to the Sources*, trans. and rev. W. Storey and N. Rasmussen (Washington, D.C., 1986), pp. 64–70 and 79–102. For Anglo-Saxon mass books that contain a mass for Cecilia's feast day, see n. 113. For a masterful interpretation of the liturgy for the celebration of Cecilia's feast and station days, and for its implications for the pagan origins of her cult, see Connolly, *Mourning into Joy*, pp. 46–54.

47 See *BHLms* under *BHL* 1495 or 'Caecilia'.

48 The entry in *Lexikon der christenlichen Ikonographie* also mentions the tympanum of a church dedicated to Cecilia that contained a bust of the pair, as does *Bibliotheca Sanctorum*, from which the reference to the art in Bourges is taken. Connolly mentions that while the

Cologne cycle itself does not survive, pictures of it do (*Mourning into Joy*, p. 201); see P. Clemen, *Die gotischen Monumentalmalereien de Rheinlande. Tafelband* (Düsseldorf, 1930), plates 22–24.

49 *Mourning into Joy*, pp. 196–261; Raphel's painting is reproduced on plate 1 following p. 176.

50 For an edition and translation of the Old English Exeter relic list and editions of two of the three other Latin lists, see P. Connor, *Anglo-Saxon Exeter: A Tenth-century Cultural History* (Boydell, 1993), pp. 171–205. Cecilia appears in the lists at pp. 184 (item 129), 197 (item 136) and 205 (item 131). Valerian and Tiburtius appear on pp. 180 (item 37), 194 (items 39 and 40) and 202 (items 30 and 31).

51 See the entry for 'Cecilia' in 'Saints' Legends', eds C. D'Evelyn and F.A. Foster, vol. 2, pt 5 of *A Manual of the Writings in Middle English, 1050–1500*, gen. ed. J. Severs, 7 vols (New Haven, 1970), pp. 574–75. Chaucer's 'Second Nun's Tale' is found on pp. 264–69 of *The Riverside Chaucer*, ed. L. Benson, 3rd ed. (Boston, 1987). The English saint Christina of Markyate recites the story of Cecilia and Valerian to her new husband in an momentarily successful attempt to dissuade him from consummating their marriage (*The Life of Christina of Markyate*, ed. and trans. C.H. Talbot [Oxford, 1959], pp. 50–51).

52 Allard, 'Chrysanthe et Daria (Saints)' [cited in n. 17], cols 1560–61.

53 See the entries for 'Crisanto e Daria', *Bibliotheca Sanctorum*, 4: cols 300–306, at col. 301 and for 'Chrysantus und Daria von Rom', *Lexikon der christenlichen Ikonographie*, 5: cols 510–11.

54 See the prayers in the *Sacramentarium Gelasianum*, eds Mohlberg, et al., p. 164, which are to be said on the feast day of 'SS Saturninus, Chrysanthus, Maurus, Daria and others'. Maurus is a character in the legend, but Saturninus was the first bishop of Toulouse, who was martyred in the third century. Since his feast day also fell on 29 November, it was apparently conflated with that of Chrysanthus and Daria. Saturninus's feast would ultimately take precedence, for the Gregorian sacramentaries commemorate him only, not Chrysanthus and Daria. Because their feast day fell on the vigil of the festival of St Andrew the apostle, it was often observed on 1 December, even 12 August or 25 October.

55 See *BHLms* under *BHL* 1787 or 'Chrysanthus et Daria'.

56 On each of the translations, except that to England, see 'Crisanto e Daria', *Bibliotheca Sanctorum*, 4: cols 302 and 305.

57 J.H. Floss studies in detail the circumstances of the translation of the relics from Rome to the monastery in Prüm and then, four years later, to the nearby dependent monastery of Münstereifel ('Romreise des Abes Markward von Prüm und Übertragung der Hl. Chrysanthus und Daria nach Münstereifel im Jahre 844', *Annalen des Historischen Vereins für den Niederrhein* 20 [1869], 96–217). On the pictorial tradition developed for the saints at Prüm, see J. Marquardt-Cherry, 'Ottonian Imperial Saints in the Prüm Troper', *Manuscripta* 33 (1989), 129–36.

58 See Connor, *Anglo-Saxon Exeter*, pp. 180 (items 50–51), 194 (items 44–45) and 202 (items 34–35).

59 See the entry for 'Crisaunt and Daria', 'Saints' Legends', eds D'Evelyn and Foster, p. 577.

60 In his recent edition of the prose version of the *De virginitate* (see next note), Scott Gwara advances the hypothesis that Aldhelm does not address the treatise exclusively to abbess Hildelith and the Barking nuns but rather several abbesses of double houses in Wessex (*Aldhemi Malmesbiriensis Prosa De virginitate: Praefatio. Indices* [Turnhout, 2001], pp. 46–55).

61 Aldhelm does not include Malchus in the verse *De virginitate*. The prose accounts are found in 'De virginitate. Prosa', *Aldhelmi Opera*, ed. R. Ehwald (Berlin, 1919), pp. 226–323: (Malchus) p. 270 (lines 4–18); (Chrysanthus and Daria) pp. 276 (line 23)–280 (line 7); (Julian and Basilissa) pp. 280 (line 8)–284 (line 17); (Amos) pp. 284 (line 18)–286 (line 16); and (Cecilia) p. 292 (lines 5–23). For the verse accounts, from which Adhelm omits Malchus, see, 'De virginitate. Carmen', pp. 350–471: (Chrysanthus and Daria) pp. 400 (line 1123)–404 (line 1250); (Julian and Basilissa) pp. 405 (line 1251)–413 (line 1449); (Amos) pp. 413 (line 1450)–415 (line 1503); and (Cecilia) pp. 424 (line 1710)–25 (line 1735). I cite from Ehwald's edition because he prints the prose and verse versions together; Scott Gwara's recent edition of the *Prosa* is *Aldhemi Malmesbiriensis Prosa De virginitate: Textus* (Turnhout, 2001). Translations of the prose and verse versions are: 'The Prose *De virginitate*', *Aldhelm: The Prose Works*, trans. M. Lapidge and M. Herren (Brewer, 1979), pp. 59–132, and 'Carmen De virginitate', *Aldhelm: The Poetic Works*, trans. M. Lapidge and J. Rosier (Brewer, 1985), pp. 120–67.

62 *Anglo-Saxon Women and the Church* (Woodbridge, 1992), p. 110.

63 'The Prose *De virginitate*', trans. Lapidge and Herren, pp. 59–60; 'De virginitate. Prosa', ed. Ehwald, p. 230, lines 2–5.

64 On Aldhelm's personification of the nuns as men, see Hollis, *Anglo-Saxon Women and the Church*, pp. 82–97.

65 As a traditional patristic symbol of virginity, the bee was believed to reproduce without intercourse, generating offspring by means of the pollen it turned into honey. On Aldhelm's use of the bee as a metaphor, see A. Casiday, 'Aldhelm's Bees (De uirginitate prosa, cc. iv-vi): Some Observations on a Literary Tradition', *ASE* 33 (2005), 1–22.

66 'The Prose *De virginitate*', trans. Lapidge and Herren, p. 62; 'De virginitate. Prosa', ed. Ehwald, p. 233, lines 3–6.

67 Hollis comments on the nuns' pastoral care in *Anglo-Saxon Women and the Church*, pp. 77 (and n. 11) and 94 (and n. 101).

68 This interpretation cannot be uniformly applied to each epitome. For example, strong evidence that Aldhelm considered the instructional and evangelizing activity of the virgin spouses as spiritual childbearing is found in his prose treatment of the legend of Cecilia, but her spiritual procreation occurs without her guardian angel's protection and without the help of Valerian. As a result, Cecilia bears more resemblance to the unmarried virgins Agatha, Lucy or Agnes, whom she joins in the Canon of the Mass and whose epitomes follow in the *De virginitate*, than she does to either Daria or Basilissa. More problematic is Aldhelm's decision to de-emphasize in the verse account Basilissa's leadership and preaching that are so prominent in the prose. I am unable to say what prompted this change; perhaps he anticipated a wider monastic audience for the verse *De virginitate* that would have included more men who were neither receptive to the camaraderie he shared with women religious nor comfortable with a model of monasticism that lacked more barriers between the sexes.

69 'The Prose *De virginitate*', trans. Lapidge and Herren, p. 96; 'De virginitate. Prosa', ed. Ehwald, p. 277, line 8.

70 *Ibid.*; 'De virginitate. Prosa', ed. Ehwald, p. 277, lines 9–12.

71 *Ibid.*, p. 97; 'De virginitate. Prosa', ed. Ehwald, p. 278, line 24.

72 *Ibid.*, p. 98; 'De virginitate. Prosa', ed. Ehwald, p. 278, lines 25–26. Aldhelm also uses 'illorum magisterio' to explain Julian and Basilissa's success at converting multitudes to the faith and the monastic life (*Ibid.*, p. 100; 'De virginitate. Prosa', ed. Ehwald, p. 281, line 19). By calling attention to Aldhelm's interest in the saints' spiritual childbearing, I do not wish to downplay his emphasis on the merits of their steadfast virginity. For Aldhelm, virginity can only be valued if it is tested in light of desire, and so virgins demonstrate the value of their virginity primarily in the midst of a struggle. Thus Chrysanthus, who in the *passio* prays earnestly for and instantly receives God's help in combatting lust when the young girls attempt to seduce him, neither asks for nor needs divine intervention in Aldhelm's account. In the final contest between Chrysanthus and his captors, however, the man whose fortitude was such that he did not need to call on God for help finds himself repeatedly protected by him, as does Daria, to whom God sends a lion, not to help her convert pagans but to devour anyone wishing to defile her.

73 *Ibid.*, p. 99; 'De virginitate. Prosa', *Aldhelmi Opera*, ed. Ehwald, p. 280, lines 5–7.

74 'Carmen De virginitate', trans. Lapidge and Rosier, p. 130; 'De virginitate. Carmen', ed. Ehwald, p. 405, line 1250. For the first two uses of the word 'throng' ('caterua'), see, respectively, 'The Prose De virginitate', trans. Lapidge and Herren, pp. 68 and 131; 'De virginitate Prosa', ed. Ehwald, pp. 240 (line 19) and 322 (line 15). The third example is cited in the next note.

75 'Carmen De virginitate', trans. Lapidge and Rosier, p. 140; 'De virginitate. Carmen', ed. Ehwald, p. 422, line 1666.

76 For these tallies, I have worked from the translation of F. Lifshitz ('Bede, *Martyrology*' in *Medieval Hagiography: An Anthology*, ed. T. Head [New York, 2001], pp. 169–97). In the absence of a critical edition of the martyrology, Lifshitz, having compared the printed text with the oldest manuscripts of the martyrology, translates from the printed edition of H. Quentin only those entries that scholars have agreed are Bede's (*Les martyrologes historiques du moyen âge* [Paris, 1908]). I cite the edition by J. Dubois and G. Renaud (*Édition pratique des martyrologes de Bède, de l'Anonyme Lyonnais et de Florus* [Paris, 1976]), which Lifshitz notes is, while flawed in some respects, 'laid out in a much more convenient, reader-friendly format than Quentin's work' (p. 175).

The total number of female saints rises to forty-six if the seven unnamed virgins of Simirium, which Bede treats in a single entry (9 April), are counted individually. The number of men nears 300 when groups of forty and forty-six soldiers (respectively, 9 Mar. and 25 Oct.) are calculated separately. Bede provides enough information to determine whether or not thirty-nine of the forty-six women are unmarried or married: twenty-six are unmarried virgins, and thirteen are married (one is a grandmother, six are mothers, and six are wives).

77 *Bede's Ecclesiastical History of the English People*, ed. and trans. B. Colgrave and R.A.B. Mynors (Oxford, 1969), pp. 390–401 (Bk 4, chs 19–20).

78 Lifshitz, 'Bede, Martyrology', p. 186; *Édition pratique*, eds Dubois and Renaud, p. 113.

79 *Ibid.*, p. 113 (translation is mine).

80 Lifshitz, 'Bede, Martyrology', p. 195; *Édition pratique*, eds Dubois and Renaud, p. 211.

81 Those without children, or whose children are not mentioned, are SS Corona (14 May), Salustia (14 Sept.) and Anastasia (25 Dec.), the last of whom joins Cecilia in the Canon of the Mass. Wives who also have children are Perpetua and Felicitas (7 March), Symphorosa (21 July), Theodota (2 Aug.) and another Felicitas (of Rome) (23 Nov.). It is worth nothing that Perpetua and Felicity also join Cecilia in the Canon of the Mass.

82 See Hollis, *Anglo-Saxon Women and the Church* [cited in n. 62], pp. 263–70, and pp. 102–05 for a comparison of Bede's view of women and the double monastery with that of Aldhelm. The locus classicus for Bede's distrust of double monasteries is his condemnation of Coldingham (*Ecclesiastical History*, ed. and trans. Colgrave and Mynors, pp. 420–27 [Bk 4, ch. 25]).

83 Bede had not only read the *De virginitate* but also praised it (*Ibid.*, p. 514 [Bk 5, ch. 18]).

84 Until Bede, all Latin martyrologies depended on and descended from a fifth-century martyrology thought to have been written by St Jerome (Lifshitz, 'Bede, *Martyrology*', pp. 169–71). As this pseudo-Hieronymian martyrology often gives several feast days for the same saint or saints, the easiest way to navigate this text is by using the index (*Martyrologium Hieronymianum* [cited in n. 32], eds Rossi and Duchesne, pp. 157–85).

85 C. Rauer, quoting D. Rollason, 'The Sources of the Old English Martyrology', *ASE* 32 (2004), 89–109, at 94.

86 *Das altenglische Martyrologium*, ed. G. Kotzor, 2 vols (Munich, 1981), 2:12–13, at lines 18, 19 and 19–20, respectively. More accessible is *An Old English Martyrology*, ed. and trans. G. Herzfeld, EETS OS 116 (London, 1900; repr. New York, 1973).

87 *Das altenglische Martyrologium*, ed. Kotzor, 2.12–13, lines 24–25.

88 *Ibid.*, 2.253–55.

89 *Ibid.*, 2.258–59.

90 Remarkably, neither Bede's nor any other known martyrology appears to have served as the Old English martyrologist's guide or source (Rauer, 'Sources of the Old English Martyrology', p. 94). Rauer lists twenty instances in which the martyrologist drew on Aldhelm's *De virginitate* ('The Sources of the Old English Martyrology [Cameron B.19]', *Fontes Anglo-Saxonici: World Wide Web Register* [2000], at <http://fontes.english.ox.uk>, accessed January 2006).

91 Rebecca Rushforth, *An Atlas of Saints in Anglo-Saxon Calendars*, ASNC Guides, Texts, and Studies 6 (University of Cambridge, Department of Anglo-Saxon, Norse, and Celtic, 2002). Rushforth's *Atlas* presents in tabular form all the contents of twenty-seven Anglo-Saxon calendars and calendar fragments. More widely available, and thus cited hereafter, is F. Wormald's edition of nineteen calendars (*English Kalendars Before A. D. 1100*, HBS 72 [London, 1934]).

92 *Anglo-Saxon Litanies of the Saints*, ed. M. Lapidge, HBS 106 (London, 1991). Lapidge prints sixty-one litanies from forty-six manuscripts. Two of these litanies, however, postdate the period: although found in an Anglo-Saxon psalter, the litany in manuscript no. 43 was written in the twelfth century (p. 84), while that in manuscript no. 27, another Anglo-Saxon psalter, was written in the fifteenth century, though it too may have been copied from an Anglo-Saxon exemplar (p. 76).

93 Four of the five entries are entered in the main hands of the calendars: *English Kalendars*, ed. Wormald, no. 3 (20 Dec.: 'Iuliani et Bassilisce uirginis'), p. 41; no. 4 (9 Jan.), p. 254; no. 5 (8 Jan.: Julian only), p. 58; and no. 10 (27 Feb.), p. 129. A fifth entry in no. 8 (9 Jan.), p. 100, has been added in a later hand, possibly of the eleventh-century (p. x, n.1). According to Rushforth, a total of twenty-four calendars and fragments contain feasts for January and February; the total is twenty-three for the month of December.

94 Lapidge, *Anglo-Saxon Litanies*, ed. Lapidge, no. 23, line 77 (Julian [J]), p. 194 and line 326 (Basilissa [B]), p. 200, and no. 44, line 123 (J), p. 290 and line 256 (B), p. 293.

95 See, for example, the *incipit* to Ælfric's Old English version of *Julian and Basilissa* (p. 54).

96 *English Kalendars*, ed. Wormald, no. 20, p. 254. The feast day is calculated according to its relationship to set days (the *Kalendae*, the first day of the month, the *Idus*, the middle of the month, and the *Nonae*, the ninth day before the *Idus*). Here the feast falls on *v Idus*, that is, the fifth day counting backwards from (and including) the Ides or 13th of January = 9 January. Saints' names usually appear in the genitive or possessive case because the entry records the feast day *of* a particular saint.

97 *Anglo-Saxon Litanies*, ed. Lapidge, no. 32, line 58, p. 236; on the date and provenance of the manuscript and litany, see p. 78. Two other litanies also invoke Julian and his companions: no. 9, line 56, p. 133 and no. 22, line 57, p. 188.

98 See entries for 1 Dec. in the following nine calendars (of nineteen printed) in *English Kalendars*: nos. 7 (p. 97), 9 (p. 125), 10 (p. 139), 11 (p. 153), 12 (p. 167), 14 (p. 195), 17 (p. 223), 18 (p. 237) and 20 (p. 265). The one calendar that singles out Chrysanthus and Daria for special veneration dates the feast day to 29 Nov. (no. 4 [p. 54]), as Ælfric does (see the *incipit* to his Old English version on p. 86). Because the feast of Chrysanthus and Daria coincided with the vigil of St Andrew, their feast day was celebrated in most Anglo-Saxon monasteries on 1 Dec. Although all ten entries in Anglo-Saxon calendars are accounted for by Wormald's edition, Rushforth's tabulation reveals that a total of twenty-three calendars preserve entries for November and December.

99 Feasts of the first rank are distinguished by an (as yet unexplained) 'F' next to the entry; those of the second rank are distinguished by an 'S'; and those of the third rank have no such mark. In this Canterbury calendar, thirty-two feasts are designated to be of the first rank, eighty of the second and 136 of the third.

100 The other graded calendars are nos. 5 (pp. 57–69) and 14 (pp. 183–95).

101 On the ownership of the book and the date of its calendar, see *The Leofric Missal*, ed. N. Orchard, HBS 114, 2 vols (London, 2002), 1:132.

102 *Ibid.*, 1:12.

103 On 'the distinctly low-key and hesitant drift of the Canterbury cathedral community towards reformed monasticism during Dunstan's pontificate', see J. Blair, *The Church in Anglo-Saxon Society* (Oxford, 2005), pp. 351–52.

104 On the additions made at Exeter, see *Leofric Missal*, ed. Orchard, 1:206–34. On the list of relics, see n. 58. Not incidentally, the feast of Cecilia and Valerian, saints whose relics are also recorded in the list, is likewise designated a feast of the second rank (*English Kalendars*, ed. Wormald, no. 4 [14 April and 22 Nov.], pp. 47 and 54, respectively).

105 *Ælfwine's Prayerbook*, ed. B. Günzel, HBS 108 (London, 1993), p. 2.

106 *English Kalendars*, ed. Wormald, no. 9, p. 125, and *Ælfwine's Prayerbook*, ed. Günzel, p. 102. For Ælfwine's litany, see *Anglo-Saxon Litanies*, ed. Lapidge, no. 21, line 64 (Chrysanthus [C]), p. 183 and line 114 (Daria [D]), p. 185, or *Ælfwine's Prayerbook*, ed. Günzel, pp. 117, line 38 (C) and 181, line 14 (D). The other litany mentioning both saints is no. 23, line 133 (C), p. 196 and line 295 (D), p. 199.

107 The dates of Ælfwine's promotion to abbot are given by Günzel, who follows D. Knowles (*Ælfwine's Prayerbook*, p. 2).

108 *The Missal of the New Minster, Winchester*, ed. D.H. Turner (London, 1962), p. 188. On the date of the manuscript, which is more specific than that given in Turner's edition, see *The Liturgical Books of Anglo Saxon England*, ed. R. Pfaff (Kalamazoo, 1995), p. 30.

109 The collect (*collecta*) was said once the congregation had collected or assembled for mass. The secret (*secreta*) was prayed in a low voice over the Eucharistic elements and also referred to as the *super oblata* ('over the sacrifice'). The preface (*praefatio*) was recited as part of the Canon of the Mass to consecrate the bread and wine. The concluding prayer (*postcommunio*) was recited after communion was completed and is sometimes called the *post communionem* or *ad complendum*, that is, the prayer said 'at the conclusion' of the mass.

Two other mass sets are found in: (1) *The Winchcombe Sacramentary*, ed. A. Davril, HBS 109 (London, 1995), pp. 203–04, where Chrysanthus and Daria share the feast day with Saturninus and Maurus (see n. 54), and (2) the *Giso Sacramentary* (London, British Library, Cotton Vitellius A. xviii, folios 145ᵛ–46ʳ). On the dates and provenance of these sacramentaries, see *Liturgical Books of Anglo-Saxon England*, ed. Pfaff, pp. 14–15 and 19–21, respectively. There is also a prayer to be said at the conclusion of the monastic office celebrating the feast day of Chrysanthus and Daria in *The Portiforium of Saint Wulstan*, ed. A. Hughes, HBS 89–90, 2 vols (London, 1958 and 1960), 1:150. It too is a general prayer of intercession that does not draw directly on the *passio*.

110 The 'per-clause' is never to my knowledge written out in the manuscripts, but the phrase 'through Jesus Christ our Lord' is a traditional conclusion to the prayer.

111 The *Corpus Orationum* [cited in n. 40] lists the collect as the only one of its kind (item 1953). The same is true of the unwieldy preface that forms part of the mass set (see item 1172 in *Corpus Praefationum*, 5 vols [Turnhout, 1980–81], Textus [Q-V] and Apparatus [Q-V]). The historical context and the relevant studies are cited in *Liturgical Books of Anglo-Saxon England*, ed. Pfaff, p. 30.

112 All nineteen Anglo-Saxon calendars printed by Wormald include entries for Cecilia (22 November) and Valerian (14 April); that total, according to Rushforth's work, increases to twenty-three when taking into consideration all calendars and calendar fragments. Cecilia appears in forty-five litanies and Valerian, together with Cecilia, in seven (nos. 1, 5, 12, 23, 24, 37.i and 44), for which see the 'Index of Saints', *Anglo-Saxon Litanies*, ed. Lapidge, pp. 302–20, at p. 306 (Cecilia) and p. 320 (Valerian). I am aware of six mass sets for Valerian's feast day, which are here arranged in chronological order: (1) *Leofric Missal*, ed. Orchard, 2:255 (Tiburtius [T], Valerian [V], Maximus [M]) (dated 860–920); (2) *Winchcombe Sacramentary*, ed. Davril, p. 154 (T, V, M) (s.xᵉˣ); (3) *The Missal of Robert of Jumièges*, ed. H.A. Wilson, HBS 11 (London, 1896; repr. Woodbridge, 1994), p. 170 (T, V, M) (s.xiⁱⁿ); (4) the Giso Sacramentary (London, British Library, Cotton Vitellius A. xviii), f. 88ʳ (T, V, M) (s.xi¹); (5) *The Missal of the New Minster*, ed. Turner, pp. 85–86 (T, V, M) (*c.*1075); and (6) *The Missal of St. Augustine's* Abbey, Canterbury, ed. M. Rule (Cambridge, 1896), p. 83 (T, V) (s.xiᵉˣ). The *Portiforium of Saint Wulstan*, ed. Hughes, also contains a concluding collect for a mass to be said on the feast day of T, V and M (p. 122) (s.xi²), while two sets of benedictions invoke T and V: (1) *The Benedictional of Æthelwold. A Masterpiece of Anglo-Saxon Art. A Facsimile*, ed. A. Prescott (London, 2002), ff. 60ᵛ–61ʳ (963–84) and (2) The Lanalet Pontifical (*Pontificale Lanaletense*, ed. G.H. Doble, HBS 74 [London,1937], p. 94) (early s.xi)

113 This list is representative not exhaustive. The seven mass, arranged chronologically, are:

(1) *Leofric Missal*, ed. Orchard, 2:306–07; (2–3) *Winchcombe Sacramentary*, ed. Davril, pp. 201–02 (vigil and feast day); (4) *The Missal of Robert of Jumièges*, ed. Wilson, p. 226; (5) the Giso Sacramentary, ff. 143ʳ⁻ᵛ; (6) *The Missal of the New Minster*, ed. Turner, pp. 182–83; and (7) *The Missal of St. Augustine's Abbey, Canterbury*, ed. Rule, p. 122. The eleven sets of benedictions are found in: (1) the Dunstan or Sherborne Pontifical, Paris, Bibliothèque Nationale, Latin MS 943, ff. 137v–38r (960–973?) (printed in *Corpus Benedictionum Pontificalium* (*CBP*), ed. E. Moeller, 4 vols [Turnhout, 1971–79], no. 1561); (2) The Ramsey Benedictional, Paris, Bibliothèque Nationale, Latin MS 987, f. 106ᵛ (*CPB* no. 659) (s.x¹?); (3) *The Benedictional of Æthelwold*, ed. Prescott, ff. 111ᵛ–12ʳ (*CBP* no. 1948) (963–84); (4) The Anderson Pontifical, London, British Library, Additional 57337, f. 144ʳ (*CBP* 1561) (*c.*1000) (for its contents, see A. Prescott, 'The Structure of English Pre-Conquest Benedictionals', *The British Library Journal*, 13 (1987), 118–58, at 134–38); (5) *The Benedictional of Archbishop Robert*, ed. H.A. Wilson, HBS 24 (London, 1903), p. 44 (980–1020), where the blessings for Cecilia's day are actually those for St Clement in the Benedictional of Æthelwold (Prescott, 'Pre-Conquest Benedictionals', p. 126); (6) *The Missal of Robert of Jumièges*, ed. H.A. Wilson, HBS 11 (London, 1896), p. 44 (*CBP* 1706) (1000–1010); (7) the Sampson Pontifical, Cambridge, Corpus Christi College 146, pp. 61–318, at p. 273 (early s.xi) (Prescott, 'Pre-Conquest Benedictionals', p. 154); (8) the Lanalet Pontifical (*Pontificale Lanaletense*, ed. Doble, p. 100) (*CBP* no. 1948) (early s.xi); (9) *The Canterbury Benedictional*, ed. R.M. Woolley, HBS 51 (London, 1917; repr. Woodbridge, 1995), p. 117 (*CBP* no. 659) (*c.*1030); (10) the Giso Benedictional, Cotton Vitellius A. xviii, ff. 216ʳ⁻ᵛ (s.xi²); and (11) the Exeter Benedictional, London, British Library, Additional 28188, ff. 158ʳ⁻ᵛ (s.xi³/⁴). The two collects are found in *The Durham Collectar*, ed. A Corrêa, HBS 107 (London, 1992), p. 198 (s.ixᵉˣ/s.x ⁱⁿ). The private prayers are found in *Ælfwine's Prayerbook*, ed. Günzel, pp. 140–41 [§16] (*c.*1030) and the Eadui Psalter (London, British Library, Arundel 155 [s.xi¹]), ed. J.J. Campbell, 'Prayers from Arundel 155', *Anglia* 81 (1963), 82–117, at 104–07. Lastly, the office is found in *Portiforium of Saint Wulstan*, ed. Hughes, pp. 114–15. V. Ortenberg, who mentions but does not cite many of the texts mentioned here, also notes that Cecilia's feast is 'distinguished with gold letters in various books', including the Benedictional of Æthelwold (*The English Church and the Continent in the Tenth and Eleventh Centuries: Cultural, Spiritual, and Artistic Exchanges* [Oxford, 1992], p. 179). For indispensable introductions and guides to these books, see the relevant sections of *Liturgical Books of Anglo-Saxon England*, ed. Pfaff (noting that Wulstan's *Portiforium* is treated under 'Daily Office Books').

114 *Leofric Missal*, ed. Orchard, 2:307.

115 The practice of reading out a blessing during the Canon of the Mass, either just before the breaking of the bread or just after the bread and wine had been mixed, is a Gallican one (J. Jungmann, *The Mass of the Roman Rite: Its Origins and Development*, trans. F. Brunner, 2 vols [New York, 1945], 2:295–96).

116 London, British Library, Additional 28188, ff. 158ʳ⁻ᵛ forms part of 'a large and beautifully-written benedictional' which 'was apparently made for Bishop Leofric's use at Exeter' (*Liturgical Books of Anglo-Saxon England*, ed. Pfaff, p. 93). The prayer reads: 'Omnipotens Deus, qui beatam Ceciliam uirg[i]nitatis et martyrii est dignatus priuilegio decorare, uos angelicæ integritatis et fidei dignetur constantia corroborare, atque euangelii Christi sui et colloquiis spiritalibus Confirmator sanctificare. Amen' (158ᵛ) (May omnipotent God, who deigned to adorn blessed Cecilia with the privilege of virginity and martyrdom, deign to strengthen you with the constancy of angelic chastity and faith, and may the Strengthener deign to sanctify you through the gospel of His Christ and divine discourse. Amen.).

117 On the idea of the *vita angelica*, see J. Bugge, *Virginitas: An Essay in the History of a Medieval Ideal* (The Hague, 1975).

118 On the contents, dating and provenance of the Eadui Psalter, see *Liturgical Books of Anglo-Saxon England*, ed. Pfaff, p. 64. A more detailed description is that of P. Pulsiano, '175. London, British Library, Arundel 155' in *Psalters I*, Anglo-Saxon Manuscripts in Microfiche Facsimile 2 (Binghamton, NY, 1994), pp. 19–37. Cecilia had been important to the Canterbury community for over two centuries (a copy of her *passio* was made at Christ Church in the early ninth century [Whatley, 'Acta Sanctorum' (cited in n. 16), p. 124]), so it is not altogether surprising to find her singled out for special veneration.

119 Translated from 'Prayers from Arundel 155', ed. Campbell, pp. 105–06.

120 *Ibid.*, p. 104, lines 8 and 12, and p. 106, line 15.

121 *Ibid.*, p. 105, line 5, and p. 107, line 7.

122 Of all the Anglo-Saxon texts surveyed above, the *De virginitate* would have been most familiar to Ælfric because Aldhelm was 'the most important curriculum author in late-tenth-century Winchester and late Anglo-Saxon England at large' (M. Gretsch, *Ælfric and the Cult of Saints in Late Anglo-Saxon England* [Cambridge, 2005], p. 24, n. 15). Indeed, it would seem that by giving such prominence to the married saints in the *Lives*, Ælfric is taking a cue from Aldhelm.

123 Basing his supposition on a rubric for *The Memory of the Saints (De memoria sanctorum)* in a Cambridge University Library manuscript of the *Lives*, P. Clemoes observes that Ælfric may have intended the sermon to introduce the collection ('The Chronology of Ælfric's Works' [cited in n. 3], p. 222). The sermon, however, survives in the most complete manuscript of the *Lives* (BL, Cotton Julius E. vii) as its fifteenth item. For a complete list of contents and a comparison of the scribal numbering to the ordering of Skeat's edition, where *De memoria sanctorum* is item 16, see Hill, 'Dissemination' [cited in n. 8], p. 241.

124 J. Hurt, 'A Note on Ælfric's *Lives of Saints*, No. XVI', *English Studies*, 51 (1970), 231–34. See also my forthcoming article, 'Homiletic Contexts for Ælfric's Hagiography: The Legend of SS Cecilia and Valerian'.

125 Respectively, *LS* (cited in n. 1) I.16, lines 9–11 (p. 336); (Job) line 36 (p. 338) and line 47 (p. 340); (Daniel) line 79 (p. 342); and (John the Baptist) lines 103–04 (p. 344), at line 103.

126 *LS* I.16, lines 221–222 (p. 352). In a similar vein, Ælfric writes earlier in the sermon that Christians are to avoid the fickleness of the plowman whom Jesus criticizes for looking back at his furrow, for 'he who desires to turn to God and turns back again to earthly possessions will not be acceptable to God' (lines 182–83 [p. 348]).

127 *Ibid.*, line 244 (p. 352).

128 See, respectively, (Agnes) *LS* I.7, line 88 (p. 174), line 122 (p. 176), and line 274 (p. 186); (Agatha) *LS* I.8, line 65 (p.198); (Cecilia) *LS* II.34, line 156 (p. 364) and line 325 (p. 374); and (Chrysanthus and Daria) *LS* II.35, line 122 (p. 384).

129 Hill, '*Imago Dei*' [cited in n. 14], p. 45.

130 *LS* I.16, lines 312–63 (pp. 358–62).

131 *The Dictionary of Old English in Electronic Form: A-F*, ed. A. Cameron, A. Amos, A. Healey and J. Holland, et al. (Toronto, 2003). On the range of meaning of *clænnyss* in Ælfric's sermons focusing on the laity, see my 'For Pastoral Care and Political Gain: Ælfric of Eynsham's Preaching on Marital Celibacy', *Traditio* 59 (2004), 39–78.

132 *LS* I.16, lines 322–23 (p. 358). I discuss each of the restrictions mentioned in the remainder of the paragraph in 'For Pastoral Care and Political Gain', pp. 44–60.

133 See the concluding lines of Ælfric's legend of Æthelthryth, *LS* I.20, lines 120–35 (p. 440). For discussions of Ælfric's purposes in adding the scenario to the legend proper, see P. Jackson, 'Ælfric and the Purpose of Christian Marriage: A Reconsideration of the *Life of Æthelthryth*, Lines 120–30', *ASE* 29 (2000), 235–60, and Gretsch, *Ælfric and the Cult of Saints* [cited in n. 122], pp. 195–231, esp. pp. 218–26.

134 See *CH* II.19 [cited in n. 6], lines 168–69 (p. 185), where Ælfric encourages couples 'to hide themselves in marriage and refrain from sexual intercourse if God so directs'.

135 See my 'Virgin Spouses as Model Christians: The Legend of Julian and Basilissa in Ælfric's *Lives of Saints*', *ASE* 34 (2005): 197–217.

136 See Ælfric's *Julian and Basilissa*, line 4 (p. 54).

137 See 'For Pastoral Care and Political Gain', pp. 60–71.

138 Respectively, Assmann 3, lines 95–100 (p. 28) and line 135 (p. 29) in *Angelsächsische Homilien und Heiligenleben*, ed. B. Assmann, Bibliothek der angelsächsischen Prosa 3 (Kassel,

1889; repr. Darmstadt, 1964). For the patristic allegory, Ælfric relies on Bede, who most likely relied on Augustine (Godden, *Commentary* [cited in n. 6], p. 277). For a representative passage of Augustine, see *De sancta virginitate*, ed. and trans. P. Walsh (Oxford, 2001), pp. 66–147, at pp. 70–73 (para. 6).

139 See my 'The Legend of Chrysanthus and Daria in Ælfric's *Lives of Saints*', *Studies in Philology* 101 (2004), 250–69, at 264.

140 *CH* II.39, lines 79–82 (p. 329).

141 Ælfric specifies that men should know the Lord's Prayer and the Creed in *LS* I.12, line 261 (p. 280). See *CH* II.3, lines 245–88 (pp. 26–27) for a passage in which he encourages Christians to be mindful of the promises made to God at their baptisms and those that they have made as godparents at the baptisms of others.

142 See *CH* II.38, lines 54–66 [p. 320], and the discussion in 'For Pastoral Care and Political Gain', pp. 68–71.

143 See also my 'Homiletic Contexts for Ælfric's Hagiography'.

144 *CH* II.6, lines 141–42 (p. 57).

145 Respectively, *CH* II.6, lines 152–53 (p. 57), and *CH* II.38, line 64 and line 57.

146 For Ælfric's advice of this sort in his first Old English pastoral letter to Wulfstan, Archbishop of York, see Fehr II, §143–213 (pp. 120–45) in *Die Hirtenbriefe Ælfrics*, ed. B. Fehr (Hamburg, 1914), pp. 68–145. Note that Fehr refers to Ælfric's Old English letters with Roman numerals and to his Latin letters with arabic numerals.

147 On marriage among Anglo-Saxon secular clergy, see Blair, *The Church in Anglo-Saxon Society* [cited in n. 103], pp. 342, 352 (and notes 287 and 288), 361 and 491. F. Tinti lists these duties in her Introduction to *Pastoral Care in Late Anglo-Saxon England*, ed. F. Tinti (Woodbridge, 2005), p. 14. On pastoral duties, see also H. Gittos, 'Is There Any Evidence for the Liturgy of Parish Churches in Late Anglo-Saxon England? The Red Book of Darley and the Status of Old English' in *Pastoral Care*, ed. Tinti, pp. 63–82, at pp. 64–65.

148 *Die Hirtenbriefe Ælfrics*, Fehr 2, §111 (p. 48).

149 *Ibid.*, Fehr 3, §41 (p. 62) and Fehr III, §81 (p.176). J. Barrow comments that 'hereditary successions to whole churches or to portions of churches or to lands associated with churches was normal and socially acceptable, however abhorrent it must have been to the Benedictine reformers' ('The Clergy in English Dioceses c.900–c.1066' in *Pastoral Care*, ed. Tinti, pp. 17–26, at p. 20).

150 See J. Wilcox, 'Ælfric in Dorset and the Landscape of Pastoral Care' in *Pastoral Care*, ed. Tinti, pp. 52–62, at 58 and 'For Pastoral Care and Political Gain', pp. 71–78. On the involvement of reformed monasteries in delivering pastoral care to the laity, see M. Clayton, 'Homiliaries and Preaching in Anglo-Saxon England', *Peritia* 4 (1985), 207–42, at 232–39.

151 On the various uses of and audiences for 'Ælfric's ideology of the supremacy of virginity', see Cubitt, *Virginity and Misogyny* [cited in n. 13], pp. 18–19, at p. 18.

152 See Wilcox, 'Ælfric in Dorset', p. 57, who for information on minsters near Cerne Abbas relies on T. Hall, *Minster Churches in the Dorset Landscape*, British Archeological Reports, British Series 304 (Oxford, 2000). Minster churches are known to have existed in Yetminster, Charminster and Puddletown, and may have existed in Sydling St Nicholas, Buckland Newton and Milton, though the last was reformed in 964 (p. 59). Wilcox acknowledges that while no records of churches in Up Cerne or Alton Pancras survive, the modern parish layout implies these two 'locally owned proprietary churches' did in fact exist only a few miles from Cerne Abbas (p. 60). His point about Sherborne Cathedral is found on p. 58. Even if we discount the evidence that points to probable religious establishments, we are left with four unreformed religious communities that would have been responsible for much of the pastoral care in the vicinity of Ælfric's monastery.

153 See, for example, *CH* I.21 [cited in n. 6], lines 218–23 (pp. 352–53); *CH* II.6, lines 136–66 (pp. 57–58); *CH* II.12, lines 548–52 (p. 125); *LS* I.10, lines 202–33 (pp. 232 and 234); *LS* I.16, line 324 (p. 358); Assmann 2 [cited in n. 138], lines 30–84 (p. 14–17); *Die Hirtenbriefe Ælfrics*, Fehr

I, §14 (p. 4) and Fehr 2, §§87–113 (pp. 46–48); and Ælfric's *Preface to Genesis*, lines 23–40 (p. 117) in *Ælfric's Prefaces*, ed. J. Wilcox (Durham, 1994).

154 Competition would have come not only from a cathedral or larger minsters but also from smaller, locally owned rural churches. Blair notes that Ælfric grouses about men who 'even sell churches for hire as if they were worthless mills' (*LS* I.19, lines 248–49 [p. 430]), and in this way registers his awareness of the 'revenue-generating capacities' of local churches that landowners may have sold to priests because of their ability to turn a profit (*The Church in Anglo-Saxon Society*, p. 494). Blair also observes that 'both churches and mills could acquire geographical spheres of influence which, even if articulated by seigneurial authority, may have depended to a large extent upon the willingness of consumers to make use of the facility' (p. 495).

155 Respectively, *LS* I.10, lines 226 and 230 (p. 234), and *CH* II.6, line 156 (p. 57).

156 It is worth remarking that the non-monastic clergy wore secular clothes when not officiating (G.R. Owen-Crocker, 'Clothing' in *The Blackwell Encyclopaedia of Anglo-Saxon England*, ed. M. Lapidge, et al. [Oxford, 1999], pp. 107–08, at p. 108).

157 For accounts of the Viking invasions in the late tenth century, see F. Stenton, *Anglo-Saxon England*, 3rd ed. (Oxford, 1971), 372–79; J. Campbell, ed., *The Anglo-Saxons* (New York, 1991), pp. 192–201; and S. Keynes, 'Æthelred II', *Oxford Dictionary of National Biography* (Oxford, 2004) at <http://www.oxforddnb.com/view/article/8915>, accessed August 2006.

158 Cubitt notes Ælfric's idealization of a social order 'in which sexuality and gender play a fundamental part' and draws upon the sermon cited in the next note as evidence ('Virginity and Misogyny', p. 21).

159 Respectively, *LS* I.13, lines 148–50 (p. 294), and lines 152–55 (p. 294).

160 *Ibid.*, line 179 (p. 296).

161 *LS* I.16, line 219 (p. 352).

162 Æthelweard, however, 'obstinately' (*LS* II.36, line 12 [p. 400]) insisted that Ælfric include the legend of St Thomas in the *Lives*.

163 H. Magennis, ed. and trans., *The Old English Life of Saint Mary of Egypt* (Exeter, 2002), pp. 35–36. The following account of the language of Cotton Julius E. vii is indebted to Magennis's discussion of the language of the Life of Mary of Egypt, a non-Ælfrician text in the same manuscript, as well as the studies cited in the next two notes. A full description of the manuscript is found in N.R. Ker, *Catalogue of Manuscripts containing Anglo-Saxon* (Oxford, 1957), pp. 206–10 (item 162). For the non-Ælfrician items, see p. 33, n. 8.

164 M. Gretsch, 'In Search of Standard Old English,' in *Bookmarks from the Past: Studies in Early English Language and Literature in Honour of Helmut Gneuss*, eds L. Kornexl and U. Lenker (Frankfurt, 2003), pp. 33–67, at p. 45. In-depth analysis of the language of Cotton Julius E. vii appears on pp. 45–55.

165 G.I. Needham, 'Additions and Alterations in Cotton Ms. Julius E VII', *The Review of English Studies* 9 (1958), 160–164, at 160. See also his remarks about the corrector in his edition of Ælfric's lives of Oswald, Edmund and Swithun (*Ælfric: Lives of Three English Saints* [Exeter, 1966; rev. ed, 1992], pp. 1 [n. 5], 9–10 [nn. 4 and 5]), as well as those of Gretsch, 'In Search of Standard Old English', eds Kornexl and Lenker, pp. 53–55.

166 A. Campbell, *Old English Grammar* (Oxford, 1959), §574.3.

167 *Ibid.*, §730.

168 *Ibid.*, §757.

169 For the possibility that *cwæþe* and *cwæþende* may represent Anglian usage, see *Ibid.*, §328 (cited by Magennis), and Magennis, ed., *Saint Mary of Egypt*, pp. 39–43.

170 Campbell notes that *æ* occurs as the dative ending in early texts (*Old English Grammar*, §571–72).

171 For the possibility that *clennysse* may represent Anglian usage, see *Ibid.*, §292.

172 *Ibid.*, §160–62, esp. 162.

173 Magennis, ed., *Life of Saint Mary*, p. 39, where D. Scragg's 'Initial *h* in Old English', *Anglia* 88 (1970), 165–96, is cited.

174 *Ibid.*, pp. 39–40, and Campbell, *Old English Grammar*, §320–22.

175 *Bibliotheca Hagiographica Latina Antiquuiae et Mediae Aetatis*, ed. Socii Bollandiani, Subsidia Hagiographica 6, 2 vols (Brussels, 1893–1901). See also *Novum Supplementum*, ed. H. Flos, Subsidia Hagiographica 70 (Brussels, 1986).

176 The printed editions of *BHL* 4529 are listed in the Selected Bibliography and in *BHL* and *Novum Supplementum* cited in the preceding note. See too Whatley's entry for Julian and Basilissa in 'Acta Sanctorum' [cited in n. 16]. The abbreviation s.xi³ᐟ⁴ means that N was written in the third quarter of the eleventh century [saeculum].

177 P. Jackson and M. Lapidge describe and list the contents of these manuscripts in 'The Contents of the Cotton-Corpus Legendary' in *Holy Men and Holy Women* [cited in n. 8], ed. Szarmach, pp. 131–46. The contents of Cotton Nero E. i, pt i are listed on pp. 135–37. For the dating of CCCC9, I follow M. Budny, who also describes the contents of the manuscript (*Insular, Anglo-Saxon, and Early Anglo-Norman Manuscript Art at Corpus Christi College, Cambridge: An Illustrated Catalogue*, 2 vols [Kalamazoo, MI, 1997], 1: 609–22), as does M.R. James, *A Descriptive Catalogue of the Manuscripts in the Library of Corpus Christi College, Cambridge* (Cambridge, 1912), pp. 21–30. On the relationship between the various parts and recensions of the legendary, and the scholarship relevant to them, see E.G. Whatley, 'Cotton-Corpus Legendary' in *Sources of Anglo-Saxon Literary Culture*, vol. 5, ed. T. Hall, et al. (Kalamazoo, forthcoming).

178 P. Zettel, 'Ælfric's Hagiographic Sources and the Latin Legendary Preserved in B.L. MS Cotton Nero E I + CCCC MS 9 and Other Manuscripts (unpublished D.Phil. dissertation, Oxford University, 1979), pp. 201–08. Another 'Cotton-Corpus' version that seems to have been copied from the same exemplar as Cotton Nero E. i is that preserved in Salisbury, Cathedral Library 221 (s.xiᵉˣ), 37ʳ–47ʳ.

179 I am aware of thirty-eight manuscripts of *BHL* 4532 as compared to nearly 100 copies of *BHL* 4529.

180 Those four manuscripts, arranged in chronological order, are: (1) Rome, Vatican City, Biblioteca Apostolica Vaticana, Reginensis latini [Regiae Sueciae] MS 516 (s.ix or x); (2) Rouen, Bibliothèque Municipale, MS U 026 (s.xi); (3) Dublin, Trinity College, MS 174 (s.xii); and (4) Munich, Bayerische Staatsbibliothek, clm 22240 (s.xii). Variants from the Rouen and Dublin manuscripts are recorded in the apparatus.

181 Zettel, 'Ælfric's Hagiographic Sources', pp. 304–05. I draw attention to these divergences in the Commentary on the Latin text.

182 Jackson and Lapidge seem to suggest a hybrid when they identify the source of the legend as *BHL* 4529 and *BHL* 4532 ('Contents of the Cotton-Corpus Legendary', p. 135).

183 See *BHLms* [cited in n. 42] under *BHL* 1495 or 'Caecilia'.

184 Whatley, 'Cotton-Corpus Legendary'. For a full description of H, see R.A.B. Mynors and R.M. Thomson, *Catalogue of the Manuscripts of Hereford Cathedral Library* (Cambridge, 1993), pp. 110–12.

185 Zettel, 'Ælfric's Hagiographic Sources', pp. 256–58, at p. 257.

186 The manuscripts in question are: Biblioteca Apostolica Vaticana, MS Latini 5771, ff. 147ᵛ–57ʳ (s.ix²-s.x¹); Douai, Bibliothèque Muncipale, MS 867, ff. 110ʳ–11ʳ (s.xi); and Montpellier, Bibliothèque de la Faculté de Médecine [Bibliothecae Scholae Medicinae], MS 30, ff. 215ʳ–20ᵛ (s.xii). Variants from MS Latini 5771 and CCCC9 are recorded in the apparatus.

187 Zettel, 'Ælfric's Hagiographic Sources', p. 257.

188 I draw attention to these instances in the Commentary on the Latin Texts.

189 On the relationship of the Hereford legendary to 'Cotton-Corpus', see Whatley, 'Cotton-Corpus Legendary'.

190 On the intercontinental contact, see, for example, M. Gretsch, *Intellectual Foundations of the Benedictine Reform* (Cambridge, 1999), pp. 275–77, and V. Ortenberg, *The English Church and the Continent* [cited in n. 113], pp. 218–63. On the date, provenance and contents of P, see *Catalogus Codicum Hagiographicorum Latinorum Antiquiorum Saeculo XVI qui asservantur in*

Bibliotheca Nationali Parisiensi, ed. Socii Bollandiani, 3 vols (Brussels, 1889–93), 3:201–02. The other two manuscripts are: Vatican City, Biblioteca Apostolica Vaticana, MS Reginensis latini [Regiae Sueciae] MS 568 (s.xii) and Brussels, Bibliothèque Royale, 206 (s.xiii). Variants from BR MS 206 are entered in the apparatus along with those from CCCC9.

191 P provides an example of intercontinental contact, for it contains not only the *passio* of Chrysanthus and Daria, and an account of their posthumous miracles (*BHL* 1791), but also the account written in Germany of the translation of their relics from Rome to Prüm in 844 (*BHL* 1793) and Aldhelm's verse epitome of the legend (*BHL* 1789). The Brussels manuscript mentioned in the previous note is the only other medieval manuscript that I am aware of that preserves a similar grouping of texts: the *passio*, the *miraculum* (though numbered *BHL* 1792), and the *translatio* (*BHL* 1793). The Bollandists do not give the provenance of BR 206 in the head note to their list of the manuscripts contents (*Catalogus Codicum Hagiographicorum Bibliothecae Regiae Bruxellensis. Pars I. Codices Latini Membranei. Tomus I*, 2 vols [Brussels, 1886], 1:108–22).

192 Ælfric's choice of possessive adjectives in the following example provides another instance in which P agrees with H rather than C. Whether or not Ælfric's immediate source followed P or H, however, is unclear. In Ælfric's version, Chrysanthus's father's friends warn that his son preaches Christ 'to plihte *þinre* æhta and *þines* agenes heafdes' ('to the peril of *your* wealth and *your* own head' [lines 23–24 (p. 86)]). In C the friends alert him about the risks to 'patrimonii *tui* et capitis *sui*' ('*your* fortune and *his* head'). In H, by contrast, Polemius is warned of the risk to 'patrimonii et capitis *tui*' ('[your] fortune and *your* head'). H's reading could have resulted in Ælfric's wording, for the Latin author can use a single possessive adjective to modify the two neuter nouns (*patrimonium* and *caput*), Ælfric must use one adjective for the feminine *æhta* and another for the neuter *heafod*. Be that as it may, P's 'patrimonii *tui* et capitis *tui*' ('your fortune and your head' [lines 70–71 (p. 222)]) corresponds exactly to Ælfric's phrasing.

193 *AS*, Oct. XI, p. 481 [§18]. The nineteenth-century *AS* text is based on a seventeenth-century transcription of the Reims manuscript (P) edited below. Except for the prologue, for which the Bollandists relied solely on P, the AS text has been collated with an unidentified manuscript of Bonus fons, Soissons; a thirteenth-century manuscript from St Maximinus, Trier (Bibliotheck des Priesterseminars [Bibliotheca Seminarii Clericalis] MS 36); and a twelfth-century manuscript from Grimbergen in Flanders (Brussels, Bibliotheca Bollandiana MS 5) [*AS*, Oct. XI, p. 470 (note b)]. Remarkably, the Bollandists omit from their Latin edition passages that have no parallel in the Greek text edited alongside the Latin one.

SELECT BIBLIOGRAPHY

Editions and Translations of the Old English Versions

Julian and Basilissa

Skeat, W.W., ed. and trans., *Ælfric's Lives of Saints*, EETS OS 76, 82, 94, 114 (London, 1881–1900; repr. as 2 vols, 1966), 1:90–115.

Cecilia and Valerian

Donovan, L., trans., *Women Saints' Lives in Old English Prose* (Cambridge, 1999), pp. 57–65.

Moloney, B., 'A Critical Edition of Ælfric's Virgin-Martyr Stories from *The Lives of Saints*' (D.Phil. dissertation, University of Exeter, 1980), pp. 320–31.

Skeat, ed. and trans., *Ælfric's Lives of Saints*, 2:356–77.

Chrysanthus and Daria

Skeat, ed. and trans., *Ælfric's Lives of Saints*, 2:378–99.

Editions of the Latin Legends

Julian and Basilissa (BHL 4529, not BHL 4532)

Acta Sanctorum, ed. J. Bollandus et al., 68 vols (Brussels, 1643–1940), Ian. I:575–87.

Grau, F., ed., *Pasionario hispánico*, 2 vols (Madrid, 1953–55), 2:118–44.

Salmon, P. ed., *Le lectionnaire de Luxeuil (Paris, ms. lat. 9427)*, 2 vols (Rome, 1944), 1 (*Édition et étude comparative*):27–57.

Cecilia and Valerian (BHL 1495)

Delehaye, H., ed., *Étude sur le légendier romain: Les saints de novembre et de décembre* (Brussels, 1936), pp. 194–220.

Grau, ed., *Pasionario hispánico*, 2:25–40.

Mombritius, B., ed., *Sanctuarium seu vitae sanctorum*, 2nd ed., 2 vols (Paris, 1910), 1:332–41.

Chrysanthus and Daria (BHL 1787)

Acta Sanctorum, Oct. XI:469–84.

Mombritius, ed., *Sanctuarium seu vitae sanctorum*, 1:271–78.

The Lives of the Virgin Spouses and their Backgrounds

Allard, P., 'Chrysanthe et Daria (Saints)' in *Dictionnaire d'archéologie chrétienne et de liturgie*, eds F. Cabrol and H. Leclercq, 15 vols (Paris, 1907–53), 3, pt 1: cols 1560–68.

Brown, P., *The Body and Society: Men, Women, and Sexual Renunciation in Early Christianity* (New York, 1988).

Connolly, T., *Mourning into Joy: Music, Raphael, and Saint Cecilia* (New Haven, 1994).

Delehaye, H., *Les Passions des martyrs et les genres littéraires*, 2nd ed. (Brussels, 1966).

Elliott, D., *Spiritual Marriage: Sexual Abstinence in Medieval Wedlock* (Princeton, 1993).

de Gaiffier, B., '*Intactam sponsam relinquens* B propos de la vie de S. Alexis', *Analecta Bollandiana* 65 (1947), 157–95 [for a seminal survey of the hagiography of chaste marriage].

McGlynn, M., and R. Moll, 'Chaste Marriage in the Middle Ages' in *Handbook of Medieval Sexuality*, eds V. Bullough and J. Brundage (New York, 1996), pp. 103–21.

Reames, S., 'The Cecilia Legend as Chaucer Inherited It and Retold It: The Disappearance of an Augustinian Ideal', *Speculum* 55 (1980), 38–57.

Salmon, P., 'Le lectionnaire de Luxeuil: ses orignes et l'église de Langres', *Revue Bénédictine* 63 (1941), 89–107 [on the cult of Julian and Basilissa].

The Old English Versions

Moloney, B., 'A Critical Edition of Ælfric's Virgin-Martyr Stories', pp. 132–62 [for an analysis of the stories, including Cecilia].

Smith, L., 'Virginity and the Married-Virgin Saints in Ælfric's *Lives of Saints*: The Translation of an Ideal' (D.Phil. dissertation, University of Toronto, 2000) [focuses on the three legends considered here].

Upchurch, R., 'The Legend of Chrysanthus and Daria in Ælfric's *Lives of Saints*', *Studies in Philology* 101 (2004), 250–69.

—, 'Homiletic Contexts for Ælfric's Hagiography: The Legend of SS Cecilia and Valerian' in *Precedence, Practice, and Appropriation: The Old English Homily*, ed. A. Kleist (forthcoming).

—, 'Married Virgins as Model Christians: Ælfric's Legend of Julian and Basilissa', *ASE* 34 (2005), 197–217.

Whatley, E.G., 'Acta Sanctorum' in *Sources of Anglo-Saxon Literary Culture*, vol. 1, ed. F. Biggs et al. (Kalamazoo, 2001), 22–486 [for overviews of the literary history of the legends in Anglo-Saxon England].

Ælfric and Saints' Lives in Late Anglo-Saxon England

Cubitt, C., 'Virginity and Misogyny in Tenth- and Eleventh-Century England', *Gender and History* 12 (2000), 1–32.

Gretsch, M., *Ælfric and the Cult of Saints in Late Anglo-Saxon England* (Cambridge, 2005).

Hill, J., 'The Dissemination of Ælfric's Lives of Saints: A Preliminary Survey' in *Holy Men and Holy Women: Old English Prose Saints' Lives and Their Contexts*, ed. P. Szarmach (Albany,1996), pp. 235–59.

Hill, T., '*Imago Dei*: Genre, Symbolism, and Anglo-Saxon Hagiography' in *Holy Men and Holy Women*, ed. Szarmach, pp. 35–50.

Hurt, J., *Ælfric* (New York, 1972) [an introduction to Ælfric's life and works].

Jackson, P., 'Ælfric and the Purpose of Christian Marriage: A Reconsideration of the *Life of Æthelthryth*, Lines 120–30', *ASE* 29 (2000), 235–60.

John, E., 'The World of Abbot Ælfric' in *Ideal and Reality in Frankish and Anglo-Saxon Society*, ed. P. Wormald (Oxford, 1983), pp. 300–16.

Kleist, A., 'An Annotated Bibliography of Ælfrician Studies: 1983–1996' in *Old English Prose: Basic Readings*, ed. P. Szarmach (New York, 2000), pp. 503–52.

Lapidge, M., 'The Saintly Life in Anglo-Saxon England' in *The Cambridge Companion to Old English Literature*, ed. M. Godden and M. Lapidge (Cambridge, 1991), pp. 242–63.

Lees, C. *Tradition and Belief: Religious Writing in Late Anglo-Saxon England* (Minneapolis, 1999).

Magennis, H. '"No Sex Please, We're Anglo-Saxons"? Attitudes to Sexuality in Old English Prose and Poetry', *Leeds Studies in English*, New Series 24 (1995), 1–27.

Moloney, B. 'Be Godes Halgum: Ælfric's Hagiography and the Cult of the Saints in England in the Tenth Century' in *Learning and Literature in Medieval and Renaissance England: Essays Presented to Fitzroy Pile*, ed. J. Scattergood (Dublin, 1984), pp. 25–40.

Ortenberg, V. *The English Church and the Continent in the Tenth and Eleventh Centuries: Cultural, Spiritual, and Artistic Exchanges* (Oxford, 1992).

Upchurch, R., 'For Pastoral Care and Political Gain: Ælfric of Eynsham's Preaching on Marital Celibacy', *Traditio* (2004), 39–78.

Whatley, E.G., 'Late Old English Hagiography, ca. 950–1150' in *Hagiographies: Histoire internationale de la littérature hagiographique latine et vernaculaire en Occident des origines B 1550*, ed. G. Philippart, 3 vols, (Turnhout, 1994–2001), 2:429–99.

—, 'An Introduction to the Study of Old English Prose Hagiography: Sources and Resources' in *Holy Men and Holy Women*, ed. Szarmach, pp. 3–32.

Zettel, P., 'Saints' Lives in Old English: Latin Manuscripts and Vernacular Accounts: Ælfric', *Peritia* 1 (1982), 17–37.

OLD ENGLISH TEXTS AND TRANSLATIONS

EDITORIAL PROCEDURE

The three Old English texts are edited from London, British Library, Cotton MS Julius E. vii (J).[1] Cotton Julius E. vii, which was written in the early eleventh century, is the fullest copy of the *Lives of Saints* to survive. The manuscript, however, lacks full copies of the treatises Ælfric appears to have appended to the collection, and J includes material not by Ælfric as well (see p. 33, n. 8). Non-standard Late West Saxon forms that reflect the work of either the scribe who copied Julius E. vii or a contemporary reviser have been allowed to stand. Departures from J are signalled with square brackets [ ]. Abbreviations have been silently expanded, and punctuation and capitalization are modernized. Accent marks have not been reproduced, for which see Skeat's edition of the *Lives* [cited in the Select Bibliography].

Numbers in parentheses (#) correspond to the numbered paragraphs in the Latin texts. The numbers, which originate in printed versions of the Latin texts, are intended to facilitate comparisons among the Old English and Latin texts in this volume and the printed editions as well.

A vertical bar (|) indicates manuscript foliation, which is given in the apparatus.

Asterisks (*) direct readers to the Commentary (pp. 100–108). For convenience, asterisks are duplicated in the translations.

Latin sentences in Ælfric's texts are italicized.

Julian and Basilissa

The Old English text of *The Passio of Saint Julian and his Wife Basilissa* is found in J on folios 26[r]–32[r]. J has been collated with portions of another text that survives in the badly burnt London, British Library, Cotton Otho B. x. (s.xi[1]) (O).[2] Kevin Kiernan, who is preparing an electronic edition of Otho B. x, has provided a 'virtual' foliation of the manuscript's disordered leaves that preserve the text of *Julian and Basilissa*, and by digitizing the manuscript he has recovered nearly thirty new variant readings ('Odd Couples in Ælfric's *Julian and Basilissa* in British Library Cotton MS Otho B. x' in *Beatus vir* [cited on p. 33, n.11], eds Wolf and Doane, pp. 85–106). Each of those variants is recorded in the apparatus.

Cecilia and Valerian

The Old English text of *The Passio of Saint Cecilia the Virgin* is found in J on folios 213^v–19^r. J has been collated with portions of another text that survives in the badly burnt London, British Library, Cotton Vitellius D. xvii, folio 11^r–11^v (s.xi^{med}) (V).[3] Instances in which I was not able to confirm B. Moloney's readings from V ('A Critical Edition of Ælfric's Virgin-Martyr Stories from *The Lives of Saints*', unpublished Ph.D. dissertation [University of Exeter, 1980]) are noted parenthetically in the apparatus.

Chrysanthus and Daria

The Old English text of *The Passio of Chrysanthus and Daria his Wife* is found in J on folios 219^r–24^r. This is the only copy of the legend to survive.

Notes

1 A full description of the manuscript is found in N.R. Ker, *Catalogue of Manuscripts containing Anglo-Saxon* (Oxford, 1957), pp. 206–10 [item 162].

2 For a full description, see *Ibid.*, pp. 224–28 [item 177].

3 For a full description, see *Ibid.*, pp. 292–98 [item 222].

IDUS IANUARII. PASSIO SANCTI IULIANI
ET SPONSE EIUS BASILISSE.*

(2) IULIANUS WÆS GEHATEN SUM ÆÐELE GODES ÐEGN ON
Egypta lande on Antiochian þære byrig.* Se wæs æðelboren of æwfestum
magum and on Cristes lare gelæred fram geogoþe.

(3) Þa wolde his fæder and his frynd ealle þæt he wifian sceolde þa ða
5   he eahtetyne gæra wæs, ac Iulianus cwæð þæt he cunnian wolde his
Drihtnes wyllan, hu he wolde be him.*

(4) He wearð þa gebysgod on his gebedum seofan niht; bæd þone ælmi-
htigan Crist þæt he his clænnysse geheolde.* Ða æteowde se Hælend hine
sylfne on swefne þam æþelan cnihte on ðære eahteoðan nihte* and cwæð
10   þæt he sceolde soðlice underfon mæden him to gemacan þe hine ne moste
ascyrian fram his clænan lufe þe he gecoren hæfde. Se Hælend him cwæð
to, 'Ic beo sylf mid þe and on þe adwesce ealle ontendnysse, and þæt
mæden ic gebige* eac to minre lufe. And on eowrum brydbedde, ic beo
eow æteowed, and þurh eow, me bið gehalgod manegra oðre clennysse, |
15   and ic þe underfo mid ðinum mædene to heofonum'.

(5) Ða awoc Iulianus gewyssod þurh his Drihten; cwæð to his freondum
þæt he onfon wolde mæden him to gemacan, and hi mycclum þæs fægn-
odon.* Þa fundon his magas sum æðelboren mæden Basilissa gehaten and
him þa begeaten.

20   (6) Þa wurdon gegearcode þa gyftu æfter gewunan, and hi butu coman
on anum bedde tosomne.* Hwæt ða Iulianus hine georne gebæd to ðam
Hælende Criste þæt he hine geheolde wið ealla ontendnysse and yfele
costnunga. Ða wearð þæt brydbed mid bræðe afylled swylce þær lagon lilie
and rose.

25   Ða cwæð Basilissa to þam clænan brydguman, 'Hit is wintertid nu, and
ic wundrie þearle hwanon þes wyrtbræð þus wynsumlice steme.* And me
nu ne lyst nanes synscipes ac þæs Hælendes geþeodnysse mid gehealdenre
clennisse'.*

Iulianus andwyrde þam æðelan mædene, 'Þes [wynsuma] bræð þe ðu
30   wundrast þearle næfð nan angin ne eac nænne ænde. Þes bræð is of Criste
se ðe is clænnysse lufigend. Gif wit þurhwuniað on ansundum mægðhade
and hine clænlice lufiað, þonne cume wit to his rice and wit ne beoð
totwæmede ac a to worulde blyssiað'.

Title] *Text begins on folio 26ʳ, thirteen lines*
    from the top, in large red capitals.
1 IULIANUS. . . ON] *in small capitals*
    occupying a full line and a red decorated
    initial I extending one line above and
    below. GODES] *above line, insertion*
    mark below

2 Egypta] e *corrected from* æ
7 gebedum] e *corrected from* æ
12 adwesce] e *corrected from* æ
14 Fol. 26ᵛ
20 coman] B beco[man]
21 bedde] e *corrected from* æ. ða] B þa

13 JANUARY. THE PASSIO OF SAINT JULIAN
AND HIS WIFE BASILISSA.*

(2) There was a certain noble thegn of God named Julian in the country of the Egyptians in the city of Antioch.* He was nobly born of a devout family and was instructed in the knowledge of Christ from his youth.

(3) Then his father and all his relatives desired that he should marry when he was eighteen years old, but Julian said that he desired to find out his Lord's will, what he intended for him.*

(4) He was then occupied in his prayers for seven nights; he asked the almighty Christ to preserve his chastity.* Then the Saviour revealed himself to the noble young man in a dream on the eighth night* and said that he indeed ought to accept a virgin as a spouse for himself who would not be allowed to separate him from his chaste love that he had chosen. The Saviour said to him, 'I myself will be with you and will extinguish all burning desire in you, and I will also turn* the virgin to my love. And in your marriage-bed, I will be revealed to you, and because of you, the chastity of many others will be consecrated to me, and I will receive you with your virgin into heaven.'

(5) Then Julian awoke guided by his Lord; he said to his relatives that he was willing to take a virgin as a spouse for himself, and they rejoiced greatly about that.* Then his kinsmen found a certain nobly born virgin named Basilissa and obtained her in marriage for him.

(6) Then the wedding was prepared according to custom, and they both came into one bed together.* So, Julian eagerly prayed to the Saviour Christ that He might preserve him from all burning desires and evil temptations. Then the marriage bed was filled with a fragrance as if a lily and rose lay there.

Then Basilissa said to the chaste bridegroom, 'It is now winter, and I wonder greatly whence this scent of flowers so pleasantly exudes.* And now marriage is not pleasing to me but rather union with the Saviour with my chastity preserved'.*

Julian answered the noble virgin, 'This pleasant fragrance at which you wonder greatly has no beginning nor any end. The fragrance is from Christ who is a lover of chastity. If we continue in uncorrupted virginity and love him purely, then we will come to his kingdom and we will not be separated but will rejoice for ever'.

---

22 geheolde] B gehælde. ontendnysse] B ontendnyssa
23 bræðe] B braþe
26 þes] e *corrected from* æ
27 synscipes] B sinscipes
28 clennisse] B [clen]nysse

29 Þes] e *corrected from* æ. (wynsuma)] wynsuman; B wynsuma
30 ænde] B ende. Þes] e *corrected from* æ.
31 se ðe] B seþe. wit] B wy[t]. ansundum] B anwealgum
32 *first* wit] B we. *second* wit] B wyt
33 a] B *omits*

Basilissa cwæð þæt heo on clænum mægðhade þurhwunian wolde for
35 ðam wynsuman behate and habban þæt ece lif and ðone Hælend to
brydguman.

Þa clypode Iulianus on cneowgebedum ðus, '*Confirma hoc Deus quod
operatus es in nobis!*', *et reliqua* ('Gefæstna þis Hælend þæt þæt ðu on us
gewyrcst!').* And Basilissa sona swa gelice dyde.

40 (7) Þa astyrede þæt brydbed and beorht leoht þær scean, I and Crist
wearð gesewen mid scinendum werode and his modur Maria mid hyre
mædenlicum heape. Crist clypode þa to ðam clænan cnihte and cwæð þæt
he hæfde oferswiðod woruldlice gælsan and þone gramlican feond. Of
Marian werode wæs þus geclypod, 'Eadig eart þu Basilissa for þan þe þu
45 gebygdest þin mod to halwendum mynegungum and middaneardlice
swæsnysse mid ealle forsihst and þe sylfe gearcost to wuldre'. Þa com to
ðam bedde boc fram þam Hælende, and twegen his halgan mid twam
cynehelmum arærdan hi þa upp and heton hi rædan. Ða rædde Iulianus
þas word on þære bec, 'Se þe for minre lufe middaneard forsihð, he bið
50 soðlice geteald to þam unbesmitenum halgum þe næran on heora life
besmitene mid wifum. Basilissa bið geteald to þæra mædena getæle þe
Marian folgiað þæs Hælendes meder'. Æfter þissere rædinge and oðrum
tihtingum, gewendon þa halgan to þam Hælende upp.

(8) Hwæt þa Iulianus ungewæmmede heold his bryde, and hi wæron
55 geðeodde mid soðre clænnysse, gastlice þeonde on Godes gewytnysse.*

(9) Heora fæderas wæron gefyrn Cristene. Hit gelamp þa raðe þæt hi
of life gewytan and læfdon heora æhta þam æðelum mannum. (10)
Iulianus þa dælde, be his Drihtnes wyssunga, heora landare þe him læfed
wæs and arærde him mynster and his mædene oðer.* He wearð þa fæder
60 ofer fæla muneca and Basilissa, modor ofer manega mynecena. And hi
þa gastlican werod under Gode gewyssodon on dæghwamlicre lare to
heora Dryhtnes wyllan (11) oþ þæt se[o] reðe æhtnysse on Egypta lande
becom fram þam I welhreowan casere þe wæs geciged Dioclytianus.

Þa gebædon þa halgan hi to þam Hælende, (12) and he him asende
65 þisne frofer þus cwæðende, 'Eala, þu Basilissa, þine gebedu synd gefyllede
þæt ealle þine mædenu of middanearde gewitað ær ðan þe seo arlease
ehtnys ofer eow becume þæt ge ne beon gewemmede þurh ða wodan
ehteras'.

---

35 ece] e *corrected from* æ. ðone] B þone
37 clypode] B cleopode. ðus] B þus
39 gewyrcst] r *above line, insertion mark
below*
40 brydbed] B brydbedd. Fol. 27ʳ.
40–41 Crist wearð] B crist sylf wearð þær.
modur] B modor
44 *second* þu] B ðu

45 gebygdest] B gebigdest
47 twegen] e *corrected from* æ
48 cynehelmum] B kyn[ehelmum]. Ða] B Þa
49 forsihð] B [fors]yhð
56 þa] B ða. raðe] B hraþe
57 gewytan] B gewitan. æðelum] B æþelum
58 wyssunga] B willan. him] B heo[m].
læfed] B gelæfed

Basilissa said that she wished to continue in pure virginity on account of that pleasant promise and to have everlasting life and the Saviour as a bridegroom.

Then Julian cried out in prayer on his knees, '*God, confirm this that you have worked in us!*', *and so on* (Confirm this, Saviour, which you work in us!') [cf. Psalm 67.29 (Septuagint)].* And Basilissa immediately did likewise.

(7) Then the marriage-bed shook and a bright light shone there, and Christ with a shining host and his mother Mary with her company of virgins were visible. Christ then called out to the chaste young man and said that he had defeated earthly pleasures and the fierce enemy. From Mary's host it was thus declared, 'Blessed are you Basilissa because you turned your mind to salutary exhortations and entirely despise the blandishment of the world and prepare yourself for glory'. Then a book came to the bed from the Saviour, and two of his holy ones with two crowns then raised them up and commanded them to read. Then Julian read these words in the book, 'He who on account of my love despises the world, he will truly be reckoned among the undefiled saints who never in their lives were defiled with women [cf. Revelation 14.4]. Basilissa will be reckoned among the number of virgins who follow Mary, the Saviour's mother'. After this reading and other exhortations, the holy ones went up to the Saviour.

(8) Then Julian preserved his bride undefiled, and they were united with true chastity, spiritually thriving in the knowledge of God.*

(9) Their parents were already Christians. Then it soon happened that they departed from life and left their wealth to the noble ones. (10) According to the Lord's instruction, Julian then distributed their landed estate that was left to them and built himself a monastery and another for his virgin.* He then became a father over many monks and Basilissa, a mother over many nuns. And they guided the spiritual hosts in subjection to God according to their Lord's will with daily instruction (11) until the cruel persecution came into the land of the Egyptians from the bloodthirsty emperor who was named Diocletian.

Then the saints prayed to the Saviour, (12) and he sent them this comfort saying thus, 'O, Basilissa, your prayers are fulfilled so that all your virgins will depart from the world before the wicked persecution comes over you in order that you will not be defiled by the mad persecutors'.

---

59 oðer] B oþer
60 fæla] B fela
61 gewyssodon] B well gewissodan
62 Dryhtnes] B drihtnes. wyllan] B willan.
    oþ] B Oð. se(o)] se; B seo. reðe] B reþe.
    æhtnysse] B ehtnys[se]
63 Fol. 27ᵛ. welhreowan] B wælhreowan
65 gebedu] *second* e *corrected from* æ

(15) Hit wearð þa gefylled swa swa him foresæde God, þæt ealle ða
70 femnan þe folgodon Basilissan gewytan of worulde to þam wuldorfullan
Hælende. And Basilissa siððan, soðlice gelaðod, gewat on mægðhade of
middanearde to Criste, and Iulianus mid blisse hi bebyrgde mid his
munecum. And he abad on life mid his leofan gebroðrum, tihtende hi
geornlice to ðam towerdan gecampe.

75 (17) Ða com Martianus se manfulla cwællere into Antiochian þære
Egyptiscan byrig mid ormettre ehtnysse fram þam arleasan casere. He
sette þa gebann þæt nan mann bicgan ne moste oððe ænig þing syllan
buton he onsægednysse geoffrode þam leasum deofolgyldum and his
Drihten wiðsoce. Him wearð þa gesæd be ðam soðan geleafan þe Iulianus
80 heold mid his halgum gebroðrum and sende to ðam heape; het hi gebugan
to his deofolgyldum þe læs þe hi fordemede wurdon. Ac Iulianus ne rohte
þæs reðan þywrace, ne nan his geferena forht næs on mode, ac wæron
lustbære for þone leofan Drihten wita to þrowienne and eac wælhreowne
deað.

85 (19) Þa gecyrde se ærendraca and þis sæde þam deman. Martianus þa
het þone halgan Iulianum him to gelangian to langsumum wytum and het
siððan forbernan ealle his gebroðra samod binnan I þam ylcan huse þe hi
heora beda beeoden.* Þa wearð se halga heap þam Hælende geoffrod and
þurh þæt hate fyr to heofonan rice becom. On ðere stowe beoð gehælede
90 gehwilce untrume þurh þæra martyra geearnunga þe on þære stowe
ðrowodon.

(20) Hwæt ða Martianus se manfulla cwellere hæfde langsum gewinn
wið þone æðelan Iulianum and cwæð þæt he geare wiste his æðelboren-
nysse, 'And Ic þe forði tihte þæt ðu þam godum geoffrige æfter þinre
95 gebyrde þæt hi þe blyðe beon'.

(21) Iulianus him sæde, 'Þu eart soðlice ablend mid þinre yfelnysse,
and forþi me þus olæcst. Ge habbað manega godas and manega gydena.
We soðlice wurðia[þ] ænne soðne God. Eower godas synd agotene oððe
agrafene. Hu magon hi beon gegladode þurh ænige bigencgas oþþe þam
100 gemyltsian þe hi mid gedwylde wurðiað?'

Þeos race is swiðe langsum fullice to gereccenne, ac we hit sæcgað eow
on þa scortostan wisan.

(23) Hwæt þa Martianus het his manfullan cwelleras þone halgan
beatan mid heardum saglum. Þa bærst sum sagol into anes beateres eagan
105 swa þæt his eage wand ut mid þam slæge. Se man wæs þam deman þearle
nydbehefe and cuð þam casere and him eallum gecweme.

---

70 femnan] e *corrected from* æ
76 Egyptiscan] e *corrected from* æ
77 sette] e *corrected from* æ
87 Fol. 28ʳ
98 wurðia(þ)] wurðian

(15) It was then fulfilled just as God said to them earlier, so that all the virgins who followed Basilissa departed from the world to the glorious Saviour. And afterwards Basilissa, truly invited, departed in virginity from the world to Christ, and Julian together with his monks buried her with rejoicing. And he went on living together with his beloved brothers, exhorting them eagerly towards the future warfare.

(17) Then Martianus the evil executioner came into Antioch the Egyptian city with heavy persecution from the wicked emperor. He set forth a decree that no man be allowed to buy or sell anything unless he offered a sacrifice to the false idols and renounce his Lord. He was then told about the true faith that Julian kept with his holy brothers and sent a message to the company; he commanded them to turn to his idols lest they be condemned. But Julian did not care about the cruel threat, nor was one of his companions fearful in mind, but they were joyful about suffering torments and also cruel death for the beloved Lord.

(19) Then the messenger returned and told this to the judge. Martianus then commanded the holy Julian to be summoned to him for long-lasting torments and afterwards commanded all his brothers to be burned alive together inside the same house in which they said their prayers.* Then the holy company was offered to the Saviour and through the hot fire went to the kingdom of heaven. In that place all the sick are healed by the merits of the martyrs who suffered there.

(20) So Martianus the evil executioner had a long conflict with the noble Julian and said that he knew well his noble pedigree, 'And I thus urge you to sacrifice to the gods according to your rank so that they will be well-disposed towards you'.

(21) Julian said to him, 'You are indeed blinded by your wickedness, and therefore you flatter me like this. You have many gods and many goddesses. We truly honour the one true God. Your gods are cast or carved. How can they be propitiated by any rites or be merciful to those who honour them with false belief?'

This account is very long to narrate in its entirety, but we will tell it to you in the shortest way.

(23) So Martianus commanded his evil executioners to beat the saint with hard clubs. Then one club smashed into the eye of one of the beaters so that his eye flew out because of the blow. The man was very necessary to the judge and known to the emperor and pleasing to them all.

Ða cwæð Martianus mid mycclum graman, 'Swa micel is þin drycræft
þæt ðu þas dyntas naht ne gefretst, and, þærtoeacan, ablendst þone þe þe
beaton sceolde!'

110 Iulianus þa cwæð to þam welhreowan þus, 'Clypiað to eowrum godum
and to eallum gydenum þæt hi nu gehælan þises hæðenan eage, and gif hi
ne magon, ic hine gehæle þurh Crist'.

(24) Þa eoden þa hæðengyldan | into heora temple clypigende hlude
to ðam leasan gode. Ða andwerdan þa deofla of þam dædan anlicnyssum,

115 'Gewitað fram us! We synd wraðe geswæncte and mid fyre fornumene for
Iulianes intingan æfre fram ðam dæge þe ge hine ærest dræhton. Hu mage
we blinde þone blindan gehælan?'

Þa cwæð Iulianus, þe þæt eal wyste, to Martiane mid micelre blisse,
'Gang into þinum godum. Þe hi clypiað to him.'

120 Þa eode se ehtere into ðam temple and geseah þa anlicnyssa ealle
tocwysede, gyldena and sylfrena, and sume of smyltinga, sume of
cristallan, tobrytte mid ealle. Þa sæde Martianus þæt ða soðfæstan godes
mid geþylde forbæron þone bysmorfullan teonan þæt hi swa Iulianum to
him gebigan mihton. (25) He bæd swa þeah Iulianum þæt he his gebeot

125 gelæste and þæs cnihtes eage þurh his Crist gehælde.

(26) Þa mærcode Iulianus þæs mannes eage mid Cristes rodetacne, and
se cniht wearð gehæled swylce his eage nære næfre ær gederod. Ða
clypode se cniht and cwæð to Martiane, 'Se God is to gelyfanne þe ða
Cristenan on gelyfað, and þine godas synd soðlice deoflu!'

130 Martianus þa het hine beheafdian for ðan þe he gelyfde on þone lyfi-
gendan God þe his eage onlihte and eac his heortan. (27) He het eac
geswencean mid swarum witum þone halgan Iulianum and het hine lædan
geond ealle þa burh gebundene mid racenteagum.

Martianus hæfde his sunu ær befæst to woruldlicre lare and to uðwite-

135 gunge on þære ylcan byrig þe se gebundene eode. His nama wæs Celsus,
and se geseah þone halgan and hu godes | ænglas him mid flugon. (29)
Awearp þa his larboc and mid geleafan arn to þam halgan were and his
fet gesohte; cwæð þæt he wiðsoce þam sceandlicum godum and Crist
andette mid ealre heortan. (30) Ne mihte hine nan man of þam geleafan

140 gebringan ne fram Iuliane þurh ænig þing ateon.

(31) Þa wæarð Martianus and eac seo modor dreorige on mode and
heora men ealle. And Martianus befran þone mæran Iulianum, 'Hwi
woldest þu amyrran min ancennedan sunu þurh þinne drycræft and to
þinum Criste geweman. Beheald ure sarnysse and urne sunu forlæt, and

145 ic ðe geþingie to urum kasere'.

---

113 Fol. 28ᵛ
127 gederod] *second e corrected from* æ
132 geswencean] ge *above line, insertion*
    mark below

136 Fol. 29ʳ
143 þurh] *above line, insertion mark below*

Then Martianus spoke with great anger, 'So great is your magic that you do not feel these blows at all, and, moreover, you blind the one who must beat you!'

Julian then spoke to the bloodthirsty one in this way, 'Call out to your gods and to all your goddesses so that they may now heal this heathen's eye, and if they are not able, I will heal him through Christ'.

(24) The heathen priests then went into their temple calling loudly to the false god. Then the devils answered from the dead images, 'Depart from us! We are fiercely afflicted and have been continually consumed by fire on account of Julian from the day you first persecuted him. How can we who are blind heal the blind?'

Then Julian, who knew all that, said to Martianus with great joy, 'Go into your gods. They summon you to themselves'.

Then the persecutor went into the temple and saw the images completely crushed, gold and silver ones, and some of amber, some of crystal, entirely broken into pieces. Then Martianus said that the just gods endured the shameful injury with patience so that they could thus turn Julian to themselves. (25) He nevertheless asked Julian to fulfil his boast and to heal the young man's eye through his Christ.

(26) Then Julian marked the man's eye with the sign of Christ's cross, and the young man was healed as if his eye had never before been injured. Then the young man cried out and said to Martianus, 'The God in whom the Christians believe must be believed in, and your gods are truly devils!' [cf. Psalm 95.5 (Septuagint)]

Martianus then commanded him to be beheaded because he believed in the living God who gave light to his eye and his heart as well. (27) He also commanded the holy Julian to be afflicted with grievous torments and commanded him to be led throughout all the city bound with chains.

Martianus had earlier set his son to learning earthly knowledge and philosophy in the same city in which the bound one went. His name was Celsus, and he saw the saint and how God's angels flew with him. (29) Then he threw away his book of instruction and with faith ran to the holy man and sought his feet; he said that he renounced the shameful gods and confessed Christ with all his heart. (30) No one was able to draw him away from the faith nor take him away from Julian by any means.

(31) Then Martianus and also the mother and all their men became anguished in spirit. And Martianus asked the glorious Julian, 'Why do you wish to lead astray my only-begotten son with your magic and to entice him to your Christ? Consider our sorrow and leave our son alone, and I will intercede for you with our emperor'.

(32) Celsus se sunu sæde þam swicolan fæder þus, 'Ic wiðsace þe, fæder, for þinum gedwylde, and ic gelyfa on Crist þe me gecoren hæfð. Witna, gif þu wylle, mid wælhreowum tintregum þinne agenre sunu for þinra goda bigencge. Gif þu nelle me ofslean, asend me to þam casere þæt ic 150 þær deað þrowige for minum Drihtne, Criste'.

(33) Þa halgan wurdon gebrohte on blindum cwearterne syððan, be Martianes hæse, þær manna lic lagon þe wæran ær acwealde on ðam cwearterne gefyrn, þa weollon eall maðon and egeslice stuncon. Þa foresceawode Godes gifu þæt þær scean mycel leoht, and se stenc wearð 155 awend to wynsummum bræðe and eall se[o] unwynsumnyss him wearð to blysse.

(34) Þa cwædon þa cempan þe se cwellere gesette þam halgum to weardmannum (þæra wæron twentig), 'Unrihtlic us bið þæt we æft gecyrron fram þysum beorhtan leohte to blindum þystrum, fram life to 160 deaðe, fram soðe to leasunga'. Hi feollon þa ealle to Iulianes fotum mid geleafan, herigende þæs Hælendes naman. Iulianus þa bæd mid | onbryrd-nysse his Drihten þæt he foresceawode hu hi gefullode wurdon.

(35) Þær wæron binnan þære byrig seofan gebroðra Cristena þæs caseres cynnes (and heora fæder wæs Cristen), þam alyfde se casere heora 165 Cristendom to healdenne butan ælcere ehtnysse for ðam arwurðan cynne. Hi hæfdon ænne mæssepreost swiðe mæres lifes, Antonius gehaten, þe him mæssan gesang. Þas geneosode se Hælend and het hi gan to þam cwearterne mid heora mæssepreoste þæt þa men wurdon gefullode. Hi eoden þa on niht, and Godes ængel hi lædde and þæt cweartern geope-170 nade mid his handa hrepunge. Þa sædon þa gebroðra þæt se Hælend hi asende mid heora mæssepreostæ þa men to fullienne. Iulianus þa sona þæs þancode Gode, and wearð þa gefullod se foresæda cnapa and his fæder cempan on Cristes naman endemes.

(36) Þis wæarð þa gecyd þam cwellere Martiane, þæt þa seofan 175 gebroðra butan ælcere ehtnysse woldan for Cristes naman on þam cwear-terne þrowian. Þa het se cwellere hi of þam cwearterne gelædan and axode hwi hi woldan butan ehtnysse þrowian.* Þa cwæð se yldesta broðor to þam arleasan deman, 'Andsæte bið þæt treow þe æfre grewð on leafum and næfre nænne wæstm his Scyppende ne bringð; swa synd we Cristene gif 180 ure Cristendom ne bið acunnod'.

---

155 se(o)] se
158 þæra] B Þær[a]
159 gecyrron] B gecirron
160 leasunga] B leasu[n]ge
161 Fol. 29ᵛ
168 cwearterne] cwearterterne, *first* ter *dotted for deletion*

169 eoden] B eodon. þa] B ða. þæt] B ð[æt]
171 asende] B asænde. fullienne] B [fu]llienne
172 þancode] B ða[ncode]
174 cwellere] *first* e *corrected from* æ. *second* þa] B ða

(32) Celsus the son spoke to his deceitful father in this way, 'I renounce you, father, for your false belief, and I believe in Christ who has chosen me. Punish, if you will, your own son with cruel tortures for the sake of the worship of your gods. If you are unwilling to kill me, send me to the emperor so that I there may suffer death for my Lord, Christ'.

(33) The saints were afterwards led into a dark prison, at Martianus's command, where lay the bodies of men who were earlier killed in the prison, which utterly boiled with maggots and smelled horribly. Then God's grace saw to it that a great light shone there, and the stench was changed into a pleasant fragrance and all the unpleasantness was made for them a source of pleasure.

(34) Then the soldiers whom the executioner set as guards for the saints (of whom there were twenty) said, 'It will be wrong for us to turn again from this bright light to obscure darkness, from life to death, from truth to falsehood'. They all then fell at Julian's feet with faith, praising the Saviour's name. Then Julian prayed with zeal to his Lord to see to it that they were baptized.

(35) There were within the city seven Christian brothers of the emperor's family (and their father had been a Christian), whom the emperor allowed to practice their Christianity without any persecution on account of their distinguished family. They had a priest of an exceedingly glorious life named Antonius, who sang masses for them. The Saviour visited these men and commanded them to go to the prison with their priest so that the men might be baptized. They went then at night, and God's angel led them and opened the prison with the touch of his hand. Then the brothers said that the Saviour had sent them with their priest to baptize the men. Julian then thanked God for that at once, and the aforementioned young man and his father's soldiers were baptized together in the name of Christ.

(36) This was then made known to the executioner Martianus, that the seven brothers without any persecution wished to suffer in the prison for Christ's name. Then the executioner commanded them to be led from the prison and asked why they wished to suffer without any persecution.* The oldest brother then said to the wicked judge, 'Hateful is the tree that always sprouts into leaf and never brings forth any fruit for its Creator; so are we Christians if our Christianity is not tested'.

---

175 butan] B [bu]ton. ehtnysse] B [eh]tnesse.
      woldan] B woldon. þam] B ðam
176–77 Þa. . . þrowian] B *omits.*
177 þam] B ðam

(37) Þa het se cwellere hi to þam cwearterne gelædan and sende his gewrit to þam wælhreowan casere: 'Gehelp urum godum and hat to þe gefeccan þisne dry Iulianum, þe ure goda anlicnysse mid ealle tobrytte and minne sunu gebygde fram me to his Criste and þa seofan cnihtas þe
185 be þinre leafa lyfedan buton ehtnysse on þyssere byrig for hyra mycclum | gebyrde'. Þa asende se casere þisne cwide ongean, 'Gif Iulianus þurhwunað mid his geferum on þysum, nim fela tunnan and do hi þæron innan. Onæl hi siððan ealle oðrum mannum to bysne.* And gif he þurh his drycræft þæt fyr adwescan mæg, gewitna hi ealle loca hu þu wylle'.
190 (38) Þa het Martianus þa Godes menn gefeccan and axode Iulianum hweðer hi aht smeadon ymbe hyre agene þearfe on þære hwile oð þæt. Iulianus sæde, 'Ure geþanc is swa swa hit wæs. Gif þu ænig wite beþohtest, we synd gearwe to þam'.

(39) Þa mid þyssere spræce, bæron menn on ðære stræt anes hæðenes
195 mannes lic, and se heardheorta dema het beran þone deadan to his domsetle. Cwæð þa to Iuliane, 'Eower Crist arærde þa deadan to life. Læt nu geswutelian gif he soð God sy, and ge þisne aræran'.

Þa andwyrde Iulianus þam arleasan deman, 'Hwæt fremað þam blindan seo beorhta sunbeam? Is swa þeah tima þæt Godes miht beo
200 geswutelod'.

Iulianus ða hof to heofonum his eagan, biddende his Drihten þæt he þone deadan arærde. Þa æfter anre tida aras se deade and clypode ofer eall*, 'Eala, hu andfæncge gebed and hu clæne mægðhad is on þisum mæran Iuliane! Eala, hwider ic wæs gelæd and hwanon ic eom nu
205 gebroht!'

(40) Þa het Martianus mid his hospwordum þæt he ful sæde his sið him eallum.

Þa cwæð se geeadcucoda, 'Me coman to Silhearwan atelices hiwes, swa heage swa entes, mid byrnendum eagum and egeslicum toðum. Heora
210 earmes wæron swylce ormæte beames, heora clawa scearpe and hi sylfa unmildheorta. Þas þyllice me tugon to þære sweartan helle. Ða mid þam þe Iulianus his Drihten gebæd þæt he me eft arærde, þa unrotsodon helware, | and of Godes þrymsetle wearð þus geclypod, "Beo se man ongean gelæd for minum leofan Iuliane.* Nelle ic hine geunrotian on
215 ænigum þincge". Þa coman twegen englas and me of ðam deoflum genamon and me gebrohtan to life þæt ic nu on God gelyfe æfter minum deaðe, þone þe ic ær wiðsoc'.

---

181 cwellere] *first* e *corrected from* æ
184 þa] B ða
185 lyfedan] B [l]eofodo[n]. ehtnysse] *first* e *corrected from* æ. hyra] B heo[ra]
186 Fol. 30ʳ
189 adwescan] e *corrected from* æ

190 menn] B [me]n
194 þyssere] B þissere
197 aræran] B aræron
203 gebed] *second* e *corrected from* æ
209 entes] *first* e *corrected from* æ
212 eft] e *corrected from* æ

(37) Then the executioner commanded them to be led into the prison and sent his letter to the bloodthirsty emperor: 'Help our gods and order to be fetched to you this sorcerer Julian, who has entirely destroyed the images of our gods and turned my son from me to his Christ as well as the seven young men who by your permission lived without persecution in this city on account of their great rank'. Then the emperor sent back this word of reply, 'If Julian persists with his companions in this, take many casks and put them inside. Afterwards burn them all as an example to other men.* And if through his magic he is able to extinguish the fire, punish them all however you wish'.

(38) Then Martianus commanded the men of God to be fetched and asked Julian whether they had thought of anything concerning their own good in the meantime. Julian said, 'Our will is just as it was. If you have thought of any punishment, we are ready for it'.

(39) Then as this was said, men carried into the market-place the body of a heathen man, and the hard-hearted judge ordered the dead man to be carried to his judgement seat. He then said to Julian, 'Your Christ raised the dead to life. Let it now be revealed if he is the true God, and let this man be raised too'.

Then Julian answered the wicked judge, 'What use is the bright sunbeam to the blind man? Nevertheless it is time for God's power to be revealed'.

Julian then lifted up his eyes to heaven, asking his Lord to revive the dead man. Then after a time the dead man arose and cried out above everything*, 'O, how acceptable a prayer and how pure a virginity is in this glorious Julian! O, the place to which I was led and whence I am now brought!'

(40) Then Martianus commanded with his scornful speech that he fully give an account of his journey to them all.

Then the one restored to life said, 'Ethiopians of hideous appearance came to me, as tall as giants, with burning eyes and terrifying teeth. Their arms were like enormous beams, their claws sharp and they themselves merciless. Such as these dragged me into the dark hell. Then, when Julian prayed to his Lord to revive me again, the inhabitants of hell grieved, and from the throne of God was declared in this way, "Let the man be led back for the sake of my beloved Julian.* I do not wish to sadden him in any way". Then two angels came and took me from the devils and led me to life so that now after my death I believe in God, whom I earlier renounced'.

---

213 Fol. 30ᵛ
215 twegen] *first* e *corrected from* æ. englas]
  e *corrected from* æ

Þa wearð Martianus mycclum gedrefed and het hi ealle gebringan
binnan þam cwearterne eft (41) and het gearcian ða tunnan to heora
220 bærnette swa swa se kasere het þurh his ærendgewrit. Þa wearð se edcu-
code man betwux þysum gefullod binnan þam cwearterne and gebad mid
þam Cristenum oð þæt Martianus hi to þam martyrdome gefette.
(42) Hi wurdon þa gebrohte gebundene on racenteagum ealle to þam
tunnum and to þære ontendnysse. (43) Þa cwæð Martianus mid mycelre
225 angsumnysse to þam halgum werum and to his agenum suna, 'Eala, hwilc
anwilnys and geortruwad wylla, þurh ða þeos fægre geogað nu forwurðan
sceall? Eala, þu Iuliane, þe awendest minne sunu swa þæt he min ne ræcð
ne eac þære meder!' Þa com seo modor mid mycelre sarnysse and ealle
hyre hyredmen to þære heofunga, and manega oðre menn to þære
230 mycclan wæfersyne.
(44) Þa cwæð þæs deman sunu to his dreorigan fæder, 'Ne þurfe ge us
bemænan ne urne siþ bewepan. Bewepaþ eow sylfe. We siðiaþ to
heofonum. We farað ðurh þæt fyr unforhte þurh God, and we ansunde
becumað eft to eowrum gesihþum. Þonne þu me eft gesihst gesundne of
235 þam fyre, geþafa þæt min modor me gespræcan and sume þreo niht on
minum ræde beon. Ic wene þæt þu ne forleosa naðor ne hi ne me'. Þa
wearð seo modor on mode geblissod, and se fæder cwæð | þæt he þæs
cnapan willan wolde gefremman gif he of þam fyre come.
(45) Þa het se dema his gingran þis don and eode mid his wife aweg to
240 his huse for þan þe he ne mihte geseon hu his sunu forburne. Þa het se
undergerefa* hi ealle gebringan into ðam tunnum and ontendan hi mid
acuman and mid wuda belecgan swa þæt se lig astah ma þone ðryttig
fæðma on þæs folces gesihþe oð þæt þæt ad wæs forburnen and ealle þa
tunnan. Ða stodan þa halgan hale of þam fyre, glitiniende swa swa gold,
245 þus herigende God, *'Transiuimus per ignem et aquam et eduðisti nos in
refrigerium!'* ('We ferdon þurh fyr and wæter, and þu us læddest on
celincge!') (46) Þis geaxode se dema and þyder efste mid his wife, and
æfter langsumre spræce (47) let þa modor to þam suna on synderlicre
clysincge þæt heo þone sunu gebigde.
250 Þa gebædon þa halgan binnan þam cwearterne for þæt hæðene wif þæt
se Hælend hire gemiltsode. (48) Þa wearð þær eorðstyrung and eall seo
stow byfode and þær scean mycel leoht, and mære bræð þær stanc swa þæt
þæt wif wundrode þæs wynsuman bræþes and cwæð þæt heo næfre ær naht
swilces ne gestunce. Þa gelyfde heo sona on þone lifigendan God and (50)
255 wearð gefullod æt þam foresædan preoste and fullice gecyrred to ðam
soðan geleafan.

---

221 gefullod] u *written as* v
225 agenum] *barred* u *above line, insertion*
     mark below
226 fægre] B fægere

229 hyre] B heo[re]. to þære] to þæ *in left*
     margin. heofunga] B [heogun]ge
232 Bewepaþ] B [be]wepað
233 ðurh þæt fyr] B þurh ðæt fir

Then Martianus was greatly vexed and ordered that they all be led inside the prison again (41) and ordered the casks to be prepared for their burning just as the emperor had commanded in his letter. Then the man restored to life was baptized among those inside the prison and remained with the Christians until Martianus fetched them to martyrdom.

(42) They were then brought bound entirely in chains to the casks and to the burning. (43) Then Martianus said with great anguish to the holy men and to his own son, 'O, what sort of obstinacy and desperate will is this, on account of which this fair youth will now perish? O, Julian, you turned my son so that he does not care about me or his mother either!' Then the mother and all of her household came with great sorrow to the lamentation, and many other men (came) to the great spectacle.

(44) Then the son of the judge said to his anguished father, 'You need not lament or bewail our lot. Weep for yourselves. We journey to heaven. We will go through the fire unafraid because of God, and we shall come again unharmed into your sight. When you see me again sound from the fire, allow my mother to speak to me and counsel with me for about three nights. I expect that you will lose neither her nor me'. Then the mother was happy in spirit, and the father said that he would be willing to do the young man's will if he came out of the fire.

(45) Then the judge commanded his aide to do this and went away with his wife to his house because he could not watch how his son would be burned alive. Then the deputy* commanded them all to be put into the casks and set them on fire with oakum and surrounded them with wood so that the fire ascended more than thirty cubits in sight of the people until the pyre and all the casks were burned up. Then the saints came out of the fire sound, glittering like gold, praising God in this way, '*We have passed through fire and water and you have brought us into cool relief!*' ('We went through fire and water, and you led us into coolness!' [Psalm 64.12]) (46) The judge discovered this and hastened to that place with his wife, and after a long conversation (47) he left the mother to the son in a private prison so that she might turn her son.

Inside the prison the saints prayed then for the heathen woman so that the Saviour might have mercy on her. (48) Then there was an earthquake and the whole place shook and there shone a great light, and a glorious fragrance rose there so that the woman wondered at the pleasant fragrance and said that she never before had smelled anything like it. She then believed at once in the living God and (50) was baptized by the aforementioned priest and fully turned to the true faith.

---

234 *second* eft] e *corrected from* æ
235 geþafa] B [ge]ðafa
236 þu] B ðu
237 Fol. 31ʳ
238 þam] B ðam

240 for þan þe] B fo[r] ðan ð[e]
241 tunnum] *bar over* u *is very faint, perhaps erased*
242 belecgan] *second* e *corrected from* æ
251 seo] o *above line, insertion mark below*

(51) Þa geaxode se dema þis þus gedon, and het hi ealle gelædan to his laðan andweardnysse and cwæð to his suna Celse mid graman, 'Bæde þu forþi þinre modor spræce þæt þu hi gebigdest to þinum bigenge fram me'.

260 Se cnapa þancode Gode þe hi swa gebigde to his soðan geleafan þæt heo ne losode mid him. Þa het Martianus þæt man hi gelæhte, ac hi | wurdon ablende þe þæt bebod begunnon.

(52) Æfter þisum het se heardheorta dema beheafdian þa cempan þe on Crist gelyfdan, and þa seofon gebroðra he het ealle forbernan and

265 heold gyt þa feower mid þam foresædan wife. Wolde hi gelædan to his leofestan godum þe him to lafe wæron þa ða oðre losodon þæt hi huru þam godum heora lac geoffrodon.

(54) He het þa gedæftan þæt deofles templ and þa halgan coman þider on bendum and ealle þa hæðengildan þe þæs huses gimdon coman to þam

270 temple togeanes þam Cristenum.* (57) Þa bed Iulianus gebigedum cneowum mid his geferum þone heofonlican God þæt he his mihte geswutelode mannum to geleafan and þæt templ towurpe mid his awyrigedum godum.* Æfter þære bene tobærst seo eorðe and þæt templ asanc mid eallum his sacerdum, and fela þære hæðenra forferdon samod.

275 Þa cwæð Iulianus to þam cwellere þus, 'Hwær is nu seo fægernys þines gefrætowodan temples? Hwær synd þa anlicnyssa þe þu on wuldrodest? Swa swa hi besuncon on ðone sweartan grund, swa sceole ge hæðene on helle grund besincan þær bið æfre ece fyr and undeadlic wyrm þe eowre lichaman cywð, and ge þeah ne sweltað, ac bið æfre se lichama geedniwod

280 to ðam witum. Þær ge biddað mildsunga, ac eow biþ forwyrned'.*

Git þa Martianus for his manfulnysse nolde on God gelyfan ac wearð mid graman afylled and cwæð þæt he wolde wrecan his godas. (59) Het þa bewindan heora handa and fet mid gesmyredum flexe and fyr under betan. Þa barn þæt fyr and þa bendas samod, and þære halgena lichaman

285 belifon ungederode. Þa wolde se manfulla hi mislice getintregian, ac God hi ahredde fram þam reðum witum | and sume eac ablende of þam bysmor-fullum þenum.

(60) Þa geseah se arleasa aidlian his smeagunge and wolde þa gyt cunnian anes cynnes wite þurh reþe deor þa þa his reðnyss ne mihte þurh

290 manna dæda gedon swa he wolde. He het þa gelædan leon and beran, manega and mycele, to þam halgum martyrum, ac þa reðan deor ne dorston hi reppan ac bigdon heora heafda to ðære halgena fotum and heora liða liccodon mid liðra tungan.*

261 Fol. 31ᵛ

274 fela] e *corrected from* æ

275 cwellere] *first* e *corrected from* æ

285 ungederode] *second* e *corrected from* æ

286 Fol. 32ʳ

288 smeagunge] a *above line, insertion mark below*

(51) The judge then learned this had happened in this way, and he ordered that they all be led into his hateful presence and said to his son Celsus with anger, 'You thus asked for a conversation with your mother with the result that you turned her from me to your religion'. The young man thanked God who thus turned her to His true faith so that she might not be lost with him. Then Martianus commanded someone to seize her, but they who undertook that command were blinded.

(52) After this the hard-hearted judge commanded the soldiers who believed in Christ to be beheaded, and he ordered the seven brothers to be burnt completely up and still kept the four with the aforementioned woman. He wished to lead them to his most beloved gods who were left to him when the others perished so that they at least might offer their sacrifices to those gods.

(54) He then ordered the devil's temple to be prepared and the saints to come there in bonds and all the heathen priests who took care of the building to come to the temple to oppose the Christians.* (57) Then Julian prayed on bended knees with his companions to the God of heaven that by his power he might be revealed to provide faith for men and that he would destroy the temple with its accursed gods.* After that prayer, the earth burst asunder and the temple sank into the ground with all its priests, and many of the heathens perished at the same time.

Julian then spoke to the executioner in this way, 'Where now is the beauty of your adorned temple? Where are the images that you gloried in? Just as they sank into the dark depth, so will you heathens sink into the depth of hell where there will always be everlasting fire and the immortal worm that will chew your bodies, and yet you will not die, but (your) body will continually be renewed for the torments. There you will pray for mercy, but it will be refused you'.*

Still Martianus on account of his wickedness was not willing to believe in God but was filled with anger and said that he wished to avenge his gods. (59) He then commanded their hands and feet to be wrapped with greased flax and a fire to be kindled under them. Then the fire and the bonds burned together, and the saints' bodies remained unharmed. The evil one wished then to torture them in various ways, but God saved them from the cruel torments and also blinded some of the shameful servants.

(60) The wicked one then saw his plan brought to nothing and wished still to try out a kind of torture with fierce wild animals when his ferocity could not accomplish what he wanted by means of the deeds of men. He commanded lions and bears, lots and large, to be brought to the holy martyrs, but the fierce wild animals dared not touch them but bowed their heads to the feet of the saints and licked their limbs with lithe tongues.*

(61) Þa het Martianus his manfullan cwelleras þa halgan beheafdian,
295   and hi þæs fægnodon, þanciende Gode ealra his godnyssa. Iulianus þa and
se geonga cniht, Martianes sunu, and his modor samod, Antonius se
preost and se geedcu[c]ode man wurdon tosomne ofslagene for Criste
and ferdon mid wuldre to þam welwillendan Hælende and to heora
geferum þe him forestopon, þæt is, Basilissa mid hyre beorhtum
300   mædenum and se halga heap þe on ðam huse forbarn and þa twentig
weardmenn þe se wælhreowa beheafdode and þa seofan gebroðra þe he
forbernan het. And hi ealle nu mid Gode on ecnysse blyssiað.*

(62) Hit gelamp þa, sona swa hi ofslagene wæron, þæt mycel liget com
ofer þa manfullan hæðenan and swiðlic eorðstyrung and egeslic þunor
305   swa þæt þæra manfulra mycel dæl forwearð, and nan stow ne ætstod mid
þam stænenum godum ne nan hæðengyld se hagol ne belæfde. Þa fleah
Martianus, fornean adyd, and he wearð fornumen æfter feawum dagum
swa þæt wurmas crupon cuce of his lice, and se arleasa gewat mid wite to
helle.
310   (63) Þæra halgan lic þurh geleaffulle menn wurdon gebyrigde sona mid
blisse binnan Godes cyrcan. Sy him a wuldor on ecere worulde, we
cweþað, AMEN.

---

297 geedcu(c)ode] geedcutode
304 egeslic] *first* e *corrected from* æ
312 AMEN] *in small capitals*

(61) Then Martianus commanded his evil executioners to behead the saints, and they rejoiced about this, giving thanks to God for all his goodness. Then Julian and the young boy, Martianus's son, and his mother too, Antonius the priest and the man restored to life were killed together for the sake of Christ and went with glory to the benevolent Saviour and to their companions who preceded them, that is, Basilissa with her bright virgins, and the holy crowd that was burned alive in the house, and the twenty guards whom the cruel one beheaded and the seven brothers whom he ordered to be burned to death. And they all now rejoice for ever with God.*

(62) It then happened, as soon as they were killed, that much lightning and a powerful earth-quake and terrifying thunder came upon the evil heathens so that a great number of the evil ones perished, and no place with stone gods remained standing nor did the hail spare any heathen shrine. Then Martianus fled, nearly killed, and he was destroyed after a few days so that worms crawled alive out of his body, and the wicked one departed with torture to hell.

(63) The bodies of the saints were at once buried with rejoicing by believing men inside God's church. To him be glory for ever in the life everlasting, we say, AMEN.

X KALENDAS DECEMBRIS.
PASSIO SANCTAE CECILIE VIRGINIS.

IU ON EALDUM DAGUM WÆS SUM ÆÐELE MÆDEN Cecilia
gehaten, fram cildhade Cristen on Romana rice þa þa seo reðe ehtnys stod
on þæra casera dagum þe Cristes ne gymdon. (3) Þeos haliga fæmne hæfde
on hire breoste swa micele lufe to þam ecan life þæt heo dæges and nihtes
5   embe Drihtnes godspel and embe Godes lare mid geleafan* smeade and
on singalum gebedum hi sylfe gebysgode.

    Heo wearð swa þeah beweddod, swa swa hit woldon hire frynd, anum
æþelan cnihte se næs Cristen þa git, Ualerianus gehaten, se is nu halig
sanct. Hwæt ða Cecilia hi sylfe gescrydde mid hæran to lice and gelome
10 fæste, biddende mid wope þæt heo wurde gescyld wið ælce
gewemlmednysse oððe weres gemanan. Heo clypode to halgum and to
heahenglum, biddende heora fultumes to þam heofonlican Gode þæt heo
on clænnysse Criste moste þeowian. Hit gewearð swa þeah þæt se
wurðfulla cniht þa brydlac geforþode and gefette þæt mæden mid
15 woruldlicum wurðmynte swa swa heora gebyrde wæron.

    Þa betwux þam sangum and þam singalum dreamum, sang Cecilia
symle þus Gode, '*Fiat cor meum et corpus meum inmaculatum ut non
confundar*' ('Beo min heorte and min lichama þurh God ungewemmed
þæt ic ne beo gescynd'). And sang symle swa.

20   (4) Hi wurdon þa gebrohte on bedde ætgædere*, and Cecilia sona, þæt
snotere mæden, gespræc hire brydguman and þus to Gode tihte, 'Eala þu
min leofa man, ic þe mid lufe secge, ic hæbbe Godes encgel þe gehylt me
on life,* and gif þu wylt me gewemman, he went sona to ðe and mid
graman þe slihð þæt þu sona ne leofast. Gif þu þonne me lufast and butan
25 laðe gehylst on clænum mægðhade, Crist þonne lufað þe and his gife
geswutelað þe sylfum swa swa me'.

    (5) Se cniht wearð þa afyrht* and cwæð to þam mædene, 'Do þæt ic geseo
sylf þone engel gif þu wylt, þæt ic gelyfe þinum wordum be þam, and gif
þe oþer cniht cuþre is þonne ic, hine ic ofslea and þe samod mid him'.

30   Cecilia þa cwæð, 'Gif þu on Crist gelyfst and þu gefullod bist fram fyrn-
licum synnum, þu miht sona geseon þone scinendan engel'.

    Ualerianus andwyrde þa eft þam mædene, 'Hwa mihte me fullian þus
færlice nu þæt ic mihte geseon þone scinendan engel?'

    Seo fæmne þa lærde swa lange þone cniht oð þæt he gelyfde on þone
35 lifilgendan God, and (6) ferde to þam papan, þe ðær ful gehende wæs,
Urbanus gehaten, and him fulluhtes bæd.

Title] *Text begins on folio 213ᵛ, seventeen*   1 IU…MÆDEN] *in small capitals occupying*
*   lines from the top, in large red capitals.*   *a full line and a red decorated initial I*
*   extending two lines above and below*

22 NOVEMBER.
THE PASSIO OF SAINT CECILIA THE VIRGIN

Formerly in days of old there was a certain noble virgin named Cecilia, a Christian from childhood in the empire of the Romans when the fierce persecution existed in the days of the emperors who took no heed of Christ. (3) This holy virgin had in her breast so great a love for the everlasting life that day and night she pondered with faith* the Lord's gospel and God's doctrine and occupied herself in constant prayers.

Nevertheless, she was betrothed, just as her kinsmen wanted it, to a noble young man who was not yet a Christian, called Valerian, who is now a holy saint. So Cecilia clothed herself with a hairshirt against her body and frequently fasted, praying with weeping that she might be shielded from any defilement or intercourse with a man. She cried out to saints and to archangels, praying to the God of heaven for their help so that she could serve Christ with chastity. It happened nevertheless that the honourable young man offered a marriage ceremony and fetched the virgin with worldly honour as became their ranks.

Then in the midst of the songs and the constant melodies, Cecilia sang continually to God in this way, '*Let my heart and my body be unstained so that I might not be put to shame*' ('Let my heart and my body be undefiled through God so that I might not be put to shame' [Psalm 118.80 (Septuagint)]. And she always sang in this way.

(4) They were then brought into bed together*, and immediately Cecilia, the wise virgin, spoke to her bridegroom and thus allured him to God, 'Oh, my beloved husband, I say to you with love, I have an angel of God who guards me while (I am) alive*, and if you wish to defile me, he will turn to you at once and strike you in anger so that instantly you will not live. Therefore if you will love me and will guard me without harm in pure virginity, then Christ will love you and will reveal his grace to you just as to me'.

(5) The young man was then frightened* and said to the virgin, 'Cause me to see the angel for myself if you wish, so that I may believe your words about that, and if another young man is more familiar with you than I, I will kill him and you together with him'.

Cecilia then spoke, 'If you will believe in Christ and will be baptized from wicked sins, you will at once be able to see the shining angel'.

Valerian then replied to the virgin once more, 'Who could baptize me now so suddenly so that I could see the shining angel?'

The virgin then instructed the young man for a long time until he believed in the living God, and (6) he went to the pope, named Urban, who was very nearby and asked him for baptism.

---

11 Fol. 214ʳ
35 Fol. 214ᵛ

Se papa þa blissode þæt he gebeah to Gode and bæd þone ælmihtigan God þæt he, for his arfæstnysse, þam cnihte gewissode þæt he wurde geleafful. (7) Efne, þa færlice ætforan heora gesihþum com Godes engel
40 mid anum gyldenum gewrite, and Ualerianus feoll afyrht to eorðan. Þa aræurde hine se engel and het hine rædan þa gyldenan stafas þe him God tosende. On þam gewrite wæron þas word gelogode, '*Unus Deus, una fides, unum baptisma*' ('An ælmihtig God is and an geleafa and an fulluht'), and he feng to rædene.
45 Þa cwæð se engel, 'Gelyfst þu þises oððe licað þe elles hwæt?'
Ualerianus andwyrde, 'Hwæt bið æfre soðlicre oððe to gelyfenne ænigum lifigendum menn?'*
And se engel þa gewende mid þam worde him fram. Se papa ða siððan hine sona gefullode and his geleafan him tæhte and let hine eft faran ham
50 to Cecilian þam halgan mædene.
(8) Þa funde se cniht þa fæmnan standende on hire gebedum on hire bure ane and Godes engel standande mid gyldenum fyþerhaman mid twam cynehelmum gehende þam mædene. Þa cynehelmas wæron wundorlice scinende on rosan readnysse and on lilian hwitnysse, and he
55 forgeaf þa ænne þam æþelan mædene and oþerne þam cnihte and cwæð him þus to, 'Healdað þas cynehelmas mid clænre heortan for þam þe ic hi genam on neorxnewange.* Ne hi næfre ne forseariað, ne heora swetnysse ne forleosað, ne heora wlita ne awent to wyrsan hiwe, ne hi nan man ne gesihð butan se þe I clænnysse lufað. And þu, Ualeriane, for ðan þe ðu
60 lufast clænnysse, se Hælend þe het biddan swa hwilce bene swa þu wille'.
Þa cneowode se cniht and cwæð to þam engle, 'Næs me nan þing swa leof on þysum life wunigende swa me wæs min broþor, and bið me uneaþe þæt ic beo alysed and he losige on witum. Þas bene ic bidde, þæt min broþor Tiburtius beo alysed þurh God and to geleafan gebiged, and he
65 do unc begen him to biggengum'.
Þa cwæð se engel eft mid blisse him to, 'For þan þe þu þæs bæde, þe bet Gode licað þin broðor Tiburtius bið gestryned þurh þe to þam ecan life, swa swa þu gelyfdest on God þurh Cecilian lare; and git sceolan, begen þu and þin broðor, beon gemartyrode samod', and (9) se engel þa
70 gewende up to heofonum.*
Hi smeadon þa mid glædnysse and embe Godes willan spræcon oþ þæt his broþor com bliðe on mergen him to and cyste hi butu and cwæð mid blisse, 'Ic wundrige þearle hu nu on wintres dæge her lilian blostm oþþe rosan bræð swa wynsumlice and swa werodlice stincað. Ðeah þe ic hæfde
75 me on handa þa blostman, ne mihton hi swa wynsumne wyrtbræð macian, and ic secge to soþan þæt ic swa eom afylled mid þam swetan bræða swylce ic sy geedniwod'.

---

42 wæron] *An erasure of approximately four   there is an erasure of approximately four*
letters follows at the end of the line, and   letters at the beginning of the next line.

The pope then rejoiced that he had turned to God and asked almighty God, on account of his graciousness, to guide the young man to become a believer. (7) Lo, then suddenly before their vision came an angel of God with a golden piece of writing, and Valerian fell frightened to the ground. Then the angel raised him and commanded him to read the golden letters that God had sent him. In the piece of writing were arranged these words, *'There is One God, one faith, one baptism'* ('There is one almighty God and one faith and one baptism' [Ephesians 4.5]), and he began to read.

Then the angel said, 'Do you believe this or does something else please you?'

Valerian answered, 'What will ever be truer or must be believed by any living person?'*

And the angel then departed from him with that word. The pope afterwards baptized him at once and taught him the faith and allowed him to go home again to Cecilia the holy virgin.

(8) Then the young man found the woman standing alone in her prayers in her chamber and God's angel with golden wings standing with two crowns near the virgin. The crowns were shining miraculously with the redness of a rose and the whiteness of a lily, and he then gave one to the noble maiden and the other to the young man and spoke to them in this way, 'Guard these crowns with a pure heart because I received them in Paradise.* They will never wither, nor lose their sweetness, nor will their beauty change to a worse colour, nor will any one see them except he who loves chastity. And you, Valerian, because you love chastity, the Saviour has commanded you to make whatever request you wish'.

Then the young man knelt and said to the angel, 'There was nothing so dear to me remaining in this life as was my brother, and it will be difficult for me that I will be delivered and he will perish in torments. I make this request, that my brother Tiburtius be delivered by God and be turned to the faith, and that he make us both his worshippers'.

Then the angel spoke to him again with joy, 'Because you asked for this, it pleases God the better that your brother Tiburtius be born to everlasting life through you, just as you believed in God through Cecilia's instruction; and you two, both you and your brother, shall be martyred together', and (9) the angel went up to heaven.*

They pondered then with delight and talked about the will of God until his brother came cheerfully to them in the morning and kissed them both and said with joy, 'I am very amazed how now, on a winter's day, the blossom of the lily and the scent of the rose waft here so pleasantly and so sweetly. Even if I had the blooms in my hands, they would not be able to produce so pleasant a fragrance, and I say truly that I am so filled with the sweet smell it is as if I were made anew'.

---

59 Fol. 215ʳ

Þa cwæð se broðor, 'Þurh mine bene þe com þæs wynsuma bræð to þæt
þu wite heonanforð hwæs blod ræadaþ on rosan gelicnysse and hwæs
80   lichama hwitað on lilian fægernysse. We habbað cynehelmas halige mid
us, scinende swa swa rose and snawhwite swa swa lilie, þa þu ne miht
geseon þeah þe hi scinende beon'.

Þa cwæð Tiburtius, 'Sege me, | broþor min, gehyre ic þis on slæpe oððe
þu hit sægst on eornost?'

85   Se oðer him cwæð to, 'Oð þis we leofodon swilce we on slæpe wæron,
ac we synd nu gewende to soðfæstnysse. Þa godas þe we wurþodon syndon
gramlice deofla'.

Þa cwæð se oþer, 'Hu wearð þe þæt cuð?'

Ualerianus andwyrde, 'Godes engel me tæhte, and þone þu miht
90   geseon gif þu soðlice bist on fulluhte aþwogen fram þam fulum deofol-
gilde'.

(10) Hi spræcon þa swa lange oð þæt he to geleafan beah and se broðor
wolde þæt he wurde gefullod.

(11) Þa befran Tiburtius hwa hine fullian sceolde. Se oðer him cwæð
95   to, 'Urbanus se papa'.

Eft þa Tiburtius him andwyrde and cwæð, 'Se is geutlagod and lið him
on digelan for his Cristendome, and gif we cumað him to, we beoð
gewitnode gif hit wyrð ameldod. And þa hwile þe we secað, swa swa hit
gesæd is, godcundnysse on heofonum, we graman gemetað and lifleaste
100   on eorðan gif we his lare folgiað'.

Þa cwæð Cecilia sona mid gebylde, 'Gif þis lif wære ana and oþer nære
selre, þonne mihte we ondrædan us deaðes rihtlice'.

Þa axode Tiburtius, 'Is ænig oþer lif?'

Cecilia him cwæð to, 'Cuð is gehwilcum menn þæt þis lif is geswincful
105   and on swate wunað. Þis lif bið alefed on langsumum sarum and on hætum
ofþefod; and on hungre gewæht, mid mettum gefylled; and modig on welum,
mid hafenleaste aworpen; and ahafen þurh iugoðe, mid ylde gebiged; and
tobryt mid seocnysse, mid unrotnysse fornumen and geangsumod þurh
cara. Þonne cymð him deað to and deð of gemynde ealle þa blysse þe he
110   breac on his life. And on þam ecan life, þe æfter þysum cymð, bið þam
rihtwisum for|gifen rest and gefea, and þam unrihtwisum þa ecan wita'.*

(12) Þa cwæð Tiburtius, 'Hwa com þanon hider þe mihte us secgan gif
hit swa wære?'*

Cecilia þa aras and mid anrædnysse cwæð, 'Ealle gesceafta Scyppend
115   ænne Sunu gestrynde and forðteah þurh hine sylfne þone Frofergast. Þurh
þone Sunu he gesceop ealle gesceafta þe syndon and hi ealle gelyffæste
þurh þone lifigendan Gast'.*

---

83 Fol. 215ᵛ   117 Gast] *above line, insertion mark below*
111 Fol. 216ʳ

Then his brother said, 'On account of my request, this pleasant fragrance came to you so that you may know henceforth whose blood reddens in the form of the rose and whose body whitens in the beauty of the lily. We have holy crowns with us, shining like a rose and snow-white like a lily, which you cannot see although they are shining'.

Then Tiburtius said, 'Tell me, my brother, do I hear you in my sleep or are you really saying it?'

The other said to him, 'Up to now we have lived as if we were asleep, but we are now turned towards truth. The gods that we honoured are fierce devils' [cf. Psalm 95.5 (Septuagint)].

Then the other said, 'How did that become known to you?'

Valerian answered, 'God's angel taught me, and you can see him if you truly will be washed clean in baptism from despicable idolatry'.

(10) They spoke then for a long time until he turned to the faith and the brother desired to be baptized.

(11) Then Tiburtius asked who ought to baptize him. The other said to him, 'Urban the pope'.

Once more Tiburtius replied to him and said, 'He is outlawed and lies in hiding on account of his Christianity, and if we come to him, we will be punished if it is revealed. And while we are seeking, as it is said, divinity in heaven, we will find trouble and death on earth if we follow his teaching'.

Then Cecilia spoke at once with assuredness, 'If there were only this life and if there were none better, then we rightly might be afraid of death'.

Then Tiburtius asked, 'Is there another life?'

Cecilia said to him, 'It is known to every man that this life is toilsome and continues in sweat. This life is weakened by long-lasting pains and is made exceedingly hot by heat; and exhausted by hunger, filled with foods; and made proud by wealth, humbled by poverty; and raised up by youth, bent by old age; and destroyed by illness, overpowered by unhappiness and made anxious by cares. Then death comes to him and puts out of memory all the pleasure that he enjoyed in his life. And in the everlasting life, which comes after this one, rest and joy will be given to the righteous and everlasting punishments to the unrighteous'.*

(12) Then Tiburtius said, 'Who has come here from there who could tell us that it is so?'*

Cecilia then stood up and said with steadfastness, 'The Creator of all creatures begot a Son and brought forth by his own means the Comforting Spirit. Through the Son he created all created things that exist and endowed them all with life through the living Spirit'.*

Þa andwyrde Tiburtius, 'Ænne God gebodiað, and humeta namast þu
namcuðlice þry godas?'
120 Cecilia him andwyrde, 'An God is ælmihtig on his mægenþrymnysse
wunigende. Ðone arwurðiað we Cristenan æfre on þrynnysse and on soðre
annysse for þan þe Fæder and Sunu and se Frofergast an gecynd habbað
and ænne cynedom, swa swa on anum men synd soðlice þreo þing —
andgit and wylla and gewittig gemynd, þe anum men gehyrsumiaþ æfre
125 togædere'.*

Þa feoll Tiburtius forht to hire cneowum and clypode hlude and cwæð
mid geleafan, 'Ne þincð me þæt þu spræce mid menniscre spræce, ac swilce
Godes engel sylf spræce þurh þe! (13) Ac ic axie git be þam oþrum life,
hwa þæt gesawe and siððan come hider?'
130 (13–14) Hwæt þa Cecilia him snoterlice andwyrde and sæde hu se
Hælend of heofonum com to us, and hwylce wundra he worhte on þisre
worulde fela, and hu he þa deadan arærde of deaðe to life and hu he sylf
of deaðe on þam þriddan dæge aras, and fela þincg him sæde swutellice
be Criste.*

135 (16) Þa weop Tiburtius and gewilnode georne þæt he gefullod wurde
æt þam foresædan papan, and se broþor siþode sona forð mid him and
cydde þam papan hwæt hi gecweden hæfdon.

Se papa ða Urbanus blis|sode on Gode and gefullode sona þone
gesæligan cniht and sæde him his geleafan geond seofon dagas on an oþ
140 þæt he fulfremod ferde eft ongean. He beget þa æt Gode þa gastlican
gesælþa swa þæt he dæghwamlice Drihtnes englas geseh, and swa hwæs
swa he gewilnode him ne forwyrnde God, and worhte gelome wundra
þurh hine and þurh his broðor swa swa bec secgað.

(17) Þa wæs on Romebyrig sum reðe cwellere Almachius gehaten se
145 wæs heahgerefa, and he mid manegum witum gemartyrode þa Cristenan
þa ða he ofaxian mihte, and man ne moste hi bebyrigan. Ualerianus þa
and his foresæda broþor bebyrigdon þa martyras þe se manfulla acwealde,
and ælmyssan dældon dæghwamlice þearfum oð þæt se arleasa ehtere
ofaxode heora dæda. Hwæt þa Almachius het þa men gelangian* and
150 axode hi sona mid swiðlicre þreatunge hwi hi þa bebyrigdon þe his beboda
forsawon and for heora scyldum ofslagene lagon, oþþe hwi hi dældon
dearnunga heora æhta waclicum mannum unwislicum ræde.

Þa andwyrde Tiburtius þam arleasan and cwæð, 'Eala, gif þa halgan
þe þu hete ofslean and we bebyrigdon woldon us habban huru him to
155 þeowum to heora þenungum'.

---

138 Fol. 216ᵛ
140 gastlican] t *above line, insertion mark*
  below

Then Tiburtius answered, 'They preach one God, and why do you mention three gods individually?'

Cecilia answered him, 'There is one God almighty dwelling in his majesty. We Christians always honour him in Trinity and in true unity because the Father and the Son and the Comforting Spirit have one nature and one supreme authority, just as in one person there are actually three things — understanding and will and conscious memory, which always serve one person together'.*

Then Tiburtius fell down frightened at her knees and exclaimed loudly and said with faith, 'It does not seem to me that you speak with human speech, but it is as if God's angel himself speaks through you! (13) But still I ask about the other life, who has seen it and afterwards has come to this world?'

(13–14) Then Cecilia wisely answered him and spoke about how the Saviour came from heaven to us, and about some of the many miracles he performed in this world, and about how he raised the dead from death to life and how he himself arose from the dead on the third day, and she told him clearly many things about Christ.*

(16) Then Tiburtius wept and urgently desired to be baptized by the afore-mentioned pope, and his brother went forth at once with him and reported to the pope what they had said.

Pope Urban then rejoiced in God and immediately baptized the blessed young man and continually explained to him his faith over the course of seven days until he went back again perfected. He then obtained spiritual prosperity from God so that he daily saw the Lord's angels, and whatever he desired God did not refuse him, and He frequently performed miracles through him and through his brother just as the books say.

(17) At that time there was in the city of Rome a certain cruel executioner named Almachius who was high-reeve, and he martyred the Christians with many tortures when he could discover them, and no one was allowed to bury them. Then Valerian and his aforementioned brother buried the martyrs whom the wicked man put to death, and they daily distributed alms to the needy until the wicked persecutor discovered their deeds. Almachius then ordered the men to be summoned* and asked them at once with violent threatening why they buried those who scorned his commands and who lay killed for their offences, or why they secretly distributed their wealth to lowly men on account of foolish advice.

Then Tiburtius answered the wicked one and said, 'Oh, if only the saints whom you ordered to be killed and whom we buried had wished to have us as slaves in their service'.

(17–20) Hi þa swa lange motodon oþ þæt (21) se manfulla het mid saglum beatan þone oþerne broþor, and (22) sum rædbora þa to þam reðan þus cwæð, 'Hat hi, leof, acwellan nu*; hi Cristene synd. Gif þu þonne elcast, heora æhta hi dælað þearfum and wædlum, and þu witnast hi siðða

160   and næfst þa æhta for þinre ælcunge'.

Almachius þa het his manfullan I cwelleras lædan þa gebroðra on bendum togædere to þam hæþengilde and het hi geoffrian oþþe hi man ofsloge mid swurde þærrihte. Hi lædde þa Maximus, swa se manfulla het, mid oþrum cwellerum to þære cwealmstowe.

165   Þa weop Maximus for þan þe hi woldon sweltan and axode þa gebroðra hwi hi swa bliþelice eodon to heora agenum slege swylce to gebeorscipe.

Þa cwæð se yldra broþor, 'Noldon we efstan to deaþe mid swa mycelre blisse gif we to beteran life soðlice ne becomon siððan we ofslagene beoð, to þam ecan life swa swa we leornodon to soþan'.

170   (23) Betwux þære tihtinge þa þa hi tengdon forð, þa cwæð se Maximus to þam martyrum þus, 'Ic wolde eac forseon þisre worulde swæsnysse gif ic wiste to gewissan þæt eowre word wæron soþe'.

Þa cwæð se gingra broðor of þam bendum him to, 'Ure Drihten Crist deð þæt þu gesihst, þonne we ofslagene beoð, hu ure sawla farað mid

175   wuldre to him gif þu wylt nu behatan þæt þu mid eallum mode þin man behreowsige'.

Maximus þa cwæð to þam martyrum þus, 'Fyr me forbærne gif ic ne buge to Criste siþþan ic geseo hu eowre sawla farað to þam oþrum life þe ge embe sprecað'.

180   Þa cwædon þa halgan gebroþra þe he on bendum lædde, 'Bebeod þysum cwellerum þæt hi us cuce healdan on þinum agenum huse nu þas ane niht oð þæt þu sy gefullod fram fyrnlicum synnum þæt þu mote geseon þa gesihðe þurh God'.

Hi wurdon þa gebrohte on bendum to his huse, and Cecilia seo eadige

185   mid arwurðum sacerdum þider com sona, and hi sæton þa niht embe Crist sprecende oþ þæt þa cwelleras gelyfdon and wurdon gefullode æt þam foresædum I preostum. Hwæt þa on dægræd þæt deorwurðe mæden Cecilia clypode and cwæð to him eallum, 'Nu, ge la Godes cempan, awurpað caflice eow fram þæra þeostra weorc and wurðað ymbscrydde

190   mid leohtes wæpnum to þysum gewinne nu. Ge habbað gecampod swiðe godne campdom, eowerne ryne ge gefyldon and geleafan geheoldon. Gaþ to þam wuldorbeage þæs wynsuman lifes, [þone] se rihtwisa dema deð eow to edleane'.

---

158 þu] *above line, insertion mark below*   178 siþþan] V syþþan (Moloney). eowre] V
161 Fol. 217ʳ   eowra
177 þam] V þa (Moloney). forbærne] V   180 halgan] V halgon (Moloney)
    forbearne   181 þysum] V þisum

(17–20) They disputed then for a long time until (21) the wicked one ordered the other brother to be beaten with clubs, and (22) then a certain adviser then spoke to the cruel one in this way, 'Order them, sir, to be put to death now*; they are Christians. If you delay thus, they will distribute their wealth to the needy and the poor, and you will punish them afterwards and will not have their wealth because of your delay'.

Almachius then ordered his wicked executioners to lead the brothers in fetters together to the heathen shrine and ordered them to offer a sacrifice or someone would kill them immediately with the sword. Then, as the wicked one had commanded, Maximus led them with other executioners to the place of execution.

Then Maximus wept because they wished to die and asked the brothers why they so cheerfully went to their own slaughter as if to a feast.

Then the older brother said, 'We would not wish to hasten to death with such great joy if after we are killed we would not actually come to a better life, to the everlasting life just as we have truly learned'.

(23) In the midst of that exhortation as they hurried forward, Maximus then spoke to the martyrs in this way, 'I might also desire to despise the blandishment of this world if I could know as a certainty that your words were true'.

Then the younger brother from his bonds said to him, 'Our Lord Christ will cause you to see, when we are killed, how our souls go to him with glory if you will now promise to repent of your sin with all your heart'.

Maximus then spoke to the martyrs in this way, 'May fire consume me if I do not turn to Christ after I see how your souls go to the other life that you speak about'.

Then the holy brothers whom he led in bonds said, 'Command these executioners to keep us alive in your house now this one night until you are baptized from wicked sins so that you may be allowed by God to see the vision'.

They were then brought in bonds to his house, and the blessed Cecilia came at once to that place with worthy priests, and they sat that night talking about Christ until the executioners believed and were baptized by the aforementioned priests. Then at daybreak the precious virgin Cecilia called out and said to them all, 'Now, O soldiers of God, boldly cast away from yourselves the works of the darkness and be now clothed for this conflict with the armour of light [cf. Romans 13.12]. You have fought an exceedingly good fight, have completed your course and have kept the faith. Go to the crown of glory of the pleasant life, which the righteous judge will give you as a reward [cf. 2 Timothy 4.7–8].

---

184 his] *above line, insertion mark below.*
    eadige] V eadiga
187 Fol. 217ᵛ. dægræd] V dægred
192 (þone)] þonne; V þone

(24) Hi wurdon þa gelædde for heora geleafan to slege and mid swurde
195 beheafdode. Þa beheold Maximus and sæde mid aþe to þam
ymbstandendum, 'Ic geseah soðlice, mid þam þe hi ofslagene wurdon,
Godes englas scinende on sunnan gelicnysse fleogende him to, and under-
fengon heora sawla. And þa sawla ic geseah swiðe wlitig faran forð mid
þam englum on heora fiðerum to heofonum'. Þa þa Maximus sæde swa
200 soðlice þas word weopendum eagum, þa gewendon þa hæþenan manega
to geleafan fram heora leasum godum.

Almachius þa ofaxode þæt se arwurða Maximus mid eallum his hiwum
on þone Hælend gelyfde and wæron gefullode, wearð þa him gram and
het hine swingan mid leadenum swipum oþ þæt he gewat of worulde to
205 Criste. Cecilia þa sona þone sanct bebyrigde on stænenre þryh on þam
stede þe lagon þa twegen gebroþra bebyrigde on ær.

(25) Heo dælde þa siððan digellice þearfum hire brydguman æhta and
his broþor þing. And Almachius wolde witan ymbe þa æhtan, swylce heo
wydewe wære, and heo wearð þa geneadod þæt heo offrian sceolde þam
210 arleasum godum. Þa weopon þa hæðenan þæt swa wlitig fæmne and swa
æþelboren wimman mid wisdome afylled wolde I deað þrowian on witum
swa [i]ung.

(26) Þa cwæð Cecilia and sæde him eallum, 'Ne bið se forloren þe lið
for Gode ofslagen. He bið swa awend to wuldre of deaðe, swilce man lam
215 sylle and sylf nime gold, swilce he sylle wac hus and wuldorful underfo,
sylle gewitendlic and ungewitendlic underfo, sylle wacne stan* and
wurðfulne gym underfo'. Heo tihte þa swa lange þa ungeleaffullan
hæðenan oð þæt hi ealle cwædon mid anre stemne þus, 'We gelyfað þæt
Crist, Godes Sunu, soðlice God is, þe þe þyllice underfeng him to þinenne
220 on worulde'. (27) Þa wurdon gefullode feower hund manna on Cecilian
huse þam Hælende to lofe, and se papa mæssode þam mannum gelome
on þam ylcan huse and se hæðenscipe wanode.

(28) Almachius se arleasa het þa ardlice gefeccan þa eadigan Cecilian
and hi axode sona hwylcere mægðe heo wære, and hi motodon lange oþ
225 þæt þam deman ofþuhte hyre dyrstignyss and cwæð orhlice eft to þam
mædene, 'Nast þu mine mihte?'

And þæt mæden him cwæð to, 'Ic secge, gif þu hætst, hwilce mihte þu
hæfst. Ælces mannes miht þe on mōdignysse færð is soðlice þam gelic
swilce man siwige ane bytte and blawe hi fulle windes and wyrce siððan
230 an þyrl þonne heo toþunden bið on hire greatnysse; þonne togæð seo
miht'.

---

207 siððan] V syðð[an] (Moloney). hire] V
    hyre
211 æþelboren] V æþelboran. wisdome] V
    wysdo[me] (Moloney). Fol. 218ʳ
212 (i)ung] Iung
214–15 swilce (*both instances*)] V swylce
    (*both instances*)
217 gym] V gim (Moloney)

(24) They were then led to death on account of their faith and were beheaded with a sword. Then Maximus watched and said with an oath to those standing nearby, 'I truly saw, when they were killed, angels of God shining in the likeness of the sun flying to them, and they received their souls. And then I saw their exceedingly beautiful souls go forth to heaven on the wings of the angels'. When Maximus thus spoke these words in truth with weeping eyes, the many heathens then turned to the faith from their false gods.

When Almachius discovered that the worthy Maximus with all the members of his household believed in the Saviour and had been baptized, he then became angry and ordered him to be beaten with leaden whips until he departed from the world to Christ. Cecilia then buried the saint at once in a stone tomb in the place where the two previously buried brothers lay.

(25) Then she afterwards secretly distributed to the needy her husband's wealth and his brother's things. And Almachius wished to know about the possessions, as she was a widow, and she was then urged that she ought to offer a sacrifice to the wicked gods. Then the heathens wept that so beautiful a virgin and a woman of such high birth filled with wisdom wished to suffer death by torments while so young.

(26) Then Cecilia spoke and said to them all, 'He will not be lost who lies slain for God. He will thus be changed from death into glory, as one might give clay and get gold for himself, as he might give a mean house and receive a glorious one, might give the transitory and receive the permanent, might give a stone of little worth* and receive a valuable gem'. She then exhorted the unbelieving heathens for a long time until they all spoke with one voice in this way, 'We believe that Christ, the Son of God, is truly God, he who has taken for himself one such as you as his maidservant on earth'. (27) Then four hundred people were baptized in Cecilia's house as praise to the Saviour, and the pope celebrated mass frequently for the people in the same house and the heathen faith waned.

(28) Almachius the wicked one then commanded the blessed Cecilia to be quickly fetched and asked her at once what sort of family she belonged to, and they argued for a long time until her presumption offended the judge and he once more spoke arrogantly to the virgin, 'Do you not know my power?'

And the virgin said to him, 'I will say, if you command, what sort of power you have. The power of every man who acts with pride is similar to when a man stitches together a wineskin and blows it full of air and afterwards makes a hole when it is swollen to its fullest; then its power departs'.

(30) Almachius hire cwæð to þa þa hi campodon mid wordum, 'Hwæt, þu ungesælige, nast þu þæt me is geseald anweald to ofsleanne and to edcucigenne? And þu spræcst swa modelice, mine mihta tælende'.

235   Þæt mæden him cwæð to, 'Oþer is modignyss, oþer is anrædnyss, and ic anrædlice spræc na modelice for þan þe we modignysse eallunga onscuniað. And eft heo cwæð him to, | 'Þu cwæde þæt þu hæfdest to acwellene anweald and to edcucigenne, ac ic cwæðe þæt þu miht þa cucan adydan and þam deadan þu ne miht eft lif forgifan; ac þu lyhst openlice'.

240   Almachius hire andwyrde, 'Awurp þine dyrstignysse and geoffra þam godum arwurðlice onsægednysse'.

    Cecilia him cwæð to, 'Cunna mid grapunge hwæðer hi stanas synd and stænene anlicnysse þa þe þu "godas" gecigst begotene mid leade, and þu miht swa witan gewislice mid grapunge (gif ðu geseon ne miht) þæt hi synd

245 stanas. Hi mihton wel to lime gif man hi lede on ad. Nu hi ne fremiað him sylfum ne soðlice mannum, and hi mihton to lime gif hi man lede on fyr'.

    (31) Þa wearð se arleasa dema deoflice gram and het hi lædan sona and seoðan on wætere on hire agenum huse for þæs Hælendes naman.* Þa dydon þa hæþenan swa swa hi het Almachius, and heo læg on þam bæðe

250 bufan byrnendum fyre ofer dæg and niht ungederodum lichaman swa swa on cealdum wætere, þæt heo ne swætte furðon.

    Hi cyddon þa Almachie hu þæt mæden þurhwunode on þam hatum baðe mid halum lichaman and furþon butan swate. Þa sende he ænne cwellere to and het hi beheafdian on þam hatan wætere.* Se cwellere hi

255 sloh þa mid his swurde æne, eft and þryddan siðe, ac hire swura næs forod, and he forlet hi sona swa samcuce licgan for þam þe witan cwædon þæt nan cwellere ne sceolde feower siðan slean to þonne man sloge scyldigne.*

    Heo leofode þa þry dagas and þa geleaffullan tihte and hire mædena betæhte þam mæran papan, and hire hus wearð gehalgod to haligre

260 cyrcan. Þær wurdon þurh God wundra gellome, and (32) Urbanus se papa bebyrigde hi arwurðlice to wuldre þam Ælmihtigan þe on ecnysse rixað. AMEN.

---

237 Fol. 218ᵛ
260 Fol. 219ʳ
262 AMEN] *in small capitals*

(30) Almachius said to her as they waged war with words, 'Well, wretched one, do you not know that I have been given the power to kill and to restore to life? And you speak so proudly, mocking my powers'.

The virgin said to him, 'Pride is one thing, steadfastness is another, and I spoke steadfastly not pridefully because we shun pride altogether'. And again she said to him, 'You said that you had the power to kill and to restore to life, but I say that you can kill the living and cannot give life again to the dead; on the contrary you lie openly'.

Almachius answered her, 'Cast away your presumption and offer a reverent sacrifice to the gods'.

Cecilia said to him, 'Test by touching whether those that you call "gods" are stones and figures made of stone covered with lead, and thus you can know for certain by touching (if you cannot see) that they are stones. They would completely turn into lime if someone laid them on a pyre. Presently they do not help themselves nor indeed men, and they would become lime if someone laid them in a fire'.

(31) Then the wicked judge became devilishly angry and ordered that she be taken immediately and boiled in water in her own house for the sake of the Saviour's name.* Then the heathens did just as Almachius ordered them, and she lay throughout the day and night in the bath above a blazing fire with her body unharmed as if (she were) in cold water, so that she did not even sweat.

They reported then to Almachius how the virgin remained in the hot bath with a sound body and without even sweating. Then he sent an executioner to that place and commanded him to behead her in the hot water.* The executioner then struck her with sword once, again and a third time, but her neck was not severed, and he immediately left her lying thus half-dead because the chief counsellors had said that no executioner ought to strike four times when he struck a guilty person.*

She lived then three days and exhorted the faithful and entrusted her virgins to the glorious pope, and her house was consecrated as a holy church. Miracles were frequently performed there by God, and (32) Urban the pope buried her honourably as glory to the Almighty who reigns for ever. AMEN.

III KALENDAS DECEMBRIS.
PASSIO CHRISANTI ET DARIĘ SPONSE EIUS.

(2) ON ÐAM TIMAN ÐE NUMERIANUS CASERE RIXODE þa,
ferde sum æðelboren man fram Alexandrian byrig to Romebyrig
Polemius gehaten. Se wæs hæþengilda, and he hæfde ænne sunu gehaten
Crisantus. Se kasere hine underfeng ða mid fullum wurðmynte, and þa
5   Romaniscan witan hine wurðodon swyðe.

Þa befæste he his sunu sona to lare to woruldwisdome þæt he uðwita
wurde for ðam þe on þam dagum ne mihte nan man beon geþogen buton
he hæþene bec hæfde geleornod and þa cræftas cuþe þe kaseres þa
lufodon. Crisantus þa leornode mid leohtum andgite and mid gleawum
10   mode grammatican cræft and þa hæðenan bec oþ þæt þa halgan godspel
him becomon to hande; þa cwæð he to him sylfum, 'Swa lange ic leornode
þa ungeleaffullan bec mid þeostrum afyllede oþ þæt ic færlice becom to
soðfæstnysse leohte, and ic snotor ne beo gif ic cyrre to þeostrum fram
þam soðan leohte. Uton healdan fæste þone fægeran goldhord. Nelle ic
15   hine forleosan nu ic swa lange swanc. Unnyt ic leofode gif ic hine nu
forlæte'.

(3) He began þa to secenne swyðe ða Cristenan oð þæt he ofaxode
ænne arwurðne mæssepreost on fyrlenum wunigende, and he fægnode
þæs. He wearð þa gefullod æt þam foresædan preoste and leornode his
20   geleafan mid þam halgan lareowe swa þæt he þone Cristendom cuðe be
fullan and began to bodigenne bealdlice þone Hælend.

(4) Þa gestodon I his frynd his fæder and cwædon, 'To plihte þinre æhta
and þines agenes heafdes bodað þes þin cnapa swa bealdlice be Criste.
Wurðe hit þam casere cuþ, ne canst þu þe nænne ræd'. Þa gebealh hine
25   se fæder and gebrohte þone sunu on leohtleasum cwearterne and beleac
hine þær and on æfen symle sende him bigleofan, lytelne and wacne, and
he wunode þær swa.

Þa sædon þa magas eft sona þam fæder, 'Gif þu wille þinne sunu
geweman fram Criste, þonne most þu him olæcan and estmettas beodan
30   and do þæt he wifige. Þonne wile he forgitan — siððan he wer bið — þæt
he wæs Cristen. Þas geswencednyssa and þas sweartan þeostra þe þu him
dest to wite awendaþ þa Cristenan him sylfum to wuldra na to witnunge'.

Title] *Text begins on folio 219ʳ, three lines*
  from the top, in large red capitals.
1 ON. . . RIXODE] *in small capitals occu-*
  pying a full line and a red decorated initial
  O *extending one line above and below*
22 Fol. 219ᵛ
26 on] *above line, insertion mark below*

29 NOVEMBER.
THE PASSIO OF CHRYSANTHUS AND DARIA HIS WIFE.

(2) In the time when Numerianus the emperor reigned, a certain noble man named Polemius went from the city of Alexandria to the city of Rome. He was an idolater, and he had a son named Chrysanthus. The emperor received him at that time with abundant honour, and the Roman senators honoured him exceedingly.

Then he immediately set his son to learning earthly wisdom so that he might become a philosopher because in those days no one could be prosperous unless he had learned heathen books and was practised in the arts that the emperors then loved. Chrysanthus then learned with an agile intellect and with a wise mind the art of grammar and the heathen books until the holy gospels came into his possession; then he said to himself, 'For such a long time I have learned faithless books filled with darkness until I suddenly came to the light of truth, and I will not be wise if I turn to the darkness from the true light. Let us hold firmly to the beautiful treasure. I do not wish to lose it since I have toiled for such a long time. I have lived uselessly if I abandon it now'.

(3) He began then to look widely for the Christians until he discovered a worthy priest living at a distance, and he rejoiced at that. He was then baptized by the aforementioned priest and learned his faith with the holy teacher so that he fully knew the Christian faith and began to proclaim the Saviour boldly.

(4) Then his relatives assailed his father and said, 'To the peril of your wealth and your own head this boy of yours preaches very boldly about Christ. Should it become known to the emperor, you will know no advantage for yourself'. Then the father became angry and put the son into a lightless prison and confined him there, and in the evening he always sent him food, a little and of low quality, and he thus remained there.

Then the kinsmen spoke once more to his father, 'If you wish to entice your son away from Christ, then you must treat him well and offer him delicacies and make him marry. Then he will be willing to forget — after he is a husband — that he was a Christian. These afflictions and black darkness that you inflict on him as torture the Christians turn into glory for themselves not punishment'.

(5) Se fæder þa het feccan of þam fulum cwearterne þone geswenctan cniht and hine sona scrydde mid deorwurðum reafum, and het dæftan his
35 bur mid pællum and mid wahryftum wurðlice þam cnihte. He funde eac sona fif mædena him to, wlitige and rance, to wunigenne mid him and het þæt hi awendon mid heora wodlican plegan his geþanc fram Criste and cwæð þæt hi sceoldon sylfe hit gebicgan gif hi ne bigdon his mod. He sende him eac gelome sanda and estas, ac se cniht forseah þa sanda and drencas
40 and þa mædena onscunode swa swa man deþ næddran.

He læg on gebedum and forbeah heora cossas and bæd þone Hælend þæt he geheolde his clænnysse swa swa he heold Iosepes on Aegipta lande. He andette eac Gode mid eallum mode and cwæð, (6) 'Ic bidde þe Drihten þæt þu do þæs næddran þæt hi ealle slapon on minre gesihðe nu
45 þæt hi awræccan ne magon mid heora wodlican plegan ænige galnysse on me for ðan þe ic truwige on þe'.

(7) Mid þam þe Crisantus clypode þas word to Gode, þa slepon þa mædene swa swarum slape þæt man hi awreccan ne mihte butan man hi awurpe ut of þæs cnihtes bure þe ða clænnysse lufode. Wiðutan þam bure
50 hi æton and wacodon, and swa hraðe swa hi in eodon, hi wurdon on slæpe. Þis wearð þa gesæd sona þam fæder, and he beweop þone sunu swilce he dead wære.

Þa cwæð sum rædbora þæt Chrisantus leornode drycræft æt þam Cristenum and ofercom mid þam þa bylewitan mædene on þam bure swa
55 eaþelice, and tihte þone fæder þæt he funde sum mæden on cræftum getogen þe cuþe him andwyrde.* Þa wæs sum mæden, wundorlice cræftig, on þære ylcan byrig æþelborenre mægðe, Daria gehaten, on hæþenscipe wunigende, wlitig on wæstme and on uðwitegunge snoter. Polemius þa sona sende his frynd to þam mædene Darian and micclum wæs biddende
60 þæt heo Chrisantum gewemde fram Criste mid spræce and þæt heo hæfde hine hire to were syððan.

Him gewearð þa æt nextan þæt heo wolde swa don, and (8) com þa geglenged mid golde to þam cnihte and scinendum gymstanum — swilce sunbeam færlice — and hine frefrode mid hire fægerum wordum.
65 Þa cwæð Crisantus hire to mid clænum mode þus, 'Swyðe þu geglengdest mid golde þe sylfe þæt þu mid þinre wlite minne willan aidlige, ac þu mihtest habban þone Hælend to brydguman gif þu hine lufodest and heolde þe clænlice on ungewemmedum mægðhade, and þu wurde swa wlitig wiþinnan on mode swa swa þu wiðutan eart'.
70 (9) Daria him andwyrde, 'Ne | dyde ic for galnysse þæt ic þus gefretewod ferde in to þe, ac þines fæder wop ic wolde gestillan þæt þu him ne losige ne huru þam godum'.

---

45 Fol. 220ʳ   70 Fol. 220ᵛ
51 þam] *bar above* a *is very faint, perhaps
erased*

(5) The father then ordered the oppressed young man to be fetched from the foul prison and immediately clothed him in precious garments, and he ordered his chamber to be fittingly prepared for the young man with silk cloths and curtains. He also immediately found five virgins for him, beautiful and showy, to remain with him, and ordered them to turn his thoughts from Christ with their foolish play and said that they would pay for it if they did not turn his mind. He also frequently sent him dishes of food and delicacies, but the young man despised the food and drinks and avoided the virgins as one does snakes.

He lay in his prayers and turned aside from their kisses and asked the Saviour to preserve his chastity just as he had preserved Joseph's in the land of the Egyptians. He also professed his faith in God with all his heart and said, (6) 'I ask you Lord to cause all these serpents to fall asleep now in my sight so that they cannot arouse any sexual desire in me with their foolish playing because I trust in you'.

(7) When Chrysanthus had spoken these words to God, the virgins then fell into so heavy a sleep that no one was able to arouse them unless he threw them out of the chamber of the young man who loved chastity. Outside the chamber they ate and stayed awake, and as soon as they walked in, they were asleep. This was then told to the father at once, and he wept over his son as if he were dead.

Then a certain adviser said that Chrysanthus had learned magic from the Christians and had subsequently overcome the simple-minded virgins in the chamber very easily, and he urged the father to find some virgin educated in the arts who knew how to answer him.* There was a certain virgin, named Daria, (who was) wonderfully learned, born in the same city of a noble family, living as a pagan, beautiful in form and wise in philosophy. Polemius then sent his friend at once to the virgin Daria and kept entreating her to entice Chrysanthus from Christ with her eloquence and to have him as a husband for herself afterwards.

Then it finally happened for him that she was willing to do so, and (8) she came then to the young man adorned with gold and glittering jewels — suddenly like a sunbeam — and comforted him with her winning words.

Then Chrysanthus spoke to her with a pure mind in this way, 'You have exceedingly adorned yourself with gold so that with your beauty you may frustrate my intent, but you could have the Saviour as a bridegroom if you loved him and would preserve yourself chastely in undefiled virginity, and you would become as beautiful inwardly, in your spirit, as you are outwardly'.

(9) Daria replied to him, 'It was not on account of sexual desire that I, thus adorned, made my way to you, but I desired to silence your father's weeping so that you might not be lost to him or, in any case, to the gods.

Crisantus þa axode betwux oþrum spræcum, 'Hwilce godnysse hæfde eower god Saturnus, þe abat his suna þonne hi geborene wæron, swa swa
75 his biggengan on heora bocum awriton? (10) Oþþe hwylce godnysse hæfde se gramlica Iouis, se þe on fulum forligre leofode on worulde and his agen swustor him geceas to wife and manega manslihtas and morðdæda gefremode, and drycræft arærde to bedydrigenne þa unwaran? (11) Oððe hwylc halignyss wæs on þam hetelan Ercule, þam ormætan
80 ente, þe ealle acwealde his nehgeburas and forbærnde hine sylfne swa cucenne on fyre siððan he acweald hæfde men and þa leon and þa micclan næddran? Hwilc beoð þa lytlan godas on to gelyfenne nu þa fyrmestan godas swa fullice leofodon?'

(14) Crisantus þa swa lange to geleafan tihte Darian mid wordum oþ
85 þæt heo gewende to Gode forlætenum gedwylde deoflicra biggenga.* Hi wurdon þa anræde and wunodon ætgædere gehiwodum synscipe and gehealdenre clænnysse oþ þæt Daria underfeng fulluht on Gode and Godes bec leornode æt þam gelæredum cnihte and hire mod gestrangode on mægðhade wunigende.

90 Wurdon þa, on fyrste, fela men gebigde þurh heora drohtnunge fram deofles biggengum to Cristes geleafan and to clænum life. Cnihtas gecyrdon þurh Crisantes lare and mædenu þurh Darian manega to Drihtne (15) forlætenum synscipe and geswæsum lustum oþ þæt sume men astyrodon sace be þysum and hi wurdon gewrehte to þam wælhre-
95 owan deman þe | on þone timan geweold þære widgillan Romebyrig.* Hwæt þa se hæðena dema het gehæftan Crisantum and Darian samod for Drihtnes geleafan and mid mislicum witum het hi gewitnian oð dead gif hi noldon geoffrian þam arwurðum godum.

Crisantus wearð betæht hundseofontigum cempum, (16) and hi hine
100 bundon hetelice swiðe, ac þa bendas toburston sona swa he gebunden wæs. Hi gebundon hine eft, oft and gelome, ac þa bendas toslupon swa swyðlice him fram þæt man ne mihte tocnawan hwæðer hi gecnytte wæron. Þa yrsodon þa cempan ongean þone Cristenen cniht and gesettan hine þa on ænne heardne stocc and his sceancan gefæstnodon on þam
105 fotcopsum, bysmrigende mid wordum þone halgan wer, ac se fotcops awende wundorlice to þrexe and eall to duste þurh Drihtnes mihte. Þa wendon þa cempan þæt he cuðe drycræft and beguton hine ealne mid ealdum miggan; wendon þæt se migga mihte aidlian ealne his scincræft, ac hi swuncon on idel for ðan þe se migga þurh Godes mihte wearð to
110 swetum stence sona awend. Hi behyldon þa ardlice ænne oxan mid graman and besywodon Crisantum swa mid þære hyde to his nacodum

---

90 gebigde] g *above line, insertion mark*
below
95 Fol. 221ʳ
102 man] *above line, insertion mark below*

105 bysmrigende] s *above line, insertion*
mark below

Chrysanthus then asked, among other questions, 'What sort of virtue did your god Saturn possess, he who devoured his sons when they were born, just as his worshippers have written in their books? (10) Or what sort of virtue did the angry Jove possess, he who lived in the world in wicked adultery and chose his own sister as a wife and perpetrated many murders and destructive deeds, and fostered magic to deceive the unwary? (11) Or what sort of holiness was there in the hostile Hercules, the huge giant, who killed all his neighbours and thus burned himself alive in a fire after he had killed men and the lion and the great serpent? Which of the lesser gods must be believed in since the foremost gods lived so wickedly?'

(14) For a long time Chrysanthus then exhorted Daria to the faith with words until she turned to God having abandoned the error of devilish worship.* They then became steadfast and lived together in feigned marriage and with their chastity being preserved until Daria received baptism in God and learned God's books from the learned young man and strengthened her mind while she lived in chastity.

Then, in due course, on account of their way of life many men were turned from the worship of the devil to faith in Christ and to a chaste life. Many young men on account of Chrysanthus's teaching and virgins on account of Daria's turned to the Lord (15) having abandoned marriage and pleasing desires until certain men stirred up strife about these (two) and they were accused before the cruel judge who at that time governed the vast city of Rome.* The pagan judge then ordered Chrysanthus and Daria to be taken prisoner together for their faith in the Lord and ordered them to be tortured to death with various torments if they did not wish to sacrifice to the worthy gods.

Chrysanthus was delivered over to seventy soldiers, (16) and they bound him very fiercely, but the bonds broke as soon as he was bound. They bound him again, often and repeatedly, but the bonds were loosened so quickly from him that no one could make out whether they had been tied. Then the soldiers became angry with the Christian young man and tied him to a hard post and fastened his legs in foot shackles, insulting the holy man with words, but the fetter changed miraculously into rotten wood and entirely into dust through the Lord's power. Then the soldiers believed that he knew magic and drenched him all over with old urine; they believed the urine could bring his sorcery to nothing, but they laboured in vain because the urine through God's power was changed at once into a sweet smell. Then they quickly flayed an ox in anger and so sewed Chrysanthus in the hide with it next to his naked body and laid him facing the

lice and ledon hine ongean þa sunnan. He læg swa ealne dæg on þære
ormætan hætan, ac seo hyd ne mihte aheardian him abutan ne þam halgan
derian on þære hatan sunnan. Hi tigdon þa his swuran swiðe mid racen-
115   teagum and his handa samod mid heardum isene and þa fet togædere mid
gramlicum anginne and wurpon hine swa gebundene into anum blindum
cwearterne. Þa toslupon þa bendas on his swuran and handum, and þær
scean mi|cel leoht swa swa of manegum leohtfatum.

   (17) Þa cempan þa cyddon þæt Claudio heora ealdre, and he sylf com
120   þærto and geseah þæt leoht and het hine utgan, and began hine to axienne,
'Hwæt is seo micele miht þinre morðcræfte þæt þu þyllic gefremast þurh
feondlicne drycræft? Ic gewylde foroft þa anrædan drymen, and ælcne
wiccecræft ic eaðelice oferswiðde, and þa Chaldeiscan wigleras and þa
wurmgaleras ic mihte gewyldan to minum willan æfre and ic næfre ne
125   afunde swa fæstne drycræft. Ic wille nu swa þeah þæt þu awende þe sylfne
fram þinum Cristendome and gecweme urum godum mid arwurðum
offrungum'.

   Him andwyrde þa Crisantus, 'Þu mihtest tocnawan, gif þu cuþest ænig
god, þæt ic mid drycræfte ne dyde þas þing ac me fylste God sylf mid
130   godcundre mihte. Þine godas ne geseoþ ne soðlice ne gehyrað ac syndon
andgitlease, mid leade gefæstnode'.

   Claudius þa het hine hetelice swingan mid greatum gyrdum for his
goda teonan. Þa wurdon þa gyrda wundorlice gehnexode færlice on heora
handum swilce [hi] fæðera wæron. Þa þa hi man heold, hi wæron hearde
135   and hostige; þonne man sloh, sona hi hnexodon.

   (18) Claudius þa het þone halgan forlæton and hine siððan scrydan
and he sylf clypode, 'Nis þeos miht of mannum ac is Godes mærð þe ealle
þas wita gewylde swa eaðelice! Hwæt wille we leng don buton licgan ealle
æt his arwurþum cneowum and eadmodlice biddan þæt he us geþingie to
140   þyllicum Gode þe his biggengan macaþ swa mihtige on gewinne'. Hi
feollon þa ealle mid fyrhte to his cneowum, and Claudius him cwæð to,
'Ic oncneow to soþan þæt þin God is soð God, and ic I sylf nu bidde þæt
þu me geþingie hu ic wurðe his biggenga'.

   Crisantus him andwyrde, 'Ne þearft þu yrnan on fotum ac mid geleafan
145   gan þæt þu God oncnawe. Swa micclum he bið andwerd anum gehwilcum
men swa micclum swa he hine secð mid soþum geleafan'.

---

118 Fol. 221ᵛ   131 andgitlease] *only top third of* g *visible*
123 Chaldeiscan] e *above line, insertion mark*   134 (hi)] hit
   below   142 Fol. 222ʳ
126 þinum] *above line, insertion mark below.*   144 þearft] r *above line, insertion mark*
   gecweme] *letter erased between* m *and* e,   *below*
   which are connected by underscoring

sun. He lay in this manner all day in the great heat, but the hide could not harden around him nor injure the saint in the hot sun. Then they violently tied his neck with chains and at the same time with hard iron (tied) his hands and feet together with angry intent and threw him bound in this way into a dark prison. Then the bonds on his neck and hands were loosened, and a great light shone there as if from many lamps.

(17) The soldiers then reported that to Claudius their leader, and he himself came to that place and saw that light and ordered him to come out, and he began to ask him, 'What is the great power of your destructive art that you perform such things through diabolical magic? I have very often overcome resolute magicians, and I have easily defeated all witchcraft, and I was always able to subdue the Babylonian sorcerers and the snake charmers to my will and never have I come across magic so intractable. Nevertheless, I now want you to turn yourself from your Christianity and to propitiate our gods with worthy sacrifices'.

Chrysanthus then replied him, 'You could understand, if you had any good sense, that I did not do these things by means of magic but that God himself helped me with divine power. Your gods do not actually see or hear but are senseless, fixed in lead'.

Claudius then ordered him to be beaten fiercely with large rods because of his insult to the gods. Miraculously the rods then softened suddenly in their hands as if they were feathers. When a man held them, they were hard and knotty; when he struck, they softened at once.

(18) Claudius then ordered them to leave the saint alone and afterwards to clothe him, and he himself exclaimed, 'This power is not from men but is a glorious act of God who has so easily overcome all these torments! What shall we longer wish to do except to lie down at his worthy knees and humbly ask him to intercede for us to such a God who makes his worshippers so powerful in a conflict'. They all then fell with fear at his knees, and Claudius said to him, 'I have truly understood that your God is true God, and I now pray that you intercede for me about how I may become his worshipper'.

Chrysanthus replied to him, 'You need not run with your feet but to walk with faith so that you may come to know God. He will be as present to each one as much as he seeks him with true faith'.

(19) Crisantus hi lærde þa oþ þæt hi gelyfdon on God. Claud[i]us and
his wif Hilaria gehaten and heora twegen suna Nason* and Maurus and
heora maga fela to fulluhte hi gebugon, and þa hundseofontig cempan þe
150   Claudius bewiste wurdon gefullode mid heora freondum þæs dæges. Hi
ealle þa wunodon, wuldrigende heora Drihten and geornlice leornodon
heora geleafan æt Crisante, and wiscton þæt hi moston wite þrowian for
Criste.

Hit bið langsum to awritene þa wundra þe hi gefremodon ealle be
155   endebyrdnysse for þan þe we efstað swyðe eow mannum to secgenne hu
hi gemartyrode wæron.*

(20) Numerianus se casere, þære Cristenra ehtere, þa þa him wearð
cuð þæt Claudius gelyfde and ealle þa cempan Cristene wæron, þa het he
niman Claudium and lædan to sæ and wurpan hine ut mid anum weorc-
160   stane. He het beheafdian siððan þa hundseofontig cempan butan heora
hwilc wolde awegan his geleafan, ac hi ealle efston anrædlice to slæge,
and Claudies twegen suna cwædon þæt hi wæron on Criste gefullode and
underfon woldon deað mid þam cempum for Cristes geleafan. Hi wurdon
þa ofslagene samod for Criste, (21) and Hilaria se[o] eadiga eac wearð
165   gelæht to þam martyrdome fram þam manfullan. Þa bæd heo þa cwelleras
þe hi to cwale læddon þæt heo moste ærest hi ardlice gebiddan, and heo
swa dyde and Drihtnes l lichaman underfeng and on þam gebedum gewat
of worulde to Criste.

(22) Efter þysum wearð se halga wer Crisantus on cwearterne gebroht
170   swa swa se casere het þæt he mid Darian for Drihtnes geleafan on
mislicum witum gemartyrod wurde. Þæt cweartern wearð afylled mid
fulum adelan and butan ælcum leohte atelice stincende. Daria seo eadiga
fram þam arwurþan wæs onsundran gehæft, and hi man sende þa to
myltestrena huse þam manfullan to gamene, ac God hi gescylde wið þa
175   sceandlican hæðenan. Þæt anþræce cweartern þe Crisantus on wæs wearð
onliht sona wundorlice þurh God and þær wynsum bræð werodlice
stemde, and an leo* ætbærst ut of þære leona pearruce and arn to Darian,
þurh Drihtnes sande, þær heo læg on gebedum, and alæt to eorðan
astræhtum limum wið þæt geleaffulle mæden.
180   (23) Þa woldon ða hæðenan habban hi to bysmore and nyston þæt se
leo læg inne mid hire. Eode þa heora an into þam mædene, ac seo leo hine
gelæhte and alede hine adune and beseah to Darian swylce heo axian
wolde hu he[o] wolde be him þa he gewyld læg. Daria þa cwæð to þam
deore þus, 'Ic þe halsige þurh Crist þæt þu þam cnihte ne derige ac læt hine
185   butan ege hlystan minre spræce'. (24) Þa forlet seo leo þone ungeleaf-
fullan cniht and forstod him þa duru þæt he Darian gespræce and þæt nan
oþer man ne mihte in to him.

---

147 Claud(i)us] Claudus   152 moston] n *above line, insertion mark*
                                           below

(19) Chrysanthus taught them then until they believed in God. Claudius and his wife named Hilaria and their two sons Nason* and Maurus and many of their kinsmen submitted themselves to baptism, and the seventy soldiers of whom Claudius had charge were baptized with their kinsmen on that day. They all remained there, glorifying their Lord and eagerly learning their faith from Chrysanthus, and they wanted to be allowed to suffer punishment for Christ.

It will take a long time to write down in chronological order the miracles that they all did because we hasten quickly to tell you men how they were martyred.*

(20) When it was made known to Numerianus the emperor, a persecutor of Christians, that Claudius believed and all the soldiers had become Christians, he then ordered Claudius to be seized and led to the sea and thrown out tied to a building-stone. He afterwards ordered the seventy soldiers to be beheaded unless any of them desired to renounce his faith, but they all hastened steadfastly to death, and Claudius's two sons said that they had been baptized in Christ and desired to accept death with the soldiers on account of their faith in Christ. They were then killed together for Christ, (21) and the blessed Hilaria also was snatched away from the wicked one to her martyrdom. She then asked the executioners who led her to her death that she first be able to pray hastily, and she did so and received the Lord's body and in her prayers departed from the world to Christ.

(22) After this the holy man Chrysanthus was put into prison just as the emperor commanded so that with Daria he might be martyred with various torments on account of their faith in the Lord. The prison was filled with foul-smelling muck and without any light stunk horribly. The blessed Daria was imprisoned separately from the honourable man, and someone then sent her to a house of prostitutes as sport for the wicked, but God defended her against the shameful heathens. The terrible prison Chrysanthus was in was at once illuminated miraculously by God and a pleasant fragrance wafted sweetly there, and a lion* escaped out of the lion's enclosure and ran to Daria, because the Lord sent it, where she lay in prayer, and the lion bent down to the ground with its limbs outstretched toward the faithful virgin.

(23) Then the heathens desired to have her shamefully and did not know that the lion lay inside with her. Then one of them went in to the virgin, but the lion seized him and laid him down and looked at Daria as if it wished to ask what she intended to do about him as he lay there overpowered. Daria then spoke to the animal in this way, 'I beseech you for Christ's sake not to injure the young man but to let him listen to my speech without fear'. (24) Then the lion released the unbelieving young man and blocked the door against him so that he might talk to Daria and so that no other man would be able to come inside to them.

---

164 se(o)] se
167 Fol. 222ᵛ

183 he(o)] he

Daria þa cwæð to þam ofdræddan men, 'Efne, þeos reþe leo arwurðað nu God, and þu, gesceadwisa man, þe sylfne fordest, and þu fægnast,

190 earmincg, on þinre fulan galnysse þurh þa ðu scealt weopan and wite þrowian'. Þa gesohte he hi | and sæde mid fyrhte, 'Læt me gan gesund ut, and ic syððan bodige mannum þone Hælend þe þu mærsast and wurðast'. Þa het Daria þæt deor him ryman ut, and he arn ut arwurðigende God and þæt halige mæden, hire mihte cyðende.

195 Þa woldon þa hæþenan hetan þære leo[n], ac heo gelæhte æfre ænne and ænne and brohte hi to Darian þurh Drihtnes mihte. (25) Þæt mæden þa cwæð to þam mannum þus, 'Gif ge wyllað gelyfan on þone lifigendan Crist, þonne mage ge gan unamyrrede heonan. Gif ge þonne nellað þone geleafan habban, nat ic gif eowre godas eow gehelpan magon'. Hi ealle

200 þa clypodon swilce mid anre stemne, 'Se ðe on Crist ne gelyfe, ne cume he cucu heonon!' And hi eodon þa ut ealle clypigende, 'Eala ge Romaniscan leoda, gelyfað to soþan þæt nan oþer God nys buton Criste anum!'

Þa wearð se heahgerefa hearde gegremod and het ontendan fyr

205 ætforan þære dura þær Daria inne wæs mid þam deore samod; wolde hi forbærnan butu ætgædere. Þa forhtode seo leo for þam fyre þearle, ac Daria cwæð to þam deore þus, 'Ne beo þu afyrht. Þis fyr þe ne derað, ne þu ne bist ofslagen ær þan þe þu sylf acwele. Gang þe nu orsorh aweg, and God ahret þone þe ðu wurðodest mid þinum weorcum todæg'. Þa eode

210 seo leo alotenum heafde tomiddes þæs folces freolice aweg and þa þe heo ær gefeng wurdon gefullode siððan hi oncneowan Crist þurh ða leon.

(26) Þis wearð þa gecyd þam casere sona, and he het mid graman his heahgerefan geniman Crisantum and Darian and acwellan hi mid witum gif hi noldon offrian þam arleasum godum. Se heahgerefa þa het on

215 hengene astreccan þone halgan Crisantum and mid candelum bærnan buta | his sidan. Þa tobærst seo hengen mid eallum ðam cræfte, and þa candela acwuncon. Ealswa þa oþre men þe yfelian woldon þa halgan Darian Drihten hi gelette swa þæt heora sina sona forscruncon, swa hwa swa hi hrepode, þæt hi hrymdon for ece. Hwæt ða Celerinus se forscylde-

220 goda gerefa mid fyrhte wearð fornumen and ferde to þam casere and sæde him be endebyrdnysse þa syllican tacne.

Numerianus þa se manfulla casere tealde þæt to drycræfte na to Drihtnes tacnum and het lædan buta þa halgan togædere to anum sand-pytte and setton hi þæron and bewurpan mid eorþan and mid

225 weorcstanum. Hi wurdon þa buta bebyrigde swa cuce swa swa se casere het, and hi mid clænnysse ferdon of worulde to wuldre to wunigenne mid Criste.

---

191 Fol. 223ʳ   209 eode] *above line, insertion mark below*
195 leo(n)] leo   216 Fol. 223ᵛ

Daria then said to the frightened man, 'Behold, this fierce lion now honours God, and you, a rational man, destroy yourself, and you, wretched one, rejoice in your wicked sexual desire on account of which you will weep and suffer torment'. Then he approached her and said with fear, 'Let me go out unharmed, and afterwards I will proclaim to men the Saviour whom you glorify and honour'. Daria then ordered the animal to make room for him to go out, and he ran out honouring God and the holy virgin, making known her power.

Then the heathens wished to attack the lion, but it always seized them one by one and brought them to Daria through the Lord's power. (25) The virgin then spoke to the men in this way, 'If you are willing to believe in the living Christ, then you may go unharmed from here. Yet if you are not willing to have that faith, I do not know if your gods will be able to help you'. They all then exclaimed as if with one voice, 'He who does not believe in Christ, let him not leave here alive!' And they all then went out exclaiming, 'O Roman people, truly believe that there is no other God save Christ alone!'

The prefect was then vehemently angered and ordered a fire to be kindled in front of the door where Daria was inside together with the animal; he wanted to burn them both together.

Then the lion was very afraid of the fire, but Daria spoke to the animal in this way, 'Do not be afraid. This fire will not injure you, nor will you be killed before you die naturally. Go away now without anxiety, and God, whom you honoured with your actions today, will set you free'. Then with its head bowed the lion went away freely into the midst of the crowd, and those whom it earlier seized were baptized after they acknowledged Christ because of the lion.

(26) This was then immediately made known to the emperor, and in anger he ordered his prefect to take Chrysanthus and Daria and to kill them with tortures if they did not wish to sacrifice to the wicked gods. The prefect then ordered the holy Chrysanthus to be stretched out on a rack and burned with candles on both his sides. Then the rack with all its ingenuity shattered, and the candles went out. Likewise, the Lord hindered the other men who wished to harm the holy Daria so that whoever touched her, their sinews immediately shrivelled up with the result that they cried out on account of the pain. Then Celerinus the wicked officer was seized with fear and went to the emperor and told him in turn about the strange signs.

Numerianus the wicked emperor then ascribed it to magic not to the signs of the Lord and ordered both the saints to be led together to a sandpit and put therein and covered with earth and building stones. Then they were thus buried alive just as the emperor commanded, and with chastity they departed from this world to glory to live with Christ.

(27) Þær wurdon gefremode fela wundra þurh God, and þæt folc
gewurðode þa wuldorfullan halgan and gelome sohton mid geleafan
230   þider. Hit gelamp þa on fyrste, þa þa þæt folc þider sohte to þam micclan
screfe þær þa martyras lagon, þæt se casere het ahebban ænne wah to þæs
scræfes ingange þæt hi ut ne mihton, and het afyllan þæt clyf færlice him
onuppan þæt hi ealle togædere heora gastas ageafon, mid eorðan
ofhrorene. And hi rixiað mid Gode on þam ecan life, for heora geleafan
235   acwealde.

We wurþiað Godes halgan, ac wite ge swa þeah þæt þam halgum nis
nan neod ure herunge on þam life, ac us sylfum fremað þæt þæt we secgað
be him, ærest to gebysnunge þæt we þe beteran beon and eft to þingræ-
dene þonne us þearf bið.* Mycel ehtnys wæs þa ða hi wæron gemartyrode,
240   ac git cymð earfoþre ehtnys on Antecristes tocyme, for þan þe þa martyras
l worhton manega wundra þurh God and on Antecristes timan ateoriað
þa wundra and se deofol wyrcð þonne wundra þurh his scincræft mid
leasum gedwimorum to dweligenne þa geleaffullan. Mycel angsumnys
bið þam arwurðum halgum þæt se feondlica ehtere fela tacna wyrce and
245   hi sylfe ne moton swa þa martyras dydon, wundra æteowigende on þam
wyrstan timan. Hi beoð swa þeah gehealdenne þurh þæs Hælendes mihte
gif hi heora geleafan gehealdað oð ende on þam earfoðum ehtnyssum þæs
arleasan deofles, swa swa se Hælend cwæð on his halgan godspelle*, se
þe þone Antecrist eaðelice fordeð. Þam sy wuldor and lof a to worulde.
250   AMEN.

---

241 Fol. 224^r
250 AMEN] *in small capitals*

(27) Many miracles were performed there by God, and the people honoured the glorious saints and frequently visited that place with faith. It then happened in due course, when the people came there to the great cave where the martyrs lay, that the emperor commanded a wall to be raised at the entrance of the cave so that they could not go out, and he commanded a mountain of earth to be thrown suddenly down on top of them so that they all gave up their spirits at the same time, buried with dirt. And they reign with God in the everlasting life, killed for their faith.

We honour God's saints, but know nevertheless that the saints do not need our praise while we are living, but that which we say about them benefits us, first as an example that we might be the better and then for intercession when we need it.* There was great persecution when they were martyred, but a more difficult persecution will yet come with the arrival of Antichrist, because the martyrs performed many miracles through God and in the time of Antichrist miracles will cease and the devil will then perform miracles through his sorcery with false delusions to lead astray the faithful. It will be great anguish to the worthy saints that the devilish persecutor will perform many signs and that they themselves cannot do as the martyrs did, exhibiting miracles in the worst time. They will nevertheless be preserved through the Saviour's power if they preserve their faith until the end in the difficult persecutions of the wicked devil, just as the Saviour said in his holy gospel*, he who will easily destroy Antichrist. To him be glory and praise for ever. AMEN.

COMMENTARY

ON THE OLD ENGLISH TEXTS

The Passio of Saint Julian and his Wife Basilissa

Title The date 13 January is not attested in Anglo-Saxon calendars, which variously date the feast to 20 December, 8 January, 9 January and 27 February (see p. 40, n. 93). 13 January, however, is a date common to thirty-one of the thirty-three manuscripts of *BHL* 4532 that I have examined, including N (see line 925 [p. 170]). Part of Ælfric's *incipit*, 'Sancti Iuliani et sponse eius Basilisse', corresponds exactly to the calendar entry discussed earlier (Introduction, p. 15).

2 As indicated in the apparatus, *Egypta* has been corrected from *Ægypta*. G. Needham concludes that such corrections reflect 'an attempt to bring [the early eleventh-century manuscript] up to date' after 1032, when a new church Cnut ordered to be built at Bury St Edmunds, where the manuscript may have originated, was finished ('Additions and Alterations in Cotton Ms. Julius E VII' [cited on p. 45, n. 165], 160).

4–6 Ælfric's treatment of Julian's encounter with his parents differs markedly from that in the *passio* (lines 14–32 [p. 114]). Concerning the effect of his revisions on the meaning of Julian's vision of Christ and of the newlywed's heavenly visitation, see the Introduction, pp. 21–22. Line 123 (p. 120) in the Latin text explains Ælfric's comment here that Julian's parents were *æwfastum* ('devout'), whereas line 27 (p. 116) of the Latin accounts for the role of Julian's *frynd* ('relatives') in urging him to marry.

7–8 As is common in Old English prose, the subject of the second independent clause is not expressed since it is identical to the subject of the preceding sentence (B. Mitchell and F. Robinson, *A Guide to Old English*, 6th ed. [Oxford, 2001], p. 107 [§193.7]).

9 See note on the Latin, lines 35–36 (pp. 251–52).

13 This is the first of eight times Ælfric uses the verb *gebigan* ('to turn, bend, convert'): see also lines 45, 124, 184, 249, 259, 260 and 292 (though the final instance refers to wild animals bending their heads

to lick the saints' feet). His repetition of *gebigan*, and use of *gebugan* ('to turn, submit' [line 80]), *wiþsacan* ('to renounce, reject, deny' [line 146]), *geweman* ('to seduce, entice, persuade, lead' [line 144]), *gecyrran* ('to turn, turn aside' [lines 159 and 302]) and *awendan* ('to turn' [line 227]) draw attention to the theme of spiritual purity and steadfastness in the Old English version.

17–18   Neither N nor any other text of *BHL* 4532 that I have seen can account for Ælfric's 'hi mycclum þæs fægnodon' ('they rejoiced greatly about that'), which corresponds to the phrase 'exhilarantur genitores' ('the parents were cheered') of *BHL* 4529 (*AS*, Ian. I, p. 576). Zettel notes this discrepancy and all others discussed below ('Ælfric's Hagiographic Sources' [cited on p. 46, n. 178], pp. 304–05).

20–21   In both *Julian and Basilissa* and *Cecilia*, Ælfric sets the initial conversations between the brides and grooms in the bed rather than the bed chamber (see *Cecilia*, line 20 [p. 72]).

25–36   Compare these lines with lines 67–80 (p. 118) of the Latin text, noting the preponderance of Old English words with the stem *clæn*. *Clænnyss* ('chastity' or 'purity') has a greater semantic range in Ælfric's lexicon than *mægðhad* ('virginity'), and his word choice may represent an effort to make the legend as widely applicable to his audience as possible.

26–28   See note on lines 69–70 of the Latin text (p. 253).

37–39   The numbering of Psalms 9–147 in the medieval Latin Bible known as the Vulgate differs from the numbering in Protestant translations. Protestant translations treat verses 22–39 of Psalm 9 in the Vulgate as a separate psalm, Psalm 10. Therefore, to locate Vulgate Psalms 10–145 in a Protestant translation, add one to the numbering of the Vulgate. Protestant translations also treat Vulgate Psalms 146–47 as a single psalm, Psalm 147.

The Catholic *Douay Rheims Bible* (Baltimore, MD, 1899; repr. Rockford, IL, 2000) is a rather literal rendering of the Vulgate (*Biblia Sacra Vulgata*, ed. R. Weber, 3rd ed. [Stuttgart, 1983]). All biblical citations and translations refer to this edition and translation.

The Septuagint is the Greek version of the most ancient witnesses to the Hebrew Bible made some time between the third and first centuries BCE. Jerome (c. 345–420), whose translations of the Hebrew and Greek scriptures formed a majority of the Vulgate, is responsible for the Latin translations of the Septuagint and Hebrew versions of the psalms, which are printed on facing pages in Weber's edition of the Vulgate. As a general rule, Protestant translations follow the Hebrew text.

54–55   Ælfric focuses on the importance of Julian and Basilissa's knowledge of God at the expense of the wordplay in the Latin on spiritual and fleshly fruit (lines 117–18 [p. 120]). He also omits any mention of a secret union (lines 118–20). Worthy of note is a sermon in which Ælfric sanctions Anglo-Saxon couples to adopt chaste marriage secretly (*CH* II.19 [cited on p. 32, n. 6], lines 168–69 [p. 185]), and he appears to idealize an open arrangement here. By contrast, Chrysanthus, whose father is a pagan, keeps his chaste union with Daria a secret (Ælfric's *Chrysanthus and Daria*, lines 85–86 [p. 90]).

58–74   Ælfric drastically abbreviates the section of the *passio* that deals with Julian and Basilissa's monasteries (see lines 126–231 [pp. 122–28]). Of course, such matters would be of little concern for the laity, but Ælfric is particularly sensitive about revealing 'the inner life and moral problems of the monks' (E.G. Whatley, '*Pearls Before Swine*: Ælfric, Vernacular Hagiography, and the Lay Reader' in *Via Crucis: Essays on Early Medieval Sources and Ideas in Memory of J.E. Cross*, ed. T. Hall with T. Hill [Morgantown, 2002], pp. 158–84, at p. 181).

Whereas the *passio* mentions the emperors Diocletian and Maximian, Ælfric refers to only the former. He explains in the Latin Preface to the *Lives* that 'nollem alicubi ponere duos imperatores siue cesares in hac narratione simul, sicut in latinitate legimus, sed unum imperatorum in persecutione martyrum ponimus ubique, sicut gens nostra uni regi subditur, et usitate est de rege non de duobus loqui' (*LS* Latin Preface [cited on p. 32, n. 1], lines 18–21 [pp. 2 and 4]) ('I have not wanted to put two emperors or caesars anywhere in this narrative at the same time, as we have read in the Latin, but we have placed one emperor over the persecution of the martyrs everywhere, just as our nation is subject to one king and is accustomed to speak of one king, not of two' [*Ælfric's Prefaces* (cited on p. 45, n. 153), ed. Wilcox, p. 120, lines 16–20].

87–88   I have encountered only one version of *BHL* 4532 that can account for Ælfric's description of the house as that 'þe hi heora beda beeoden' ('in which they said their prayers'). Rome, Biblioteca Casanatense, MS 718, f. 49ʳ (s.xi), reads: 'Multitudinem vero sanctorum iussit in eodem loco in quo degebant in Dei laudibus igne copioso cremari' ('But he ordered the multitude of saints to be burned in a great fire in the same place in which they continued in the praises of God'). This manuscript, however, is among those versions of *BHL* 4532 that are least similar to Ælfric's immediate source. The reading in the Casanatense MS is most similar to that in a text of *BHL* 4529 in the late seventh- or early eighth-century Luxeuil lectionary: 'Multitudinem uero sanctorum iussit in eodem loco, in quo degebant in Dei laudibus, igni cupiosum adgregare' ('But he ordered a multitude of saints to be thrown into a great fire in the same place in which they continued in praises of God'

[*Lectionnaire de Luxeuil* (cited on p. 36, n. 38), ed. Salmon, p. 38]).

176–77 Cotton Otho B. x omits this sentence altogether, which prompts K. Kiernan to make this observation: 'The version in Otho B. x . . . appears to be a deliberate revision, removing the potentially merciful action of the judge' ('Odd Couples in Ælfric's *Julian and Basilissa*' [cited on p. 52]), p. 103.

188 N's 'ad exemplum omnium conuocata uniuersa prouincia' ('as an example to all those gathered from every province' [lines 574–75 (p. 148)]), a reading shared by all other versions of *BHL* 4532 that I have seen, cannot account for the emperor's instructions to burn the saints 'oðrum mannum to bynse' ('as an example to other men'). Ælfric's wording corresponds more closely to a reading of *BHL* 4529 preserved in *AS*, Ian. I., p. 583: 'ad exemplum aliorum conuocata uniuersa prouincia' ('as an example to others gathered from every province').

203 I know of no version of *BHL* 4532 that accounts for Ælfric's 'clypode ofer eall' ('cried out above everything'), which more closely reflects *BHL* 4529's 'uoce magna clamabat' ('he shouted in a loud voice' [*AS*, Ian. I., p. 583]) than N's 'clamabat' ('he shouted' [line 610 (p. 150)]).

214 While N's 'propter dilectum meum' ('for the sake of my beloved one' [line 620 (p. 150)]) does not account for Ælfric's 'for minum leofan Iuliane' ('for the sake of my beloved Julian'), several manuscripts of *BHL* 4532 read 'propter dilectum meum Iulianum' ('on account of my beloved Julian'), including R and D, as the variants show.

241 *Undergerefa* ('under-reeve, deputy') and *gingra* ('aide, deputy') (line 239), which translate *assessor* (lines 669–70 [p. 152]), a Latin word for an aide, counsellor or judge's assistant, represent Ælfric's attempts to make comprehensible an unfamiliar Roman social structure for his Anglo-Saxon audience. In the other two lives, see also *rædbora* ('counsel-bearer, adviser') for *assessor* (lines 157 [p. 80] and 53 [p. 88]) and *heahgerefa* ('high-reeve, prefect') for *prefectus*, a Roman civil administrator, (lines 145 [p. 78], 204 and 214 [p. 96]).

268–70 Because Ælfric emphasizes the virtue of steadfastness in the legend, Julian's commitment to God never wavers, even in jest. Compare the Latin, lines 823–36 (pp. 162–64).

270–73 N (line 851 [p. 166]) and all other copies of *BHL* 4532 that I have seen mention that Julian prays only with Antonius. Ælfric's immediate source must have preserved a reading closer to that of *BHL* 4529, where Julian prays with Antonius and 'cum sociis' ('together with his companions' [*AS*, Ian. I., p. 586]).

275–80 Of twenty passages of direct speech that occur from this point onward in the *passio*, Ælfric preserves only this one. Regarding the possibility that he intends Martianus to symbolize wayward Christians, compare this passage with *LS* I.17, lines 29–34 (p. 366), and see the note below on lines 295–302.

293   In the phrase 'mid liðra tungan', there is confusion between the adjective endings -*ra*, which is used here for the dative, singular feminine form of *lip*, and -*re*, which would be the standard Late West Saxon ending. While 'tungan' ('tongue') is singular in Old English, I have translated it as plural for sense.

    I have not been able to locate a reference to both lions and bears among copies of *BHL* 4532. There is a reference to 'liones ieiuni ad sanctorum devorationem dimissi' ('young lions released to devour the saints') in two similar sets of lections, or abbreviated readings, in two Italian manuscripts, which Guy Philippart classifies as having been taken from a text of *BHL* 4532: Rome, Biblioteca Apostolica Vaticana, Archivo di San Pietro MSS A. 9 (1339) and A. 8 (s.xv).

    Aldhelm, however, mentions both kinds of animals in his epitomes of the legend in the prose and verse *De uirginitate* when he writes that the saints were sent to the amphitheatre in order that 'ursorum genuinis carperentur et leonum rictibus roderentur' ('they might be devoured by the teeth of bears and gnawed by the jaws of lions' ['De virginitate. Prosa', *Aldhelmi Opera*, ed. Ehwald, p. 284, line 7; and *Aldhelm: The Prose Works*, trans. Lapidge and Herren, p. 102]). For the detail in the verse, see 'De virginitate. Carmen', *Aldhelmi Opera*, ed. Ehwald, p. 413, lines 1433–36 and *Aldhelm: The Poetic Works*, trans. Lapidge and Rosier, p. 134. All references to Aldhelm's works are cited on pp. 37–38, n. 61. Ælfric may be recalling Aldhelm's work, or his immediate source may have mentioned lions and bears. On the study of Aldhelm in tenth-century Anglo-Saxon schools, see p. 43, n. 122; M. Lapidge, 'The Hermeneutic Style in Tenth-Century England' in his *Anglo-Latin Literature 900–1066* (London, 1993), pp. 105–49, at pp. 111–14; and Gretsch, *Intellectual Foundations of the English Benedictine Reform* (cited on pp. 46, n. 190), pp. 332–83.

295–302 Ælfric adds this catalogue, which may have been prompted by Julian's vision in the *passio* (lines 879–83 [p. 168]). By adding the catalogue of saints, Ælfric restructures the end of the legend by treating the glorification of the saints before the destruction of the pagans. On the likelihood that Julian and Basilissa, and the rest of the saints included in the catalogue, represent Christians whom God rewards for their corporeal chastity and spiritual purity, see *LS* I.17, lines 60–66 (p. 368). For reasons why Ælfric may have made these alterations and their effects on his narrative, see my 'Virgin spouses as model Christians' [cited on p. 43, n. 135].

The Passio of Saint Cecilia the Virgin

5 Ælfric indicates the importance of true belief and truly believing by repeating the noun *geleafa* ('faith, belief'), the verb *gelyfan* ('to believe'), and the adjective *geleafful* ('believing, faithful'), twenty-one times, including this one (see lines 28, 30, 34, 39, 43, 45, 46, 49, 64, 68, 92, 127, 139, 186, 191, 194, 201, 203, 218 and 258).

20 As in *Julian and Basilissa* (lines 20–21 [p. 54]), Ælfric recasts the couple's initial encounter as a pillow talk with the result that Cecilia 'makes love' to Valerian in bed with her wisdom and language, and 'þus to Gode tihte' ('thus allured [him] to God' [line 21]).

23 Although *on life* makes sense, Skeat emends *life* to *lufe* (*LS* II.34, line 32 [p. 358]), on the grounds that the emendation would reflect more closely Cecilia's comment in line 65 of the *passio* that '"angelum Dei habeo amatorem"' ('"I have an angel of God for a lover"' [p. 176]).

27 The variant reading in V and C, which describes Valerian as 'nutu Dei *timore* correptus' ('by the will of God seized *with fear*'), accounts for Ælfric's 'se cniht wearð þa *afyrht*' ('the young man was then *frightened*') whereas H's 'nutu Dei correptus' ('seized by the will of God' [line 71]) does not. Zettel notes this discrepancy and others regarding lines 113–14 and 216 ('Ælfric's Hagiographic Sources' [cited on p. 46, n. 178], p. 314).

   On the theme of sight in the *passio*, see the Latin Commentary on lines 74–76 (pp. 256–57).

46–47 Ælfric uses the inflected infinitive (*gelyfenne*) with the verb 'to be' to express necessity or obligation' (Mitchell and Robinson, *Guide to Old English*, p. 112 [§205.2 (b)]).

56–57 Ælfric's angel requires Cecilia and Valerian to keep the crowns 'mid clænre heortan' ('with a pure heart') not, as in the *passio*, 'immaculato corde et mundo corpore' ('with an unstained heart and a pure body' [line 124 (p. 180)]). By omitting any mention of corporeal virginity, he shifts the focus to the couple's spiritual purity. For an echo of the phrase *mid clænre heortan* in a sermon where Ælfric personifies the Church as a body of believers who are holy and pure of heart, see *CH* II.40 [cited on p. 32, n. 6], lines 96–108 (p. 338).

66–70 Ælfric substitutes a metaphor of procreation for the monetary metaphor of the *passio* (lines 135–38 [p. 180]), with the result that he links ideas of spiritual rebirth and teaching, and symbolizes the fruitfulness of the church by means of the saints' conversions of others to Christianity. On Ælfric's willingness to assign to laymen the role of teaching, see *CH* II.38, lines 54–66 (p. 320) and my 'Homiletic Contexts for Ælfric's Hagiography' [cited on p. 43, n. 124].

104–11 Like many of the speeches Ælfric preserves from the *passio*, Cecilia's answers to Tiburtius's questions reinforce doctrines and practices he preaches and teaches about elsewhere. Malcolm Godden notes that speeches such as Cecilia's allow the saint to assume the role of preacher, and in light of the emphasis Ælfric places on teaching (see note above), her voice becomes that of the lay teacher as well ('Experiments in Genre: The Saints' Lives in Ælfric's *Catholic Homilies*' in *Holy Men and Holy Women* [cited on p. 33, n. 8], ed. Szarmach, p. 266). Compare Cecilia's answer here to *CH* I.32, lines 195–229 (p. 457) and *SH* II.21 [cited on p. 32, n. 1], lines 33–71 (p. 678–79), a treatise on false gods (*De falsis diis*) that Ælfric apparently appended to the *Lives* when he first issued the collection.

112–13 Ælfric's immediate source must have read, as V and C do, '"Et quibis ibi fuit et inde huc ueniens *nobis* hoc potuit indicare"' ('"And who has been there and has come from there who could disclose this *to us*"'), not 'uobis' ('to you') as H reads (line 211 [p. 184]).

114–17 Compare Cecilia's answer regarding the Trinity with similar formulations found in three texts of the *Lives*: (1) *De falsis diis* (*SH* II.21, lines 12–20 [p. 677]); (2) *Interrogationes Sigeuulfi in Genesin* ('Ælfric's Translation of Alcuin's *Interrogationes Sigwulfi Presbiteri*' [cited on p. 33, n. 8], ed. Stoneman, lines 554–65 [pp. 236–37]); and (3) *De memoria sanctorum* (*LS* I.16, lines 1–4 [p. 336] and lines 382–84 [p. 362]).

120–25 Communicating the doctrine of the Trinity was one of Ælfric's 'key concerns' notes Malcolm Godden (*Commentary* [cited on p. 33, n. 6], p. 164). Compare Cecilia's comments concerning the unity of the Trinity to *LS* I.1, lines 14–19 (pp. 10 and 12) and lines 31–41 (p. 12); *SH* II.21, lines 20–24 (p. 677); the passage from *Interrogationes Sigeuulfi* cited in the previous note; and *CH* I.8, lines 206–10 (p. 248). Ælfric employs the tri-fold comparison of the Trinity to 'understanding, will and conscious memory' in *LS* I.1, lines 112–22 (pp. 16 and 18); *Interrogationes Sigeuulfi*, lines 190–212 (p. 341–42); and *CH* I.20, lines 190–212 (p. 341–42). He often uses *froforgast* ('Comforting Spirit' [line 145]) to refer to the Holy Spirit; see, for example, *CH* I.20, line 84 (p. 338) and *CH* I.22, line 175 (p. 360).

130–34 Compare Ælfric's fifty-four-word summary to Cecilia's 854-word answer in the *passio* (lines 236–313 [pp. 186–92]). For a portion of a sermon in which he covers similar ground, see *CH* I.1, lines 236–93 (pp. 187–89).

149 Douai, Bibliothèque Municipale, MS 838 (s.xiii) preserves a reading that accounts more fully for Ælfric's 'Hwæt þa Almachius het þa men gelangian' ('Almachius then ordered the men to be summoned') than the texts of H, V or C (line 349 [p. 194]). Whereas

H reads 'Tenti ero ab apparitoribus Almachio presentantur' ('When they had been seized by the prefect's aides, they were presented to Almachius.'), the Douai text has 'Quod audiens prefectus iussit illos uenire' ('When the prefect heard about this, he ordered them to come.').

158 See note on the Latin, lines 462–63 (p. 258).

216 The reading 'lapidem uilem' ('a worthless stone') in V and C is found in a majority of manuscripts and corresponds more closely to Ælfric's 'wacne stan' ('a stone of little worth') than H's 'lapidem uiuum' ('an unwrought stone' [line 542 (p. 206)]).

247–48 Believing that the loss of bodily fluids will be fatal to Cecilia, Almachius intends to sweat the life out of her.

253–54 In the clause 'þa sende he ænne cwellere to' ('then he sent an executioner to that place'), the preposition *to* is used adverbially and thus lacks an object. In this instance, and in *slean to* in the next sentence (line 257), the preposition *to* remains untranslated due to the adverb clause that follows and functions much like the separable prefix in modern German (Mitchell and Robinson, *Guide to Old English*, p. 116 [§213]). Both *tosendan* and *toslean* are Old English verbs.

254–57 On the significance of these lines, see the Introduction, p. 30.

The Passio of Chrysanthus and Daria His Wife

56 In its entry for *and-wyrdan* (§1.a), the *Dictionary of Old English* (cited on p. 43, n. 131) queries whether or not *andwyrde* was 'written in error for *andwyrdan,* since a finite form of the verb is unlikely after *cunnan*; or perhaps a verb (of speaking, e.g. *secgan*) [was] omitted after *andwyrde* (noun)'.

84–85 The phrase 'forlætenum gedwylde deoflicra biggenga' is an example of the 'dative absolute' in which the dative case of the past participle of the verb *forlætan* modifies the dative neuter noun *gedwylde*. Because the Old English dative absolute mimics the Latin ablative absolute, this phrase may also be translated 'with the errors of devilish worship having been abandoned' (Mitchell and Robinson, *Guide to Old English*, p. 106 [§191.4]). Ælfric employs the dative absolute with the same verb several sentences later ('forlætenum synscipe and geswæsum lustum') ('with marriage and pleasing desires having been abandoned' [line 93]).

91–95 As if to downplay the potential divisiveness of chaste marriage, Ælfric mutes the public outcry from abandoned spouses and fiancées that flares up in the *passio* (lines 292–99 [p. 238]).

148 I have seen the mistake of *Nason* for *Iason* only once, in a late manuscript, Paris, Bibliothèque Nationale, Lat. 11759 (late fourteenth century), but the copy does not otherwise preserve readings closer

to Ælfric's immediate source than P does.

154–56   The phrase 'eow mannum' might also be translated as 'you people', a rendering that would imply a wider audience than the book's dedicatees, Æthelweard and Æthelmær. On possible audiences for the *Lives of Saints*, including those of mixed sexes and ranks, see J. Wilcox, 'The Audience of Ælfric's *Lives of Saints*' [cited on p. 33, n. 11].

177   The fact that *leo* can be either masculine or feminine causes some confusion in the following lines. It is not clear from this first instance whether *leo* is masculine or feminine, since *an* is an attested nominative, singular, feminine form of the adjective *an* when declined strong. *Se leo* in lines 181–82 treats the word unambiguously as masculine. However, beginning with *seo leo* at the end of line 182, the remaining references to the lion are feminine (see the Glossary for a full account).

236–50   This coda to the legend is Ælfric's, although Zettel surmises that lines 1–5 of the *passio* (p. 218) may have served as a prompt for lines 237–40 ('Ælfric's Hagiographic Sources' [cited on p. 46, n. 178], p. 258, n. 164). On the relationship of the coda to the theme of steadfastness that Ælfric develops throughout the legend, see my 'Legend of Chrysanthus and Daria' [cited on p. 44, n. 139].

248   It is not clear exactly to which passage of Scripture Ælfric is referring, but he may have in mind one similar to Matthew 24.1–31.

LATIN TEXTS AND TRANSLATIONS

EDITORIAL PROCEDURE

Abbreviations have been silently expanded, and capitalization and punctuation are modernized. Departures from the base texts are signalled in the editions by square brackets [ ]. The apparatus records differences between the texts with the exception of minor variations in spelling (*e.g.* between ę and e, ae and e, oe for e, y and i, t and tt, and conl and coll). No attempt has been made to register every erasure, addition or correction, but alterations that may help to determine a copy's relationship to another text or set of texts have been recorded.

Numbers in parentheses (#) correspond to numbered paragraphs in printed editions of the Latin texts. Paragraph numbers are also reproduced in the Old English texts to facilitate comparison between the Latin and vernacular versions. To that end, portions of the Latin texts that Ælfric treats in his Old English versions have been italicised.

A vertical bar (|) indicates manuscript foliation, which is given in the apparatus.

Asterisks (*) direct readers to the Commentary (pp. 250–59). For convenience, they are duplicated in the editions as well as the translations.

Julian and Basilissa

The text of *The Passio of the Holy Martyrs Julian and Basilissa* is based on that in London, British Library, Cotton Nero E. i, part i, folios 77va–85rb (N).[1] As was explained in the Introduction (p. 29), this text of *BHL* 4532 is not an exact match to Ælfric's source, and this manuscript of the 'Cotton-Corpus Legendary', which was copied in the third quarter of the eleventh century at Worcester, postdates the Old English *Julian and Basilissa*. Collated with N are two other copies of *BHL* 4532, one Continental and one English. Rouen, Bibliothèque Municipale, MS U 026, ff. 106^r–121^v (R) is a late eleventh- or early twelfth-century collection of saints' lives copied in France.[2] Dublin, Trinity College, MS 174, ff. 64^r–72^v (D) is a supplement to 'Cotton-Corpus' copied at Salisbury Cathedral around 1100.[3] D points to the sort of hybrid of *BHL* 4532 and 4529 that must have served as Ælfric's immediate source. Both R and D share many features with N. In one instance where N is defective (lines

266–67 [p. 130]), I have supplied a reading from the other 'Cotton-Corpus' copy in Salisbury, Cathedral Library, MS 221, ff. 37^r–47^r (s.xi^{ex}) (S), which seems to have been copied from the same exemplar as N. Paragraph numbers correspond to those in the edition of *BHL* 4529 printed in *AS*, Ian. I: 575–87.[4]

Cecilia and Valerian

The text of *The Passio of Saint Cecilia the Virgin* is based on that in Hereford, Cathedral Library, MS P.VII.6, ff. 73^v–80^r (H), a manuscript dated to the mid-twelfth century.[5] Like N above, it does not represent Ælfric's precise source, and it too postdates his Old English version of the legend. Collated with H is another 'Cotton-Corpus' copy found in Cambridge, Corpus Christi College, MS 9, pp. 323–36 (C), which was copied at Worcester around 1025–1050.[6] As mentioned in the Introduction (p. 30), H and C are significantly different texts, despite the fact that the Hereford collection is a later derivative of 'Cotton-Corpus'. Another set of readings recorded in the apparatus comes from Rome, Vatican City, Biblioteca Apostolica Vaticana, MS Latini 5771, ff. 147^v–57^r (V), a legendary of unidentified origin dated to the ninth or tenth century.[7] Paragraph numbers correspond to those in the eclectic edition of *BHL* 1495 by H. Delehaye, ed., *Étude sur le légendier romain: Les saints de novembre et de décembre* (Brussels, 1936), pp. 194–220.

Chrysanthus and Daria

The text of *The Passio of the Holy Martyrs Chrysanthus and Daria* is based on Paris, Bibliothèque Nationale, Latin MS 13764, ff. 118^v–37^r, a tenth-century manuscript of St Rémy, Reims (P).[8] Though it is a contemporary text, P does not represent Ælfric's exact source. Collated with P are the 'Cotton-Corpus' text from Cambridge, Corpus Christi College MS 9, pp. 379–89 (C) and a text from a thirteenth-century legendary of unidentified origin preserved in Brussels, Bibliothèque Royale, MS 206, ff. 121r–127r (B).[9] Paragraph numbers correspond to those in the edition of *BHL* 1787 printed in *AS*, Oct. XI: 469–84.

Notes

1 The contents of N are listed by Jackson and Lapidge, 'Contents of the Cotton-Corpus Legendary' in *Holy Men and Holy Women* [cited on p. 33, n. 8], ed. Szarmach, pp. 131–46, at 135–37.

2 The contents of R are listed by A. Poncelet, 'Catalogus Codicum Hagiographicorum Latinorum Rotomagi', *Analecta Bollandiana* 23 (1904), 129–275.

3 For a description of D and a list of its contents, see M. Colker, *Trinity College, Dublin. Descriptive Catalogue of the Medieval and Renaissance Latin Manuscripts*, 2 vols (Aldershot, 1991), 1: 320–30. Note, however, that the text of *Julian and Basilissa* is identified as *BHL* 4529 not *BHL* 4532.

4 The *AS* text, which is printed from a thirteenth-century legendary, occasionally provides some textual control for readings in *BHL* 4532, as does P. Salmon's edition of a text of *BHL* 4529 from the late seventh- or early eighth-century Luxeuil legendary (cited on p. 36, n. 38). G. Whatley notes that Aldhelm appears to have used a version of *BHL* 4529 closer to Salmon's than to the Bollandists' ('Acta Sanctorum' [cited on p. 34, n. 16], p. 280).

5 For a description and list of the contents of H, see Mynors and Thomson, *Catalogue of the Manuscripts of Hereford Cathedral Library* (cited on p. 46, n. 184).

6 C is described and its contents listed by Budny, *Insular, Anglo-Saxon, and Early Anglo-Norman Manuscript Art at Corpus Christi College, Cambridge* and James, *A Descriptive Catalogue* (both cited on p. 177, n. 177).

7 The contents of V are listed by A. Poncelet, *Catalogus Codicum Hagiographicorum Latinorum Bibliothecae Vaticanae* (Brussels, 1910), pp. 140–49.

8 The contents of P are listed in *Catalogus Codicum Latinorum Antiquiorum Saeculo XVI qui asservantur in Bibliotheca Nationali Parisiensi*, ed. Socii Bollandiani (Brussels, 1893), pp. 201–202.

9 The contents of B are listed in *Catalogus Codicum Hagiographicorum Bibliothecae Regiae Bruxellensis*, part 1, ed. Socii Bollandiani, 2 vols (Brussels, 1886), 1:108–22.

INCIPIT PASSIO SANCTORUM MARTYRUM IULIANI ET
BASILISSE .V. IDUS. IANUARIUS.

(2) *BEATVS IULIANUS nobili familia inlustris in seculo erat*; quem parentes unicum pignus uiscerum suorum dulcem susceperant sobolem. *Omni doctrina* et omni scientia *eum imbuerunt*: non dialeticam, non rethoricorum fugiebat ingenium. Omnium auctorum mundi sapientia eum imbuerant;

5 quasi bonus athleta Christi sic utebatur mundo quasi non uteretur. Legerat enim magistrum omnium Christianorum apostolum Paulum dicentem, 'Preteriit enim figura huius mundi', et ne cum ipso mundo inmundus periret, sic se De[o] carum exhibebat ut sapientiam mundi stultitiam reputaret. Optabat enim semper pretereundo sine sollicitudine esse cum Christo.* Erat

10 enim amator fidei et ecclesię sancte, adherens sanctorum ergastulis. Nullum intermittebat diem quo sanctos Dei non uidendo properaret. Quasi bonus negotiator thesaurum reponebat in corde; omnium electorum imitans actus, studens in singulorum uirtute, gratia sanctitatis florebat.*

(3) Hunc parentes cum uiderent | tanta animi intentione Christianis

15 adherere, conuocantes eum ad se dixerunt, 'Audi genitorum tuorum salubre consilium, quo [in uenerabili]* lege a magistro omnium Christianorum docemur qui dicit, "Uolo iuuenes nubere, filios procreare, patresfamilias esse, nullam dantes occasionem maligno".* Pro qua re non solum ut nobis consentias hortamur, sed tantum ut legi diuine obediens esse uidearis'.

20 Iulianus respondit, 'Non uoluntatis nec aetatis tempus est ut faciam quę hortamini'.

Parentes dixerunt, '*Annorum es decem et octo. Quomodo excusare te poteris ne coniugio sociæris?* Nolumus ut de tempore causeris; uolumus enim te unius mulieris esse uirum, et concessa procreatione letari possis cum pater

25 fueris'.

Title] *Text begins on folio 77ᵛᵃ in small capitals.*
R reads in small capitals: INCIPIT PASSIO
SANCTORUM MARTYRUM IVLIANI ET
BASLILISSĘ. MENSE IANVARII; *D reads
in large capitals* PASSIO SANCTORUM
IVLIANI ET BASILISSE VIRGINIS.

1 BEATVS IULIANUS] *large capitals spanning column with a B four lines tall; in R,*
Beatus *begins with a* B *four lines tall and
remainder of text is normal size; in D,*
BEATUS. . . ERAT *is in small capitals with
a* B *four lines tall.* parentes] D *second* e
corrected from i
2 susceperant] RD susceperunt
3 non dialeticam] RD non enim dialecticorum
4 Omnium] R omnium si quidem. auctorum] D

auctores, es *corrected from an incomplete
abbreviation for* orum. sapientia eum
imbuerant] RD sapientiam habuerat
5 quasi] RD sed ille quasi
7 Preteriit] R Præterit; D Preterit
8 De(o)] N deum; RD deo
11 properaret] RD uisitaret
12 actus] RD actus sanctorum
13 studens] R studens in bonis
14 Fol. 77ᵛᵇ
16 (in uenerabili)] NRD innumerabili. lege] D
legem
19 legi] NRD legis.
22 decem] D .x. excusare te] D *order reversed*
23 sociæris] R sociaris; D socieris
24 et] RD ut

HERE BEGINS THE PASSIO OF THE HOLY MARTYRS JULIAN AND BASILISSA. 9 JANUARY.

(2) Blessed Julian was, in the world's eyes, distinguished on account of his noble family; his parents had raised their dear offspring, the sole token of their flesh. They had instructed him in all doctrine and all knowledge [cf. Romans 15:4]: he avoided neither dialectics nor rhetoricians' ingenuity. They had introduced him to the wisdom of all the world's authors; thus, like a fit athlete of Christ he trained in this world even as he was not trained by it [cf. 1 Corinthians. 7.31a]. He had read the apostle Paul, teacher of all Christians, who said, 'The form of this world passes away'[1 Cor. 7.31b], and so that he would not perish impure with this world, he showed himself dear to God in order that he might regard as foolishness the wisdom of the world [cf. 1 Cor. 3.19].* He preferred to go along always free of anxiety and so to be with Christ [cf. Philippians 1.23]. He was a lover of the faith and holy Church, keeping close to the prison-houses of the saints. He let not a day go by without being quick to gaze upon the holy ones of God [cf. Matthew 25.36]. Like a good banker he stored up treasure in his heart; imitatiing the deeds of all the Elect and striving after the virtue of each individual, he prospered in the grace of holiness.*

(3) When his parents noticed that he associated with the Christians so purposefully, they summoned him and said, 'Heed the helpful advice of your parents, which we are taught in the venerable law* by the teacher of all Christians who says, "I want young men to marry, to produce sons, to be heads of families, giving no opportunity to the devil" [cf. 1 Timothy 5.14].* For this reason we urge you not only to follow our advice but, more than that, to be seen as obeying divine law'.

Julian answered, 'I neither desire nor am I of age to do what you urge'.

His parents said, 'You are eighteen years old. How will you explain that you are not married? We do not want you to plead time as an excuse; we want you to be the husband of one woman, and having decided to have children, you can rejoice once you have become a father'.

Agebant enim parentes quomodo aut qualiter eorum semen resus-
citaretur. Cumque parentum et amicorum molestias non sufferret, ait, 'Nec
promittendi mihi facultas est nec denegandi potestas. *Hoc quod hortamini
potestati Dei mei committo. Pro qua re septem diebus inducias peto, et quod*
30   *ipse dignatus fuerit aspirare hoc a me responsum accipietis'.* Hoc audientes
parentes erant nimio tedio afflicti et cogitationibus tabescebant quousque
dies statutus ueniret quo responsum filii reciperent.

(4) *Puer uero spatium dierum exigit et die noctuque in orationibus peruig-
ilans*; postulabat a Domino ne uirginitatem promissam qualibet occasione
35   uiolaret. *Octaua enim die noctu* corpus maceratum ieiuniis *soporans apparuit
illi Dominus.** Consolatur fidelem seruum, probatam sibi mentem corrob-
orat, et iuxta precepta ut faciat iubet et ita eum adloquitur, 'Surge, ne timeas
suasiones uerborum nec uoluntatem parentum perhorrescas. *Accipies enim
uirginem quę non polluendo te a me separet* sed per te uirgo perseueret, *et te*
40   *et ipsam in cęlis uirgines recipiam. Multorum enim mihi per uos castitas dedi-
cabitur. Adero tibi ut omnes uoluptates carnis et hostis libidines conterantur,
et ipsam quę tibi fuerit iuncta conuertam* | in meum amorem, tuamque
sequipedam faciam. *Ibique me in cubiculum preparatum uidebitis'.* Et
Dominus tetigit eum et dixit, 'Uiriliter age et confortetur cor tuum'. His
45   uirtutibus corroboratus Iulianus exsurgens gratias Deo referebat.*

(5) Et completa oratione egreditur letus de cubiculo et ait parentibus,
'*Ecce, sicut desiderastis — quia ex diuino precepto coniugium mihi non esse
peccatum sed gratie — faciam que hortamini'.* Inquiritur quę illi similis esset,
et preparante misericordia Domini *inuenitur puella* et facultate locuples et
50   *nobilis genere Basilissa*, que unica parentibus esse dinoscitur. *Ordinantur
nuptię.* Iulianus uero ita diem nuptiarum expectabat; quasi bonus athleta
deuicta libidine regi cęlorum placere studebat.

Uenit dies statutus. Sonant platęę organorum fremitus; diuerse uoces
musicorum resultant: multitudo uirginum aureis ornamentis crispantes
55   crines, ad quarum suauissimas uoces, si homo ferreus esset, solueretur delec-
tamento luxurie. Iulianus autem occulta cordis nulli manifestabat nisi
Domino a quo spem promisse uictorię tenebat. (6) *Suscepit sponsam letus et
in corde suo psallebat Domino dicens, 'Ure renes meos et cor meum*; ne in
me antiquissimus serpens libidinis suscitat bellum'.*

---

29 septem] D .vii.
31 nimio] D enim nimio
35 noctu] R u *corrected from* e
36 Consolatur] RD consolaturque. probatam] D
     probatamque
39 *first* te] RD se. separet] D separabit, *dotted* et
     and abit *above line.* perseueret] R
     perseuerat, a *above final* e; D perseuerabit,
     bi *above line*

40 cęlis] R cælum; D cęlum
41 libidines] e *corrected from* i. conterantur] D
     conuertantur
42 Fol. 78ᵐ
44 Dominus tetigit] D *order reversed.* age] D
     agite
48 gratie] D gratante, *tail of* ę *dotted and* atant
     above line. illis similis] D *order reversed*

His parents debated how and by what means their lineage might be regenerated. And when he could not bear the intrusions of his parents and friends, he said, 'I do not have the warrant to promise or the authority to deny. I am turning your request over to the authority of my God. For this reason, I ask for a delay of seven days and that you accept from me the reply that he may deign to favour'. Hearing this, his parents were greatly oppressed with sorrow and were consumed in thought until the appointed day came on which they were to receive their son's answer.

(4) The young man spent several days remaining awake in prayer day and night; he asked God not to dishonour for any reason the virginity he had vowed. On the eighth day at night, when his body was wasted by fasts, the Lord appeared to him when he was asleep.* He comforts his faithful servant, strengthens his tested will and commands that he should act according to his instructions and says to him as follows, 'Arise, do not fear verbal persuasion nor dread your parents' will. Take a virgin who will not separate you from me by defiling you but who will remain a virgin on your account, and I will receive you and her among the virgins of heaven. Many will consecrate their chastity to me through you both. I will help you so that all desires of the flesh and lusts of the enemy are crushed, and I will turn her, to whom you have been united, towards my love, and I will make her your handmaiden. And you will see me there in the bedroom that has been made ready'. And the Lord touched him and said, 'Act like a man and let your heart be comforted'. Strengthened by these miracles, Julian rose to his feet and gave thanks to God.*

(5) And when he had finished his prayer, he joyfully came out of his chamber and said to his parents, 'Look, just as you wanted — because by divine instruction marriage will not be for me sin but grace — I will do what you ask'. A woman his equal was sought out, and, the mercy of the Lord being already worked out, Basilissa was found, a young woman of extraordinary ability and noble birth who was known to be her parents' only child. The nuptials were arranged. Julian truly looked forward his wedding day; like a good athlete, he defeated his passions and focussed on pleasing the king of heaven.

The appointed day arrives. Musical instruments resound in the streets; various vocalists break out in song: a crowd of virgins, their hair plaited with golden ornaments, at whose extremely sweet voices a man, if he were made of iron, would dissolve in the enjoyment of pleasure. Julian, however, revealed the secrets of his heart to no one except the Lord, from whom he held the hope of promised victory. (6) Julian joyfully received his bride and sang in his heart to the Lord saying, 'Scorch my innermost parts and my heart [Psalm 25.2b]*; let not the most ancient serpent stir up in me a war of desire'.

---

50 Basilissa] D nomine Basilissa. Ordinantur]
   RD Ordinanturque
53 fremitus] RD fremitu

55 si] RD et si
58 meum] RD meum domine
59 suscitat] D suscitet

60   *Adpropiat hora qua thorum coniugii preparetur, traditaque sibi uirgine certus de Deo cubiculum ingreditur.* In quo oratione facta, *talis odor liliorum et rosarum apparuit ut uideretur* uirgini *locus in quo solent lilia et rosę* uernantes tempore *suo suauitatem propinare.*

    Facto silentio noctis, dixit uirgo ad iuuenem, 'Miram rem sentio; quod et
65 tu sentis, ne mihi neges'.

    Cui Iulianus respondit, 'Que sentis fideliter enarra'.

    Dixit uirgo, 'Dum tempus sit hiemis, et omnem rosarum et liliorum naturam terra nondum parturiat. Ita in hoc cubiculo odor mihi omnium famulatur ut his suauissimis odoribus satiata horream | et nunc penitus desiderem
70 *Redemptoris coniunctionem'.**

    Cui Iulianus respondit, 'Odor suauissimus qui tibi apparuit nec initium habet nec finem. Qui temporibus dat tempora, qui singulis temporibus dat gratiam, *ipse est Dominus Christus, qui est amator castitatis*, qui integritatem corporis custodientibus uitam reddit aeternam. *Si huius monita mecum uelis*
75 *suscipere ut eum amemus et uirginitatem concessam inuicem custodiamus*, efficiemur in hoc seculo uasa eius munda in quo habitet, *et cum ipso regnabimus in futuro nec ab inuicem separabimur'.*

    Basilissa respondit, 'Quid melius nisi uirginitatem custodiendo uitam ęternam adipisci? Quod credendo ita esse ut protestaris, opto tibi consentiens
80 *esse ut possideam ęternum sponsum Dominum Ihesum Christum'.*

    Haec ea dicente, *procidit in orationem Iulianus et clamabat, 'Confirma hoc Deus quod operaris in nobis!' Hęc uidens uirgo similiter fecit.*

    (7) *Et subito fundamenta cubiculi commota sunt et lux emicuit* ita ut luminaria quę preerant illius luminis magnitudine uelarentur. Fit in cubiculo
85 spectaculum magnum spiritale: *ex una parte sedebat rex ęternus, Dominus Christus, cum multitudine candidatorum, et ex alia parte innumerabilis multitudo uirginum quarum principatum uirgo gloriosa Maria tenebat. A parte regis clamabatur, 'Uicisti, Iuliane, uicisti!' A parte reginę clamabant, 'Beata es Basilissa! Quę sic consensisti salutaribus monitis et fallacis blandimenta mundi*
90 *respuens ad eternam gloriam preparasti'.* Iterum a parte regis clamabant, 'Milites mei qui uicerunt antiqui serpentis libidinem de pauimento leuentur, et intento corde in thoro quod eis preparatum est, *librum uite aeternę superpositum legant'.* Ea uoce ex utraque parte sedentes responderunt, 'Amen'.

---

60 Adpropiat] RD adpropriante; D
    Appropinquante. preparetur] R prepararetur,
    ra *above line*
61 Deo] D domino
62 locus] RD locus esse
64 Facto] RD Facto autem. et] RD et si
69 Fol. 78rb.
70 Redemptoris] R redemp *written over erasure*
72 tempora. . . dat] RD *omit*
73 Christus] D ihesus christus. integritatem] D
    integritate

75 inuicem] RD inuiolatam
76 efficiemur] D efficiaemur, *second* e *above*
    line
78 custodiendo] D custodientibus
79 ęternam] D aeternum
80 ęternum] R æternam
81 dicente] RD dicente uirgine
83 cubiculi] D cubili
86 Christus] R ihesus christus; D christus ihesus
88 parte] RD parte autem
89 fallacis] D fallacia

The time approached for which the marriage bed had been prepared, and when the girl had been given to him in marriage, Julian, confident in God, enters the chamber. In the bedroom where he had prayed, there arose such a fragrance of lilies and roses that it seemed to the girl a place in which lilies and roses flourishing in season were wont to give off their sweetness.

When it was the dead of night, the girl said to the young man, 'I smell something amazing; if you smell it too, do not hesitate to tell me'.

Julian answered her, 'Explain exactly what you smell'.

The girl said, 'It is now wintertime, and the earth does not yet bring forth various kinds of roses and lilies. Nevertheless, in this chamber the scent of all such flowers attends me so that, filled with these most delightful fragrances, I shudder with fear and now wholly long for union with the Redeemer'.*

Julian replied to her, 'The utterly delightful fragrance that you smell has neither beginning nor end. The one who sets the times for the seasons and gives each its own charm, he is Christ the Lord, who is a lover of chastity, who grants eternal life to those preserving bodily purity. If you are willing to accept his instruction with me so that we may love him and may preserve the virginity we pledge to each other, then in this world we will be made into his clean vessels in which he dwells, and in the future we will reign with him and will never be separated from each other'.

Basilissa replied, 'What can be better than to acquire eternal life by preserving virginity? By trusting what you declare to be the case, I wish to consent to you so that I may have the Lord Jesus Christ as eternal bridegroom'.

And when she said these things, Julian fell down in prayer and cried aloud, 'God, confirm what you have worked in us!' When she saw this, the virgin did likewise.

(7) And suddenly the foundations of the room shook and a light burst forth such that the lamps already burning were enveloped by the intensity of that light. There in the bedroom a great spiritual spectacle occurred: on one side sat the eternal king, Christ the Lord, with a multitude of men arrayed in white, and on the other side was an innumerable multitude of virgins, among whom the glorious virgin Mary held pride of place. On the king's side came the shout, 'You have won, Julian, you have won!' And on the queen's side they proclaimed, 'Blessed are you Basilissa! You have consented to beneficial advice and, rejecting the deceitful charms of the world, have prepared for eternal glory'. Once more on the king's side they proclaimed, 'Let my soldiers who have overcome the desire of the ancient serpent be raised up off the floor, and with an earnest heart in the bed provided for them, let them read the book of eternal life laid upon (the bed)'. To this proclamation those sitting on both sides responded, 'Amen'.

---

90 eternam] R æternum. preparasti] RD te preparasti
92 quod] D qui. preparatum est] R preparatus (tus *above* tum) esse (*above line*) dinoscitur;
D preparatum dinoscitur
93 legant] R legant *in a different hand, which continues to* ad illud quod *in line 104, at which point the main hand resumes*

Et uenerunt duo in albis induti, habentes circa corpora zonas et singulas
95 coronas | *in manibus, eleuauerunt eos dicentes,* 'Surgite quia uicistis et in
numero angelorum computati estis. Aspicite quod uidetis in thoro uestro;
legite et cognoscite quia fidelis est Dominus in uerbis suis et sanctus in
omnibus operibus suis'. Et tenentes ei[u]s manus adplicuerunt eos, et super-
positus erat liber septies splendidior argento, litteris aureis scriptus. Et in
100 circuitu thori .iiii.ᵒʳ seniores, habentes in manibus suis fialas aureas plenas
aromatibus diuersis odorem reddentes. Et respondens unus ex his dixit,
'Ecce, in his quattuor fialis continetur perfectio uestra, ex his enim in
conspectu Dei suauitatis odor ascendit. Pro qua re beati estis qui seculi bland-
imenta respuistis, properantes ad illud quod oculus non uidit, nec auris
105 audiuit, nec in cor hominis ascendit. Accede nunc, Iuliane, et lege quod una
Trinitas iubet'. *Et cepit legere, 'Qui pro amore [meo] mundum contemps[er]it
deputetur in eorum numerum qui cum mulieribus non sunt coinquinati.
Basilissa uero deputatur in numerum uirginum,* quibus uirgo mater Domini
principatum tenet'. Iterum dixit ad eos, 'In hoc libro scripti sunt ueraces et
110 sobrii, misericordes, humiles et mansueti, caritatem habentes non fictam,
aduersa tolerantes, in tribulatione patientes, qui amori Domini nihil
pretulerunt — non patrem, non matrem, non uxorem, non filios, non diuitias,
non cetera quę in hoc seculo inpedimenta sunt — qui nec ipsas animas suas
dubitauerunt tradere in mortem pro [animabus eorum].* In quo numero et
115 uos esse meruistis'. (8) Et statim uisio ab oculis eorum ablata est.

Tunc exultantes in Domino beate uirgin[e]s reliquum spatium noctis
peruigiles in hymnis et canticis peragunt. Quid multa? *Ceperunt spiritu esse
coniuncti non carne fructificantes*, et ita mysterium diuine gratiae in se
conlatum occultabant; a Domino Christo et sanctis angelis sciretur quod
120 agebant. |

(9) Ita Dominus procurauit ut *in paucum tempus utrorumque genitores de
hac uita migrarent, relinquen[te]s idoneos superstites* per quos cęlorum regna
non fraudarentur*; *fuerant enim parentes et ipsi Christiani.* Tunc beat[i]
uirgines spatium temporis lete suscipiunt licentię suę possessuri uictorię
125 palmam, quo possent [per] patrimonium terrenum migrare in superna cęlorum.

---

94 in] RD *omit.* circa] D *omits*
95 Fol. 78ᵛᵃ
97 legite] RD et legite. in] R in *above line.*
  uerbis] RD muneribus
98 ei(u)s manus] eis manus; RD eos in manibus.
  adplicuerunt] D amplicuerunt
99 septies] D species
100 circuitu thori] RD conspectu throni. .iiii.ᵒʳ]
  RD quattuor. plenas] D *omits*
101 diuersis odorem] D diuersos odores.

reddentes] R reddentibus, tibus *above line*
  between t *and* e *of* reddentes. his] RD eis
102 *second* his] D is
106 amore (meo)] amore; RD amore meo.
  contemps(er)it] contempsit; RD
  contempserit
107 numerum] RD numero
114 (animabus eorum)] anime eius; RD
  animabus eorum. quo] R quo *above line*
116 uirgin(e)s] uirginis; RD uirgines

And there came two arrayed in white with sashes around their bodies and each carrying a crown, and they raised them up saying, 'Stand up because you have won and have been reckoned among the company of angels. Reflect upon what you see in your bed; read and learn that the Lord is faithful in his words and holy in all of his deeds'. And they took their hands and led them near (the bed), and upon it was laid a book seven times brighter than silver and written in gold lettering. And standing around the bed were four elders holding in their hands golden vials full of different spices that gave off a pleasant fragrance. And one among them responded and said, 'Look, your moral perfection is contained in these four vials, from which a pleasant fragrance ascends into the presence of God. For this reason, you who have rejected the charms of the world are blessed, hastening toward what no eye has seen, no ear has heard, nor has arisen in the heart of man [cf. 1 Corinthians 2.9]. Now draw near, Julian, and read what the one Trinity commands'. And he began to read, 'Let him who has despised the world for my love be reckoned among the company who have not been defiled with women [cf. Revelation 14.4]. Basilissa is reckoned in the company of virgins among whom the virgin mother of the Lord holds pride of place'. He spoke to them once more, 'This book records the honest and the sober, the merciful, the humble and the mild, those whose love is not false, those who endure adversity and bear tribulation, those who have put nothing before their love of the Lord — not father, not mother, not wife, not children, not riches, nor the other things which are impediments in this world — and those who have not hesitated to give their very lives up for the sake of their souls.* You also deserve to be among their number'. (8) And immediately the vision faded from their eyes.

Then, exulting in the Lord, the blessed virgins spent the rest of night awake singing hymns and sacred songs. What more need be said? Having been joined in the spirit, not in the flesh, they began to be fruitful*, and they kept secret the mystery of divine grace that had been conferred upon them; what they were doing would be known to the Lord Christ and the holy angels.

(9) So the Lord ordained it that after a short while both sets of parents departed from this life and left behind capable survivors on account of whom the realms of heaven would not be cheated*; the parents themselves had been Christians too. Then the blessed virgins joyfully received a period of time with the freedom to take possession of the palm of victory, at which point they would depart into the heights of heaven on account of an earthly inheritance.

---

119 a] RD ut a. Christo] RD ihesu (R *above line*) christo

120 Fol. 78vb

121 in] RD intra (tra *above line* in R)

122 relinquen(te)s] relinquens; R ad relin-quentes, ad *very faint, perhaps erased*; D

reliquentes. regna] RD regno

123 beat(i)] beatȩ; R beati

124 lete] D lȩtitiȩ

125 (per) patrimonium] *omits* per; D per patrimonium

(10) Fit consensus quo non solum de sua salute solliciti, sed multorum animarum curam suscipiant. *Diuiduntur domicilia*, et undique uox illa suauis Domini per os eorum omnes inuitabat dicens, 'Uenite ad me omnes qui laboratis et onerati estis, et ego uos reficiam'. *Instituunt sancta monasteria*, in quę
130   m[e]ssis anima[rum] sęculi penis et tribulorum suffocatione rapiebant.* Relinquebant uxores, filii parentes, sponsi sponsas; diuitias contemnentes uiam angustam arripiebant: nec quisquam eorum manu in aratro posita respiciebat retro. *Erat autem Iulianus circiter decem milia monachorum pater.* Et sicut scriptum est, 'Generatio uadit et generatio uenit'. Quanti migrabant
135   ad cęlum, tanti conuertebantur ad Dominum. *Similiter et beata Basilissa* agmina uirginum et mulierum de squaloribus liberabat; castissimas animas premittebat ad cęlum. Erantque cum sancto Iuliano uirorum sanctorum commercia, et per sanctam Basilissam fulgebat in uirginibus, in mulieribus uictorie palma. Et qualiter de hoc seculo ad celestia regna migrauerunt
140   sequens declarat lectio.

(11) *Temporibus Diocliciani* et Maximiani *furor persecutionis inuasit* Syriam et *Egypti uicinia*, qua opinione conperta sancti uirgines [inuicem] se adloquuntur et talem *precem fundunt in conspectu Domini*: 'Domine Deus, qui es occultorum cognitor et mentium testis, scrutator cordis et renum,
145   deprecamur ut letum super nos inlumines uultum, et pium et exaudibilem prestes auditum. Non dormis neque dormitas, qui custodis nostre castitatis imaginem, in quo tu, ipse Christe, letaris. | Ne patiaris gregis tui integritatem uitiari, nec habeat potestatem insatiabilis, gregi sancto semper infestus. In nullo habeat licentiam ad dissipandum morum uigores et signum fidei quod
150   in seruos et ancillas tuas sequipedas contulisti. Cura sit tibi, Christe, de nobis et de illis, quia plus ualet dextera tua ad erigendum, quam fortitudo persecutoris ad deiciendum. Considera, et scrutare singulorum corda, et secundum prescientię tuę donum omnes perduc ad illam regionem uiuorum ubi nulla est sollicitudo moriendi sed regnat beatitudo uiuendi. Et in die illa qua
155   uenturus es magnus et manifestus presta, Domine, ut omnes famulos et famulas tuas quos per nos tibi militare fecisti integros utrosque in conspectu tuo constitu[as] ut recte exultantes dicamus, "Ecce nos et pueri quos dedisti nobis; nemo perit ex eis"'.

---

126 solliciti] D diuiduntur. sed] R Diuiduntur
    Sed, Diuiduntur *underscored with dashes for*
    deletion
129 uos reficiam] D *order reversed*
130 m(e)ssis anima(rum)] NRD missis
    animabus
131 Relinquebant] RD uiri relinquębant (R n
    above line and erasure of two letters after t).
    diuitias] D diuites diuitias

133 decem] D .x. milia] RD milium
134 uenit] RD aduenit (R ad *in right margin*).
    migrabant] D migrauerunt, erunt *above* it
    marked for deletion
138 in mulieribus] R et in (*above line*)
    mulieribus
141 Temporibus] R •K• *in left margin*
142 sancti] R sanctę. inuicem] N in inuicem;
    RD inuicem

(10) A unanimity develops in which not only are they busied about their own salvation, but they assume the care of many souls. Their dwellings are separated, and from each side that sweet voice of the Lord through their mouths summoned all saying, 'Come to me all you who labour and are burdened, and I will restore you' [Matthew 11.28]. The couple establish holy monasteries to which they quickly brought in crops of souls from the pains and choking thistles of the world.* Those who came left wives, sons left parents, and bridegrooms left brides; despising riches they laid hold of the narrow way [cf. Matt. 7.13–14]: not one of them who had put a hand to the plough looked back [cf. Luke 9.62]. Julian, moreover, was father of some ten thousand monks. And as it is written, 'A generation goes and a generation comes' [cf. Ecclesiastes 1.4]. As many as departed to heaven, that many more were being converted to the Lord. And likewise, blessed Basilissa freed an army of maidens and wives from filth; she sent on to heaven exceedingly pure souls. And they had the fellowship of holy men, among them Saint Julian, and on account of Saint Basilissa, the palm of victory gleamed among maidens and wives. And the following passage makes clear how they departed from this world to the heavenly realm.

(11) During the days of Diocletian and Maximian, the madness of persecution spread through Syria and the nearby regions of Egypt, in which, when the holy virgins had confirmed the report, they comfort each other and pour out a prayer so pious as this in the presence of the Lord: 'Lord God, you who are knowledgeable about hidden things and a witness to people's minds, an examiner of the heart and the inmost depths, we pray that you shine your bountiful countenance over us and that you grant us a benevolent and attentive hearing. You neither sleep nor tire, you who preserve the purity of our virginity in which you, very Christ, delight. Do not suffer the purity of your flock to be spoiled, nor permit the insatiable one, ever hostile to the holy flock, to hold sway. In no way give him leave to dilute the strength of our virtues and the sign of our faith that you have conferred upon your servants and handmaidens who follow you. Our care and theirs belongs to you, O Christ, because your right hand is more powerful to raise us up than the strength of the persecutor is to cast us down. Examine us, searching the hearts of us all, and according to the gift of your divine foreknowledge, lead us all to that land of the living where there is no concern for dying but where the blessedness of living holds sway. And on that day, when you will appear manifestly and greatly, see to it, O Lord, that you set each of the groups, all your male and female servants whom you have made to be your soldiers on our account, unharmed in your presence, so that exulting, we may rightly say, "Look at us and the children you have given us; not one among them has perished"'.

---

145 uultum] R uultum serenum (serenum *above line*)
147 quo] RD qua. Fol. 79ra
148 insatiabilis] RD insatiabilis lupus

154 qua] RD in qua
157 constitu(as)] constitue; R constituæ; D constituę. pueri] R puer
158 perit] R periit

(12) Et cum finem orationis co[m]plessent, redierunt ad propria domi-
160 cilia. Ea die quies aduenit, et beatam Basilissam ita per uisum adloquitur
Dominus, 'Basilissa, nominis tui digna, quę orasti hoc implere me delectat ut
omnia uasa que commendaui tibi cum adhuc es in hac uita, tu ea permittas
ad cęlum.* Habebis dimidium temporis spatium, quo possis ex omni loco
triticum colligere, et recondita messe laboris tui, tu ipsa sequaris claues accep-
165 tura horrei pleni pinguedinem animarum, ex quo cotidie odor suauitatis
ascendit ad cęlum in conspectu sanctorum angelorum. Iulianus uero ut bonus
athleta pugnabit et uincet; nec aliquando uinci poterit in quo castitas regnat.
Erit enim mihi multitudo adinquirendarum animarum. Multa enim eum
oportet pati pro nomine meo, multasque uirtutes et signa ostendam in
170 conspectu inimicorum eius. Priusquam inuocet me dicam, "Ecce adsum"'.

(13) Hęc audiens Basilissa euigilans letabatur in Domino, et conuocans
multitudinem uirginum dixit ad eos, 'Uos omnes, gaudium et corona capitis
mei, sancte uirgines, Domino nostro uitam reddamus, et sacrificium laudis in
corde contrito, hostiam iubilationis, immolemus qui dignatus est | reuelare
175 misterii uiam. Et tempus acceptum terminauit quo castas animas illi
consignemus, dilatione concessa ut unaquęque considerans cellaria cordis
sui, id est habundantiam bonorum operum, eructuantia ex hoc in illud. Hoc
est, si de hoc seculo peregrinantes, recte de hac uita migremus ad ęternam,
ut nullum in nobis habeant uel cognoscant ille potestates peccatum quę
180 animas pergentes ad celum retinent, et scrutantes et nihil inuenientes suum
reuereantur et timeant uidentes nobiscum sanctum adiutorium pergentem,
spiritum castitatis congaudentem.

'Considerate et scrutamini archana pectoris uestri ut dum tempus
habemus, liceat animam ab omni uitio culparum defecatam, splendidi
185 liquoris [actu] conprobatam retribuere Creatori.* Hanc enim optinuimus a
Domino petitionem ut omnes uos ante persecutionem inimici inmaculatas
premittam ad regna cęlorum, ubi est sponsus castitatis Dominus Ihesus
Christus. Pro qua re hortor uos, sancte sorores: ne quid malitię fermentum
cordis remaneat, sed omnes donate uobis inuicem si qua habet aduersus
190 aliam aliquid ut perfectam coronam animę et corporis uestri recipiatis, meque
matrem integro numero salutis uestrę uictricem reddatis, hoc scientes: quia
nihil ualet uirginitas carnis, ubi habitat iracundia cordis'.

---

159 co(m)plessent] coplessent; RD complessent
160 quies] RD uox
161 hoc] RD hęc. que] *above* quas
162 commendaui] RD mundaui. tibi] RD *omit*
164 tu] D *omits*
165 pinguedinem] D pinguedine
166 ut] D in
168 adinquirendarum] RD inadquirendarum
169 pati] D *omits*. meo] D *omits*
169–70 in conspectu] D *above line*

170 eius] R eius et dicam (et dicam *above line*).
    dicam] R *omits*. Priusquam...dicam] D et
    dicam priusquam inuocet me
172 eos] RD eas (R a *above dotted* o). gaudium]
    RD gaudium meum
174 hostiam] R hosstiam, stiam *above letters*
    that have been scratched out. Fol. 79rb
175 uiam] D uiuam. qu(o)] NRD qui. castas]
    RD castitatis
176 ut] D et

(12) And when they finished their prayer, they returned to their own dwellings. Blessed Basilissa is overcome by sleep during the day, and the Lord addresses her in a vision: 'Basilissa, worthy of your name ('Queen'), it delights me to fulfil what you have requested so that you may send forth to heaven all the vessels I have entrusted to you while you are alive.* You will have half the time (Julian does) to gather wheat from every place, and when the fruit of your labour has been laid up, you yourself will follow me to accept the keys of a storehouse full of an abundance of souls, from which a pleasant fragrance ascends daily to heaven into the presence of the holy angels. But Julian will compete and win, like a worthy athlete; not once will it be possible to defeat him in whom chastity reigns. A host of souls will be mine for examining. He must suffer many things for my name, and I will make known many miracles and signs in the presence of his enemies. Before he will call upon me, I will say, "Look, I am here"'.

(13) When she had heard these things, Basilissa awoke and rejoiced in the Lord, and calling together her multitude of virgins she said to them, 'All you holy virgins, my joy and crown, let us yield our lives to our Lord and with a repentant heart offer a sacrifice of praise, an offering of joyful singing, to him who deigned to reveal his secret plan. And he has fixed a welcome time at which we may hand over our chaste souls to him, and he has allowed a delay so that each one may examine the store-rooms of her heart, that is, the abundance of good works, the overflow of the heart into the store-room. In other words, if those of us who are pilgrims in this world hope to pass from this life to the eternal one, then let those powers who detain those souls making their way to heaven learn of no sin in us, and when they search and discover nothing of theirs, let them stand in awe and let them be afraid when they see holy help travelling with us and the spirit of chastity rejoicing with us.

'Reflect on and examine the secrets of your heart so that while we have the time, the soul, when it has been purified from every blemish of sin, may be permitted to return to the Creator once it has been tested by the work of the splendid liquid.* The Lord has granted our request that prior to the persecution of the enemy, I may despatch you all unstained to the kingdom of heaven where the bridegroom of chastity, the Lord Jesus Christ, is. For this reason, I admonish you, holy sisters: let no malice of spirit fester in your hearts, but forgive all among yourselves mutually if anyone holds anything against another so that you will receive a perfect crown for your soul and body and so that you may repay me, a victorious mother, with the full value of your salvation, knowing this: that virginity of the flesh counts for nothing where there is wrath in the heart'.

---

178 recte] RD regnum
179 potestates] D per potestates
180 animas] R ad animas; D ad animam.
    retinent] RD pertinent

182 congaudentem] D congaudentes
185 (actu)] NRD actum

(14) Haec prosequente Basilissa locus in quo erant commotus est, et
columna lucis in conspectu earum apparuit super se titulum aureum habens
195   scriptum, et uox de columna processit cum splendore et odore suauitatis, et
signum crucis emicuit dicens, 'Basilissa nominis auctrix quod scriptum uides
lege'. Tituli autem scriptura hęc erat, 'Hęc dicit primus et nouissimus:
"Omnes iste uirgines quibus tu ducatum prebes uasa munda et accepta sunt
oculis meis. Nec quicquam in eis reprobum | inueni quas tu olim cum igne
200   iuste probationis uelut aurum purissimum exhibuisti. Uenite ad premia uobis
parata"'. Et his lectis, uisio ab oculis eorum ablata est.

     Tunc omnes gratias referebant Domino, qui testimonio suę maiestatis
animas sanctas declarasset. Beata Basilissa exultans in Domino, dixit, 'Gratias
tibi [ago], Domine Ihesu Christe, qui pugnas carnales uicisti'. Et adiecit
205   dicens, 'Insulto tibi, diabole, quia perfecta querentes, nullis artibus, nullis
machinis, ualuisti retinere. Tu solus tua poena letare! Uides enim predam de
tuis dentibus ereptam ad cęlorum regna ascendere unde tu cecidisti. Gaudete
mecum [sanctę uirgines] regnant in nobis regna uirtutum. Contemptus mundi
regna cęlorum accepit. Renuntiatio parentum consortium sumsit angelorum.
210   Parua temporis tribulatio aeternam meruit letitiam et humilitas sicut cedrus
Libani et sicut cypressus in montibus Hermon. Deuicta libidine, castitas
fecunditas. Sola est de inimicis nostris audacia que parentum animas retinent.
Omnes ille potestates erubescent quia nihil suum cognoscent in nobis'.

     (15) Haec cum gaudio dicens, cepit uineam Domini rore iustitię matu-
215   ratam recondere. Ita diuina prouidentia adimpleuit ut intra tempus
promissum omnes migrarent ad Dominum. Beata uero Basilissa secura de
reposito thesauro hora sexta in oratione constituta soporata est et uidit multi-
tudinem uirginum — circiter mille — niueis cycladibus indute, regalibus zonis
cincte, crucem Domini in manibus gestantes. Ad Basilissam dixerunt, 'Hoc
220   responsum accepimus: Ecce, expectamus te ut tu nos offeras Christo'.
Euigilans Basilissa partus sui gloria letabatur.

     Haec referens sancto Iuliano, simul gaudebant in Domino. *Ita completum
est* ut constitutis illis in oratione beata *Basilissa migraret ad Dominum, quam
tradidit sanctus Iulianus sepulturę dignissime*, die noctuque memor eius | excu-
225   bias spiritales adimplendo.

---

193 erant] D erat
196 nominis] RD nominis tui
197 scriptura] a *above dotted* ę; RD scripturę.
   hęc] D hic
199 oculis] RD in oculis. nec] D ne. Fol. 79ᵛᵃ
199–200 tu olim cum igne iuste] RD tulerim a
   iustitiæ igne
201 parata] D perata. Et his lectis] R hæc; D Et
   hęc. eorum] RD earum (R a *above dotted* o).
   ablata] D sublata

202 maiestatis] R magestatis
204 tibi (ago)] tibi; RD tibi ago
206 retinere] R retinere *with* inretire (?) *above*.
   solus] D solis
208 mecum (sanctę uirgines)] mecum; D
   mecum sanctę uirgines (e *of* uirgines
   corrected from i). Contemptus] D contentus
209 consortium] D consortio
210 Parua] D parui
213 quia] a *added, by a different hand?*; R qui

(14) When Basilissa finished speaking, the place where they were gathered shook, and a column of light with a golden inscription above it appeared before them, and a voice came forth from the column with magnificence and a pleasant fragrance, and a sign of the cross appeared saying, 'Basilissa, paragon of your name, read what you see written'. Now that inscription read, 'The First and Last says this: "All these virgins to whom you gave guidance are pure vessels and are acceptable in my sight. I have discovered nothing false in all these whom you have already proved with the fire of just examination to be like the purest gold. Come to the reward prepared for you"'. After these words had been read, the vision faded from their sight.

Then they all gave thanks to the Lord who had declared their souls to be holy through the testimony of his majesty. Exulting in the Lord blessed Basilissa said, 'Thanks be to you, Lord Jesus Christ, who overcame the battles of the flesh'. And she added, 'I scoff at you, Devil, because you have not been able to detain those seeking eternal glories with any cunning plots or stratagems. Enjoy your punishment all by yourself! For you see the spoil snatched out of your teeth and ascending to the kingdom of heaven whence you fell. Rejoice with me, holy virgins, because the powers of the virtues reign in us. A contempt for the world has acquired the kingdom of heaven. A renunciation of parents has purchased the fellowship of angels. Brief tribulation for a time has earned eternal joy and humility, like the cedars of Lebanon and the cypresses on Mount Hermon. When desire has been defeated, chastity is fruitfulness. There remains only the boldness of our enemies who detain the souls of (your spiritual) parents. All these powers blush with shame because they recognize nothing of themselves in us'.

(15) When she had joyfully declared these things, she began to store away the Lord's vineyard that had been ripened with tears of righteousness. Thus divine providence fulfilled it so that within the promised time, all departed to the Lord. Because blessed Basilissa was untroubled about the treasure stored away, she fell asleep at the sixth hour when she finished her prayer and saw a host of virgins — around 1000 — arrayed in snow-white robes, girded with regal sashes and bearing the cross of the Lord in their hands. They said to Basilissa, 'We have received this charge: Look, we are waiting for you to present us to Christ'. When she woke up, Basilissa rejoiced in the glory of her children.

When she related this to Saint Julian, they rejoiced together in the Lord. So it came to pass that when they had determined those things through prayer, blessed Basilissa departed to the Lord and Saint Julian handed her over with a most fitting burial ceremony and remembered her day and night by carrying out spiritual vigils.

---

219 in manibus] D *omits*

221 Euigilans] RD Et euigilans. partus sui] R proparata sibi; D preparata sibi

224 Fol. 79vb

225 adimplendo] o *over dotted* um; R adimplens

(16) Sanctus uero Iulianus florebat in Domino; gratia Domini concessa ut nullus esset inferior qui non alterum precederet in uirtutibus. Nullius iracundiam ibi sol inuenit aut reliquid; ut adsolet aliquis cuiquam in uerbo superbus non accipiebat cibum, sed humilitati et fletui insistentes, quoadusque cari-

230 tatem renecterent. Letabatur [pater] in hoc studio filiorum; tunc se unusquisque dicebat incipere quando finiebat.

(17) *Hęc agebantur in ciuitate Antiochia, que est metropolis Aegypti. Adueniente autem Marciano preside in eandem ciuitatem, ita in furorem sacrilegus exarsit ut non uilla, non uicus remaneret ubi non idolum poneret, ut si*

235 *quis emere uel uendere uellet, primum idolis immolaret.* Cum urgeretur iussio presidis ut unusquisque imaginem Iouis erigeret, *cumque de fide sancti Iuliani audisset et multos secum de hac religione haberet socios qui pararent se ad mortem magis quam idolis immolare, tunc iratus preses conuocans assessorem suum iussit eum conueniri ut cum omnibus suis secundum decreta*

240 *principum idolis immolaret ne diuersas luerent pęnas.*

Assessor uero cum principe et corniculario pergunt ad Iulianum, ad quem multitudo sacerdotum et leuitarum uel omnes ministri aecclesię confugerant, rabiem persecutoris declinantes. Tunc nuntiatur sancto Iuliano adsessorem et principem cum primario ciuitatis aduenisse. Dixitque ad eos qui erant

245 congregati, 'Nunc fratres quia adpropiauerunt persequentes nos, qui querunt uelut aqua [absorbere] nos'. Armat[us] fronte uexillo et scuto fidei firmato pectore, iussit eos ingredi. Et qui[a] erat prioris ciuitatis filius, digne honorabat eum ordo ciuitatis.

(18) Dixit ei assessor, 'Puto non latere [te], Iuliane, principum statuta ut

250 una sit aput nos omnis deorum cultura. Nam preses, audiens natiuitatem tuam — nobili stirpe ort[a]m — hoc decreuit ut secundum moderationem legum, cum gratia conueniaris. Quam legem pre manibus habeo tibi recenlsændam. Ex quibus [ueritate] conperta, reddas te genitor[i] tuo ut proprio bono tuo fruaris et principum amicitiam consequaris'.

255 Iulianus respondit, 'Sapientiam tuam non credo fugere quia serpens non mouetur ex propria sede nisi ex ore incantantis uera cognouerit carmina. Nam sicut [non] proficit nec preualet mouere serpentem qui carmina nescit, ita nec decreta principum nec philosophia iudicis, qui in temporibus temporalis cognoscitur, ualere poterit Christicolas mentes ad demonum culturam

260 declinare'.

---

228 ibi] R ubi. superbus] RD superbus ullus
229 quoadusque] D quodusque
230 renecterent] D renecterent. Hoc studio laborabant ut oratione fructum deo sacrificium laudis offerent. Letabatur (pater)] Letabatur; D Lętabatur pater
231 finiebat] D finiebat. In hac sancta congregatione nunquam potuit diabolus aliquem inretire.
234 *second* non] D nec

235 Cum] R Tum, t *above dotted* C. urgeretur] D urgetur
238 immolare] RD immolarent
240 immolaret] D immolarent
244 Dixitque] R Dixit uero
245 Nunc] D Huc. quia] R *underscored for deletion;* D *omits*
246 (absorbere)] absorberet; RD absorbere. armat(us)] armati; RD armatus
247 qui(a)] N qui; RD quia

(16) Saint Julian truly flourished in the Lord; he was granted the Lord's grace that no one (in his community) would be inferior nor did anyone surpass another in spiritual virtues. The sun did not rise or set on the wrath of any one there; in the same way, it was customary that anyone who spoke disdainfully to another did not take a meal, but they entreated each other with humility and tears until they fully restored their love. The father rejoiced in such zeal in his sons; in those days each said that his ending was his beginning.

(17) These things took place in the city of Antioch, which is a chief city of Egypt. But when the governor Martianus arrived in the same city, the profaner burned with such fury that there was no villa or village without an idol, with the result that if anyone wished to buy or sell anything, he first had to sacrifice to idols. When the governor's order was enforced, everyone set up an image of Jupiter, and when he heard of Saint Julian's faith and that he had many of this religion in his company who were preparing to die rather than sacrifice to idols, the enraged governor sent for his aide and ordered Julian to be summoned so that he could sacrifice to the idols with all his followers according to the decrees of the emperors or else they would suffer various punishments.

So, an aide together with a ranking official and a tribune went to see Julian, to whom a multitude of priests and deacons as well as all the clerks of lower orders had fled for protection to avoid the persecutor's fury. Then it was reported to Saint Julian that the aide and ranking official together with the tribune had arrived. And he said to those gathered with him, 'Now, brothers, because those seeking us have approached, they would like to swallow us like water'. Armed with the sign of the cross on the forehead and with his chest strengthened with the shield of faith, Julian ordered them to go in (to the tribunal). And because (Julian) was the son of a rather important citizen, the group from the city honoured him worthily.

(18) The aide said to him, 'I suppose the emperors' decree that there is to be among us all one form of worship of the gods is not unknown to you, Julian. Now the governor, hearing about your origins — that you are born of noble stock — has decided that, according to the moderation of law, you should be approached with goodwill. I have at hand the law to be reviewed for you. When the law has made clear the truth, you may return to your father to enjoy your rightful benefit and to acquire the emperors' friendship'.

Julian responded, 'I do not believe it escapes your understanding that the serpent is not moved from his proper place unless he recognizes as genuine the songs from the singer's voice. Now just as one who does not know the songs is unable and incapable of stirring the serpent, so neither the emperors' decrees nor the philosophy of a judge, who is known to be temporary in his own time, can be strong enough to twist Christian minds to the worship of demons'.

---

249 latere (te)] latere; RD latere te
251 ort[a]m] ortum; RD ortam
253 Fol. 80ᵃ. recensændam] R recensendam,
  third e *over dotted* a. (ueritate)] ueritatem;

RD ueritate. genitor(i)] genitore; RD genitori
256 propria] i *above second* p *is redundant*
257 (non)] *omits*; RD non
259 proterit] RD potuit

Assessor dixit, 'Ergo contemnis principum iussa?'

Iulianus respondit, 'Audiunt principum iussa qui ipsis militant; nos autem qui regem habemus in caelo terrenorum principum iussa non audiemus'.

Assessor dixit, 'Et potes hoc gestis dicere?'

265 Iulianus respondit, 'Ipsis gestis prosequantur qui in hac uita spem habent. Nobis autem, quibus crucifixus est mundus, quid nobis cum [foro?'

Assessor dixit, 'Vt uideo desperasti de te: ne uiuas; uel] istius multitudinis quam tibi adgregasti, miserere'.

Iulianus respondit, 'Istius multitudinis uoluntas simul mecum pendet in
270 Dei arbitrio. Nam qualem me uides loquentem, tales sunt omnes isti tacentes: Unus Dominus quem confitemur, qui est filius Dei uiui'.

Assessor dixit, 'Haec quę prosequeris renuntio presidi'.

Iulianus respondit, 'Quę cognouisti occultare non debes. Nos uero parati sumus temporalem suscipere mortem ut in eternum uiuamus quam uitam
275 temporalem eterne uitę mancipemur'.

Assessor dixit, 'Audio etiam episcopum et omnem clerum adgregatum tecum. Numquid et ipsi discipuli tui sunt?'

Respondit, 'Non sunt discipuli sed parentes. Per illos enim ueram natiui-tatem suscepimus. Pro qua re dignum est ut filii cum patre pergant ad regna
280 cęlorum'.

(19) *Rediens ad presidem Marcianum, assessor quę gesta sunt intimauit. Tunc Marcianus consilio diaboli armatus talem dedit auctoritatem Iulianum solum suis obtutibus audientię reseruari, illos autem omnes iussit in eodem loco in quo erant igne | copioso cremari. Impletur ergo iussio presidis, et omnes*
285 *sancti ibidem consumpti sunt.* In quo loco diuina gratia concessit ut usque in hodiernum diem omnibus aduenientibus tempore psallendi tertiam, sextam, nonam, uespertinos, et matutinos*, ita audiant multitudines psallentes sicut in corpore manentes, ut *si quis his temporibus aeger aduenerit, quacumque fuerit aegritudine oppressus, sanus abscedat in nomine Domini nostri Ihesu*
290 *Christi.*

(20) Finitum martyrium sanctorum in nomine Domini, postea quam sancti martyres uelut aurum per ignem probati migrassent ad regna cęlorum, nuntiatur presidi Martiano impleta esse omnia quę preceperat, Iulianum autem custodia retineri. Tunc iussit in foro preparari sibi tribunal, et concurrit
295 undique omnis aetas omnisque sexus aduenit ut beatum Iulianum, in cuius amore pendebat, uideret cum diabolo dimicantem.

---

262 Audiunt] D Audiant
263 audiemus] D audiamus
266 cum [foro...uel] istius (line 267)] *reading supplied from* S. quid nobis cum foro?] RD quid iuuat dominum celęstem (D cęleste) derelinquere et demonia adorare?
267 de] D *omits*
268 adgregasti] D agregasti
271 Unus] D Unus est

273 cognouisti] D cognouistis
274 temporalem...uitam] D *omits*
277 tui] D *struck through*
278 Respondit] RD Iulianus respondit.
279 patre] D parentes
284 Fol. 80rb. copioso] R copiosa
285 ibidem] RD ibidem igne
287 nonam] D *omits*

The aide said, 'So do you despise the emperors' orders?'

Julian answered, 'Those who fight for the emperors heed their orders; we, however, who have a king in heaven will not heed the orders of earthly emperors'.

The aide said, 'And will you be able to express this with deeds (not just words)?'

Julian responded, 'Let those who put hope in this life attend to these deeds for themselves. But for those of us for whom the world has been crucified, what have we to do with the affairs of this world?' [cf. Galatians 6.14]

The aide said, 'I see that you have given up hope for yourself: you shall not live; but as for that multitude you have gathered to yourself, have compassion on them'.

Julian responded, 'As with me, the will of that multitude depends upon God's will. Now you will hear me say out loud what all these say silently: there is one Lord in whom we believe, who is the Son of the living God'.

The aide said, 'I will report to the governor the things you maintain'.

Julian replied, 'You must not conceal what you have learned. We are prepared to accept temporary death to live eternally rather than be delivered over to temporal life in lieu of the eternal one'.

The aide said, 'I also hear that a bishop and all sorts of clerics are gathered with you. Is it really possible that they are your disciples too?'

He answered, 'They are not disciples but parents. Through them I have obtained my true birth. For that reason, it is fitting that sons make their way to the kingdom of heaven with their father'.

(19) When he returned to the governor Martianus, the aide made known what had happened. Then Martianus, armed with the counsel of the devil, gave the command that Julian alone be kept back for a private audience, but he ordered all those to be burned alive in a raging fire on the spot where they were. The order of the governor was then carried out, and all of the saints were burned on the spot. Divine grace was granted in that place so that today all who come there at the time when they would sing the offices of terce, sext, nones, vespers and matins* hear hosts of voices singing psalms as if they were alive in the flesh, with the result that if anyone now who is ill goes there at those times, oppressed by any sickness whatsoever, he will leave cured in the name of our Lord Jesus Christ.

(20) When the martyrdom of the saints was completed in the name of the Lord, after which the holy martyrs like gold proved by fire departed to the kingdom of heaven, it was announced to the governor Martianus that all his orders had been carried out but that Julian had been confined to prison. He then ordered a judgment seat to be made ready for him in the city centre, and people of all ages and both sexes came hurriedly from all over and arrived to see the blessed Julian, on whose love each hung, contend with the devil.

289 Domini nostri] R domini postea quam
    sancti nostri
291 Finitum martyrium] R Finito martyrio; D
    finitio martirio

293–94 Iulianum autem custodia retineri] RD
    Audiens autem hæc iudex ilico iulianum in
    custodia precepit retineri

Tunc preses sub uoce terribili iussit eum intromitti. Quem cum uidisset prẹses dixit, 'Tu es, Iuliane, preceptorum principum rebellis et diuinorum numinum contumax? Tu es qui innocentium multitudinem magicis artibus
300   tibi congregas et omnium mentes inmutas?'

Ad hẹc Iulianus studebat silentium.

Ad quem iterum preses dixit, 'Ut uideo, reatu tuo obpressus, nihil ad ea que te interrogo respondes'.

Iulianus respondit, 'Ego rebellis nec sacrilegus umquam fui, sed legi
305   diuine in qua regula uitae continetur semper parui. Quod autem me studentem silentium miraris; tecum loqui confundor, quem uideo mendacio et fallacia sic inuolutum. Nam horum imperatorum lex quomodo poterit esse sacra qui sacrilegium operatur?'

Preses dixit, 'Doleo super te quod sic magicis artibus occupatus sis ut non
310   intellegas quantam uim habeant principum iussa. Per quẹ oboediens consequitur laudem et imperatorum meretur amicitias, contemptor autem sicut tu dinosceris, pen[ae] subiacet et tormenti et mortis heres I efficitur. *Nam audio te nobili familia ortum, ut adhuc natalibus tuis parcere uidear. Pro qua re hortor te, ut filium meum, ad laudem generis tui diis tura offerre letus propera'.*

315   (21) *Iulianus dixit, 'Malitia tua cecatus es.* Ideo non recte ordinem prosequeris ut non intellegas quẹ sit laus generis mei. *Tu mihi false blandiendo suades ut amicitiam principum merear adipisci.* Uos estis multorum deorum dearumque cultores, nos uero Trinitatis unice uere sumus cultores. Dii uestri aut lapidei sunt aut aeriei. Si eriei sunt, satis meliores sunt illis cucumẹ, quẹ
320   ad usus hominum ex ipso metallo fiunt. Si lapidei sunt, respuendi sunt quia ex ipsis lapidibus plateẹ sternuntur ad euadendum lutum. *Et cum sicut omnes quos colitis imagines uanẹ ex quolibet metallo aut conflati aut sculpti, dicitis eos sacrificiis cælestibus placari ut per hẹc sint propitii his qui eos colunt.* Nos autem, qui uiuum Deum colimus qui est in cẹlis dicitis nos magicis artibus
325   occupatos; pro qua re torqueri nos iubetis uerum Dominum confitentes, unde debes scire quod nescis: quia sicut non est societas luci et tenebre, iam non potest fides nostra subiugari imperio uestro uel demoniis uestris'.

Preses dixit, 'Mihi non uerbis iussum est agere tecum; sed audi quid iubeant inuictissimi principes ut ex eorum lege cognoscas quid te agere
330   oporteat'.

---

300 et] R ut
304 respondit] RD dixit. Ego] D Ergo
307 fallacia] D fallatio
308 qui] RD quẹ. operatur] *stroke above* a *suggests* operantur *but* operatur *is correct*
312 pen(ae)] pena; R poene, *second* e *corrected from* i; D pẹna. Fol. 80ᵛᵃ
313 ut] RD et ut. adhuc] D *omits*. Pro qua re] RD *omit*
316 laus] D lux. blandiendo] D blandimento

317 ut amicitiam] D ut diis quos colitis thura offeram ut amicitiam
319 sunt illis] D *order reversed*.
321 sicut] R sint
322 imagines uanẹ] D *order reversed*
324 uiuum] D unum
325 torqueri] D torquere. nos] D uos
326 scire quod] D *order reversed*. luci] R lucis, s *above line*. et] D ad. tenebre] RD tenebras. iam] R Ita; D ita

Then in a frightening voice the governor ordered him to be sent in. When the governor saw him, he said, 'Julian, are you a rebel against the emperors' orders and an opponent of the holy gods? You are the one who gathers around you an innocent group by the power of sorcery and warps everyone's mind?'

At this Julian remained deliberately silent.

And so the governor said to him once again, 'It would appear that, overwhelmed by the charge against you, you say nothing in reply to the things I ask you'.

Julian responded, 'I have never ever been a rebel or a sacrilegious person, but have always been obedient to the divine law in which the rule of life is contained. Yet you are amazed that I am deliberately silent; I am confounded about how to converse with you whom I perceive to be wrapped up in falsehood and deception. For how may the law of these emperors, which perpetrates sacrilege, be sacred?'

The governor said, 'I feel sorry for you because you have been so possessed by sorcery that you do not appreciate how much power the emperors' orders possess. Through them obedient people win praise and merit the emperors' friendship, but disobedient ones, as you are recognized to be, are subject to punishment and become the heirs of death and torment. I hear that you have come from a noble family, so, even now, I am at pains to show consideration for your lineage. For this reason, I urge you, as I would my own son, to think of your family's renown and be quick joyfully to offer incense to the gods'.

(21) Julian said, 'You have been blinded by your wickedness. And you have not taken an advantageous approach because you do not understand what is praiseworthy to my family. With false flattering you coax me to offer incense to the gods you worship so that I may deserve to obtain the emperors' goodwill. You are worshippers of many gods and goddesses, but we are worshippers of the one true Trinity. Your gods are made of stone and copper. If they are copper, then kettles are better suited than they, since kettles are made from the same metal for men's use. If they are stones, they are to be rejected because the same stones are laid in streets so that we can avoid the mud.

And when all those hollow images you worship have been cast or sculpted from any metal whatsoever, then you say they are placated by divine sacrifices so that their worshippers may win them over with offerings. By contrast, you say that we who worship the living God in heaven have been possessed by sorcery; for this reason you order those of us who acknowledge the true Lord to be tortured, whence you ought to know what you do not: namely, that just as there is no affinity between light and darkness, so our faith cannot be subjected to your emperor or your demons'.

The governor said, 'I have not been ordered to spar verbally with you; rather I have followed the orders of the utterly invincible emperors so that in accordance with their law you may recognize what you ought to do'.

---

327 imperio uestro] D *order reversed*   329 principes] D e *corrected from* i. quid] D qui

(22) Iulianus respondit, 'Quid iubeant audiui quid autem oporteat me facere consilio salutari definiui. Turpe est enim grege præmisso pastorem minime sequi'.

Preses dixit, 'Illi quos memoras pro errore suo dignam consecuti sunt
335 mortem. Tu autem ut euadas tormenta quę contemptoribus debentur et generi tuo et natalibus tuis restituaris, hoc elaboro'.

Iulianus respondit, 'Labora pro te uel pro tuis quos | ita sibi fecit heredes diabolus, pro me autem ille sollicitus est Dominus Ihesus Christus qui me ex limo terre formauit'.

340 Preses dixit, 'Sic tecum agere debeo quasi cum infirmo medicus usque dum sanitatem recipias. Quod si te sanum et diuinorum deorum cultorem reddidero, magnum mihi agonem et honorem aput principes conlocabo. Nam ipsi domini rerum multum tuę uesanię condolent'.

Iulianus respondit, 'Numquam auditum est ut cecus inluminet uidentem,
345 et morbidus curet sanum et qui errat possit corrigere recto itinere gradientem'.

Preses dixit, 'Ergo ut dicis cecus sum et morbidus et errans, qui saluti tuę cupio consultum, et tu solus optines sanitatem?'

Iulianus respondit, 'Haec omnia in te dominantur; quod si uelles te
350 agnoscere et ex toto corde requirere salutem tuam, non te horreret medicus noster, per quem omnes Christiani uerissimam optinent sanitatem. Quos autem colitis demones sunt*; liberare non possunt'.

(23) Tunc preses iratus clamabat tortoribus, 'Extendatur ad uerbera ut uel sic stultitia eius manifestetur!'

355 Iulianus respondit, 'Non est [stultitia], Dominum nosse sed gloria, tu autem secularibus oppressus inlecebris quid sit congruum non agnoscis'.

Preses dixit, 'Extendite eum et fustes rigidos afferte et omnia membra eius dissipate'.

Et cum ita facerent cedentes, unus ictu percutientis oculum amisit, qui erat
360 *necessarius presidi et imperatoribus notissimus. Haec uidens preses fremuit, dicens, 'Tantum ualuit magica ars tua ut nihil sentias et aliis oculos euellas?'*

Iulianus respondit, 'Uides, Marciane, quia hoc est, quod superius dixi: cecus, morbidus et errans. Tandem amota seuitia tua qua in me bacharis, audi quę propono'.

365 Preses dixit, 'Si pro salute tua, audiam libentissime'.

---

335 contemptoribus] D contemporibus
336 elaboro] D et laboro
337 Fol. 80vb
338 sollicitus est] D *order reversed*
341 sanitatem] D ad sanitatem
342 Nam] D Nam et

343 domini] D dii
348 et] R ut *over* et. optines] RD optineas (a *above line in* R)
352 liberare non possunt] R et neminem salute (D salutem) carentem saluare uel liberare possunt

(22) Julian replied, 'I have heard what they ordered but with beneficial counsel have settled on what I ought to do. It is shameful for a shepherd not to follow a flock that has been sent ahead'.

The governor said, 'Those whom you recall got the death they deserved for their error. However, I am taking pains with you so that you may escape the torment due those who despise the emperors and so that you may be restored to your family and your birthright'.

Julian responded, 'Work for you and yours whom the devil has made his heirs, but He who is busied on my account is the Lord Jesus Christ who formed me from the dust of the earth' [cf. Genesis 2.7].

The governor said, 'I ought to treat you like a doctor does a sick man until you recover your health. For if I restore you to health and to the worship of the heavenly gods, then I will involve myself in a great contest and win great honour in the emperors' eyes. For even those in authority are greatly moved to pity your madness'.

Julian replied, 'No one has ever heard of a blind man giving sight to him who can see, or the diseased curing the healthy or he who goes astray setting right the one who walks in a straight line'.

The governor said, 'Are you saying that I, the one who wants to have looked after your well-being, am blind, sick and errant, and that you alone are healthy?'

Julian answered, 'All these ailments dominate you; but should you decide to recognize and seek your health with all your heart, then our physician, through whom all Christians possess the truest health, will not refuse you. However, those you worship are demons [cf. Psalm 95.5 (Septuagint)]*; they cannot cure you'.

(23) Then the angered governor shouted to the torturers, 'Stretch him out for a beating to show his stupidity!'

Julian replied, 'It is not stupidity to know the Lord but glory, but you, overcome by worldly charms, do not recognize what is proper'.

The governor said, 'Stretch him out and beat him with rigid clubs and shatter all his limbs'.

And when they were beating him, one of the assailants who was a friend of the governor and very well-known to the emperors lost an eye from the blow of another flogger. When the governor saw this, he roared and said, 'Is your sorcery so powerful that you feel nothing and pluck out the eyes of others?'

Julian replied, 'You see, Martianus, what I said to you earlier is so: you are blind, sick and errant. When the rage in which you rant at me has finally subsided, listen to what I suggest'.

The governor said, 'If it is for the sake of your well-being, I will most gladly listen'.

---

355 (stultitia)] iustitia; RD stultitia. nosse] R
   above line; D nosce
360 fremuit] RD ut leo fremuit

363 bacharis] R baccaris
364 propono] R præpono
365 pro] RD de. tua] RD tua tractare uelis

Iulianus respondit, 'Conuoca omnes deorum dearumque probatissimos sacerdotes, et inuocent omnes deos suos super oculum euulsum ut restituant cultori suo uisum. Cum ergo non ualuerint, ego nomen Domini mei Ihesu Christi inuocabo et non solum oculum euulsum sed et cordis inluminabo
370   oculos'.*

(24) Tunc Marcianus iubet omnes | pontifices adesse et dixit eis, 'Ite et inmortales deos sacrificiis optimis honorate ut [huic] rebelli suo Iuliano ostendant uirtutem suam, et homini necessario oculum reformantes et ipsum suę culturę inclinent'. Ingrediuntur lapides ad lapides, iussum lapidis
375   implentes. *Qui cum ritu illo nequissimo demonia appellarent, ita accipiunt responsum in templis, 'Discedite a nobis quia igni perpetuo mancipati sumus!* Nam tantum ualet Iuliani deprecatio ad Dominum ut *a die quo ad hanc passionem est conprehensus nobis pęna conduplicata est. Cum in tenebris clausi retineamur, quomodo lumen reddimus quod non habemus?'* Tunc
380   egrediuntur sacerdotes falsa promittentes.

Sanctus autem *Iulianus, quem nihil latebat,* oratione facta *dixit ad presidem, 'Festina celeriter ingredere templum'. Uidit omnia simulacra cristallina, et electrina, et aurea,* et ex omni metallo — quę amplius quingenta dinoscebantur — *ita comminuta et in puluerem redacta,* ut quia fuerant,
385   omnino non parerent. Preses ita uidens cęcatus a diabolo clamabat, 'O maleficia! Sic [preualent] carmina ut uirtutes deorum superent et pretiosa numina in puluerem redigerent. *Sed hic deorum patientia laudabilis est; iniurias sibi inrogatas sustinent ut rebelles suos patiendo sibi subiciant.* Nunc autem [magum] uideamus si pollicitationis sue implet effectum ut oculum ictu
390   percutientis extinctum sola inuocatione dei sui restituat'.

(25) Et dixit ad Iulianum, 'Patientissimos deos te superasse gloriaris, quorum pietatem circa te minime cognoscis. *Nunc* sopito multiloquio *promissum adimple,* sed ne hoc magicis artibus exerceas, lotio te perfundi iubeo, per quod omnes malefici fugantur'.

395   Iulianus respondit, 'Hoc quod facturus es non ad iniuriam meam sed ad laudem Domini mei pertinet ut oculum pristinę sanitat[i] restituat et lotium in odorem nectareum conuertat'.

Cumque eum perfunderet, ita completum est ut dixerat, | ut non lotio sed balsamo aut cinnamonio eum putarent perfusum. Ad quod miraculum, licet
400   incredulus, Martianus tabescebat.

---

366 probatissimos] D cultores probatissimos
368 ualuerint] RD ualuerint ei adiutorium
   impendere
369–70 inluminabo oculos] RD *order reversed*
371 Fol. 81ᵐ. pontifices] R e *corrected from* i
372 (huic)] uhic; RD huic
374–75 Ingrediuntur...implentes] R Ingrediuntur
   (*above line:* pontifices lapideum co...[rest is
   unreadable]) lapides (*above line:* ad lapidea

metalla) ad lapides iussum lapides (*above line:* presides)
378 est conprehensus] *above line;* RD *order reversed.* pęna conduplicata est] R poena centuplicata sit (sit *over* est); D centuplicata pęna est
379 retineamur] RD retinemur. quomodo] R *erasure of* ergo *following;* D quomodo ergo. reddimus] RD reddere possumus

Julian replied, 'Summon together the most esteemed priests of your gods and goddesses, and let them invoke all their gods concerning the eye that was plucked out so that the gods may restore sight to their worshipper. When they do not succeed, I will invoke the name of my Lord Jesus Christ and will illuminate not only the plucked out eye but also the eyes of his heart'.*

(24) Then Martianus orders all the priests to assemble and said to them, 'Go and honour the immortal gods with the choicest sacrifices so that they may reveal their power to this rebel, their Julian, and, restoring the eye of my indispensable man, may incline Julian to worship them'. The stones go in to stones, carrying out the order of a stone. When the priests called upon their demons with that utterly worthless rite, they receive an answer in the temples: 'Get away from us because we have been handed over to unremitting fire! Julian's prayer to the Lord is so powerful that our punishment has doubled from the day he was arrested for this suffering. Since we are shut away in darkness, how can we who have no light restore it?' The priests then came out making false promises.

But Saint Julian, from whom nothing was hidden, said to the governor when the priests had made their speech, 'Hurry and go into the temple'. He saw that all the images of crystal, amber, gold and every metal — he discerned more than 500 — had been smashed and reduced to dust, and that the idols had been so completely shattered that they were not visible at all. Seeing this was so, the governor was blinded by the devil and cried out, 'O the wickedness! The spells are so superior that they surpass the gods' powers and reduce the precious divinities to dust. Yet this patience of the gods is praiseworthy; they endure the injuries inflicted on them to make their rebels submit to them by being patient. But now let us see if the sorcerer can make good on his promise to restore the eye put out by the beater's blow with only an invocation of his god'.

(25) And he said to Julian, 'You boast that you have defeated the most patient gods whose kindness concerning you, you do not even recognize. Now, quiet your senseless chatter and fulfil your promise, but so you do not perform it with sorcery, I order you to be drenched with urine, which drives away all evil'.

Julian replied, 'What you are about to do will not injure me but will bring glory to my Lord with the result that he will restore the eye to its former health and will turn the urine into the fragrance of nectar'.

And when they drenched him, it came to pass just as he had said, so that they thought he had been soaked not in urine but in balsam and cinnamon. At this miracle, Martianus, although unbelieving, grew weak.

380 egrediuntur] D ingrediuntur
382 templum. Uidit] RD templum uocant te dii tui. Tunc martianus licet non uoluntate sed inuitus perrexit ad templum. Cumque ingrederetur templum uidit
385 parerent] R apparetent, t *above second* r; D apparerent. ita] D hoc ita. cęcatus] RD factum cæcatus
386 (preualent)] ND preualentes; R pręualent

387 in puluerem] D impulverem
388 subiciant] a *above dotted* e; RD subiugent
389 (magum)] ND magnum; R magum. implet] RD impleat
393 lotio] R lio otio
394 malefici] R maleficiæ; D malaficię
396 sanitat(i)] sanitatis; RD sanitati (R *final* s *dotted*)
398 Fol. 81ʳᵇ

(26) *Tamen sanctus Iulianius super oculum extinctum crucem Saluatoris faciens, statim ita restitutus est oculus quasi nihil fuisset passus,* sed hẹc omnia non Dei uirtute facta esse credebat Martianus. Ille uer[o] oculum recipiens *clamabat, 'Uere Deus est Christianorum ipse solus adorandus!* Dii autem tui*
405 *uere demonia manifestantur'. Qui cum talia prosequeretur iussit eum Martianus gladio interimi.* Quem nullus dubitet quod rosei sui sanguinis perfusum rubore, Dominus Ihesus Christus sibi martyrem consecrauit ad laudem et gloriam nominis sui. Amen.

(27) *Sanctum uero Iulianum iussit impius Marcianus diuersis penis*
410 *afflictum et uinculis ferreis per omnes artus oneratum,* sub uoce preconia circuire ciuitatem, dicens, 'Hoc merentur rebelles deorum et principum contemptores!' *Cumque uenisset ad locum ubi filius presidis studebat,* tunc puer ad condiscipulos suos dixit, 'Rem uideo inauditam'.

Qui dixerunt, 'Quid uides?'

415 'Reum illum Christianum quem ducunt ore frenato *uideo multitudinem albatorum cum illo loquentem,* et coronam de lapidibus pretiosis super caput eius cuius splendor aeris lumen obtundit, *et alios tres uiros cum comis aureis,* qui uultum in similitudinem aquilarum *super eum excubias celebrantes.* Et mihi dignum uidetur quia oportet huic tali Deo credere qui sic suos cultores
420 tuetur. Et credite mihi quia in eius confessione delector et talia pati desidero si uoluerit Deus eius esse Deus meus'.

(28) Hẹc audientes, condiscipuli eius uel magistri turbati sunt ualde. Quem blando sermone corripientes ab intentione reuocare uolebant. Timebant autem quia unicus erat patri.

425 Dixit puer, 'Uere magnus est Deus Christianorum, quem credere consilio salutari decreui. Ipse est uerus Deus, qui credentes | in se non deserit. Talis est enim gloria uitẹ huius: sicut uter uento extensus plenus apparens et intus est uacuus; ita et gloria seculi huius in qua nos temporalem habemus letitiam et ẹternam Dei potentiam non agnoscimus. Uolumus elati dominationem
430 exercere, et dominatorem uerum qui est in celis corde incredulo non agnoscimus. Quanto meliora nobis sunt pecora, iumenta et canes, que uocem dominorum suorum cognoscunt! Nos uero facti rationales Creatorem nostrum colendo lapides et ligna non agnoscimus.

---

403 uer(o)] uere; RD uero
404 Uere] D Uerus
412 tunc] D *omits*
415 Reum] RD Ille respondens ait, Reum. ore frenato] RD ore infrenato
417 comis] RD coronis (R ro *above line and first minim of* m *erased for* n)
418 aquilarum] RD aquilarum tenent (tenent *above line in* R)
419 sic suos] D *order reversed*

422 magistri] RD magister
424 erat] D *omits*
425 Dixit] DR dixit uero (uero *above line in* R)
426 Fol. 81ᵛᵃ
430 uerum] D *omits*
431 Quanto] Rº Quanto; D O quanto. meliora] a *above dotted* es; RD meliores. nobis] D *omits*. que] e *corrected from* i; RD qui
432 cognoscunt] NR u *above dotted* e; D secuntur

(26) Nevertheless, when Saint Julian made the sign of the Saviour's cross over the eye that had been put out, it was instantly restored as if it had suffered nothing, but Martianus did not believe this had been done by God's power. In fact, that man who received his sight cried out, 'Truly, the very God of the Christians should alone be worshipped!* But your gods are truly shown to be demons' [cf. Psalm 95.5 (Septuagint)]. When he carried on like this, Martianus ordered him to die by the sword. The healed man did not hesitate one bit because when the redness of his rose-coloured blood was poured out, the Lord Jesus Christ consecrated a martyr for himself to the praise and glory of his name. Amen.

(27) Now when Julian had been afflicted with various punishments and loaded down with iron chains on each limb, the wicked Martianus ordered him to be led around the city in the company of a herald who declared, 'This is what rebels against the gods and those contemptuous of the emperors deserve!' And when they approached the place where the governor's son was studying, the boy said to his schoolmates, 'I see something unheard of'.

They said, 'What do you see?'

(He said), 'I see a multitude arrayed in white conversing with that Christian convict whom they lead around with his mouth bridled, I see above his head a crown of precious stones whose brilliance outshines the daylight and I see three other men with golden hair and faces like eagles keeping watch over him. And it seems right to me that I ought to believe in this God who protects his worshippers in this way. And believe me, I am delighted by that man's acknowledgement of Christ and will suffer such punishments if his God will be my God'.

(28) When his schoolmates and teachers heard this, they were utterly confounded. They rushed to him with coaxing words and tried to dissuade him from his purpose. Moreover, they were afraid because he was his father's only son.

The boy said, 'Truly, the God of the Christians is great, and with beneficial advice I have decided to believe in him. He is the true God and does not forsake those who believe in him. Such is the glory of this life: it is like a wineskin inflated with air, appearing to be full but empty inside; so too is the glory of this world in which we have temporal joy but do not recognize the eternal power of God. Filled with pride we want to exercise earthly authority and with unbelieving hearts do not recognize the true authority in heaven. How much better than we are the sheep, mules and dogs that recognize the voice of their masters! We who have been made rational do not acknowledge our Creator when we worship stones and wooden things.

'Sufficiat mihi huc usque errasse, iam itaque non errabo. Quod mihi defuit
435 ostensum est; mihi tempus acceptum inueni. Quare non laborem et accipiam
tempus sine tempore, fruar gloria sine fine, contempnendo diuitias laudabiles
aeternas adquiram? Nam inpedimenta huius mundi separant a Deo. Potestas
uero temporalis uel quælibet dignitas successione finitur, et uita ipsa tempo-
ralis quibuslibet casibus subiacet et morte finitur.
440 'Illi debeo credere Deo uero et uiuo Christo. Cui si militauero, nullus mihi
ueniet successor. Cuius aeternitati si sociatus fuero, casibus malignis non
subiacebo, nec mortem pertimesco. Hęc est uera gloria et nobilitas generis
mei pro tali Deo pati. Quem cum torqueor, numquam amitto. Quem dum
confessus fuero, a bono non derelinquor, et pro ipso in me omnia tolerare
445 non dubito'.
(29) Hęc cum dixisset *filius presidis proiecit uolumina doctorum* et ipsas
uestes quibus indutus erat iactauit a se et dixit, 'Cum pollutione uestimenti
mei ad Dei hominem properare non est necesse. Nudum me mater huic
seculo de utero suo fudit. Quod mundi est, mundo relinquam'. Et per plateas
450 ciuitatis cursus arripuit usque dum ad locum ubi sanctus Iulianus torquebatur
ueniret quia iusserat impius ut per omnes plateas et uicos ciuitatis diuersas
penas pateretur. *Tunc puer prostratus pedibus sancti Iuliani* clamabat, 'Te
agnosco patrem secunde natiuitatis, quem mihi Dominus Christus sic clarifi-
catum ostendit! Marcianum uero genitorem meum, | inimicum ueritatis, Dei
455 [cultorum] persecutorem, abnego et despicio. Tibi adherens, opto pro
Christo salutari meo quem usque modo ignoraui, simili modo pati quo et tu'.
Haec uidentes qui illum torquebant milites contremuerunt, statim sermo
eorum de sensu defecit. Doctores uero studiorum fugerunt. Tota quoque
ciuitas utriusque sexus ad spectaculum tante rei cognoscende concurrebat,
460 omnes [cognoscentes] presidis filium sancto Iuliano adherentem, talia
proclamantem, 'O uniuersi populi, agnoscite quia ego sum pręsidis filius, qui
cum patre sanctorum ueneranda corpora paterne potestatis elatus
despiciebam, sed hęc quę miramini inmutatio dextere excelsi laudabilis est.
Hęc feci ignorans Dominum; audiui, cognoui Dominum, immo cognitus sum
465 ab eo. *Diis abrenuntio*; patrem et matrem abnego; diuitias superfluas respuo;
Christum confiteor; beati Iuliani me sequipedam testor. Quid tardatis ministri
uel milites? Ite, nuntiate parentibus meis me Deum uiuum cognouisse.
Demonia execro'.

434 huc] D huic. itaque] RD iam
436 gloria] *added in left margin*; R luce; D
    luc
438 quælibet] R qualibet. finitur] D finit
439 quibuslibet] D quibuslibet uel. finitur] D
    finit
440 si militauero] *first i of* militauero *above
    erased letter*; R similata uero; D simili uero

443 torqueor] D torquear
453 Christus] R ihesus (*above line*) christus
454 Fol. 81vb
455 (cultorum)] cultor; RD cultorum.
    despicio] NR e *corrected from* i
456 quo] quo *above* que; R quæ; D quę
457 statim] R statimque
458 Tota quoque] D totaque

'Let it suffice for me to have erred thus far, but I will not err now. What I needed has been revealed; I have discovered the right moment for me. Why would I not work to receive timeless time, to enjoy glory without end and to acquire everlasting valuables by despising wealth? Now the impediments of this world separate me from God. But temporal power or any earthly honour whatsoever comes to an end by turns, and temporal life itself is subject to any number of accidents and ends in death.

'I have to believe in him who is the true God and the living Christ. If I am his soldier, no successor will come to take my place. If I share in his immortality, I will not be at the mercy of harmful accidents, nor will I be terrified of death. It is true glory and renown for my family that I suffer for the sake of such a God. Though I be tortured, I will never lose Him. While I confess him, I will not be abandoned by the Good, and I have no doubt that I can bear all things by myself for his sake'.

(29) When the governor's son had said these things, he threw down his teachers' books and threw off the very clothes in which was dressed and said, 'It is essential that I not hasten to the man of God with polluted garments. My mother sent me forth naked from her womb into this world [cf. Job 1.21]. What belongs to the world, I leave to the world'. And he raced through the streets of the city until he came to the place where Saint Julian was being tortured because the wicked one had ordered him to be subjected to various punishments throughout all the city's streets and quarters. Then, when the boy had fallen at Saint Julian's feet, he cried out, 'I acknowledge you, whom the Lord Christ revealed to me after he made you famous, to be the father of my second birth! I truly reject and despise Martianus my father, an enemy of the truth and a persecutor of God's worshippers. I cling to you and want to suffer like you for the sake of Christ my Saviour whom I failed to recognize until now'.

When the soldiers torturing Julian saw this, they trembled with fear and suddenly became speechless. The boy's teachers fled. The whole city, both men and women, ran to the spectacle when they found out about the momentous affair, and all recognized the governor's son clinging to Saint Julian and declaring loudly, 'O all you people, know that I am the governor's son who, proud of my father's power, despised with my father the bodies of the saints who ought to have been venerated, but this change from favourable high status that astonishes you is praiseworthy. I did those despicable things when I did not know the Lord; now I have heard, have known the Lord, or rather have been known by him. I renounce the gods; I reject my father and mother; I spurn excess wealth; I confess Christ; I declare that I am a follower of the blessed Julian. Why do you officials and soldiers delay? Go, report to my parents that I have acknowledged the living God. I curse the devils'.

---

460 (cognoscentes)] ND *omits*; R
  cognoscentes. adherentem] R adher-
entem *with* mirabantur *above line*; D

adherentem et mirabantur
466 sequipedam] D sequipedum
468 execro] D execrasse

(30) Parentes uero hęc audientes ut cera in igne tabescunt, confluxerat
470 enim innumerabilis multitudo populi. Iubent filium suum a Iuliano segre-
gatum sibi restitui. Domini uero misericordia adfuit ut *si quis uellet manum
suam mittere ut eum separaret a conplexibus sancti Iuliani, statim contrahe-
bantur manus et brachia eius.*

(31) Iubet eos simul ad se perduci, et dixit ad Iulianum, '*Tu es qui spei*
475 *meę fructum magicis artibus auferre contendis*? Qui tenerum pectus inlicitis
carminibus alienasti, et genitorum affectum negare conpellis?' *Huc pater
pueri et mater aduenit cum omni familia* sua utriusque sexus — circiter
quinque milia — crinibus solutis, uberibus nudatis, lacerato pectore; *uoces
dabant ad cęlum.*

480 Tunc preses, hęc uidens, scidit uestimenta sua. Lacerata facie clamabat ad
Iulianum, 'Iuliane crudelis, *aspice dolorem patris et matris*! Aspice tante
familię planctum et a magicis artibus *absolue innocentem*! Et ut nobis unicum
reddas filium et tante familię dominum ut *et ego pro te imperatoribus
suggeram* et culpam bacchantem abscidas'.

485 Iulianus respondit, | 'Suffragia tua opus non habeo, nec ab imperatoribus
tuis dimitti desidero. Sed hoc rogo Dominum Ihesum Christum, ut una cum
isto agno de luporum uisceribus nato uel omnibus qui credituri sunt martyrio
conpleto, suscipiar in eorum numero, quos tu in innocentia igne consump-
sisti. Nam iste qui ex te natus fuerat modo mecum renatus est credendo.
490 Aetatem habet; ipse pro se tibi responsum det. Ipse genitricis aspiciat
lacrimas, ipse uberibus quibus nutritus est doleat'.

(32) *Celsus puer dixit*, 'Contingere solet ut de spinis rosę nascantur. Nec
amittit odorem suauissimum rosa nata de spinis, nec frondes que genuit
rosam spinarum remittit aculeos. Ergo, ut consuestis parentes, pungite et
495 odorem suauitatis credentibus preparate. Uobis oboediant qui perire parati
sunt. Me imitentur qui de tenebris ad lucem transire contendunt. Hoc scire
debetis: quia *ego pro Christo Domino meo nego* uos parentes, *et uos uero
propter deorum uestrorum culturam filium tormentis affligite.* Credo enim per
ista tormenta et temporalem mortem uitam aeternam adquirere. Nec plus
500 faciam uos quam me, nec amorem uestrum prepono aeterne lętitiae. Quid
moram differtis? Accede tu, Marciane, quasi incredulus et crudelis pater non
quasi uere pater Abraham, adprehende gladium, Christo filium uictimam
offer. *Sed si te uiscerum pietas uincit, dirige me ad seuissimum principem tuum
ut ego pro Domino meo Ihesu Christo ornamenta martyrii poenis adimpleam*'.

---

470 Iubent] ent *above dotted* et; R hec
  audiens præses iubet; D iubet
471 adfuit] R ita adfuit
472–73 contrahebantur] R contrahæbantur;
  D contrahabantur
474 dixit ad Iulianum] D ad Iulianum dixit
475 Qui] R et qui
478 quinque] D .v.
480 Lacerata] D et lacerata

482 ut] D *omits*
483 reddas] a *above dotted* e; R reddes; D
  redde. ut et] R *order reversed*; D et
485 Fol. 82ra. Suffragia tua] RD suffragiis tuis
487 luporum] D luporibus
488–89 consumpsisti] D consupsisti
490 tibi responsum] D *order reversed*
492 solet] RD assolet
493 genuit] RD generant

(30) Hearing these things, his parents melt like wax in the fire, for an innumerable multitude of people had flocked together. They order their son to be returned to them once he had been separated from Julian. But the mercy of the Lord was present there so that if anyone decided to grab the boy to separate him from the embrace of Saint Julian, then immediately the assailant's hands and arms were constricted.

(31) Then the governor orders them to be brought to him together, and he said to Julian, 'Are you the one who is striving to steal away the fruit of my hope with sorcery? Have you alienated his tender heart with illicit spells, and do you force him to deny his love for his parents?' The mother as well as the father came to the place with all her household — about 5000 men and women — with her hair unbound, her breasts exposed and her chest scratched bloody; they all uttered cries to the heavens.

Then, when the governor saw this, he tore his clothes. When he had bloodied his face with scratches, he shouted at Julian, 'Cruel Julian, look at a father and mother's anguish! Look at the grief of such a great household and release the innocent boy from your sorcery! And when you give us back our only son and this great household its master, then I will intercede with the emperors on your behalf, and you may cut short an impetuous mistake'.

Julian replied, 'I have no need of your help, nor do I want to be released by your emperors. Rather I ask the Lord Jesus Christ to receive me, together with that lamb born from a family of wolves and with all those about to be handed over to a perfected martyrdom, into the company of those innocents whom you destroyed with fire. Now this son born of you has just been born again with me by believing. He is of age; let him answer you for himself. Let him look at his mother's tears, and let him grieve for the breasts which nourished him'.

(32) The boy Celsus said, 'Roses usually are produced among thorns. Neither does the rose produced among thorns lose its most pleasing fragrance, nor do the branches producing the rose shed their pointy thorns. Therefore, as you my parents have been accustomed to do, prick and prepare a sweet fragrance for those who believe. Let those who are prepared to perish obey you. Let those who hasten to cross over from darkness to light imitate me. Know this: I deny you father and mother for the sake of Christ my Lord, so afflict your son with torments on account of your reverence for your gods. I believe that through those torments and temporal death, I will acquire everlasting life. I will not value you more than myself, nor will I put your love before eternal joy. Why do you delay? You, Martianus, approach like an unbelieving and cruel father not in fact like father Abraham, take up the sword and offer your son as a sacrifice to Christ [Genesis 22.1–19]. However, should fatherly feeling get the better of you, send me straight to your most violent emperor so that for the sake of my Lord Jesus Christ I may complete the glories of martyrdom through punishments'.

---

494 remittit] RD remittent. consuestis] RD   498 filium] RD filium uestrum
consueti estis (R eti *above line*)   500 prepono] RD propono

505   (33) Haec audiens pręses dixit, 'Custodia priuata recludantur et quę necessaria sunt ministrentur eis'.

    Iulianus respondit, 'Hęc quę preparari iubes, tibi et [consentientibus] tibi impende'.

    Haec audiens preses fremit ut leo. Estimans eos poena terreri quos bland-
510 imentis obtinere non ualuit, *iussit eos in carceris ima concludi ubi dampnatorum membra diurni temporis consumpta horribilium uermium examina bulliebant et odor pessimus.* Qui, dum introducti essent, *gratia Domini precedens eos, locum horrendum delectabilem reddidit. Tenebras conuertit in lumen, exhibens cereorum officia, nectareum odorem reddens:*
515 ebulliens uero pena euanuit.

    (34) Haec uildentes *milites — circiter uiginti — qui eos custodię mancipauerunt omnes ad inuicem dixerunt,* 'Pudoris est ut ferreum possideamus pectus. *Numquid iustum est ut de hac luce ad tenebras reuertamur, de uita ad mortem,* et de odore nectareo ad sanguinis effusionem, et [a tali patre
520 monente] ad iudicem irascentem, *a ueritate ad mendacium,* a sobrietate ad ebrietatem, a castitate ad libidinem? Turpe est esse quod fuimus et negligere salutem quam inuenimus'.

    Haec uero dicentes, *ad pedes sancti Iuliani se uolutabant, laudantes* et confitentes *Christi nomen.* Tunc Iulianus et puer gratias Domino referebant.
525 Audiens itaque hoc Martianus preponit custodes crudelissimos quoadusque tormenta prepararentur et omnibus penis inferret. *Sanctus uero Iulianus* sollicitus pro salute eorum quos Christo adquisierat, *orabat Dominum qualiter procuraret ut baptismi gratiam consequerentur.**

    (35) Nec hoc silebo aliud magnum miraculum in eadem ciuitate
530 concessum ante tempus persecutionis. *Imperatores Dioclicianus et Maximianus priorem ciuitatis unice diligebant quia de genere Carini imperatoris descendebat. Hoc defuncto Christiano* cum uxore sua, *septem filios Christianos reliquerunt. Quos imperatores retinentes amore patris eorum, iusserunt eos sine aliqua persecutione Christiane religioni deseruire. Hi*
535 *habuerunt secum presbiterum qui eis mysteria sancta celebrabat.*

    Isti uisitantur a Domino et iubentur ut una cum presbitero carcerem peterentut baptismi gratiam uenerabilis puer Celsus et milites consequerentur. Statim ad carcerem ueniunt nocte et uident angelum Domini ante se precedentem; qui mox ut tetigit ianuas, omnia claustra aperta sunt.

---

505 Custodia] D In custodia
507 (consentientibus)] C conscientibus; RD
    consentientibus. tibi] D te
510 obtinere] *final* e *corrected from* i; R
    obtineri. iussit] R iussit autem
511 consumpta] RD labore consumpta
512 bulliebant] R ebulliebant; D ebuliebant.
    Quidum] D Quicum
513 horrendum] D horridum

514 reddens] RD reddentes
516 Fol. 82rb. uiginti] D .xx.ti
519–20 (a tali patre monente)] *reading is
    from* S; N ad talem patrem monentem;
    RD de patre bona ad monentem (R ad
    above line)
521 negligere] i *above dotted* e; RD
    neglegere

(33) When the governor heard this, he said, 'Shut them away in a private prison and provide them with what is necessary'.

Julian replied, 'Use for yourself and those who sympathize with you the things you order to be prepared'.

Hearing this, the governor roared like a lion. Judging that those he was not strong enough to win by enticements would be terrified by punishment, he ordered them to be confined in the depths of the jail where swarms of horrible maggots boiled out from the bodies of the condemned that had been wasting away day after day, and where there was the foulest stench. When they were being led in, the Lord's grace went before them and rendered the dreadful place a delightful one. His grace changed darkness into light, furnishing candlelight and sending forth the fragrance of nectar: in fact, the punishment bubbling up vanished.

(34) When the soldiers who had imprisoned them saw this — there were about twenty — they said to each other, 'It is shameful that we have hearts of iron. How can it be right for us to return from this light to darkness, from life to death, from the odour of nectar to the shedding of blood, from a father who gives instruction to a judge who flies into a rage, from truth to falsehood, from sobriety to drunkenness, from chastity to lust? It is disgraceful to continue to be what we have been and to ignore the salvation we have discovered'.

When they said this, they fell at the feet of Saint Julian, praising and confessing the name of Christ. Then Julian and the boy gave thanks to the Lord. And when the governor heard about this, Martianus put his cruelest guards in charge until torments could be prepared and he could inflict punishment on each of them. Saint Julian was anxious about the salvation of those whom he had acquired for Christ and asked the Lord how He would see to it that they might receive the grace of baptism.*

(35) I will not be silent about another great miracle that was granted in the same city before the time of persecution. The emperors Diocletian and Maximian specially loved a governor of the city because he was a descendant of the emperor Carinus. When this Christian man and his wife died, they left seven Christian sons. The emperors remembered their love of the boys' father and ordered that they devote themselves to the Christian religion without fear of persecution. They had with them a priest who celebrated the holy mysteries for them.

They were visited by the Lord and were ordered to go to the jail together with the priest so that the venerable boy Celsus and the soldiers might acquire the grace of baptism. They go immediately to the jail at night and see preceding them an angel of the Lord; as soon as he touched the doors, all the bolts were opened.

---

526 prepararentur] RE preparentur. penis] R penas; D p nas

529 Nec] •K• *in right margin.* hoc] RD *omit*

530 concessum] R factum *above* concessum *marked for deletion*; D factum. persecutionis] D *second* i *corrected from* e

531–32 imperatoris] D *second* i *corrected from* e

532 septem] D .vii.

534 Christiane] e *corrected from* i

540   Quibus orantibus ingressi septem fratres una cum presbitero Antonio, uidentibus splendorem Domini clamauerunt dicentes, 'Adsumus! *Dominus nos huc direxit cum sacerdote suo ut baptismi gratiam [omnes] consequantur et nos tyrones per te, pater Iuliane, ueraces milites Christo militemus'.*

     Tunc Iulianus dixit, 'Gratias tibi ago, Christe Ihesu, | qui dignatus es ita
545 implere desiderium meum, ut quos per me adquisisti per baptismi gratiam et ueram fidem membra confirmentur. Et [hos] quos impietas imperatoris quasi agnos inter tanta agmina luporum reliquerat ad tui nominis confessionem adgregasti'.

     (36) *Nuntiatur hoc factum* impio *Martiano, septem germanos sine aliqua*
550 *persecutione Iuliano sociatos optantes pro Christo mori. Quos iubet educi de custodia, dicens ad eos,* 'Quid uobis contulit infantuli quos ita principes tuentur et diligunt ut arbitrio nostro essetis et fidei uestre cultores? *Qui patimini sine aliqua persecutione optantes mori quibus concessum est uiuere?* Si ergo maleficiis filium amisi et nescio quibus carminibus militum mentes
555 mutate sint, quare uos qui in uestro estis arbitrio constituti? Audite me et estote securi'.

     Respondens frater senior dixit, 'Massa auri naturę suę claritatem continet, et nisi per manum artificis et per ignem et malleum partibus secretur. Et ipso metallo auri, industria artificis, diuersarum margaritarum et lapidibus
560 pretiosis conponitur diadema, ita enim sumus, et nos de Christianis. Sed ipsa natiuitas nisi in publico fuisset manifestata, in occulto non potuit coronari.* Et nisi sancti Iuliani uestigia inmaculato calle secuti fuerimus, in diadema regis esse non possumus. *Satis horrenda est arbor quę foliis uernat et Creatori suo poma non affert'.*

565   *Et iussit eos* preses *in custodiam recipi* (37) et fecit suggestionem imperatoribus dicens, 'Piissimi principes, subuenite legibus uestris, et *diuinis numinibus* qui remanserunt *prebete munimen, et Iulianum [magum] uestris obtutibus presentate, qui* magicis artibus amplius quam quingenta *deorum simulacra* per quos floret mundus *comminuit. Filium unicum a me separauit;*
570 militum mentes nescio qua magica arte inmutauit; nam *et septem fratres quos clementia uestra iusserat esse* | *legis suę cultores ad se persuasit,* et beneficiis uestris fecit esse ingratos. Quos iussu uestro determinetis decernite'.

---

540 septem] D .vii. cum] D *omits*. Antonio]
  R antonino, *second* n *above line*
541 uidentibus] RD uidentes
542 (omnes)] omi; RD omnes
544 Christe Ihesu] D *order reversed*. Fol. 82ᵛᵃ
546 membra] D *omits*; (hos)] NRD hi
549 septem] D .vii.
551 infantuli] RD o infantuli
552 nostro] D uestro
555 mutate] e *corrected from* i. constituti]
  RD constituti uultis mori (R m[ori])

558 nisi] D misi. partibus secretur] R part-
  ibus non (*above line*) secretur; D partibus
  non seccetur. ipso] D ipsum
559 auri] RD auri et (R et *above line*)
560 sumus et nos] D et nos sumus
567 (magum)] magnum; RD magum
569 floret] D libet. comminuit] D
  comminitur. Filium] RD filium meum (R
  meum *above line*)
570 septem] D .vii.
571 Fol. 82ᵛᵇ

While Julian and the others were praying, the seven brothers and the priest Antonius entered, and when they saw the radiance of the Lord, they shouted and said, 'We are here! The Lord directed us to this place with his priest so that all might acquire the grace of baptism and that we, new recruits on your account, father Julian, may serve as true soldiers for Christ'.

Then Julian said, 'Thank you, Christ Jesus, who deigned to fulfil my request, so that those who have been acquired on my account might be confirmed as members of the Christian body through the grace of baptism and true faith. And those whom the emperor's wickedness left behind like lambs among a great pack of wolves you have now added to the flock to confess your name'.

(36) It was reported to the wicked Martianus that the seven brothers had joined Julian in prison without being persecuted and wanted to die for Christ's sake. The governor orders them to be brought out of the prison and said, 'What happened to you children whom the emperors safeguarded and so loved that you have been under our protection and worshippers of your own religion? Why do you suffer without being persecuted and want to die at the hands of those who have allowed you to live? If I have lost my son to sorcery and if by some spell or other my soldiers' minds have been changed, then how have I lost you who have been made your own masters? Listen to me and you will be safe'.

The oldest brother answered and said, 'A lump of gold is naturally brilliant, but only if it is broken into pieces by the craftsman's hand and the fire and the mallet. And just as a crown is made by the craftsman's industry from gold, different kinds of pearls and precious gems, so are we, and we are descended from Christians. But our very birth, unless it had been made public, could not be crowned in secret.* And unless we follow Saint Julian's footsteps in this pure path, we cannot be in the king's crown. The tree that puts forth leaves and does not bring forth fruit for its Creator is utterly loathsome'.

And the governor ordered them to be led back to prison (37) and made a suggestion to the emperors saying, 'Most upright emperors, come to the defence of your laws, and provide protection for the heavenly gods who are left and see for yourselves the sorcerer Julian, who with his magic shattered more than 500 images of the gods through whom the world prospers. He has separated my only son from me; by some spell or other he has altered the minds of my soldiers; and now he has won over to himself the seven brothers whom your clemency established as worshippers of their own religion, and he has made them ungrateful for your kindnesses. Judge them according to your decree'.

Tunc imperatores hanc dederunt licentiam Marciano ut 'si Iulianus cum sociis suis in hac obstinatione maneret, ad exemplum omnium conuocata
575 uniuersa prouincia, *singul[os] in singulas cupas* repletas pice, sulphure et bitumine *concremare. Quod si aduersus hęc magicis artibus preualuerint carmina, habeas licentiam qualicumque uelis eos affligere poena'.*

(38) Accepta auctoritate pręses iussit sibi in foro sedem parari, et *accersito Iuliano cum sociis suis dixit ad eos, 'Nihil de uestra salute tanto temporis*
580 *spatio cogitastis?'*

Iulianus respondit, 'Cogitatus noster, qui fuit ab initio, in quo cepit in hoc finiuit. Sed si aliquid excogitasti penarum, exerce'.

Preses dixit, 'Audistis quid de uobis determinauerunt inuictissimi principes?'

585 Puer Celsus respondit, 'Audisti — nec dicende pater — poenam quam preparauit Deus diabolo et uobis qui effecti estis angeli eius?'

Et Iulianus respondit, 'Quod iusserunt principes tu exerce'.

(39) *Cumque hoc diceret corpus ferebatur per plateam ad sepulchrum. Tunc* pręses cęcato *corde iussit reuocari corpus et in medio foro deponi, et*
590 dixit ad Iulianum, *'Magister uester Christus* antequam crucifigeretur *dicitur mortuos suscitasse. Hic parebit si uere Deus est si uos istum mortuum suscitaueritis ad uitam'.*

Iulianus respondit, 'Quid prodest cęco quando sol oritur?'

Preses dixit, 'Parce fabulis, et si quid preuales aut deus tuus, istum
595 mortuum suscitet'.

Iulianus respondit, 'Licet infidelitas uestra hoc non mereatur a Domino, sed quia *tempus est ut manifestetur uirtus Domini,* nec inpos[s]ibile est. Fidele promissum habeo a Domino, credens quia quicquid eum peto, non mihi negabit'.

600 Statim autem *Iulianus oculos in cęlum defigens* per unius hore spatium, facies eius mutata est et facta est sicut nix, et his uerbis coram omnibus uidentibus *fudit orationem ad Dominum*: 'Domine Ihesu Christe, qui es uerus filius Dei uiui, qui in principio natus es de Patre et in nouissimo mundi | carnem de uirgine adsumpsisti sine semine, aspice de summitate cęlorum, et ad confu-
605 sionem inimicorum tuorum, ad coroborandam fidem credentium in te et quę operatus es positus in terris, exaudi nunc in celis et *suscita hunc mortuum* ut uiui non moriantur sed mortui reuiuiscant'.

---

574 maneret] D premaneret
575 prouincia] R c *above dotted* t. singul(os)]
   ND singulis; R singulos, o *above dotted* i
576 concremare] R concremaret
579 tanto] D *omits*
582 finiuit] RD finit
588 corpus] RD corpus alicuis (R alicuis
   above line)

597 Domini] RD domini mei (R mei *above line*). inpos(s)ibile] inposibile; RD inpossibile
600 per] D *omits.* spatium] D spatio
601 mutata] D immutata
601–02 uidentibus] R *erased;* D *omits.* orationem] D orationem dicens. ad Dominum] D *omits*

Then the emperors gave Martianus this leave: 'If Julian persists in this obstinacy with his companions, then, as an example to all those gathered from every province, burn each in individual barrels filled with pitch, sulphur and bitumen. But if in the face of this sentence the spells prevail through sorcery, then you have permission to inflict on Julian and his companions whatever punishment you choose'.

(38) When the authorization had been received, the governor ordered the judgment seat prepared for him in the city centre, and when Julian had been fetched with his companions, the governor said to them, 'Have you thought of nothing concerning your well-being after such a long time?'

Julian answered, 'Our way of thinking, which has not changed from the outset, has ended where it began. But if you have devised any punishments, carry them out'.

The governor said, 'Have you heard what the utterly invincible emperors have decided about you?'

The boy Celsus answered, 'Have you — who ought not to be called 'father' — heard about the punishment God has prepared for the devil and those of you who have become his messengers?'

And Julian responded, 'Carry out what the emperors have ordered'.

(39) As he said this, a corpse was being carried along the street to its tomb. The governor, whose heart had been blinded, then ordered the corpse to be brought back and put down in the middle of the square, and he said to Julian, 'It is said that your teacher Christ raised the dead before he was crucified. It will be revealed here whether or not he truly is God if you raise this dead man to life'.

Julian replied, 'What use is it to the blind when the sun rises?'

The governor said, 'Do not tell stories, but if you or your god has power over anything, let him raise this dead man'.

Julian replied, 'Although your unbelief does not merit this from the Lord, because it is time for his power to be revealed, it is not impossible. I have a faithful promise from the Lord, believing that whatever I ask him, he will not refuse me' [cf. John 14.13].

Then Julian immediately fixed his eyes on heaven for an hour, and his appearance was changed and became like snow, and in front of all the onlookers he poured out a prayer to God in these words: 'Lord Jesus Christ, true Son of the living God, born of the Father in the beginning and incarnated from a virgin without seed in the last age of the world, look down from the summit of heaven, and confuse your enemies, and strengthen the faith of those who believe in you and that which you worked when you had been put on earth, listen now in heaven and raise this dead man so that the living may not die but so that the dead may be restored to life'.

---

603 Fol. 83ʳᵃ   605 fidem] D fidemque
604 de uirgine] D *omits*

Et conpleta oratione dixit ad mortuum, 'Tibi dico, terra arida, in ipsius nomine qui quatriduanum Lazarum suscitauit, ipse tibi imperat, surge super
610 te!' Et cum dixisset, *surrexit mortuus et clamabat, 'O acceptabilis oratio et inmaculata uirginitas! Ubi ducebar? Et unde reductus sum?'*
(40) *Inridebat eum pręses, 'Unde reductus es expone'.*

Respondit qui resurrexerat, 'Ducebar a nescio quibus *Aethiopibus, quorum status erat ut gigas, aspectus horridus, oculi ut fornacis ignis ardentis,*
615 *dentes eorum ut dentes leonum, brachia sicut trabes, ungues ut aquilarum in quibus nulla misericordia est.* Hi ducebant me in infernum; et iam prope putei abyssum cum essem, adhuc expectabatur ut caro mea terre redderetur ex qua sumpta est. At ubi fecisti corpus meum reuocari et beatus *Iulianus orationem fudit ad Dominum, infernus omnis turbatus est, et uox de throno Dei audita*
620 *est dicens, "Propter dilectum meum reducatur quia in nullo eum uolo contristari* in quo sic et Pater et ego et Spiritus letamur". *Et aduenerunt duo albis induti et tulerunt me de dominatu eorum et* huic luci *reddiderunt ut per eum qui me suscitauit agnoscam uerum Deum post mortem quem ante denegabam'.*

Hęc audiens preses turbatus est ita ut dissensio fieret, *iussit eum cum sanctis*
625 *recludi* et claustra anulo suo signari. *Quem Iulianus fecit baptismi gratiam consequi.*

(41) *Marcianus uero fecit poenam quam imperatores iusserunt preparari.* Ordinantur cupe triginta, mediantur pice et bitumine, adgregantur onera lignorum et sarmentorum. (42) *Et cum educerentur de custodia, Iulianum et*
630 *filium presidis unum uinculum tenebat. Ceteri uero oneratis uinculis catenis trahebantur ad hoc expectaculum.* Omnes | una uoce ymnum cantabant, 'Bonum mihi quod humiliasti me, Domine, ut discam iustificationes tuas'.

Quorum aspectu omnis etas nouas pulchritudines mirabatur. Quorum mentes ad fletum conuersa pietas inclinabat. Clamabatur ab omni aetate.
635 Inconfuse uiri clamabant, 'O iniustitia impietatis!' et 'Nos filios habemus!' Mulieres solutis crinibus clamabant, 'O gemitus amarior felle! Ut quid iubentur tales igne cremari? O potestas cęca, que nec uiuis parcit nec mortuos resurgentes audit!'

---

609 imperat] R imperet, *second* e *above dotted* a
609–10 super te] R *omits*
610 cum] R cum hæc; D cum hoc
612 pręses] R pręses dicens
613 a nescio] RD nescio a
617 adhuc] D illuc
619 turbatus] D turbata
620 meum] RD meum iulianum (R iulianum *above line*)
621 *first* et] RD *omit*
623 agnoscam] D cognoscam. uerum Deum] D *order reversed*

627 iusserunt] R iusserant; D iusserat
628 triginta] D .xxx.^{ta}. mediantur] RD replebantur (*above* mediantur *marked for deletion in* R)
629 lignorum] o *above dotted* a; R lignarum
631 hoc] R *above* hunc. expectaculum] RD spectaculum. Fol. 83rb. cantabant] D *second* a *corrected from* e
633 mirabatur] D mirabantur
635 iniustitia impietatis] D iniusta impietas
636 amarior felle] D fellę amariorum

And when he had finished the prayer, he said to the dead man, 'I say to you, dust of the earth, in the name of him who raised Lazarus after four days, he who has authority over you, stand up!' And when he had spoken, the dead man rose to his feet and shouted, 'O, acceptable prayer and unstained virginity! Where was I being led? And whence have I been brought back?'

(40) The governor mocked him, 'Describe whence you have been brought back'.

The resurrected man replied, 'I was being led away by some black men or other who were as tall as giants, whose appearances were horrible, whose eyes were like flaming fiery furnaces, whose teeth were like those of lions, whose arms were like tree trunks, whose nails were like eagles' in which there is no mercy. They were leading me to hell, and then when I was near the depths of the chasm, the expectation was that my flesh would be returned to the earth from which it had been made. And when you had my corpse brought back and when blessed Julian poured out a prayer to the Lord, all hell was confounded, and a voice from the throne of God was heard saying, "On account of my beloved one, let him be brought back, because I do not in any way want to disappoint Julian in whom the Father and I and the Spirit rejoice". And two arrayed in white came and took me out of the demons' dominion and restored me to this light so that on account of him who raised me I acknowledge after death the true God whom I earlier denied'.

Hearing this, the governor was confounded so that when dissension developed, he ordered the man who had been raised from the dead to be imprisoned with the saints and the bolts to be sealed with his signet ring. Julian had the resurrected man acquire the grace of baptism.

(41) Martianus had the punishment the emperors ordered made ready. Thirty barrels were set out, half-filled with pitch and bitumen, and loads of wood and twigs were piled on. (42) And when they were led out from prison, a single chain bound Julian and the governor's son. But the rest, having been loaded down with shackles, were dragged by their chains to the spectacle. All were singing a hymn in one voice: 'It is good for me that you have humbled me, Lord, so that I might know your decrees' [Psalm 118.71 (Septuagint)].

At the sight of the prisoners, people of every age were astonished at their new beauty. Their sympathy, having shifted, turned their thoughts to lamentation. There was shouting from people of all ages. Men shouted in an orderly way, 'O the injustice of wickedness!' and 'Let us have our sons!' Women with hair unbound shouted, 'O the sorrow more bitter than bile! How is it that such as these are ordered to be consumed by fire? O blind power that neither spares the living nor listens to the dead who are raised!'

Tunc Iulianus petit silentium et dixit ad populum, 'Uidete ne prohibeatis
640 fieri. Sinite nos splendidiores effici auro per ignem, hoc scientes: quia uideb-
itis nos omnes creduli et increduli igne consummatos sicut nunc uidistis'.

(43) *Quibus dixit preses, 'O desperata uoluntas per quam decus iuuentutis*
ad interitum properat. Nescio quo carmine sic alienate mentes conuertimini,
etsi tandem pro uestra salute diis inmortalibus qui laborant pro uobis ceruices
645 flectite. Quod si uolueritis, ego obtinebo ab imperatoribus, sine aliqua perse-
cutione religionis uestre esse cultores, tantum ne unicum mihi filium dulcem
cum talibus ac tantis in ipso flore uernant[ibus] igne cremari [uideam]'. Et
dixit, 'O insanabilis dolor pectori meo! Quem primum plangam cum omnium
decora sint corpora? Filii dulcissimi plus considero uultum. *O Iuliane,*
650 omnium malorum magister, quam multa bona tecum trahes ut *filiu[s] per te*
negando patrem nec matrem agnoscat'. Et ad filium conuersus dixit, 'Uel ante-
quam pereas, fili dulcissime, ex ore tuo uerbum audiam. Ecce, *uenit* et *mater,*
quę partus sui dolores quos non sperauerat inuenit. Ecce, *et* innumerosa
familia que te sibi dominum gaudebat funeri tuo ualedicturi *aduenerunt'.*

655 (44) Audiens puer *Celsus dixit, 'Lugeant te et se. Nos autem quos*
conspicitis *ad regna celorum pergere lugere non debetis. Nam nos omnes | tran-*
sibimus per ignem et inlesi uobis apparebimus. Demones uero quos colitis et
illos quos imperatores dicitis ac si purgamenta despicimus'.

Preses dixit, 'Ipsa est contumax audacia uestra; quę uos non dimittit
660 uiuere'.

Celsus puer dixit, 'Quod [postulo] intrepido corde petitioni meę tribuas
effectum'.

Preses dixit, 'Quicquid uolueris pete'.

Celsus puer respondit, '*Cum uideris inlesum de igne exire, permitte ad me*
665 *uenire matrem meam ut habeam cum ea consilium triduo* dilatione concessa,
et *forsitan nec me nec illam amittis'.*

Haec audiens mater urguebat fieri. Impius preses *dixit ei, 'Si igne inlesus*
exieris, quod fieri non credo, faciam quod desideras'.

(45) *Qui dum non poterat tolerare nec uidere incendium filii sui, asses-*
670 *sorem reliquid qui iussa impleret. Ipse* uero scissis uestibus *cum uxore* prope
mortua *domum reuersi sunt.* Fit luctus ingens. Lugebant parentes filium, serui
dominum; nec erat qui consolaretur.

---

641 consummatos] R consummato
644 etsi] RD et (R si *scratched out*)
647 uernant(ibus)] ND uernantes; R uernan-
   tibus, ib *corrected from* es. igne] R igne
   non liceat (R non liceat *above line*).
   (uideam)] NRD *omit*; reading is from
   Rome, Biblioteca Apostolica Vaticana,
   Reginensis latini MS 516 (s.ix[ex] or x[in])

650 filiu(s)] NR filium; D filius, *above line*
   corrected from bar over u
656 conspicitis] C conspici. Fol. 83[va]
661 (postulo)] totulo; RD postulo
664 Cum] RD Cum me
667 urguebat] D urgebat. igne] D ex igne
671 domum] RD domo

Then Julian called for silence and said to the people, 'See that you do not prevent this from occurring. Permit us to be made more brilliant than gold by the fire, knowing this: you all, believing and unbelieving, will see us having been perfected by the fire even as you see us now'.

(43) The governor said to them, 'O the hopeless wish by which the glory of youth hastens to an untimely death. Some spell or other has made you mad, but for the sake of your well-being, bend your necks at last to the immortal gods who work on your behalf. But if you so desire, I will obtain from the emperors that the worshippers of your religion live without any persecution, provided that I not see my only dear son burned by fire along with such and so many people flourishing in the very flower of youth'. And he said, 'O the incurable anguish of my heart! Whom will I mourn first when all these handsome ones are corpses? I will gaze longer at the face of my dearest son. O Julian, master of all wickedness, you carry off so many good things with you that a son admits to rejecting his father and mother because of you'. And having turned to his son the governor said, 'Perhaps before you die, dearest son, I may hear a word from your own mouth. Look, your mother, who meets with the unexpected sorrows of her child, comes too. Look, the innumerable household who rejoiced in you as their master have also come to your funeral to say goodbye'.

(44) When the boy heard this, Celsus said, 'Let them grieve for you and for themselves. But you ought not grieve for us whom you see proceeding to the kingdom of heaven. Now, we all will pass through the fire and will appear to you unharmed. We despise the demons you worship and those whom you call emperors as if they were rubbish'.

The governor said, 'This very audacity of yours, which will not permit you to leave here alive is defiant'.

The boy Celsus said, 'I ask with an untroubled heart that you allow my request to be carried out'.

The governor said, 'Ask whatever you want'.

The boy Celsus replied, 'When you see me come out of the fire unharmed, permit my mother to come to me so that I may talk to her for three days once the delay has been granted, and perhaps you will lose neither me nor her'.

When his mother heard this, she urged that it be done. The wicked governor said to him, 'If you come out of the fire unharmed, which I do not believe will happen, then I will do what you want'.

(45) In the meantime, unable to bear or witness his son's burning, the governor left an aide who carried out the order. The governor, his clothes torn, returned home with his wife who was nearly dead. A great sorrow arises. The parents mourned their son, the servants their master; there was no one to comfort them.

Assessor uero munus sibi iniunctum adimplet: iussit singulos in singulas cupas deponi. Puer uero Celsus, qui a latere Iuliani nunquam fuerat

675 deiunctus, dans illi pacem ad preparatum supplicium properabat intrepidus. *Cumque mitterentur in cupas, supposita stuppa et accenso igne eructuabat flamma excelsior obolisco amplius cubitos triginta.* De medio igne, ita multitudo psallentium resonabat quasi uox aquarum multarum. *Consumptas autem cupas in igne subito, apparent sancti sicut aurum rutilantes, canebant,*

680 *'Transiuimus per ignem et aquam, et induxisti nos in refrigerium'.* Ignis uero ardens atque coruscans uim uirtutis suę oblitus ne sanctos Dei lederet Domino adiuuante.

(46) *Haec audiens preses* quia igne consumpto nullus de sanctis lesus est, *cum uxore* et familia *ad expectaculum properat* exitum rei cognoscere, et dixit

685 ad Iulianum, 'Obtestor te per deum tuum, unde tantam uirtutem maleficiorum nosti?'

Iulianus respondit, 'Quia per Deum meum me adiuratus es qui est I horum mirabilium auctor, referam qualiter possint discere, qui talia "maleficia" desiderant sicut ego, ut huius "carminis" sancti efficiantur auctores. Si quis

690 se lauerit ab omnibus actionibus sęculi et facit alienum, ut solam uocem Domini audiat, imperantis et dicentis, "Si quis uult post me uenire, abneget semetipsum". Nihil amori Christi preponat. Nihil aliud desideret nisi quod ipse Dominus promittit. Non consideret patrem, nec matrem, nec cetera, quę nouerunt intellegentes.* Ante omnia uero qui pauperum curam sollicite

695 agunt; qui contenti sunt esurire ut alii saturentur. Satis Deo acceptum est munus, quo indigens saturatur, quod ira non perficitur et malum pro malo non redditur, qui non dicitur sanctus antequam sit. Multi enim dicuntur quod non sunt, et multi sunt sancti et non de his dicitur quod sunt; sed humilitate et gratia ab omnibus [se] scire nolunt ut ab illo recipiant mercedem qui nouit

700 quod sunt.

'Hi tales a caritate quem ego noui discere possunt. Non solum in hoc corpore degentes hanc merentur gratiam, sed eternam cum Domino conlocant amicitiam. Qui primum edocti a Christo, aliis subministrant donum in se conlatum, se primum lucrantes, deinde proximis. Facientes quę dicant, qui

705 inlatam sibi iniuriam pro laude putant; qui iniurię tempus non reseruant; qui reconciliantes sed proximo obtinent quod est culmen omnium bonorum'.

---

674 latere] D latare
675 deiunctus] RD disiunctus (R is *over erased* e)
677 triginta] D .xxx.
677–78 multitudo psallentium] D *order reversed.* consumptas] RD consumptis (R i *over* a)
679 cupas] RD cupis. canebant] RD et canebant
681 oblitus] D oblitus est
684 expectaculum] RD spectaculum

(*preceding* ex *erased in* R). cognoscere] RD cognoscere uolens (R uolens *above line*)
687 Quia] R *underscored for deletion;* D *omits.* me adiuratus es] R me *erased;* D *omits.* Fol. 83ᵛᵇ
689 huius] D hius
696 munus] D quo munus
697 sit] D fiat
698 et multi sunt...quod sunt] R et multi non (*above line*) sunt sancti et de his dicitur

The aide fulfilled the duty imposed on him: he ordered each of the prisoners to be put in individual barrels. The boy Celsus, who had never been separated from Julian's side, gave him the kiss of peace and hurried bravely to the punishment that had been prepared. And when they were thrown into the barrels and when the flax had been placed under them and a flame kindled, the fire leapt up higher than an obelisk more than thirty cubits high. In the middle of the fire, the host of those singing resounded like the voice of many waters. And then after the barrels had been quickly consumed in the fire, the saints appeared glowing like gold and singing, 'We have passed through fire and water, and You have led us to cool relief' [Psalm 64.12]. The fiercely hot and flashing fire forgot the force of its power and did not injure the saints of God with the Lord protecting them.

(46) When the governor heard that none of the saints was harmed after the fire had consumed itself, he hurried to the spectacle with his wife and household to learn the final outcome, and he said to Julian, 'I implore you by your god, where have you learned such power of sorcery?'

Julian answered, 'Because on account of my God you have earnestly asked me who is the source of these miracles, I will tell you how those wishing for such "sorcery" as I have can learn about it, so that they may become workers of this holy "spell". If anyone washes himself of all the activity of the world and becomes a stranger in it, then he may hear the lone voice of the Lord who commands and says, "If anyone wishes to come after me, let him deny himself" [Luke 9.23]. He should place nothing before the love of Christ. He should long for nothing other than what the Lord himself promises. He should not consider his father, or mother, or the rest of those things the understanding are aware of.* In fact, before all things followers of Christ constantly care for the poor; they are content to go hungry so that others are fed. The gift truly acceptable to God is that by which the needy are fed, that anger is not acted upon and evil is not returned for evil, and that one not be called "holy" before he truly is this. In fact, many are called what they are not, and many are holy but are not said to be so; but with humility and grace they do not want to be known by everyone so that they may receive their gift from Him who knows that they are holy.

'Such people out of love can learn of Him whom I know. Not only do they earn this favour while living here in this earthly body, but they also acquire eternal friendship with the Lord. Having first been taught by Christ, they give the gift bestowed on them to others, profiting first themselves and then those around them. Making good their word, they consider harm inflicted on them as glory; they do not dwell on a moment of injury; and reconciling with those around them, they acquire the height of all good things'.

---

quod non sunt; D et multi non sunt sancti et multi sunt sancti et de his dicitur quod sunt
699 (se) scire] secire; RD se scire
701 quem] R quam
702–03 conlocant] RD collocant (R first l

over dotted n; D n *above line*)
705–06 *second* qui...obtinent] RD Qui reconciliantes (D reconcilientes) sed (D se) proximo et proximum sibi sic offerre Christi munera debent (R *above line*) qui humilitatem optinent

Prẹses dixit, 'Ut qui[s] ita insipiens est ut huius uitẹ letitiam fugiat ut ad tantam iniuriam semetipsum inclinet?'

Iulianus respondit, 'Dominus noster paratus est omnibus dare, sed pauci
710 dignos se exhibent dona eius accipere'.

Preses dixit, 'A te, Iuliane, meus sermo finem accipiet'. Iulianus respondit, 'Hoc ego semper optaui'.

(47) Tunc preses ad filium suum dixit, '*Ecce matrem tuam do tibi sicut postulasti*. Triduo cum ea habeas induciam. Hẹc enim tibi ad omnia parata
715 est; te ne unicum filium amittat'.

Celsus respondit, 'Isto triduo matre mihi concessa, nulli licebit interesse'.

Preses dixit, 'Sicut uis ita concedo. *Recludantur in custodia priuata*'.

Tunc sancti recluduntur custodia cum matre pueri. *Sancti uero hanc orationem fundunt ad Dominum*, 'Tu, Domine, | qui prescius es futurorum,
720 qui transacta uelud presentia conspicis, qui mentes probas non ẹtatem. Tu, Domine, aperi oculos cordis eius et acceptabilem fac terram ex qua suscepisti fructum in quo letari dinosceris'.

(48) *Et statim commotus est locus* in quo erant sancti orantes, et *fulgor* argent[o] septies splendidior *emicuit*. Nec *odor* defuit sanctis ut uox psallen-
725 tium in aere sona[bat]: 'Uere pius Deus, qui iustificat animas peccatrices pro quibus operibus'. *Hẹc uidens mulier clamabat, 'Numquam in diebus meis hunc tantum suauissimum odorem sensi!* Nam sicut liliorum et rosarum et croceos nectar balsami et nardi redundant. His tantis suauissimis odoribus ita sum refecta. Nec aliquid aliud in corde meo cognosco nisi ipsum Dominum
730 uerum fateor pro quo filius meus agonizatur'.

(49) Hẹc audiens beatus Iulianus dixit, 'Beata tu credentibus arbor [dinosceris], quẹ sic fructui meo medicinam celeriter consequeris.* Nam talis et medicus est qui tuam suscipit sanitatem ut non secando uulnera tua curet sed probando'.

735 Celsus puer subsecutus dixit, 'Ueram te matrem modo profiteor; ueram genitricem agnosco. Nec tu amittis filium, nec ego matrem, si una mecum ad illum contendas'.

Respondit mulier cuius intima pectoris diuina gratia iam inluxerat, 'Cognosce me, fili: iam nihil amori eius prẹpono quem tu sic diligis. Pro qua
740 re quicquid necessarium saluti meẹ agnoscis exerce'.

---

707 qui(s)] NR quid; D quis, s *above line*
   corrected from d
713 do tibi] RD *omit*
714 postulasti. Triduo] RD postulasti ad te
   uenire faciam ut triduo. cum ea habeas]
   D habeas cum ea. tibi] RD *omit*. omnia]
   RD omnia tibi. te ne] RD *order reversed*
716 respondit] D respondet. nulli] D nulli
   tuorum
717 in] R *omits*

719 Fol. 84ra
720 ẹtatem] D ẹtates
721 acceptabilem] D acceptalem
724 argenti] o *above* i.
725 sona(bat)] NRD sonabant. Uere] D
   Uerus
731 beatus] D *omits*
732 (dinosceris)] N dinossceris; RD
   dinosceris
733 tuam] D ẹtiam. secando] D sectando

The governor said, 'How is anyone so stupid that he would flee the joy of this life to incline himself to such harm?'

Julian answered, 'Our Lord is ready to give to all, but few show themselves worthy to receive his gifts'.

The governor said, 'My conversation with you, Julian, is over.'

Julian replied, 'I have always desired this.'

(47) The governor then said to his son, 'Look, I give you your mother just as you asked. You may have a delay of three days with her. She has in fact been prepared for you in all matters; let her not lose her only son'.

Celsus replied, 'For these three days granted to me with my mother, no one will be allowed to be present'.

The governor said, 'I allow it as you wish. Let them be shut them away in a private cell'.

Then the saints were locked in the prison with the boy's mother. And the holy ones poured out this prayer to the Lord, 'You, Lord, are prescient about the future, you see the past as well as the present, you value hearts not rank. Lord, open the eyes of her heart and make acceptable the ground from which you have received fruit in which you are known to rejoice'.

(48) And immediately the place where the saints were praying shook, and a flash seven times brighter than silver burst forth. Nor did the saints lack a fragrance while singing voices resounded in the air: 'You are truly faithful, O God, justifying sinful souls through such deeds.' When the woman experienced these things, she cried out, 'Never in my life have I smelled so utterly pleasing a fragrance! For it is as if the nectar of lilies and roses and crocuses and balsam and spikenard pours forth. I have been renewed by these most pleasant fragrances. I will not acknowledge anything else in my heart when I confess the true Lord himself for whose sake my son struggles'.

(49) Hearing this, blessed Julian said, 'You are recognized by those who believe to be a blessed tree, you who so quickly obtains a cure from my spiritual fruit'.* For He who cures you is so great a physician that he heals your wounds not by making an incision but by examining you'.

Having followed immediately the boy Celsus said, 'I now declare you to be a true mother; I acknowledge you as my true mother. You will not lose a son nor I a mother if you hasten as one with me to Him'.

The woman into the depths of whose heart divine grace had shone replied, 'Look at me, son: already I place nothing before His love whom you love so. For this reason, do whatever you think is necessary for my salvation'.

Respondit puer, 'Corde creditur ad iustitiam, et quia ore confessio fit ad salutem, hoc deest, ut purificationem baptismi accipias, per quod possis esse habitaculum Spiritus Sancti'.

Respondit mulier, 'Ecce, nos omnes claustra obtinent et militum custodie
745   circumuallant. Nec introitus nec exitus permittitur. Quomodo inueniemus hunc talem hominem qualem mihi proponis?'

Iulianus respondit, 'Hic habemus sanctum et uerum Christi sacerdotem qui te purificet. Tantum est ut tu abneges deos patrię tuę et unum credas qui regnat in cęlis, qui est unus in trinitate et trinus in unitate. Sub cuius imperio
750   I imperant principes, cuius gratia confirmantur duces, cuius tremore contremiscunt gentes, cuius imperio operiuntur cęli nubibus et dant terre pluuiam. Ipsius splendore inluminantur ceci, tenebre incredulitatis fugantur'.

Mulier respondit, 'Qui hęc non ita credit ferreum possidet pectus; nec humanum sensum gerit sed pecudum'.

755   Tunc sancti gratias referebant Domino, qui dignatus est de luporum faucibus ouem perditam liberare.

Cui iterum Iulianus dixit, 'Ita credis ut audisti'.

Respondit mulier, 'Ipsum uiuum Deum credo, quem per tuam predicationem cognoui. Qui certis limitibus fixit mare, qui cęlum suspendit, ipse est
760   Dominus Ihesus Christus, quem relicta uanitate credo, cupiens hac uita temporali carere ut ad illam eternam uitam merear uobiscum attingere'.

(50) Cumque hęc dixisset mulier, locus in quo erant contremuit, et audita est uox in aeræ dicens, 'Credidi propter quod locutus sum'. Responderunt omnes sancti, 'Amen'.

765   *Tunc beatusAntonius presbiter baptizauit eam*quam uenerabilis Celsus filius suscepit, et pater eius in baptismi gratia factus est, prestante Domino nostro Ihesu Christo. Cumque baptizata fuisset et omnes de salute eius gauderent, uox de cęlo audita est dicens, 'Uiriliter agite et confortetur cor uestrum in Domino'. Hęc audiens sanctus Iulianus dixit, 'Uox quę intonuit auribus
770   nostris pronuntiat nobis futuram passionem et diuersa genera tormentorum quę aduersus nos cogitat inimicus. Pro qua re fidei nostre cursum Domino commendemus qui potens est fidem nostram seruare ut cursu consummato repositam coronam recipiamus'.

(51) *Cumque hoc factum cognouisset* impius *Marcianus* uxorem suam
775   martyribus sociatam, *iubet illos intra domum exhiberi, et dixit ad Celsum,* '*Matrem tuam sub hac ratione postulasti ut tibi consentiret?* Quid gestum sit agnoscere cupio'.

---

745 inueniemus] D inuenimus
750 Fol. 84ʳᵇ
750–51 contremiscunt] R contremescunt
753 hęc] D hęc monita. ita] D *omits*
757 iterum Iulianus] D *order reversed*
758 quem] RD quam

760 uanitate] D unitate
761 carere] D carcere
769 audiens] *MS is damaged*
770 tormentorum] *MS is damaged*
771 cogitat] D excogitat. inimicus] *MS is damaged*

The boy answered, 'Confession with the heart is credited as righteousness and because confession with the mouth brings one to salvation, you need only to receive the purification of baptism, through which you can become a dwelling-place of the Holy Spirit' [cf. Romans 10.10].

The woman replied, 'Look, bolts confine and watches of soldiers surround us all. Neither entry nor exit is permitted. How will we find the sort of man you mention to me?'

Julian answered, 'We have here a holy and true priest of Christ who can purify you. It is very important that you deny the gods of your native land and believe in the one God who reigns in heaven, who is one in three and three in one. Under his rule emperors hold sway, with his favour leaders are established, under his dread nations tremble, by his authority the skies are overspread with clouds and bring forth rain for the earth. His splendour gives sight to the blind and puts shadows of unbelief to flight'.

The woman replied, 'Anyone who does not believe these things has a heart of iron; he reasons like animals not men'.

Then the saints gave thanks to the Lord who deigned to free the lost sheep from the wolves' jaws.

Julian spoke to her once more, 'Do you believe what you have heard?'

The woman answered, 'I believe in the living God himself, whom I have known through your affirmation. He who has set the sea within fixed boundaries and who hung the sky, he is himself the Lord Jesus Christ in whom I, having forsaken foolishness, believe, and I hope to be deprived of this temporal life so that I might deserve to attain that everlasting life with you all'.

(50) And when the woman had said this, the place they were in shook, and a voice was heard in the air saying, 'I have believed, so I have spoken' [Psalm 115.10 and 2 Corinthians 4:13]. All the saints replied, 'Amen'.

Then blessed Antonius the priest baptized her whom the venerable Celsus, her son, received into the family (of Christ), and in the grace of baptism he became her father with our Lord Jesus Christ seeing to it. And when she had been baptized and all were rejoicing in her salvation, a voice from heaven was heard saying, 'Act manfully and may your hearts be comforted in the Lord'. Hearing this, Saint Julian said, 'The voice that has thundered in our ears announces our impending martyrdom and the various torments the enemy plans against us. For this reason, let us entrust the course of our faith to the Lord who is powerful to preserve our faith so that when we complete the course, we may receive the crown set aside for us' [cf. 2 Timothy 4.7].

(51) When the wicked Martianus learned that his wife had joined the martyrs, he orders them to be presented inside his house, and he said to Celsus, 'Did you ask for your mother under this pretense so that she might assent to you? I want to know what happened'.

---

776 Quid] D et quid *and no interrogative*
   mark after preceding consentiret

Puer respondit, 'Gratias ago Domino qui uoluntatis meę fructum | ita compleuit ut in eternum possideam matrem et illa me filium a modo cognoscat.
780 Nos pro amore Christi in hac uita spem non proponimus. Pro qua re nec ego te agnosco patrem, nec illa maritum'.

Tunc preses ira repletus iussit comprehendi mulierem. Ad qu[a]m cum adpropiassent ministri, facti sunt cęci. Audiens autem hęc Marcianus iussit eos in ima carceris recludi.

785 (52) Alia uero die sedens pro tribunali, *iussit* uiginti *milites* adduci et tradidit *decollandos. Septem uero fratres igni tradi precepit.* Quod cum factum fuisset, martyrium consummauerunt in pace, cum gaudio et exultatione pergentes ad Christum. *Sanctum uero Iulianum cum Antonio presbitero, et matrem cum filio et puerum quem infernus reddiderat, suo iudicio reseruauit.*

790 (53) Et sedens pro tribunali in foro, iussit eos adduci et conuersus preses ad Iulianum dixit, 'Tecum, Iuliane, sermonem penitus non habeo'. Et iterum dixit ad Antonium, 'Tu es Antonius quem isti papam suum esse testantur? Constat te huius magice artis esse auctorem'.

Beatus Antonius dixit, 'Gratias ago Domino meo Ihesu Christo qui huius
795 gratię suę me fecit esse ministrum'.

Preses dixit, 'Uel tu, mihi dic que sit magica uestra ut sic coniugia separetis, et filios ac parentes deiungatis, bona ipsa uita abnegare et horrere persuadetis; dii inmortales per uos blasphemantur. Quę est audacia uestra qui tantum preualuistis ad decipiendum populum ut et gloriemini uos
800 mortuum suscitasse et innocentum pectora inretitis?'

---

778 uoluntatis] ND s *above line*; R uoluntati.
 Fol. 84ᵛᵃ
781 te] D *omits*
782 iussit] D iussit corpus. mulierem] D
 mulieris. qu(a)m] quem; RD quam.
783 adpropiassent] D adpropinquassent.
 autem] RD *omit*
785 uiginti] D .xx.
786 septem] D .vii.

793 Constat] RD Nam (R *above line*) constat
796 magica] RD ars magica (R ars *and* c
 above line). ut] D qua, a *corrected from*
797 et] D ut. ac parentes] c *above line*; RD a
 parentibus. deiungatis] RD disiungatis.
 ipsa] RD ipsam. uita] RD uitam
799 gloriemini] D glorie ymni
800 inretitis] R inretitis; D inretietis

The boy replied, 'I thank the Lord who brought my desire to fruition so that I may have my mother in eternity and so that she henceforth may know me as her son. On account of a love for Christ, we express no hope in this life. For this reason, I do not acknowledge you as my father, nor does she acknowledge you as her husband'.

Then, filled with anger, the governor ordered the woman to be seized. When the servants rushed to her, they were blinded. And when Martianus heard about this, he ordered them to be shut away in the depths of the prison.

(52) Now another day when the governor was presiding from his judgment seat, he ordered the twenty soldiers to be led out and handed over to be beheaded. He ordered the seven brothers to be handed over to be burned in the fire. When these things had been done, they accomplished martyrdom in peace, making their way to Christ with joy and exultation. The governor reserved for his own judgement Saint Julian with Antonius the priest, the mother with her son and the young man whom hell had given back.

(53) And while the governor was presiding from the judgment seat in the city centre, he ordered them to be brought out and turning towards Julian said, 'I will not exchange one word with you, Julian'. And then he said to Antonius, 'Are you the Antonius whom these call their father? It is plain that you are a source of this sorcery'.

Blessed Antonius said, 'I thank my Lord Jesus Christ whose grace has made me his minister'.

The governor said, 'If you will, tell me about this sorcery of yours that divides husbands and wives, severs sons and parents, and persuades people to deny and loathe this good life; even the immortal gods are blasphemed on your account. What is this audacity of yours by which you have been so successful in deceiving people that you boast you have raised the dead and that you have ensnared the hearts of the innocent?'

Antonius presbiter respondit, 'Optaueram quidem ut ducem huius agonis nostri Iulianum tibi prouocares et ab eo acciperes responsum, sed quia unus est Dominus Ihesus Christus qui tangit organa cordis nostri percunctatus es quę uoluisti. Audi nunc et a me quę inquiris: magister et auctor "magicę",
805 quam a nobis dicis exercere, hoc nobis dedit preceptum: | ne margarite pretiose a nobis ante porcos mittantur. Qui non uenit mittere pacem sed gladium, uenit autem separare filios a parentibus. Et alio loco, "qui plus fecerit matrem aut patrem aut uxorem aut filios uel diuitias quam me non potest esse meus discipulus". Hanc uocem audiens filius tuus non fecit te plus
810 carnalem genitorem quam Christum Creatorem. Similiter et quam dicis tuam uxorem, hac uoce conperta contempsit te mortalem et horum temporalem ut per Christum inmortalem aeternam requiem consequatur. Ecce, nihil tam uerius [cognoscere] poteris'.

Haec audiens preses iussit eos recludi, (54) *et conuocans ad se sacerdotes*
815 *et dixit ad eos*, '*Ornate uenerandum locum* Iouis — cuius est consuetudo semel in anno patefieri — ubi ueneranda nomina dinoscuntur Iouis, Iunonis, Ueneris et Minerue, ex uitro puro constructas imagines, quibus Cupido delectamenta ministrat et incensa preparat'. Hęc audientes consuetas preparant hostias, et patefacto templo uniuersa multitudo conuenit ad mirac-
820 ulum. Tal[is] enim erat fabric[a] ut non marmoreis tabulis sed argenteis parietes et pauimentum stratum splendere, auro purissimo uel margaritis et lapidibus pretiosis crispantes.

(55) Ingressus Marcianus templum *iussit sanctos Dei adduci*, quibus dixit, 'Ecce nunc, Iuliane, et tu, Antoni, tempus aduenit ut et uos et socii uestri
825 salutem consequamini. Hoc enim eligite pro uestra salute ut in isto templo deorum tam terribili inmortalibus numinibus tura incendatis. Quod si adhuc in ipsa contumacia perseueratis, abnegantes deos, diuersis tormentis uos affi- ciam. Pro qua re Iuliane quia te constat esse auctorem huius sceleris, accede, repropitia tibi deos inmortales'.

---

801 ducem] D duce
802 nostri] D uestri
804 magicę] c *above line*; RD magicæ artis
(R c *and* artis *above line*)
805 exercere] RD exerceri. hoc] ND o *over dotted* un; R hunc. Fol. 84ᵛᵇ. margarite] e *above dotted* as; RD margaritas
806 pretiose] e *above dotted* as; RD pretiosas
807 plus] R *struck through*
808 fecerit] RD diligit. matrem aut patrem] D *order reversed.* quam] R plus quam
809 esse meus] D *order reversed*
811 uoce] R uocem, m *partially erased*

813 (cognoscere)] cognoscerit; RD cognoscere
815 et] R *omits*
818 delectamenta] R dilecta libidinis
820 Tal(is)] Talem; RD Talis. fabric(a)] fabrice; RD fabrica
821 splendere] D splendore. margaritis] *second* i *over undotted or faintly dotted* a; R i *over dotted* a
826 numinibus] R nominibus
828–29 accede, repropitia] RD accede et propitia

The priest Antonius answered, 'I had really hoped you would call out for yourself Julian, the leader of our struggle, and that you would receive an answer from him, but because there is one Lord Jesus Christ who touches our hearts, you have asked what you have wanted. Now, hear from me what you desire to know: the master and source of the "magic" you say we practise gave us this teaching: we should not cast precious pearls before swine [cf. Matthew 7.6]. He did not come to bring peace but the sword, and he came to divide sons from parents [cf. Matt. 10.34–35]. And in another place (he said), "Anyone who values mother or father or wife or sons or riches more than me cannot be my disciple" [cf. Luke 14.26]. When your son heard this teaching, he did not value you, a fleshly parent, more than Christ his Creator. Likewise, just as you say, when your wife learned this teaching, she despised you, a mortal man, and temporal marriage so that through the immortal Christ she might acquire eternal rest. Look, you cannot know anything truer'.

Hearing this, the governor ordered them to be locked away (54) and summoning the priests to himself, he said to them, 'Prepare the venerable temple of Jupiter — which is customarily opened once a year — where the venerable names of Jupiter, Juno, Venus, and Minerva are seen and where their statues are constructed from pure glass, for which Cupid serves up amusements and prepares sacrifices'. When the priests heard this, they prepared the customary sacrifices, and a whole multitude assembled for the amazing event in the opened temple. It was so great a work of art that its walls and paved floors shone not with marble but silver panels and swirled with the purest gold and even pearls and precious gems.

(55) When Martianus entered the temple, he ordered the saints of God to be led in and said to them, 'Now look, Julian, and you, Antonius, the time has come for you and your companions to attend to your well-being. In the interests of your safety, choose to burn incense to the immortal gods in this awesome temple. But if you still persist in this obstinacy and reject the gods, I will visit you with various torments. Because you, Julian, are known to be the cause of this villainy, approach, win over the immortal gods again to you'.

830   Iulianus respondit, 'Tu iam nomen haberis, sed, quia uideo tempus ut et
nos salutem consequamur et numina a nobis honorentur, fac omnes deorum
sacerdotes intus adesse ut cognoscant quale sacrificium illis offerimus'. Et
iterum dixit, 'Bene ualeas obtime preses! | Qui tale tempus nobis laudem et
gloriam accepturi persuades, et omnibus in uno commanentibus diis uestris
835   precipias immolare, quod nos facere non pigeat. Nam ideo distulimus ut in
isto templo mirabili quod habetis magnum sacrificemus'.

        (56) Tunc preses quo ordine diceretur non intellegens dixit illis, 'Gaudeo
quod, et si tarde, respuistis uanitatem diis immolantes'. Tunc iussit omnium
sanctorum uincula auferri dicens, 'Turpe est uinculis teneri quia dii ceperunt
840   esse propitii'. Cumque exonerati fuissent uinculis, dixit ad Celsum et matrem
eius, 'Accedite et repropitiate uobis deos'.

        Respondit mulier, 'Non mihi faciat Deus uerus quem cognoui ut ultra
tecum conloquium habeam. Hęc autem quę dicis per ignorantiam feci'.

        Preses dixit, 'Est hora si uultis'.

845   Sanctus Iulianus dixit, 'Adpropiemus ut salutem consequamur, et sit in
notitia seculi superuenturi que facturi sumus hodie'.

        Ingressi autem in templo, uexillo crucis armata fronte et ait Iulianus,
'Quid precipis? Omnibus diis offerimus sacrificium?'

        Preses dixit, 'Omnes quos uidetis inmortales sunt et presentes sunt in
850   uirtute, et non inuident sibi in cultoribus suis'.

---

830 nomen haberis] R nominaberis *with space between* n *and* a, *which are connected by underscoring*
831 numina] R nomina
833 Fol. 85ra
834 accepturi] D accepturis, s *above line*
836 magnum] R agnum, *faint initial* m
837 illis] D *omits*
839 quia] RD quibus
841 repropitiate] D propitiate

842 Non] RD Nam (R Non *corrected to* Nam)
843 habeam] RD non habeam
846 superuenturi] D semper uenturi
847 Ingressi] RD Ingressi sunt (R *barred* s *inserted after* Ingressi). templo] RD templum (R barred u *above dotted* o). uexillo] D o *corrected from* a. armata] a *above undotted* o; RD armato
848 offerimus sacrificium] D *order reversed*

Julian replied, 'At present you are judged to be a man of renown, but, because I see that it is time we attend to our well-being and honour the gods, see to it that all their priests are here inside so that they may see what sort of sacrifice we offer to the gods'. And then he said, 'I wish you well, most excellent governor! You persuade us at this moment to receive praise and glory, and you may instruct all those who remain together how to sacrifice to your gods, which we are pleased to do. We have delayed thus far so that we may offer a great sacrifice in this wondrous temple you have'.

(56) Now the governor did not understand what Julian intended by this plan and said to them, 'I am happy that, even if slowly, you have rejected stupidity by sacrificing to the gods'. Then he ordered the chains removed from all the saints and said, 'It is shameful to be held in chains since the gods have begun to be appeased'. And when they had been freed from the chains, he said to Celsus and his mother, 'Draw near and win the gods over again to you'.

The woman replied, 'May true God whom I have acknowledged see to it that I do not speak to you any more. However, those sacrifices you mention I offered in ignorance'.

The governor said, 'It is time if you so choose'.

Saint Julian said, 'Let us approach so that we may attain our salvation, and let what we are about to do today be done in the knowledge of the world to come'.

And when they had entered the temple, Julian, his forehead armed with the sign of the cross, also said, 'What do you command? Are we to sacrifice to all the gods?'

The governor said, 'All those you see are immortal and mighty in power and will not refuse themselves to their worshippers'.

(57) *Tunc sanctus Iulianus* et Antonius presbiter *fixis genibus talem fundunt orationem ad Dominum,* 'Deus, qui es ab initio sine fine, sine tempore quia eternum possides nomen. Qui non in manufactis hominum delectaris; requiescis in corde mundo. Qui per prophetam dixisti, "Omnes dii gentium demonia", Deus autem tu solus. Deus Abraham, Isaac et Iacob, qui in sapientia tua fecisti celos, fundasti terram, congregasti aquam, mari terminum posuisti qu[e]m non transgreditur. Quem murmura undarum sua uoce conlaudant, quem diuersarum uolatilium garrulę suaui uoce laudantes. Qui in Christi arbitrio creasti uniuersa, aspice nunc in subuersione profani huius et ad tantas demonum tegas, et tantorum iniustorum cultoribus frange audaciam *et ad nihilum redigantur hęc omnia in quibus gloriantur ut te solum agnoscant.* Et glorientur in te, qui credunt nomini tuo et Ihesu Christo I filio tuo, quem cognoscimus tibi coaequalem et coeternum in unitate Spiritus Sancti et in secula seculorum'.

Cumque dixissent omnes Christiani 'Amen', statim *templum submersum est* et qui adfuerat non pareret, et *multitudo sacerdotum —* circiter mille — *cum templo dimersi sunt et maxima pars paganorum s[i]mul interiit.* Ignis uero eructuans usque in hodiernum diem.

Tunc beatus Iulianus dixit ad presidem, '*Ubi sunt manufacte imagines* demonum *in quibus gloriabaris? Ubi templi pulchritudo?* Inuocato nomine Christi, hec omnia in terra dimersa sunt. *Sicut illa uterus terre recepit, ita et uos* et imperatores uestros *et omnes cultores demonum perpetuum accipiet infernus, ubi ignis ęternus et uermis non moritur, ubi corpus ad poenam semper renouatur, ubi misericordia queritur et non inuenitur.* Uos et auctorem uestrum diabolum hic talis locus expectat'.

Preses dixit, '*O uirtus et carmina magię, sic preualere ut etiam terre sinus aperiat et tanta bona auferat! Iam non miserebor; iam non parcam; antequam gladio pereant, de eorum poena me satiabo'.*

Line numbers: 855, 860, 865, 870, 875

853 manufactis] R fabritaculunt (?)
854 requiescis] D quiescis
857 *first* qu(e)m] quę, ę *barred*; RD quem.
   murmura] R murmuritus, final u *above
   dotted* i; D murmuricius
858 garrulę] D gargulę
859 subuersione] RD subuersionem. profani]
   R pro *is faint*
860 tegas] RD togas (R o *above dotted* e).
   iniustorum] RD istorum
862 Fol. 85ʳᵇ
864 et] RD et nunc et (R nunc et *above line*)

866 qui adfuerat] R qui afuerat, d *after initial
   a erased;* D qui affuerat
867 dimersi] R demersi, first e *corrected
   from* i. s(i)mul] smul; RD simul
868 eructuans] RD eructuans apparet
871 dimersa] R demersa, *first* e *corrected
   from* i. illa] R illud templum; D illum
872 perpetuum] R in perpetuum; D imper-
   petutum
873 moritur] R morietur
876 magię] RD magicæ artis (R c *and* artis
   above line)

(57) Then Saint Julian and Antonius the priest knelt and poured out a pious prayer to the Lord: 'God, you exist from the beginning without end and without time because you have an eternal name. You do not delight in the works of men; you take comfort in a pure heart. You have said through the prophet David, "All the gods of the nations are demons" [Psalm 95.5 (Septuagint)], and you alone are God. You are the God of Abraham, Isaac and Jacob, who in your wisdom made the heavens, laid the foundations of the earth, collected the waters and set a limit for the sea which it does not cross. The waves' roars extol you with their voices, while various chirping birds praise you with their sweet song. You who have created everything by the will of Christ, see now to the destruction of this wickedness and these coverings of demons, and destroy the audacity of so many unrighteous worshippers and let all that they glory in be reduced to nothing so that they may acknowledge you alone. And let those who believe in your name and in Jesus Christ your Son, whom we acknowledge to be coequal and coeternal with you in the unity of the Holy Spirit for ever, glory in you'.

And when all the Christians said 'Amen', the temple instantly sank and was no longer visible, and a host of priests — about 1000 — sank with the temple and a large majority of the pagans were killed at the same time. Fire erupts there even to this day.

Then blessed Julian said to the governor, 'Where are the manmade images of demons you gloried in? Where is the beauty of the temple? When I invoked the name of Christ, all these sank into the earth. Just as the belly of the earth swallowed them up, so will hell hold you and your emperors and all the worshippers of demons for all time, where the fire and maggot do not die, where the body is always renewed for punishment, where mercy is sought and not found. Such a place awaits you and your master, the devil'.

The governor said, 'O, to think that his power and magic spell are so strong that even the belly of the earth opens up and carries off so many good things! I will not take pity on them; nor will I spare them; before they die by the sword, I will sate myself with their punishment'.

Iubet impius sanctos Dei in carcere cludi, (58) et cum in laudibus
880 epulentur, ipso medio noctis silentio aduenit multitudo sanctorum cum sacer-
dotibus qui iam martyrii palmam triumphant, omnes stolis albis induti. Inter
quos uiginti milites et septem germani fratres et beata Basilissa cum choro
uirginum. In qua multitudine sola uox 'Alleluia' declarabatur. Tunc sancta
Basilissa alloquitur ad sanctum Iulianum. Dixit, 'Regna cęlorum patefact[a]
885 sunt, et hoc preceptum accepimus a Rege aeterno: ut hodie te cum sociis tuis
recipiat cum patriarcharum et apostolorum gloriosus chorus in numero sanc-
torum cum perpetua letitia conlocabit'. Et tertio 'Alleluia', et uisio ab oculis
eorum ablata est.

(59) Alia die sedit in foro et excogitat nequissimus serpens noua et infinita
890 genera tormentorum. | *Iubet ut eis digitos [de manibus et pedibus] licinio et
oleo infuso ligari, et igne subponi precepit. Cumque factum fuisset, licini[is]
consumptis, inmaculata permanebat sanctorum caro.* Tunc impius Marcianus
iussit sancto Iuliano et Celso filio suo cutem capitis auferri, Antonio uero
presbitero et Anastasio, quem infernus reddiderat, oculos effodiri. Sanctam
895 autem matrem Celsi, quam Deus sciebat tolerare non posse, cum iuberetur
aculeo applicari; si quis uoluisset de ministris ad eam attingere manus,
*[cæcus] efficiebatur. Sanctos autem suos Dominus ita inluminauit et curauit
ut omnibus apparerent quasi nihil passi fuissent.*

(60) *Tunc uidit se uinci Marcianus* fecit amphiteatrum preparari et *iubet*
900 *sanctos intromitti et dimitti multitudinem ferarum. Quę nullum ex eis ledentes,
sed singule currentes pedes sanctorum lingebant.* (61) Haec uidens *Marcianus*
conuocans magistratus ciuitatis et *iubet* omnes custodia[s] perscrutari et
personas iam morte dignas in amphiteatro indu[c]i et *sanctos* Dei inter sacri-
legas personas *decollari.* Tunc sanctus Iulianus dixit, 'Gloria tibi, Christe, qui
905 nos usque in hac hora salutis perduxisti'. Et uenerabilis puer cum sancta
matre sua ad presidem dixit, 'Nota tibi facies nostras quas in hoc seculo per
gratiam Christi si uides inmutat[as]. Perpetua enim perfidia tua fuit, ita te
nobis conaberis inponere. Gratia uero et pietas Christi inbuit nos magnam
gloriam cum decore ut illa die cognoscas nos in gloria cum tu fueris in
910 infernum'. Tunc Marcianus iussit eos inter noxios commisci et intromisso
spiculatore iussit eos decollari.

---

879 cludi] D recludi
880 epulentur] RD epularentur (R ar *above
line*)
881 martyrii palmam] D *order reversed.*
stolis albis] R stolis abbis
882 uiginti] D .xx.^{ti}. septem] D .vii.^{tem}
884 ad] R *very faint.* Dixit] RD et dixit (R et
above line). patefact(a)] patefacte; R
patefacta; D patęfacte
885 accepimus] D *omits*
886 patriarcharum et apostolorum] D *order
reversed.* gloriosus] D gloriosis

887 conlocabit] R *first* l *of* collocabit *above
dotted.* tertio] RD tertio canebant (R
both words above *line*)
889 infinita] RD inaudita (R audita *written
above* finita)
890 Fol. 85va. (de manibus et pedibus)] de
manus et pedes; RD manuum et pedum
891 ligari] RD ligarent (R e *corrected from* i
and nt *inserted between* e *and* et).
licini(is)] N licini; RD licinis
895 tolerare] D pnas tolerare
896 aculeo] D ęculeo. manus] D *omits.*

The wicked one orders God's saints to be shut away in prison, (58) and as they were feasting on praises, there came in the dead of night a multitude of saints and priests who now triumph with the palm of martyrdom, all arrayed in white robes. Among them were the twenty soldiers and the seven full brothers and blessed Basilissa with a company of virgins. Among the multitude the single word 'Alleluia' was being proclaimed. Then Saint Basilissa speaks to Saint Julian. She said, 'The realms of heaven have been opened, and we have received this proclamation from the eternal King: today he will receive you and your companions when a glorious band of patriarchs and apostles will place you in the company of the saints with everlasting joy'. And with a third 'Alleluia', the vision faded from their sight.

(59) Another day the utterly depraved serpent sat judging in the city centre and contrived new and infinite kinds of torments. He orders their fingers and toes wrapped in lint and soaked in oil, and commanded that they be subjected to fire. And when that was done, once the lint had been consumed, the saints' skin remained unblemished. The wicked Martianus then ordered Saint Julian and Celsus his son to be scalped, and the eyes of Antonius the priest and Anastasius, whom hell gave back, to be gouged out. Then the holy mother of Celsus, whom God knew could not endure, was ordered to be put on the rack; if any attendant tried to grab her, he was struck blind. But the Lord made his saints illustrious and watched over them so that they appeared to everyone to have suffered nothing.

(60) When Martianus saw himself defeated, he had the amphitheatre made ready and orders the saints to be led in and a multitude of wild animals to be released. The animals did not hurt any of the saints, but as each ran around it licked the saints' feet. (61) Seeing this, Martianus assembles the city's magistrates and orders all the prisons to be searched high and low, the people who deserved death to be led into the amphitheatre and the saints of God to be beheaded among the sacrilegious. Then Saint Julian said, 'Glory be to you, O Christ, who has led us all the way to this hour of salvation'. And the venerable boy and his holy mother said to the governor, 'Look for yourself at our appearances if you think them unchanged in this world by the grace of Christ. Your treachery has been unceasing, so you will try to deceive us. But Christ's grace and goodness has imbued us with great glory and beauty so that you will recognize us in glory on that day when you are in hell'. Martianus then ordered them to be mingled among the guilty and ordered them to be beheaded by the executioner who had been sent in.

---

897 (cæcus)] C *omits*; RD cæcus
899 uidit] R uidens
902 magistratus] D magistrates. custodia(s)]
    NR custodia; D custodias
903 amphiteatro] D amphiteatrum. indu(c)i]
    induti; RD induci
905 hac] DR hanc (R n *above line*)

907 si] D sic. inmutat(as)] N inmutatos; RD
    inmutatas
908 conaberis] R conabaris. Gratia] D
    gratias. inbuit] RD induit. nos] D nobis
909 illa] RD in illa
909–10 in infernum] R in inferno, o *corrected
    from* u *and* m *dotted for deletion*

(62) *Cumque factum fuisset, factus est terre motus* ut prope tertia pars ciui-
tatis a fundamento subuerteretur. *Nec qualiscumque locus permissus est stare
ubi idolum colebatur. Fulgura et tonitrua et grando* intolerabilis *extiterunt, qui*
915   *maximam partem incredulorum consumpsit. Ipse autem impiissimus semi-
uiuus euasit; qui non post multos dies | uermibus ebulliens exspirauit.*

(63) Eadem nocte *uenerunt populi Christiani et sacerdotes* ut corpora sanc-
torum colligerent, et pre [multitudine] cadauerum, sanctorum corpora non
cognoscebantur. Positis genibus oratione completa, apparuerunt in specię
920   uirginum anime sanctorum, et unaqueque eorum super corpora ueneranda
resedit. Sancte reliquie collecte sunt, Domino adiuuante ita ut sanguis eorum
quasi lacteus panis circa suum aperire ad sanguinem recipiendum. *Sepulti
sunt autem in ecclesia* sub sacro altare ex quo loco Dominus fontem indefi-
cientem prodere precepit, ex quo sanctum baptisterium inundetur. Passi sunt
925   autem Idus Ianuarias regnante Domino Ihesu Christo, qui est gloriosus in
secula seculorum.* Amen. EXPLICIT PASSIO SANCTORUM IULIANI
ET BASILISSE.

---

912 Cumque] R que *above line*. ut] D et
914 Fulgura] R fulgora
915 incredulorum] RD incredulam
916 Fol. 85vb
918 (multidudine)] C multitudinem; RD
    multitudine
920 eorum] R earum
921 Sancte] D Sanct uero
922 lacteus] R lactantis, *second* a *corrected*

from e. circa suum] RD circa unum quem
    (D quemque) eorum colligeretur ut nec
    terra auderet os suum
923–24 indeficientem] D indesinantem.
    sanctum] D *omits*. inundetur] D inun-
    daretur, a *corrected from* e
925 Idus Ianuarias] D .v. Idus Ianuarii.
    Domino] D domino nostro
926–27 EXPLICIT...BASILISSE] RD *omit*

(62) When that had been done, an earthquake occurred and nearly a third of the city was toppled from its foundations. No place whatsoever where idols were worshipped was allowed to remain standing. There was lightning and thunder and insufferable hail, which destroyed the great majority of unbelievers. But the utterly impious one himself escaped more dead than alive; he died a few days later boiling with maggots.

(63) On the same night, the Christian community and their priests came to gather the bodies of the holy ones, and on account of the piles of corpses, the saints' bodies were unrecognisable. When the Christians had said a prayer on bended knees, the saints' souls appeared in the likenesses of virgins, and each of the souls sat above its venerable body. The holy remains were collected, with God helping in such a way that the saints' blood appeared to those recovering it like milk-white bread around the corpses. Moreover, the saints were buried beneath the sacred altar in the church where the Lord commanded an ever-flowing spring to bubble up, from which a sacred baptistry is filled. They suffered on the thirteenth day of January with the Lord Jesus Christ reigning, he who is glorious for ever.* Amen. HERE ENDS THE PASSIO OF SAINTS JULIAN AND BASILISSA.

172 Latin Texts and Translations

INCIPIT PASSIO SANCTE CECILIE UIRGINIS
DECIMO KALENDAS DECEMBRIS.

(1) HUMANAS laudes et mortalium infulas uidemus aut ere inciso conscriptas aut auro radiantibus litteris ad posteritatis memoriam commendatas. Et ista attendentes, miror quare non erubescimus militum Christi uictorias silentio tegere, et non ad laudem imperatoris eorum qualiter
5 pugnauerint contra hostes et uicerint — [sc]edulis saltem uilibus — tradere et ad incitandos animos bellatorum diligentius explicare.

Multa dona talium narrationum scripta conuectant. Laus Dei est cum ista leguntur, memoria sanctorum excolitur, edificatio mentibus traditur, honor martyribus exhibetur. Hinc infidelibus nascitur meror, incredulis liuor, indis-
10 ciplinatis angustia, et sanctis omnibus cum Christo gaudentibus leticia.

Solus diabolus ingemiscit qui uidet pugnam suam eo usque armis celestibus debellatam ut ex ipsa pugna ille melius uictor existeret qui putatus est uictus. Denique putabat se tunc hostis sanctos Dei occidendo uincere, illi autem melius occisi uincebant. Interrogati ilico confitebantur; damnati
15 gratias referebant. Sic denique legimus antiquas Domini uictorias celebratas, quando dixit inimicus, 'Persequens comprehendam, partibor spolia, replebo animam meam, interficiam gladio meo; dominabitur manus mea'. Sed extendit Deus dexteram suam, et deuorauit eos terra et populum uero suum sanguinis sui pretio liberauit.

20 (2) Denique iacet nunc sub sanctorum pedibus captiuus inimicus, et dans mugitum per lunaticos et inlerguminos clamat, et penas incendii quas patitur indicat, atque se flammarum attrocitate aduri commemorans, approbat quod omnes sancti quos pro Christi nomine persecutus est regnant. In tantum denique non sunt mortui, ut morituris uitam donent, tristibus gaudium
25 exhibeant, languentibus prebeant medicinam atque, ipsum humani generis inimicum ex obsessis corporibus propellentes, in ipsum reuocant tormenta que passi sunt. Et illi, quidem momentaneum perpessi dolorem, eternam gloriam tenent; illum uero nunquam finiendis ardentem incendiis uident perpetue ignominie mancipatum.

Title] *in small capitals. Text begins on folio*
73ᵛᵃ. V *reads in small capitals* INCIPIT
MARTIRIUM SANCTAE
CAECILIAE UIRGINIS QUOD EST
DECIMO KALENDS DECEMBRIS; C
reads in small capitals INCIPIT PASSIO
SANCTE CECILIĘ QUOD EST X
KALENDS DECEMBRIS.
1 HUMANAS] *in small capitals with a large*
decorated H six lines tall. V Humanas,
with an H four lines tall. C HUMANAS
LAUDES ET MORTALIUM *in small*
capitals spanning the column with a

simply decorated H five lines tall.
mortalium] V mortales. uidemus] VC
uidimus
5 (sc)edulis] edulis; VC scedulis. saltem] C
saltim
6 incitandos] V intimos
7 dona] C bona. conuectant] C conuertant
8 traditur] V *omits*
10 leticia] VC *omit*
11 eo usque] V *omits*
12 existeret] V exierit
14 uincebant] V uincebant dum accusati non
negabant

HERE BEGINS THE PASSIO OF SAINT CECILIA THE VIRGIN.
22 NOVEMBER.

(1) We see human praises and mortals' marks of distinction that have been recorded with a bronze inscription or committed to the memory of future generations in shining golden letters. And while we pay close attention to those things, I am amazed why we are not ashamed to cloak in silence the victories of the soldiers of Christ, and are unashamed not to pass on — even on ordinary sheets of paper — how they fought against and overcame their enemies for the glory of their emperor, and are unashamed not to make this known more diligently for rousing the spirits of the warriors.

Written works of such accounts bring together many benefits. God is praised when they are read, the memory of the saints is honoured, minds are edified, honour is shown to the martyrs. Thus sorrow arises in the unbelieving, envy in those without faith, distress among the undisciplined, and joy arises among all the saints who rejoice with Christ.

The devil laments alone seeing his warfare so completely vanquished by heavenly arms that He who was believed to have been defeated has more fittingly emerged from this fight as the victor. And then the devil supposed that he might overcome the saints of God, his enemy, by slaughtering them, but those slaughtered more fittingly prevailed. When they were interrogated, they confessed at once; when they were condemned, they gave thanks. Accordingly, we thus read about the celebrated, ancient victories of the Lord, when the enemy said, 'When I pursue, I will seize, divide the spoils, sate my soul, kill them with my sword; my hand will rule' [cf. Exodus 15.9]. But God stretched out his right hand, and the earth swallowed them, and truly he freed his people at the price of his blood [cf. Ex. 15.12–13].

(2) Now at last the enemy lies captive under the feet of the saints, and making his moan he cries out through lunatics and the possessed, and reveals the fiery punishments that he suffers, and recalling that he had been burned in the fury of the flames, he proves that all the saints whom he has persecuted for the sake of Christ's name prevail. To that extent, then, they have not died, so that they may give life to those about to die, may provide joy to the sorrowful, may offer medicine to the sick and, expelling the enemy of humanity himself from possessed bodies, they renew in him the torments that they suffered. And having suffered a measure of momentary pain, they possess eternal glory; they, in fact, see him burning in never ending fire, subjected to unremitting disgrace.

---

15 antiquas] V et antiquas
18 *second* et] V *omits*. uero] C *omits*
20 sub] V *omits*. captiuus] C *omits*
21 inerguminos] V inergumines. Fol. 73vb
23 sancti] V *omits*
24 uitam] C *omits*
25 atque] C a que

26 propellentes] VC proferentes. ipsum] C ipsa
27 dolorem] C laborem
28 ardentem] C agentem. incendiis uident] C incendii sui
29 perpetue] V perpetua

30 Clamat se ardere diabolus ut tu intelligas quia Christus bene refrigerat
sanctos. Clamat se saluatum infirmus ut tu intelligas sanctos Saluatori coniunctos. Sic enim ad Patrem dixisse legimus ipsum Dominum Saluatorem:
'Pater, uolo ut ubi ego sum et ipsi sint mecum'. Excitatur ergo per hec animus
ad medelam quando sue restaurationis attendit indicium. Patulum sui
35 pectoris prebet auditum dum sue salutis probamenta per eos qui uere sunt
saluati cognoscit.

Hanc fidem tenuerunt sancti apostoli. Quos e uestigio exercitus martyrum
persecuti uictorias suas ad regem uictoriosissimum reportauerunt. Ipse enim
triumphali crucis sue labaro usque hodie antecedit omnium in se credentium
40 mentes. Hunc secuti sunt priores apostoli; post apostolos, martyres; post
martyres, confessores; post confessores, sacerdotes; post sacerdotes,
uirgines; post uirgines, uidue; post uiduas, continentes; omnibusque patent
uestigia Christi.* Ideo denique cotidie omnibus clamat, 'Venite ad me omnes
qui laboratis et onerati estis, et ego uos requiescere faciam'.

45 (3) Huius uocem audiens *Cecilia, uirgo* clarissima, absconditum semper |
euangelium Christi gerebat in pectore et non diebus non noctibus a colloquiis
diuinis et *oratione cessabat. Hec Ualerianum quendam iuuenem habebat
sponsum. Qui iuuenis in amore uirginis perurgens animum, diem constituit
nuptiarum. Cecilia uero subtus ad carnem cilitio induta* desuper auratis
50 uestibus tegebatur. Parentum enim tanta uis et hortatus sponsi circa illam
erat exestuans ut non posset amorem sui cordis ostendere et quod solum
Christum diligeret indiciis euidentibus aperire.

Quid multa? Venit dies in qua thalamus collocatus est. Et *cantantibus
organis, illa* in corde suo *soli Domino decantabat dicens, 'Fiat Domine cor
55 meum et corpus meum immaculatum ut non confundar'.* Et biduanis ac triduanis *ieiuniis orans,* commendabat Domino quod timebat. *Inuitabat angelos
precibus et lacrimis interpellabat apostolos. Sancta omnia Christo famulantia
exorabat ut suis eam deprecationibus adiuuarent suam Domino puditiciam
commendantem.*

30–31 ut...infirmus] V *omits*
31 intelligas] V intellegas
33 ego sum] C *order reversed.* ipsi] VC isti
34 attendit] V accendit. indicium] VC
   indicia. sui] VC enim sui
37 sancti] VC *omit*
37–38 martyrum persecuti] V martyrum
   prosecutus; C *omits*
38 reportauerunt] VC reportarunt
39 triumphali] V triumphale. labaro] V
   labore; C lauacro
42 omnibusque] VC omnibus

43 uestigia Christi] VC *order reversed.*
   cotidie] C *omits*
44 uos requiescere] V *order reversed*
45 Fol. 74ra
46 euangelium] V euuangelium. gerebat] V
   gestabat
47 oratione] V orationibus
48 amore] C amorem. perurgens] V perur
   guens
50 hortatus] VC *omit*
51 amorem] V ardorem
53 qua] C quo

The devil cries out that he is burning so that you may understand that Christ has duly refreshed the saints. The sick man cries out that he has been healed so that you may understand that the saints have joined the Saviour. Thus we read that the Lord Saviour himself said to the Father, 'Father, it is my will that where I am, they too will be with me' [cf. John 17.24]. Therefore, the soul is stirred to healing on account of these things when it observes evidence of its restoration. It gives a willing hearing with its heart when it recognizes the proofs of its salvation in those who truly have been saved.

The holy apostles kept this faith. Armies of martyrs who followed them forthwith brought back their victories to the most victorious king. For He himself, in the triumphant sign of his cross, to this day marches before the minds of all those who believe in him. The first apostles followed him; after the apostles, martyrs; after the martyrs, confessors; after the confessors, priests; after the priests, virgins; after the virgins, widows; after the widows, the continent; and to all the footsteps of Christ are evident.* And so he daily cries out, 'Come to me all you who labour and are oppressed, and I will give you rest' [cf. Matthew 11.28].

(3) Hearing this voice Cecilia, the most celebrated virgin, carried the gospel of Christ always hidden in her heart and did not cease day or night from divine discourse and prayer. She had as a fiancé a certain young man named Valerian. Since the spirit of the young man was pressed by his love of the young woman, he set the day of the wedding. Cecilia was covered outwardly in a garment woven with gold but wore a hairshirt underneath next to her skin. Her parents' excitement and her fiancee's incitement welled up so high that she was not able to reveal the love in her heart and could not make known by clear signs that she loved Christ alone.

What more is there to say? The day came in which the marriage chamber was prepared. And while the instruments played, she sang in her heart to God alone, saying 'Lord, let my heart and my body be unstained so that I might not be put to shame' [cf. Psalm 118.80 (Septuagint)].* And praying with two and three day fasts, she entrusted the things she feared to the Lord. With prayers she summoned the angels and with tears importuned the apostles. She who had entrusted her chastity to the Lord implored all the holy servants of Christ to help her by their prayers.

---

54 Domine] V *omits*
54–55 cor meum et corpus meum] V corpus
  et cor meum
55–56 ac triduanis] V *omits.* commendabat]
  V commendat; C commendabat se (se
  inserted). quod] C quem

57 et] V *omits.* Sancta] VC et sancta. omnia]
  V agmina
58–59 Domino puditiciam commendantem]
  C commendantem domino pudicitiam

60   (4) Sed cum hec agerentur, uenit nox in qua suscepit una cum sponso suo cubiculi secreta silentia, et ita *eum alloquitur*, 'O dulcissime atque *amantissime* iuuenis, est mysterium quod tibi confitear si modo tu iuratus asseras tota te illud obseruantia custodire'. Iurauit Ualerianus sponsus se illud nulla omnino prodere ratione nulla necessitate detegere.

65   Tunc illa ait, '*Angelum Dei habeo* amatorem *qui* nimio zelo *custodit corpus meum*. Hic *si* uel leuiter senserit quod *tu me polluto* amore *contingas*, *statim* circa te suum *furorem exagitabit*, et amittes florem tue gratissime iuuentutis. *Si* autem cognouerit quod *me* sincero et immaculato amore *diligas et uirginitatem meam integram* illibatamque *custodias*, *ita te quoque diliget*
70 *sicut et me et ostendet tibi | gratiam suam*'.

     (5) *Tunc Ualerianus* nutu Dei correptus *ait*, '*Si uis ut credam sermonibus tuis, ostende michi ipsum angelum* ut probem quod uere angelus Dei sit, et faciam que hortaris. *Si autem uirum alterum diligis, et te et illum gladio feriam*'.

     Tunc beata *Cecilia dicit* ei, '*Si* consiliis meis promittas te adquiescere et
75 *permittas te purificari* fonte perhenni, et credas unum Deum esse in celis uiuum et uerum, *poteris eum uidere*'.*

     Dicit ei Ualerianus, '*Et quis est qui me purificet ut ego angelum Dei uideam?*'

     Respondit Cecilia, 'Est senior qui nouit purificare homines ut mereantur
80 uidere angelum Dei'.

     Dicit ei Ualerianus, 'Et ego ubi hunc senem requiram?'

     Respondit Cecilia, 'Vade in tercium miliarium ab urbe uia que Appia nuncupatur; illic inuenies pauperes a transeuntibus elemosine petentes auxilium. De his enim michi semper cura fuit, et optime huius mei secreti
85 conscii sunt.

     'Hos tu cum uideris, dabis eis benedictionem meam dicens, "Cecilia me misit ad uos, ut ostendatis michi senem Urbanum quia ad ipsum habeo eius secreta mandata que perferam". Hunc ut uideris, indica ei omnia uerba mea. Et dum te purificauerit, induet te uestibus nouis et candidis. Cum quibus mox
90 ut ingressus fueris istud cubiculum, uidebis angelum Domini etiam tui amatorem effectum, et ea que ab eo poposceris, impetrabis'.

---

61 cubiculi] V *omits.* silentia] V silentio
63 Iurauit] VC iurat
64 omnino] C *omits*
65–66 custodit corpus meum] VC corpus
    meum custodit. me polluto amore] C
    polluto amore me
67 exagitabit] VC exagitat
68 et immaculato] C *omits*
69 te quoque] V *order reversed*
70 *first* et] V *omits.* Fol. 74rb
71 Valerinanus] uelerianus. correptus] VC
    timore correptus. credam] C uere credam

72 angelum] C *omits.* ut probem] VC et si
    probauero. Dei] C *omits.* et] VC *omit*
73 que] V quod. alterum] C alium. *first* et] V
    omits
74 dicit ei] C dixit ad eum
74–75 adquiescere et permittas] C *omits.* et]
    V ut
77 est] V erit. Dei] V *omits*
79 Respondit] VC respondit ei
80 Dei] C *omits*
82 Respondit] C respondit ei. tercium] V
    tertio (o *above line*)

(4) But while these things took place, the night came in which she ventured by herself upon the silent secrets of the bed chamber with her husband, and she addresses him in this manner, 'O sweetest and most beloved young man, there is a mystery that I will reveal to you provided that you, having given your word, promise to keep it to yourself with all vigilance'. Valerian her husband swore that he would not reveal it for any reason nor disclose it under compulsion.

Then she said, 'I have an angel of God for a lover who guards my body with extraordinary jealously. If he supposes even a little bit that you might touch me with an impure love, he will immediately kindle his fury around you, and you will lose the flower of your most charming youth. If, however, he recognizes that you love me with a pure and unstained love, and that you will guard my virginity untouched and intact, then he will love you in the same way as he does me and will show you his favour'.

(5) Then, seized by the will of God, Valerian said, 'If you want me to believe your words, then show me the angel himself so that I may prove that he really is an angel of God, and I will do what you urge. However, if you love another man, I will put both you and him to the sword'.

Then blessed Cecilia says to him, 'If you promise willingly to heed my advice and to allow yourself to be purified in the everlasting font, and if you believe that there is one living and true God in heaven, then you can see him'.*

Valerian says to her, 'And who might purify me so that I may see the angel of God?'

Cecilia answered, 'There is an old man who knows how to purify men so that they may deserve to see the angel of God'.

Valerian says to her, 'And where might I look for this old man?'

Cecilia answered, 'Go three miles from the city on the road called Appia; there you will find the poor begging for charitable alms from those passing by. I have always taken care of these people, and they are very well aware of my secret.

'When you see them, give them my blessing saying, "Cecilia sent me to you, so that you might show me the old man Urban because I have for him her secret instructions that I am delivering". When you see him, make known to him my every word. And when he has purified you, he will clothe you in new and snow-white garments. As soon as you have entered this chamber in these, you will see the angel of the Lord and he will become your lover as well, and whatever you ask of him, you will obtain'.

---

83 nuncupatur] V nunccupatur. illic] C illuc. elemosine] V alimonię; C *omits*.
84 enim] C *omits*. michi semper] V semper mihi. cura] V curę.
84–85 secreti conscii sunt] V secreti sunt conscii; C conscii secreti sunt
86 cum] C dum. dicens] V et dicens

87 senem] VC sanctum senem. quia] V quem; C quam. eius] C *omits*
88 ut] V cum; C tu cum
90 ut] V *omits*. istud cubiculum] V tuum cubiculum; C *omits*. Domini] VC sanctum
91 ea que] VC omnia quę

(6) Tunc *Ualerianus perrexit, et* secundum ea signa que acceperat, *inuenit* sanctum *Urbanum* episcopum, qui iam bis confessor factus inter sepulchra martyrum latitabat. Cui cum dixisset omnia uerba Cecilie, *gauisus est gaudio* 95   *magno.* Et ponens genua sua in terram, expandit manus suas ad celum cum lacrimis et dixit, 'Domine Ihesu Christe, seminator casti consilii, suscipe seminum fructus quos in Cecilia | seminasti. Domine Ihesu Christe, pastor bone, Cecilia famula tua quasi apes tibi argumentosa deseruit.* Nam sponsum, quem quasi leonem ferocem accepit, ad te quasi agnum mansuetis- 100   simum destinauit. Iste huc, nisi crederet, non uenisset. *Aperi ergo, Domine, cordis eius ianuam sermonibus tuis ut te Creatorem suum esse cognoscens, renuntiet diabolo et pompis eius et idolis eius'.*

(7) Hec et his similia orante sancto Urbano episcopo, *subito ante faciem ipsorum apparuit* senior *indutus uestibus niueis, tenens titulum in manibus* 105   *aureis litteris scriptum.* Quem uidens *Ualerianus, nimio terrore correptus est et cadens in terram* factus est quasi mortuus.

Tunc senior eleuauit eum dicens, '*Lege huius tituli textum* et crede ut purificari merearis et uidere angelum cuius tibi aspectum Cecilia uirgo deuotissima repromisit'.

110   Tunc Ualerianus respiciens, *cepit intra se legere. Scriptura autem tituli, hec erat,* 'Vnus Deus, una fides, unum baptisma. Unus Deus et Pater omnium, qui super omnia et in omnibus nobis'.* Cumque hoc intra se legisset, *dicit* ei senior: '*Credis ita esse, an adhuc dubitas?'*

Tunc *Ualerianus* uoce magna clamauit *dicens,* '*Non est aliud quod uerius* 115   possit credi sub celo!'

Cumque hec dixisset Ualerianus, ille senior ab oculis eorum elapsus est. Tunc sanctus *Urbanus baptizauit eum et edocens eum omnem fidei regulam, remisit eum ad Ceciliam* diligenter instructum.

(8) Veniens igitur Ualerianus indutus candidis uestimentis, *Ceciliam intra* 120   *cubiculum orantem inuenit, et stantem iuxta eam angelum Domini, pennis fulgentibus* alas habentem et flammeo aspectu radiantem, *duas coronas ferentem in manibus choruscantes rosis et liliis albescentes.*

---

94 latitabat] V latebat
95 sua] V *omits.* terram] C terra. suas] V
    omits. cum] C et cum
96 et] VC *omit.* casti] V sancti
97 Fol. 74va
98 Cecilia famula tua] V cecilię famulę tuę
    quę. apes] V ouis; C *above line above*
    erasure
104 uestibus niueis] VC *order reversed*
105 correptus est] V corripitur
107 eleuauit] V leuauit. tituli] C libri. et

crede] C *omits*
108 aspectum] C aspectus
110 cepit intra se legere] C intra se legere
    coepit
112 super omnia] V super omnes et per
    omnia
116 hec] V hoc. elapsus] C eleuatus
117 eum] V *omits*; C *barred* u *above erased* i.
    omnem fidei] C *order reversed*
121 radiantem] V *omits*
122 albescentes] C albentes

(6) Then Valerian departed and, when he had followed the signs he had received from her, he found Saint Urban the bishop, who now had become a confessor for a second time and was hiding among the tombs of the martyrs. When Valerian had told him Cecilia's every word, he rejoiced with great joy. And kneeling on the ground, he spread out his hands towards heaven with tears in his eyes and said, 'Lord Jesus Christ, sower of chaste counsel, accept the fruits of the seeds which you have sown in Cecilia. Lord Jesus Christ, good shepherd, your servant Cecilia, like a busy bee, has devoted herself to you.* For her husband, whom she received like a ferocious lion, she sent to you like the gentlest lamb. Had he not believed, he would not have come here. Therefore, Lord, open the door of his heart with your words so that recognizing you to be his Creator, he might renounce the devil and his pomps and his idols'.

(7) When Saint Urban the bishop prayed these and similar things, suddenly in their presence appeared an older man arrayed in snow-white garments, holding in his hands an inscription written in gold lettering. When Valerian saw him, he was overcome with fear and fell to the ground as if dead.

Then the older man raised him up saying, 'Read the text of this inscription and believe so that you may deserve to be purified and to see the angel, the sight of whom the most faithful virgin Cecilia promised to show you'.

Then looking at the text, Valerian began to read to himself. And the text of the inscription read, 'There is one God, one faith, one baptism. There is one God and Father of all, who is above all things and in all of us' [cf. Ephesians 4.5–6].* And when he had read this to himself, the old man says to him, 'Do you believe this to be so, or do you still doubt?'

Then Valerian cried out in a loud voice saying, 'There is nothing else truer under heaven that can be believed!'

And when Valerian had said these things, that old man disappeared from their sight. Then Saint Urban baptized him, and when he had instructed him in the whole rule of the faith, he sent Valerian back to Cecilia diligently taught.

(8) So when Valerian arrived clothed in white garments, he found Cecilia praying in the bed chamber and standing next to her an angel of the Lord, with wings of gleaming feathers and who radiated with a fiery countenance, carrying in his hands two crowns shimmering with roses and glowing with lilies.

Quique unam | *dedit Cecilie alteram Ualeriano dicens*, 'Istas coronas
immaculato corde et mundo corpore *custodite quia de paradiso* Dei eas *attuli*
125 uobis. Et hoc uobis signum erit: *Nunquam marcescent, nunquam aspectus sui
adiment uel perdent florem, nunquam sui minuent suauitatem odoris, nec ab
alio uideri poterunt nisi ab eis quibus ita castitas placuerit*, sicut et in uobis
probata est placuisse. *Et quia tu, Ualeriane*, consentis consilio castitatis, misit
me Christus filius Dei ad te ut *quam uolueris petitionem insinues'*.

130   At ille hec audiens, *adorauit et dixit*, 'Nichil michi in ista uita dulcius extitit
quam unicus *mei fratris* affectus. Et impium michi est, *ut me liberato
germanum meum in periculo perditionis aspiciam*. Hoc solum omnibus peti-
tionibus meis antepono et *deprecor, ut fratrem meum Tiburtium* sicut me
liberare dignetur et faciat nos ambos in sui nominis confessione perfectos'.

135   Audiens hec *angelus letissimo uultu dixit ad eum*, 'Quoniam hoc petisti
quod melius quam te Christum implere delectat, sicut te per famulam suam
Ceciliam lucratus est Dominus, ita per te quoque tuum lucrabitur fratrem, *et
cum eodem ad martyrii palmam attinges'*.

        (9) His itaque finitis sermonibus, *aspectus angelici luminis migrauit ad
140 celos. Et illis epulantibus in Christo atque in edificatione sancta sermocinan-
tibus*, Tiburtius, *Valeriani frater, aduenit*, et ingressus quasi ad cognatam
suam, *osculatus est* caput sancte Cecilie *et ait*, 'Miror hoc tempore roseus hic
odor et liliorum unde respiret. Nam si tenerem ipsas rosas aut ipsa lilia in
manibus meis, nec sic poterant odoramenta tante michi suauitatis infundere.
145 Confiteor uobis quia ita sum refectus ut putem me totum subito renoua|tum'*.

        Dicit ei *Ualerianus, 'Odorem iam meruisti me interpellante suscipere,
modo te credente, promereberis etiam ipso roseo aspectu gaudere et intelligere
cuius in rosis ipsis sanguis florescit et in liliis corpus albescit. Coronas enim
habemus quas tui oculi uidere non preualent floreo rubore et niueo candore
150 uernantes'*.

        Dicit ei *Tiburtius, 'In somnis hec audio, an in ueritate ista loqueris*,
Ualeriane?'

        Respondit Ualerianus, *'In somnis nunc usque uiximus, nam modo in ueri-
tate sumus* et fallatia in nobis nulla est.* *Dii enim quos colimus ad omnem
155 fidem demonia comprobantur'*.

---

123 Fol. 74vb   130 hec] VC *omit*. in ista uita dulcius] C
124 corde et mundo] C *omits*   dulcius in ista uita. extitit] C existit
124–25 attuli uobis] V ad uos adtuli; C attuli   131 mei fratris] V *order reversed*
    ad uos. marcescent] VC marcidum.   135 hoc] VC *omit*
    nunquam] VC *omit*   136 quam te] C *omits*. Christum] C christus
126 adiment] VC adhibent. uel perdent] VC   138 attinges] V a *between* e *and* s *erased*; C e
    omit. minuent] VC minuunt   *corrected from* i
127 alio] VC aliis. ita] C *omits*. et in] V   139–40 sermonibus...sancta] C *omits*.
    omits; C et   luminis] V numinis
128 consentis] VC consensisti   140 edificatione] V eruditione

He gave one to Cecilia and the other to Valerian saying, 'Guard these crowns with an unstained heart and a pure body because I have brought them to you from the paradise of God. This will be a sign to you: never will they wither, never will they be deprived of their hue nor lose their bloom, never will the pleasantness of their fragrance abate, nor can they be seen by another unless it is by those for whom chastity is pleasing, just as it has proved pleasing to you. And because you, Valerian, accept the counsel of chastity, Christ the Son of God sent me to you so that you may make whatever request you want'.

And when he heard these things, Valerian begged him and said, 'There has been nothing in this life dearer to me than my singular love for my brother. And it seems ungodly to me that having been set free, I should see my brother in danger of damnation. This alone I place before all my requests and pray that He deign to free my brother Tiburtius just as he freed me and that he perfect us both in the confession of his name'.

When the angel heard these things, he said to him with a most joyful countenance, 'Because you have asked for something that it pleases Christ to fulfil even better than it pleases you, just as the Lord redeemed you through his servant Cecilia, so in the same way will he redeem your brother through you, and you will attain the palm of martyrdom together with him'.

(9) When this conversation ended, the angel's luminous presence departed to heaven. And while they were rejoicing in Christ and talking about holy edification, Tiburtius, Valerian's brother, arrived, and having approached Cecilia as his kinswoman, kissed her on the head and said, 'I am amazed that at this season the fragrance of roses and lilies wafts forth. For if I were to hold roses and lilies themselves in my hands, they would not give off such a pleasant smell to me. I confess to you I am so refreshed that I believe my whole self has been suddenly renewed'.

Valerian says to him, 'Since I requested it, you have deserved to receive the fragrance, but by believing, you will also deserve to rejoice in the sight of the roses themselves and to understand whose blood blooms in those very roses and whose body glows in the lilies. We have two crowns flourishing with rosy redness and snowy whiteness that you do not have the power to see with your eyes'.

Tiburtius says to him, 'Do I hear these things in my sleep or are you really saying them, Valerian?'

Valerian answered, 'Until now we have lived in sleep, but presently we live in the truth and there is no deception in us.* The gods that we worship in all faith are shown to be demons' [cf. Psalm 95.5 (Septuagint)].

140–41 sermocinantionibus] C tionibus
   above line above erasure
145 quia] C *omits.* Fol. 75ʳᵃ
147 ipso roseo aspectu] C ipsum roseum
   aspectum. et intelligere] V *omits*

148 ipsis] C *omits.* corpus] V cuius corpus
149 floreo] C flore. rubore] VC colore
151 loqueris] C tu loqueris
154 colimus] V coluimus

Dicit ei Tiburtius, '*Vnde hoc nosti?*'

Respondit Ualerianus, 'Angelus Dei docuit me. Quem et tu uidere poteris si purificatus fueris ab omni sorde idolorum'.

Dicit ei Tiburtius, 'Et si potest fieri ut uideam angelum Dei, que mora est
160   purificationis?'

Respondit Ualerianus, 'Nulla. Hoc tantum tu michi sponde: quod omnia idola deneges et credas unum Deum esse in celis'.

Tiburtius respondit, 'Non intelligo qua intentione ista prosequeris'.

(10) Cecilia dixit, 'Miror ut non intelligas figuras fictiles gipseas, ligneas,
165   ereas atque lapideas, uel cuiuscunque metalli, deos esse non posse, quas aranee intexunt et aues stercorant, in quorum capitibus solent sibi ciconie nidos struere, quos dampnati faciunt. Nam ad omne metallum pro criminibus damnati mittuntur. Ergo a damnatis initium accipientes quomodo possunt dii uel estimari uel credi?

170   'Inter mortuum denique et simulacrum nulla distantia est. Sicut enim mortuus omnia membra habet, flatum tamen et uocem non potest habere nec sensum, sic et ista uana numina omnia quidem membra halbent, sed omnia fatua et ceca esse noscuntur et deteriora quam homines mortui comprobantur quia hominum membra, dum uiuerent, et oculis uiderunt et auribus
175   audierunt, ambulauerunt pedibus, ore locuti sunt, manibus palpauerunt et odorem naribus attraxerunt. Ista autem et a morte ceperunt et in morte perdurant quia nunquam nec uixisse nec uiuere posse comprobantur'.

Tunc cum omni alacritate Tiburtius ait, 'Qui ista non credit pecus est!'

Hec dicente Tiburtio, sancta Cecilia osculata est caput eius et dixit, 'Hodie
180   meum te fateor esse cognatum. Sicut enim amor Dei michi fratrem tuum coniugem fecit, ita te michi cognatum faciet contemptus idolorum. Vnde quia paratus es ad credendum, uade cum fratre tuo ut purificationem accipias per quam merearis angelicos uultus aspicere et omnium tuarum ueniam inuenire culparum'.

185   (11) *Tunc dicit fratri suo Tiburtius, 'Obsecro te mi frater ut dicas michi ad quem me ducturus es'.*

---

157 Respondit Ualerianus] C *order reversed*
158 fueris] V *omits.* idolorum] V idolorum fueris
159 est] V erit
161 Respondit Ualerianus] C *order reversed.* tu michi] V *order reversed*
162 credas] C crede. Deum esse] C *order reversed*
164 Miror] V Miror te frater. gipseas] C cypseas
164–65 ligneas ereas] C *order reversed.* metalli deos] C metallis, *blank space*

between i *and* s, *which is from an erased word*
166 intexunt] V texerunt; C texunt. et] V *omits.* sibi ciconie] V *order reversed*; C *omits* sibi
167 struere] VC instruere. dampnati] VC damnaticii
168 damnati mittuntur] C damnaticii mittunt. damnatis] C damnaticiis. accipientes] C accipiens
169 estimari] V dici

Tiburtius says to him, 'From whom have you learned this?'

Valerian replied, 'An angel of God taught me. You too can see him if you are purified from all the filth of the idols'.

Tiburtius says to him, 'And if it is possible for me to see the angel of God, then why put off the purification?'

Valerian answered, 'There is no reason. Just promise me this: that you will reject all the idols and will believe that there is one God in heaven'.

Tiburtius replied, 'I do not understand why you pursue these things'.

(10) Cecilia said, 'I am amazed that you do not understand that figures made of clay, plaster, wood, bronze and stones, or any metal whatsoever, which spiders cover with webs and birds soil with droppings, on whose heads storks are accustomed to build nests for themselves, which the condemned construct, cannot be gods. For the condemned are sent to every sort of mine for their misdeeds. Therefore, how can things taking their origins from the condemned either be judged to be or believed to be gods?

'In point of fact, there is no difference between a dead man and an image. Just as a dead man has all his limbs and yet cannot have breath, voice or feeling, so also these hollow gods have every single one of their limbs, but all are known to be foolish and blind and are proven to be worse than dead men because the limbs of men, while they were alive, both saw with their eyes and heard with their ears, walked on their feet, talked with their mouths, felt with their hands and breathed in fragrances through their noses. But these gods begin in death and continue in death because they are never shown to have lived or to be able to live'.

Then with utter joy Tiburtius said, 'Anyone who does not believe this is an animal!'

When Tiburtius said these things, Saint Cecilia kissed his head and said, 'Today I declare you to be my kinsman. Just as the love of God has made your brother my husband, a contempt of idols will make you my kinsman. Thus because you are ready to believe, go with your brother so that you may receive the purification on account of which you will deserve to gaze upon the angelic faces and to find forgiveness for all your sins'.

(11) Then Tiburtius says to his brother, 'I beg you my brother to tell me to whom you are going to take me'.

---

170 denique] V *omits*; C quoque. enim] V *omits*

171 tamen et] C tunc nec

172 numina] V nomina. Fol. 75rb

173 ceca] VC caduca. esse] VC *omit*

176 attraxerunt] V adsumpserunt; C assumserunt. Ista] VC isti. *first* et] VC *omit*

177 uiuere posse] VC *order reversed.* comprobantur] V noscuntur

178 ista] C ita. est] V esse conprobatur

179 caput] VC pectus

180 meum] C *omits.* esse] V uere esse; C esse meum. amor Dei] V deus; C maiorum deus

180–81 coniugem] V coniugi

181 faciet contemptus] VC *order reversed*

185 mi] VC *omit*

Respondit Ualerianus, 'Ad magnum uirum nomine *Urbanum* in quo est angelicus aspectus, ueneranda canicies, sermo uerus et sapentia conditus'.

Dicit ei Tiburtius, 'Tu illum Urbanum dicis quem papam suum Christiani
190   nominant? Hunc ego audio iam secundo damnatum et iterum pro ipsa re qua *damnatus est, latebram sui fouendo precauere.* Iste si inuentus fuerit, sine dubio atrocibus dabitur flammis et, ut dici solet, centenas exoluet, et *nos* simul cremabimur *si apud illum fuerimus inuenti. Et dum querimus diuinitatem in celis latentem, incurrimus furorem exurentem in terris'.*

195   *Dicit* ei *Cecilia,* '*Si ista sola esset uita et non esset alia, iuste istam perdere timeremus.* Est autem uita satis ista melior que nunquam finiri potest. | Vt quid istam perdere timemus quando per huius perditionem ad illius adquisitionem attingimus?'

Respondit Tiburtius, 'Adhuc nunquam aliam audiuimus. *Ergo est altera*
200   *preter istam?'*

Dicit ei Cecilia, 'Et hoc quod in isto mundo uiuitur "uita" est? Quam humores humidant, *dolores extenuant, ardores exsiccant,* egritudines morbidant, *esce inflant, ieiunia macerant,* ioca soluunt, tristicie consumunt, *sollicitudo coartat,* securitas hebetat, *diuitie iactant, paupertas deicit, iuuentus*
205   *extollit, senectus incuruat, frangit infirmitas,* meror consumit, *et his omnibus mors furibunda succedit, et ita uniuersis gaudiis carnalibus finem imponit,* ut cum esse desierit, nec fuisse putetur! Pro nichilo enim computatur iam omne quod non est. *Illa autem uita que isti uite succedit aut perpetuis tribulationibus datur iniustis, aut eternis gaudiis iustis offertur'.*

210   (12) Respondens ad hec *Tiburtius dixit, 'Et quis ibi fuit et inde huc ueniens* uobis *hoc potuit indicare* ut merito possimus ista uobis asserentibus credere?'*

Tunc beata *Cecilia* erigens se *stetit et cum magna constantia dixit,* 'Celi terreque, maris et hominum ac uolucrum serpentium pecudumque *Creator*
215   ex se ipso antequam ista omnia faceret *genuit Filium et protulit ex uirtute sua Spiritum Sanctum: Filium ut crearet omnia, Spiritum ut uiuificaret uniuersa.* Omnia autem que fecit Pater, Filius ex Patre genitus condidit. Vniuersa autem que condita sunt ex Patre procedens Spiritus Sanctus animauit'.

---

187 Respondit Ualerianus] C *order reversed.*
   nomine Urbanum] VC *order reversed*
188 angelicus aspectus] VC *order reversed*
190 ego] C ergo
191 latebram] V latebra. sui] V se.
   precauere] C predicare
192 centenas] V cæntenas; C certe, te *written
   over erasure of several letters and a blank
   space for four letters following.* exoluet] C
   omits
193 apud illum] V ab illo; C cum illo.
   inuenti] V edocti inuenti
194 incurrimus] V incurremus

195 sola] VC una
196 Est autem] C si autem est. que] C et que.
   Fol. 75va
197 timemus] V timeamus
197–98 adquisitionem] C inquisitionem.
   attingimus] V attingemus
199 Respondit Tiburtius] V respondit ei
   tiburtius; C *order reversed.* Adhuc
   nunquam aliam] VC Adhuc hoc
   numquam. audiuimus] VC audiui. altera]
   VC altera uita
200 istam] V istam quam prędicatis
201 Quam] C quod

Valerian replied, 'To a great man named Urban who has an angelic presence, venerable white hair, truthful speech and seasoned wisdom'.

Tiburtius says to him, 'Are you talking about that Urban whom the Christians call their pope? Now I hear that he has been condemned for a second time, and that he has again withdrawn into a hiding place for his own protection because he was condemned. If he is discovered, he will undoubtedly be given over to the fierce flames, and, as is commonly said, will pay a hundred times over, and we will be burned at the same time if we are found with him. And while we are searching for the divinity hidden in heaven, we will rush into a consuming fury on earth'.

Cecilia says to him, 'If this were the only life and there were no other, then we would rightly be afraid to lose this one. However, there is a life sufficiently better than this one that can never end. Why are we afraid to lose this life when we achieve the acquisition of that other life through the loss of this one?'

Tiburtius responded, 'Up to now we have never heard of this other life. Is there then another life besides this one?'

Cecilia says to him, 'And is living in this world "life"? How fluids swell us, pains shrivel us, passions dry us out, diseases make us ill, foods bloat us, fasts weaken us, trifles enervate us, unhappiness consumes us, anxiety constricts us, freedom from worry dulls us, wealth puffs us up, poverty brings us low, youth exalts us, old age enfeebles us, illness crushes us, grief consumes us, and furious death comes after all of these things and thus puts an end to all fleshly joys, so that when life ceases to be, it is thought not to have existed! All that does not exist is now reckoned as nothing. However, that life which comes after this one either is given to the unrighteous with unending tribulation, or it is conferred on the righteous with everlasting joys'.

(12) Replying to these things Tiburtius said, 'And who has been there and has come here from there who could disclose this to you so that with good cause we can believe you when you assert these things?'*

Then rising to her feet, blessed Cecilia stood up and said with great constancy, 'The Creator of heaven and earth, of the sea and men and birds, of serpents and animals, before he made all these things, begot out of himself the Son and by his power brought into existence the Holy Spirit: the Son so that he might create all things, the Spirit so that he might give life to all. Moreover, the Son, begotten of the Father, formed all that the Father had made. And the Holy Spirit proceeding out of the Father quickened all that had been formed'.

---

202 humidant] V tumidant
202–03 egritudines morbidant] V *omits*; C aures morbidant. ioca] V ioci; C a *corrected from* i
204 hebetat] C euertat. iactant] V superbiunt
205 extollit] C Extollitur
206 ut] V et
207 desierit] V desierint. putetur] V putantur. enim] V *omits*

210 Respondens] C Respondit. dixit] C dicens
211 *first* uobis] VC nobis. hoc] V *omits*. *second* uobis] VC *omit*
214 ac uolucrum] V *omits*. serpentium pecudumque Creator] V repentiumque creator et pecudum
215 ista] V *omits*
217 fecit] VC sunt. Pater] VC *omit*

Dicit ei Tiburtius, 'Certe *unum Deum* in celis credendum asseritis.
220   *Quomodo nunc tres esse testaris?'*

Respondit Cecilia, 'Vnus est Deus in maiestate sua quem ita in sancta
Trinitate diuidimus: *ut in uno homine* dicimus I esse sapientiam unam, quam
sapientiam dicimus habere *ingenium, memoriam et intellectum.* Nam ingenio
adinuenimus quod non didicimus; memoria tenemus quod docemur; intel-
225   lectu aduertimus quicquid uel uidere nobis contigerit uel audire. Quid modo
faciemus? Nunquid non ista tria una sapientia in homine possidet? Si ergo
homo in una sapientia trinum possidet nomen, quomodo non Deus
omnipotens in una deitate Trinitatis optineat maiestatem?'

Tunc Tiburtius prostratus in terram, cepit clamare dicens, 'Non michi
230   *uidetur humana lingua rationem reddere, sed puto quod angelus Dei per os*
tuum loquatur!'

Et cum multas gratias ageret quod breuiter unum Deum esse in tribus
personis euidentius ostendisset, conuersus ad fratrem suum dixit, 'De Deo
uno satis michi factum esse confiteor; superest ut ad inquisitionem meam ut
235   ceperat sermo percurrat'.

(13) Cecilia dixit, 'De his mecum loquere quia tirocinii tempus fratrem
tuum tibi prohibet dare responsum, me autem quam ab ipsis cunabulis Christi
sapientia docuit, ad quamcumque causam querere uolueris imparatam
habere non poteris'.

240   Dicit ei Tiburtius, '*Hoc inquisiui: quis inde huc ueniens aliam uobis quam*
predicatis uitam ostenderit?'

Cecilia dixit, 'Vnigenitum filium suum de celis pater per uirginem misit
ad terras, qui stans super montem sanctum clamauit uoce magna dicens,
"Venite ad me omnes populi". Cucurritque ad eum omnis sexus, omnis etas
245   omnisque conditio.

---

219 Deum] V esse deum
222 uno] V *omits.* dicimus esse] V *order*
    reversed. Fol. 75ᵛᵇ
223 ingenium] C *letter erased between* i *and*
    barred u. et] V *omits*
224 quod non didicimus] V *omits.* docemur]
    V docemus
225 nobis contingerit] C uis contingere
226–27 Nunquid...nomen] V numquid non
    ista unum sapientię in homine possidet
    nomen. trinum] C tria. nomen] C nomina
228 Trinitatis] C sua trinitas
229 terram] C terra

230 angelus] V angelum
231 loqatur] C loquitur
232 in] V *omits*
234 superest] V nunc superest; C in super.
    ut] V *omits*
236 Cecilia] V Respondens cecilia
238 querere] V loquere
239 poteris] V potueris
240 inquisiui] V inquisi (*final letter* i?)
241 predicatis] C iudicatis. ostenderit] VC
    ostendit
244 omnis] C omnisque

Tiburtius says to her, 'Without any doubt, you maintain believing that there is one God in heaven. How do you now affirm that there are three?'

Cecilia replied, 'There is one God in his majesty whom we thus divide into the holy Trinity: just as in one man we say there is a single faculty of reason, which possesses intellect, memory and intelligence. Now with the intellect, we find out what we have not learned; with the memory we retain what we are taught; with intelligence we perceive by sight or hearing whatever happens to us. What are we to make of this? Does not the single faculty of reason in a man possess these three? If a man has three names under one faculty of reason, how may not almighty God possess the majesty of the Trinity in one divine nature?'

Then when Tiburtius had prostrated himself on the ground, he began to cry out saying, 'It does not seem to me that a human tongue utters this explanation, but I believe that an angel of God speaks through your mouth!'

And when he had thanked her abundantly for clearly revealing in so few words that there is one God in three persons, he turned to his brother and said, 'I acknowledge that what has been put forth concerning one God is sufficient for me; my question that began the conversion remains to be addressed'.

(13) Cecilia said, 'Speak with me about these things because a time of catechization prohibits your brother from answering you, but the wisdom of Christ has instructed me from the cradle itself, and you will not find me unprepared for any matter you wish to ask about'.

Tiburtius says to her, 'I have asked about this: who in coming here from there has made known to you the other life that you proclaim?'

Cecilia said, 'The Father through a virgin sent from heaven to earth his only begotten Son, who stood on the holy mountain and cried out in a loud voice saying, "Come to me all peoples" [cf. Matthew 11.28]. And each sex, every age and every rank ran to him.

Tunc omnibus dixit, "Penitentiam agite pro ignorantia uestra quia appropinquabit regnum Dei, quod auferet regnum hominum. Regnum autem suum uult Deus participari credentibus, in quo eo excelsior quisque erit, quo I fuerit sanctior. Ibi peccatores eternis cruciatibus et sempiternis
250 incendiis consumentur, iusti uero perpetue glorie splendorem accipient et gaudiis que nullo fine poterunt concludi succedent. Nolite itaque, o filii hominum, istius uite gaudia fugitiua querere ut illic uite gaudia eterna teneatis que isti uite succedunt. In ista enim uita paruo tempore uiuitur, in illa autem uiuetur in eternum".

255 'Audientes hec increduli populi, omnes una uoce dixerunt, "Et quis ibi fuit qui inde ueniens potuit docere uera esse que asseris?"

'Tunc filius Dei dixit eis, "Si ostendam uobis mortuos qui surrexerunt ignorantes quod mortui fuerint, non credetis ueritati. Ite ergo nunc et mortuos quantos inueneritis afferte ut resurgentes, ipsi uobis asserant uerum
260 esse omne quod dixi."

'Tunc populi attulerunt infinita corpora mortuorum, que ille quasi dormientia sola uoce excitans suscitabat, clamauitque omnibus dicens, "Si uerbis meis non creditis, uel uirtutibus credite!"

'Denique ne uel occasionis uestigium dubietati remaneret, cum populis
265 ad sepulchra pergebat et triduanis et quatriduanis atque fetentibus mortuis uitam quam amiserant reuocabat. Transmeabat maria, super undas ambulans pedibus siccis, imperabat uentis, tempestates arcebat atque seuientes procellas ac turbines compescebat. Restituebat cecis uisum, mancis dexteram, claudicantibus gressum. Mutis uocem, surdis auditum reddebat.
270 Paraliticos uerbo sanabat, leprosos mundabat, infirmos curabat, lunaticos instaurabat et demones effugabat.

---

246 Tunc] C Tum. quia] V *omits*
247 appropinquabit] V adpropinquabit enim. auferet] VC auferat
248 uult Deus] VC *order reversed.* participari credentibus] C participare credentibus se. excelsior] VC fit excelsior
249 erit] VC *omit.* Fol. 76ra. sanctior] constantior. Ibi] C Ibique
249–50 sempiternis incendiis consumentur] C his consumuntur sempiternis incendiis. accipient] C accipiunt

251 gaudiis] V gaudia. succendent] C succenduntur
252 illic] VC illius
253 que isti uite succedunt] V *omits;* C que isti uite succedit, *erasure between* e *and* d *of* succedit. paruo] pauco
254 uiuetur] C dabitur
255 Audientes] V te *above line;* C Audiens. Et] C *omits*
256 qui inde] V quis inde; C et quis inde huc. esse] C ęsse

Then he said to all of them, "Do penance for your sins because the kingdom of God, which will take away the kingdom of men, will be at hand. Moreover, God wishes to share his kingdom with those who believe, a kingdom in which the holier one will have been, the higher he will be exalted. At that time sinners will be consumed by eternal torments and perpetual flames, but the righteous will receive the splendour of everlasting glory and will be inflamed by joys that can never end. Therefore, do not, O sons of men, seek the fleeting joys of this life in order that you may there take hold of that life's eternal joys, which come after this life. For in this one, life is lived for a short while, but in that one, it will be lived for eternity".

'When the unbelievers heard these things, they all said in one voice, "And has anyone been there who, coming from there, could show what you say to be true?"

'Then the Son of God said to them, "If I show you dead men who have risen unaware that they were dead, you will not believe the truth. Yet go now and bring as many dead as you can find so that when they rise again, they may themselves affirm for you that all I have said is true."

'Then the people brought countless bodies of the dead which he raised, rousing them only with his voice as if they had been sleeping, and he cried out to all saying, "If you do not believe my words, then believe my miracles!"

'And so that no trace of doubt might remain, he made his way toward the tombs with the people and restored to the dead, who had been stinking for three or four days, the life that they had lost. He crossed the seas, walking on the waves with dry feet. He exercised authority over the winds. He kept the storms at bay and calmed the raging gales and whirlwinds. He restored sight to the blind, dexterity to the crippled, the power of walking to the lame. He gave back voices to the mute, hearing to the deaf. He healed paralytics with a word, cleansed lepers, cured the sick, restored the lunatics and expelled demons.

---

258 fuerint] V fuerunt. nunc] V *omits*
261 attulerunt] V adduxerunt
262 sola] V sua. clamauitque] V Clamabat; C clamabatque. omnibus] V omnibus hominibus
263 meis] VC *omit*
264 ne] C *omits*
265 ad] C a. *second* et] C atque. atque] C ac
267 arcebat] V quiescere faciebat; C acerbas, s *above dotted* t
268–69 mancis dexteram] V mancis reddebat

dexteras; C mancis inpendebat dextras. claudicantibus] V claudis. Mutis uocem, surdis auditum reddebat] V mutis dabat uocem et surdis auditum; C mutis uocem dabat et surdis auditum
270 sanabat] V saluabat. mundabat] C uerbo mundabant, u *of* mundabant *written as* v *above dotted* a
271 instaurabat] VC restaurabat. effugabat] V fugabat; C expugnabat

'Sed quia hunc impii Iudei zelati sunt eo quod ipsos populi rel[i]nquentes eius uestigia sequerentur, sternentes ue|stimenta sua ante pedes eius et clamantes, "Benedictus qui uenit in nomine Domini!" Inflammati aduersus
275 eum Pharisei cuidam Pilato eum presidi tradiderunt, magum eum esse et sceleratissimum asserentes, atque tumultuosa seditione egerunt ut eum crucifigerent.

(14) 'Quod ille preuidens mundo proficere ad salutem, permisit se et teneri et illudi et uerberari pariter et occidi. Sciebat enim non nisi per
280 passionem suam diabolo captiuitatem inferri et immundis spiritibus ardua irrogari supplicia. Ideo denique ille tentus est qui peccatum non fecit ut dimitteretur genus humanum quod tenebatur uinctum in nodo peccati.* Benedictus maledicitur ut nos a maledictionibus tolleret. Illudi se passus est ut nos ab illusione demonum qui in hoc mundo uersantur auferret. Spineam
285 in capite coronam accepit ut sententiam capitalem que ex spinis peccatorum nostrorum nobis debebatur eriperet. Fel in escam suscepit ut dulcem gustum primi hominis unde mors mundum inuaserat commutaret. Aceto potatus est ut acredinem quam sanguis noster efferbuerat in se susciperet, et ipse biberet passionis calicem qui nostris passionibus debebatur. Expoliatus est ut nudi-
290 tatem parentum nostrorum quam serpentis consilio factam doluerat niueo uestimentorum tegmine operiret. In ligno suspensus est ut ligni preuaricationem ligno sue tolleret passionis. Mortem quoque ad se uenire permisit ut eam aduersum se colluctantem prosterneret et que, per serpentem regnum inuenerat, cum ipso serpente prostrata fieret captiua per Christum.
295 'Denique cum uniuersa elementa | Creatorem suum in cruce leuatum aspicerent, horrore nimio tremuerunt. Nam ex uno latere terra mouebatur, ex alio templa scindebantur et saxa. Fugit dies. Sol expauit et fuscatus lugubrem totum prebuit mundum. Luna pallidos sui luminis uultus sanguinea nube contexit. Stelle sidereo radiantes aspectu omnes pariter obscurate sunt.
300 Dedit mugitum terra et quasi parturiens cepit multos sanctos parere de sepulchris qui darent testimonium hoc quod descensus Saluatoris ad inferos diabolo regnum eripuit et moriendo mortem optinuit et edomuit et ligauit et suorum subdidit pedibus famulorum.

---

272 hunc] V tunc. Iudei] VC *omit.*
  rel(i)nquentes] relnquentes; VC
  relinquentes
273 *first* eius] V huius. Fol. 76rb
274 Inflammati] V Inflati sunt; C Inflati
275 Pharisei] V pharisẹi et. eum] V *omits*; C
  enim
279 uerberari] C era *above underscored* a.
  Sciebat] VC sciuit
280 inferri] C inferre
281 irrogari] V et inenarrabilia inferri
282 humanum] V hominum
284 qui] V quẹ. uersantur] VC uersatur.

285 que] V omits
286 nostrorum] VC *omit.* nobis] V *omits.*
  gustum] V gustu
288 acredinem] C acerbitatem. efferbuerat]
  C efferuerat, *insertion mark between* r
  and u *but nothing above line.* biberet] C
  bi *above dotted* li *and first* e *dotted but*
  letter above erased
292 tolleret] V *omits.* passionis] V passionis
  eriperet. quoque] V *omits*
293 aduersum] C aduersus. colluctantem] C
  colluctante, *first* l *above dotted* n

'But the wicked Jews were jealous of him, because the people, deserting them, were following in his footsteps, spreading their clothes before his feet and were crying out, "Blessed is He who comes in the name of the Lord!" [cf. Matthew 21.9] Having been inflamed against him, the Pharisees handed him over to a certain governor named Pilate, alleging that he was a most accursed sorcerer, and they stirred up turbulent civil unrest so that they might crucify him.

(14) 'Foreseeing that he would bring salvation to the world, he allowed himself to be taken and mocked and at the same time scourged and killed. He knew that except through his suffering he would not bring the devil into captivity and that heavy punishment would not be inflicted on the unclean spirits. For this reason then, he who had not committed any sin was held captive so that the human race held in the bond of sin might be set free.* The blessed one is cursed so that he might spare us from curses. He permitted himself to be mocked so that he might remove us from the mocking of demons who whirl about in this world. He accepted a thorny crown on his head so that he might snatch away the capital sentence due us on account of the thorns of our sins. He took gall for his food so that he might replace the first man's sweet taste by which death invaded the world. He drank vinegar so that he might take into himself the bitterness that boiled up in our, and he drank himself the cup of suffering due us for our passions. He was stripped so that he might cover in snow-white garments the nakedness of our parents, which grieved him when the serpent's counsel caused it. He was hung on a tree so that he might remove the transgression of the tree through the tree of his suffering. Likewise, he allowed death to approach him so that he might overthrow her as she struggled against him and so that she, who had managed to get a kingdom through the serpent, might, together with the serpent, be made a vanquished captive through Christ.

'Finally, when all the elements saw their Creator raised up on the cross, they trembled with great dread. For on one side the earth was shaken, on another temples and stones were rent asunder. The light of day fled. The sun was frightened and made all the world mournful when it became darkened. The moon covered the pale surfaces of her light with a bloody cloud. All the stars radiating with shining hue were likewise darkened. The earth gave a groan and as if giving birth began to bring forth from the tombs many holy ones who gave testimony that the Saviour's descent into the underworld had snatched the kingdom from the devil and that by dying he had gained control over death and had subjugated and bound her and had put her under his subjects' feet.

---

294 inuenerat] C inuenit. cum ipso serpente
   prostrata] V *omits*; C *follows* H *except for*
   prostrato
295 Fol. 76va
296 horrore] C terrore
297 alio] C altero. scindebantur] VC
   findebantur
298 lugubrem] C et lugubrem. pallidos] V
   pallidum. uultus] V uultum
299 contexit] C texit. obscurate sunt] VC
   migrauerunt
300 Dedit] V Dat. parere] V reddere
301 quod] V quia
302 optinuit] C tenuit
303 subdidit pedibus] V *order reversed*

'Inde est quod pro nomine eius uerberari gaudemus et in persecutionibus
305 gloriamur quia uite nostre isti caduce et misere et terrene eterna uita succedit
illa quam Dei filius resurgens a mortuis suis apostolis demonstrauit quibus
uidentibus ascendit in celos. Hoc si trium testium doceret assertio, sapien-
tium mentes dubitare non poterant. At uero cum non solum duodecim
apostolis sed plusquam quingentis simul se demonstrare dignatus est, ambi-
310 guitatis nulla penitus uestigia dereliquit. Hi autem qui hec in uniuersum
mundum missi sunt predicare signis et uirtutibus magnis sua dicta firmabant.
Nam et omnes egritudines in eius nomine curauerunt, effugauerunt demonia,
et uitam mortuis reddiderunt.

(15) 'Nichil puto tibi remansisse quod queras nisi ut istam uitam et animo
315 et corde despicias, et illam uehementer et fortiter queras. Qui enim filium
Dei crediderit et preceptis eius adheserit, dum deposuerit corpus, a morte
non tangitur sed a sanctis angelis in gremio suscipitur et | ad Paradisi
perducitur regionem. Inde est quod ipsa mors cum diabolo agit ut diuersis
occupationibus obliget mentes et uariis incautos necessitatibus occupet.
320 Nunc de damno timidat, nunc de lucro incitat, nunc de pulchritudine illicit,
nunc de gula exagitat, et diuerso genere suasionis de ista sola uita facit
miseros homines cogitare, ut eos exeuntes de corpore inueniant nudos nichil
secum preter peccata portantes.

'Hec breuiter explicaui [tibi]; si quid tibi deesse consideras, quere'.

325 (16) *Tunc Tiburtius* pedibus eius prostratus cum ingenti gemitu et *lacrimis*
dixit, 'Si de ista uita ulterius uel mente tractauero uel cogitatione quesiero,
in illa uita non inueniar. Habeant stulti lucrum labentis temporis; ego qui
usque hodie sine causa uixi, iam non sit sine causa quod uiuo'.

Et his dictis ad fratrem suum conuersus ait, 'Miserere mei frater karissime,
330 et rumpe moras quarum nexus non patior. Dilationes timeo. Pondus ferre
non possum. *Obsecro te, perduc me ad hominem Dei ut me purificans illius
uite participem faciat*'.

---

304 Inde] V Unde. uerberari] V fatigati; C
uerberati. et] V *omits*
305 et terrene] VC *omit*
307 assertio] C *dotted* ti *above line*
308 uero cum] *double slashes signal
transposition of* cum uero. solum] V solis
308–09 duodecim apostolis] V duodecim
discipulis; C xii· discipulis. demonstrare]
C demonstrauit
310 derelinquit] C derelinqui. Hi] V Ispi
311 missi sunt predicare] VC predicare missi
sunt. signis] C set signis
312 et] C *omits*. effugauerunt] V fugauerunt
314 et] VC *omit*
315 uehementer et fortiter] C uehementius
et fortius

316 dum] V cum
317 Fol. 76vb
319 occupationibus] VC occupationibus
hominum. obliget] V inplicet
320 Nunc] VC Et nunc. damno] V mundo.
pulchritudine] V pulchro. illicit] C illicitat
321 suasionis] V suasioni
322 miseros homines] VC *order reversed*.
inueniant] VC inueniat
324 (tibi)] tu; VC *omit*
325 gemitu] VC fletu
327 labentis] V presentis
330 rumpe] C erumpe. non patior] C
compatior
331 illius] C illi

'So it is that we rejoice to be scourged for his name's sake and glory in persecutions because following this transitory and wretched and earthly life of ours is that eternal life which the Son of God, rising from the dead, revealed to his apostles, who were watching as he ascended into heaven. If the testimony of three witnesses were to affirm this, then the minds of the wise could not doubt it. But since he deigned to show himself not only to the twelve apostles but to more than five hundred people at the same time, he left no trace of uncertainty. Moreover, those who were sent to proclaim these things to all the world affirmed what they said by mighty signs and miracles. For they healed all illnesses in his name, cast out demons, and they restored life to the dead.

(15) 'I think that nothing remains you might seek except to despise this life with both mind and heart, and to seek that other life vigorously and zealously. He who believes in the Son of God and remains steadfast in his teachings, when he lays down this body, is not touched by death but is taken up by holy angels into their bosom and is led into the realm of paradise. That is why death herself works with the devil to bind minds with various preoccupations and to seize the unwary with different obligations. At one moment she makes us afraid of loss, at another incites us with gain, now entices with beauty, now harasses with gluttony, and with various sorts of persuasions makes wretched men think only about this life, so that when they leave the body, they will discover themselves nude, bearing nothing with them except sins.

'I have explained these things to you briefly; if you think of anything that you need, ask'.

(16) Then, when Tiburtius had prostrated himself at her feet, he said with great groaning and weeping, 'If I try to find out more about that life either through lengthy reflection or deliberation, I will not be found in that life. Let fools have the material gain of time that is passing away; let me, who has lived until today without good reason, not go on living without good reason'.

And with these words, he turned to his brother and said, 'Have mercy on me dearest brother, and end the delays whose hindrances I cannot bear. I am afraid of putting it off. I cannot bear the burden. I beg you, take me to the man of God so that when he purifies me, he might make me a sharer in that life'.

Tunc Ualerianus perduxit fratrem suum ad papam Urbanum. Cui cum narrasset uniuersa que fuerant acta uel dicta, gratias referens Deo, suscepit
335 Tiburtium cum omni gaudio. *Et baptizans eum*, secum esse precepit quoad-usque albas deponeret. *Quem perfectum doctrina sua per septem dies*, Christo militem consecrauit. *Tantam deinceps gratiam consecutus est Domini ut et angelos Dei uideret cotidie, et omniumque poposcisset a Deo protinus eueniret effectus.*
340 Verum quam multum est ut omnia per ordinem prosequentes que et *quanta per eos Dominus fecerit* conscribamus; ad gloriosas passiones eorum articulum reuocemus.

| (17) [T]unc *Almachius, urbis Rome prefectus, sanctos Dei fortiter lani-abat et inhumata iubebat eorum corpora derelinqui. Tiburtius uero et*
345 *Ualerianus ad hoc uacabant cotidie ut preciosas martyrum facerent sepulturas elemosinis* et pietatibus *insistentes.* Interea, ut solitum est, bonos odiunt mali et indicant uniuersa Almachio que per eos Dominus circa egentes ageret uel quam studiose quos ille occidi iusserat sepelirent.

Tenti ergo ab apparitoribus Almachio presentantur. *Quos Almachius his*
350 *protinus aggressus est uerbis,* 'Cum uos nobilitatis titulus clarissimo genere fecerit nasci, cur nescio per quam superstitionem infelices uos et degeneres exhibetis? *Nam facultates uestras uos audio nescio in quas uiles personas expendendo consumere ac pro sceleribus suis punitos cum omni gloria tradere sepulture.* Vnde datur intelligi quod conscii uestri sint quibus pro coniura-
355 tione honestam traditis sepulturam'.

Respondens Tiburtius dixit, '*Vtinam dignentur nos ut seruos suos computare,* quorum tu existimas nos esse collegas; qui contempserunt quod uidetur esse et non est, et inuenerunt illud quod uidetur non esse et est'.

Almachius dixit, 'Quid est quod uidetur esse et non est?'
360 Tiburtius dixit, 'Omnia que in isto mundo sunt que mutant animos ad mortem perpetuam per leticiam temporalem'.

Almachius dixit, 'Quid est quod uidetur non esse et est?'

---

334 acta uel dicta] VC dicta uel facta
336 Quem perfectum] V *omits.* septem] C
   vii· *and* t *written above*
337 deinceps] C denique
338 angelos] V angelum. omniumque] C
   omniaque. Deo] C domino
340 quam] VC quia. prosequentes] C
   prosequamur
341 fecerit] V mirabilia fecerat; C mirabilia
   fecerit

343 Fol. 77ra. (T)unc] unc *is indented for a*
   space of five letters to accommodate the
   right side of a crossbar of a large T *that*
   was never executed; V Turbidus; C
   Turicius. Rome] C *omits.* Dei] C domini.
345 uacabant] C uocabantur. cotidie] C
   omits
347 circa] C *erased.* egentes] C *omits.*
   studiose] V studiosi
349 ergo] VC *omit*

Then Valerian led his brother to pope Urban. When he told him all the things that had been done and said, he gave thanks to God and received Tiburtius with utter joy. And when he had baptized him, he commanded him to remain with him until he had taken off his albs. When Tiburtius had completed his instruction over the course of seven days, Urban consecrated him a soldier of Christ. After that, such grace from the Lord followed that he daily saw the angels of God, and whatever he asked of God was immediately carried out.

But it is too much for us to write down in order everything that happened and all the many things that the Lord did through them; let us recount the part about their glorious martyrdoms.

(17) Then Almachius, the prefect of the city of Rome, violently butchered the saints of God and ordered their bodies to be left unburied. Tiburtius and Valerian devoted themselves daily to providing costly burials for the martyrs while continuing their almsgiving and works of piety. Meanwhile, as is usual, evil men hated the good and made known to Almachius all that the Lord did through them for those in need and how zealously they buried those he had ordered to be killed.

When they had been seized by the prefect's aides, they were presented to Almachius. Almachius immediately accosted them with these words, 'When a noble name has by birth put you in the ranks of the most illustrious, why for some trifling superstition or other do you show yourselves to be foolish and ignoble? For I hear that you waste your wealth by spending it on some worthless people or other and that you bury with all honour those punished for their crimes. By this deed it is given to be understood that those you bury with honour are your accomplices in a conspiracy'.

Tiburtius replied and said, 'If only they would deign to count us as their slaves, those whom you suppose to be our conspirators; they have despised what seems to exist and does not, and have discovered that which seems not to exist and does'.

Almachius said, 'What is it that seems to exist and does not?'

Tiburtius said, 'All the things in this world that draw our souls to everlasting death through temporal joy'.

Almachius said, 'What is it that seems not to exist and does?'

---

350 clarissimo] VC clarissimos. genere] VC *omit*

351 nescio per quam superstitionem] V nescio per qua superstitione; C nuper nescio qua superstitione

352 nescio in quas] V *omits* in; C in nescio quas

353 suis] V *omits*

355 honestam] C honestas. sepulturam] C sepulturas

356 Respondens] C Respondit. dixit] C dicens

357 existimas nos esse] V nos aestimas esse; C aestimas nos esse

359 Almachius dixit] V Almatius prefectus dixit; C Almachius prefectus dixit

360 mutant animos] V incitant animas; C inuitant homines

362 Quid] VC Et quid. uidetur non] V *order reversed*; C non uidetur non

Tiburtius dixit, 'Vita que uentura est iustis et pena que debetur iniustis. Et utroque latere uerum nouimus esse quod ueniant, et infelici dissimula-
365   tione quod oculos cordis nostri scimus uidere oculis corporis nostri subducimus ut, contra conscientiam nostram, que bona sunt malis sermonibus obumbremus et que mala sunt bonis sermonibus adornemus'.

Almalchius dixit, 'Non puto quod mente tua loquaris'.

Tiburtius dixit, 'Non mea mente loquor sed eius quem in uisceribus mee
370   mentis accepi'.

Almachius dixit, 'Nunquid tu ipse scis quid loquaris?'

Tiburtius dixit, 'Et noui et didici et credo quod uniuersa que a me dicta sunt ita ut dicta sunt permanebunt'.

Almachius dixit, 'Ego quare non aduerto quo ordine ista prosequaris?'
375   Tiburtius dixit, 'Quia animalis homo non percipit ea que sunt spiritus. Spiritualis homo iudicat omnia et ipse a nemine iudicatur'.

(18) Tunc ridens prefectus iussit amoueri Tiburtium et applicari Ualerianum. Cui et dixit, 'Quoniam non est sani capitis frater tuus, tu saltem potes sapienter dare responsum'.
380   Dicit ei Ualerianus, 'Auditus tuus errorem patitur quia uim sermonis nostri non potes intueri'.

Prefectus dixit, 'Nullus sic errat sicut uos erratis. Qui relictis rebus necessariis et utilibus, ineptias sectamini et otium. Respuentes gaudia, execrantes leticiam atque contempnentes omne quod uite blandimento concessum est,
385   illud tota mentis auiditate suscipitis quod saluti est contrarium, gaudiis inimicum'.

Valerianus ad hec respondit, 'Iocantes et ridentes et uariis deliciis affluentes uidi glaciali tempore transire per campos. In quibus campis stabant rustici pastinantes, et cum omni studio sarmenta pangentes atque spinosa
390   surcula rosarum animose et cautissime componentes. Alii quoque taleas inserebant, alii radicitus noxia queque truncabant cunctaque ruris opera labore nimio excolebant.

---

363 uentura] VC futura
365 quod...uidere] V *omits.* corporis] V
    cordis
368 Fol. 77rb. dixit] V respondit. mea mente]
    V *order reversed*
371 quid] V quę; C qua, *corrected from* quas.
    loquaris] VC loqueris
372 dixit] C respondit. quod] V quia

374 Ego] VC Et ego. aduerto] V auerto.
    prosequaris] VC prosequeris
375 ea] VC *omit*
376 homo] V autem di; C autem. et] VC
    omit. ipse] VC ipse autem
379 potes] VC poteris. responsum] C
    responsa

Tiburtius said, 'The life that is to come to the righteous and the punishment that is owed to the unrighteous. And we know to be true what will come for both sides, and with foolish pretended ignorance we look away with our bodily eyes from that which we know how to see with the eyes of our heart so that, against our own conscience, we conceal with evil words that which is good and embellish that which is evil with good words'.

Almachius said, 'I do not think that you are speaking in your right mind'.

Tiburtius said, 'I do not speak with my mind but with the mind of Him whom I have received in the innermost parts of my mind'.

Almachius said, 'Do you yourself really know what you are saying?'

Tiburtius said, 'I have come to know and have learned and believe that all the things I have said will endure just as I have said them.'

Almachius said, 'Why do I not turn to that course you follow?'

Tiburtius said, 'Because the sensual man does not perceive the things that are of the spirit. The spiritual man judges all things, and he himself is judged by no one' [cf. 1 Corinthians 2.15].

(18) Then as he was laughing, the prefect ordered Tiburtius to be led away and Valerian to be led in. And he said to him, 'Because your brother is not right in the head, maybe you can sensibly give an answer'.

Valerian says to him, 'There is something wrong with your hearing since you cannot grasp the weight of our words'.

The prefect said, 'No one errs as greatly as you err. You have abandoned what is essential and profitable, and chase after what is absurd and useless. Spurning joys, abhorring delight and despising all that has been given for pleasure in this life, you have ardently embraced what is contrary to well-being and hateful to enjoyment'.

Valerian replied to this, 'I have seen those joking and laughing and abounding in comforts crossing the fields during winter. Rustics stood in those fields preparing the ground, and planting twigs with their full attention and eagerly and very carefully arranging the thorny canes of roses. Some were grafting cuttings, others were cutting off each harmful plant by the roots and all were tending to the work of the countryside with extraordinary industry.

---

380 tuus] C i *between* u *and* s *erased.* uim] C
  uiam
381 potes] C poteris. intueri] V intuere
382 errat] C erat. uos] C et uos. rebus] C
  erasure between e *and* b, *and after* s
383 ineptias] VC inepta. et otium] V *omits.*
  execrantes] V et execrantes
384 omne] V *omits.* est] C *omits*

385 suscipitis] V suspicitis. est contrarium]
  VC contrarium inueniri (C inuenire)
  potest et
387 Valerianus ad hec] V Ad hęc ualerianus
389 studio] V gaudio. sarmenta] C armenta
391 cunctaque] C cunctique. ruris] C ruri
392 excolebant] V explentes; C excolentes

'Tunc illi qui diliciabantur et epulabantur ceperunt laborantes irridere ac dicere, "Infelices et miseri, istum superfluum laborem abicite et nobiscum
395 gaudentes | deliciis uos ac uoluptatibus exhibete. Quare sicut insani duro labore deficitis et uite uestre tempora tristissimis occupationibus fatigatis?" Et hec dicentes soluebantur super eos risu et dabant plausus manuum, multis increpationibus insultantes.

'Hec illis agentibus imbriferis atque algidis mensibus, serena tempora
400 successerunt. Et ecce floribus roseis uernantes campi nemoribus pampineis ornabantur, et crispas botrionum sertas exhibebant suo partu sarmenta et uario genere talee arborum melliflua poma gignebant. In quibus uidimus usque hodie habundare gratiam et fructum pariter et decorem.

'Tunc gaudentibus illis qui putabantur uani, ceperunt flere qui uidebantur
405 urbani. Et qui in sua fuerant sapientia gloriati in nimia pestilentia perierunt, et sera penitudine mugitum sui otii gemitumque reddentes, sibi inuicem loquebantur, "Isti sunt quos habuimus in derisum; laborem ipsorum putabamus opprobrium; uitam eorum execrabamus ut miseram; personam eorum iudicauimus indignam et conuentus eorum sine honore. Isti autem
410 inuenti sunt sapientes, et nos probamur miseri tunc fuisse et insipientes et uani quando nec ipsi laborauimus nec laborantibus auxilium pro labore prestitimus. Quinimno eos in deliciis positi risimus et credidimus dementes quos fulgentes nunc aspicimus et florentes"'.

(19) Ad hec prefectus ait, 'Sapienter quidem te uideo prosecutum, sed
415 non ad interrogationem meam uideris dedisse responsum'.

Valerianus respondit, 'Stultos nos et insipientes esse dixisti quod facultates nostras egentibus damus, aduenas suscipimus, uiduis opem ferimus, orphanis subuenimus, inhumata corpora tegimus et honestas Dei martyribus tradimus sepulturas. | Insipientes nos esse et insanissimos iudicas quod non
420 cum letantibus letamur, neque cum uoluptuosis deliciis resoluimur aut ignobilis uulgi oculis nos illustres et nobiles ostendimus.

'Veniet tempus in quo fructum huius nostre tristicie colligemus, et nobis gaudentibus, lugeant hi qui nunc in suis gaudiis extolluntur. Tempus enim seminandi modo est. Qui in ista uita seminauerit gaudia in illa uita luctum et
425 gemitum metet. Qui autem nunc seminauerint lacrimas temporales in illa uita gaudia sunt sempiterna messuri'.

---

395 Fol. 77va
397 risu] C risus
400 nemoribus] et nemoribus
401 botrionum] C butronum
402 talee] V talia; C tabus
403 habundare] V abundare et
405 urbani] C uani. in nimia pestilentia
  perierunt] V in nimia facti sunt
  pestilentia nubulati
406 et sera penitudine] V in sua poenitentia.
  sui otii gemitumque] V *omits*; C sui ut hii

gemitumque
408 putabamus] V putamus
408–09 ut...iudicauimus] C *omits*.
  iudicauimus] V iudicabamus. conuentus]
  VC conuentum
410 inuenti sunt] C *omits*. probamur] C
  probamui, r *above line and erasure of*
  abbreviatory mark over i
411 quando] C quedum
413 fulgentes] V gaudentes. florentes] V
  fulgentes

'Then those who were living in luxury and enjoying themselves began to make fun of those working and to say, "Unhappy and wretched ones, give up this unnecessary labour and rejoicing with us, devote yourselves to comforts and delights. Why like madmen do you weaken yourselves with hard work and weary yourselves during your lifetime with most unpleasant pursuits?" And as they were saying these things they dissolved into laughter at them and applauded them, jeering at them with many reproaches.

'They did these things in the rainy and cold months, but fair weather followed. And, lo, the fields flowering with rosy blooms were adorned with leafy groves, and the vines in their fruitfulness produced twisted garlands of clustered grapes and the grafts from different kinds of trees brought forth sweet fruits. Even today we see the trees overflowing with charm and both fruit and beauty in equal measure.

'Then while those who were thought to be foolish rejoiced, those who seemed sophisticated began to weep. And those who had gloried in their own reasoning perished in a great pestilence, and uttering groans and moans with belated regret for their idleness, they said among themselves, "There are those whom we held in scorn; we considered their work to be a source of shame; we detested their way of life as wretched; we judged their position to be unworthy and their community to be without honour. But these are found to be wise, and we are thus proved wretched and unwise and foolish when we neither worked ourselves nor offered help to the workers. Rather, we laughed amid our comforts and believed them to be insane whom we now see radiant and flourishing"'.

(19) To these things the prefect said, 'If nothing else I see that you have intelligently pursued a theme, but you seem not to have answered my question'.

Valerian said, 'You said that we are stupid and unwise because we give our wealth to the poor, take in strangers, give aid to widows, provide relief for orphans, bury unburied corpses and give honourable burials to God's martyrs. You pronounce us unwise and utterly insane because we do not rejoice with those who rejoice, nor are weakened with pleasurable delights, nor present ourselves as illustrious and distinguished to the eyes of the undistinguished crowd.

'A time will come in which we will harvest the fruit of our austerity, and while they are rejoicing with us, those who are now exultant in their joy will lament. Now is the time for sowing. He who sows joy in this life will reap grief and groaning in that life. But those who now sow temporal tears will reap everlasting joy in that life'.

---

414 quidem te] C *order reversed*
416 respondit] VC dixit
417 suscipimus] C suscepimus
419 Fol. 77vb. Insipientes...iudicas] V *omits*
420 resoluimur] C resoluamur
422 fructum] V fructus. colligemus] C colligamus

423 lugeant] V lugent. nunc in suis] VC in suis nunc
424 seminauerit] V seminauerint; C seminauerunt
425 metet] V metent; C metunt. seminauerint] C seminauerunt
426 gaudia sunt] C *order reversed.* messuri] C mansuri

(20) Prefectus dixit, 'Ergo nos et inuictissimi principes eternum habebimus luctum, uos uero perpetuum possidebitis gaudium?'

Valerianus respondit, 'Vos enim quid estis aut quid principes uestri?
430　Homuntiones estis tempore uestro nati, tempore uestro expleto morituri, tantum Deo reddituri rationem quantam uobis potestatis tradidit summam'.

Almachius dixit, 'Quid uerborum circuitu moramur? Offerte diis libamina et abscedite illesi'.

Responderunt ambo et dixerunt, 'Non nos diis sed Deo cotidie sacrifi-
435　cium exhibemus'.

Almachius dixit, 'Quis est Deus cui uestrum uos dicitis tradere famu-latum?'

Responderunt ambo et dixerunt, 'Et quis est deus alius ut de Deo nos interroges? Est enim alius preter unum?'

440　Almachius dixit, 'Ipsum unum quem dicitis, nomen ipsius edicite'.

Valerianus respondit, 'Nomen Dei non inuenies, etiam si pennis uolare possis'.

Almachius dixit, 'Ergo Iouis nomen Dei non est?'

Valerianus respondit, 'Nomen est hominis, corruptoris uxorum et stupra-
445　toris puerorum. Homicidam illum uestri auctores commemorant, et criminosum littere uestre demonstrant. Hunc tu "Deum" miror qua fronte locutus sis cum Deus dici non possit nisi ab omni | peccato alienus sit et sit omnibus uirtutibus plenus'.

Almachius dixit, 'Ergo omnis mundus errat, et tu cum fratre tuo uerum
450　"Deum" nosti?'

Valerianus respondit, 'Innumerabilis multitudo Christianitatis sancti-tatem suscepit, et magis uos pauci estis qui sicut hastule de naufragio remansistis ad nichil aliud nisi ut in ignem mittamini'.

(21) *Tunc iratus Almachius iussit eum fustibus cedi.* Ille autem statim ut
455　exutus est, cepit gaudere dicens, 'Ecce dies et hora quam sitienter optaui, ecce dies omni michi festiuitate iocundior!' Cumque cederent eum, uox preconia super eum clamabat dicens, 'Deos et deas blasphemare noli!'

---

427 nos] C et nos
429 Vos enim quid estis] VC Quid enim estis
　　uos. aut] C *omits.* quid] V *omits*
430 Homuntiones] V humum; C
　　humunciones. nati tempore uestro
　　expleto] V *omits*
431 reddituri rationem] V *order reversed.*
　　potestatis tradidit summam] V
　　potestatem suam; C tradidit summam
　　potestatis

432 circuitu] V circuitum. moramur] V
　　inmoramur; C immoramur
434 et dixerunt] VC *omit.* Non nos] C *order*
　　reversed
438 et dixerunt] VC *omit*
439 unum] V unum deum
440 dicitis] C dicis. edicite] C edicito
441 respondit] V dixit. nomen Dei] VC *order*
　　reversed
444 respondit] V dixit

(20) The prefect said, 'So while we and the utterly invincible emperors will have everlasting grief, you will have unending joy?'

Valerian answered, 'What are you or your emperors in fact? You are little men born in your time, who will die when your time is up, who will repay God in proportion to all of the power he gave to you'.

Almachius said, 'Why do we delay in a round of words? Offer sacrifices to the gods and leave unharmed'.

Both responded and said, 'Not to the gods but to God we daily offer a sacrifice'.

Almachius said, 'Who is the God to whom you say you give your service?'

Both answered and said, 'And who is another god that you ask us about our God? Is there another besides the One?'

Almachius said, 'This One you speak about, declare his name'.

Valerian responded, 'You will not discover the name of God for yourself even if you had wings to fly.'

Almachius said, 'So Jupiter is not the name of God?'

Valerian replied, 'That is the name of a man, a seducer of wives and a ravisher of boys. Your own authors write that he is a murderer, and your literature shows him to be guilty. I am amazed how with boldness you have called this one "God" since he cannot be called God unless he is a stranger to all sin and is filled with all virtues'.

Almachius said, 'So the entire world is wrong, and you and your brother know the true "God"?'

Valerian replied, 'An innumerable multitude has accepted the holiness of Christianity, and, what is more, there are hardly any of you left, like splinters of wood left over from a shipwreck, with which there is little to be done except to throw them onto the fire'.

(21) Enraged, Almachius then ordered Valerian to be beaten with clubs. But as soon as he was stripped, he began to rejoice saying, 'Behold the day and the hour that I have ardently hoped for, behold the day that is more delightful to me than any festivity!' And while they were beating him, the voice of the herald rang out above him saying, 'Do not blaspheme the gods and goddesses!'

444–45 uxorum et stupratoris puerorum] V *omits* et; C *omits*. commemorant] V fuisse commemorant

447 sis] es. possint] C posse. Fol. 78ʳᵃ. *both instances of* sit] V *omits*

451–52 sanctitatem] V sanctitate. hastule de naufragio] V tabulę naufragii; C astule de manu naufragio

454 Ille autem] V *omits*

455 dies et] VC *omit*. sitienter] VC semper

456 omni] V omnium. festiuitate] V festiuitatum; C te *above line*. iocundior] C *first* o *corrected from* u

457 et deas] V deasque

Ille autem clamabat populo dicens, 'Ciues Romani, uidete ne uos a ueritate ista mea plaga reuocet, sed state uiriliter et deos lapideos quos colit
460   Almachius in calcem conuertite quia in eterna tribulatione erunt omnes qui colunt eos'.

(22) *Tunc assessor* prefecti Tarquinius *dixit* prefecto, '*Prefecte*, inuenisti occasionem.* Tolle eos. *Nam si moras feceris et de die in diem protraxeris, omnes facultates suas erogabunt. Et punitis eis, tu nichil inuenies*'.

465   *Tunc Almachius prefectus iussit carnificibus ut ab eis ducerentur ad pagum* ubi erat idolum Iouis, *et iussit ut si noluissent sacrificare, ambo fratres sententiam capitalem exciperent*. Tunc gloriosi martyres, *tenti a Maximo*, corniculario prefecti, *ducebantur* ad pagum.

Qui Maximus cepit flere super eos dicens, 'O iuuentutis flos purpureus! O
470   germanus fraternitatis affectus! Qua uos impia definitione uultis amittere, *ad interitum uestrum quasi ad epulas festinantes*?'

Tiburtius *dixit*, '*Nos nisi pro certo didicissemus alteram, uitam esse perpetuam | que isti uite presenti succedit, nunquam istam nos amittere gauderemus*'.

475   Dicit ei Maximus, 'Ergo potest esse altera uita?'

Respondit Tiburtius, 'Sicut uides homo constat anima et corpore, et sicut uestitur uestimentis corpus, ita uestitur anima corpore. Et sicut expoliatur uestimentis corpus, ita expoliatur anima corpore. Et corpus quidem, quod terrenum semen per libidinem dedit, terreno uentri redditur, in puluerem
480   redactum sicut fenix donec futuri luminis aspectu resurgat. Anima uero ad paradisi delicias, si sancta est, perducetur ut in deliciis affluens tempus sue resurrectionis expectet'.

(23) *Dicit ei Maximus, 'Optarem et ego contempnere uitam istam si certum apud me haberem quod loqueris'*.

---

459 ista] V *omits.* sed] C set
460 eterna] V ęternam. tribulatione] V tribulationem
462 Tarquinius] C Tarquinus. Prefecte] VC *omit*
463 moras] V moram
464 nichil inuenies] VC *order reversed* (C inuenies *corrected from* inuenitis, ti *underscored for deletion and* e *above line*)
465 Almachius prefectus] VC *omit*
466 idolum Iouis] V statunculum iouis; C statu uinculus ionius, u *of* ionius (*written as* v) *above line.* fratres] VC fratres pariter

467 exciperent] C susciperent
469 purpureus] V purpureum
470 Qua] V quem; C quia. impia definitione] C impiam diffinitionem. uultis] VC uolentes
470–71 ad interitum uestrum] C et. festinantes] VC festinatis
472 Tiburtius] VC Tunc tiburtius
473 Fol. 78ᵗᵇ. isti] V istę. uite presenti] V *order reversed*
475 ei] V eis. Ergo] V Et quę; C et que. altera uita] V alteram uitam
476 Respondit] V dicit.

But Valerian cried out to the crowd saying, 'Citizens of Rome, see that this flogging of mine does not dissuade you from the truth, but manfully stand firm and render the stony gods whom Almachius worships into lime because those who worship them will live in everlasting tribulation'.

(22) Then the prefect's aide Tarquinius said to the prefect, 'Prefect, you have happened upon an opportune moment.* Get rid of them. For if you create delays and prolong this from day to day, they will give away all their wealth. And when you punish them, you will find nothing left for yourself'.

Then the prefect Almachius ordered the torturers to lead them to the countryside where there was an idol of Jupiter, and he ordered that if they did not wish to sacrifice, then both brothers were to receive the death sentence. When the illustrious martyrs had been seized by Maximus, the prefect's adjutant, they were led to the countryside.

This Maximus began to weep over them saying, 'O the rosy flower of youth! O the genuine love of brotherhood! Do you wish to lose these for the sake of an impious pronouncement, hastening to your destruction as if to a feast?'

Tiburtius said, 'If we had not learned for certain there is another, everlasting life that follows this present one, we would not rejoice to lose this one'.

Maximus says to him, 'So what can this other life be?'

Tiburtius answered, 'Now you know that a man is made of a body and soul, and just as the body is clothed with garments, so is the soul covered by the body. And just as the body is stripped of clothing, so is the soul stripped from the body. And indeed the body, which earthly seed produced by means of lust, is returned to the belly of the earth, reduced to dust like the phoenix until it rises again in the sight of the coming light. Truly the soul, if it is holy, may be led to the delights of paradise so that abounding in delights, it may look forward to (the body's) resurrection'.

(23) Maximus says to him, 'I too would choose to despise this life if I could be certain in my own mind about what you say'.

476–77 Sicut...corpore.] V Anima hominis ita uestitur corpore ut corpus induitur uestimento; C *omits* Sicut uides homo constat anima et corpore et. uestitur uestimentis] *double slashes signal transposition of* uestimentis uestitur. Et] C *omits*

478 corpore] V a corpore
480 redactum] V redigitur. donec] C *omits*. futuri] V *omits*. luminis aspectu] C *order reversed*

481 perducetur ut] V ducitur et; C perferatur ut. sue] V *omits*
482 resurrectionis] C restaurationis. expectet] V expectat
483 certum] VC poteram certum
484 haberem] VC habere. quod] V quę; C que

485   *Dicit ei* Ualerianus, 'Quia nichil tibi superesse dicis nisi ut probes uera esse que diximus, in hora qua nos Dominus faciet istam corporis tunicam in gloriosa nominis sui confessione deponere, *aperiet oculos tuos et faciet te uidere cum quanta gloria illa uita suscipitur, si tamen promittas nobis quod ex animo ad penitentiam erroris tui uenias'.*

490   *Tunc Maximus deuotauit se dicens, 'Fulmineis ignibus consumar si* ex hac hora *non illum Dominum confitear* qui alteram uitam facit isti uite suc[c]edere. Hoc tantum uos michi quod promisistis ostendite'.

       Dicunt ei ambo fratres, 'Impera carnificibus ut ad domum tuam nos ducant, hodierna die inducias explicans ita *ut custodiant nos in domo tua,* et illic ad

495   te uenire faciemus purificatorem qui, te ista nocte statim ut purificauerit, faciet te uidere hoc quod tibi promisimus'.

       Quod cum imperasset Maximus, *duxit eos in domum suam.* Ad quorum predicationem et ipse Maximus cum omni domo sua | *et ipsi carnifices crediderunt.* Tunc sancta *Cecilia uenit ad eos nocte cum sacerdotibus, et*

500   *uniuersi baptizati sunt. Igitur cum aurora* nocti finem daret, facto magno silentio *Cecilia dixit, 'Eia milites Christi, abicite opera tenebrarum, et induimini arma lucis. Certamen bonum certastis, cursum consummastis, fidem seruastis. Ite ad coronam uite quam dabit uobis iustus iudex,* non solum autem uobis sed et omnibus qui diligunt aduentum eius'.

505   (24) Locus igitur qui uocabatur pagus quarto miliario ab urbe positus erat, in quo per templi ianuam transitus erat, ut omnes qui ingrederentur si Ioui thura non imponerent, punirentur. *Venientibus ergo sanctis,* offeruntur thura, et recusant recusantes, ponunt genua, *feriuntur gladio.* Proiciunt corpus temporale et martyrium suscipiunt sempiternum.

510   *Tunc Maximus iuratus asserebat dicens, 'Vidi angelos Dei fulgentes sicut sol in hora qua uerrati sunt gladio et egredientes animas eorum de corporibus* quasi ornatas uirgines de thalamo suo. *Quas in gremio suo suscipientes angeli, remigio alarum suarum ferebant ad celos'. Itaque cum lacrimis talia prosequente Maximo, plurimi crediderunt, et ab idolorum cultura conuersi,* suo se

515   Artifici reddiderunt.

---

485 superesse dicis] C *order reversed*
486 diximus] C dicimus
487 confessione] C confessionem. aperiet]
      VC aperiet dominus
488 cum] V eum. quanta] V qua. illa uita] V
      order reversed. quod] C quo
490 deuotauit] VC deuotabat. se dicens] V
      se et animam suam dicens
491 Dominum] V solum deum; C deum
492 suc(c)edere] sucedere; VC succedere
493 Impera] V Inpetra; C Impetra.
      carnificibus] VC a carnificibus

494 hodierna die] V et hodierna die; C et
      hodierni diei. explicans] VC explica. et]
      VC *omit.* illic] C illuc
496 faciet] V faciat
497–98 Ad quorum predicationem et ipse
      Maximus] V A quorum prędicatione
      carnifices ipsi et Maximus. domo] C
      domu. Fol. 78ᵛᵃ. et ipsi carnifices] V *omits*
500 nocti] V nocte; C noctis
502 certastis] VC certati estis
503 dabit] C dabit dominus. uobis] V *omits.*
      autem] VC *omit*

Valerian says to him, 'Since you say that nothing remains for you except to prove what we have said to be true, in the hour in which the Lord makes us lay down this bodily tunic in glorious confession of his name, he will open your eyes and will make you see with what glory that other life is taken up, if only you promise us that you will sincerely come to repent of your error'.

Then Maximus made a vow saying, 'May I be consumed by fiery lighting bolts if from this hour I do not confess that Lord who makes another life to follow this one. Just show me what you have promised'.

Both brothers say to him, 'Command the torturers to lead us to your house, arranging a delay for today so that they may guard us in your house, and we will have a purifier come there to you who, as soon as he has purified you this very night, will make you see what we have promised you'.

When Maximus had ordered that, he led them into his house. On account of their preaching, Maximus himself together with his household and even the torturers believed. Then Saint Cecilia came to them at night with priests, and all were baptized. Thus when dawn brought an end to the night, amid a great silence Cecilia said, 'O soldiers of Christ, throw away the works of darkness, and put on the armour of light [cf. Romans 13.12]. You have fought the good fight, you have finished the race, you have kept the faith. Go to the crown of life that the just judge will give to you, not only to you but to all those who love his coming' [cf. 2 Timothy 4.7–8].

(24) Now located four miles from the city was the place called the country-side, into which there was a passage through the gate of a temple, so that all who entered were punished if they did not offer incense to Jupiter. And so when the saints arrived, they were offered incense, and being unwilling they refused, kneeled and were struck with the sword. They cast aside the temporal body and accepted eternal martyrdom.

Then, having sworn an oath, Maximus made a declaration and said, 'I saw angels of God shining like the sun when they were swept away by the sword and their souls ascending from their bodies like richly adorned virgins from their bridal chamber. Receiving them into their bosoms, the angels carried them to heaven on the oarage of their wings'. And when Maximus accompanied such things with tears, a great many believed, and having been turned from the worship of idols, they returned to their Creator.

---

504 et] C *omits*

505 qui uocabatur] C *omits.* quarto] C iiii·. postius erat] V situs erat; C situs

506 omnes] V omnis. ingrederentur] VC ingrederetur

507 imponeret] VC poneret. offeruntur] V non offeruntur

508 et] V sed. recusant recusantes] V recusant; C recussant (*first* s *dotted for deletion*) recussantes (*first* s *dotted for*

deletion). genua] VC genu

510 iuratus] C iratus

511 uerrati] V percussi; C uerberati

512 ornatas] V *omits.* suo] VC *omit*

513 ferebant] V ferebantur. Itaque] V Ista; C Ita

513–14 talia prosequente] VC narrante. cultura] V errore; C cultura plurimi. suo se] C *order reversed.* artifici] C creatori

IGITUR dum comperisset Almachius quod Maximus cornicularius *cum suis omnibus factus fuisset Christianus, iussit eum tam diu plumbatis tundi* quam diu spiritum redderet. *Quem* sancta *Cecilia iuxta Tiburtium et Ualerianum sepeliuit in* nouo *sarcofago* et iussit ut in sarcofago eius
520 sculperetur fenix ad indicium fidei eius qui resurrectionem se inuenturum fenicis | exemplo credidit.

(25) *Factumque est post hec cepit Almachius querere facultates amborum.* Pro qua inquisitione sanctam Ceciliam quasi Ualeriani coniugem fecit artari. *Que cum uniuersa que remanserant ex eorum facultatibus pauperibus fideliter*
525 *tradidisset, ipsa quoque ut thura imponeret cepit impelli.*

Tunc apparitoribus qui eam hoc facere compellebant dixit, 'Audite me ciues et fratres. Vos ministri estis iudicis uestri, et uidetur uobis quod ab eius impietate alieni esse mereamini. Michi quidem gloriosum est et ualde obtabile omnia pro Christi confessione perferre tormenta quia cum hac uita
530 nunquam dignata sum habere amicicias; sed de uestra satis doleo iuuentute quam sine sollicitudine geritis, facientes quod uobis fuerit ab iniusto iudice imperatum'.

Tunc illi dabant fletus et uoces *quod tam elegans puella et* tam sapiens et *nobilis* etiam *optaret occidi.* Et rogabant eam dicentes ne tale decus amitteret,
535 nec talem pulchritudinem uersaret in mortem.

(26) Quibus flentibus atque animum eius reuocare uolentibus, ita *respondit,* 'Hoc non est iuuentutem perdere sed mutare. *Dare lutum et accipere aurum. Dare habitaculum paruum et accipere domum magnam* et amplissimam ex lapidibus preciosis et auro constructam. Dare angulum
540 breuem et opacum et accipere forum lucidum margaritis celestibus choruscantem. Dare rem perituram et accipere rem que finem nescit et mortem ignorat. *Dare lapidem uiuum** qui pedibus conculcatur *et accipere lapidem preciosum* qui in diademate regio radiante splendet aspectu.

---

516 Igitur] *large* I *in left margin is five lines tall with remainder of word in small capitals.* dum comperisset Almachius] V dum peruenisset ad Almatium; C cum peruenisset ad Almachius
518 spiritum redderet] V ad uitam ęternam cuius amore crediderat peruenisset. iuxta] C iuxta ubi
519 sepeliuit] V quos ipsa sepelierat; C sepelierat. *first* sarcofago] VC sarcophago sepeliuit

520 sculperetur] V indicium fidei eius sculperetur. ad indicium fidei eius] V *omits.* se] VC *omit.* iuenturum] VC inuentorum
521 Fol. 78vb. credidit] VC suscepit
522 Factumque est] VC Factum est autem. cepit] V ut. querere] C quęreret
523 fecit artari] VC pręcepit artari (C artare)
524 remanserant] V remanserunt
525 ipsa] V a pręfecto ipsa; C ipsam. thura] V tura; C h *above line.* imponeret] VC poneret

Then when Almachius had discovered that his adjutant Maximus together with all of his dependents had become Christians, he ordered him to be beaten with leaden scourges until he gave up the ghost. Saint Cecilia buried him next to Tiburtius and Valerian in a new sepulchre and ordered a phoenix to be carved on his tomb as a symbol of the faith of him who believed he would meet with resurrection in the manner of the phoenix.

(25) And after these things happened, Almachius began to make inquiries about the wealth of both brothers. In the interests of the investigation, he ordered Saint Cecilia as the wife of Valerian to be imprisoned. Since she had given away to the poor all that remained of their wealth, she too began to be compelled to offer incense.

Then to the aides who were urging her to do this she said, 'Listen to me citizens and brothers. You are servants of your judge, and it seems to you that you deserve to be unassociated with his wickedness. For me it is a glorious thing and exceedingly desirable to suffer all tortures for the sake of confessing Christ because I have never deigned to have affinities with this life; but I am quite grieved by your youth, which you spend without care, doing whatever you have been commanded by the unjust judge'.

Then they gave themselves over to weeping and crying out because such a graceful and wise and noble young woman should choose to be killed. And they begged her not to forfeit such attractiveness nor to fling such beauty into death.

(26) While they were weeping and were trying to change her mind, she replied in this way, 'This is not to destroy my youth but to exchange it. To hand over clay and receive gold. To hand over a small dwelling and receive a large and most spacious house made of precious stones and gold. To hand over a narrow and dark corner and receive a light-filled piazza gleaming with heavenly pearls. To hand over a thing that will die and to receive a thing that knows no end and has no knowledge of death. To hand over an unwrought stone* trampled under foot and to receive a precious stone that shines with radiance in the royal crown.

---

529 confessione] C nomine. perferre] V ferre
530 de] C *omits*
531 sine] C *omits*. geritis facientes quod] VC
   gerentes facitis quicquid. iniusto] V isto
533 et uoces] V *omits*
534 optaret] C optare. amitteret] VC
   omitteret
535 nec talem] V nec tantum; C ne tantum
536 reuocare uolentibus] C reuocantibus

538 habitaculum paruum] V cellulam uilem
   et paruam; C habitaculum uile. magnam
   et] C *omits*
540 et opacum] V *omits*. margaritis] C
   margar(et)is, *ampersand erased?*
540–41 choruscantem] C coruscans. *second*
   rem] VC *omit*
542 uiuum] VC uilem
543 radiante splendet] VC uibrante
   resplendet. aspectu] V affectum

'Hodie si uobis aliquis offerret solidos aureos ita ut parem summam a
545   uobis nummorum offerret oblatam, nunquid non et uos curreretis ad tale |
mercatum et omnes parentes et notos et affines et propinquos et caros et
amicos faceretis uobiscum currere? Quicumque autem uos lacrimis reuo-
carent eo quod omnes nummorum uestros daretis intrepidi, nunquid non
irrideretis eos ut ignaros et nescios; uos autem curreretis, exultantes quod
550   daretis ad commutationem auri preciosi eramentum uile et nullius summe
iacturam? Et tamen pondus ad pondus uos accipere gauderetis. Deus autem
non dat pondus ad pondus; simplum accipit et centuplum reddit insuper
uitam eternam'.

Et his dictis ascendit super lapidem qui erat iuxta pedes eius et dixit
555   omnibus, 'Creditis his que dico?'

*At illi omnes una uoce dixerunt, 'Credimus Christum filium Dei uerum
Deum esse, qui talem te possidet famulam'.*

Dicit [eis] Cecilia, 'Ite ergo et dicite infelici Almachio quod ego inducias
peto ut non urgeat passionem meam, et intra domum meam faciam uenire
560   qui uos omnes faciat uite eterne participes'.

Et ita Domino procurante completur.

(27) Nam ueniens *papa* Urbanus *baptizauit intra domum eius quadrin-
gentos* promiscui sexus ex quibus unus clarissimus uir erat nomine Gordianus.
Hic sub umbratione nominis sui domum sancte Cecilie suo nomine titulauit,
565   et in occulto *ex illa die ibi baptisma Christi celebratum est* quousque ecclesia
fieret, ita ut etiam papa Urbanus illic moraretur et licet occulte tamen cotidie
Dominice redemptionis crescerent lucra et *infinita fierent diaboli detrimenta.*

(28) Sed cum hec agerentur, *Almachius Ceciliam sibi presentari iubet.
Quam interrogans ait,* 'Quod tibi nomen est?'
570   Illa respondit, 'Cecilia uocor'.

Almachius dixit, *'Cuius conditionis es?'*

Cecilia dixit, 'Ingenua, nobilis, clarissima'.

---

544 solidos] V tot solidos. aureos] C *omits*
544–45 ita ut parem summam a uobis
    nummorum offerret oblatam] V quantos
    nummos traderetis. nummorum] C
    numerum grantanter. nunquid] C *erasure
    of* quem *preceding.* non] C *omits.*
    curreretis] VC curreretis gaudentes. Fol.
    79ra
546 *first* et] C *omits*
547 Quicumque] V Aut quicumque. autem]
    V *omits*
547–48 reuocarent] C reuocaret. eo] V *omits.*
    nummorum] VC nummos. intrepidi] V
    omits
549 irrideretris] C irridetris
550 ad commutationem] C *notation mark in*

left margin. summe] C sū *erased*
551 tamen] C *omits.* uos] C *omits.* gaud-
    eretis] V gratularemini; C gratulamini
552 simplum] VC sed quod simplum. accipit
    et] V acceperit; C accipiet. reddit] VC
    reddet
553 uitam eternam] V et uitam ęternam; C et
    uitam aęternam
554 dixit] VC dicit
555 his] VC hęc. dico] V dixit; C dixi
557 talem te] VC *order reversed*
558 (eis)] ei; VC eis
558–59 quod ego inducias peto] V quasi
    consenserim uobis (quasi *or* quos *before*
    quasi *erased*); C *follows* H *except for*
    petam. et] V et hic; C et huc

'Today if someone offered you gold coins so that he offered you an equal number of gold coins as you offered him pennies, would you not run to such a deal and make all your family and acquaintances and neighbours and kinsmen and loved ones and friends run with you? But if anyone called you back in tears because you were freely giving away all your pennies, you would certainly laugh at them as being ignorant and unaware; rather would you not run about, exulting that you handed over common copper and an outlay of a trifling sum in exchange for precious gold? And you would rejoice that you received pound for pound. But God does not give pound for pound; he accepts the simple sum and gives back a hundredfold in addition to everlasting life'.

And with these words she got up on top of a stone that was next to her feet and said to all, 'Do you believe these things that I say to you?'

And they all said in one voice, 'We believe that Christ the Son of God is the true God, who has in you so worthy a maidservant'.

Cecilia says to them, 'Go then and say to the unhappy Almachius that I request a delay so that he might not hurry along my suffering, and I will have one who will make you sharers in the everlasting life come to my house'.

And so with the Lord attending to the matter, it was done.

(27) Now when pope Urban came, he baptized in her house a group of four hundred of both sexes, among whom was man of the highest rank named Gordianus. Under the cover of his name, Urban consecrated the house of Saint Cecilia in Gordianus's name, and in secret from that day the baptism of Christ was celebrated there until it became a church, and so pope Urban remained there and, though in secret, the profits of the Lord's redemption nevertheless daily increased and brought about infinite losses for the devil.

(28) But while these things were happening, Almachius ordered Cecilia to be presented to him. Questioning her he said, 'What is your name?'

She replied, 'I am called Cecilia'.

Almachius said, 'What is your legal status?'

Cecilia said, 'Free-born, noble, of the highest rank'.

---

560 faciat] V faciet
562 Nam] VC Tunc. Urbanus] C sanctus urbanus. eius] V cecilie
562–63 quadringentos promiscui sexus] V super quadringentas animas sexus promiscui; C amplius quam quadringentos promiscui sexus et conditionis et aetatis. ex quibus] V in quibus; C Inter quos.
nomine] V e *corrected from* i
564 umbratione] V ombratione; C umbrationem
565 et] C ut. ibi] VC ex quo ibi. quousque] VC *omit*

566 papa Urbanus] V supra dictus papa nomine urbanus; C papa urbis urbanus. occulte] V occulto. tamen cotidie] V omni die; C *order reversed*
567 Dominice] *added in left margin*; C *omits.* redemptionis] C redemptionis christi. crescerent] VC ibi crescerent. diaboli] V diabolo
568 Sed cum hec agerentur Almachius] V Almatius tamen his quę gerebantur auditis; C *follows* H *except for* hęc
570 Illa respondit Cecilia uocor] V respondit illa Cecilia; C Respondit cęcilia
571 dixit] VC respondit. nobilis] C nobili

Almachius dixit, 'Ego te de | religione interrogo'.

Sancta Cecilia dixit, 'Interrogatio tua stultum sumpsit initium qua duas
575   responsiones una putasti inquisitione concludi'.

Almachius dixit, '*Vnde tibi tanta presumptio respondendi?*'

Cecilia dixit, 'De conscientia bona et fide non ficta'.

Almachius dixit, 'Ignoras cuius potestatis sim?'

Cecilia dixit, 'Tu ignoras cuius sis potestatis. *Nam ego, si me interrogas de*
580   *tua potestate, ueris tibi assertionibus manifestabo*'.

Dicit ei Almachius, 'Dic si quid nosti'.

Cecilia dixit, '*Omnis potestas hominis sic est quasi uentus in utre conclusus:
quem si una acus pupugerit, omnis tumor ceruicis eius follescit, et quicquid in
se rigidum habere cernitur incuruatur*'.

585   Almachius dixit, 'Ab iniuriis cepisti, et in iniuriis perseueras'.

Cecilia dixit, 'Iniuria non dicitur nisi quod uerbis fallentibus irrogatur.
Vnde aut iniuriam doce si falsa locuta sum, aut te ipsum corripe calumpniam
inferentem'.

(29) Almachius dixit, 'Ignoras quia domini nostri, inuictissimi principes,
590   iusserunt ut qui se non negauerint Christianos puniantur, qui uero negauerint
dimittantur?'

Cecilia dixit, 'Sic imperatores uestri errant sicut et nobilitas uestra.
[Sententia] enim quam ab eis prolatam esse testaris uos seuientes et nos inno-
centes ostendit. Si enim malum esset hoc nomen, nos negaremus, uos uero
595   ad confitendum suppliciis nos cogeretis'.

Almachius dixit, 'Pietate sua hoc uoluerunt statuere ut quo quomodo uite
uestre possit esse consultum'.

Cecilia dixit, 'Nichil tam impium, nichil tam innocentie inimicum quam
ut reis omnibus tormenta adhibeatis et ad confitendum quantitatem sceleris
600   locum, tempus, conscios omni examinatione perquiratis, nobis | uero, quos
innocentes scitis, nominis tantum crimen inpingatis. Sed nos scientes sanctum
Christi nomen omnino negare non possumus. Melius est enim feliciter mori
quam infeliciter uiuere. Nos uera dicentes uos torquemus qui mendatium
elaboratis audire'.

---

573 Fol. 79rb   582 dixit] VC respondit. uentus in utre
574 Sancta] VC *omit*. dixit] VC respondit.   conclusus] C uter uento repletus
   qua] V Quẹ; C que   583 acus] V acu. pupugerit] V pungeris.
575 responsiones] V res. putasti] VC putat   tumor] C rigor. follescit] C mollescit. in
576 respondendi] V *omits*   se] V *omits*
577 dixit] VC respondit   584 habere] V *omits*. incuruatur] C *omits*
578 sim] V sum   585 dixit] VC respondit
579 dixit] VC respondit. interrogas] C   586 fallentibus] C falla cybus
   interroges   587 aut] C autem
580 ueris] C uerius. manifestabo] C   589 nostri] C uestri
   manifestatem   590 se non] V *order reversed*

Almachius said, 'I am interrogating you about your religion'.

Saint Cecilia said, 'Your interrogation has taken a foolish starting point in that you have supposed two answers can be derived from one question'.

Almachius said, 'Whence comes such presumption in your answers?'

Cecilia said, 'From a good conscience and an unfeigned faith'.

Almachius said, 'Are you unaware what power I have?'

Cecilia said, 'You are unaware what power you have. Now, if you ask me about your power, I will show you clearly the truths of your assertions'.

Almachius says to her, 'Speak if you know anything'.

Cecilia said, 'All human power is like a wind bottled up in a wineskin: if a needle punctures it, all the swelling in its neck goes slack, and anything in it seen to be rigid is made to droop'.

Almachius said, 'You began with insults, and you persist in insults'.

Cecilia said, 'It is not considered an insult unless it is proposed in false words. Either point out the insult if I have spoken falsely, or rebuke yourself for making a false statement'.

(29) Almachius said, 'Are you unaware that our lords, the utterly invincible emperors, have ordered those who do not deny they are Christians to be punished and those who deny it to be set free?'

Cecilia said, 'So your emperors are wrong just like your nobility. The decree you attest that they issued shows you to be savage and us to be innocent. If this name were evil, we would deny it, yet you compel us with tortures to confess'.

Almachius said, 'In their kindness they have wanted to resolve this such as way that your life might be spared'.

Cecilia said, 'There is nothing so wicked, nothing so hateful to the innocent than when you torture all the defendants and when for the confession of a multitude of crimes you search diligently in every trial for a place, a time and accomplices, but you charge us, whom you know to be innocent, only with the crime of the name. But we, knowing it to be holy, cannot deny the name of Christ in any way. It is better to die happily than to live unhappily. Speaking things that are true, we torture you who take pains to hear a lie'.

---

592 dixit] VC respondit
593 (Sententia)] HV sententiam; C
   Sententia. enim] V *omits.* ab eis] V
   illorum ore
595 ad confitendum suppliciis nos cogeretis]
   V suppliciis urgueretis; C ad confitendum
   suppliciis urgeretis
596 Pietate] C Pro pietate. quo quomodo] V
   commodo; C quomodo
598 dixit] VC respondit. impium] C pium.
   second nichil] C nihilque

599–600 omnibus...perquiratis] V hominibus
   socios omni examinatione perquiratis
599 et] C *omits.* confitendum] C
   confitendam. quantitatem] C qualitatem
600 conscios omni examinatione perquiratis]
   C conscios socios omni examinatione
   perquiritis. Fol. 79va
601 impingatis] C inpingitis
602 Christi] VC *omit*
603 Nos] VC Nos enim. uos torquemus] V
   apud uos torquemur

605   Almachius dixit, 'Elige tibi unum e duobus: aut sacrifica aut nega te
Christianam esse ut facias te euadere supplicium'.

Tunc ridens beata Cecilia dixit, 'O iudicem necessitate confusum! Vult ut
negem me innocentem ut ipse faciat me nocentem. Parcit et seuit, dissimulat
et aduertit. Si uis dampnare, cur hortaris negare? Si uis absoluere, quare non
610   uis inquirere?'*

Almachius dixit, 'Accusatores presto sunt qui te Christianissimam esse
testantur. Si negaueris, compendiosum dabis accusantibus finem. Si negare
nolueris, dementie tue deputabis quando sententie subiacebis'.

Cecilia respondit, 'Horum michi accusatio uotiua est, et tua pena uictoria.
615   Noli me ut dementem arguere sed te ipsum, qui me cogis Christum dene-
gare'.

(30) *Almachius dixit, 'Infelix, ignoras quoniam uiuificandi et mortificandi
michi ab inuictissimis principibus potestas est data? Vt quid cum tanta
superbia loqueris?'*

620   *Cecilia dixit, 'Aliud est esse superbum, aliud esse constantem. Ego
constanter locuta sum non superbe quia superbiam et nos fortiter execramus.*
Tu autem si uerum audire non times, iterum docebo te falsissime prose-
cutum'.

Almachius dixit, 'Quid sum falsissime prosecutus?'

625   Cecilia dixit, 'Hoc quod principes tuos uiuificandi et mortificandi tibi
tradidisse asseris potestatem'.

Almachius dixit, 'Ergo mentitus sum?'

Cecilia dixit, 'Contra ueritatem publicam, si iubes, probo te esse
mentitum'.

630   Almachius dixit: 'Proba'. |

*Cecilia dixit, 'Dixisti principes tuos et uiuificandi et mortificandi tibi
copiam tribuisse.* Mortificandi tibi scias traditam potestatem, *uitam enim
uiuentibus tollere potes*; *mortuis dare non potes.* Dic ergo quia imperatores
tui mortis te ministrum esse uoluerunt. Nam si quid plus dixeris, *uideberis*
635   *frustra mentitus'.*

---

605 tibi] C *omits.* e] V de
605–06 te Christianam] V *order reversed.*
   facia te euadere supplicium] V copiam
   euadendi accipias; C copiam euadendi
   suscipias
608 me innocentem] V me nocentem; C me
   esse nocentem. faciat me] VC *order
   reversed.* nocentem] VC innocentem
608–09 Parcit...aduertit] C *omits*
612 accusantibus] C accusans
613 deputabis] V inputabis; C reputabis.
   subiacebis] V subiacueris
614 respondit] C dixit

615 Noli] V Non potes. ipsum] C ipsum
   increpa
615–16 qui me cogis Christum denegare] V
   qui me Christum estimas negare; C qui
   Christum me aestimas denegare
617 Infelix] V *omits.* uiuificandi et
   mortificandi] V et mortificandi et
   uiuificandi; C *order reversed*
618 est data] V *order reversed*
620 dixit] VC respondit. aliud esse] V aliud;
   C aliud est esse
621 et] V *omits.* execramus] V execramur
622 si uerum] V falsum

Almachius said, 'Choose for yourself one of two things: either sacrifice to the gods or deny that you are a Christian so that you may escape torture'.

Then blessed Cecilia laughed and said, 'O the judge is confused by necessity! He wishes me to deny that I am guiltless so that he might make me guilty. He forebears and then is savage, feints and then concentrates. If you wish to condemn me, why urge me to deny that I am a Christian? If you wish to set me free, why do you not wish to look further into the matter?'*

Almachius said, 'Informers are here who will testify that you are very much a Christian. If you deny it, you will bring about a quick end to the informers. If you do not wish to deny it, then you will attribute it to your insanity when you submit to your sentence'.

Cecilia responded, 'Their accusation is what I have longed for, and your punishment is my victory. Do not accuse me of being insane but yourself, who compels me to deny Christ'.

(30) Almachius said, 'Unhappy one, are you unaware that the utterly invincible emperors have granted me the power of giving life and death? So why do you speak with such pride?'

Cecilia said, 'It is one thing to be prideful, another to be steadfast. I spoke steadfastly not pridefully because we also intensely detest pride. But if you are not afraid to hear the truth, I will show again that you have proceeded most falsely'.

Almachius said, 'How have I proceeded most falsely?'

Cecilia said, 'You allege that your emperors have granted you the power to give life and death'.

Almachius said, 'So I have lied?'

Cecilia said, 'If you wish, I will prove that, contrary to accepted truth, you have lied'.

Almachius said, 'Prove it'.

Cecilia said, 'You have declared that your emperors have granted you the means of giving life and giving death. You know that the power of death has been conferred on you, for you are in fact able to take life from the living; you are not able to give life to the dead. State then that your emperors wanted you to be an agent of death. For if you say more than that, you will appear to have been lying for no reason'.

622–23 iterum docebo te falsissime prosecutum] V iterum uitiosissime docebo te nunc locutum; C iterum docebo te falsissime nunc locutum
624 Quid] V Quę; C Que
625 dixit] VC respondit
628 Cecilia dixit] V respondit cecilia; C cecilia respondit. publicam] C publice. probo te] V te probabo
630 Proba] VC Doce. Fol. 79ᵛᵇ
631 dixit] VC respondit. et uiuificandi et

mortificandi] V mortificandi et uiuificandi; C *omits first* et
632 Mortificandi tibi scias traditam potestatem] V cum tantum mortificandi acceperis; C cum solam mortificandi tibi scias traditam potestatem
633 mortuis dare non potes] V mortuis dare eam non potes; C uitam dare non potes mortuis
634 te ministrum] V te immo homicidii ministrum; C *order reversed*

Almachius dixit, 'Depone iam audatiam tuam et sacrifica diis'.

Cecilia dixit, 'Nescio ubi tu oculos amiseris. Nam quos tu deos dicis, ego et omnes qui sanos oculos habemus saxa uidemus esse et eramentum et plumbum'.

640 Almachius dixit, 'Meas iniurias philosophando contempsi, sed deorum ferre non possum'.

Cecilia dixit, 'Ex quo os aperuisti, non fuit sermo quem non probarim iniustum, stultum et uanum. Sed ne quid deesset, etiam exterioribus oculis te cecum ostendis, cum quod omnes lapidem uidemus et saxum inutile hoc 645 tu deum tuum esse testaris. Do, si iubes, consilium. *Mitte manum tuam et tangendo disce saxum esse si uidendo non nosti.* Nefas est enim ut omnis populus de te risum habeat. Omnes enim sciunt Deum in celis esse. *Istas autem figuras saxeas per ignem melius in calcem posse conuerti,* quia modo sui otio pereunt et *nec quid tibi proderunt neque sibi si uero in ignem mittantur* 650 *poterunt subuenire'.*

(31) *Tunc iratus uehementer Almachius iussit eam in domum suam reduci et in sua domo flammis balnearibus concremari. Cumque fuisset in calore balnei sui inclusa et subter incendia lignorum pabula ministrarent, die integro et nocte tota quasi in frigido loco integra illibataque permansit ita ut nulla pars* 655 *membrorum eius saltem sudoris signo lassaretur.*

Quod cum audisset Almachius, misit qui eam in ipsis balneis decollaret. Quam spiculator tertio ictu percussit et caput amputare non potuit. | *Et quam legibus tunc ratum erat ne quartam percussionem decollandus acciperet, sic seminecem truculentus carnifex dereliquit.**

660 Cuius sanguinem omnes Christiani bibleis lintheaminibus extergebant. *Per triduum autem quod superuixit, non cessauit* omnes puellas quas nutrierat *confortare.* Quibus et diuisit uniuersa que habuit et sancto Urbano urbis *pape tradidit commendatas.* Cui et dixit, 'Ad hoc triduanas michi a Domino poposci inducias ut et istas beatitudini tue commendarem et hanc domum 665 meam ecclesie nomini consecrarem'.

---

637 dixit] VC respondit. quos] C *omits.* ego] VC et ego
638 sanos oculos] VC *order reversed.* habemus] VC habent
642 dixit] V respondit. Ex] C Ex eo. probarim] V arguere; C probarem
643 stultum] V et stultum. Sed] V se
644 cecum] V cecatum. ostendis] V ostendi. cum] V *omits.* uidemus] VC uidemus esse
645 Do si iubes] V Docebis
646 esse] C hoc esse. omnis] VC totus
647 habeat] C habeant
648 quia] C qui.
649 otio] C uitio. nec quid] VC neque. proderunt] VC pereunt. uero] V *omits.* si uero in ignem mittantur] C *omits*

651 uehementer Almachius] V almatius uehementer. eam] C *omits.* in] VC ad. reduci] C duci
652 et] V *omits.* sua] VC sua sibi. balnearibus] V balnealibus
653 subter incendia] V super incendia nimia; C subter incendia nimia. pabula] V pabulo
654 frigido loco] VC *order reversed.* integra illibataque permansit] VC inlibata perstitit sanitate. nulla] C una
655 saltem] V *omits*; C saltim. signo] V signa. lassaretur] V lassasent; C lassesceret
656 eam] V eam ibidem. in ipsis balneis] C in ipso balneo

Almachius said, 'Now cease your audacity and sacrifice to the gods'.

Cecilia said, 'I do not know where you lost your eyes. For you call gods what I and all those who have healthy eyes recognize to be stone and bronze and lead'.

Almachius said, 'I have disregarded insults to me by philosophising, but I cannot endure those of the gods'.

Cecilia said, 'From the time that you opened your mouth, there has not been a word that I have not proved unjust, foolish and false. But so that nothing is lacking, you demonstrate that you are also blind in your external eyes, since you testify that what we all see to be stone and useless rock is your god. If you wish, I give this advice. Stretch out your hand and learn that it is stone by touching it if you do not know it by seeing it. It is wrong for all the people to be laughing at you. They all know that God is in heaven. But it would be better if these stone figures were turned into lime in the fire, since they only perish by their idleness and neither offer anything to you nor are able to help themselves if they are thrown into the fire'.

(31) Violently angered, Almachius then ordered her to be taken back to her house and to be burned in her house with flames from her bath. And when she had been enclosed in the heat of her bath and flames from the firewood were providing fuel, she survived unharmed and unimpaired for a whole day and an entire night as if in a cold place so that no part of her body was weakened by even so much as a sign of sweat.

When Almachius heard that, he sent someone to behead her in her bath. The executioner struck her three blows and could not cut off her head. And as it was then legally established that one could not receive a fourth stroke when being beheaded, the savage butcher left her half-dead.*

All the Christians wiped up her blood with pieces of linen paper. During the three days that she remained alive, however, she did not cease to strengthen all the young women she had nurtured. She divided all that she had among them and when they had been entrusted to his care, handed them over to Saint Urban, pope of the city. And she said to him, 'I asked the Lord for a delay of three days for myself that I might commit these to your blessedness and might consecrate this house of mine with the name of a church'.

---

657 spiculator] C i *above underscored* e. caput] C caput eius. Fol. 80ra. quam] V quia

657–58 Et quam legibus tunc ratum erat ne quartam percussionem decollandus acciperet] C *omits*.

658 tunc ratum erat] V caput eius truncatum erat. sic] C sic autem

659 seminecem] VC seminecem eam. truculentus] C cruentus

660 Christiani] C *omits*. lintheaminibus extergebant] C linteaminibus populi qui per eam crediderant et tergebant

661 quod] V quo. puellas] C *omits*. quas] C quos

661–62 nutrierat confortare] C nutrierat et quos docuerat in fide dominica confortare

662–63 sancto Urbano urbis pape] C sancto papę urbano. commendatas] V commendata; C commendatos. hoc] VC huc. a Domino] VC *omit*

664 beatitudini tue] VC *order reversed*. commendarem] C traderem

665 ecclesie] VC in ęternum ęcclesię. nomini] C *omits*. consecrarem] C consecrare

(32) Tunc sanctus *Urbanus* corpus eius auferens cum diaconibus nocte *sepeliuit eam* inter collegas suos episcopos ubi omnes sunt confessores et martyres collocati. *Domum autem eius sancte ecclesie nomine consecrauit, in qua beneficia Dei exuberant* ad memoriam sancte Cecilie usque in hodiernum diem prestante Domino nostro Ihesu Christo, qui cum Patre et Spiritu Sancto uiuit et regnat, Deus in secula seculorum. Amen. EXPLICIT PASSIO SANCTE CECILIE VIRGINIS.

670

---

668 sancte ecclesie nomine consecrauit] V in ęternum sanctę ęcclesię nomini tradidit; C in aetęrnum sanctę aecclesię nomini tradidit
669 Dei] VC domini. sancte] C beatę
670–71 prestante...Amen] V In gratia domini nostri ihesu christi. Cui gloria et imperium cum patre et spiritu sancto in secula seculorum. Amen; C *omits*

671–72 EXPLICIT...VIRGINIS] V *omits*; C *in small capitals* EXPLICIT PASSIO SANCTĘ CECYLIĘ ET ALIORVM MARTIRUM (*followed by an erased space of approximately ten small capitals*)

(32) Then removing her body during the night with the deacons, Saint Urban buried her among his fellow bishops where all the confessors and martyrs had been placed. Moreover, he consecrated her house with the name of a holy church, in which the blessings of God abound in memory of Saint Cecilia even now with our Lord Jesus Christ providing them, he who lives and reigns with the Father and the Holy Spirit, God forever and ever. Amen. THE PASSIO OF SAINT CECILIA THE VIRGIN IS ENDED.

INCIPIT PASSIO SANCTORUM MARTYRUM CHRYSANTI ET DARIAE. MENSE [OCTOBRE] XXV DIE*

(1) *Historiam priorum sanctorum ad œdificationem nostram Deus uoluit peruenire, non ut laudibus mortalium pasceret eos quos inmortalitatis dapibus reficit, sed ut nos exemplo eorum doceat prœsentis sœculi blandimenta contempnere et ad inquisitionem sempiternœ gloriœ labentem ac momen-*
5 *taneam angustiam non timere.** Omnis enim dolor aut leuis est et sufferri potest, aut grauis et finem imponit. Sed si uterque timendus est, ratio est ut ille qui æternus est non contempnatur. Si enim isti dolores, qui hodie minantur et cras uacuantur, qui hodie exardescunt et cras refrigescunt, qui hodie oriuntur cras finiuntur tam diri, tam sæui sunt, quam graues erunt illi
10 dolores qui sic inchoant ut crescant cotidie, sic initium capiunt ut omnino finiri non possint? Hanc denique imaginem tenent, qui se permittunt aut setari a medicis aut igniri cauteriis aut amaris|simis potionibus sautiari. Mortis enim timore perterriti et amaritudines appetunt et ignes non metuunt et ferrum non perhorrescunt. Si ergo amore huius uitæ, quę fidem seruare
15 non nouit, amantibus se auro comparantur dolores ignis et amaritudines, gratulandum est gratuitis passionibus; quæ ultro uenientes, faciunt nos temporaliter humiles ut in perpetuum exaltemur. Faciunt nos amaritudines momentaneas incurrere ut sempiternas dulcedines capiamus. Faciunt nobis ardores fugitiui incendii ut refrigerii nos faciant participes sempiterni.
20 Hoc intuitu omnes martyres Christi, ut triumphum ex hostibus caperent, omnium passionum genera ridendo potius quam metuendo perpessi sunt, credentes quod et gloriam sempiternam adquirerent temporalem respuendo et æternum ignem euaderent præsens incendium perferendo. Horum itaque gloriis delectati respuamus mundum cum omnibus delectamentis suis, et
25 sanctorum | gesta absque incredulitatis nubilo serenissimam recitemus; hystoriam Chrisanti tam nobis qui credidimus quam omnibus qui credituri sunt profuturam.

(2) *Polemius uir inlustrissimus Alexandriæ urbis, honoratus et primus ad urbem Romam cum filio Chrisanto ueniens,* a Romano senatu susceptus est;
30 et *magnis honoribus a Numeriano imperatore illustratus, cathedram in curia Romana suscepit.*

Title] *in small capitals taking up the width of the folio. Text begins on* 118ᵛ. *The specific month has been erased, but see Commentary [p. 258].* C *reads in small capitals,* INCIPIT PASSIO SANC-TORUM CHRISANTI ET DARIAE; B *reads* Incipit prologus in passionem sanctorum Crisanti et Darie virginis.
1 Historiam] *a large* H *four lines tall;* B Hystoriam *with a decorated* H *seven lines*

tall Historiam…ædificationem] C *an* H *four lines tall and* HISTORIAM…EDIFI *in small capitals spanning the width of one column.* ad] B ob
3 reficit] C pascit
4 ad inquisitionem] C adquisitionem
6 grauis] C grauis est
9 cras] C et cras
10 incohant ut crescant] C *omits*
12 Fol. 119ʳ. potionibus] C potationibus

HERE BEGINS THE PASSIO OF THE HOLY MARTYRS CHRYSANTHUS AND DARIA. 25 OCTOBER*

(1) God wanted the story of earlier saints to be known for our edification, not that he might nourish with mortal praises those whom he feeds with immortal feasts, but to teach us by their example to despise the charms of this present age and not to fear pain and momentary distress in the search for everlasting glory.* For all pain is either light and can be endured, or it is severe and inflicts death. But if we fear either of these, it is only because we pay no heed to the pain that lasts forever. If those pains that threaten us today and tomorrow disappear, that flare up today and tomorrow subside, that arise today and end tomorrow are so frightful and so harsh, then how much more severe will those pains be that begin and increase daily, that start and cannot ever stop? Those who finally get the picture allow doctors to cut them open, burn them with cauterizing irons or wound them with the most bitter potions. Terrified by a fear of death they seek the bitters and are not afraid of the fires and do not dread the iron. If fiery pains and bitters are compared to gold by those who indulge their lust for this life, which does not know how to keep faith, then we ought to rejoice in sufferings that cost nothing; when they arrive unprovoked, they humble us temporarily so that we may be exalted in perpetuity. They cause us momentary bitterness so that we might enjoy everlasting sweetness. They afflict us with the flames of a fleeting fire to make us sharers in everlasting coolness.

With this in mind, all the martyrs of Christ, to seize the victory from their enemies, endured all manner of suffering by laughing rather than cowering in fear, and believed that they would win everlasting glory by rejecting temporal glory and would escape eternal fire by preferring the present burning. And so having been delighted by the martyrs' glories, let us reject the world with all its pleasures, and free from the cloud of unbelief, let us read aloud the deeds of the saints; the utterly joyful story of Chrysanthus will be as beneficial to us who have believed as to all those who will believe.

(2) When Polemius, a most distinguished, respected and eminent man from the city of Alexandria, arrived in Rome with his son Chrysanthus, he was received by the Roman Senate; and when the emperor Numerianus had distinguished him with great honours, Polemius received a seat in the Roman Senate-house.

---

15 auro] *in left margin*; B *omits.* ignis] C
  ignes. amaritudines] C e *corrected from* i;
  B amaritudinis
17 perpetuum] CB perpetuo
22 et] C *omits*
24 delectati] C delectatione
25 Fol. 119ᵛ. nubilo] C nube, e *corrected from* i *and erasure of two letters following.* serenissimam] CB serenissima

26 hystoriam Chrisanti] C historiamque
  CHRISANTI (*in small capitals*); B
  hystoria chrisanti et dariȩ. credidimus]
  CB credimus
27 profuturam] B profutura. Finit prologus.
  Incipit passionis cordem
28 Polemius] *large* P *in left margin three lines tall*
29 susceptus est] B *order reversed*

Hic filium suum unicum Chrisantum cum omnibus liberalibus studiis imbuisset etiam *philosophorum studiis tradidit. Erat enim ardentis ingenii, ita ut omnia quecumque ei ab oratoribus aut a philosophis fuissent tradita capaci animo fortiter retineret.* Cuius prudentiæ cuiusque fuerit intellegentiæ rerum exitus docet.

Nam uniuersa librorum uolumina cum animo curiosus discuteret, *ad euuangelicos apices peruenit*, et figens curiositatis suæ cursum, *ad semetipsum | ait, 'Tamdiu te decuit, Chrisante, per librorum tenebras curarum tuarum frena laxare, quamdiu ad lumen pertingeres ueritatis. Non est prudentiæ ut ad tenebras redeamus a lumine.* Perdimus quod laborauimus si fructum laboris amittimus. Fructus autem laboris hic est, quem a Deo datum querentibus legimus. Sic enim legimus Deum hominibus præcepisse, "Querite ut inueniatis." Si quod quesiuimus et inuenimus dimiserimus, erimus fatuis et stultissimis comparandi. *Teneamus ergo quod tenendum est animo*, et omnia quæ respuenda sunt relinquamus. *Fit enim iactura laboriosæ inquisitionis meae, si non teneam uiriliter quod inueni. Diu laboraui querendo. Inueni aurum. Inueni argentum. Inueni lapides prætiosos.* Si ideo quæsiui ut inuenirem, ideo inueni ut teneam. Iam non patiar mihi eripi quod inueni. Teneam, utar, perfruar, quia hæc erit summa laboriosæ inquisiti|onis meæ. *Quam si amisero, uidebor sine causa uixisse*, sine causa quesisse'.

(3) Et hæc dicens, coepit querere quis esset litterarum diuinarum expositor, et sicut audierat ante grammaticos et oratores magistros, sic desiderabat rusticos doctores et piscatores adquirere.* Legerat enim dixisse apostolum, 'Ubi sapiens, ubi scriba, ubi conquisitor huius sæculi? Et quia per sapientes mundus Deo displicuit, placuit Deo per insipientes saluos facere credentes in se'.

---

32 Chrisantum] C *in small capitals.* liberal-
   ibus studiis] *order reversed*
33 imbuisset...tradidit] C *omits.* ingenii ita]
   ingenii et tamen memoriæ capax ita, *with*
   et...capax *dotted for deletion;* B *reads the
   same but* et...capax *not marked for
   deletion.*
34 capaci] C capax
38 euuangelicos] CB ęuangelicos
39 Fol. 120ʳ. decuit] C docuit. Christante] C
   in small capitals

42 autem] C *omits*
44 fatuis] C fatui
46 quæ] C que. Fit] C Si
47 querendo] C querens
50 laboriosę inquisitionis meæ] C laboris me.
   Fol. 120ᵛ
51 amisero] C amittere
52 litterarum diuinarum] CB *order reversed*
54 piscatores] C pastores. dixisse apostolum]
   order reversed
56 Deo displicuit] C displicuit

He introduced his only son Chrysanthus to all liberal studies and handed him over to the study of philosophy. The son had so fierce an intellect that he retained firmly in his capacious mind whatever the orators and philosophers taught him. It was a mark of his intelligence and understanding that he would teach them the solutions to problems.

Now when he, being curious, had eagerly investigated every book, he came to the gospel writings, and when he had trained his inquisitiveness on them, he said to himself, 'It was fitting, Chrysanthus, that you loosened the bridle of your cares through the darkness of books while you were reaching for the light of truth. It is not wise to return to darkness from light. We waste what we have worked for if we lose the fruit of our labour. But we have read that God gives the fruit of the labour to those who seek it. In fact, we have read that God commanded men, "Seek so that you will find" [cf. Matthew 7.7]. If we let go of what we sought and found, then we ought to be compared to a stupid and utterly foolish man. Let us then hold on to what ought to be eagerly held, and let us abandon everything that ought to be rejected. I will squander my toilsome search, if I do not manfully hold on to what I have found. I worked hard for a long time in searching for it. I found gold. I found silver. I found precious gems. If I searched to find, then I found to keep. I cannot bear to have what I found snatched away from me. Let me keep, make use of and enjoy what I found because this will be the sum total of my toilsome search. If I lose it, then I will appear to have lived without good reason, to have searched without good cause'.

(3) And when he said these things, he began to look for someone who was an interpreter of the divine scriptures, and just as he had earlier listened to teachers of grammar and oratory, so he wanted to add rustic instructors and fishermen to his list of teachers.* For he read that the apostle had said, 'Where is the wise man, where is the scribe, where is the philosopher of this age? Because the world displeased God through the wise, God was pleased to save those who believe in him through the unwise' [cf. 1 Corinthians 1.20–21].

Hæc secum cotidie reuoluenti animo et cotidie *Christi famulos requirenti,*
occurrit qui diceret nosse se quendam Carpoforum nomine *uirum per omnia*
60   *eruditum, Christianum et sanctum,* sed persecutionis atrocitate seuiente in
quodam montis speleo collocatum, uix posse a paucissimis ac fidelissimis uisi-
tari. Audiens hæc Chrisantus coepit esse feruentior, et genibus referentis
fusis precibus, aduolutus etiam cum lacrimis postula|bat ut ad eius mereretur
notitiam peruenire. Fit prouidente Deo quod ex fidei desiderio flagitabat, et
65   *peruveniens ad* sanctum *Carpoforum,* quintæ regionis *presbiterum.* Cum quo
intra paucos menses *omnibus diuinis litteris imbutus, ita coepit esse diligenter*
instructus, ut statim post septem dies baptismatis sui Ihesum Christum filium
Dei uoce publica prædicaret.

(4) *Tunc adfines eius,* uiri nobiles et potentes, comprehendentes patrem
70   eius Polemium, *coeperunt eum arguere dicentes, 'Periculo patrimonii tui et*
capitis tui iste iuuenis contra deos deasque nostras uociferat clamoribus uanis
*dicit*que nescio quem *Christum uerum Deum esse.* Quem si audierit imper-*
ator ista prosequentem, *nec tibi poterit* nec nobis *esse consultum.* Quis enim
audeat ista præsumere nisi qui se aut sine rege aut sine lege Romana agere
75   credat impune?'

*Tunc iratus pater eius*Polemius *fecit eum in tenebroso et squalido loco*
claudi, et uespertinis | horis paruissimo *cibo refici.* Hoc autem uir Dei
Chrisantus magis ad exercitationem sibi quam ad supplicium dicebat inferri.
Cumque hoc factum publica confabulatio detexisset, dicit patri eius unus ex
80   audientibus, 'Si filium tuum ab hac usurpatione conaris eripere, magis *eum*
deliciis et uoluptatibus *occupa, et* cuicumque elegantissimæ puellæ atque
prudentissimæ *coniugio trade ut cum didicerit esse maritus,* obliuiscatur esse
Christianus. Nam istas tenebras et afflictiones quas tu ad supplicium illi te
credis inferre, Christiani hæc ad laudem *et perpetuam gloriam sibi estimant*
85   *euenire'.*

---

58 secum cotidie] C *order reversed.* Christi
   famulos] B *order reversed*
59 Carpoforum] *blank space of approxi-*
   mately four letters between Carpo *and*
   forum
62 Chrisantus] C *in small capitals*; B
   crisantus. esse] C enim
63 Fol. 121ʳ
63–64 mereretur notitiam] B *order reversed.*
   et] B *omits*
65 cum quo] C *omits*

66 imbutus] C inbuitur. ita] C Et ita. esse
   diligenter] B *order reversed*
67 septem] C .vii. Ihesum Christum] C *order*
   reversed
71 tui] C sui. uociferat] B uociferatur
73 poterit] C proderit. esse] C potest esse
74 audeat] C audet, i *erased between* d *and*
   ampersand (et). first aut] B *omits*
77 Fol. 121ᵛ
79 patri eius] C patricius
81 cuicumque] C cuiuscumque
84 credis] C credas

While he daily turned this over in his mind and daily searched for the servants of Christ, he ran into someone who said he knew a certain Carpoforus who was learned in all things, Christian and holy, but who, because the fury of persecution was raging, was lodged in a certain cave, scarcely able to be visited except by the very few and most faithful. Hearing this, Chrysanthus became very upset, and with prayers poured out at the man's knees, he threw himself at his feet and asked him with tears that he might have the right to make Carpoforus's acquaintance. With God seeing to it, that for which Chrysanthus was begging on account of his desire for faith was fulfilled, and he got through to the holy Carpoforus, a priest of the fifth district. When Chrysanthus had been instructed by him in all the divine scriptures in a few months, Chrysanthus was so thoroughly instructed that immediately after the seventh day of his baptism, he publicly proclaimed Jesus Christ as the Son of God.

(4) Then when his neighbours, noble and powerful men, found his father Polemius, they began to criticize him and said, 'Risking your fortune and your head that boy cries out against our gods and goddesses with foolish outbursts and says that "Christ" or whatever he is called, is the true God.* If the emperor hears him carrying on like that, he will not look after your interests nor you after ours. Who would dare to presume such things unless he believes that he acts with impunity, independent of the king or Roman law?'

Then Chrysanthus's enraged father Polemius had him locked away in a dark and filthy place, and fed him the smallest bit of food in the evenings. But the man of God Chrysanthus said that this brought him practice rather than punishment. And when a public discussion revealed that this happened, one of those listening said to his father, 'If you are trying to deliver your son from practising his Christianity, then distract him instead with delights and pleasures, and marry him to any very elegant and very wise young girl so that when he devotes himself to being a husband, he will forget that he is a Christian. As for those dungeons and torments that you believe will inflict punishment on him, the Christians think they are allotted to them for praise and everlasting glory'.

(5) Audiens hæc Polemius *iubet triclinia uestibus sericis strata preparari.**
Ipsum quoque auferens de squalenti illa et tetra habitatione, induit uestibus
pretiosis, et ponens eum in triclinio, elegit quinque pulcherrimas uirgines ex
ancillis suis *et accuratissimis uestibus et ornamentis composuit. Et simul | eas*
90   *cum Chrisanto constituens, iussit cotidiana conuiuia affluentissimis dapibus*
exhiberi. Puellis autem interminatus est dicens, 'Nisi eum iocis uestris et
amplexibus ab intentione Christianitatis separaueritis, *diuersis uos faciam*
interire suppliciis'. Aguntur inter hæc ludibria.

Uir Dei immobilis animo *delicias* quasi stercora *contemnebat; puellas*
95   *autem uirgines quasi uiperas perhorrebat. Iacebat* autem *in oratione* immo-
bilis animo, et amplexus earum et *oscula* quasi sagittarum ictus scuto suæ
fidei *excipiens, clamabat ad Dominum dicens*, (6) 'Exurge, Domine, in adiu-
torium mihi. Dic animę meæ, "Salus tua ego sum." Quis enim istam pugnam
a diabolo excitatam uincere præualet nisi tua pro eo fuerit dextera dimicata?
100   Errat qui se putat castitatem perfectam suis uiribus optinere; nisi enim tuo
imbre flammæ fuerint hæc corporales extinctæ, non potest animus peruenire
| quo pergitur.

'Libido enim est bestia maligna quæ in silua huius sæculi ad deuorandas
animas per carnem et diabolum incitatur. Qui eius morsus euaserit tibi, Deo,
105   gratias referet quia tuum est quod euasit, sicut beatissimus famulus tuus
Ioseph, quem plangebat pater suus dicens, "Bestia maligna comedit illum.
Bestia maligna rapuit Ioseph". Et nolebat penitus consolari in eo. Certe hic
est Iacob famulus tuus, Domine, quem nichil latebat. Quare ergo, dum dixis-
sent ei filii sui, "Agnosce si tunica filii tui est", non manifestasti ei quod
110   fallerent eum? Sed ideo dissimulasti quia patriarchas prophetico sermone
patrem alloqui præuidisti.

---

86 sericis] C syricis
87 de squalenti illa] C de squalidido loco.
 tetra] C tenebrosa
88 quinque] C .v.
89 Fol. 122ʳ. eas] C omits
90 Chrisanto] C *in small capitals.*
 affluentissimis] C fluentissimis
93 ludibria] B *a notation mark (.x.) follows*
 above the line which appears to have been
 made in a much later hand, perhaps of the
 seventeenth century. Judging from the
 notation marks and marginalia elsewhere
 in the legend, which are not recorded here,
 and in the account of the saints'
 translation that follows in the MS, it seems
 that B may have been consulted by the
 Bollandists.

94 delicias] CB et dilicias
95 perhorrebat] B perhorrescebat
96 animo] C omits
99 pro eo fuerit] B fuerit pro eo. dimicata] B
 dimicatum (?), *final a of* dimicata *dotted*
 and t barred
100 uiribus] C nisibus
101 hæc] C omits. peruenire] C pergere.
102 Fol. 122ᵛ. pergitur] C pergit; B tendit
103 in silua] B *struck through*
106 comedit] C rapuit
107 maligna] B mala
108 tuus] C omits. Domine] C domini sui; B
 omits
108–09 quem...filii sui] C omits. Agnosce] B
 Nunquid (*written over erasure*) agnosce
111 præuidisti] C prouidisti

(5) When Polemius hears this, he orders dining-rooms to be made ready by hanging them with silk tapestries.* Taking Chrysanthus out of that filthy and foul dwelling, he dressed him in costly garments, and putting him in a dining-room, he chose five very beautiful young maidens from among his maidservants and arrayed them in very elaborate garments and accoutrements. And when Polemius put the girls with Chrysanthus, he ordered that they be provided with daily banquets of the most sumptuous foods. He also threatened the girls and said, 'If you do not part him from his zeal for Christianity with your jests and embraces, I will have you killed with various tortures'. Meanwhile, the girls became playful.

The man of God, unmoved in spirit, despised the delights as if they were dung; he likewise recoiled in terror from the maidens as if they were vipers. But unmoved in spirit, he lay in prayer, and with his shield of faith he intercepted the girls' embraces and kisses as if they were shots of arrows and cried out to the Lord saying, (6) 'Rise up, O Lord, to help me. Say to my soul, "I am your salvation" [cf. Psalm 34.2–3]. Who will have strength to win this fight stirred up by the devil unless your right hand fights for him? Anyone who thinks he can maintain perfect chastity by his own strength is mistaken; for unless you extinguish these bodily flames with your rain showers, the spirit cannot arrive where it is led.

'Sexual desire is a malicious beast that is incited by the flesh and the devil to devour souls in the forest of this world. Anyone who escapes its teeth gives thanks to you, O God, because he belongs to you, just like your most blessed servant Joseph whom his father mourned and said, "A malicious beast ate him. A malicious beast snatched Joseph away" [cf. Genesis 37.33]. And in the depths of his being he refused to be comforted about him. Certainly, this is your servant Jacob, O Lord from whom nothing was hidden. Why then, when his sons said to him, "See if this is the tunic of your son" [cf. Gen. 37.32], did you not reveal to him that they were tricking him? But you pretended not to notice because you foresaw that the patriarchs would speak to the father with a prophetic word [cf. Gen. 46.2–4].

'Denique occurrit ei bestia maligna et quasi leena ita eum suis unguibus arpaxauit.* Et quod peius, insidiata est ut solum inueniret et unicum. Sed solus non erat quia patris eius lacrimis iam fuerat interpellatus. Ideo eum

115 permisisti lugere et mugitum imi cordis emittere ut iustis eum adiutolriis subleuares. Libido enim erat bestia maligna, per quam contra eum diabolus et mulier luctabantur. Ibi caro et sanguis, ibi iuuentus et pulcher aspectus, ibi pubertas et irritatio oculorum, ibi potestas dominationis, ibi delectatio obscenitatis, ibi inuitamenta potestatis, ibi ornamenta suadentis oculos, ibi

120 caput auro et gemmis instructum, ibi odoramenta exhalantia, ibi amplexus ipsi deuorationi et morti iam proximus. Inter hæc omnia et solum inuenit leena et tenuit.

'Hunc tua manus, Domine, iam ante ora positum liberauit. Unde et nunciantibus quod filius eius uiueret, Iacob dixit, "Mirum mihi est si bestiam

125 illam malignam sic euasit ut uiueret". Quare? Quoniam Deus inquit erat cum Ioseph, et omnia quecumque faciebat Deus benedicebat in manibus eius. *Et ego, Domine, tibi confiteor, et a te auxilium contra istas uiperas deprecorut, sicut serpentes obdormiscunt ad uocem | incantantis, ita iste obdormiscant in conspectu meo, et nullum in me libidinis excitent bellum quia te didici,* uerum

130 Deum, qui in hominibus in te credentibus operaris uirtutem quæ penitus uinci non potest'.

(7) *Igitur dum complesset Chrisantus orationem suam, ita graui somno correptae sunt uirgines ut nisi fuissent foras de triclinio eiectæ, penitus excitari non possent. Euigilabant autem foris et capiebant cybum. Statim autem ut*

135 *ingresse fuissent* ubi orabat Chrisantus, *sopore nimio artabantur. Nunciantur hæc patri* ab his quorum fuerat curæ commissus, *et coepit eum quasi iam mortuum flere.*

Tunc dicit ei quidam ex amicis suis, '*Hic artem magicam a Christianis didicit, et ideo aduersus puellas simplicissimas facile præualuit* incantando.*

140 *Sed si eruditam aliquam miseris ad eum,* poterit eum et ad tuum arbitrium et ad suos libitus inclinare'.

Dicit ei Polemius, 'Et ego ubi inuenturus sum talem feminam | quæ hoc possit implere?'

---

113 arpaxauit] C arpaxabat; B arpagauit.
  peius insidiata est] C peius est
  insidiabatur; B peius est insidiata
114–15 eum permisisti] B *order reversed.*
  imi] C intimi. iustis] iussisti. Fol. 123ʳ
116 subleuares] C subleuari. enim] C *omits*
119 inuitamenta] CB incitamenta.
  ornamenta] B ornamenta forme

121 ipsi] C ipse. iam proximus] B *double
  slashes signal transposition of* proximus
  iam. *second* et] C *omits*
123 Hunc] B sed hunc. ante ora] C
  interiorem
124 dixit, Mirum] C dixit, Mirum mihi est
  ioseph filius meus uiuit. Quasi qui
  diceret, Mirum...; B *nearly identical to* C,
  except B reads ait *for* dixit *and* Quasi
  diceret *for* Quasi qui diceret

'At last, the malicious beast rushed him and like a lioness seized him with her claws.* And what is worse, she lay in wait to find him alone. But he was not alone because his father's tears had already interceded for him. You allowed Jacob to lament and groan from the depths of his heart so that you might help Joseph with support that was well deserved. Sexual desire was a malicious beast through whom the devil and the woman fought against him. There was flesh and blood, youth and beauty, virility and provocation for the eyes, the power of authority, the pleasure of indecency, the allurement of power, ornaments to entice the eyes, a head bedecked with gold and jewels, wafting spices, and an embrace to devour and later to kill. Amid all these things the lioness found him alone and seized him.

'Your hand, O Lord, freed the one brought to your attention. And when they brought word that his son was alive, Jacob said, "I am astonished if he escaped from that malicious beast and lived" [cf. Gen. 45.26]. Why? For God said that he was with Joseph, and God blessed everything he put his hand to [cf. Gen. 39.3]. And I acknowledge you, O Lord, and ask for your help against these vipers so that, just as serpents fall asleep to the snake-charmer's song, so might these maidens fall asleep in my presence, and let none of them stir up in me a war of desire because I have known you, the true God, who gives a strength that utterly cannot be overcome to those believing in you'.

(7) When Chrysanthus finished his prayer, the virgins were overcome by a sleep so deep that had they not been thrown outside the dining-room, they never would have been roused. But outside they woke up and ate. However, as soon as they went in where Chrysanthus was praying, they were weakened by an overpowering sleep. Those entrusted with Chrysanthus's care reported this to his father, and Polemius began to weep for his son as if he were already dead.

Then a certain one of his friends says to him, 'Chrysanthus has learned sorcery from the Christians, and for that reason he easily prevailed against the very simple-minded girls by uttering magic spells.* But if you send him some learned female, she will be able to incline him to your will and her whims'.

Polemius says to him, 'And where am I going to find such a woman to do this?'

---

126 eius] C suis
127 tibi] C te. auxilium] C consilium.
  uiperas] C ut feras
128 Fol. 123ᵛ. ita] C ita et
131 potest] C possit
132 Chrisantus] C *in small capitals*. suam] C
  omits
133 foras] C foris

135 Chrisantus] C *in small capitals*
136 patri] C patricio. commissus] C
  commissum
138 quidam] B unus. suis] C eius
139 et ideo] C *omits*
140 *first* et] C *omits*
142 Fol. 124ʳ

Respondit ei amicus eius, 'Est inter uirgines quæ deæ uestæ inseruiunt
145   *quędam uirgo super omnem pulchritudinem*, elegantior, et ita *sapiens* ut illi
nec ipsi oratores occurrant. Hæc iam ad nubiles annos, quantum ætas
ostendit, admittit, et necesse erit ut quicumque eam nobilis sortiatur uxorem.
Hanc itaque nos, ut consuetudo est, per supplicationem mereamur, et *agamus*
cum ea quatinus et tibi filium reddat et sibi eum maritum accipiat'.
150   *Facta sunt omnia quæ isti consilio erant necessaria, et ad consensum*
uirginis peruenitur.

(8) *Tunc uirgo nomine Daria gemmis et auro radians repente ad*
Chrisantum quasi sol radians constanter *ingreditur*, et quasi sub specie conso-
lationis, tanta *eum elegantia sermonis alloquitur* tantamque ingenii artem
155   interserit ut si esset ferro durior, pluma mollior redderetur.

Sed Chrisantus Domini fretus auxilio sagittas diaboli scuto suæ | fidei
repellebat. Et medium inter se atque illam Sanctum Spiritum postulans, *allo-*
quiis suis hoc initium dedit, 'Si mihi mortali homini per temporale conubium
tantam tuæ pulchritudinis elegantiam exhibes tantamque dulcedinem
160   melliflui sermonis ostendis — *ut etiam ab intentione propositi te animum*
meum reuocare credas, aliis amoribus occupatum, et cogas mentem uelle
quod non uult — quanto magis amantem te et desiderantem inmortalem regis
filium poteris si uolueris optinere? *'Nam si ei animam tuam in corporis tui*
integritate custodias, sicut corpore pulchra es ita pulchra eris et mente. Et sicut
165   *extrinsecus gemmis et auro resplendes, ita intrinsecus in tuis uisceribus*
perorneris. Erunt de te proximi angeli laudatores, archangeli paranimphi,
apostoli amici, martyres coheredes, Christus sponsus, qui tibi thalamum in
cælis construit æternis margaritis instructum, tradat tibi | possessiones para-
disi, dotem tibi sempiternam tribuat, constituat tibi incomparabiles reditus
170   et florem in te cotidie gratissime renouet iuuentutis'.

(9) Ad hæc *Daria* conpuncta *respondit*, *'Nulla me, O iuuenis, petulantis*
animi cum his uestibus ad te signa perduxerunt, sed patris tui lacrimis miserata,
cupio te et patri reddere et deorum reuocare culturæ'.

Chrisantus respondit, 'Si nosti aliqua quæ uera mihi ratio manifestet,
175   ponam animum et diligenter auscultem ita ut ex alterna disputatione libenter
et audias et loquaris'.

---

145 pulchritudinem] C pulchritudine
146 ad] B *dotted for deletion.* nubiles] C
   nobiles
148 et] B ut
150 isti] B huic
152 uirgo] C uirgo ueste. Daria] C *in small*
   capitals. radians] B fulgens. ad] C *omits*
153 Chrisantum] C *in small capitals*
154 ingenii] B ingenii sui. artem] CB arte
155 pluma] C flamma

156 Chrisantus] C *in small capitals.* fretus
   auxilio] C *order reversed.* suæ] C *omits.*
   Fol. 124ᵛ
158 per] B spe. temporale conubium] C
   temporales conubii; B temporalis conubii
159 elegantiam exhibes] B *order reversed*
160 propositi te] C proposita
164 ita pulchra eris] *slash between* a *and* e,
   and ri *above line between* e *and* s; C ita
   eris *above line*; B ri *of* eris *above line*

His friend replied to him, 'Among the virgins who serve the goddess Vesta, there is a certain girl more beautiful than any other, very elegant and so wise that not even the orators oppose her. She admits that she is now of a marriageable age, what age shows, and it is true that any nobleman would choose her for a wife. So, let us win her favour by offering a sacrifice, as is the custom, and let us work with her, seeing that she may restore a son to you and take him as a husband for herself'.

All the essentials for this plan were arranged, and they reach an agreement with the girl.

(8) Then the girl named Daria, who was sparkling with gems and gold, unexpectedly goes in calmly to Chrysanthus sparkling like the sun, and under the pretense of consoling him, she addresses him with such elegant words and interjects with such intelligent artfulness that had he been harder than iron, he would have been rendered softer than a feather.

But Chrysanthus was confident in the Lord's help and repelled the devil's arrows with his shield of faith. And asking the Holy Spirit stand between himself and her, he began his speech in this way, 'If for a temporal marriage, you display your beauty so exquisitely and express yourself so charmingly with sweet words to me a mortal man — believing that you may dissuade my spirit from its chosen purpose after it has been seized by other loves, and compelling my mind to choose what it does not want — then how much more lovely and charming would you be if you wanted to win the immortal son of the king who loves and longs for you? For if you guard your soul in the chastity of your body, then you will be as beautiful in mind as you are in body. And just as you glitter with gems and gold on the outside, so you will be adorned inwardly in your innermost parts. There will be angels around you who praise you, archangels will be your groomsmen, apostles your friends, martyrs your co-heirs, and Christ your bridegroom, who will build you a bridal chamber outfitted with everlasting pearls in heaven, who will hand over to you the estate of paradise, who will give you an eternal dowry, who will allot you unequalled revenue and who will most willingly renew your flower of youth each day'.

(9) Stung, Daria replied to this, 'O young man, no hints of wantonness drew me to you in these clothes, but I felt sorry for your father's tears and want to restore you to him and call you back to the worship of the gods'.

Chrysanthus responded, 'If you know something that genuine reasoning would make clear to me, then I will consider it and will listen carefully so that you might willingly hear and respond to the other side of the argument'.

---

166 perorneris] B perornaberis, be *above line.* laudatores] C laudantes
167 coheredes] C *omits*
168 cælis] C cęlo; B cęlestibus. construit] B construat. Fol. 125ʳ
170 florem] C flores. cotidie] C *omits*
171 Daria] C *in small capitals*
172 perduxerunt] C perduxit, *but* it *dotted and barred* r *above line.* lacrimis

miserata] C *order reversed*; B lacrimas (a *over dotted* i) miserata
173 deorum] C ad deorum. culturæ] C culturam
174 Chrisantus] C *in small capitals.* quæ uera] B *double slashes signal transposition of* uera que
176 et audias] CB exaudias

Daria respondit, 'Inter omnia quæ humanis commodis necessaria nouimus, nichil tam utile tamque primum agnoui quam diuinitatem excolere et supernas uires deorum nequaquam per contemptum ad iracundiam
180   concitare'.

Chrisantus ad hæc ait, 'O uirgo prudentissima, quam putas nos idolis exhibere culturam?'

Respondit Daria, 'Hanc quæ nobis faciat | esse custodes'.

Et Chrisantus, 'Quomodo,' inquit, 'nobis possunt esse custodes, qui nisi
185   custoditi fuerint a canibus, nocte rapiuntur a furibus? Et ne ab aliquo deiciantur inpulsu, uinculis ferreis coartantur et plumbo?'

Daria respondit, 'Si uulgus ignobile posset absque his imaginibus uirtutem deorum nostrorum credere et eorum sanctitatem ex celeberrima cultura ueraciter agnoscere, nulla esset necessitas similitudinis exhibendæ. Hæ
190   autem imagines aut in ære et marmore et in auro atque argento funduntur et finguntur ut oculis cultor attendat eum quem doceatur mente excolere et timere'.

Respondit Chrisantus, 'Inquiramus ergo quorum sunt istæ ipsæ imagines, et uideamus si his merito honorem debeamus exhibere culturæ. Deus enim
195   non potest nec estimari nec credi nisi qui omnem sanctitatem omnemque supergreditur maiestatem. (10) | *Quæ ergo bona Saturnus* falcifer *habuit, qui proprios filios* quotienscumque *nascebantur* occidit — ut non dicam *comedit sicut eius cultores scribunt? Quæ bona in Ioue fuisse existimas*, qui quot dies uixit tot inaudita incesta, tot *adulteria*, tot *homicidia perpetrauit*, eneruator
200   patris, puerorum incestor, maritorum adulter, *sororum maritus*, usurpator imperii, *magorum adinuentor*, transfigurationis arbiter, massa dæmonum, metator mortis et *omnium* inauditorum *criminum perpetrator*? Hunc tu talem esse non credas si non de eo ista scripta sunt; quorum testimonio dii memorantur et reges nati tamen leguntur et mortui, tempore quo rudes homines
205   deos putabant quoscumque fortes in proelio comprobassent.

---

177 Daria] C *in small capitals*
178 agnoui] C *omits*
179 deorum] C eorum
181 ait] C dicit. nos] C *omits*
182 exhibere] C exhiberi
183 Fol. 125ᵛ
184 Et Chrisantus] C Crisantus respondit.
    inquit] C *omits*
186 inpulsu] B impulsu et
187 ignobile] C nobile. absque] C et absque

187–88 uirtutem deorum] B *double slashes
    signal transposition of* deorum uirtutem
187–89 uirtutem...agnoscere] C deorum
    cęlebrare culturam
189 exhibendæ] C exhibendo. Hæ] C Hęc; B
    Heę
190 imagines] C imagines. aut] C *omits*. et
    marmore] C et in marmore; B aut in
    marmore. *third* et] B atque

Daria replied, 'Among all that we know to be essential for the benefit of man, there is nothing I am aware of so useful and so fundamental as worshipping a divinity and not rousing the gods' divine powers to anger by showing contempt for them'.

Chrysanthus replied to this, 'O most intelligent young woman, what reverence do you think we show to idols?'

Daria replied, 'Such reverence that makes them our guardians'.

And Chrysanthus said, 'How can they be our guardians who are carried off by thieves at night unless they are guarded by dogs? And are they not held in place with iron chains and lead so that they are not knocked over by some blow?'

Daria answered, 'If low-born common people could believe in the power of our gods without these images and if they could truly recognize the gods' holiness from a most solemn rite, then displaying likenesses of the gods would not even be necessary. However, these images are cast and moulded either in bronze or marble or gold or silver so that a worshipper may see with his eyes the god he is taught to worship and fear with his mind'.

Chrysanthus responded, 'Let us investigate the gods represented by these statues and see if we ought to honour them with worship. For a god is not to be valued or trusted unless he excels in all holiness and excellence. (10) Therefore, what goodness did sickle-bearing Saturn possess who killed his sons whenever they were born — and I do not mention his worshippers write that he ate them. What good do you think was in Jupiter, who committed as many unheard acts of incest, adultery and murder as he lived days, murderer of his father, defiler of boys, cuckolder of husbands, husband to his sisters, usurper of authority, inventor of sorcery, master of transfiguration, mass of demons, one who metes out death and a perpetrator of all unheard of crimes? You would not believe him to be such had not these things been written about him; by their testimonies the gods are remembered and kings read about who were born and nevertheless have died, any of whom unlearned men over time come to consider to be a god if he proved brave in battle.

---

191 finguntur ut oculis] C oculos suos.
    doceatur mente] C doceat tormenta
193 sunt] B sint
194 exhibere] re *above dotted* amus
196 Fol. 126ʳ
197 proprios filios] C proprium filium.
    quotienscumque] C quotiescumque
198 Ioue] C iouem. existimas] C estimas
199 incesta] C ingesta

200 patris, puerorum incestor] C *omits*.
    maritorum] B maritatarum
201 transfigurationis] C transfiguratione
202 mortis] C morti. tu] C *omits*.
203 *second* non] C non eorum. testimonio] C
    testimonium
203–04 memorantur] C memorator. rudes] C
    rudeos, o *above line*
205 deos] C *erased*. comprobassent] B
    probassent

'Nam quid in Ioue diuinum esse potuit, qui omni castitati ita usque ad mortem extitit inimicus ut aerem ipsum in Ganimedis sanguilne pollueret, et terram, ut dixi, in suis sororibus inquinaret? Quid etiam in Mercurio diuini- tatis inuentum putas, cuius capitalis aspectus sycofanticum indicat monstrum

210 cum in eius uertice simul cernimus et capillos et pennas? Hic maleficiis suis absconditas terræ pecunias reperiebat, et incantationibus suis serpentium iras mitigabat ad uirgam. (11) Hæc autem omnia dęmonum patrocinio perpe- trabat quibus porcinum ficatum cotidie sacrificabat et gallum. *Quæ autem in Hercule sanctitas, qui,* uicinorum suorum omnium interfectione fatigatus,

215 *etiam ipse uiuum* se nutu dei *ignibus tradidit concremandum* et arsit, miser, simul cum mathera quam gestabat et pelle? *Et licet leonem necauerit, hydram truncauerit,* canem infernalem ligauerit, ipse tamen redactus in cynerem nusquam omnino comparuit sed periit. Quæ in Apolline sanctitas, cum mysteriis Dionysialibus et inebriatis confusionibus et diuinationibus Delficis

220 et luxuriis I poculorum?

'Iam si ad reginam Iunonem et ad castissimam Uenerem ueniamus, inue- niemus eas idcirco inter se acriter litigantes quia ad usus turpes una alteram præcedebat. Clamant omnium poetarum et oratorum et historiographorum scripta iudicium Paridis spreteque iniuriam formæ.* Quid enim illa indignata

225 est, quid illa lætata, nisi quod una impudicitiæ usibus aptior pastoris iudicio eligitur, alia denegatur?

'His itaque diuinitatis honoribus supplosis, quibus diuinitatis priuilegium imperitum uindicat uulgus de ceteris eorum minoribus sileamus. Unum enim caput est, quod uniuersa sequitur compago membrorum: quicumque enim

230 deus quæcumque dea esse iactatur Saturno, Iunoni, Ioui et Ueneri, non erit præponendus. *Si enim priuilegia tenentes tam miseri probantur et turpes, quanto miseriores sunt quos inferiores eorum annuntiant esse cultores?'*

---

206 castitati] C castitate
207 inimicus] B contrarius. Ganimedis] C
  Ganimedem. Fol. 126ᵛ. sanguine] C
  omits. pollueret] C polluit
208 terram, ut dixi, in suis] C terram in suis
  ut dixi. inquinaret] C inquinauit
211 reperiebat] C repperebat
212 omina] C *omits.* dęmonum patrocinio] C
  patricidio demonum
214 Hercule] h *above line*; C herculem
216 hydram] C hydrum
219 Dionysialibus] C dyonisalibus; B
  dyonisii olimpii. Delficis] C delfilcis
220 Fol. 127ʳ

221 Iam] C Nam. *second* ad] C *omits.*
  Uenerem ueniamus] B *double slashes*
  signal transposition of ueniamus uenerum
221–22 inueniemus] C inuenimus. alteram] C
  altera
223 Clamant] CB Clamabant.
  historiographorum] C p *corrected from
  another letter*
224 iniuriam] C iniuria
225 una] C illa
227 honoribus] C honores
228 uindicat] C indicat
230 esse] C se
231 præponendus] C preponenda
232 quos] C qui

'Now what can be divine about Jupiter, who was so opposed to all chastity that until he died he polluted the very sky with Ganymede's blood and, as I mentioned, defiled the earth with his sisters? And what mark of divinity do you think is found in Mercury, whose deadly appearance reveals a monstrous trickster when we see hair and wings together on his head? With his deceptions he discovered the earth's hidden riches, and with his spells he soothed the serpents' anger with his staff. (11) What is more, he perpetrated these things through the patronage of demons to whom he offered a pig's liver and a rooster each day. What holiness, moreover, is there in Hercules, who, when he had been wearied by the slaughter of all his neighbours, handed himself over to the will of a god to be consumed alive and was burned to death, the wretched one, with the spear he carried and the hide he wore? Although Hercules killed the lion, chopped off the hydra's head and bound the infernal dog, he, having been reduced to ashes, is nowhere to be seen but has perished. What holiness is there in Apollo, with his Dionysian rites and besotted confusions and Delphian oracles and drunken excesses?

'Now if we consider the queen Juno and the most chaste Venus, we find them quarrelling bitterly because one outdid the other in shameful practices. The writings of all the poets and orators and historians cry out about Paris's judgement and the injustice to her scorned beauty.* Was Juno aggrieved and Venus delighted by the decision in so far as one is chosen in the judgment of a shepherd to be better at shameless conduct while the other is rejected?

'Now that I have refuted their honours of divinity, I will not mention other lesser gods for whom the unlearned claim the prerogative of divinity. There is one main point, namely that the entire pantheon follows suit: whatever god or goddess is mentioned, it must not be valued more highly than Saturn, Juno, Jupiter and Venus. For if these who hold the privilege of divinity are proved to be so wretched and so shameless, then how much more wretched are the gods whom worshippers declare to be their inferiors?'

(12) Ad hæc Daria respondit, 'Quoniam poetarum figmenta nulla sunt
uirtulte subnixa, ad philosophos eamus quorum ingenia uniuersa uitia dese-
235   cant et uirtutibus colla submittunt. Qui licet uaria interpretatione de mundi
machina disputare uideantur, deorum tamen ista nomina allegorica inter-
pretatione distinguunt. "Saturno" denique tempus ostendunt si quidem
"Chronos", quod est eius in Græco uocabulum, non aliud posse quam tempus
intellegi. "Iouem" uero substantiam feruidam, "Iunonem" aerem uocant,
240   "Uestam" ignem, "Neptunum" mare, "Matrem Magnam" terram, et ceteras
deorum dearumque personas his et huiusmodi asserunt uelaminibus coop-
ertas'.

Chrysantus ad hæc respondit: 'Illorum', inquit, 'effigies per simulachrum
aliquod representari solet qui possunt aliquando non esse presentes. Terra
245   uero, quæ absens esse numquam potest, et ignis, qui in presenti semper est,
et aer, qui aperte omnium oculis patet, cur per nescio quas effigies coli iuste
putentur ignoro. Nec omnino considero quare malgis imago eorum sit
colenda quam ueritas. Numquid est in regibus aut in iudicibus, qui se ipsum
iubeat derelinqui et suam imaginem uenerari? Quod si nulla hoc ratio patitur,
250   restat ut istæ effigies non sint elementorum, potius sed defunctorum et
mortuorum magis hominum quam deorum imagines comprobentur'.

(13) Ad hæc Daria respondit, 'Dictis meis assertio tua probamentum
exhibuit. Docuisti enim ut si imperiti imagines colunt, nos ipsas res quorum
illi colunt imagines adoremus et unicuique honorem maiestatis suae sapien-
255   tius quam alii exhibent præbeamus'.

'Optime', ait Chrysantus, 'ad clausulam definitionis attingis. Adducamus
ergo ante oculos elementorum omnium diuersa uoluntate cultores. Et colat
unus terram ut deam, sed ut deam tantum, obsecrationibus, sacrificiis atque
omni cultu, quod ei conuenit promereri, cesset uero ab araltri uel rastri
260   cultura.* Alter econtra negans eam deam, solum uomeris in ea cultum
ostendat et rastri, nec ut sacerdos uenerando eam excolat sed ut rusticus
operando. Cui magis fructum proferre credenda est? Illi sine dubio qui eam
ut terram tantum coluerit, non ei qui eam quasi deam uanissima fuerit super-
stitione ueneratus. Si enim uere dea esset, illi potius uberes fructus qui eam
265   religionis titulo honorabat afferret.

---

234 Fol. 127ᵛ
234–35 desecant] C c *erased between* e *and* c
238 uocabulum] C uocabulo. posse] C possit
239 aerem] C uero aerem
240 Matrem Magam terram] C mater magna
terra. ceteras] C cetera
241 et huiusmodi] B *omits.* uelaminibus] B
nominibus
241–42 coopertas] C cooperta
243 Chrysanthus] C Chrisantus

244 qui] C Quid
245 absens] C ab *followed by erasure.*
presenti] B presentia
247 Fol. 128ʳ
248 Numquid] B Numquis
249 derelinqui] C relinqui. uenerari] C
honorari. Quod] C quid. hoc ratio] B
order reversed
250 potius sed] B *order reversed*
252 probamentum] C promertis

(12) Daria replied to this, 'Because none of the poets' inventions depend on moral excellence, let us move to the philosophers whose intellects prune away all their imperfections and who bend their necks under the yoke of moral excellence. Although they are seen to debate the workings of the universe with different explanations, they nevertheless distinguish among the gods' names by interpreting them allegorically. In point of fact, they denote time by the name "Saturn" if, for instance, "Chronos", the Greek word for time, cannot be understood as anything but time. So, the philosophers call "Jupiter" hot matter, "Juno" sky, "Vesta" fire, "Neptune" sea and the "Great Mother" earth, and they set free other personas of the gods and goddesses that have been veiled by such names and coverings of this sort'.

Chrysanthus replied to this: 'It is customary', he said, 'for the likenesses of those things that can never be present to be represented by some image. But I fail to see how the earth, which can never be absent, and fire, which is always present, and the sky, which is patently evident to everyone's sight, can justifiably be thought to be worshipped through some statue or another. Nor can I see at all how a representation of the earth, fire and sky should be worshipped instead of the actual element. Is it not the case among kings and judges that one can decree he is not to be forgotten and that his image is to be venerated? But if this is not admissible to your way of thinking, then I must still prove that those statues are not symbols of elemental substances but are images of men who are dead and gone rather than of gods'.

(13) To this Daria replied, 'Your assertion proves what I said. You have shown that if the unlearned worship images, then we revere the very elements whose images the unlearned worship, and we honour an element's majesty more wisely than the others do'.

Chrysanthus said, 'You have most aptly put your finger on the conclusion of my explanation. Therefore, let us imagine worshippers of all the elements who have different purposes. One worships the earth as a goddess, but tries so intently to win over the earth as a goddess with prayers, offerings and every means of cultivating her favour that he stops cultivating the ground with the plough or hoe.* The other worshipper, by contrast, denies that the earth is a goddess and makes a show of cultivating it only with the plough and hoe, so that he does not cultivate the earth like a priest by venerating it but like a farmer by working it. Who should be trusted to produce the bigger crop? Without a doubt the one who only cultivated the earth as earth, not the one who venerated it as a goddess with an utterly empty superstition. If the earth really were a goddess, then she would have instead bestowed abundant crops on the one who honoured her with a religious rite.

---

254 illi] C illic. adoremus] a *corrected from* æ
256 clausulam] B clausuram. definitionis] C
   meae difinitionis
259 cultu] C culturam. quod] B quo, quo
   letter following erased. ei] C eadem.
   aratri] C abaratri. Fol. 128ᵛ. uel] C et

260 eam] C eandam. solum] C solam. in ea]
   C *omits.* cultum] C cultu illam
261 rastri] C rastrine. nec ut] C Cui
262 sine] qui sine. qui] C *omits*
263 tantum coluerit] C *order reversed.* ei] C
   enim. uanissima] C uanissimam

'Similiter et alius Neptunum, id est mare, diuino cultu ueneretur, et aut in tempestiuo tempore nauiget aut copias eius ac si religiosus cultor expectet. Alius uero quasi exanime elementum omni diuinitatis reuerentia arbitretur indignum, et hic non nisi certo et oportuno tempore se fluctibus credat, et
270 marinas copias non adorando sed piscando perquirat. Quem ex his duobus aut felicius nauigare aut piscium dapibus habundare existimas? Illum | procul dubio, qui hæc rationabiliter procurauerit, non illum qui uanissimo ritu hæc speranda crediderit.

'Hoc etiam de ceteris elementis credendum est, quod nichil se colentibus
275 prestent quia non suo motu sed diuino iussu hominum usibus famulantur. Iussu uero Dei calores solis terræ concipiunt, aeris temperie pariunt, cæli clementia et imbribus nutriuntur, qualitate temporum coalescunt. Ille tamen digna ratione dignus est honorari qui prestat ea, non per quæ prestantur. Neque enim qui litteras discunt, tabulis et codicibus potius gratias referunt
280 quam magistro, aut ægrotantes liberati a medico ferramentis aut medicamentis eius honorem quam ipsi medico estimant rependendum'.

(14) Hæc et his similia prosequente Chrysanto, _credidit Daria. Et quasi simulata uoluntate inter se et Chrysantum habens consilium, nomen coniugii assumpserunt_ ita ut ambo in Dei timore _et castitatis gloria perdurarent._
285 At ubi Chrysantus libenter ministerium paternæ uoluntatis accepit, _fecit baptizari | Dariam_ intra domum suam. Et ita facta est sacratissima uirgo Christi ut intra dies paucos et _omnes diuinas scripturas arriperet_ et sanctæ uirginitatis suæ uelamen sanctitatis aptaret.* Erat tamen iuncta Chrysanto non calore corporeo, sed Sancti Spiritus feruore sociata. _Et tam per_
290 _Chrysantum multitudo uirorum quam per Dariam feminæ innumerabliles ad Christi gratiam confluebant._

---

268 omni] C omne
269 et oportuno tempore] B tempore et oportuno
271 Fol. 129ʳ
272 procurauerit] C procurauit
273 speranda] B sperando. crediderit] C credit
275 hominum usibus] C hominibus uiuis
276 solis] C _omits._ concipiunt] C capiunt
277 clementia et imbribus] C uberibus
278 digna ratione dignus est honorari] C ueneratione dignus est
280–81 medico…estimant] _insertion mark above line between the words and_ ferramentis…ipsi medico _in right margin, several letters of which are not visible in the gutter; unreadable letters are supplied from_ C _and_ B. rependendum] C respuendum _corrected to_ rependendum

282 credidit] C credit
285 libenter] B libertatem. ministerium] CB _omit._ accepit] C decretum (_above line_) accepit
286 Fol. 129ᵛ
287 dies paucos] B _order reversed. first_ et] C _omits._ diuinas scripturas] C _order reversed_
288 uirginitatis] B uirginitati. uelamen] C uelamenta
289 Sancti Spiriti] C _order reversed._ feruore] feruore _above_ uirtute _underscored for deletion_
290 per Dariam] CB _omit_

'Likewise, let another worshipper venerate Neptune, that is to say the sea, with a divine rite, and if he is a devout worshipper, he should either sail at the right time or expect the sea's abundance. Another, however, considers the sea to be a lifeless element, unworthy of any godly respect, and he does not entrust himself to the waves unless it is with certainty and at a favourable time, and searches everywhere for a big catch not by worshipping but by fishing. Which of the two do you think sails more successfully and has an abundance of fish to feast on? No doubt the one who sensibly manages his affairs, not the one who believes by putting his hopes in an utterly empty rite.

'This too should be believed about the other elements: they offer nothing to those who worship them because they do not serve the needs of men by their own doing but by divine command. By the order of God the earth absorbs the sun's heat, brings forth temperate air, is nourished by the sky's mildness and its rain-showers, and is strengthened by the nature of the seasons. By right reason, he who provides these benefits is worthy to be honoured, not the elements through which the benefits are provided. To be sure, those who learn from what has been written do not thank the documents and books instead of the teacher, nor do the sick, once the physician has cured them, think the honour goes to the cauterizing irons or remedies rather than the physician'.

(14) When Chrysanthus continued these arguments and others like them, Daria believed. And once she had taken his advice, as if there had been one will between her and Chrysanthus, they took up the pretense of marriage in order that they both might endure to the end in reverence for God and the glory of chastity.

And when Chrysanthus gladly took charge of the administration of his father's will, he had Daria baptized in their house. She thus became a most blessed virgin of Christ so that within a few days she had learned all the divine Scriptures and as a mark of her holy virginity took the veil of holiness.* She was not joined to Chrysanthus by the heat of the body but was united to him in the passion of the Holy Spirit. And just as a host of men flocked to the grace of Christ through Chrysanthus, so did innumerable women flock to Him through Daria.

(15) Igitur cum *multæ uirgines, relicto per Dariam amore sponsorum,* Christo se traderent, *nunc iuuenes, relicto uoluptatum studio* et carnali commertio, sese castimonio manciparent, *excitata est in urbe seditio,* et
295   Celerino prefecturam urbis administranti, interpellatio publica exhibetur. Iuuenes clamabant, 'Sponsas nostras per Dariam amittimus!' Uiri clamabant, 'Coniugia perdimus!' Mulieres clamabant, 'Maritos amisimus per Chrysantum, et iam filios non habemus!' Et erat interpellantium uaria et | seditiosa confusio.
300   *Iubentur itaque a prefecto ambo constringi et diuersis poenis interfici si sacrificiorum cerimonias contempsissent.* Traditur itaque tribuno Claudio Chrysantus, qui *Claudius tradidit eum septuaginta militibus* dicens, 'Ducite eum extra ciuitatem ad fanum inuicti Herculis, ubi si sacrificare noluerit, diuersis eum penis agite quoadusque consentiat'.
305   (16) *Tunc milites crudis eum neruis adstringunt* ut sensim siccantibus neruis ad ossa eius uis pertingeret ligamenti. *Statim autem ut constrictus est, ita omnia sunt in manibus eius ligamenta resoluta ut non occurrerent oculi eius uidere celeritatem resolutionis eorum.* Et quasi luctantes contra se ligaturas, *diuerso modo diuersi eum milites constringebant nouis et exquisitis ingeniis.*
310   Mox autem ut manus ligantis cessassent a uinculo, dicto citius quicquid ligauerant soluebatur. Tunc irati milites | *mittunt eum in cippum* nouum et nodosissimum ita ut in tertio puncto *eius tibias coartarent. Igitur cum starent ante eum et insultarent ei, ita putrefactum est lignum totius cippi ut in cinerem conuerteretur. Tollentes autem milites Chrysantum perfundunt eum lotio*
315   *humano* dicentes, 'Maleficia tua modo amittes!' *Statim autem ut perfusus est lotio putentissimo, ipsa aqua putens ita est in nectareum odorem conuersa* ut putares eum non lotio sed rosato esse perfusum. Auferentes autem eum ex eodem loco, *excoriauerunt uitulum, et corio retenti cingunt eum nudum et posuerunt eum ad solem. Sed per totum diem in æstu nimio et flagrantissimo*
320   *sole nulla omnino potuit calefactione siccari, sed eadem qua fuerat uiriditate perdurans corium in nullo potuit Dei famulum uiolare. Item posuerunt in collum eius catenas ferreas, et simul manus et pedes constringentes, clauserunt eum in obscurissimo loco. Statim autem ex manibus eius soluta sunt uin|cula, et tanta lux refulsit in loco ut putarentur illic esse lampades multe fulgentes.*

---

294 sese] C se. castimonio] B castimonie
295 prefecturam] C prefecto. administranti] C administrante
297–98 Coniugia...Chrysantum] C uxores amittimus per chrisantum. Fol. 130ʳ
303 ubi] C ibi
304 eum] B *omits.* quoadusque] C quousque

305 crudis] C nodosis. eum neruis] B *order reversed*
306 uis] C uix. ligamenti] C ligamentum
307 *second* eius] C *omits*
308 se] C *omits*. ligaturas] C liguturas et
309 nouis] C nodis. ingeniis] C ingentibus
310 ligantis] C ligantes. dicto] C *omits*

(15) Consequently, when many young girls, who had given up their fiancees, gave themselves over to Christ on Daria's account, and now when young men, who had given up their eagerness for pleasure and sex, surrendered themselves to chastity, then turmoil was stirred up in the city, and the public outcry was shown to Celerinus, who served the prefect of the city. Young men shouted, 'We lose our fiancees because of Daria!' Husbands shouted, 'We are deprived of wives!' Wives shouted, 'We have lost husbands because of Chrysanthus, and now we have no sons!' And there was varied and riotous disorder from those creating the disturbance.

Then the prefect ordered Chrysanthus and Daria to be bound and killed with various punishments if they scorned the sacrificial rites. Chrysanthus was handed over to the tribune Claudius, who handed him over to seventy soldiers and said, 'Take him outside of the city to the temple of the invincible Hercules where, if he will not offer a sacrifice, you are to ply him with various punishments until he does'.

(16) Then the soldiers bound him with rawhide strips so that as the thongs gradually dried out, they would shrink and cut Chrysanthus to the bone. But as soon as he was bound, all the strips came untied so fast that the soldiers could not figure out how it had happened. And as if they fought against themselves to tie him up, different soldiers bound him in different ways with novel and meticulously contrived knots. But once those who were tying him up removed their hands from the bond, no sooner was it said than done that whatever they bound him with came untied. Then the angered soldiers threw him into a freshly cut and very knotty set of wooden stocks to squeeze his legs into a third small hole. When they stood in front of him and jeered at him, every bit of the (green) wood was made to disintegrate and turned to ashes. The soldiers then picked him up, drenched him in human urine and said, 'Now give up your sorcery!' But as soon as they drenched him with the very foul urine, the stinking water was turned into the fragrance of nectar so that you would have thought he had been drenched in rose wine not urine. And then those who were holding him prisoner took him away from that place, skinned a calf, sewed him up naked in the hide and positioned him facing the sun. Not only would the hide not shrink after drying all day in the scorching heat and under the hottest sun, but the hide Chrysanthus was in retained its original freshness and could not harm God's servant in any way. In addition, the soldiers chained him around the neck, and likewise bound his hands and feet, and locked him away in a very dark place. But instantly the chains were loosened from his hands, and such light shone in the place that the soldiers thought many torches were ablaze there.

---

311 Fol. 130ᵛ. cippum nouum] C cyppo nouo
312 nodosissimum] C nodosissimo
314 milites] C *omits*
315 amittes] C amittis
317 rosato esse] C rosa
319 flagrantissimo] C in flagrantissimo

320 nulla] C nullam. calefactione siccari] C calefactionem sentire
322 collum] CB collo. *first* et] C sed. manus] C manus eius
323 ex] C in. Fol. 131ʳ
324 refulsit] C infulsit. in] C *omits*

325 (17) *Nuntiantur omnia hæc a* septuaginta *militibus Claudio tribuno suo. Et ipse ueniens ad locum uidit lumen* inmensum *et iubens eum ad se egredi, dixit ei, 'Quæ ista tanta uis maleficiorum tuorum est ut ista perficias?* Nam omnes *magos* et hierofantas *et Chaldeos* et ariolos *et incantatores ego edomui, et adhuc istam potentiam in maleficis non inueni. Omnibus tamen imperaui*
330 *quod uolui et eorum consensum ad meos libitus inclinaui.* Nunc uero te uirum nobilem et sapientem ad hanc solam partem accepi, ut *contempta superstitione Christianę temeritatis*, de qua murmur populi Romani et seditio excitata est, reddas te generi tuo et *diis* omnipotentibus debita *sacrificia* clementer *exhibeas'.*
335 *Cui respondens Chrysantus* ait, '*Si esset in te uel scintilla prudentiæ, cognosceres me non maleficiorum argumentis | sed diuinis adminiculis adiuuari*; sed sic ad me respicis sicut ad deos, quos colere iniusto iudicio comprobaris. Si enim oculi tui sapienter aspicerent, uiderent quia *dii tui non uident.* Si aures tuæ reciperent ueritatem, aduerteres *illos* uoces clamantium
340 *audire non posse.* Si interiora tua intellectum alicuius prudentiæ caperent, considerares *istos in interioribus suis nichil habere aliud preter argillam et plumbum'.*

Tunc tribunus *Claudius iussit eum fustibus cædi. Statim autem ut allate sunt uirgę durissimę, coeperunt in manibus cædentium quasi plume mollescere.*
345 *Denique dum tenerentur uirgæ, quasi ferreę essent ita erant nodosæ et solidæ, dum uero percuterent, quasi ex papyro essent ita mollissime reddebantur et lenes.*

(18) *Tunc Claudius* tribunus *iussit eum erigi et indui uestimentis suis.* Et conuersus ad milites suos, omnes | hac uoce alloquitur dicens, 'Bene nostis
350 me et incantatorum et magorum deprehendisse prestigia. *Hic humanę artes penitus non sunt, ubi uirtutum diuinarum potestas apparet.* Nam uincula neruorum sponte soluta cesserunt. Ligni fortitudo repentina defectione conputruit. Corii uiriditas in solis nimio ardore in eadem qua de uitulo ablata fuerat nouitate permansit. Catenarum quoque nexus inuisibilis potestas
355 exsoluit. Tenebrarum locus nimia illustratione perfulsit. Fustes in manu tenentis rigescunt, in ferientis ictu mollescunt. In aspectu patientis ista sinceritas apparet. In uerbo etiam ipso rationabilis ueritas conprobatur. *Quid superest nisi omnes huius hominis genibus aduoluti* ueniam postulemus

---

325 Nuntiantur] C Nuntiant. a septuaginta
   militibus] C lxx (septuaginta *above*)
   milites
326 ipse] C *omits.* uidit] C uidens. iubens] C
   iussit, ssit *written over erasure.* ad se
   egredi] B egredi ad se
327 dixit] C et (*inserted*) dixit. tanta] B *omits*
328 *first* et] C *omits.* hierofantas] B ihero-

   fantas. ego edomui] C secta domui
331 contempta] C contenta
335 Cui respondens Chrysanthus] C
   respondit chrisantus et ait
336 Fol. 131ᵛ
337 respicis] C respice
339 reciperent ueritatem] C *order reversed*
341 considerares] C considerare

(17) The seventy soldiers reported all this to their tribune Claudius. And when he came to the place himself, he saw the great light, ordered Chrysanthus to be brought out to him and said to him, 'What is so powerful about your sorcery that enables you to do this? For I have overcome all sorcerers and high-priests and Babylonian astrologers and diviners and enchanters, and so far I have not discovered this power among the magicians. Yet I have mastered all whom I have wanted to and have inclined them to agree with what I chose. Now I was in fact told that you are high-born and knowledgeable with respect to this particular sorcery, so once you have scorned your irrational belief in Christian superstition, which has stirred up an outcry and disorder among the Roman people, then you may return to your family and quietly offer the sacrifices owed to the omnipotent gods'.

Chrysanthus replied to him and said, 'If you possessed a glimmer of good sense, then you would see that I am aided by divine assistance not sorcery. But yet you look to me just as you look to the gods, whom you have sanctioned to be worshipped by an unjust judgment. If your eyes were to see with true understanding, then they would see that your gods do not see. If your ears were to accept the truth, then you would discover that your gods cannot hear the voices of those who cry out to them. If the innermost fibres of your being were to grasp the meaning of any bit of knowledge whatsoever, then you would notice that your gods have nothing in their interiors except clay and lead'.

Then the tribune Claudius ordered him to be beaten with clubs. But as soon as the soldiers swung the very hard sticks, they began to soften in their hands like feathers. Indeed, when the soldiers held the sticks ready, they were as knotty and rigid as if made of iron, but when the soldiers struck, they became very soft and light as if they were made of paper.

(18) Then the tribune Claudius ordered Chrysanthus to be helped to his feet and dressed in his clothes. And after he had turned to his soldiers, he addresses them all with these words and says, 'You know well that I have uncovered the tricks of enchanters and sorcerers. Where the power of divine miracles appears, there is no human artifice whatsoever. For the rawhide strips, spontaneously loosened, failed. The strong wood rotted and suddenly collapsed. In the sun's scorching heat the hide remained as fresh as it had been when it was removed from the calf. An unseen power also undid a knot of chains. A place of darkness shone brightly with a great light. Clubs harden when held ready in the hand, then soften when the beater strikes a blow. The soundness of the one who suffers is evident from his appearance. The rational truth is borne out in his very words. What is left except that we all, once we have fallen

344 plume] B pluma
345 uirgæ] C *omits*
349 Fol. 132ʳ. dicens] C *omits*
350 incantatorum] C incantatores. prestigia]
  C fastigia
353 *second* in] C *omits*
354 potestas] C *omits*

356 tenentis] i *corrected from* e; C
  tenentium. ferientis] C inferientis, *final* i
  corrected from e. ista] B ipsa
357 rationabilis] C r (?) *in right margin of*
  column
358 nisi] CB nisi ut (B ut *above line*)

sceleris et *rogemus ut nos quoque talem Deum faciat colere qui cultores suos*
360 *in omni faciat pugna uin\centes?** Ecce etenim et nos et iudices et omnes qui
contra eum uenerunt; numquid non eos ita superat ut probastis?'

Igitur cum hæc et alia fuisset perlocutus militibus, *cum uniuersis militibus*
ipse Claudius genibus eius aduolutus, orabat dicens, 'In *ueritate probaui quia*
Deus tuus Deus uerus est. Peto itaque ut facias me cognoscere eum et *ad noti-*
365 *tiam cultur[ę eius aliqua ratione pertingere'.*

Cui Chrisantus dixit, 'Ad notitiam peruenire desideras, *non pedibus tibi*
sed corde pergendum est.] *Tantum enim unicuique presens efficitur Deus,*
quantum eum fide mentis et cordis integritate *quæsierit'.*

(19) Hæc et his similia prosequente Chrysanto *credidit Claudius* tribunus;
370 *credidit Hylaria uxor eius*; *credunt et duo filii eius Iason et Maurus*; *crediderunt*
omnes amici et familiares eius; credidit omnis familia eius; *credunt omnes illi*
septuaginta milites cum suis, et uniuersi eodem die baptizati. Per singulos dies
a sancto *Chrisanto eruditionem ueritatis desiderantissime audiebant,* et
uerbum Christi cum omni reuerentia et timore capientes, *optabant pro Dei*
375 *nomine etiam aduersa perferre.*

Uerum quia longum est mirabilia quæ Deus per eos fecerit enarrare, rerum
exitum intimemus.

(20) *Cum omnes credidis\sent Deo et imperator Numerianus audisset, iussit*
Claudium tribunum, *ingenti saxo constrictum, in medio mari dari precipitem*;
380 *omnes autem milites singillatim audiri, et quicumque se negasset Christianum*
dimitti, qui uero negare noluisset, caput amputari. Tantam autem gratiam
Dominus credentibus se concessit ut primus Iason et Maurus, *filii Claudii,*
etiam non interrogati Christum se colere dicerent et *pro eius nominis confes-*
sione mortem libenter optarent. Hos imitantes omnes unanimiter intra unam
385 horam martyrium Domino consecrarunt.

Erat autem in loco ubi decollati sunt cuniculus antiquus; hunc emun-
dantes per noctem Christiani simul in unum omnia corpora sepelierunt non
longe ab urbe uia quæ Salaria nuncupatur. Corpora autem filiorum suorum
collegit sancta Hilaria, relicta martyris Claudii, et singillatim condiens, id est
390 Mauri et Iasonis, in sarcofagis singulis collocauit.

---

360 Fol. 132ᵛ
361 eos] B *omits*
362 alia] C talia. perlocutus militibus] C
    militibus prolocutus
364–67 est. ... Tantum] *insertion mark above*
    line between these words and text to be
    inserted at bottom of page. On the photo-
    copy from the manuscript, some lines of
    the text to be inserted have been cut off,
    and some of what appears is faint. I read
    only: Peto itaque ut facias me cognoscere
    eum et ad noticiam cultur.... *The*
    remaining text is provided from the AS
    edition, which is based on a seventeenth-

century transcription of P and which also
agrees with B. C differs only in one
instance, reading tibi est...pergendum
(*line* 367).

364–65 notitiam] B noticiam dei
366 peruenire] B si peruenire
367 enim] C *omits.* Deus] C *omits*
369 prosequente] C docente
370 credidit] B credi[dit], *hole in manuscript.*
    Hylaria] C illaria. *first* et] C *omits.*
    credunt] B crediderunt. crediderunt] C
    credunt
371 credit omnis familia eius] C *omits.*
    credunt] B crediderunt, ider *above line*

at this man's knees, ask forgiveness for our crimes and beg him to enable us to worship this God who makes his worshippers victorious in every battle?* Look at us and the judges and all those who have opposed him; is it not true that he overcomes them, just as you have discovered?'

Then, when he had spoken these and other words to his soldiers, Claudius himself, with all the soldiers, fell at Chrysanthus's knees, and Claudius begged him and said, 'I have learned the truth that your God is true God. And now I ask you to enable me to know him and somehow learn to worship him'.

Chrysanthus said to him, 'If you want to come to that knowledge, then you should pursue it with your heart not your feet. For God makes himself known to each person to the extent that he seeks him with the faith of the mind and a purity of heart'.

(19) When Chrysanthus continued these words and others like them, Claudius the tribune believed; Hilaria his wife believed; and his two sons, Jason and Maurus, also believe; all Claudius's friends and acquaintances believed; all his household believed; all seventy soldiers believe with them, and they all were baptized on the same day. Over successive days, they listened to Saint Chrysanthus teach about the truth they longed for, and they seized the word of Christ with all reverence and fear, and wanted to endure adversity for the sake of God's name.

But because it will take too long to recount the marvellous things that God did through them, we will make known their final moments.

(20) When all these had believed in God and when the emperor Numerian had heard about it, he ordered the tribune Claudius to be tied to an enormous rock and thrown headlong into the middle of the sea; moreover, he ordered all the soldiers to be given an audience one by one, and those who denied they were Christians to be released and those who did not choose to deny it to have their heads chopped off. But the Lord granted such grace to those who believed in him that the young Jason and Maurus, Claudius's sons, also declared that they worshipped Christ, though they had not been questioned, and said that they would gladly choose death for the sake of confessing his name. Within an hour, all those unanimously imitating the brothers devoted their martyrdom to the Lord.

Now there was an old mine tunnel in the place where they were beheaded; after the Christians had cleaned it during the night, they buried all the bodies together in one group not far from the city along a road called the Salarian Way. Then the holy Hilaria, the widow of the martyr Claudius, gathered up the bodies of her sons, and embalming them one by one, that is to say Jason and Maurus, and she placed them in individual tombs.

---

372 septuaginta] C .lxx. uniuersi] C uniuersis
 eorum
373 sancto] B beato. Chrisanto] C *in small
 capitals*
375 etiam] C *omits*
378 Fol. 133ʳ
379 dari precipitem] C *order reversed*, dari
 above line

380 omnes] C Cum. audiri, et] C audiret
381 caput] C capite. autem] C *omits*
382 se] B in se. concessit] C cessit. primus] B
 primum
383 et] C ei. nominis confessione] C nomine
 confessionem
384 optarent] C optare
387 noctem] C noctanter

(21) Quæ dum assiduis obsequiis circa sanctorum confessionem oraret Deum, | tenta est. *Quæ dum traheretur, rogauit eos qui se trahebant dicens, 'Obsecro uos permittite me prius orationem meam complere, et ueniam quocumque uolueritis'.* Igitur dum fixisset gradum, *accepit sacramentum*
395 *Dominic*et expandens manus suas dixit, 'Domine Ihesu Christe, quia te toto corde confiteor, modo me associa cum filiis meis quos ex utero meo ad tuum martyrium conuocasti'. *Et hæc dicens proiecit se in orationem, et dum oraret emisit spiritum.* Tunc illi ipsi qui eam tenuerant dolentes super repentinum obitum eius, reliquerunt duas ancillas eius que cum ea erant. Illę autem sepe-
400 lierunt eam diligentissime sepulturæ et super eam breuissimam ecclesiam fabricauerunt, quia locus in quo defuncta fuerat eiusdem erat hortus Hilariæ, et ex quo sancti passi fuerant ibidem sibi mansiunculam collocauerat.

(22) *Interea Chrysantum iussit infernali retineri custodia ut simul cum Daria diluersis tormentorum generibus ageretur.* Erat autem ima custodia in
405 carcere Tulliano unde putor horribilis ascendebat quia cloacarum cuniculi digesta domorum stercora illic iugiter decurrebant. Et in hoc decursorio, ut diximus, *erat ima, et lutea et ita tenebrosa custodia ut penitus lucifluus aer, nec signum ibidem diei nec uestigium aliquod lucis ostenderet.* In hanc ergo habi- tationem ferro uinctus Chrysantus mittitur nudus. *Daria uero ponitur in*
410 *publico contubernio meretricum.* Sed diuersis his sanctorum passionibus diuerso genere Christus occurrit: nam *Chrysanto lux diuina et odoramenta sancta prestantur; Dariæ uero leo fugiens de cauea amphiteatri dirigitur. Qui ingressus cellulam illam in qua Daria prostrata in oratione iacebat, ipse quoque leo prostrauit se iuxta eam protinus, ut uideretur etiam ipse illam |*
415 adorare qui suam præsentiam deprecanti uirgini exhibebat.

(23) *Nescientes itaque leonem intus esse, miserunt ad eam quendam* turpis- simum qui in scelere corruptionis opinatissimus habebatur. Qui ut ingressus est, *insiliuit in eum leo et prosternens eum sub pedibus suis, coepit ad faciem uirginis Christi Dariæ respicere quasi interrogans quid de eo iuberet.* Quod
420 intellegens beata *Daria dixit, 'Adiuro te per filium Dei,* pro quo martyrii passionem libenter complector, *ut non eum in aliquo ledas, sed permitte eum sermonem meum absque terrore suscipere'. (24) Tunc leo, relinquens eum, posuit se in ipso introitu* ut nec ille remissus copiam fugiendi arriperet nec *alius posset intrare.*

---

392 Fol. 133ᵛ
393 complere] C implere
395 expandens] C expandit
396 associa] C associare, re *above line*
397 conuocasti] C ti *above line*
398 repentinum] B repentino
399 que] *corrected to* ę *by later hand*
400 diligentissime] B diligentissima. sepul- turæ] C *omits*; B sepultura
401 erat hortus] B *order reversed*

402 mansiunculam] C mansionem. collacauerat] C collocauit
403 infernali] C in carcerali, carcerali (*in a different hand?*) *above* fernali *that has been struck through.* retineri] C retinere
404 Daria] C *in small capitals.* Fol. 134ʳ. ageretur] C necaretur, neca *above dotted* age; B angeretur, n *above line.* autem] C igitur. ima] B *erased*
405 putor] C fetor

(21) While Hilaria prayed to God near the saints' tomb with unceasing prayers, she was seized. When she was being dragged off, she made a request of those who hauled her away and said, 'I beg you to allow me to finish my prayer first, and then I will come wherever you want'. And when she had situated herself, she received the Lord's sacrament, spread out her hands and said, 'O Lord Jesus Christ, because I confess you with all my heart, let me now join my sons whom you summoned from my womb to be martyred for you'. And as Hilaria said this, she fell face down in prayer and as she was praying, sent forth her spirit. When those who had detained her felt sorry about her sudden death, they left behind two of her maidservants who were with her. And they buried her most lovingly in a tomb and built a very small church over it, because the garden where she died belonged to this same Hilaria and was the same place in which she had built a little dwelling for herself after the saints had been killed.

(22) Meanwhile Numerian ordered Chrysanthus to be confined in a cell in the depths of the prison so he might suffer various tortures with Daria. Now there was the lowest cell in the Tullian jail whence an awful stench arose because the excrement carried away from houses flowed through the tunnels of the sewers there. And in the path of this downward flow, as we have said, was the bottommost cell, both smeared with excrement and so dark that no light-filled air, no sign of day nor any trace of light could be seen inside. So when Chrysanthus had been shackled with iron, he was thrown naked into this room. Daria on the other hand was put in a public whorehouse. But Christ countered the various sufferings of his saints in different ways: he provided Chrysanthus with a divine light and a holy fragrance; however, he sent a lion who escaped from a cage at the amphitheatre straight to Daria. When the lion entered that tiny room in which Daria lay face down in prayer, he too stretched himself out next to her at once, so that the lion, which presented himself to the virgin while she was praying, seemed to be adoring her.

(23) Not knowing a lion was inside, they sent to Daria a certain utterly indecent man who was held to be most accomplished in the wicked art of seduction. When he had entered, the lion pounced on him, knocked him down underneath his paws and began to look at the face of Daria, the virgin of Christ, as if to ask what she would do about the man. When she understood that, the blessed Daria said, 'I beg you by the Son of God, for whose sake I willingly embrace the suffering of martyrdom, do not harm him at all, but permit him to listen without fear to what I have to say'. (24) Then the lion moved away from the man and placed himself right in the doorway so that the man might not seize the opportunity to flee once he had been released and so that no one else could enter.

---

406 domorum] C a domibus. hoc] B *not visible because of hole in manuscript.* decursorio] C decursori
407 lucifluus] C luctifluus
408 hanc] C hac
408–09 habitationem] C habitatione. uinctus] C *erased and* ligatus *above line.* ponitur] C datur ut ponatur
413 cellulam] C cellam

414 illam] B illum. Fol. 134ᵛ
418 insiliuit] C insiliut
419 Dariæ] B *omits.* interrogans] C interrogans eam. de eo] C *omits*
420 dixit] B ait
421 passionem] C passiones. complector] CB amplector. ut] C *omits*
423 fugiendi] C fugendi

425   *Tunc dicit ad eum Daria, 'Ecce, ferocitas leonis* audito Christi nomine *dat reuerentiam Deo. Et tu, homo rationabilis,* in tantis criminibus te exerces ut etiam in hoc quo, *miser,* lugendus I *es glorieris?' Tunc ille prosternens se ante, eam cepit clamare dicens, 'Iube me hinc egredi sanum ut et ego clamem omnibus Dei filium Christum quem colis* ipsum solum uerum esse Deum!'

430   *Tunc Daria iussit leoni ut amoueret se ab ingressu. Qui cum fuisset egressus, clamare coepit* et per totam ciuitatem currere dicens, '*Sciatis omnes Dariam deam esse!'*

    Igitur diuersi uenatores et diuersi populi dum ad leonem capiendum pergerent, hanc Deus uirtutem leoni concessit: ut omnes caperet, et quasi manu

435 tenens, ita conprehensos sine aliqua lesione *ante pedes* sanctæ *Dariæ poneret.* (25) *Tunc Daria omnes alloquebatur dicens, 'Si promiseritis uos Christo credituros, inlesi poteritis abscedere. Sin alias, nescio si dii uestri auxilientur uobis'. Tunc illi omnes una uoce clamabant, 'Qui non credit Christum uerum Deum esse uiuus hinc non exeat!'* Et hæc dicentes, *coeperunt omnes egredi* una uoce

440 clamantes, '*Credite, populi Romani,* I *non esse alterum Deum preter Christum!'*

    Tunc prefectus Celerinus nomine *iussit ignem accendi copiosum in ingressu cellulæ in qua erat Daria cum leone.* Quod cum fieri uideret, *coepit leo expauescere* et rugitum dare. *Cui* beata *Daria ait, 'Noli timere. Nec*

445 *incendio cremaberis,* neque capieris, *neque interfici poteris, sed morte tua morieris. Egredere securus* et uade quia *ille quem* in me *honorasti ipse te liberat'. Tunc inclinato capite leo egreditur per medias turbas populorum.* Nullus eum umquam coepit; numquam neminem lesit. *Hi autem qui ex ore eius incolumes euaserant uniuersi baptizati sunt.*

450   (26) *Nuntiata sunt omnia hæc* Numeriano *imperatori, et iussit* Celerino *prefecto ut ambos, id est* Chrysantum et Dariam, *si non consensissent sacrificiis, diuersis tormentorum cruciatibus puniret.* Igitur cum cogeret eos I Celerinus ad sacrificandum, et diuersa diceret et audiret, *iussit sanctum Chrisantum eculeo ingenti suspendi et torqueri. Cumque inponeretur eculeo*

455 *Chrysantus, ligna omnia eculei comminuta sunt;* uincula uero uniuersa disrupta sunt. *Lampades quoque quæ erant lateribus eius applicande extinctæ sunt. Quicumque autem misissent manum ad sanctam Dariam stupebant nerui eorum, et pre dolore mugitum* cordis gemitumque *reddebant.* Uidens itaque hæc, *Celerinus* præfectus *uehementer expauit,* et cursu rapidissimo *ad imper-*

460 *atorem properans, cuncta quæ gesta fuerant enarrauit.*

---

425 Daria] C *omits*
426 te] C *omits*
427 etiam] B etiam quod, *but* quod *dotted for deletion.* Fol. 135ʳ
429 esse Deum] B *order reversed*
433 uenatores] C ueneratores
436 dicens] C *omits*

440 Fol. 135ᵛ
443 ingressu cellulæ] C ingressum cellẹ
444 Daria] C *in small capitals*
445 cremaberis] C caperis
448 numquam] C umquam. Hi] B Hii
450 hæc] C *omits.* imperatori] C prefecto

Then Daria says to the man, 'Look, when the fierce lion heard the name of Christ, he showed reverence for God. And do you, a rational man, busy yourself in such crimes that you even boast about this, for which you, wretched one, ought to be deplored?' Then he fell face down in front of her and began to cry out saying, 'Order that I leave here unharmed so that I too may declare to all that the Son of God, Christ, whom you worship, is himself the only true God!' Daria then ordered the lion to move away from the entrance. When the man had left, he began to shout and to race through the entire city declaring, 'Know that Daria is a goddess!'

When various hunters and different people came to capture the lion, God granted the lion this miracle: he captured them all and, as if he held them with human hands, placed the captives unharmed at the feet of Saint Daria. (25) Then Daria spoke to them and said, 'If you promise to believe in Christ, then you can leave unharmed. But if not, I do not know if your gods can help you'. Then they all shouted with one voice, 'Do not let anyone who does not believe that Christ is true God leave here alive!' And when they said this, they all began to go out shouting in one voice, 'Believe, people of Rome, that there is no other God except Christ!'

Then the prefect named Celerinus ordered a huge fire kindled in the doorway of the room where Daria was with the lion. When the lion saw what had been done, he began to be afraid and to roar. The blessed Daria said to him, 'Do not be afraid. You will not be burned alive in the fire, nor captured, nor killed, but you will die a natural death. Go out fearlessly and be on your way because He whom you have honoured in me will himself free you'. Then with his head bowed, the lion goes out through the middle of the crowds of people. No one ever captured him; he never harmed anyone. What is more, all those who escaped uninjured from his mouth were baptized.

(26) All these things were reported to emperor Numerian, and he ordered the prefect Celerinus to punish both of them, that is to say Chrysanthus and Daria, with different tortures should they not agree to sacrifice. Then when Celerinus had summoned them to sacrifice, and had addressed and listened to the opposing side, he ordered Saint Chrysanthus to be strapped to a huge rack and tortured. And when Chrysanthus was put on the rack, all its wooden parts were smashed; all its chains were shattered too. Likewise, the torches applied to his sides were extinguished. Whoever tried to grab Saint Daria was paralysed, and in their pain they let loose moans and groans from the heart. When the prefect Celerinus saw this, he was utterly terrified, and rushing to the emperor by the quickest way, he recounted everything that had happened.

450–51 Celerino prefecto] C *omits*. ambos] C ambo. Dariam] C daria
452 diuersis] C diuersorum. cruciatibus] B generibus. puniret] C puniretur. Fol. 136ʳ.
453 Celerinus] C prefectus nomine celerianus; B *omits*
454 et torqueri] C *omits*. inponeretur] B imponeretur

456 disrupta] B dirupta, *dotted* s *between* i *and* r
457 autem] C *omits*; B ergo. misissent] C mittebant. Dariam] C *in small capitals*
458 dolore] C doloribus. mugitum] C gemitum. gemitumque] C *omits*. reddebant] C *first* d *above line*

Tunc Numerianus imperator, non uirtutibus diuinis hæc sed maleficiis imputans, iussit eos duci in uiam Salariam atque *in arenario deponi illic utrosque simul,* id est Chrysantum et Dariam, *ac uiuos terra et lapidibus obrui.* Tunc beatissimus | Chrysantus cum beata uirgine Daria deponuntur in
465 foueam psalmis et orationibus insistentes. Facti sunt in passione sociati sanguine sicut fuerant mente etiam coniuges, quasi in uno lectulo ita in una fouea in una uoluntate durantes. Talis fuit passio quæ magis sepulturam Dei famulis intulit quam poenam ingessit. Accepit autem Deus hostiam uiuentem, cuius gratia hoc factum est ut qui *simul fuerant in uirginitate*
470 *durantes* simul pertingerent ad coronam sine fine uiuentes.

(27) *Igitur cum multa beneficia Deus uenientibus ad eorum sepulturam prestaret, euenit ut* die natalis eorum *infinita populi multitudo concurreret,* uiri simul ac mulieres pariter et infantes et innuptæ puellæ et iuuenes. *Hoc cum fuisset Numeriani auribus intimatum, iussit ut in introitu per quem introierant*
475 *in cripta paries leuaretur. Quod cum fuisset adimpletum, desuper ad s[a]blonem super eos* | *montem deiecit.* Omnes ergo pariter dum communionis sacramenta perciperent et martyrum gloriam cælebrarent, ipsi quoque ad coronam martyrii pertinxerunt. Inter quos erat Diodorus presbiter, et diaconus Marianus et plurimi clericorum. Populi autem multitudo, nec
480 numero nec nomine collecta est, quia et laciniosum esse et superfluum iudicauimus.

(28) Hæc omnia sicut gesta sunt scripsimus Uirinus et Armenius fratres, a sancto Stephano papa Romano in sede apostolica facti presbiteri, et direximus ad omnes ecclesias per orientem et occidentem ut sciat omnis mundus
485 quia martyres suos Dominus Chrysantum et Dariam cum multis filiis in triumpho martyrii et gloria perpetuæ coronę suscepit, qui uiuit et regnat in secula seculorum. Amen. EXPLICIT PASSIO SANCTI CHRISANTI MARTYRIS ET DARIAE UIRGINIS.

---

462 uiam Salariam] C uia salaria
462–63 illic utrosque simul] C simul et illic
    utrosque. et Dariam] C cum daria. ac]
    CB *omit*
464 beatissimus] C beatus. Fol. 136ᵛ
465 foueam] C fouea. Facti sunt] C Facta est
465–66 sociati sanguine] C socia sanguinis
470 sine fine uiuentes] C *omits*
471 sepulturam] C sepulchra
472 euenit] C et uenit. die] C dies.
    concurreret] C concurrerent
473 *first* et] C *omits*
475 cripta] B criptam. adimpletum] C
    impletum
475–76 desuper ad s(a)blonem] PC
    sublonem; B de sabulone. Fol. 137ʳ

478 pertinxerunt] C perrexerunt, re *above
    dotted* ti; B pertigerunt
479 Marianus] *second* a *above line;* C
    maurianus; B marinus
480 numero nec nomine] C numerus nec
    nomina. est] C sunt. laciniosum] C
    latinitiosum
482 Armenius] B armenus
483 Romano] B *each* o *over dotted* a
485 Dominus] B *omits.* multis filiis] C multis;
    B *order reversed.* in] C *omits*
486 martyrii] C martyris. gloria] C gloriam
486–87 qui...Amen.] CB *omit*
487–88 C EXPLICIT PASSIO
    SANCTORUM CHRISANTI. ET
    DARIE., *in small capitals;* B Finit passio
    sanctorum Crisanti et Darie martyrium.

Emperor Numerian did not attribute these things to divine miracles but to sorcery, and he ordered the saints to be led to the Salarian Way, put into a sand-pit there and both together, that is to say Chrysanthus and Daria, to be buried alive with dirt and rocks. Then the most blessed Chrysanthus and the blessed virgin Daria were put in a pit as they continued singing psalms and saying prayers. They were united by blood in their suffering just as they had also been joined in spirit as husband and wife, enduring to the end in one desire, in one pit, as if in one bed. Their suffering was such that it provided God's saints a burial rather than heaping punishment on them. Moreover, God accepted the living sacrifice, and his grace enabled those who had endured together in virginity to attain the crown together and live for ever.

(27) When God had provided many favours to those who arrived at their tomb, it happened that an innumerable crowd of people flocked together for their feast-day, men together with women in equal numbers and children and unmarried girls and young men. When this had been made known to Numerian, he ordered a wall to be raised at the entrance through which the crowd had entered the crypt. When that was done, he hurled down on top of them a towering heap of gravel. Thus while they all were receiving the sacrament of communion and celebrating the glory of the martyrs, they also attained the crown of martyrdom for themselves. Among them were Didorus the priest, the deacon Marianus and a great many clerics. However, we have not listed the total number of people in the crowd or their names because we decided that it would take too long and is not essential.

(28) We, brothers Uirinus and Armenius, made priests in the papal church by the holy Stephen, pope of Rome, have written these things just as they occurred, and we have directed them to all the churches throughout the East and West so that the whole world may know that the Lord has received his martyrs Chrysanthus and Daria with many of their children in the triumph of martyrdom and with the glory of an ever-lasting crown, he who lives and reigns forever and ever. Amen. HERE ENDS THE PASSIO OF SAINT CHRYSANTHUS THE MARTYR AND OF DARIA THE VIRGIN.

COMMENTARY ON THE LATIN TEXTS

The Passio of the Holy Martyrs Julian and Basilissa

2–9   The Scriptures alluded to in these lines, particularly those verses from 1 Corinthians 7, may provide a justification of sorts for the spiritual marriage that is to follow. 1 Cor. 7 is the apostle Paul's celebrated and influential chapter on marriage in which he declares that those who are unmarried may give undivided attention to the Lord whereas the married must divide their attention between worldly and heavenly concerns. In 1 Cor. 7.35, he counsels men and women to remain single so that they may have 'facultatem... sine inpedimento Dominum observandi' ('power to attend upon the Lord, without impediment' [respectively, *Biblia Sacra Vulgata* and *Douay Rheims Bible* (cited in Old English Commentary, p. 101 [note on lines 37–39]), to which all biblical citations and translations refer]). On the *passio*'s concern with various 'impediments', see lines 109–14 and 693–94.

13   The phrase 'studens in singulorum uirtute' could also be translated 'striving for the virtue of the chaste' if *singulis* is taken to mean celibate (see the entry for *singulis* in A. Blaise, *Dictionnaire Latin–Français des Auteurs Chrétiens* [Turnhout, 1954]). This reading becomes more compelling if *ergastulum* of line 10 is taken to mean a 'work-house' of the saints in the sense of a monastery. Although R.E. Latham records that *ergasterium* is used for 'monastery' in Britain c. 930 (*Revised Medieval Latin Word-List from British and Irish Sources* [Oxford, 1965]), no dictionary that I consulted defines *ergastulum* as monastery. The present translation of 'studens in singulorum uirtute' sustains a focus on Julian's acumen regarding the 'business' of being a Christian.

16   N's 'innumerabili lege', which is attested in at least four other manuscripts of *BHL* 4532, might be translated loosely as the 'inestimable law' of the apostle Paul, but 'venerable law' is a better choice.

17–18   Julian's parents actually misquote Paul, although the author never calls into doubt their sincerity or questions the accuracy of their advice. However, when read in the context of 1 Timothy 4, Paul's advice to 'iuveniores' ('younger ones') to marry, bear children and oversee households in verse 14 is directed at the 'adulescentiores viduas' ('younger widows') of verse 11: 'adulescentiores autem viduas devita; cum enim luxuriatae fuerint in Christo nubere volunt (11) ... volo ergo iuveniores nubere filios procreare matres familias esse nullam occasionem dare adversario maledicti gratia' (14) ('But the younger widows avoid. For when they have grown wanton in Christ, they will marry ... I will, therefore, that the younger should marry, bear children, be mistresses of families, give no occasion to the adversary to speak evil').

The substitution of 'iuvenes' ('young men') in the legend for Paul's 'iuveniores' ('younger [widows]') occurs in the Greek original of the *passio* ('La Passion Ancienne des Saints Julien et Basilisse [*BHG* 970–71]', ed. F. Halkin, *Analecta Bollandiana* 98 [1980], 241–96, at 246 [lines 8–9] and note 4 in the apparatus). In the Greek text, the author or scribe substitutes 'neous' (νέους), with its unambiguous masculine ending, 'neoteras' (νεωτερας) of verse 14, a feminine adjective used as a noun for 'young female ones' (*The Greek New Testament*, ed. K. Aland *et al.*, 3rd ed. [Stuttgart, 1983]). 'Neoteras' is translated in the Vulgate with the comparative (but either masculine or feminine) adjective 'iuveniores' (and in some manuscripts 'iuniores'). 'Matres familias' in verse 14 makes the Greek verb 'oikodespotein' (οἰχοδεσποτεῖν) ('to manage households') more gender-specific and affirms that Paul is referring to younger widows.

When the verse is taken out of context and applied to Julian, his parents appear to ignore Paul's advice to the unmarried in 1 Corinthians 7.7–9 to remain single if they are able. Also noteworthy is that while 1 Timothy 5.14 is followed faithfully for much of the time, its conclusion is altered in both the Greek and Latin texts. Paul encouraged younger widows to marry so that they might avoid becoming oath-breakers, idlers, gossips and busybodies (verses 12–13) and might avoid being lured away from their faith by the devil (verse 15). The legend, by contrast, implies that remaining single would attract Satan's attention and thus expose young men to his attacks. This too contradicts Paul's characterization of the unmarried in 1 Cor. 7.32–35 as those who are able to serve Christ most devotedly and unswervingly. I am grateful to Gordon Whatley for helping me solve this conundrum and for providing translations from the Greek.

35–36 It seems that by the phrase 'octaua...die noctu' we are to understand that Julian has reached the end of his seventh diurnal period (counting from night to night as one day), a reading that would agree with his request for a delay of seven days. More important

than the issue of how to calculate the passage of time is the fact that
Ælfric must have had a text containing the reading 'octaua...die
noctu', which explains why he writes that Julian's vision occurs 'on
ðære eahteoðan nihte' ('on the eighth night' [line 9 (p. 54)]). The
reading is significant for identifying manuscripts of *BHL* 4532 that
belong to the family of the version Ælfric must have used
(Zettel,'Ælfric's Hagiographic Sources' [cited on p. 46, n. 178], p.
203). Thirty-two manuscripts of *BHL* 4532 that I have seen record
it, the exception being Stuttgart, Württembergische Landes-
bibliothek, MS XIV 13 (s.ix), which shares a reading of the most
common version of the *passio*, *BHL* 4529: 'septimo...die adueniente
nocte' ('on the seventh day when night had come' [*AS*, Ian. I, p.
576]). No manuscripts of *BHL* 4532 that I am aware of are older
than the ninth century, so perhaps the German one represents an
early stage of the version's development. Zettel points out this and
all other variants discussed below at lines 69–70, 117–18, 404, and
924–26 ('Ælfric's Hagiographic Sources', pp. 203–08 and 304–05).

45   Most of *BHL* 4532's abbreviation of *BHL* 4529 occurs in the *vita*
portion of the *passio*, and as a result *BHL* 4532 curtails the atten-
tion *BHL* 4529 gives to Julian's ascetic behaviour. For example, N's
'Iulianus...gratias Deo referebat' ('Julian...gave thanks to God')
replaces this prayer in *BHL* 4529: 'Gratias tibi ago, Domine, qui es
scrutator cordis et renum; qui a me species et delectationes mundi
longe fecisti; ut credulo corde, castitate adjuvante et in me regnante,
ad id quod nec oculus vidit, nec auris audiuit, nec in cor hominis
ascendit, quæ præparasti diligentibus te, perueniam; qui me
dignatus es esse uiam et iter uerum his qui castitatem diligunt et
integritatem mentis ac corporis amplectuntur. Tu nosti, Domine,
quia ex die qua in te renatus sum, usque in horam qua me accersire
dignatus es, nihil præposui amori tuo. Hoc enim desidero ut quod
et ore meo procedit, tu confirmes; quia me tunc credo incipere
quando finio' (*AS*, Ian. I, p. 576). ('I give thanks to you, O Lord,
examiner of the heart and innermost being, you who have made
worldly allures and delights to be far from me, so that with a
believing heart, with chastity sustaining and reigning in me, I will
come to what you have prepared for those who love you, which no
eye has seen, no ear has heard, nor has arisen in the heart of man
[1 Corinthians 2.9]. You have deigned me to be a way and a true
path for those who love chastity and delight in the purity of mind
and body. You know, O Lord, that from the day I was born again
in you until the time you deigned to call out to me, I have put nothing
before your love. I want you to confirm what proceeds from my
mouth: I believe my ending is my beginning'.) In *BHL* 4529, the
prayer links Julian's ascetic zeal as a young man to his later success

as abbot of an idyllic monastery where each of his monks avows the same eagerness for death and awaits the same reward (*AS*, Ian. I, p. 579). Furthermore, without the prayer, *BHL* 4532 does not draw attention to Julian's ability to pass on his character traits to his monastic children and postpones the initial articulation of one of the legend's major themes until lines 109–114 (see the note below).

58   On the numbering and designation of the Psalms in the Latin Vulgate and in modern translations, see the note on lines 37–39 of *Julian and Basilissa* in the Old English Commentary (p. 101).

69–70   Basilissa's comment 'nunc penitus desiderem Redemptoris coniunctionem' ('I now wholly long for union with the Redeemer') is another significant variant common to manuscripts of *BHL* 4532, and explains why in Ælfric's version Basilissa desires to have 'ðone Hælend to brydguman' ('the Saviour as a bridegroom' [lines 35–36 (p. 56)]. As Zettel points out, *BHL* 4532's error for *BHL* 4529's 'nec desiderem thori coniunctionem' ('I do not desire the [carnal] union of marriage' [*AS*, Ian. I, p. 576]) makes Basilissa's comment awkward because Julian has yet to tell her who Christ is ('Ælfric's Hagiographic Sources', p. 207).

109–14   Here begins the development of one of the major themes of the *passio*: the necessity of unswerving devotion to God. Of the 'impediments' listed here, family loyalty constitutes the greatest challenge in the legend to one's complete submission to God. For reiterations of this theme, see paragraphs 32, 46, 49 and 53, the last of which draws on Jesus's words in Luke 14.26 as a biblical basis for the legend's uncompromising, unsentimental brand of Christianity: 'si quis venit ad me, et non odit patrem suum et matrem et uxorem et filios et fratres et sorores adhuc autem et animam suam non potest esse meus discipulus' ('If any man come to me, and hate not his father and mother and wife and children and brethren and sisters, yea and his own life also, he cannot be my disciple').

It is worth remarking that Ælfric neither translates or paraphrases any speech in which a character iterates this theme, as if he is not eager to present to the laity so uncompromising a brand of Christianity. He does, however, find Luke 14.26 useful in his arguments against clerical marriage. Quoting selectively and deliberately, Ælfric makes it clear that they must hate their wives if they are to be Jesus's disciples (see *CH* I.21 [cited on p. 32, n. 6], lines 222–23 [p. 353] and Fehr 2 [cited on p. 44, n. 146], p. 46 [§91]).

117–18   The reading 'Ceperunt spiritu esse coniuncti non carne fructificantes' ('Having been joined in the spirit, not in the flesh, they began to be fruitful') is unique to *BHL* 4532, whose author either combined or had access to a textual tradition that combined different readings in some of the oldest manuscripts of *BHL* 4529.

Though the *AS* edition is based on a thirteenth-century legendary, its reading, 'coeperunt esse spiritu, non carne, fructificantes' ('they began to be fruitful in the spirit not in the flesh' [Ian. I, p. 577]) is also found in a late ninth- or early tenth-century copy of *BHL* 4532 (Rome, Vatican City, Biblioteca Apostolica Vaticana, Reginensis latini MS 516). Alternatively, the late seventh-, early eighth-century copy in the Luxeuil legendary reads, 'coeperunt esse spiritu coniuncti carnem mortificantes' ('having been joined in the spirit, they began to mortify their flesh' [*Lectionnaire de Luxeuil* (cited on p. 36, n. 38), ed. Salmon, p. 33]).

121–23 N's 'per quos cęlorum regna non fraudarentur', a reading also found in *BHL* 4529 (*AS*, Ian. I, p. 577), awkwardly shifts the focus from the parents to their offspring. A better reading is that of manuscripts R and D 'per quos cęlorum regno non fraudarentur' ('through whom [the parents] would not be cheated of the kingdom of heaven').

129–30 The 'choking thistles of the world' may allude to the parable of the sower wherein the seed that falls among the thorns represents a faith choked out by worldly cares and riches (Matthew 13.22, Mark 4.18–19 and Luke 8.14).

161–63 'Basilissa' (Βασίλισσα) is Greek for 'queen'.

184–85 'Splendidus liquor' ('splendid liquid') is a curious phrase that I have found attested nowhere else. Perhaps it refers to the wine of Communion, the 'blood of Christ', which will cleanse the nuns of their sins so that their souls may ascend to heaven.

285–87 Terce (9 a.m.), Sext (Noon), None (3 p.m.), Vespers (sunset), and Matins (6 p.m.–sunrise) are five of the eight worship services or 'offices' that comprise the 'Canonical Hours' or 'Divine Office' around which the day of the monastic and secular clergy is structured. The other three offices are Lauds (sunrise), Prime (6 a.m.) and Compline (after sunset prior to bed).

352 On the designation of a psalm as belonging to the Septuagint, see the note on lines 37–39 of *Julian and Basilissa* in the Old English Commentary (p. 101).

368–70 Ælfric apparently liked Julian's comment about illuminating 'non solum oculum euulsum sed et cordis...oculos' ('not only the plucked out eye but also the eyes of his heart'), for he transfers it a later point in the Old English version (lines 130–31 [p. 60]).

404 Very few manuscripts of *BHL* 4532 that I have consulted preserve the reading in which the healed man exclaims, 'Uere Deus est Christianorum ipse solus adorandus!' ('In truth, the very God of the Christians should alone be worshipped!'). More common is 'Uere Deus est Christus; ipse solus adorandus' ('Truly Christ is God; he alone should be worshipped!').

In addition to MSS N, S, R, and D [see pp. 110-11], I have seen only two other manuscripts of *BHL* 4532 that preserve the first reading cited above: (1) Rome, Biblioteca Apostolica Vaticana, Reg. lat. 516 (s.ix) and Munich, Bayerische Staatsbibliothek, clm 22240 (s.xii). Ælfric's immediate source must have contained it, for he renders the exclamation, 'Se God is to gelyfanne þe ða Cristenan on gelyfað...!' ('The God in whom the Christians believe must be believed in...!' [lines 128–29 (p. 60)]). Perhaps these six Latin manuscripts represent the larger family to which Ælfric's text belonged.

526–28 The importance of baptism is another major theme in the *passio*: God sends Antonius the priest, along with the seven Christian brothers, to join Julian in prison so that Celsus and the soldiers (lines 536–37), the resurrected man (lines 625–26) and Celsus's mother (lines 765–67) might be baptized.

It is worthy of note that the feast day of Julian and Basilissa was originally celebrated on Epiphany, 6 January, a day on which baptisms were performed in the early Middle Ages. One of the earliest surviving copies of the longer version of the *passio* (*BHL* 4529) is found in the late seventh- or early eighth-century Luxeuil lectionary where the legend is to be read on the eve of Epiphany in lieu of the usual lessons from Scripture (*Le lectionnaire de Luxeuil*, ed. Salmon [cited on p. 36, n. 38], pp. 27–57; he comments on the unusual nature of this choice in note 1, p. 28). With its multiple confessions of faith and baptisms, Julian's mini 'scrutiny' of Celsus's mother (the questions and response between the priest and new believer prior to baptism) and the healing of the lepers at the baptismal font that springs up where the saints are buried (a chapter omitted from *BHL* 4532), the legend would be an appropriate selection for the vigil of Epiphany and helps to explain its appearance in a French mass book designed to be used by the bishop in his church in the episcopal seat of Langres (*Ibid.*, pp. xcvi–xcvii). While Salmon suggests how the lectionary might have been used, he does not comment on or attempt to explain the choice of the legend as a preparation for the celebration of Epiphany.

560–61 The sentence is ungrammatical but is clearly meant to be in past tense. Rome, Biblioteca Apostolica Vaticana, Reg. lat. 516 constructs the sentence as 'future more vivid': 'nisi in publico fuerit manifesta...non poterit coronari' ('if our birth is not made public...it will not be crowned').

693–94 The 'cetera' ('rest of those things') seems to refer to wives, children, riches, or other 'impediments' mentioned earlier in lines 109–14 (p. 120).

731–32 The mixed metaphor plays on the double meaning of *fructus* as 'fruit' and 'offspring', and calls attention to the legend's insistence on redefining the meaning of family in primarily spiritual rather than biological terms. Celsus is the biological fruit of the tree of his mother but the spiritual fruit of Julian, whom he earlier calls 'father of my second birth' (line 453 [p. 140]). In this way Julian's spiritual son becomes 'a father in the grace of baptism' (line 766 [p. 158]) to his biological mother, the tree blessed by her own fruit. The metaphor is not as convoluted in those manuscripts wherein Julian praises the mother for so quickly obtaining healing 'tuo fructui' ('from your own fruit').

924–26 The date of 'Idus Ianuarius' (the Ides of January or 13 January) is another significant variant common to manuscripts of *BHL* 4532 and is the date Ælfric supplies in the *incipit* of his Old English version (p. 54).

The Passio of Saint Cecilia the Virgin

40–43 *Continentes* refers to husbands and wives who have adopted celibacy. Augustine wrote that martyrs, virgins and married couples earn, respectively, the hundredfold, sixtyfold and thirtyfold rewards that correspond to the yields of the seeds sown in good soil in the parable of the sower (Matthew 13.1–23) (*Quaestiones Euangeliorum* in *Patrologia Latina*, ed. J.-P. Migne, 221 vols [Paris, 1844–6], 35: cols 1321–64, at cols 1325–26 [§9], as cited by Walsh [see below], p. 132, n. 133). More conventionally these three rewards are equated with the three states of chastity: virginity (hundredfold), widowhood (sixtyfold) and marriage (thirtyfold). For an example from Augustine, see *De sancta uirginitate (On Holy Virginity)* [cited on p. 44, n. 138], ed. and trans. Walsh, pp. 66–147, at pp. 130–33 [§46]). The substitution of the continent where we would expect to find the married may indicate how the author of the *passio* may have intended its model of sanctity to apply to the laity.

53–55 Thomas Connolly hears an echo of Ephesians 5.18–19 or possibly Colossians 3.16 in the author's description of Cecilia singing in her heart to God (*Mourning into Joy* [cited on p. 34, n. 17], p. 65 and n. 17). Concerning the author's further use of Ephesians, see the note on lines 110–12.

On the numbering and designation of the Psalms in the Latin Vulgate and in modern translations, see the note on lines 37–39 of *Julian and Basilissa* in the Old English Commentary (p. 101).

74–76 Here begins the development of a prominent theme of the *passio*: the superiority of spiritual perception over literal sight. See also paragraphs 7, 8, 16, 17, 23, 24 and 30. On the implications this theme has for the pagan origins of Cecilia's cult, see Connolly, *Mourning into Joy*, pp. 23–59, a chapter that includes a masterful reading of the liturgies that were developed for the annual station day observed at Cecilia's basilica in Trastevere and for her feast day (pp. 46–54).

97–98 More literally, 'quasi apes...argumentosa' might be translated 'like a bee capable in argument', a reference to Cecilia's persuasive conversation with Valerian. The simile also anticipates her catechetical conversation with Tiburtius (lines 189–324) and her antagonistic exchange with Almachius (lines 568–650). On the conventional association of bees with intelligence and wisdom, see Casiday, 'St. Aldhelm's bees' [cited on p. 38, n. 65], pp. 6–8. A ninth-century manuscript edited by Delehaye reads, more fittingly perhaps, *ovis* ('sheep') not *apes*, a comparison that shows Cecilia to have been a faithful sheep that gives birth to new lamb, i.e. the fruit of the seed of Christ's chaste counsel that Urban mentions in the previous sentence (*Étude sur le légendier romain* [cited on p. 35, n. 21], p. 198). Still, *apes* enters the textual tradition early, for it appears as a correction in the tenth-century manuscript Delehaye also consults for his eclectic edition.

110–12 So strong is the influence of Ephesians on the author of the legend, that Connolly writes, 'One could say that the Passio represents Ephesians in action: that the author translated the doctrinal content of the epistle, and the moral admonitions that flow therefrom, into the life of a saint' (*Mourning into Joy*, 65–72 [and esp. n. 19], at 65). See also the note above on lines 53–55.

153–54 Valerian's comment represents the initial articulation of another major theme of the *passio*: the illusoriness of earthly life and the reality of an eternal one. See further paragraphs 11, 13–15, 17, 18, 19, 22 and 26. The biblical idea of exchanging earthly life and flesh for everlasting glory (see, for example, Matthew 16.25, Mark 8.34, Luke 9.24–25 and John 12:25) is also bolstered in the *passio* by a series of heavenly visions, which underscores the legend's insistence that there are more things in heaven and on earth than pagans dream of in their philosophies.

210–12 H's first *uobis* makes sense, though it likely represents a typical small error for *nobis*, a reading that Ælfric's immediate source must have contained, as V and C do: 'Et quis ibi fuit et inde huc ueniens *nobis* potuit indicare' ('And who has been there and has come here from there who could disclose this *to us*'). The presence of *nobis* in Ælfric's immediate source would correspond to his *us*: 'Hwa com þanon hider þe mihte us secgan gif hit swa wære?' ('Who has come here from there who can tell us that it is so?' [lines 112–13 (p. 76)]).

281–82 This sentence, along with the seven that follow, comprise a rhetorically heightened section of the *passio*. Much of the wordplay can be rendered in translation, but some cannot, such as Christ's willingness to bear a crown of thorns *capite* ('on his head') and a *sententiam capitalem* ('capital sentence') on his body, and his willingness to drink the *passionis calicem* ('cup of suffering') due humanity for its *passionibus* ('passions' or 'desires').

462–63   It is unusual in a *passio* for a character, even a subordinate, to use a formal term of address to initiate a dialogue, yet the vocative 'Prefecte' of H must have prompted Ælfric to write that 'sum rædbora þa to þam reðan þus cwæð, "Hat hi, leof, acwellan nu"' ('a certain adviser then spoke to the cruel one in this way, "Order them, sir, to be put to death now"' [lines 157–58 (p. 80)]). Of thirty-nine other manuscripts that I have seen that would appear to preserve a recension of *BHL* 1495 much like that from which Ælfric worked, only Douai, Bibliothèque Municipale, MS 838 (s.xiii) shares with H the reading *prefecte*.

542   Most manuscripts of *BHL* 1495 record 'lapidem uilem' ('a worthless stone') rather than 'lapidem uiuum' ('an unwrought stone').

609–10   Here Cecilia baits Almachius to 'set her free' by executing her, since her only freedom as a Christian is to be found in death.

657–59   On the significance of these lines, see p. 30.

The Passio of the Holy Martyrs Chrysanthus and Daria

Title   The month has been erased. A clue to the correct month, however, lies in the date, *die XXV*. In addition to 29 November and 1 December, the couple's feast day was often celebrated on 25 October. In fact, the *incipit* of a (now destroyed) tenth-century French manuscript from Chartres (Bibliothèque Municipale, MS 144) read 'Passio sanctorum martyrum Chrysanthi et Dariae die XXV mensis Octobris, hoc est VIII kal. Novembris' ('The passio of the holy martyrs Chrysanthus and Daria, the 25 day of the month of October, that is the eighth day before 1 November' [C. de Smedt, 'Catalogus Codicum Hagiographicorum Bibliothecae Civitatis Carnotensis', *Analecta Bollandiana* 8 (1889), 86–208, at 134 (item 71)]). Had this manuscript survived, it would have been one of the few early legendaries to have contained the lives of all three saints considered here.

1–5   Zettel suggests Ælfric may have relied on these lines from the *passio* for the opening lines of the coda that he adds to his version of the legend (see lines 236–50 [p. 98]) ('Ælfric's Hagiographic Sources' [cited on p. 46, n. 178], p. 258, n. 164).

52–54   The 'rusticos doctores and piscatores' ('rustic instructors and fishermen') presumably refer to the apostles, whose writings Chrysanthus is eager to study.

69–72   On the significance the phrase 'patrimonii tui et capitis tui' ('your fortune and your head'), see p. 47, n. 192.

86   The scene of Chrysanthus's temptation is uncommon for a *passio*, especially for a male saint. It is, however, indicative of the pronounced misogynist strain in the early part of the legend, which Ælfric downplays considerably. Compare lines 86–131 of the Latin text with lines 34–46 of the Old English one (p. 88).

112–13   Chrysanthus alludes to the story of Joseph and Potiphar's wife in Genesis 39 in this part of his prayer.

138–39   On the significance of the phrase 'ideo...præualuit' ('for that reason...he prevailed'), see p. 31.

223–24   '[I]udicium Paridis spreteque iniuriam formæ' is a quotation from Virgil's *Aeneid*: 'exciderant animo manet alta mente repostum / iudicium Paridis spretaeque iniuria formae' ('for deep within her [Juno's] mind lie stored / the judgment of Paris and the wrong done to her scorned beauty' [*Aeneid*, Book 1, lines 26–27, The Virgil Project (1995), at <http://vergil.classics.upenn.edu>, accessed 27 Jan. 2006; *The Aeneid of Virgil*, trans. A. Mandelbaum (New York, 1961; repr. 1981)]). I am grateful to Suzanne Paul for bringing this to my attention.

257–60   Chrysanthus plays on the double meaning of the word *cultor* as 'farmer' and 'worshipper', and the differences in cultivating the earth and cultivating the gods' favour.

286–88   While sense can be made of 'sanctæ uirginitatis suæ uelamen sanctitatis aptaret' ('she took the veil of holiness as a mark of her holy virginity'), B's reading of *uirginitati* is more grammatical: 'et sancte uirginitati sue uelamen sanctitatis aptaret' ('on account of her holy virginity, she took the veil of holiness').

357–60   On the significance of the phrase 'qui cultores suos in omni faciat pugna uincentes' ('who makes his worshippers victorious in every battle'), see pp. 31–32.

GLOSSARY

The Glossary records all word forms found in the Old English texts. In cases where a form occurs more than four times, the first two occurrences are cited. **A** is followed by **Æ** and **T** by **Þ**. The prefix **ge-** is ignored, and **þ** rather than **ð** is used throughout. When the symbol ~ is encountered, the headword or its root should be supplied; * indicates an emended form. Square brackets indicate unattested headwords. Weak forms of adjectives are indicated; otherwise, forms are strong.

Abbreviations

I	*Julian and Basilissa*
II	*Cecilia and Valerian*
III	*Chrysanthus and Daria*

a.	accusative	m.	masculine
adj.	adjective	n.	nominative
adv.	adverb	nt.	neuter
anom.	anomalous	num.	number
art.	article	p.	plural
comp.	comparative	part.	participle
conj.	conjunction	pers.	person, personal
correl.	correlative	poss.	possessive
d.	dative	pp.	past participle
def.	definite	prep.	preposition
dem.	demonstrative	pres.	present
f.	feminine	pret.	preterite
g.	genitive	pron.	pronoun
imp.	imperative	refl.	reflexive
impers.	impersonal	rel.	relative
ind.	indicative	s.	singular
indecl.	indeclinable	subj.	subjunctive
indef.	indefinite	superl.	superlative
inf.	infinitive	sv.	strong verb
infl.	inflected	uninfl.	uninflected
inst.	instrumental	v.	verb
interj.	interjection	w.	with
interrog.	interrogative	wk.	weak
intrans.	intransitive	wv.	weak verb

A

a, *adv.*, for ever: I.33, 311; *see also*
   woruld.
abidan, *sv.1*, to remain; (w. **on life mid**)
   to go on living: **abad** *pret.ind.3s.*,
   I.73.
abitan, *sv.1*, to devour: **abat** *pret.ind.3s.*,
   III.74.
ablendan, *wv.1*, to blind: **ablendst**
   pres.ind.2s., I.108; **ablende**
   pret.ind.3s., I.286; **ablend** *pp.*,
   (n.s.m.) I.96; ~**e** *(n.p.m.)* I.262.
abutan, *prep. w. a./d.*, about, round
   about: III.113.
ac, *conj.*, but, but rather: I.5, 27, etc.;
   II.86, 127, etc.; III.39, 67, etc.
acuma, *m.*, oakum: ~**n** *d.s.*, I.242.
acunnian, *wv.2*, to test: **acunnod** *pp.*,
   (n.s.m.) I.180.
acwelan, *sv.4*, to die, perish: **acwele**
   pres.subj.2s., III.208.
acwellan *wv.1*, to kill: *inf.*, II.158,
   III.213; **to acwellene** *infl. inf.*, II.237–
   38; **acwealde** *pret.ind.3s.*, II.147;
   III.80; **acweald** *pp.*, III.81; ~**e**
   (n.p.m.) I.152; *(n.p.m./nt.)* III.234.
acwincan, *sv.3*, to be extinguished:
   acwuncon *pret.ind.3p.*, III.217.
ad, *nt.*, pyre: *n.s.*, I.243; *a.s.*, II.245.
adela, *m.*, filth: ~**n** *d.s.*, III.172.
adune, *adv.*, down: III.182.
adwescan, *wv.1*, to extinguish: *inf.*,
   I.189; **adwesce** *pres.ind.1s.*, I.12.
adydan, *wv.1*, to kill: *inf.*, II.239; **adyd**
   pp., *(n.s.m.)* I.307.
afindan, *sv.3*, to discover, come across:
   afunde *pret.ind.3s.*, III.125.
afyllan, *wv.1*, to fill: **afylled** *pp.*, *(n.s.m)*
   I.282; II.76, 211; *(n.s.nt.)* I.23; III.171;
   ~**e** *(a.p.f.)*, III.12.
afyllan, *wv.1*, to throw down (some-
   thing *a.*): *inf.*, III.232.
afyrht, *adj.*, frightened: *n.m.s.*, II.27, 40;
   III.207.
ageafon, *see* **agyfan**
agen, *adj.*, own: *a.s.f.*, III.77; **agenre** (for
   agenne, an attested form) *a.s.m.*,
   I.148; ~**e** *a.s.f.*, I.191; ~**es** *g.s.nt.*,

III.23; ~**um** *d.s.m.*, I.225; II.166;
   d.s.nt., II.181, 248.
ageotan, *sv.2*, to cast: **agoten** *pp.*, ~**e**
   (n.p.m.) I.98.
agrafan, *sv.6*, to carve: **agrafen** *pp.*, ~**e**
   (n.p.m.) I.99.
agyfan, *sv.5*, to give up: **ageafon**
   pret.ind.3p., III.233.
aheardian, *wv.2*, to harden: *inf.*, III.113.
ahebban, *sv.6*, to raise up: *inf.*, III.231;
   ahafen *pp.*, *(n.s.nt.)* II.107.
ahreddan, *wv.1*, to save: **ahret**
   pres.ind.3s., III.209; **ahredde**
   pret.ind.3s., I.286.
aht, *nt.*, anything: *a.*, I.191.
aidlian, *wv.2*, to bring to nothing, to
   frustrate: *inf.*, I.288; III.108; **aidlige**
   pres.subj.2s., III.66.
alecgan, *wv.1.*, to put, place: **alede**
   pret.ind.3s., III.182.
alefan, *wv.1*, to weaken: **alefed** *pp.*,
   (n.s.nt.) II.105.
Alexandria, *proper name*, Alexandria;
   ~**n** *g.*, III.2.
Almachius, *proper name*, Almachius:
   n., II.144, 149, etc.; ~**e** *d.*, II.252.
alutan, *sv.2*, to bow down to (w. **to**,
   someone or something *d.*): **alæt**
   pret.ind.3s., III.178; **aloten** *pp.*, ~**um**
   (d.s.nt.) III.210.
alyfan, *wv.1*, to allow: **alyfde** (w. *d.*)
   pret.ind.3s., I.164.
alysan, *wv.1*, to redeem: **alysed** *pp.*,
   (n.s.m.) II.63, 64.
ameldian, *wv.2*, to reveal: **ameldod** *pp.*,
   (n.s.nt.) II.98.
amen, *interj.*, amen: I.312; II.262;
   III.250.
amyrran, *wv.1*, to lead astray: *inf.*, I.143.
an, *num., adj., art.*, (i) one, a, an: *n.s.m.*,
   II.43 (1st 2 occurrences), 120; III.177
   (possibly *f.*), 181; *n.s.nt.*, II.43 (3rd
   occurrence); **ænne** *a.s.m.*, I.98, 166;
   II.55, 115, etc.; III.3, 18, etc.; *a.s.nt.*,
   II.122, 230; ~**e** *a.s.f.*, II.182, 229; ~**es**
   g.s.m., I.104, 194; *g.s.nt.*, I.289; ~**um**
   d.s.m., II.7, 123, 124; III.145, 159,
   223; *d.s.nt.*, I.21; II.40; III.17, 117;

~**re** *d.s.f.*, I.202; II.218; III.200; (ii) alone, only: ~**a** *n.s.nt.*, II.101; ~**e** *a.s.f.*, II.52; ~**um** *d.s.m.*, III.203; (iii) **on an**, continuously: II.139.

ancenned, *adj.*, only-begotten: ~**an** *a.s.m.*, I.143.

and, *conj.*, and: I.3, 4, etc.; II.4, 5 (2x), etc.; III.3, 4, etc.

andettan, *wv.1*, to confess, profess one's faith: **andette** *pret.ind.3s.*, III.43; *pret.subj.3s.*, I.139.

andfæncge, *adj.*, acceptable: *n.s.nt.*, I.203.

andgit, *nt.*, understanding, intellect: *n.s.*, II.124; ~**e** *d.s.*, III.9.

andgitleas, *adj.*, incapable of sensation or perception: ~**e** *n.p.m.*, III.131.

andsæte, *adj.*, hateful: *n.s.nt.*, I.178.

andweardnyss, *f.*, presence: ~**e** *d.s.*, I.258.

andwerd (andweard), *adj.*, present: *n.s.m.*, III.145.

andwyrdan, *wv.1*, to answer, reply to (w. *d.*): **andwyrde** *pret.ind.3s.*, I.29, 198; II.32, 46, etc.; III.56? (see note), 70, 128, 144; **andwerdan** *pret.ind.3p.*, I.114.

andwyrde, *nt.*, answer, response: *a.s.*, III.56 (see note).

angin, *nt.*, beginning: *a.s.*, I.30.

anginn, *nt.*, treatment, intent: ~**e**, *d.s.*, III.116.

geangsumian, *wv.2*, to make anxious: **geangsumod** *pp.*, *(n.s.nt.)* II.108.

angsumnys, *f.*, anguish: *n.s.*, III.243; ~**se** *d.s.*, I.225.

anlicnyss, *f.*, image, figure: ~**a** *n.p.*, I.276; *a.p.*, I.120, 183; ~**e** *n.p.*, II.243; ~**um** *d.p.*, I.114.

annyss, *f.*, oneness, unity: ~**e** *d.s.*, II.122.

anræd, *adj.*, steadfast, single-minded, resolute: ~**e** *n.p.m.*, III.86; ~**an** *a.p.m.wk.*, III.122.

anrædlice, *adv.*, steadfastly, single-mindedly: II.236; III.161.

anrædnyss, *f.*, steadfastness, constancy, single-mindedness: *n.s.*, II.235; ~**e** *d.s.*, II.114.

ansund, *adj.*, uncorrupted, unharmed: ~**um** *d.s.m.*, I.31; ~**e** *n.p.m.*, I.233.

Antecrist, *proper name*, Antichrist: *a.s.*, III.249; ~**es** *g.s.*, III.240, 241.

Antiochia, *proper name*, Antioch: ~**n** *d.*, I.2, 75.

Antonius, *proper name*, Antonius: *n.s.*, I.166, 296.

anþræce, *adj.*, terrible: *n.s.nt.*, III.175.

anweald, *m.*, power: *n.s.*, II.233; *a.s.*, II.238.

anwilnys, *f.*, obstinacy: *n.s.*, I.226.

ar, *f.*, property, wealth: ~**e** *a.s.*, I.82.

aræran, *wv.1*, (i) to build, raise, restore to life: *inf.*, I.197; **arærde** *pret.ind.3s.*, I.59, 196; II.41, 132; *pret.subj.3s.*, I.202, 212; **arærdan** *pret.ind.3p.*, I.48; (ii) to foster: **arærde** *pret.ind.3s.*, III.78.

ardlice, *adv.*, quickly: II.223; III.110, 166.

arfæstnyss, *f.*, graciousness: ~**e** *d.s.*, II.38.

arisan, *sv.1*, to arise: **aras** *pret.ind.3s.*, I.202; II.114, 133.

arleas, *adj.*, wicked: ~**a** *n.s.m.wk.*, I.288, 308; II.148, 223, 247; ~**e** *n.s.f.*, I.66; ~**an** *g.s.m.wk.*, III.248; *d.s.m.wk.*, I.76, 178, 198; II.153; ~**um** *d.p.m.wk.*, II.210; III.214.

arn, *see* **yrnan**

arwurþ, *adj.*, noble, honourable, worthy: ~**a** *n.m.s.wk.*, II.202; ~**ne** *a.s.m.*, III.18; ~**an** *d.s.m.wk.*, III.173; *d.s.nt.wk.*, I.165; ~**um** *d.p.m.*, II.185; III.98, 244; *d.p.nt.*, III.139; *d.p.f.*, III.126.

arwurþian, *wv.2*, to honour: **arwurþaþ** *pres.ind.3s.*, III.188; **arwurþiaþ** *pres.ind.1p.*, II.121; **arwurþigende** *pres. part.*, III.193.

arwurþlic, *adj.*, honourable, reverent: ~**e** *a.f.s.*, III. (alternatively, see the next entry)

arwurþlice, *adv.*, honourably: II.261.

ascyrian, *wv.1/2*, to separate: *inf.*, I.11.

asendan, *wv.1*, to send: **asend** *imp.s.*, I.149; **asende** *pret.ind.3s.*, I.64, 171, 186.

asincan, *sv.3*, to sink into the ground:
  asanc *pret.ind.3s.*, I.274.
astigan, *sv.1*, to ascend:
  astah *pret.ind.3s.*, I.242.
astreccan, *wv.1*, to stretch out, extend:
  inf., III.215; **astreht** *pp.*, **astræhtum**
  (*d.p.nt.*) III.179.
astyrian, *wv.1/2*, to shake, stir up:
  astyrede *pret.ind.3s.*, I.40; **astyrodon**
  pret.ind.3p., III.94.
atelic, *adj.*, hidden: ~**es** *g.s.nt.*, I.208.
atelice, *adv.*, horribly, foully: III.172.
ateon, *sv.2*, (w. *fram*) to take away
  from: *inf.*, I.140.
ateorian, *wv.2*, to cease, fail: **ateoriaþ**
  pres.ind.3p., III.241.
aþ, *m.*, oath: ~**e** *d.s.*, II.195.
aþwean, *sv.6*, to wash clean, cleanse:
  aþwogen *pp.*, (*n.s.m.*) II.90.
awacan, *sv.6*, to awake: **awoc**
  pret.ind.3s., I.16.
aweg, *adv.*, away: I.239; III.208, 210.
awegan, *sv.5*, to put away, renounce:
  inf., III.161.
awendan, *wv.1*, to turn, change into:
  awendest *pres.ind.2s.*, I.227; **awent**
  pres.ind.3s., II.58; **awendaþ**
  pres.ind.3p., III.32; **awendon**,
  pres.subj.3p., III.37; **awende**
  pres.subj.2s., III.125; *pret.ind.3s.*,
  III.106; **awend** *pp.*, (*n.s.m.*) I.155;
  II.214; III.110.
awreccan, *wv.1*, to arouse: *inf.*, III.45
  (**awræccan**), 48.
awritan, *sv.1*, to write: **to awritene** *infl.
  inf.*, III.154; **awriton** *pret.ind.3p.*,
  III.75.
awurpan, *sv.3*, (i) to throw or cast
  (away): **awurp**, *imp.s.*, II.240;
  awurpaþ *imp.p.*, II.189; **awearp**
  pret.ind.3s., I.137; **awurpe**
  pret.subj.3s., III.49; (ii) to cast down,
  humble: **aworpen** *pp.*, (*n.s.nt.*) II.107.
awyrian, *wv.1*, to curse: **awyriged** *pp.*,
  accursed: ~**um** (*d.p.m.wk.*) I.273.
axian, *wv.2*, to ask: *inf.*, III.182; **to
  axienne** *infl. inf.*, III.120; **axie**
  pres.ind.1s., II.128; **axode**

pret.ind.3s., I.176, 190; II.103, 150,
  165, 224; III.103.
geaxian, *wv.2*, to discover, learn:
  geaxode *pret.ind.3s.*, I.247, 257.

Æ

æfen, *m.* evening: *a.s.*, III.26.
æfre, *adv.*, continually, always, ever:
  I.116, 178, 278, 279; II.46, 121, 124;
  III.124, 195.
æft, *adv.*, again: I.158.
æfter, *prep. w. d.*, after, according to:
  I.20, 52, etc.; II.110; III.169 (**efter**).
Ægipta, *see* **Egypte**
æht, *f.*, wealth: ~**a** *a.p.*, I.57; II.152, 159,
  160, 207; II.208 (**æhtan**: declined
  wk.); *g.p.*, III.22.
æhtnys, *see* **ehtnys**
ælc, *adj.*, each, every, any, all: ~**ne**
  a.s.m., III.122; ~**e** *a.s.f.*, II.10; ~**es**
  g.s.m., II.228; ~**um** *d.s.nt.*, III.172;
  ~**ere** *d.s.f.*, I.165, 175.
ælcung, *f.*, delay: ~**e** *d.s.*, II.160.
ælmihtig, *adj.*, almighty: *n.s.m.*, II.43,
  121; ~**an** *a.s.m.wk.*, I.7–8; II.37;
  d.s.m.wk., II.261.
ælmysse, *wk.f.*, alms: ~**an** *a.p.*, II.149.
ænde, *see* **ende**
æne, *adv.*, once: II.255.
ængel, *see* **engel**
ænig, *adj.*, (i) any: *a.s.nt.*, I.77, 103, 192;
  III.128; ~**e** *a.s.f.*, III.45; *a.p.m.*, I.99
  ~**um** *d.s.m.*, II.47; *d.s.nt.*, I.215; (ii)
  (w. **oþer**) any other, another: *n.s.nt.*,
  II.140.
ænne, *see* **an**
ær, *adv.*, before: I.127, 134, etc.; III.211;
  on ær previously, before: II.206.
ærendgewrit, *nt.*, letter: *a.s.*, I.220.
ærendraca, *m.*, messenger: *n.s.*, I.88.
ærest, *adv.*, first: I.116; III.166, 238.
ær þan þe, *conj.*, before: I.66; III.208.
æt, *prep. w. d.*, by, from: I.255; II.136,
  140, 186; III.19, 53, etc.
ætberstan, *sv. 3*, to escape from (w. **of**):
  ætbærst, *pret.ind.3s.*, III.177.
æteowan, **æteowian**, *wv. 1/2*, (i) to
  appear, reveal: **æteowde** *pret.ind.3s.*,

I.8; **æteowed** *pp.*, *(n.m.s.)* I.14; (ii) to
show, exhibit: **æteowigende** *pres.
part.*, III.245.

ætforan, *prep. w. d.*, before, in front of:
II.39; III.205.

ætgædere, *adv.*, together: II.20, 86;
III.206.

æton, *see* **etan**

ætstandan, *sv.6*, to remain standing:
ætstod *pret.ind.3s.*, I.305.

æþelboren, *adj.*, nobly born: *n.s.m.*, I.2;
II.211; III.2; *a.s.nt.*, I.18; ~**re** *g.s.f.*,
III.57.

æþelborennyss, *f.*, noble pedigree,
lineage: ~**e** *a.s.*, I.93–94.

æþele, *adj.*, noble: *n.s.m.*, I.1; *n.s.nt.*,
II.1; ~**an** *a.s.m.wk.*, I.93; *a.s.nt.wk.*,
II.55; *d.s.m.wk.*, I.9; II.8; *d.s.nt.wk.*,
I.29; ~**um** *d.p.m.*, I.57.

æwfest, *adj.*, pious: ~**um** *d.p.m.*, I.2.

B

gebann, *nt.*, decree, proclamation: *a.s.*,
I.77.

barn, *see* **byrnan**

Basilissa, *proper name*, Basilissa: *n.*,
I.25, 34, etc.; *a.* I.18; ~**n** *d.*, I.70.

baþe, *see* **bæþ**

bæd, *see* **biddan**

bærnan, *wv.1*, to burn: *inf.*, III.215.

bærnet, *nt.*, burning: ~**te** *d.s.*, I.220.

bæron, *see* **beran**

bærst, *see* **berstan**

bæþ, *nt.*, bath: ~**e** *d.s.*, II.249; **baþe**,
II.253.

be, *prep. w. a./d.*, by, about, according
to: I.6, 58, etc.; II.28, 128, 134; III.23,
94, etc.; **be fullan**, fully, completely,
III.20.

bealdlice, *adv.*, boldly: III.21, 23.

beam, *m.*, beam: ~**es** *n.p.*, I.210.

beatan, *sv.7*, beat: *inf.*, I.104, 109 (~**on**);
II.157.

beatere, *m.*, beater: ~**s** *g.s.*, I.104.

bebeodan, *sv.2*, to command (someone
d.): **bebeod**, *imp.s.*, II.180.

bebod, *nt.*, command: *a.s.*, I.262; ~**a** *a.p.*,
II.150.

bebyr(i)gan, *wv.1*, to bury: *inf.*, II.146
(**bebyrigan**); **bebyrgde** *pret.ind.3s.*,
I.72; **bebyrigde**, II.205, 261;
bebyrigdon *pret.ind.3p.*, II.147, 150,
154; **bebyriged** *pp.*, ~**e** *(n.p.m.)*
II.206; *(n.p.m.)* III.225.

bec, *see* **boc**

becuman, *sv.4*, to come, arrive (at):
becumaþ *pres.ind.1p.*, I.234; **becume**
pres.subj.3s., I.67; **becom** *pret.ind.3s.*,
I.63, 89; III.12; **becomon** *pret.ind.3p.*,
III.11; *pret.subj.3p.*, II.168.

bed, *nt.*, prayer: ~**a** *a.p.*, I.88.

gebed, *nt.*, prayer: *n.s.*, I.203; ~**u** *n.p.*,
I.65; ~**um** *d.p.*, I.7; II.6, 51; III.41,
167, 178.

bedd, *nt.*, bed: ~**e** *d.s.*, I.21, 47; II.20.

bedydrian, *wv.2*, to deceive, delude: **to
bedydrigenne** *infl. inf.*, III.78.

beeoden, *see* **began**

befæstan, *wv.1*, (w. **to lar**) to set to
learning: **befæste** *pret.ind.3s.*, III.6;
befæst *pp.*, *(n.s.m.)* I.134.

befrinan, *sv.3*, to ask: **befran**
pret.ind.3s., I.142; II.94.

began, *anom. v.*, to perform, do:
beeoden *pret.ind.3p.*, I.88.

begen, *pron.*, both: *n.*, II.69; *a.*, II.65.

begeotan, *sv.2*, (i) to cover: **begoten**
pp., ~**e** *(a.p.m.)* II.243; (ii) to drench:
beguton *pret.ind.3p.*, III.107.

beginnan, *sv.3*, (i) to begin (w. *infl.
inf.*): **began** *pret.ind.3s.*, III.17, 21,
120; to undertake (to perform) a
command (w. **bebod**): **begunnon**
pret.ind.3p., I.262.

begytan, *sv.5*, to obtain (someone *a.*) in
marriage: **beget** *pret.ind.3s.*, II.140;
begeaten *pret.ind.3p.*, I.19.

behat, *nt.*, promise: ~**e** *d.s.*, I.35.

behatan, *sv.7*, to promise: *inf.*, II.175.

beheafdian, *wv.2*, to behead: *inf.*, I.130,
263, 294; II.254; III.160; **beheafdode**
pret.ind.3s., I.301; **beheafdod** *pp.*, ~**e**
(n.p.m.) II.195.

behealdan, *sv.7*, to consider, watch:
beheald *imp.s.*, I.144; **beheold**,
pret.ind.3s., II.195.

behreowsian, *wv.2*, to repent of: **behre-owsige**, *pres.subj.2s.*, II.176.

behyldan, *wv.1*, to flay, skin: **behyldon** *pret.ind.3p.*, III.110.

belǣfan, *wv.1*, to spare: **belǣfde** *pret.ind.3s.*, I.306.

belecgan, *wv.1*, to surround (something or someone *a.*): *inf.*, I.242.

gebelgan, *sv.3*, to become angry (w. *refl. pron.*): **gebealh** *pret.ind.3s.*, III.24.

belifan, *sv.1*, to remain: **belifon** *pret.ind.3p.*, I.285.

belucan, *sv.2*, to confine, lock: **beleac** *pret.ind.3s.*, III.25.

bemǣnan, *wv.1*, to lament: *inf.*, I.232.

ben, *f.*, prayer, request: ~**e** *a.s.*, II.60, 63, 78; *d.s.*, I.273.

bend, *m.*, bond, fetter: ~**as** *n.p.*, I.284; III.100, 101, 117; ~**um** *d.p.*, I.269; II.162, 173, 180, 184.

beodan, *sv.2*, to offer (something *a.* to someone or something *d.*): *inf.*, III.29.

beon, *anom. v.*, be: *inf.*, I.99, 235; II.69; III.7 *pres.subj.1p.*, III.238; *pres.subj.2p.*, I.67; *pres.subj.3p.*, I.95; II.82; **beo** *imp.s.*, III.207; **eom** *pres.ind.1s.*, I.282, II.76; **eart** *pres.ind.2s.*, I.44, 96; III.69; **is** *pres.ind.3s.*, I.25, 31, etc.; II.8, 29, etc.; III.121, 137, 143; **synd** *pres.ind.1p.*, I.115, 179, 193; II.86; *pres.ind.3p.*, I.65, 98, 129, 276; II.123, 158, 242, 244; **syndon** *pres.ind.3p.*, II.86, 116; III.130; **sy** *pres.subj.1s.*, II.77; *pres.subj.2s.*, II.182; *pres.subj.3s.*, I.197, 311; III.249; **beo** *pres.ind.1s.*, I.12, 13, etc.; II.63; III.13; *pres.subj.1s.*, II.19; *pres.subj.3s.*, I.199, 213; II.18, 64; **bist** *pres.ind.2s.*, II.30, 90; III.208; **biþ** *pres.ind.3s.*, I.14, 49, etc.; II.46, 62, etc.; III.30, 145, etc.; **beoþ** *pres.ind.1p.*, I.32; II.97, 168, 174; *pres.ind.3p.*, I.89; III.82, 246; **wæs** *pret.ind.1s.*, I.282; *pret.ind.3s.*, I.1, 2 etc.; II.1, 35, etc.; III.3, 31, etc.; **wære** *pret.subj.3s.*, II.101, 113, 209, 224;

III.52; **wæron** *pret.ind.3p.*, I.54, 56, etc.; II.15, 42, etc.; III.74, 103, etc.; I.152 (**wæran**); **nis, nys** (= ne is) *pres.ind.3s.*, III.137, 202, 236; **næs** (= ne wæs) *pret.ind.3s.*, I.82; II.8, 61, 255; **næran** (= ne wæron) *pret.ind.3p.*, I.50; **nære** (= ne wære) *pret.subj.3s.*, I.127; II.101.

beorht, *adj.*, bright: *n.s.nt.*, I.40; ~**a** *n.s.f.wk.*, I.199; ~**an** *d.s.nt.wk.*, I.159; ~**um** *d.p.nt.wk.*, I.299.

gebeorshipe, *m.*, feast, party: *d.s.*, II.166.

gebeot, *n.*, boast: *a.s.*, I.124.

bera, *m.*, bear: ~**n** *a.p.*, I.290.

beran, *sv.4*, to carry: *inf.*, I.195; **bæron** *pret.ind.3p.*, I.194.

geberan, *sv.4*, to give birth to: **geboren** *pp.*, ~**e** *(n.s.m.)* III.74.

berstan, *sv.3*, to burst, (w. **into**) enter: **bærst** *pret.ind.3s.*, I.104.

beseon, *sv.5*, to look at (w. **to** and someone or something *d.*): **beseah** *pret.ind.3s.*, III.182.

beseowian, *wv.2*, to sew up: **besywodon** *pret.ind.3p.*, III.111.

besincan, *sv.3*, to sink: *inf.*, I.278; **besuncon** *pret.ind.3p.*, I.277.

besmitan, *sv.1*, to defile: **besmiten** *pp.*, ~**e** *(n.p.m.)* I.51.

bet, *comp. adv.*, better, (w. *pron.* **þe**, *inst.s.nt.*) the better: II.67.

betan, *wv.1*, to kindle: *inf.* I.284.

betǣcan, *wv.1*, (i) to deliver, hand over (to someone *d.*): **betǣht** *pp.*, *(n.s.m.)* III.99; (ii) to entrust for safekeeping (someone/something *a.* to someone *d.*): **betǣhte** *pret.ind.3s.*, II.259.

betera, *adj.* (*comp.* of **god**), better: ~**n** *d.s.nt.wk.*, II.168; *n.p.m.wk.*, III.238.

betwux, *prep. w. d.*, among: I.221; II.16, 170; III.73.

beþencan, *wv.1*, to think of (something *a.*): **beþohtest** *pret.ind.2s.*, I.192.

beweddian, *wv.2*, to betrothe: **beweddod** *pp.*, *(uninfl.)* II.7.

bewepan, *sv.7*, (i) to weep over: **bewepaþ** *imp.p.*, I.232; **beweop**

pret.ind.3s., III.51; (ii) to bewail (one's) lot (w. **siþ**): *inf.*, I.232.

bewindan, *sv.3*, to wrap: *inf.*, I.283.

bewitan *pret. pres. v.*, to have charge of: **bewiste** *pret.ind.3s.*, III.150.

bewurpan, *sv.3*, (w. **mid**) to cover over (something or someone *a.*) w. (something thrown *d.*): **bewurpan** *inf.*, III.224.

(ge)bicgan, *wv.1*, (i) to buy: *inf.*, I.77 (**bicgan**); (ii) to pay for (w. *a.*): *inf.*, III.55 (**gebicgan**).

gebidan, *sv.1*, to remain: **gebad** *pret.ind.3s.*, I.221.

biddan, *sv.5*, (i) to ask, pray (w. **þæt** clause): *inf.*, III.13; **bidde** *pres.ind.1s.*, III.143; **biddende** *pres. part.*, II.10; III.59; (ii) to ask, pray (for something *a.* or *g.*): *inf.*, II.60; **biddaþ** *pres.ind.2p.*, I.280; **bæde** *pret.ind.2s.*, I.258; II.66; **bæd** *pret.ind.3s.*, II.36; (iii) to ask, pray (for something *a.* w. **þæt** clause): **bidde** *pres.ind.1s.*, II.63; (iv) to ask, pray to (someone *a.* or *d.* w. **þæt** clause): **bidde** *pres.ind.1s.*, III.43; **bæd** *pret.ind.3s.*, I.7, 124, 161; II.37; III.41, 165; **bed** I.270; **biddende** *pres. part.*, I.201; (v) to ask, pray to (someone *a.* or *d.* for something *a.* or *g.* w. **þæt** clause): **biddende** *pres. part.*, II.12.

gebiddan, *sv.5*, (i) to ask, pray (w. *refl. pron.* in *a.* or *d.*): *inf.*, III.166; **gebædon** *pret.ind.3p.*, I.64; (ii) to pray (w. *refl. pron.* in *a.* or *d.* and **þæt** clause): **gebæd** *pret.ind.3s.*, I.21; (iii) to ask, pray (to someone *a.* or *d.* w. **þæt** clause): **gebæd** *pret.ind.3s.*, I.212; (iv) to pray for (w. **for** and someone *a.*): I.250.

bifian, *wv.2*, to shake: **byfode** *pret.ind.3s.*, I.252.

bigan, *wv.1*, (i) to bow: **bigdon** *pret.ind.3p.*, I.292; (ii) to turn: **bigdon** *pret.ind.3p.*, III.38.

gebigan, *wv.1*, to turn, bend: *inf.*, I.124; **gebige** *pres.ind.1s.*, I.13; **gebygdest**

pret.ind.2s., I.45, 259 (**gebigdest**); **gebygde** *pret.ind.3s.*, I.184, 260 (**gebigde**); **gebigde** *pret.subj.3s.*, I.249; **gebiged** *pp.*, *(n.s.m.)* II.64; *(n.s.nt.)* II.107; **~gde** *(n.p.m.)* III.90; **~um** *(d.p.nt.)*, I.270.

big(g)eng, *m.* and *nt.*, rite, worship, religion: **bigencge** *d.s.*, I.149, 259; **bigencgas** *a.p.*, I.99; **~a** *g.p.*, III.85; **~um** *d.p.*, III.92.

biggenga, *m.*, worshipper: *n.s.*, III.143; **~n** *n.p.*, III.75; *a.p.*, III.140; **~um** *d.p.*, II.65.

bigleofa, *wk.m.*, food: **~an** *a.s.*, III.26.

(ge)bindan, *sv.3*, to bind: **(ge)bundon** *pret.ind.3p.*, III.100, 101; **gebunden**, *pp.*, *(n.s.m)* III.100; **~e** *(n.s.m.)* I.135; *(a.s.m.)* I.133; III.116; *(n.p.m.)* I.223.

binnan, *prep. w. d.*, inside: I.87, 163, etc.

blawan, *sv.7*, to blow: **blawe** *pres.subj.3s.*, II.229.

blind, *adj.*, blind:; **~an** *a.s.m.wk*, I.117; *d.s.m.*, I.199; **~um** *d.s.nt*, I.151; III.116; *d.p.nt.*, I.159; **~e** *n.p.m.*, I.117.

bliss, **blyss**, *f.*, bliss, joy, happiness, gladness: **~e** *a.s.*, II.109; *d.s.*, I.72, 118, 156, 311; II.66, 73, 168.

blissian, *wv.2*, to rejoice: **blyssiaþ** *pres.ind.1p.*, I.33; *pres.ind.3p.*, I.302; **blissode**, *pret.ind.3s.*, II.37, 138; **geblissod**, *pp.*, *(uninfl.)* I.237.

bliþe, *adv.*, cheerfully: II.72.

bliþelice, *adv.*, cheerfully: II.166.

blod, *nt.*, blood: *n.s.*, II.79.

blostm, *m.*, blossom: *n.s.*, II.73; **~an** *a.p.*, II.75.

blyss, *see* **bliss**

blyþe, *adj.*, well-disposed: *n.p.m.*, I.95.

boc, *f.*, book: *n.s.*, I.47; **bec** *d.s.*, I.49; *n.p.*, II.143; *a.p.* III.8, 10, 12, 88; **bocum** *d.p.*, III.75.

(ge)bodian, *wv.2*, to preach: **to bodigenne** *infl. inf.*, III.21; **bodige**, *pres.ind.1s.*, III.192; **bodaþ** *pres.ind.3s.*, III.23; **gebodiaþ** *pres.ind.3p.*, II.118.

geborene, *see* **geberan**

bræþ, *m.*, fragrance, scent: *n.s.*, I.29, 30, 252; II.74, 78; III.176; ~**es** *g.s.*, I.253; ~**e** *d.s.*, I.23, 155; ~**a**, II.76 (variant spelling attested).

breac, *see* **brucan**

breost, *nt.*, breast: ~**e** *d.s.*, II.4.

(ge)bringan, *sv.3*, (i) to lead: *inf.*, I.218; **gebrohte** *pret.ind.3s.*, III.25, 196 (**brohte**); **gebrohtan** *pret.ind.3p.*, I.216; **gebroht** *pp.*, *(n.s.m.)* I.205; III.169; ~**e** *(n.p.m.)* I.151, 223; II.20, 184; (ii) (w. **of geleafan**) to draw away from the faith: *inf.*, I.140; (iii) to bring forth, produce: **bringþ** *pres.ind.3s.*, I.179; (iv) (w. **into**) to put into: *inf.*, I.241.

broþor, *m.*, brother: *n.s.*, I.177; II.62, 64, etc.; *a.s.*, II.143, 157; *g.s.*, II.286.

gebroþru, *m.p.*, brothers, members of a monastic community, fellow-Christians: ~**a** *n.*, I.163, 170, etc.; II.180, 206; *a.*, I.264; II.161, 165; *g.*, I.87; ~**m** *d.*, I.73, 80.

brucan, *sv.2*, to enjoy: **breac**, *pret.ind.3s.*, II.110.

bryd, *f.*, bride: ~**e** *a.s.*, I.54.

brydbedd, *nt.*, marriage-bed: *n.s.*, I.23, 40; ~**e** *d.s.*, I.13.

brydguma, *m.*, bridegroom, husband: ~**n** *g.s.*, II.207; *d.s.*, I.25, 36; II.21; III.67.

brydlac, *nt. p.*, marriage ceremony ('bride-gift' = dowry?): *a.*, II.14.

bufan, *prep. w. d.*, above: II.250.

(ge)bugan, *sv.2*, (w. **to**) to turn to, submit to (something *d.*): *inf.*, I.80; **buge** *pres.subj.1s.*, II.178; **(ge)beah** *pret.ind.3s.*, II.37, 92; **gebugon** *pret.ind.3p.*, III.149.

gebun~, *see* **gebin~**

bur, *nt.*, chamber: *a.s.*, III.35; ~**e** *d.s.*, II.52; III.49 (2x), 54.

burh, *f.*, city: *a.s.*, I.133; **byrig** *d.s.*, I.2, 76, etc.; II.196; III.2, 57.

buta, *see* **butu**

butan, buton, (i) *conj.*, unless: I.77; III.7, 48, 160; (ii) *prep. w. d.*, without, except: I.165, 175, etc.; II.24, 59, 253;

III.138, 172, 185, 202.

butu, *adj.*, both: *n.p.m.*, I.20; III.225 (**buta**); *a.p.m.*, II.72; III.206, 223 (**buta**); **buta** *a.p.f.* III.216.

byfode, *see* **bifian**

gebygde, *see* **gebigan**

gebyldu, *f.*, boldness, assuredness: ~**e** *d.s.*, II.101.

bylewite, *adj.*, simple-minded, naive: ~**an** *a.p.nt.wk.*, III.54.

gebyrd, *f./nt.*, rank: ~**e** *d.s.f*, I.95; *d.s.nt.*, I.186; *n.p.f.*, II.15.

(ge)byrgan, *wv.1*, to bury: **gebyrged** *pp.*, **gebyrigde** *(n.p.nt.)* I.310.

byrig, *see* **burh**

byrnan, *sv.3*, to burn: **barn**, *pret.ind.3s.*, I.284; **byrnende** *pres. part.*, ~**um** *(d.s.nt.)* II.250; *(d.p.nt.)* I.209.

bysen, *f./nt.*, example: **bysne** *d.s.*, I.188.

gebysgian, *wv.2*, (i) occupy, busy: **gebysgode** *pret.ind.3s.*, II.6; (ii) (in the passive) to be engaged, occupied: **gebysgod** *pp.*, *(n.s.m.)* I.7.

bysmor, *m./nt.*, shame, disgrace: **to bysmore** *(d.s.)*, shamefully, III.180.

bysmorian, *wv.2*, to insult: **bysmrigende** *pres. part.*, III.105.

bysmorful, *adj.*, shameful: ~**lan** *a.s.m.wk.*, I.123; ~**lum** *d.p.m.wk.*, I.286–87.

bysmrigende, *see* **bysmorian**

bysne, *see* **bysen**

gebysnung, *f.*, example: ~**e** *d.s.*, III.238.

bytt, *f.*, skin, wineskin: ~**e** *a.s.*, II.229.

C

caflice, *adv.*, boldly: II.189.

gecamp, *m./nt.*, warfare: ~**e** *d.s.*, I.74.

campdon, *m.*, fight, battle: *a.s.*, II.191.

campian, *wv.2*, to fight, wage war: **campodon** *pret.ind.3p.*, II.232; **gecampod** *pp.*, *(uninfl.)* II.190.

candel, *f.*, candle: ~**a** *n.p.*, III.217; ~**um** *d.p.*, III.215.

caru, *f.*, anxiety, care: **cara** *a.p.*, II.109.

casere, *m.*, emperor: *n.s.*, I.164, 186, 220 (**kasere**); III.1, 4 (**kasere**), etc.; *d.s.*, I.63, 76, etc.; I.145 (**kasere**); III.24,

212, 220; ~s *g.s.*, I.164; *n.p.*, III.8
(**kaseres**); ~a *g.p.*, II.3.

ceald, *adj.*, cold: ~**um** *d.s.nt.*, II.251.

Cecilia, *proper name*, Cecilia: *n.*, II.1, 9, etc.; ~**n** *a.*, II.223; *g.*, II.68, 221; *d.*, II.50.

Celerinus, *proper name*, Celerinus: *n.*, III.219.

celing, *f.*, coolness: **celincge** *a./d.s.*, I.247.

Celsus, *proper name*: *n.*, I.135, 146; **Celse** *d.*, I.258.

cempa, *m.*, soldier: ~**n** *n.p.*, I.157, 173; II.188; III.103, 107, etc.; *a.p.*, I.263; III.160; ~**um** *d.p.*, III.99, 163.

geceosan, *sv.2*, to choose: **geceas** *pret.ind.3s.*, III.77; **gecoren** *pp.*, *(n.s.m.)* I.11, 147.

ceowan, *sv.2*, to chew: **cywþ** *pres.ind.3s.*, I.279.

Chaldeisca, *adj.*, Babylonian: ~**n** *a.p.m.*, III.123.

gecigan, *wv.1*, to call, name: **gecigst** *pres.ind.2s.*, II.243; **geciged** *pp.*, *(n.s.m.)* I.63.

cildhad, *m.* childhood: ~**e** *d.s.*, II.2.

Claudius, *proper name*, Claudius: *n.*, III.132, 136, etc.; ~**um** *a.*, III.159; ~**es** *g.*, III.162; ~**o** *d.*, III.119.

clawu, *f.*, claw: **clawa** *n.p.*, I.210.

clæne, *adj.*, chaste, pure: *n.s.m.*, I.203; ~**re** *d.s.f.*, II.56; ~**an** *d.s.m.wk.*, I.25, 42; *d.s.f.wk.*, I.11; ~**um** *d.s.m.*, I.34; II.25; *d.s.nt.*, III.65, 91.

clænlice, *adv.*, purely, chastely: I.32; III.68.

clænnyss, *f.*, chastity, purity: *n.s.*, I.14 (**clennysse**); ~**e** *a.s.*, I.8; II.59, 60; III.42, 49; *g.s.*, I.31; *d.s.*, I.28 (**clennisse**), 55; II.13; III.87, 226.

clyf (clif), *nt.*, mountain of earth: *a.s.*, III.232.

clypian, *wv.2*, to cry out, to summon: **clypiaþ** *imp.p.*, I.110; *pres.ind.3p.*, I.119; **clypode** *pret.ind.3s.*, I.37, 42, etc.; II.11, 126, 188; III.47, 137; **clypodon** *pret.ind.3p.*, III.200; **clypigende** *pres. part.*, I.113; III.201.

geclypian, *wv.2*, to declare: **geclypod** *pp.*, *(uninfl.)* I.44, 213.

clysing, *f.*, prison: **clysincge** *d.s.*, I.249.

cnapa, *m.*, young man: *n.s.*, I.172, 260; III.23; ~**n** *g.s.*, I.238.

cneow, *nt.*, knee: ~**um** *d.p.*, I.271; II.126; III.139, 141.

cneowgebed, *nt.*, prayer on one's knees: ~**um** *d.p.*, I.37.

cneowian, *wv.2*, to kneel: **cneowode** *pres.ind.3s.*, II.61.

cniht, *m.*, young man: *n.s.*, I.127, 128, etc.; II.14, 27, etc.; III.39; *a.s.*, II.34, 139; III.34, 103, 186; ~**e** *d.s.*, I.9, 42; II.8, 38, 55; III.35, 63, 88, 184; ~**es** *g.s.*, I.125; III.49; ~**as** *n.p.*, III.91; *a.p.*, I.184.

(ge)cnyttan, *wv.1*, to tie up, bind: **gecnytt** *pp.*, ~**e** *(n.p.m.)* III.102.

com~, *see* **cum**~

coss, *m.*, kiss: ~**as** *a.p.*, III.41.

costnung, *f.*, temptation: ~**a** *a.p.*, I.23.

cræft, *m.*, art, skill, ingenuity: *a.s.*, III.10; ~**e** *d.s.*, III.216; ~**as** *a.p.*, III.8; ~**um** *d.p.*, III.55.

cræftig, *adj.*, learned: *n.s.nt.*, III.56.

creopan, *sv.2*, to crawl: **crupon** *pret.ind.3p.*, I.308.

Crisantus, *proper name*, Chrysanthus: *n.* III.4, 9, etc., 53 (**Chrisantus**); ~**es** *g.*, III.92; ~**um** *a.*, III.60, 96, etc.; ~**e** *d.*, III.152.

Crist, *proper name*, Christ: *n.*, I.40, 42, etc.; II.25, 173, 219; *a.*, I.7, 112, etc.; II.30, 185; III.184, 197, 200, 211; ~**es** *g.*, I.3, 126, etc.; II.3; III.91, 163; ~**e** *d.*, I.22, 30, etc.; II.13, 134, 178, 205; III.23, 29, etc.

cristalla, *m.*, crystal: ~**n** *d.s.*, I.122.

Cristen, *adj.*, Christian: *n.s.m.*, I.164; II.8; III.31; *n.s.nt.*, II.2; ~**en** (where ~**an** expected) *a.s.m.wk.*, III.103; ~**e** *n.p.m.*, I.56, 179; II.158; III.158; ~**a** *n.p.m.* I.163; ~**an** *n.p.m.wk.*, I.129; II.121; III.32; *a.p.m.wk.*, II.145; III.17; ~**ra** *g.p.m.*, III.157; ~**um** *d.p.m.*, I.222, 270; III.53.

Cristendom, *m.*, Christianity: *n.s.*, I.180;

a.s., I.165; III.20; ~e *d.s.*, II.97; III.126.

cucu, *adj.*, alive, living: *n.s.m*, III.201; **cucenne** *a.s.m.*, III.81; ~e *n.p.m.*, I.308; III.225; *a.p.m.*, II.181; ~an *n.p.m.wk.*, II.238.

cuman (coman), *sv.4*, to come: **coman** *inf.*, I.268, 269; **cymþ** *pres.ind.3s.*, II.109, 110; III.240; **cumaþ** *pres.ind.1p.*, II.97; **cume** *pres.subj.3s.*, III.200; *pres.subj.1p.*, I.32; **com** *pret.ind.3s.*, I.46, 75, 228, 303; II.39, 72, etc.; III.62, 119; **coman** *pret.ind.3p.*, I.20, 208, 215; **come** *pret.subj.3s.*, I.238; II.129.

cunnan, *pret. pres. v.*, (i) to know: **canst** *pres.ind.2s.*, III.24; **cuþest** *pret.ind.2s.*, III.128; **cuþe** *pret.ind.3s.*, III.20, 56; *pret.subj.3s.*, III.107; (ii) to be practised in an art: **cuþe** *pret.ind.3s.*, III.8; **cuþ** *pp.*, well-known, known, familiar: *(n.s.m)* I.106; *(n.s.nt.)* II.104; ~re *comp.n.s.m.*, II.29; (iii) *pp.*, (w. **weorþan**) to become known: **cuþ** *(n.s.nt.)* II.88; III.24, 158.

cunnian, *wv.2*, (i) to find out (w. clause): *inf.*, I.5; (ii) to try out (w. *a.*): *inf.*, I.289; (iii) to test: **cunna** *imp.s.*, II.241.

cuþ, *see* **cunnan**

cwalu, *f.*, death: ~e *d.s.*, III.166.

cwealmstow, *f.*, place of execution: ~e *d.s.*, II.164.

cweartern, *nt.*, prison: *n.s.*, III.171, 175; *a.s.*, I.169; ~e *d.s.*, I.151, 153, etc.; III.25, 33, 117, 169.

cwellere, *m.*, executioner: *n.s.*, I.75 (**cwællere**), 92, etc.; II.144, 254 (2nd instance), 257; *a.s.*, II.254 (1st instance); *d.s.*, I.174, 275; ~as *n.p.*, II.186; *a.p.*, I.103, 294; II.161; III.165; ~um *d.p.*, II.164, 181.

gecweman, *wv.1*, to please, propitiate (w. *d.*): **gecweme** *pres.subj.2s.*, III.126.

gecweme, *adj.*, well-pleasing: *n.s.m.*, I.106.

cweþan, *sv.5*, to say, speak: **cwæþe** *pres.ind.1s.*, II.238; **cweþaþ** *pres.ind.1p.*, I.312; **cwæde** *pret.ind.2s.*, II.237; **cwæþ** *pret.ind.3s.*, I.5, 9, etc.; II.27, 30, etc.; III.11, 38, etc.; **cwædon** *pret.ind.3p.*, I.157; II.180, 218, 256; III.22, 162; **cwæþende** *pres. part.*, I.65; **gecweden** *pp.*, *(uninfl.)* II.137.

cwide, *m.*, word of reply: *a.s.*, I.186.

cydde/cyddon, *see* **cyþan**

cymþ, *see* **cuman**

gecynd, *nt.*, nature: *a.s.*, II.122.

cynedom, *nt.*, supreme authority: *a.s.*, II.123.

cynehelm, *m.*, crown: ~um *d.p.*, I.48; II.53; ~as *n.p.*, II.53; *a.p.*, II.56, 80.

cynn, *nt.*, (i) family: ~es *g.s.*, I.164; ~e *d.s.*, I.165; (ii) kind, sort: ~es *g.s.*, I.289.

cyrce, *wk.f.*, church: ~an *d.s.*, I.311; II.260.

(ge)cyrran, *wv.1*, to turn, return: **cyrre** *pres.ind.3s.*, III.13; **gecyrron** *pres.subj.1p.*, I.159; **gecyrde** *pret.ind.3s.*, I.85; **gecyrdon** *pret.ind.3p.*, III.92; **gecyrred** *pp.*, *(uninfl.)* I.255.

cyssan, *wv.1*, to kiss: **cyste** *pret.ind.3s.*, II.72.

cyþan, *wv.1*, to report, make known: **cydde** *pret.ind.3s.*, II.137; **cyddon** *pret.ind.3p.*, II.252; III.119; **cyþende** *pres. part.*, III.194.

gecyþan, *wv.1*, to make known: **gecyd** *pp.*, *(n.s.nt.)* I.174; III.212.

D

dagum, *see* **dæg**

Daria, *proper name*, Daria: *n.*, III.57, 70, etc.; ~n *a.*, III.84, 92, etc.; *d.*, III.59, 170, etc.

dæd, *f.*, action: ~a *a.p.*, I.290; II.149.

dædan, *see* **dead**

(ge)dæftan, *wv.1*, to prepare: *inf.*, I.268; III.34.

dæg, *m.*, day: *a.s.*, II.250; III.112; ~e *d.s.*, I.116; II.73, 133; ~as *a.p.*, II.139, 258;

dagum *d.p.*, I.307; II.1, 4; III.7; **þæs dæges** *(g.s.)*, on that day: III.150.
dæges, *adv.*, by day: II.5.
dæghwamlic, *adj.*, daily: **~re** *d.s.f.*, I.61.
dæghwamlice, *adv.*, daily: II.141, 148.
dægræd, *nt.*, daybreak: *a.s.*, II.187.
dæl, *m.*, number: *n.s.*, I.305.
dælan, *wv.1*, to divide, distribute: **dælaþ** *pres.ind.3p.*, II.159; **dælde** *pret.ind.3s.*, I.58; II.148, 207; **dældon** *pret.ind.3p.*, II.151.
dead, *adj.*, dead: *n.s.m.*, III.52; **~e** *n.s.m.*, I.202; **~an** *a.s.m.wk.*, I.195, 202; *a.p.m.wk.*, I.196; II.132; *d.p.m.wk.*, II.239; *d.p.f.wk.*, I.114 (**dædan**).
dearnunga, *adv.*, secretly: II.152.
deaþ, *m.*, death: *n.s.*, II.109; *a.s.*, I.84, 150; II.210; III.97, 163; **~es** *g.s.*, II.102; **~e** *d.s.*, I.160, 217; II.132, 133, 166, 214.
dema, *m.*, judge: *n.s.*, I.195, 239, etc.; II.192, 247; III.96; **~n** *g.s.*, I.231; *d.s.*, I.85, 105, etc.; II.225; III.95.
deoflic, *adj.*, devilish: **~ra** *g.p.m./nt.*, III.85.
deoflice, *adv.*, devilishly: II.247.
deofol, *m.* in *s.* / *nt.* in *p.*, devil: *n.s.*, III.242; **deofles** *g.s.*, I.268; III.91, 248; **deoflu** *n.p.*, I.129, 114 (**deofla**); II.87; **deoflum** *d.p.*, I.215.
deofolgyld, *nt.*, idolatry, idol,: **~e** *d.s.*, II.90–91; **~um** *d.p.*, I.78, 81.
deor, *nt.*, animal: *a.s.*, III.193; *n.p.*, I.291; *a.p.*, I.289; **~e** *d.s.*, III.184, 205, 207.
deorwurþ, *adj.*, precious: **~e** *n.s.f.*, II.187; **~um** *d.p.nt.*, III.34.
(ge)derian, *wv.1/2*, to injure (w. *d.*): *inf.*, III.114; **deraþ**, *pres.ind.3s.*, III.207. **derige** *pres.subj.2s.*, III.184; **gederod** *pp.*, *(n.s.nt.)* I.127.
digelan, *see* **digol**
digellice, *adv.*, secretly: II.207.
digol, *nt.*, concealment, hiding: **digelan** *d.p.*, II.97.
Dioclytianus, *proper name*, Diocletian: *n.*, I.63.

domsetl, *nt.*, judgment seat: **~e** *d.s.*, I.196.
don, gedon, *anom. v.*, (i) to do, cause, make: *inf.*, I.239, 290; III.62, 138; **do** *imp.s.*, II.27, III.30; *pres.subj.2s.*, III.44; *pres.subj.3s.*, II.65; **dest**, *pres.ind.2s.*, III.32; **deþ** *pres.ind.3s.*, II.174, 192; III.40; **dyde** *pret.ind.1s.*, III.70, 129; *pret.ind.3s.*, I.39; III.167; **dydon** *pret.ind.3p.*, II.249; III.245; **gedon** *pp.*, *(n.s.nt.)* I.257; (ii) to put: **do** *imp.s.*, I.187; **deþ** *pres.ind.3s.*, II.109.
dorston, *see* **durran**
dræhton, *see* **dreccan**
dream, *m.*, melody, music: **~um** *d.p.*, II.16.
dreccan, *wv.1*, to persecute: **dræhton** *pret.ind.2p.*, I.116.
gedrefan, *wv.1*, to vex: **gedrefed** *pp.*, *(n.s.m.)* I.218.
drenc, *m.*, drink: **~as** *a.p.*, III.39.
dreorig, *adj.*, anguished: **~an** *d.s.m.wk.*, I.231; **~e** *n.p.m.*, I.141.
Drihten, *m.*, the Lord: *n.s.*, II.173; III.218; *a.s.*, I.16, 79, etc.; III.44, 151; **Drihtnes** *g.s.*, I.6, 58, etc., I.62 (**Dryhtnes**); II.5, 141; III.97, 106, etc.; **Drihtne** *d.s.*, I.150; III.93.
drohtnung, *f.*, way of life: **~e** *a.s.*, III.90.
dry, *m.*, sorcerer: *a.s.*, I.183.
drycræft, *m.*, magic: *n.s.*, I.107; *a.s.*, I.143, 189; III.53, 78, etc.; **~e** *d.s.*, III.129, 222.
drymann, *m.*, magician, sorcerer: **drymen** *a.p.*, III.122.
[durran], *pret. pres. v.*, to dare: **dorston** *pret.ind.3p.*, I.292.
duru, *f.*, door: *a.s.*, III.186; **~a** *d.s.*, III.205.
dust, *nt.*, dust: **~e** *d.s.*, III.106.
dwelian, *wv.2*, to lead astray: **dweligenne** *infl. inf.*, III.243.
gedwimor, *nt.*, delusion: **~um** *d.p.*, III.243.
gedwyld, *nt.*, false belief, error: **~e** *d.s.*, I.100, 147; III.85.
dynt, *m.*, blow, stroke: **~as** *a.p.*, I.108.

engel, *m.*, angel: *n.s.*, I.169 (**ængel**); II.39, 41, etc.; *a.s.*, II.22 (**encgel**), 28, 31, 33; *d.s.*, **engle**, II.61; ~**as** *n.p.*, I.136 (**ænglas**), 215; *a.p.*, II.141, 197; **englum** *d.p.*, II.199.

ent, *m.*, giant: ~**e** *d.s.*, III.80; ~**es** *n.p.*, I.209.

eoden, *see* **gan**

eornost, *nt.*, (w. **on**) really, in fact: *a.s.*, II.84.

eorþe, *wk.f.*, (i) earth: *n.s.*, I.273; ~**an** *d.s.*, II.40, 100; (ii) ground, dirt, earth: ~**an** *d.s.*, III.178, 224, 233.

eorþstyrung, *f.*, earthquake: *n.s.*, I.251, 304.

eow, *see* **þu**

eower, *poss. adj.*, your (p.): *n.s.m.*, I.196; III.74; *n.p.m.*, I.98; **eowerne** *a.s.m.*, II.191; **eowrum** *d.s.nt.*, I.13; *d.p.m.*, I.110; *d.p.f.*, I.234; **eowre**, *n.p.m.*, III.199; *n.p.nt.*, II.172; *n.p.f.*, II.178; *a.p.m.*, I.278.

[Ercul], *proper name*, Hercules: ~**e** *d.*, III.79.

estas, *m. p.*, delicacies: *a.*, III.39

estmett, *m.*, choice food, delicacy: ~**as** *a.p.*, III.29.

etan, *sv.5*, to eat: **æton** *pret.ind.3p.*, III.50.

F

faran, *sv.6*, (i) to go: *inf.*, II.49, 198; **faraþ** *pres.ind.1p.*, I.233; *pres.ind.3p.*, II.174, 178; (ii) to act, behave: **færþ** *pres.ind.3s.*, II.228.

fæder, *m.*, (i) father: *n.s.*, I.4, 59, etc.; II.122; III.25, 33; *a.s.*, I.146 (2nd instance); III.22, 55; *g.s.*, I.173; III.71; *d.s.*, I.146 (1st instance), 231; III.28, 51; (ii) parents (in *p.*): ~**as** *n.p.*, I.56.

fæger, *adj.*, fair, pleasing: **fægre** *n.s.f.wk.*, I.226; ~**an** *a.s.m.wk.*, III.14; ~**um** *d.p.nt.*, III.64.

fægernys, *f.*, fairness, beauty: *n.s.*, I.275; ~**se** *d.s.*, II.80.

fægnian, *wv.2*, to rejoice (w. *g.*): **fægnast** *pres.ind.2s.*, III.189; **fægnode** *pret.ind.3s.*, III.18; **fægnodon**

pret.ind.3p., I.17–18, 295.

fæla, *see* **fela**

fæmne, *wk.f.*, virgin: *n.s.*, II.3, 34, 210; ~**an** *a.s.*, II.51; **femnan** *n.p.*, I.70.

færlice, *adv.*, immediately, without delay, suddenly: II.33, 39; III.12, 64, 133, 232.

færþ *see* **faran**

fæst, *adj.*, intractable: ~**ne** *a.s.m.*, III.125.

fæstan, *wv.1*, to fast: **fæste** *pret.ind.3s.*, II.10.

fæste, *adv.*, firmly: III.14.

gefæstnian, *wv.2*, (i) to fasten, fix: **gefæstnodon** *pret.ind.3p.*, III.104; **gefæstnod** *pp.*, ~**e** *(n.p.m.)* III.131; (ii) to confirm: **gefæstna** *imp.s.*, I.38.

fæþera *see* **feþer**

fæþm, *f.*, fathom: ~**a** *a.p.*, I.243.

fea, *adj.*, few: **feawum** *d.p.m.*, I.307.

gefea, *m.*, joy: *n.s.*, II.111.

feallan, *sv.7*, to fall: **feoll**, *pret.ind.3s.*, II.40, 126; **feollon** *pret.ind.3p.*, I.160; III.141.

feawum, *see* **fea**

(ge)feccan, *wv.1*, to fetch: *inf.*, I.183, 190; II.223; III.33; **gefette** *pret.ind.3s.*, I.222, II.14.

fela, *indecl. adj.* (often w. *g.*) and *pron.*, many: I.60 (**fæla**), 187, 274; II.132, 133; III.90, 149, 228, 244.

feond, *m.*, enemy: *n.s.*, I.43.

feondlic, *adj.*, diabolical: ~**a** *n.s.m.wk.*, III.244; ~**ne** *a.s.f.*, III.122.

feower, *num.*, four: I.265; II.220, 257.

gefera, *m.*, companion: ~**ena** *g.p.*, I.82; ~**um** *d.p.*, I.187, 271, etc.

feran, *wv.1*, to go: **ferde** *pret.ind.3s.*, II.35, 140; III.2, 71; III.220; **ferdon** *pret.ind.1p.*, I.246, *pret.ind.3p.*, I.298; III.226.

fet, *see* **fot**

feþer, *f.*, feather: **fæþera** *a.p.*, III.134.

fif, *number*, five: III.36.

findan, *sv.3*, to find: **funde**, *pret.ind.3s.*, II.51; III.35; *pret.subj.3s.*, III.55; **fundon** *pret.ind.3p.*, I.18.

fiþer, *nt.*, wing: ~**um** *d.p.*, II.199.

fleogan, *sv.2*, to fly: **flugon** *pret.ind.3p.*,
  I.136; **fleogende** *pres.part.*, II.197.
fleon, *sv.2*, to flee: **fleah** *pret.ind.3s.*,
  I.306.
flex, *nt.*, flax: **~e** *d.s.*, I.283.
folc, *nt.*, people: *n.s.*, III.228, 230; **~es**
  g.s., I.243; III.210.
folgian, *wv.2*, to follow (w. *d.* object):
  folgiaþ *pres.ind.3p.*, I.52; II.100;
  folgodon *pret.ind.3p.*, I.70.
fon, *sv.7*, to take up, to begin (w. *infl.
  inf.*): **feng**, *pret.ind.3s.*, II.44.
gefon, *sv.7*, to seize, catch hold of:
  gefeng, *pret.ind.3s.*, III.211.
for, *prep. w. d./a.*, for, on account of,
  because of, for the sake of: I.34, 83,
  etc.; II.38, 97, etc.; III.70, 96, etc.
forbærnan, *wv.1*, to be put to death by
  burning, burned alive: *inf.*, III.206;
  forbernan *inf.*, I.87, 264, 302;
  forbærne *pres.subj.3s.*, II.177;
  forbærnde *pret.ind.3s.*, III.80.
forbeah, *see* **forbugan**
forberan, *sv.4*, to endure: **forbæron**
  pret.ind.3p., I.123.
forbugan, *sv.2*, to turn aside from,
  avoid: **forbeah** *pret.ind.3s.*, III.41.
forbyrnan, *sv.3*, to burned to death,
  burned alive: **forbarn** *pret.ind.3s.*,
  I.300; **forburne** *pret.subj.3s.*, I.240;
  forburnen *pp.*, *(n.s.nt.)* I.243.
fordeman, *wv.1*, to condemn: **fordemed**
  pp., **~e** *(n.p.m.)* I.81.
fordon, *anom. v.*, to destroy: **fordest**
  pres.ind.2s., III.189; **fordeþ**
  pres.ind.3s., III.249.
foresæd, *see* **foresecgan**
foresceawian, *wv.2*, to see (to it):
  foresceawode *pret.ind.3s.*, I.154;
  pret.subj.3s., I.162.
foresecgan, *wv.3*, to foretell: **foresæde**
  pret.ind.3s., I.69; **foresæd** *pp.*, afore-
  mentioned: **~a** *(n.s.m.wk.)* I.172;
  II.147; **~an** *(d.s.m.wk.)* I.255; II.136;
  III.19; *(d.s.nt.wk.)* I.265; **~um**
  (d.p.m.wk.) II.187.
forestæppan, *sv.6*, to precede
  (someone/something *a.* or *d.*):

forestopon *pret.ind.3p.*, I.299.
forferan, *wv.1*, to perish: **forferdon**
  pret.ind.3p., I.274.
forgifan, **forgyfan**, *sv.5*, to give: *inf.*,
  II.239; **forgeaf** *pret.ind.3s.*, II.55;
  forgifen *pp.*, *(uninfl.)* II.111.
forgitan, *sv.5*, to forget: *inf.*, III.30.
forht, *adj.*, fearful, frightened: *n.s.*, I.82;
  II.126.
forhtian, *wv.2*, to be afraid of (w. **for**):
  forhtode *pret.ind.3s.*, III.206.
forlætan, *sv.7*, to leave, leave alone,
  abandon, let go: *inf.*, III.136
  (forlæton); **forlæt** *imp.s.*, I.144;
  forlæte *pres.ind.3s.*, III.16; **forlet**
  pret.ind.3s., II.256; III.185; **forlæten**
  pp., (as *d.* absolutes) **~um** *(d.s.m.)*
  III.93; *(d.s.nt.)* III.85.
forleosan, *sv.2*, to lose: *inf.*, III.15;
  forleosaþ *pres.ind.3p.*, II.58; **forleosa**
  pres.subj.2s., I.236; **forloren** *pp.*,
  (n.s.m.) II.213.
forligr, *nt.*, adultery, fornication: **~e** *d.s.*,
  III.76.
forloren, *see* **forleosan**
fornean, *adv.*, nearly: I.307.
forniman, *sv.4*, (i) to seize, consume:
  fornumen *pp.*, *(n.s.m.)* I.307;
  III.220; *(n.s.nt.)* II.108; **~e** *(n.p.m.)*
  I.115.
forod, *adj.*, broken, severed: *n.s.m.*,
  II.255.
foroft, *adv.*, very often: III.122.
forscrincan, *sv.3*, to shrivel up, wither:
  forscruncon *pret.ind.3p.*, III.218.
forscyldigian, *wv.2*, *(pp.* only)
  forscyldigod, guilty, wicked:
  forscyldegoda *(n.s.m.wk.)* III.219–20.
forsearian, *wv.2*, to wither: **forseariaþ**,
  pres.ind.3p., II.57.
forseon, *sv.5*, to despise, scorn: *inf.*,
  II.171; **forsihst** *pres.ind.2s.*, I.46;
  forsihþ *pres.ind.3s.*, I.49; **forseah**
  pret.ind.3s., III.39; **forsawon**
  pret.ind.3p., II.150.
forstandan, *sv.6*, to block, obstruct
  (door *a.* against someone *d.*): **forstod**
  pret.ind.3s., III.186.

forþ, *adv.*, forth, forward: II.136, 170, 198.

for þam þe, *conj.*, for, because: II.56, 256; III.7.

for þan þe, *conj.*, for, because: I.44, 130, 240; II.59, 66, etc.; III.46, 109, 155, 240.

forþi, *adv.*, therefore, for that reason: I.94, 97, 259.

geforþian, *wv.2*, to offer: **geforþode** *pret.ind.3s.*, II.14.

forþteon, *sv.2*, to bring forth: **forþteah** *pret.ind.3s.*, II.115.

forwurþan, *sv.3*, to perish: *inf.*, I.226; **forwearþ** *pret.ind.3s.*, I.305.

forwyrnan, *wv.1*, to refuse (w. d. of pers.): **forwyrnde** *pret.ind.3s.*, II.142; **forwyrned** *pp.*, *(uninfl.)* I.280.

fot, *m.*, foot: **fet** *a.p.*, I.138, 283; III.115; **~um** *d.p.*, I.160, 292; III.144.

fotcops, *m.*, foot shackle, fetter: *n.s.*, III.105; **~um** *d.p.*, III.105.

fram, *prep. w. d.*, from: I.3, 11, etc.; II.2, 30, etc.; III.2, 13, etc.

gefrætwian, *wv.2*, to adorn: **gefrætwod** *pp.*, **gefretewod** *(uninfl.)* III.71; **gefrætowodan** *(g.s.nt.wk.)* I.276.

gefredan, *wv.1*, to feel: **gefretst** *pres.ind.2s.*, I.108.

frefrian, *wv.2*, to comfort: **frefrode** *pret.ind.3s.*, III.64.

fremian, *wv.1/2*, to be of use (w. d.): **fremaþ** *pres.ind.3s.*, I.198; **fremiaþ** *pres.ind.3p.*, II.237.

gefremman, *wv.1/2*, to do, perform, carry out: *inf.*, I.238; **gefremast** *pres.ind.2s.*, III.121; **gefremode** *pret.ind.3s.*, III.78; **gefremodon** *pret.ind.3p.*, II.154; **gefremod** *pp.*, **~e** *(n.p.nt.)* III.228.

freolice, *adv.*, freely: III.210.

freond, *m.*, kinsman, relative, friend: **frynd** *n.p.*, I.4; II.7; III.22; *a.p.*, III.59; **~um** *d.p.*, I.16; III.150.

gefretst, *see* **gefredan**

frofer, *m.*, comfort: *a.s.*, I.65.

Frofergast, *m.*, Comforting Spirit: *n.s.*, II.122; *a.s.*, II.115.

frynd, *see* **freond**

ful, *adj.*, despicable, foul: **~an** *d.s.f.wk.*, III.190; **~um** *d.s.m.*, III.172; *d.s.nt.*, II.90; III.33, 76.

ful, *adv.*, fully, very: I.206; **ful gehende**: very nearby, II.35.

fulfremian, *wv.2*, to make perfect, complete: **fulfremod** *pp.*, *(n.s.m.)* II.140.

full, *adj.*, full, abundant: **~e** *a.s.f.*, II.229; **~um** *d.s.m.*, III.4.

fullan, *see* **be**

(ge)fullian, *wv.2*, to baptize: *inf.*, II.32, 94; **to fullienne** *infl. inf.*, I.171; **gefullode** *pret.ind.3s.*, II.49, 138; **gefullod** *pp.*, *(uninfl.)* I.255; *(n.s.m.)* I.172, 221; II.30, 93, 135, 182; III.19; **~e** *(n.p.m.)* I.162, 168; II.186, 203, 220; III.162, 211; *(n.p.nt.)* III.150.

fullice, *adv.*, wickedly: III.83.

fullice, *adv.*, entirely, fully: I.101, 255.

fulluht, *nt.*, baptism: *n.s.*, II.44; *a.s.*, III.87; **~es** *g.s.*, II.36; **~e** *d.s.*, II.90; III.149.

fultum, *m.*, help: **~es** *g.s.*, II.12.

furþon, *adv.*, even: II.251, 253.

gefyllan, *wv.1*, to fulfil, complete: **gefyldon** *pret.ind.3p.*, II.191; **gefylled** *pp.*, *(n.s.nt.)* I.69; II.106; **~e** *(n.p.nt.)* I.65.

fylstan, *wv.1*, to help (w. d.): **fylste** *pret.ind.3s.*, III.129.

fyr, *nt.*, fire: *n.s.*, I.278, 284; II.177; III.207; *a.s.*, I.89, 189, etc.; II.246; III.204; **~e** *d.s.*, I.115, 235, etc.; II.250; III.81, 206.

fyrhtu, *f.*, fear, awe: **~e** *d.s.*, III.141, 191, 220.

fyrlen, *nt.*, (a) distance: **~um** *d.p.*, III.18.

fyrmest, *adj.*, foremost: **~an** *n.p.m.*, III.82.

gefyrn, *adv.*, already, earlier: I.56, 153.

fyrnlic, *adj.*, wicked: **~um** *d.p.f.*, II.30–31, 182.

fyrst, *m./nt.*, time: **on fyrste** *(d.s.)*, in due course, III.90, 230.

fyþerhama, *m.*, wing: **~an** *d.p.*, II.52.

G

galnyss, *f.*, sexual desire: ~e *a.s.*, III.45, 70, 190.

gamen, *nt.*, sport: ~e *d.s.*, III.174.

gan, *anom. v.*, to go: *inf.*, I.167; III.145, 191, 198; **gaþ** *imp.p.*, II.191; **eode** *pret.ind.3s.*, I.120, 135, 239; III.181, 209; **eoden** *pret.ind.3p.*, I.113, 169; **eodon**, II.166; III.50, 201.

gangan, *sv.7*, to go: **gang** *imp.s.*, I.119; III.208.

gast, *m.*, (i) spirit: ~as *a.p.*, III.233; (ii) (Holy) Spirit: *a.s.*, II.117.

gastlic, *adj.*, spiritual: ~an *a.s.nt.wk.*, I.61; *a.p.f.wk.*, II.140.

gastlice, *adv.*, spiritually: I.55.

gælsa, *m.*, pleasure: ~n *a.p.*, I.43.

ge, *see* þu

ge, *conj.*, also: I.197.

gear, *m./nt.*, year: **gæra** *g.p.*, I.5.

(ge)gearcian, *wv.2*, to prepare: *inf.*, I.219; **gearcost** *pres.ind.2s.*, I.46; **gegearcod** *pp.*, ~e *(n.p.nt.)* I.20.

geare, *adv.*, well: I.93.

gearwe, *adj.*, ready: *(n.p.m.)* I.193.

gecoren, *see* ceosan

gegladian, *wv.2*, to propitiate: **gegladod** *pp.*, ~e *(n.p.m.)* I.99.

geogaþ, *f.*, youth: *n.s.*, I.226; **iugoþe** *a.s.*, II.107; **geogoþe** *d.s.*, I.3.

geond, *prep. w. a.*, through, throughout, over the course of: I.133; II.139.

geong, *adj.*, young: ~a *n.s.m.wk.*, I.296; **iung** *n.s.m.*, II.212.

georne, *adv.*, eagerly: I.21, II.135.

geornlice *adv.*, eagerly: I.74; III.151.

gif, *conj.*, if: I.31, 111, etc., II.23, 24, etc.; III.13, 15, etc.

gifu, *f.*, grace: *n.s.*, I.154; ~e *a.s.*, II.25.

gimdon, *see* gyman

gingra, *n.s.m.wk.*, II.173; *adj. (comp.* of **geong**), younger.

gingra, *m.*, aide, deputy: ~n *a.s.*, I.239.

git, *see* gyt, þu

glædnyss, *f.*, delight: ~e *d.s.*, II.71.

gleaw, *adj.*, wise: ~um *d.s.nt.*, III.9.

geglengan, *wv.1*, to adorn: **geglengdest**, *pret.ind.2s.*, III.66; **geglenged** *pp.*,

(uninfl.) III.63.

glitenian, *wv.2*, to glitter: **glitiniende** *pres. part.*, I.244.

god, *m.*, god, God: *n.s.*, I.69, 128, etc.; II.41, 43, etc.; III.74, 129, etc.; *a.s.*, I.98, 131, etc.; II.18, 35, etc.; III.145, 147, etc.; ~es *g.s.*, I.1, 55, etc.; II.5, 22, etc.; III.88, 109, 137, 236; ~e *d.s.*, I.61, 114, etc.; II.11, 17, etc.; III.43, 47, etc.; ~as *n.p.*, I.98, 129; I.122 (**godes**); II.86; III.82, 83, 130, 199; *a.p.*, I.97, 282; II.119, 243; ~a *g.p.*, I.149, 252; III.133; ~um *d.p.*, I.94, 110, etc.; II.201, 210, 241; III.72, 98, 126, 214.

god, *nt.*, good, good thing: *a.s.*, III.129.

god, *adj.*, good: ~ne *a.s.m.*, II.191.

godcund, *adj.*, divine: ~re *d.s.f.*, III.130.

godcundnyss, *f.*, divinity: ~e *a.s.*, II.99.

godnyss, *f.*, goodness, virtue: ~e *a.s.*, III.73, 75; ~a *g.p.*, I.295.

godspel, *nt.*, Gospel: *a.s.*, II.5; *n.p.*, III.10; ~le *d.s.*, III.248.

gold, *nt.*, gold: *n.s.*, I.244; *a.s.*, II.215; ~e *d.s.*, III.63, 66.

goldhord, *m.*, treasure, gold-hoard: *a.s.*, III.14.

gram, *adj.*, angry: *n.s.m.*, II.203, 247.

grama, *m.*, anger, trouble: ~n *a.s.*, II.99; *d.s.*, I.107, 258, 282; II.24; III.111, 212.

gramlic, *adj.*, fierce, angry: ~a *n.s.m.wk.*, III.76; ~an *a.s.m.wk.*, I.43; ~um *d.s.nt.*, III.116; ~e *n.p.nt.*, II.87.

grammatic, *adj.*, grammatical, of grammar: ~an *a.m.s.wk.*, III.10.

grapung, *f.*, touching: ~e *d.s.*, II.242, 244.

great, *adj.*, large: ~um *d.p.f.*, III.132.

greatnyss, *f.*, fullness: ~e *d.s.*, II.230.

gegremian, *wv.2*, to anger: **gegremod** *pp.*, *(n.s.m.)* III.204.

grewþ, *see next entry*

growan, *sv.7*, to grow: **grewþ** *pres.ind.3s.*, I.178.

grund, *m.*, depth: *a.s.*, I.277, 278.

gydenu, *f.*, goddess: ~ena *a.p.*, I.97; ~um *d.p.*, I.111.

gyftu, *nt.p.*, wedding: *n.*, I.20.
gylden, *adj.*, made of gold: ~**um** *d.s.nt.*,
II.40; *d.p.m.*, II.52; ~**an** *a.p.m.wk.*,
II.41; ~**a** *a.p.f.*, I.121.
gym, *m.*, gem: *a.s.*, II.217.
gyman, *wv.1*, care for, take care of (*w.
g.*): **gimdon** *pret.ind.3p.*, I.269;
gymdon II.3.
gymstan, *m.*, jewel: ~**um** *d.p.*, III.63.
gyrd, *f.*, rod: ~**a** *n.p.*, III.133; ~**um** *d.p.*,
III.132.
gyt, git, *adv.*, still, yet: I.265, 281, 288;
II.8, 128; III.240.

H

habban, *wv.3*, (i) to have: *inf.*, I.35;
II.154; III.67, 180, 199; **hæbbe,**
pres.ind.1s., II.22; **hæfst** *pres.ind.2s.*,
II.228; **habbaþ** *pres.ind.1p.*, II.80;
pres.ind.2p., I.97; *pres.ind.3p.*, II.122;
hæfdest *pret.ind.2s.*, II.237; **hæfde**
pret.ind.3s., I.92; II.3; III.3, 73, 76;
pret.subj.1s., II.74; *pret.subj.3s.*,
III.60; **hæfdon** *pret.ind.3p.*, I.166;
(ii) as auxiliary w. *pp.*, **habbaþ**
pres.ind.2p., II.190; **hæfþ** *pres.ind.3s.*,
I.147; **hæfde** *pret.ind.3s.*, I.11, 43,
etc.; III.81; *pret.subj.3s.*, III.8;
hæfdon *pret.ind.3p.*, II.137.
hafenleast, *f.*, poverty: ~**e** *d.s.*, II.107.
hagol, *m.*, hail: *n.s.*, I.306.
hal, *adj.*, sound: ~**um** *d.s.m.*, II.253; ~**e**
n.p.m., I.244.
halga, *m.*, holy one, saint: ~**n** *a.s.*, I.103,
136; III.136; *d.s.*, III.113; *n.p.*, I.47,
53, etc.; II.153; *a.p.*, I.268, 294;
III.223, 229, 236; *g.p.*, I.310 (**halgan**);
~**ena** *g.p.*, I.284, 292; ~**um** *d.p.*, I.50,
157; II.11; III.236, 244; *see also* **halig**.
gehalgian, *wv.2*, to consecrate:
gehalgod *pp.*, (*n.s.m.*) I.14; (*n.s.nt.*)
II.259.**halig**, *adj.*, holy: *n.s.m.*, II.8;
halga *n.s.m.wk.*, I.88, 300; III.169; ~**a**
n.s.f., II.3; ~**e** *a.s.nt.*, III.194; *a.p.m.*,
II.80; **halgan** *a.s.m.wk.*, I.86, 132, 137;
III.104, 215; *a.s.f.wk.*, III.217;
d.s.m.wk., I.190; III.20; *d.s.nt.wk.*,
II.50; III.248; *n.p.m.wk.*, II.180;

n.p.nt.wk., III.10; **haligre** *d.s.f.*,
II.259; **halgum** *d.p.m.*, I.80;
d.p.m.wk., I.225, 291.
halignyss, *f.*, holiness: *n.s.*, III.79.
halsian, *wv.2*, to beseech: **halsige**
pres.ind.3s., III.184.
halwende, *adj.*, salutary: ~**um** *d.p.f.*,
I.45.
ham, *m.*, home: *a.s.* (w. adverbial force:
home, homewards), II.49.
hand, *f.*, hand: ~**a** *d.s.*, II.75; ~**e** *d.s.*,
III.11; ~**a** *a.p.*, I.283; III.115; *g.p.*,
I.170; ~**um** *d.p.*, III.117, 134.
hat, *adj.*, hot: ~**e** *a.s.nt.wk.*, I.89; ~**um**
d.s.nt., II.252; ~**an** *d.s.nt.wk.*, II.254;
d.s.f.wk., III.114.
hatan, *sv.7*, (i) to name, call: **gehaten**
pp., (*n.s.m*) I.1, 166; II.8, 36, 144;
III.3 (2x), 148; (*n.s.nt.*) I.18, II.2;
III.57, 211. (ii) to command: **hat**
imp.s., I.182; II.158; **hætst**
pres.ind.2s., II.227; **hete** *pret.ind.2s.*,
II.154; **het** *pret.ind.3s.*, I.80, 86 (2x),
etc.; II.41, 60, etc.; III.33, 34, etc.;
heton, *pret.ind.3p.*, I.48.
gehæftan, *wv.1*, to take prisoner,
imprison: *inf.*, III.96; **gehæft** *pp.*,
(*uninfl.*) III.173.
gehælan, *wv.1*, to heal: *inf.*, I.117;
gehæle *pres.ind.1s.*, I.112; **gehælan**
pres.subj.3p., I.111; **gehælde**
pret.subj.3s., I.125; **gehæled** *pp.*,
(*n.s.m.*) I.127; ~**e** (*n.p.nt.*) I.89.
Hælend, *m.*, Saviour: *n.s.*, I.8, 11, etc.;
II.60, 131; III.248; *a.s.*, I.35; II.203;
III.21, 41, 67, 192; ~**es** *g.s.*, I.27, 52,
etc.; II.248; III.246; ~**e** *d.s.*, I.22, 47,
etc.; II.221.
hære, *wk.f.*, hairshirt: ~**an** *d.s.*, II.9.
hæs, *f.*, command: ~**e** *d.s.*, I.152.
hæte, *wk.f.*, heat: ~**an** *d.s.*, III.113; ~**um**
d.p., II.105.
hæþen, *adj.*, heathen: ~**a** *n.s.m.wk.*,
III.96; ~**e** *a.s.nt.wk.*, I.250; *n.p.m.*,
I.277; *a.p.f.*, III.8; ~**es** *g.s.m.*, I.194;
~**an** *g.s.m.wk.*, I.111; *n.p.m.wk.*,
II.200, 210, 249; III.180, 195;
a.p.m.wk., I.304; II.218; III.175;

a.p.f.wk., III.10; **~ra** *g.p.m.*, I.274.
hæþengyld, **~gild**, *nt.*, heathen shrine:
  a.s., I.306; **~e** *d.s.*, II.162.
hæþengylda, **~gilda**, *m.*, heathen priest,
  idolater: *n.s.*, III.3; **~n** *n.p.*, I.113; **~an**
  a.p., I.269.
hæþenscipe, *m.*, heathen faith,
  paganism: *n.s.*, II.222; *d.s.*, III.57.
he, heo, hit, *pers. pron.*, he, she, it: **he**
  n.s.m., I.4, 5 (2x), etc.; II.23, 34, etc.;
  III.3, 6 (2x), etc.; **hit** *n.s.nt.*, I.25, 56,
  etc.; II.13, 98, etc.; III.24, 154, 230;
  a.s.nt., I.101; II.7, 84; III.38; **heo**
  n.s.f., I.34, 249, etc.; II.4, 7, etc.;
  III.60 (2x), 62, etc.; **hine** *a.s.m.*, I.8,
  10, etc.; II.29, 41 (2x), etc.; III.4, 5,
  etc.; **hi** *a.s.f.*, I.72, 236, etc.; II.6, 9,
  etc.; III.166 (2x), 173, etc.; *n.p.m.*,
  I.17, 20, etc.; II.20, 57, etc.; III.74, 85,
  etc.; *n.p.nt.*, III.37, 38 (2x), etc.;
  n.p.f., I.277; III.44, 45, etc.; *a.p.m.*,
  I.48 (2x), 73, etc.; II.56, 58, etc.;
  III.97, 147, etc.; *a.p.nt.*, III.48 (2x);
  a.p.f., II.116; III.134 (2nd instance);
  his *g.s.m.*, I.4 (2x), 5, etc.; II.25, 38,
  etc.; III.6, 19, etc.; *g.s.nt.*, I.272, 274;
  hyre *g.s.f.*, I.41, 229, 299; II.225; **hire**,
  II.4, 7, etc.; III.64, 88, 194; **him**
  d.s.m., I.6, 10, etc.; II.29, 36, etc.;
  III.11 (2x), 26, etc.; *d.p.m.*, I.58, 64,
  etc.; II.154, 188, 213; III.32, 187, 232;
  hire *d.s.f.*, I.251; II.232, 240; III.61,
  65, 181; **heora** *g.p.m.*, I.50, 56, etc.;
  I.185 (**hyra**), 191 (**hyre**); II.12, 15,
  etc.; III.75, 90, etc.; *g.p.nt.*, III.37, 41,
  etc.; *g.p.f.*, III.45, 75.
heafod, *nt.*, head: **~e** *d.s.*, III.210; **~es**
  g.s., III.23; **heafda** *a.p.*, I.292.
heage, *see next entry*
heah, *adj.*, tall: **heage** *n.p.m.*, I.209.
heahengel, *m.*, archangel: **~glum** *d.p.*,
  II.12.
heahgerefa, *m.*, prefect ('high-reeve' for
  Latin *prefectus*): *n.s.*, II.145; III.204,
  214; **~n** *a.s.*, III.213.
(ge)healdan, *sv.7*, to preserve, keep,
  hold: *inf.*, III.14; **to (ge)healdenne**
  infl. inf., I.165; **healdaþ** *imp.p.*, II.56;

gehylst, *pres.ind.2s.*, II.25; **gehylt**
  pres.ind.3s., II.22; **gehealdaþ**
  pres.ind.3p., III.247; **healdan**
  pres.subj.3p., II.181; **heold**
  pret.ind.3s., I.54, 80, 265; III.42, 134;
  geheoldon *pret.ind.3p.*, II.191;
  (ge)heolde *pret.subj.3s.*, I.7, 22;
  III.42, 68; **gehealden** *pp.*, **~re** *(d.s.f.)*
  I.27; III.87; **~ne** *(n.p.m.)* III.246.
heap, *m.*, company: *n.s.*, I.88, 300; **~e**
  d.s., I.42, 80.
heard, *adj.*, hard: **~ne** *a.s.m.*, III.104;
  ~um *d.s.m.*, III.115; *d.p.m.*, I.104; **~e**
  n.p.f., III.134.
hearde, *adv.*, vehemently, greatly:
  III.204.
heardheort, *adj.*, hard-hearted: **~a**
  n.s.m.wk., I.195, 263.
hebban, *sv.6*, lift up: **hof** *pret.ind.3s.*,
  I.200.
hell, *f.*, hell: **~e** *d.s.*, I.211, 278, 309.
gehelpan, *sv.3*, to help (w. *d.*): *inf.*,
  III.199; **gehelp** *imp.s.*, I.182.
helware, *m.p.*, inhabitants of hell: *n.*,
  I.213.
gehende, *adj.*, nearby, close: *n.m.s.*,
  II.35; *see also* **ful**.
gehende, *prep. w. d.*, near: II.53.
hengen, *f.*, rack: *n.s.*, III.216; **~e** *d.s.*,
  III.215.
heofon, *strong m. / wk. f.*, heaven,
  Heaven: **~an** *g.s.wk.*, I.89; **~um** *d.p.*,
  I.15, 201, 233; II.70, 99, 131, 199.
heofonlic, *adj.*, of heaven: **~an**
  a.s.m.wk., I.271; *d.s.m.wk.*, II.12.
heofung, *f.*, lamentation: **~a** *d.s.*, I.229.
heonan, *adv.*, from here, III.198, 201
  (**heonon**).
heonanforþ, *adv.*, henceforth: II.79.
heorte, *wk.f.*, heart: *n.s.*, II.18; **~an** *a.s.*,
  I.131; *d.s.*, I.139; II.56.
her, *adv.*, here: II.73.
herian, *wv.1/2*, to praise: **herigende**
  pres. part., I.161, 245.
herung, *f.*, praise: **~e** *g.s.*, III.237.
het, *see* **hatan**
hetan, *(sv.5?)*, to attack: *inf.*, III.195.
hetel, *adj.*, hostile, hateful: **~an**

d.s.m.wk., III.79.
hetelice, *adv.*, fiercely: III.100, 132.
hider, *adv.*, here, to this world: II.112, 129.
Hilaria, *proper name*, Hilaria: *n.*, III.148, 164.
hiw, *nt.*, appearance, form: ~es *g.s.*, I.208; ~e *d.s.*, II.58.
hiwan, *m.p.*, members of a household: **hiwum** *d.*, II.202.
(ge)hiwian, *wv.2*, to feign, pretend: **gehiwod** *pp.*, ~um *(d.s.m.)* III.86.
hlude, *adv.*, loudly: I.113; II.126.
hlystan, *wv.1*, to listen to (w. *g.* or *d.*): *inf.*, III.185.
(ge)hnexian, *wv.2*, to soften: **hnexodon** *pret.ind.3p.*, III.135; **gehnexod** *pp.*, ~e *(n.p.f.)* III.133.
hospword, *nt.*, scornful word: ~um *d.p.*, I.206.
hostig, *adj.*, knotty: ~e *n.p.f.*, III.135.
hraþe, *adv.*, quickly, soon: **swa hraþe swa**, as soon as, III.50.
hreppan, *wv.1*, to touch: **reppan** *inf.*, I.292; **hrepode** *pret.ind.3s.*, III.219.
hrepung, *f.*, touch: ~e *d.s.*, I.170.
hryman, *wv.1*, to cry out, shout: **hrymdon** *pret.ind.3p.*, III.219.
hu, *adv.*, how: I.6, 99, etc.; II.73, 88, etc.; III.143, 155, 183; *see also* **loca hu**.
humeta, *adv.*, why: II.118.
hund, *nt.*, hundred (w. noun in *g.*): *n.p.*, II.220.
hundseofontig, *number*, seventy: *n.p.m.*, III.149; *a.p.m.*, III.160; ~um *d.p.m.*, III.99.
hungor, *n.*, hunger: **hungre** *d.s.*, II.106.
huru, *adv.*, at least, if only, even: I.266; II.154; (ii) in any case: III.72.
hus, *nt.*, house: *n.s.*, II.259; *a.s.*, II.216; ~es *g.s.*, I.269; ~e *d.s.*, I.87, 240, 300; II.181, 184, etc.; III.174.
hwa, (i) *interog. pron.*, *m./f.*, who: *n.s.m.*, II.32, 94, 112, 129; **hwæs**, *g.m.s.*, II.79 (2x); (ii) **swa hwa swa**, *indef. pron.*, whoever, whatever: III.218–19; **swa hwæs swa** *g.s.nt.*, II.141–42.

hwanon, *adv.*, whence, from where: I.26, 204.
hwær, *adv.*, where: I.275, 276.
hwæs, *see* **hwa**
hwæt, *interrog. pron.*, *nt.*, what: *n.s.*, II.46; III.121; *a.s.*, I.198; II.137; III.138; (ii) *indef. pron.*, something, (w. **elles**) something else: *n.s.*, II.45.
hwæt, *interj.*, so, well, so then (often w. **þa** as an introductory interj.): I.21, 54, etc.; II.9, 130, etc.; III.96, 219.
hweþer, *conj.*, whether: I.191; II.242; III.102.
hwi, *adv.*, why: I.142, 177; II.150, 151, 166.
hwider, *adv.*, where, to which place: I.204.
hwil, *f.*, time: ~e *d.s.*, I.191 (w. **oþ þæt** to mark a limit or extent); **þa hwile þe**, *conj.*, while: II.98.
hwilc, **hwylc**, (i) *interrog. pron.* and *adj.*, which, what sort of: *n.s.f.*, I.225; III.79; *n.p.m.*, III.82; ~e *a.s.f.*, II.227; III.73, 75; *a.p.nt.*, II.131; ~ere *g.s.f.*, II.224; (ii) *indef. pron.*, some, any: *n.s.m.*, III.161; (iii) *rel. adj.* **swa hwilce . . . swa**, whatever: *a.s.f.*, II.60.
gehwilc, *pron.* and *adj.*, each, all: ~um *d. s.m.*, III.145; *d.p.m.*, II.104; ~e *n.p.m.*, I.90.
hwitian, *wv.2*, to be or become white: **hwitaþ** *pres.ind.3s.*, II.80.
hwitnyss, *f.*, whiteness: ~e *d.s.*, II.54.
hyd, *f.*, hide: *n.s.*, III.113; ~e *d.s.*, III.111.
hyredman, *m.*, member of a household: ~men *n.p.*, I.229.
gehyrian, *wv.1*, to hear: **gehyre** *pres.ind.1s.*, II.83; **gehyraþ** *pres.ind.3p.*, III.130.
gehyrsumian, *wv.2*, to serve (w. *d.*): **gehyrsumiaþ** *pres.ind.3p.*, II.124.

I

ic, *pers. pron.*, I: *n.s.*, I.12, 13, etc.; II.19, 22 (2x), etc.; III.11, 12, etc.; **me** *a.s.*, I.97, 147, etc.; II.22, 23, etc.; III.191; *d.s.*, I.14, 26, etc.; II.26, 61; III.46,

129, 143; **min** *g.s.*, I.227; **wit** *n. dual*,
I.31, 32 (2x); **we** *n.p.*, I.98, 101, etc.;
II.80, 85, etc.; III.138, 155, etc.; **unc** *a.
dual*, II.65; **us** *a.p.*, I.231, 246; II.154,
181; *d.p.*, I.38, 115, etc.; II.81, 102,
112, 131; III.139, 237, 239.
idel, *nt.*, futility: **on idel** (*a.s.*): in vain,
III.109.
in, *adv.*, in: III.50, 71, 187.
ingan, *anom. v.*, to enter: **ineodon**
pret.ind.3p., III.72.
ingang, *m.*, entrance: ~**e** *d.s.*, III.232.
innan, *adv.*, within: I.188.
inne, *adv.*, within, inside: III.181, 205.
intinga, *m.*, sake, account: ~**n** *d.s.*, I.116.
into, *prep. w. d.*, into: I.75, 104, etc.;
III.116, 181.
Ioseph, *proper name*, Joseph: ~**es** *g.s.*,
III.42.
Iouis, *proper name*, Jove: *n.*, III.77.
isen, *nt.*, iron: ~**e** *d.s.*, III.115.
iu, *adv.*, formerly: II.1.
iugoþ, see **geogaþ**
Iulianus, *proper name*, Julian: *n.*, I.1, 5,
etc.; ~**um** *a.*, I.86, 93, etc.; ~**es** *g.*,
I.116, 160; ~**e** *d.*, I.140, 271, etc.;
vocative, I.227.
iung, *see* **geong**

K
kasere, *see* **casere**

L
la, *interj.*, now: II.188.
lac, *nt./f.*, sacrifice: *a.p.*, I.266.
laf, *f.*, remainder; **to lafe**, left,
remaining: I.266.
lagon, *see* **licgan**
lam, *nt.*, clay: *a.s.*, II.214.
land, *nt.*, land: ~**e** *d.s.*, I.2, 62; III.43.
landar, *f.*, landed estate: ~**e** *a.s.*, I.58.
lange, *adv.*, long, for a long time: II.224;
(w. swa) II.34, 92, 156, 217; III.11, 15,
84.
gelangian, *wv.2*, to summon: *inf.*, I.86;
II.149.
langsum, *adj.*, long, long-lasting: *n.s.nt.*,
III.154; *n.s.f.*, I.101; *a.s.nt.*, I.92; ~**re**

d.s.f., I.248; ~**um** *d.p.nt.*, I.86; II.105.
lar, *f.*, doctrine, instruction, learning,
teaching: ~**e** *a.s.*, II.5, 68, 100; III.92;
d.s., I.4, 61, 134; III.6.
larboc, *f.*, book of instruction: *a.s.*,
I.137.
lareow, *m.*, teacher: ~**e** *d.s.*, III.20.
laþ, *adj.*, hateful: ~**an** *d.s.f.wk.*, I.258.
laþ, *nt.*, harm, enmity: ~**e** *d.s.*, II.25.
gelaþian, *wv.2*, to invite: **gelaþod** *pp.*,
(uninfl.) I.71.
gelæccan, *wv.1*, to seize, snatch:
gelæhte *pret.ind.3s.*, III.182, 195;
pret.subj.3s., I.261; **gelæht** *pp.*,
(uninfl.) III.165.
(ge)lædan, *wv.1*, to lead, take: *inf.*,
I.132, 176, etc.; II.161, 247; III.159,
223; **læddest** *pret.ind.2s.*, I.246; **lædde**
pret.ind.3s., I.169; II.163, 180;
læddon *pret.ind.3p.*, III.166; **gelæd**
pp., *(n.s.m.)* I.204, 214; ~**de** *(n.p.m.)*
II.194.
læfan, *wv.1*, to leave (behind): **læfdon**
pret.ind.3p., I.57; **læfed** *pp.*, *(uninfl.)*
I.58.
læg, *see* **licgan**
gelæt(e), *see* **gelæccan**
læran, *wv.1*, to instruct: **lærde**,
pret.ind.3s., II.34; III.147; **gelæred**
pp., *(n.s.m.)* I.3; (ii) *adj.*, learned:
~**um** *(d.s.m.)* III.88.
læs, see **þe læs þe**
gelæstan, *wv.1*, to fulfil: **gelæste**
pres.subj.3s., I.125.
lætan, *sv.7*, to let, allow, leave: **læt**
imp.s., I.196; III.184, 191; **let**
pret.ind.3s., I.248; II.49.
lead, *nt.*, lead: ~**e** *d.s.*, II.243; III.131.
leaden, *adj.*, made of lead, leaden: ~**um**
d.p.f., II.204.
leaf, *nt.*, leaf: ~**um** *d.p.*, I.178.
leaf, *f.*, permission: ~**a** *d.s.*, I.185.
geleafa, *m.*, belief, faith: *n.s.*, II.43; ~**n**
a.s., II.49, 139, 191; III.20, 152, etc.;
d.s., I.79, 137, etc.; II.5, 64, etc.;
III.84, 91, etc.
geleafful, *adj.*, believing, faithful: *n.m.s.*,
II.39; ~**lan** *a.p.m.wk.*, II.258; III.243;

~**le** *a.s.nt.*, III.179; *a.p.m.*, I.310.
leas, *adj.*, false: ~**an** *d.s.m.wk.*, I.114;
~**um** *d.p.m.wk.*, II.201; *d.p.nt.*,
III.243; *d.p.nt.wk.*, I.78.
leasung, *f.*, falsehood: ~**a** *d.s.*, I.160.
lecgan, *wv.1*, to lay: **lede** *pret.ind.3s.*,
II.245, 246; **ledon** *pret.ind.3p.*,
III.112.
lede, ledon, *see* **lecgan**
leng, *adv.* (*comp.* of **lange**), longer:
III.138.
leo, *m./f.*, lion: *n.s.*, III.177 *(m./f.)*, 181
(m.), 181 *(f.)*, 185 *(f.)*, 188 *(f.)*, 206
(f.); 210 *(f.)*; ~**n** *a.s.f.*, III.81, 211;
g./d.s.f., III.195*; *a.p.m./f.*, I.290; ~**na**
g.p., III.177.
[leod], *f.*, people, nation: ~**a** *n.p.*,
III.202.
leof, *adj.*, dear, beloved: *n.s.m (voca-
tive)*, II.158; *n.s.nt.*, II.62; ; ~**a**
n.s.m.wk., II.22; ~**an** *a.s.m.wk.*, I.83;
d.s.m.wk., I.214; *d.p.m.wk.*, I.73;
~**estan** *superl.d.p.m.wk.*, I.266.
leofodon, see **lybban**
leogan, *sv.2*, to lie, speak falsely: **lyhst**
pres.ind.2s., II.239.
leoht, *nt.*, light: *n.s.*, I.40, 154, etc.;
III.118; *a.s.*, III.120; ~**es** *g.s.*, II.190;
~**e** *d.s.*, I.159; III.13, 14, 172.
leoht, *adj.*, bright, agile: ~**um** *d.s.nt.*,
III.9.
leohtfæt, *nt.*, lamp: ~**fatum** *d.p.*, III.118.
leohtleas, *adj.*, lightless: ~**um** *d.s.nt.*,
III.25.
(ge)leornian, *wv.2*, to learn: **leornode**
pret.ind.1s., III.11; *pret.ind.3s.*, III.9,
19, 53, 88; **leornodon** *pret.ind.1p.*,
II.169; III.151; **gelornod** *pp.*, *(uninfl.)*
III.8.
gelettan, *wv.1*, to hinder: **gelette**
pret.ind.3s., III.218.
lic, *nt.*, body: *a.s.*, I.195; *n.p.*, I.152, 310;
~**e** *d.s.*, I.308; II.9; III.112.
gelic, *adj.*, like, similar to (w. *d.*): *n.s.nt.*,
II.228.
liccian, *wv.2*, to lick: **liccodon**
pret.ind.3p., I.293.
gelice, *adv.*, likewise: I.39.

licgan, *sv.5*, to lie (down): *inf.*, II.256;
III.138; **liþ** *pres.ind.3s.*, II.96, 213;
læg *pret.ind.3s.*, II.249; III.41, 112,
etc.; **lagon** *pret.ind.3p.*, I.23, 152;
II.151, 206; III.231.
lichama, *m.*, body: *n.s.*, I.279; II.18, 80;
~**n** *a.s.*, III.167; *d.s.*, II.250, 253; *n.p.*,
I.284; *a.p.*, I.279.
lician, *wv.2*, to please (w. *d.*): **licaþ**
pres.ind.3s., II.45, 67.
gelicnyss, *f.*, likeness: ~**e** *d.s.*, II.79, 197.
lif, *nt.*, life: *n.s.*, II.101, 103, 104, 105;
a.s., I.35; II.239; ~**es** *g.s.*, I.166;
II.192; ~**e** *d.s.*, I.50, 57, etc.; II.4, 62,
etc.; III.91, 234, 237; **on life**, while
alive: I.73; II.23.
geliffæstan, *wv.1*, to endow with life:
gelyffæste, *pret.ind.3s.*, II.116.
lifigendan, *see* **lybban**
lifleast, *f.*, death: ~**e** *a.s.*, II.99.
lig, *m.*, fire: *n.s.*, I.242.
liget, *m./nt.*, lightning: *n.s.*, I.303.
lilie, *wk.f.*, lily: *n.s.*, I.23; II.81; ~**an** *g.s.*,
II.54, 73, 80.
lim, *m.*, lime: ~**e** *d.s.*, II.245, 246.
lim, *nt.*, limb: ~**mum** *d.p.*, III.179.
gelimpan, *sv.3*, to happen: **gelamp**
pret.ind.3s., I.56, 303; III.230.
liþ, *m./nt.*, limb: ~**a** *a.p.*, I.293.
liþe, *adj.*, lithe: **liþra** (where ~*re* is
expected) *d.s.f.*, I.293.
loca hu, *interj.*, however: I.189.
lof, *nt.*, praise: *n.s.*, III.249; ~**e** *d.s.*,
II.221.
gelogian, *wv.2*, to arrange; **gelogod** *pp.*,
~**e** *(n.p.nt.)* II.42.
gelome, *adv.*, frequently, repeatedly:
II.9, 142, 221, 260; III.39, 101, 229.
losian, *wv.2*, to be lost, perish: **losige**
pres.subj.2s., III.72; *pres.subj.3s.*,
II.64; **losode** *pret.ind.3s.*, I.261;
losodon *pret.ind.3p.*, I.266.
lufian, *wv.2*, to love: **lufiaþ** *pres.ind.1p.*,
I.32; **lufast**, *pres.ind.2s.*, II.24, 60;
lufaþ *pres.ind.3s.*, II.25, 59; **lufodest**
pret.ind.2s., III.67; **lufode**
pret.ind.3s., III.49; **lufodon**
pret.ind.3p., III.9.

lufigend, *m.*, lover: *n.s.*, I.31.
lufu, *f.*, love: ~**e** *a.s.*, II.4; *d.s.*, I.11, 13, etc.; II.22.
lust, *m.*, desire, pleasure: ~**um** *d.p.*, III.93.
lustbære, *adj.*, joyful: *n.p.m.*, I.82–83.
lybban, *wv.3*, to live: **leofast**, *pres.ind.2s.*, II.24; **leofode** *pret.ind.1s.*, III.15; *pret.ind.3s.*, II.258; III.76; **leofodon** *pret.ind.1p.*, II.85; *pret.ind.3p.*, III.83; **lyfedan** *pret.ind.3p.*, I.185; **lifigende**, **lyfigende** *pres. part.*, ~**dan** *(a.s.m.wk.)* I.130–31, 254; II.35, 117; III.197; ~**um** *(d.s.m.)* II.47.
gelyfan, *wv.1*, to believe; w. **on**, to believe in: *inf.*, I.281; III.197; **to gelyfanne** *infl. inf.*, I.128, II.46 (**gelyfenne**); III.82 (**gelyfenne**); **gelyfaþ** *imp.p.*, III.202; **gelyfa** *pres.ind.1s.*, I.147; **gelyfe**, *pres.ind.1s.*, I.216; *pres.subj.1s.*, II.28; *pres.ind.3s.*, III.200; **gelyfst**, *pres.ind.2s.*, II.30, 45 (w. g. object); **gelyfaþ** *pres.ind.1p.*, II.218; *pres.ind.3p.*, I.129; **gelyfdest** *pret.ind.2s.*, II.68; **gelyfde** *pret.ind.3s.*, I.130, 253; II.34, 203; III.158; **gelyfdan** *pret.ind.3p.*, I.264; **gelyfdon**, II.186; III.147.
lyfedan, *see* **lybban**
gelyffæste, *see* **geliffæstan**
lystan, *wv.1* (*impers.* w. *d.* or *a.*), to please: **lyst** *pres.ind.3s.*, I.27.
lytel, *adj.*, (i) little: ~**ne** *a.s.m.*, III.26; (ii) lesser: **lytlan** *n.p.m.wk.*, III.82.

M

ma, *adv.* (*comp. of* **micle**), more: I.242.
gemacca, *m./f.*, spouse: **gemacan** *d.s.*, I.10, 17.
macian, *wv.2*, to make: *inf.*, II.75; **macaþ** *pres.ind.3s.*, III.140.
magan, *pret. pres. v.*, (i) to be able, can (w. *inf.*): **miht** *pres.ind.2s.*, II.31, 81, etc.; **mæg** *pres.ind.3s.*, I.189; **magon** *pres.ind.3p.*, I.99, 112; III.199; *pres.subj.3p.*, III.45; **mage**

pres.subj.1p., I.116; *pres.subj.2p.*, III.198; **mihtest** *pret.ind.2s.*, III.67, 128; **mihte** *pret.ind.3s.*, I.139, 240, 289; II.199; III.7, 48, etc.; *pret.subj.1s.*, II.33; *pret.subj.3s.*, II.32, 112; III.108, 187; *pret.subj.1p.*, II.102; **mihton** *pret.subj.3p.*, I.124; II.75; III.232; (ii) to be good for (w. **to**): **mihton** *pret.ind.3p.*, II.245, 246.
magas, *see* **mæg**
man, mann (i) *m.*, man, person, human being: *n.s.*, I.77, 105, etc.; II.22, 58, 296; III.2, 187, 189; ~**es** *g.s.*, I.126, 195; II.228; **men** *d.s.*, II.123, 124; III.146, 188; *n.p.*, I.142, 168; III.90, 94, 217; *a.p.*, I.171; II.149; III.81,217; **menn** *d.s.*, II.47, 104; *n.p.*, I.194, 229; *a.p.*, I.190, 310; **manna** *g.p.*, I.152, 290; II.220; **mannum** *d.p.*, I.57, 188, 272; II.152, 221, 246; III.137, 155, 192, 197;
(ii) *indef. pron.*, one, someone: **man** *n.s.*, I.261; II.146, 162, etc.; III.7, 40, etc.
man, *nt.*, sin: *a.s.*, II.175.
gemana, *m.*, sexual intercourse: ~**n** *a.s.*, II.11.
manega, ~**ra**, ~**um**, *see* **manig**
manful, *adj.*, wicked, evil: ~**la** *n.s.m.wk.*, I.75, 92, 285; II.147, 156, 163; III.222; ~**lan** *d.s.m.wk.*, III.165; *a.p.m.wk.*, I.103, 294, 304; II.161; *d.p.m.wk.*, III.174; ~**ra** *g.p.m.*, I.305.
manfulnyss, *f.*, wickedness: ~**e** *d.s.*, I.281.
manig, *adj.*, many: **manega** *n.p.m.*, I.229; II.200; III.92; *a.p.m.*, I.97 (1st instance); III.77; *a.p.nt.*, III.241; *a.p.f.*, I.60, 97 (2nd instance), 291; **manegra** *g.p.m.*, I.14; **manegum** *d.p.nt.*, II.145; III.118.
mansliht, *m.*, murder: ~**as** *a.p.*, III.77.
maran, *see* **mære**
Maria, *proper name*, Mary: *n.*, I.41; ~**n** *a.*, I.52; *g.*, I.44.
Martianus, *proper name*, Martianus: *n.*, I.75, 85, etc.; ~**es** *g.*, I.152, 296; ~**e** *d.*, I.118, 128, etc.

martyr, *m.*, martyr: ~**as** *n.p.*, III.231,
240, 245; *a.p.*, II.147; ~**a** *g.p.*, I.90;
~**um** *d.p.*, I.291; II.171, 177.
martyrdom, *m.*, martyrdom: ~**e** *d.s.*,
I.222; III.165.
gemartyrian, *wv.2*, to martyr: **gemarty-
rode** *pret.ind.3s.*, II.145; **gemartyrod**
pp., *(n.s.m.)* III.171; ~**e** *(n.p.m.)*
II.69; III.156, 239.
Maurus, *proper name*, Maurus: *n.*,
III.148.
maþa, *m.*, maggot, worm: **maþon** *d.p.*,
I.153.
Maximus, *proper name*, Maximus: *n.*,
II.163, 165, etc.
mæden, *nt.*, virgin, maiden: *n.s.*, II.1, 21,
etc.; III.56, 196; *a.s.*, I.10, 13, etc.;
II.14; III.55, 179, 194; ~**e** *d.s.*, I.15,
29, etc.; II.27, 32, etc.; III.59, 181;
n.p., III.48; *a.p.*, III.54; ~**u** *n.p.*, I.66;
III.92; ~**a** *a.p.*, II.258; III.36, 40; *g.p.*,
I.51; ~**um** *d.p.*, I.300.
mædenlic, *adj.*, of virgins: ~**um** *d.s.m.*,
I.42.
mæg, *m.*, kinsman, parent: **magas** *n.p.*,
I.18; III.28; **maga** *g.p.*, III.149;
magum *d.p.*, I.3.
mægenþrymnyss, *f.*, majesty: ~**e** *d.s.*,
II.120.
mægþ, *f.*, family: ~**e** *g.s.*, II.224; III.57.
mægþhad, *m.*, virginity: *n.s.*, I.203; ~**e**
d.s., I.31, 34, etc.; II.25; III.68, 89.
mærcode, *see* **mearcian**
mære, *adj.*, glorious: *n.s.m.*, I.252; ~**an**
a.s.m.wk., I.142; *d.s.m.wk.*, I.204;
II.259; ~**s** *g.s.nt.*, I.166.
mærsian, *wv.2*, to glorify: **mærsast**
pres.ind.2s., III.192.
mærþ, *f.*, glorious act: *n.s.*, III.137.
mæsse, *wk.f.*, mass: **mæssan** *a.p.*, I.167.
mæssepreost, *m.*, priest, mass-priest:
a.s., I.166; III.18; ~**e** *d.s.*, I.168; 171
(~**æ**).
mæssian, *wv.2*, to celebrate mass:
mæssode *pret.ind.3s.*, II.221.
mearcian, *wv.2*, to mark: **mærcode**
pret.ind.3s., I.126.
meder, *see* **modor**

mennisc, *adj.*, human: ~**re** *d.s.f.*, II.127.
mergen, *m.*, morning: *a.s.*, II.72.
gemetan, *wv.1*, to find: **gemetaþ**
pres.ind.1p., II.99.
mete, *m.*, food: ~**tum** *d.p.*, II.106.
mettum, *see previous entry*
micel, **mycel** *adj.*, great: *n.s.m.*, I.107,
305; *n.s.nt.*, I.154, 252; III.118;
n.s.m./nt., I.303; *n.s.f.*, III.239, 243;
~**e** *n.s.f.wk.*, III.121; *a.s.f.*, II.4; ~**re**
d.s.f., I.118, 224, 228; II.167; ~**clum**
d.s.m., I.107; *d.s.nt.*, I.185; ~**clan**
a.s.f.wk., III.81; *d.s.nt.wk.*, III.230;
d.s.f.wk., I.230; ~**e** *a.p.f.*, I.291; *see
also* **mycclum**.
mid, *prep. w. d.*, with, because of, filled
with: I.12, 15, etc.; II.5, 9, etc.; III.4, 9
(2x), etc.; **mid ealle**, *adv.*, entirely:
I.46, 122, etc.; **mid þam**, *adv.*, at that,
subsequently: III.54; **mid þam þe**,
conj., when: I.211–12; II.196; III.47.
middaneard, *m.*, the world: *a.s.*, I.49; ~**e**
d.s., I.66, 72.
middaneardlic, *adj.*, of the world: ~**e**
a.s.f., I.45.
migga (**micga**), *wk.m.*, urine: *n.s.*, I.108,
109; ~**n** *d.s.m.*, III.108.
miht, *f.*, power: *n.s.*, I.199; II.228;
III.121, 137; ~**e** *a.s.*, I.271; II.226,
227; III.106, 109, etc.; ~**e** *d.s.*, III.130;
~**a** *a.p.*, II.234; (ii) greatness: *n.s.*,
II.231.
mihtig, *adj.*, poweful: ~**e** *n.p.m.*, III.140.
mildsung, *f.*, mercy: ~**a** *a.s.*, I.280.
min, *poss. adj.*, my: *n.s.m.*, II.18 (2nd
instance), 22, etc.; *n.s.f.*, I.235; II.18
(1st instance); *a.s.m.*, I.143; ~**ne**
a.s.m., I.184, 227; III.66; ~**e** *a.s.f.*,
II.78, 226; *a.p.f.*, II.234; ~**um** *d.s.m.*,
I.150, 214, etc.; III.124; ~**re** *d.s.f.*,
I.13, 49; III.44, 185; *see also* **ic**.
mislic, *adj.*, various: ~**um** *d.p.nt.*, III.97,
171.
mislice, *adv.*, in various ways: I.285.
mod, *nt.*, mind, spirit: *a.s.*, I.45; III.38,
88; ~**e** *d.s.*, I.82, 141, etc.; II.175;
III.10, 43, 65, 69.
modelice, *adv.*, proudly: II.234, 236.

modig, *adj.*, proud: *n.s.nt.*, II.106.

modignyss, *f.*, pride: *n.s.*, II.235; ~**e** *a.s.*, II.236; *d.s.*, II.228.

modor, *f.*, mother: *n.s.*, I.41 (**modur**), 60, 141, etc.; *a.s.*, I.248; *g.s.*, I.228 (**meder**); *d.s.*, I.52 (**meder**), 259 (**modor**).

modur, *see* **modor**

morþcræft, *f.*, destructive art: ~**e** *g.s.*, III.121.

morþdæd, *f.*, destructive deed: ~**a** *a.p.*, III.78.

motan, *pret .pres. v.*, to be allowed to, may: **most** *pres.ind.2s.*, III.29; **mote** *pres.subj.2s.*, II.182; **moton** *pres.ind.3p.*, III.245; **moste** *pret.ind.3s.*, II.146; *pret.subj.3s.*, I.10, 77; II.13; III.166; **moston** *pret.subj.3p.*, III.152.

motian, *wv.2*, to dispute: **motodon**, *pret.ind.3p.*, II.156, 224.

munuc, *m.*, monk: **muneca** *g.p.*, I.60; **munecum** *d.p.*, I.73.

mycclum, **micclum** *adv.*, greatly: I.17, 218; III.59; **swa micclum. . . swa micclum swa** as much. . . as much as, III.145–46; *see also* **micel**.

myltestre, *f.*, prostitute: ~**ena** *g.p.*, III.174.

gemyltsian, *wv.2* (w. *d.*), to have mercy: *inf.*, I.100; **gemiltsode** *pret.subj.3s.*, I.251.

gemynd, *nt.*, memory: *n.s.*, II.124; ~**e** *d.s.*, II.109.

mynecen, *f.*, nun: ~**a** *a.p.*, I.60.

mynegung, *f.*, exhortation: ~**um** *d.p.*, I.45.

mynster, *nt.*, monastery: *a.s.*, I.59.

N

na, *adv.*, not: II.236; III.32, 222.

nabban, *wv.3*, (= ne habban) not to have: **næfst**, *pres.ind.2s.*, II.160; **næfþ** *pres.ind.3s.*, I.30.

nacod, *adj.*, naked: ~**um** *d.s.nt.*, III.111.

naht, (i) *indef. pron.*, nothing: *a.s.*, I.253; (ii) *adv.*, not at all: I.108.

nama, *m.*, name: *n.s.*, I.135; ~**n** *a.s.*,

I.161; *d.s.*, I.173, 175 (or *a.*); II.248.

namcuþlice, *adv.*, individually: II.119.

namian, *wv.2*, to mention, mention by name: **namast** *pres.ind.2s.*, II.118.

nan, (i) *adj.*, no: *n.s.m.*, I.77, 139, etc.; II.58, 257; III.7, 186, 202; *n.s.nt.*, I.41; II.61; *n.s.f.*, I.305; III.237; *a.s.nt.*, I.30, 306; **nænne** *a.s.m.*, I.30,179; III.24; ~**es** *g.s.m.*, I.27; (ii) *pron.*, none: *n.s.m.*, I.82.

Nason, *proper name*, Nason (for Iason, i.e. Jason): *n.*, III.148.

nast, *see* **nytan**

naþor ne. . . ne *conj.*, neither. . . nor: I.236.

næddre, *wk.f.*, serpent: ~**an** *a.s.*, III.82; *a.p.*, III.40, 44.

næfre, *adv.*, never: I.127, 179, 253; II.57; III.124.

næran, see **beon**

næs, *see* **beon**

ne, *adv.*, not, nor: I.10, 27, etc.; II.3, 13, etc.; III.7, 19, etc.

geneadian, *wv. 2*, to compel, urge: **geneadod** *pp.*, *(uninfl.)* II.209.

nehgebur, *m.*, neighbour: ~**as** *a.p.*, III.80.

nellan, *anom. v.*, (= ne willan) to be unwilling: **nelle** *pres.ind.1s.*, I.214; III.14; *pres.subj.2s.*, I.149; **nellaþ** *pres.ind.2p.*, III.198; **nolde** *pret.ind.3s.*, I.281; **noldon** *pret.ind.3p.*, III.214; *pret.subj.3p.*, II.167; III.98.

neod, *f.*, need: *n.s.*, III.237.

neorxnewang, *m.*, Paradise: ~**e** *d.s.*, II.57.

geneosian, *wv.2*, to visit: **geneosode** *pret.ind.3p.*, I.167.

next, *adj.*, last: **æt nextan**, at last, finally: III.62.

niht, *f.*, night: *a.s.*, I.169; II.182, 185, 250; *a.p.*, I.7, 235; ~**e** *d.s.*, I.9.

nihtes, *adv.*, by night: II.5.

(ge)niman, *sv.4*, to take, receive, get: *inf.*, III.159, 213; **nim** *imp.s.*, I.187; **nime** *pres.subj.3s.*, II.215; **genam** *pret.ind.1s.*, II.57; **genamon** *pret.ind.3p.*, I.216.

nolde, *see* **nellan**

nu, (i) *adv.*, now: I.25, 27, etc.; II.8, 33, etc.; III.15 (2nd instance), 44, etc.; (ii) *conj.*, now that, since: III.15 (1st instance), 118.

Numerianus, *proper name*, Numerian: *n.*, III.1, 157, 222.

nydbehefe, *adj.*, necessary: *n.s.m.*, I.106.

nytan, *pret. pres. v.*, (= **ne witan**) not to know: **nat**, *pres.ind.1s.*, III.199; **nast** *pres.ind.2s.*, II.226, 233; **nyston** *pret.ind.3p.*, III.180.

O

of, *prep. w. d.*, from, of, out of, made of: I.2, 30, etc.; II.109, 131, etc.; III.33, 49, etc.

ofaxian, *wv.2*, to discover: *inf.*, II.146; **ofaxode**, *pret.ind.3s.*, II.149, 202; III.17.

ofdræd, *adj.*, frightened: **~dan** *d.s.m.wk.*, III.188.

ofer, *prep. w. a./d.*, over, throughout: I.60 (2x), 68, 202, 355; II.250.

ofercuman, *sv.4*, to overcome: **ofercom** *pret.ind.3s.*, III.54.

oferswiþan, *wv.1*, to defeat: **oferswiþde** *pret.ind.3s.*, III.123; **oferswiþod** *pp.*, *(uninfl.)* I.43.

(ge)offrian, *wv.2*, to offer: *inf.*, II.162, 209; III.98, 214; **geoffra**, *imp.s.*, II.240; **geoffrige** *pres.subj.2s.*, I.94; **geoffrode** *pret.subj.3s.*, I.78; **geoffrodon** *pret.subj.3p.*, I.267; **geoffrod** *pp.*, *(n.s.m.)* I.88.

offrung, *f.*, sacrifice, offering: **~um** *d.p.*, III.127.

ofhreosan, *sv.2*, to bury: **ofhroren** *pp.*, **~e** *(n.p.m./nt.)* III.234.

ofhroren *see* **ofhreosan**

ofslean, *sv.6*, to kill: *inf.*, I.149; II.154; **to ofsleanne** *infl. inf.*, II.233; **ofslea**, *pres.ind.1s.*, II.29; **ofsloge** *pret.subj.3s.*, II.163; **ofslagen** *pp.*, *(n.s.m.)* II.214; *(n.s.m./f.)* III.208; **~e** *(n.p.m.)* I.297, 304; II.168, 174, 196; III.164. *(n.p.nt.)* II.151.

oft, *adv.*, often: III.101.

[ofþefian], *wv.2*, to dry up: **ofþefod** *pp.*, *(n.s.nt.)* II.106.

ofþyncan, *wv.1*, to offend (w. *d.*): **ofþuhte** *pret.ind.3s.*, II.225.

olæcan, *wv.1*, to flatter, treat well, give pleasure to: *inf.*, III.29; **olæcst** *pres.ind.2s.*, I.97.

on, *prep. w. a./d.*, in, into, on: I.1, 2, etc., II.1, 2, etc.; III.1, 7, etc.

on, *adv.*, in: III.175.

onælan, *wv.1*, to burn: **onæl** *imp.s.*, I.188.

onbryrdnyss, *f.*, zeal: **~e** *d.s.*, I.161–62.

oncnawan, *sv.7*, (i) to learn, understand: **oncneow** *pret.ind.1s.*, III.143; (ii) to know **oncnawe** *pres.subj.2s.*, III.145; **oncneowan** *pret.ind.3p.*, III.211.

ondrædan, *sv.7*, to fear, be afraid of (w. *d. refl. pron.* and *g.* object): *inf.*, II.102.

onfon, *sv.7*, to take: *inf.*, I.17.

ongean, *prep. w. d./a.*, towards: III.103, 112.

ongean, *adv.*, back: I.186, 214; II.140.

onlihtan, *wv.1*, to give light, illuminate: **onlihte** *pret.ind.3s.*, I.131; **onliht** *pp.*, *(n.s.nt.)* III.176.

onsægednyss, *f.*, sacrifice: **~e** *a.s.*, I.78; II.241.

onscunian, *wv.2*, to shun, avoid: **onscuniaþ** *pres.ind.1p.*, II.237; **onscunode** *pret.ind.3s.*, III.40.

onsundran, *adv.*, separately, apart: III.173.

ontendan, *wv.1*, to set on fire, to kindle: *inf.*, I.241; III.204.

ontendnyss, *f.*, burning desire, burning: **~e** *a.s.*, I.12; *d.s.*, I.224; *a.p.*, I.22.

onuppan, *prep. w. d.*, on top of: III.233.

geopenian, *wv.2*, to open: **geopenade** *pret.ind.3s.*, I.169–70.

openlice, *adv.*, openly: II.239.

orhlice, *adv.*, arrogantly: II.225.

ormæte, *adj.*, (i) enormous, heavy, huge: *n.p.m.*, I.210; **~an** *d.s.m.wk.*, III.79; **ormettre** *d.s.f.*, I.76; (ii) great, intense: **~an** *d.s.f.wk.*, III.113.

orsorh, *adj.*, without anxiety: *n.s.m./f.*,
III.208.

geortruwian, *wv. 2*, to despair:
geortruwad *pp.*, desperate: *(n.s.m.)*
I.226.

oþ, *prep. w. d./a.*, up to, until: II.85;
III.97, 247; *see also* **oþ þæt**.

oþer, *adj.* and *pron.*, other, another:
n.s.m., II.29, 85, 88, 94; III.187, 202;
n.s.nt., II.101, 103; *a.s.nt.*, I.59; **~ne**
a.s.m., II.55, 157; **oþre** *n.p.m.*, I.229,
266; *a.p.m.*, III.217; *g.p.m.*, I.14;
oþrum *d.s.nt.*, II.128, 178; *d.p.m.*
I.188; II.164; *d.p.f.*, I.52; III.73;
oþer. . . oþer, one thing. . . another:
II.235.

oþ þæt, *conj.*, until: I.62, 222, 243; II.34,
71, etc.; III.10, 12, etc.; *see also* **hwile**.

oþþe, *conj.*, or: I.77, 98, 99; II.11, 45,
etc.; III.75, 79.

oxa, *m.*, ox: **~n** *a.s.*, III.110.

P

papa, *m.*, pope: *n.s.*, II.37, 48, etc.; **~n**
d.s., II.35, 136, 137, 259.

pæll, *m.*, silk cloth, rich cloth: **~um** *d.p.*,
III.35.

pearruc, *m.*, enclosure: **~e** *d.s.*, III.177.

plega, *m.*, play, playing: **~n** *d.s.*, III.37,
45.

pliht, *m./f.*, danger, risk: **~e** *d.s.*, III.22.

Polemius, *proper name*, Polemius: *n.*,
III.3, 58.

preost, *m.*, priest: *n.s.*, I.297; **~e** *d.s.*,
I.255; III.19; **~um** *d.p.*, II.187.

R

race, *f.*, account: *n.s.*, I.101.

[racentege, -teah], *f.*, chain: **~teagum**
d.p., I.133, 223; III.114–15.

ranc, *adj.*, showy: **~e** *a.p.nt.*, III.36.

raþe, *adv.*, quickly: I.56.

ræadaþ, *see* **readian**

ræcþ, *see* **rec(c)an**

ræd, *m.*, (i) counsel, advice: **~e** *d.s.*,
I.236; II.152; (ii) benefit, advantage:
a.s., III.24.

rædan, *wv.1*, to read: *inf.*, I.48, II.41; **to**

rædene *infl. inf.*, II.44; **rædde**,
pret.ind.3s., I.48.

rædbora, *m.*, adviser ('counsel-bearer'
for Latin *assessor* 'aide'): *n.s.*, II.157;
III.53.

ræding, *f.*, reading: **~e** *d.s.*, I.52.

readian, *wv.2*, to be or become red:
ræadaþ *pres.ind.3s.*, II.79.

readnyss, *f.*, redness: **~e** *d.s.*, II.54.

reaf, *nt.*, clothing, garment: **~um** *d.p.*,
III.34.

[rec(c)an], *wv.1*, to care about (w. *g.*):
ræcþ *pres.ind.3s.*, I.227; **rohte**
pret.ind.3s., I.81.

gereccan, *wv.1*, to narrate: **to gerec-
cenne** *infl. inf.*, I.101.

gerefa, *m.*, officer: *n.s.*, III.220.

reppan, *see* **hreppan**

rest, *f.*, rest: *n.s.*, II.111.

reþe, *adj.*, fierce, cruel: *n.s.m.*, II.144;
n.s.f., I.62; II.2; III.188; *a.p.nt.*, I.289;
~an *g.s.m.wk.*, I.82; *d.s.n.wk.*, II.158;
n.p.nt.wk., I.291; **~um** *d.p.nt.wk.*,
I.286.

reþnyss, *f.*, ferocity: *n.s.*, I.289.

rice, *nt.*, kingdom: *d.s.*, I.32, 89; II.2.

rihtlice, *adv.*, rightly: II.102.

rihtwis, *adj.*, righteous: **~a** *n.s.m.wk.*,
II.192; **~um** *d.p.m.*, II.111.

rixian, *wv.2*, to reign: **rixaþ** *pres.ind.3s.*,
II.261; **rixiaþ** *pres.ind.3p.*, III.234;
rixode *pret.ind.3s.*, III.1.

rodetacen, *nt.*, sign of the cross: **~tacne**
d.s., I.126.

rohte, *see* **rec(c)an**

Romani, *m.p.*, the Romans: **Romana**
g.p., II.2.

Romanisc, *adj.*, Roman: **~an** *n.p.m.wk.*,
III.5; *n.p.f.wk.*, III.202.

Romeburh, *f.*, city of Rome: **Romebyrig**
g.s., III.95; *d.s.*, II.144; III.2.

rose, *wk.f.*, rose: *n.s.*, I.24, II.81; **~an**
g.s., II.54, 74, 79.

ryman, to make way for (w. *d.* of pers.):
inf., III.193.

ryne, *m.*, course: *a.s.*, II.191.

S

sace, *see* **sacu**

sacerd, *m.*, priest: ~**um** *d.p.*, I.274; II.185.

sacu, *f.*, strife: **sace** *a.s.*, III.94.

sagol, *m.*, club: *n.s.*, I.104; **saglum** *d.p.*, I.104; II.157.

samcucu, *adj.*, half-dead: ~**e** *a.s.f.*, II.256.

samod, *adv.*, together, at the same time, as well: I.87, 274, 284, 296; II.29, 69; III.96, 115, 164, 205.

sanct, *m.*, saint: *n.s.*, II.9; *a.s.*, II.205.

sand, *f.*, dish of food: ~**a** *a.p.*, III.39 (2x).

sand, *f.*, sending: ~**e** *a.s.*, III.178.

sandpytt, *m.*, sandpit: ~**e** *d.s.*, III.223–24.

sang, *m.*, song: ~**um** *d.p.*, II.16.

(ge)sang, *see* **singan**

sar, *nt.*, physical pain: ~**um** *d.p.*, II.105.

sarnyss, *f.*, sorrow: ~**e** *a.s.*, I.144; *d.s.*, I.228.

Saturnus, *proper name*, Saturn: *n.*, III.74.

sawl, *f.*, soul: ~**a** *n.p.*, II.174, 178; *a.p.*, II.271 (2x).

sæ, *f.* (*indecl.*) sea: *d.s.*, III.159.

sæcgaþ, *see* **secgan**

(ge)sæd, *see* **secgan**

gesælig, *adj.*, blessed: ~**an** *a.s.m.wk.*, II.139.

gesælþ, *f.*, prosperity: ~**a** *a.p.*, II.141.

gesceadwis, *adj.*, rational: ~**a** *n.s.m.wk.*, III.189.

gesceaft, *f.*, created thing: ~**a** *a.p.*, II.116; *g.p.*, II.114.

sceal, *pret. pres. v.*, must, ought; (w. *inf.*) ought to, will, shall, must, should: **scealt** *pres.ind.2s.*, III.190; **sceall** *pres.ind.3s.*, I.3, 11, 227; **sceolan** *pres.ind.2p.*, II.68; **sceole** *pres.subj.2p.*, I.277; **sceolde** *pret.ind.3s.*, II.257; *pret.subj.3s.*, I.4, 10, 109; II.94, 209; **sceoldon**, *pret.ind.3p.*, III.38.

sceanca, *m.*, leg: ~**n** *a.p.*, III.104.

sceandlic, *adj.*, shameful: ~**an** *a.p.m.wk.*, III.175; ~**um** *d.p.m.wk.*, I.138.

scearpe, *adj.*, sharp: *n.p.f.*, I.210.

gesceop, *see* **gescyppan**

scinan, *sv.1*, to shine, glitter: **scean** *pret.ind.3s.*, I.40, 154, 252; III.118; **scinende** *pres. part.*, II.197; *(n.p.m.)* II.54, 82; *(a.p.m.)* II.81; ~**an** *(a.s.m.wk.)* II.31, 33; ~**um** *(d.s.nt.)* I.41; *(d.p.m.)* III.63.

scincræft, *m.*, sorcery, magic: *a.s.*, III.108, 242.

scortost, *adj.*, (*superl.* of **scort**), shortest: ~**an** *a.s.f.wk.*, I.101.

scræf, *nt.*, cave: **scræfes** *g.s.*, III.232; **screfe** *d.s.*, III.231.

(ge)scrydan, *wv.1*, to clothe: *inf.*, III.136; **gescrydde** *pret.ind.3s.*, II.9; III.34 (**scrydde**).

scyld, *m.*, offence: ~**um** *d.p.*, II.151.

gescyldan, *wv.1*, to shield: **gescylde** *pret.ind.3s.*, III.174; **gescyld**, *pp.*, (*uninfl.*) II.10.

scyldig, *adj.*, guilty: ~**ne** *a.s.m.*, II.257.

gescyndan, *wv.1*, to put to shame: **gescynd** *pp.*, (*uninfl.*) II.19.

gescyppan, *sv.6*, to create: **gesceop** *pret.ind.3s.*, II.116.

Scyppend, *m.*, Creator: ~**e** *d.s.*, I.179; II.114.

se, seo, þæt, (i) *def. art.*, the: **se** *n.s.m.*, I.8, 11, etc.; II.13, 27, etc.; III.4, 24, etc.; **þæt** *n.s.nt.*, I.23, 40, etc.; II.20, 187, etc.; III.171, 175, etc.; *a.s.nt.*, I.12, 35, etc.; II.14; III.120, 179, 193, 232; **seo** *n.s.f.*, I.62*, 66, 141, 155*, etc.; II.2, 34, 184, 230; III.113, 121, etc.; **þone**, *a.s.m.*, I.7, 35, etc.; II.28, 31, etc.; III.14, 20, etc.; **þa** *a.s.f.*, I.102, 133, etc.; II.51, 109, etc.; III.49, 81 (2x), etc.; **þæs** *g.s.m.*, I.27, 52, etc.; II.248; III.49, 150, 246, 247; *g.s.nt.*, I.243, 269; II.192; III.210, 231; **þære** *g.s.f.*, I.228; III.95, 195 (or *d.*); **þam** *d.s.m.*, I.9, 21, etc.; II.12, 35, etc.; III.1, 19, etc.; *d.s.nt.*, I.29, 35, etc.; II.4, 27, etc.; III.14, 33, etc.; **þære** *d.s.f.*, I.2, 9, etc.; I.89 (**þere**); II.164, 170; III.57, 111, etc., 195 (or *g.*); **þe** (for **þy**) *inst.s.nt.*, II.66; III.238; **þa**

siþian, *wv.2*, to travel, go: **siþiaþ** *pres.ind.1p.*, I.232; **siþode** *pret.ind.3s.*, II.136.

siþþan, syþþan, (i) *adv.*, subsequently, afterwards: I.72, 87, etc.; II.48, 129, etc.; III.61, 136, 160, 192; (ii) *conj.*, after: II.168, 178; III.30, 81, 211.

siwian, *wv.2*, to stitch, sew: **siwige** *pres.subj.3s.*, II.229.

slapan, *sv.7*, to fall asleep, sleep: **slapon** *pres.subj.3p.*, III.44; **slepon** *pret.ind.3p.*, III.47.

slæge, *see* **slege**

slæp, *m.*, sleep: **~e** *d.s.*; III.48 (**slape**); **on slæpe**, alseep: *d.s.*, II.83, 85; III.50.

slean, *sv.6*, to strike: *inf.*, II.257; **slihþ** *pres.ind.3s.*, II.24; **sloh** *pret.ind.3s.*, II.255; III.135; **sloge** *pret.subj.3s.*, II.257.

slege, *m.*, (i) blow: **slæge** *d.s.*, I.105; (ii) slaughter, death: **slege** *d.s.*, II.166, 194; III.161.

sloh, *see* **slean**

smeagan, *wv.1*, to think of, ponder: **smeade** *pret.ind.3s.*, II.5; **smeadon** *pret.ind.3p.*, I.191; II.71.

smeagung, *f.*, plan: **~e** *a.s.*, I.288.

smylting, *f.*, amber: **~a** *d.s.*, I.121.

(ge)smyrian, *wv.1/2*, to smear, grease: **gesmyred** *pp.*, **~um** *(d.s.nt.)* I.283.

snawhwhit, *adj.*, snow-white: **~e** *a.p.m.*, II.81.

snoter, *adj.*, wise: *n.s.m.*, III.13 (**snotor**), *n.s.nt.*, III.58; **~e** *n.s.nt.wk.*, II.21.

snoterlice, *adv.*, wisely: II.130.

sona, *adv.*, at once, immediately: I.39, 171, etc., II.20, 23, etc.; III.6, 28, etc.; **sona swa**, as soon as: I.303; III.100.

soþ, *adj.*, true: *n.s.m.*, I.197; III.143; **~ne** *a.s.m.*, I.98; **~um** *d.s.m.*, III.146; **~an** *d.s.m.wk.*, I.79, 256, etc.; *d.s.nt.wk.*, III.14; **~re** *d.s.f.*, I.55; II.121; **~e** *n.p.nt.*, II.172.

soþ *nt.*, truth: **~e** *d.s.*, I.160; **to soþan**, truly: II.76, 169; III.143, 202.

soþfæst, *adj.*, just: **~an** *n.p.m.wk.*, I.122.

soþfæstnyss, *f.*, truth: **~e** *g.s.*, III.13; *d.s.*, II.86.

soþlic, *adj.*, true: **~re** *comp.n.s.nt.*, II.46.

soþlice, *adv.*, indeed, truly, actually: I.10, 50, etc.; II.90, 123, etc.; III.130.

spræc, *f.*, conversation, speech, eloquence: **~e** *a.s.*, I.259; *d.s.*, I.194, 248; II.127; III.60, 185; **~um** *d.p.*, III.73.

gespræcan, *see* **gesprecan**

sprecan, *sv.5*, to speak, talk: **spræcst** *pres.ind.2s.*, II.234; **sprecaþ** *pres.ind.2p.*, II.179; **spræce** *pres.subj.2s.*, II.127; *pres.subj.3s.*, II.128; **spræc** *pret.ind.1s.*, II.236; **spræcon** *pret.ind.3p.*, II.71, 92; **sprecende** *pres. part.*, II.186.

gesprecan, *sv.1*, to speak to: *inf.*, I.235 (**gespræcan**); **gespræce** *pres.subj.3s.*, III.186; **gespræc** *pret.ind.3s.*, II.21.

stafas, *see* **stæf**

stan, *m.*, stone: *a.s.*, II.216; **~as** *n.p.*, II.242, 245.

standan, *sv.6*, (i) to come out, stand: **stodan** *pret.ind.3p.*, I.244; **standende** *pres. part.*, II.51, 52 (**standande**); (ii) to exist: **stod** *pret.ind.3s.*, II.2.

gestandan, *sv.6*, to oppose, assail: **gestodon** *pret.ind.3p.*, III.22.

stæf, *m.*, letter: **stafas** *a.p.*, II.41.

stænen, *adj.*, stone, made of stone: **~re** *d.s.f.*, II.205; **~e** *n.p.f.*, II.243; **~um** *d.p.m.wk.*, I.306.

stede, *m.*, place: *d.s.*, II.206.

steman, *wv.1*, to exude, waft: **steme** *pres.ind.3s.*, I.26; **stemde** *pret.ind.3s.*, III.177.

stemn, *f.*, voice: **~e** *d.s.*, II.218; III.200.

stenc, *m.*, (i) smell: **~e** *d.s.*, III.110; (ii) stench: *n.s.*, I.154.

gestillan, *wv.1*, to silence: *inf.*, III.71.

stincan, *sv.3*, to smell, rise (*intrans.*): **stincaþ** *pres.ind.3p.*, II.74; **stanc** *pret.ind.3s.*, I.252; **stuncon** *pret.ind.3p.*, I.153; **stincende** *pres. part.*, III.172.

gestincan, *sv.3*, to smell (*trans.*): **gestunce** *pret.ind.3s.*, I.254.

stocc, *m.*, wooden post: *a.s.*, III.104.

stow, *f.*, place: *n.s.*, I.252, 305; ~**e** *d.s.*, I.89, 90.

gestrangian, *wv.2*, to strengthen: **gestrangode** *pret.ind.3s.*, III.88.

stræt, *f.*, market-place: *d.s.*, I.194.

gestrynan, *wv.1*, to beget, to acquire: **gestrynde**, *pret.ind.3s.*, II.115; **gestryned** *pp.*, *(n.s.m.)* II.67.

sum, *adj.*, (i) a, a certain one, some: *n.s.m.*, I.1, 104; II.144, 157; III.2, 5, 53; *n.s.nt.*, II.1; *a.s.nt.*, I.18; III.55, 56; ~**e** *n.p.m.*, III.93; *a.p.m.*, I.286; *a.p.f.*, I.121 (2x); (ii) about (qualifying a number): *a.p.f.*, I.235.

sunbeam, *mf.*, sunbeam, sunshine: *n.s.f.*, I.199; III.64.

gesund, *adj.*, unharmed: *n.s.m.*, III.191; ~**ne** *a.s.m.*, I.234.

sunne, *wk.f.*, sun: ~**an** *a.s.*, III.112; *g.s.*, II.197; *d.s.*, III.114.

sunu, *m.*, son: *n.s.*, I.146, 231, etc.; II.122, 219; *a.s.*, I.134, 143, etc.; II.115, 116; III.3, 6, etc.; **suna** *d.s.*, I.225, 248, etc.; *n.p.*, III.148, 162; *a.p.*, III.74.

swa, (i) *adv.*, so, thus, in this way: I.39, 107, etc.; II.4, 19, etc.; III.11, 15, etc.; (ii) *conj.*, as: I.290, 303; II.163; **swa swa**, just as: I.69, 192, etc.; II.7, 15, etc.; III.40, 42, etc.; (iii) **swa... swa** *correl. conj.*, as ... as: I.208–09; **swa... swa swa**, III.97/98; (iv) **swa þæt** *conj.*, so that: I.105, 227, etc.; II.141; III.20, 218; (v) **swa þeah** *adv.*, nevertheless: I.124, 199; II.7, 13; III.125, 236, 246.

swa hwæs swa, *see* **hwa**

swar~, *see* **swær~**

swat, *nt.*, sweat: ~**e** *d.s.*, II.105, 253.

geswæncte, *see* **geswencan**

swær, *adj.*, grievous, heavy: **swarum** *d.s.m.*, III.48; *d.p.nt.*, I.132.

geswæs, *adj.*, pleasing: ~**um** *d.p.m.*, III.93.

swæsnyss, *f.*, blandishment: ~**e** *a.s.*, I.46; II.171.

swætan, *wv.1*, to sweat: **swætte**

pret.ind.3s., II.251.

sweart, *adj.*, dark: ~**an** *a.s.m.wk.*, I.277; *d.s.f.wk.*, I.211; *n.p.nt.wk.*, III.31.

swefn, *nt.*, dream: ~**e** *d.s.*, I.9.

sweltan, *sv.3*, to die: *inf.*, II.165; **sweltaþ** *pres.ind.2p.*, I.279.

geswencan, *wv.1*, to afflict, oppress: **geswencean** *inf.*, I.132; **geswenct** *pp.*, ~**e** *(n.p.m.)* I.115 (**geswæncte**); ~**an** *(a.s.m.wk.)* III.33.

geswencednyss, *f.*, affliction, tribulation: ~**a** *n.p.*, III.31.

swete, *adj.*, sweet: ~**an** *d.s.m.wk.*, II.76; ~**um** *d.s.m.*, III.110.

swetnyss, *f.*, sweetness: ~**e** *a.s.*, II.57.

swicol, *adj.*, deceitful: ~**an** *d.s.m.wk.*, I.146.

swilc, *pron.*, such: ~**es** *g.s.nt.*, I.254.

swilce, **swylce**, *conj.*, as if, like, as: I.23, 127, etc.; II.76, 85, etc.; III.51, 63, etc.

swincan, *sv.3*, to toil, labour: **swanc** *pret.ind.3s.*, III.15; **swuncon** *pret.ind.3p.*, III.109.

geswincful, *adj.*, toilsome: *n.s.nt.*, II.104.

swingan, *sv.3*, to beat: *inf.*, II.204; III.132.

[**swipe**], *f.*, whip: ~**um** *d.p.*, II.204.

swiþe, *adv.*, (i) very, exceedingly: I.101, 166; II.190, 198; III.5, 62, 100; (ii) widely: III.17; (iii) violently: III.114; (iv) quickly, III.155.

swiþlic, *adj.*, powerful, violent: *n.s.f.*, I.304; ~**re** *d.s.f.*, II.150.

swiþlice, *adv.*, quickly: III.102.

swura, *m.*, neck: *n.s.*, II.255; ~**n** *a.s.*, III.114; *d.s.*, III.117.

swurd, *nt.*, sword: ~**e** *d.s.*, II.163, 194, 255.

swustor, *f.*, sister: *a.s.*, III.77.

geswutelian, *wv.2*, to reveal: *inf.*, I.197; **geswutelaþ** *pres.ind.3s.*, II.26; **geswutelode** *pret.subj.3s.*, I.272; **geswutelod** *pp.*, *(uninfl.)* I.200.

swutellice, *adv.*, clearly: II.133.

swylce, *see* **swilce**

sylf, *pron.*, self, oneself, himself, herself, itself, etc.: *n.s.m.*, I.12; II.28, 128, 132, 215; III.119, 129, etc.; ~**ne**

a.s.m., I.9; II.115; III.80, 125, 189; ~e
a.s.f., I.46; II.6, 9; III.66; *n.p.m.*,
III.245; *n.p.nt.*, III.38; *a.p.m.*, I.232;
~**um** *d.s.m*, II.26; III.11; *d.p.m.*,
II.246; III.32, 237; ~**a** *n.p.m.*, I.210.
sylfren, *adj.*, made of silver: ~**a** *a.p.f.*,
I.121.
syllan, *wv.1*, to sell, to give: *inf.*, I.77;
sylle *pres.subj.3s.*, II.215 (2x), 216
(2x); **geseald** *pp.*, *(n.s.m.)* II.233.
syllic, *adj.*, strange: ~**an** *a.p.nt.wk.*,
III.221.
symle, *adv.*, continually, always: II.17,
19; III.26.
synderlic, *adj.*, private: ~**re** *d.s.f.*, I.248.
synn, *f.*, sin: ~**um** *d.p.*, II.31, 182.
synscipe, *m.*, marriage: ~**s** *g.s.*, I.27; ~**e**
d.s., III.86, 93.

T

tacn, *nt.*, sign: ~**e** *a.p.*, III.221; ~**a** *g.p.*,
III.244; ~**um** *d.p.*, III.223.
tæcan, *wv.1*, to teach (w. *d.* of pers. and
a. object): **tæhte** *pret.ind.3s.*, II.49,
89.
getæl, *nt.*, number: ~**e** *d.s.*, I.51.
tælan, *wv.1*, to mock: **tælende** *pres.
part.*, II.234.
tellan, *wv.1*, to reckon, count, ascribe:
getealde *pret.ind.3s.*, III.222; **geteald**
pp., *(n.s.m.)* I.50, *(uninfl.)* I.51.
templ, *nt.*, temple: *n.s.*, I.273; *a.s.*, I.268,
272; ~**es** *g.s.*, I.276; ~**e** *d.s.*, I.113, 120,
270.
tengan, *wv.1*, to hasten, hurry: **tengdon**,
pret.ind.3p., II.170.
(ge)teon, *sv.2*, (i) to drag: **tugon**
pret.ind.3p., I.211; (ii) to educate:
getogen *pp.*, *(a.s.nt.)* III.56.
teona, *m.*, (i) injury: ~**n** *a.s.*, I.123; (ii)
insult ~**n** *a./d.s.* *(or a.p.)*, III.133.
Tiburtius, *proper name*, Tiburtius: *n.*,
II.64, 67, etc.
tid, *f.*, time: ~**a** *d.s.*, I.202.
tigan, *wv. 1*, to tie: **tigdon** *pret.ind.3p.*,
III.114.
tihtan, *wv.1*, to incite, exhort, urge:
tihte *pres.ind.1s.*, I.94; *pret.ind.3s.*,

II.21, 217, 258; III.55, 84; **tihtende**
pres. part., I.73.
tihting, *f.*, incitement, exhortation: ~**e**
d.s., II.170; ~**um** *d.p.*, I.52.
tima, *m.*, time: *n.s.*, I.199; ~**n** *a.s.*, III.95;
d.s., III.1, 241, 246.
tintreg, *nt.*, torture: ~**um** *d.p.*, I.148.
getintregian, *wv.2*, to torture: *inf.*, I.285.
to, *prep. w. d.*, (i) to, for, as, to provide:
I.10, 12, etc.; II.4, 11 (2x), etc.; III.2,
6, etc.; (ii) towards: II.9; (iii) for, as
(*w. g.*): III.46 (2x).
toberstan, *sv.3*, to burst asunder, break:
tobærst *pret.ind.3s.*, I.273; III.216;
toburston *pret.ind.3p.*, III.100.
tobrytan, *wv.1*, to destroy, break into
pieces: **tobrytte** *pret.ind.3s.*, I.183;
tobryt *pp.*, *(n.s.nt.)* II.108; ~**te** *(a.p.f.)*
I.122.
tocnawan, *sv.7*, make out, discern,
understand: *inf.*, III.102, 128.
tocwysan, *wv.1*, to crush: **tocwysed** *pp.*,
~**e** *(a.p.f.)* I.121.
tocyme, *m.*, coming, arrival: *d.s.*,
III.240.
todæg, *adv.*, today: III.209.
togan, *anom. v.*, to depart, disperse:
togæþ *pres.ind.3s.*, II.230.
togædere, *adv.*, at the same time,
together: II.125, 162; III.115, 223,
233.
togeanes, *prep. w. d.*, against, to meet
(in opposition): I.270.
tomiddes, *prep. w. g.*, in the midst of:
III.210.
tosendan, *wv.1*, to send: **tosende**
pret.ind.3s., II.42.
toslupan, *sv.2*, to become loose:
toslupon *pret.ind.3p.*, III.101, 117.
tosomne, *adv.*, together: I.21, 297.
totwæman, *wv.1*, to separate:
totwæmed *pp.*, ~**e** *(n.p.nt.)* I.33.
toþ, *m.*, tooth: ~**um** *d.p.*, I.209.
toþindan, *sv.3*, to swell, inflate:
toþunden *pp.*, *(uninfl.)* II.230.
toþunden, *see previous entry*
towerd, *adj.*, future: ~**an** *d.s.m./nt.wk.*,
I.74.

towurpan, *sv.3*, to destroy: **towurpe** *pret.subj.3s.*, I.272.

treow, *nt.*, tree: *n.s.*, I.178.

truwian, *wv.2*, to trust: **truwige** *pres.ind.1s.*, III.46.

tugon, *see* **teon**

tunge, *wk.f.*, tongue: **tungan** *d.s.*, I.293.

tunne, *wk.f.*, cask, barrel: **~an** *n.p.*, I.244; *a.p.*, I.187, 219; **~um** *d.p.*, I.224, 241.

twam, *see next entry*

twegen, *num.*, two: *n.*, I.47, 215; II.206; III.148, 162; **twam** *d.*, I.47; II.53.

twentig, *num.*, twenty: I.158, 300.

Þ

þa, (i) *adv.*, then, at that time: I.4, 7, etc.; II.8, 9, etc.; III.1, 4, etc.; (ii) *conj.*, when, as: I.367; III.183; **þa þa** I.4, 289; II.2, 146, etc.; III.134, 157, 230, 239; *see also* **se** *and* **hwæt**.

geþafian, *wv.2*, to allow: **geþafa** *imp.s.*, I.235.

geþanc, *m.*, will, mind, thought: *n.s.*, I.192; *a.s.*, III.37.

þancian, *wv.2*, to give thanks (w. *d.* of pers. and *g.* of that for which thanks are given): **þancode** *pret.ind.3s.*, I.172, 260; **þanciende** *pres. part.*, I.295.

þanon, *adv.*, from there: II.112.

þær, (i) *adv.*, there: I.23, 40, etc.; II.35, 260; III.26, 27, etc.; (ii) *conj.* where: I.152, 278; III.178, 205, 231.

þæron, *adv.*, inside, therein, in that place: I.187; III.224.

þærrihte, *adv.*, immediately: II.163.

þærto, *adv.*, to that place: III.120.

þærtoeacan, *adv.*, moreover: I.108.

þæt, *conj.*, that, so that, in order that: I.4, 5, etc.; II.4, 10, etc.; III.6, 30, etc.; *see also* **se**.

þe, *rel. particle (indecl.)*, who, which, that: I.10, 11, etc.; II.3, 22, etc.; III.1, 8, etc.

þeah, *adv.*, yet: I.279.

þeah þe, *conj.*, though, although: II.74, 82.

þearf, *f.*, need, good, benefit: *n.s.*, III.239; **~e** *a.s.*, I.191.

þearfa, *m.*, a poor or needy person: **~um**, *d.p.*, II.148, 159, 207.

þearft, *see* **þurfan**

þearle, *adv.*, very, greatly: I.26, 30, 105; II.73; III.206.

þegn, *m.*, thegn: *n.s.*, I.1.

þe læs þe, *conj.*, lest: I.81.

þen, *m.*, servant: **~um** *d.p.*, I.287.

þenung, *f.*, service: **~um** *d.p.*, II.155.

geþeodan, *wv.1*, to unite: **geþeoded** *pp.*, **geþeodde** *(n.p.m.)* I.55.

geþeodnyss, *f.*, union: **~e** *g.s.*, I.27.

þeon, *sv.2*, to thrive, to be prosperous: **~de** *pres. part.*, I.55; **geþogen** *pp.*, *(n.s.m.)* III.7.

þeostru, *nt. p.*, darkness: **~a** *n.*, III.31; *g.*, II.189; **~m** *d.*, I.159 (**þystrum**); III.12, 13.

þeow, *m.*, servant, slave: **~um** *d.p.*, II.155.

þeowian, *wv.1/2*, to serve (w. *d.*): *inf.*, II.13.

þere, *see* **se**

þes, þis, þeos, (i) *dem. adj.*, this: **þes** *n.s.m.*, I.26, 29, 31; III.23; **þæs**, II.78; **þis** *n.s.nt.*, II.101, 104, 105; III.207; **þeos** *n.s.f.*, I.101, 226; II.3; III.137, 188; **þisne** *a.s.m.*, I.65, 183, 186; **þas** *a.s.f.*, II.63, 181; **þises** *g.s.m.*, I.111; **þisre**, *g.s.f.*, II.171; **þisum** *d.s.m.*, I.203; **þysum** *d.s.nt.*, I.159; II.62, 190; **þissere** *d.s.f.*, I.52; **þyssere** I.185, 194; **þisre**, II.131; **þas** *n.p.nt.*, II.42; III.31 (2nd instance); *n.p.f.*, III.31 (1st instance); *a.p.m.*, I.108; II.56; *a.p.nt.*, I.49; II.200; III.47, 129, 137; **þæs** *a.p.f.*, III.44; **þysum** *d.p.m.*, II.181; (ii) *dem. pron.*, this: **þis**, *n.s.nt.*, I.174, III.51, 212; *a.s.nt.*, I.38, 85, etc.; II.83, 85; **þisne**, *a.s.m.*, I.197; **þises** *g.s.nt.*, II.45; **þysum, þisum** *d.s.m.*, III.94; *d.s.nt.*, I.187, 263; II.110; III.169; **þas** *n.p.m.*, I.211; *a.p.m.*, I.167; **þysum** *d.p.m.*, I.221.

þider, þyder *adv.*, there, to that place: I.247, 268; II.185; III.230 (2x).

þin, *poss. adj.*, your *(s.)*: *n.s.m.*, I.107;
II.67, 69; III.142; *a.s.nt.*, I.45; II.175;
~**ne** *a.s.m.*, I.143, 148; III.28; ~**e** *a.s.f.*,
II.240; ~**es** *g.s.m.*, III.71; *g.s.nt.*, I.275;
III.23; ~**um** *d.s.m.*, I.144, 259 (or
d.s.nt.); III.126; *d.s.nt.*, I.15, 147;
II.181; *d.p.m.*, I.119; *d.p.nt.*, II.28;
III.209; ~**re** *g.s.f.*, III.121; *d.s.f.*, I.94,
96, 185, 259; II.160; III.66, 190; ~**e**
n.p.m., I.129; III.130; *n.p.nt.*, I.65, 66;
~**ra** *g.p.m.*, I.148; ~**re** *g.p.f.*, III.22;
see also **þu**.

þincan, *wv.1*, to seem: **þincþ**
pres.ind.3s., II.127.

þinen, *f.*, maidservant: ~**ne** *d.s.*, II.219.

þing, *nt.*, thing: *n.s.*, II.61; *a.s.*, I.77, 140;
n.p., II.123; *a.p.*, II.208; III.129,
þincg, II.133; **þincge** *d.s.*, I.215.

geþingian, *wv.2*, to intercede (w. *d.*):
geþingie *pres.ind.1s.*, I.145;
pres.subj.2s., III.143; *pres.subj.3s.*,
III.139.

þingræden, *f.*, intercession: ~**e** *d.s.*,
III.238–39.

þissere, see **þes**

geþogen, *see* **þeon**

þone, *conj.* (w. *comp.*), than: I.242; II.29
(**þonne**).

þonne, *adv.*, (i) then, thus: I.32; II.24,
25, etc.; III.29, 30, etc.; (ii) *conj.*,
when: I.234; II.174, 230, 257; III.74,
135, 239.

þreatung, *f.*, threatening: ~**e** *d.s.*, II.150.

þreo, *see* **þrie**

þrex (þreax), *nt.* (?), rottenness, rotten
wood: ~**e** *d.s.*, III.106.

þrie, *num.*, three: **þreo** *n.*, II.123; *a.*,
I.235; **þry** *a.*, II.119, 258.

þrowian, *wv.2*, to suffer: *inf.*, I.176, 177;
II.211; III.153, 191; *infl. inf.* **to**
þrowienne, I.83; **þrowige**
pres.subj.1s., I.150; **þrowodon**
pret.ind.3p., I.91.

þruh, *f.*, tomb, sarcophagus: **þryh** *d.s.*,
II.205.

þry, *see* **þrie**

þrydda, *adj.*, third: ~**n** *d.s.m.*, II.133,
255.

þryh, *see* **þruh**

þrymsetl, *nt.*, judgement seat: ~**e** *d.s.*,
I.213.

þrynnyss, *f.*, Trinity: ~**e** *d.s.*, II.121.

þryttig, *num.*, thirty: I.242.

þu, *pers. pron.*, you: *n.s.*, I.29, 38, etc.;
II.21, 23, etc.; III.24, 28, etc.; **þe** *a.s.*,
I.15, 46, etc.; II.24, 25, etc.; III.43, 66,
etc.; *d.s.*, 12 (2x), 95; II.22, 23, etc.;
III.24, 46, 71; **þin** *g.s.*, III.23; **git** *dual
n.*, II.68; **ge** *n.p.*, I.67, 97, etc.; II.179,
188, 190, 191; III.197, 198 (2x), 201,
236; **eow** *a.p.*, I.14 (2nd instance), 67,
etc.; *d.p.*, I.14 (1st instance), 101,
etc.; II.189, 193; III.155, 199.

þunor, *m.*, thunder: *n.s.*, I.304.

þurfan, *pret. pres. v.*, to need: **þearft**,
pres.ind.2s., III.144; **þurfe**
pres.subj.2p., I.231.

þurh, (i) *prep. w. a./d.*, through, by, by
means of, because of, by the agency
of, on account of: I.14, 16, etc.; II.18,
64, etc.; III.90, 92, etc.; (ii) *conj.*,
whereby: I.226.

þurhwunian, *wv.2*, to continue, persist,
remain: *inf.*, I.34; **þurhwunaþ**
pres.ind.3s., I.187; **þurhwuniaþ**
pres.ind.1p., I.31; **þurhwunode**
pret.ind.3s., II.252.

þus, *adv.*, so, thus, in this way: I.26, 37,
etc.; II.17, 21, etc.; III.65, 70, etc.

þyder, *see* **þider**

geþyld, *nt.*, patience: ~**e** *d.s.*, I.123.

þyllic, *pron.*, such: *a.s./p.(?)nt.*, III.17;
~**e** *a.s.f.*, II.219; *n.p.m.*, I.211; ~**um**
d.s.m., III.140.

þyrl, *nt.*, hole: *a.s.*, II.230.

þystrum, *see* **þeostru**

þywracu, *m.*, threat: **þywrace** *g.s.*, I.82.

U

unamyrred, *adj.*, unharmed: ~**e** *n.p.m.*,
III.198.

unbesmiten, *adj.*, undefiled: ~**um**
d.p.m., I.50.

unc, *see* **ic**

undeadlic, *adj.*, immortal: *n.s.m.*,
I.278.

under, *prep. w. d./a.*, in subjection to, under: I.61, 283.
underfon, *sv.7*, to take, take in, receive: *inf.*, I.10; III.163; **underfo** *pres.ind.1s.*, I.15; *pres.subj.3s.*, II.215, 216, 217; **underfeng**, *pret.ind.3s.*, II.219; III.4, 87, 167; **underfengon** *pret.ind.3p.*, II.197–98.
undergerefa, *m.*, deputy, aide ('under-reeve' for Latin *assessor*, 'aide'): *n.s.*, I.241.
uneaþe, *adj.*, difficult: *n.s.m.*, II.62.
unforht, *adj.*, intrepidly: ~**e** *n.p.m.*, I.233.
ungederod, *adj.*, unharmed, sound: ~**um** *d.s.m.*, II.250; ~**e** *n.p.m.*, I.285.
ungeleafful, *adj.*, unbelieving, faithless: ~**lan** *a.p.m.wk.*, II.217; III.185–86; *a.p.f.wk.*, III.12.
ungesælig, *adj.*, wretched, unhappy: ~**e** *n.s.f.wk.*, II.233.
ungewemmed, *adj.*, undefiled: *n.s.m.*, II.18; ~**e** *a.s.f.*, I.54 (**ungewæmmede**); ~**um** *d.s.m.*, III.68.
ungewitendlic, *adj.*, permanent: *a.s.nt.*, II.216.
unmildheort, *adj.*, merciless: ~**a** *n.p.m.*, I.211.
unnyt, *adj.*, useless: *n.s.m.*, III.15.
unrihtlic, *adj.*, wrong: *n.s.m.*, I.158.
unrihtwis, *adj.*, unrighteous: ~**um** *d.p.m.*, II.111.
geunrotian, *wv.2*, to make sad: *inf.*, I.214.
unrotnyss, *f.*, unhappiness: ~**e** *d.s.*, II.108.
unrotsian, *wv.2*, to grieve: **unrotsodon** *pret.ind.3p.*, I.212.
untrum, *adj.*, sick: ~**e** *n.p.m.*, I.90.
unwar, *adj.*, unwary: ~**an** *a.p.m.wk.*, III.78.
unwislic, *adj.*, foolish: ~**um** *d.s.m.*, II.152.
unwynsumnyss, *f.*, unpleasantness: *n.s.*, I.155.
up, **upp**, *adv.*, up: I.48, 53; II.70.
Urbanus, *proper name*, Urban the pope: *n.*, II.36, 95, 138, 260.

ure, *poss. adj.*, our: *n.s.m.*, I.180, 192; II.173; *a.s.f.*, I.144; *n.p.f.*, II.174; *g.p.m.*, I.184; **urne** *a.s.m.*, I.144, 232; **urum** *d.s.m.*, I.145; *d.p.m.*, I.182; III.126; **ure** *d.s.f.*, III.237.
ut, *adv.*, out: I.105; III.49, 159, etc.
utgan, *anom. v.*, to go out: *inf.*, III.120.
geutlagian, *wv.2*, to outlaw: **geutlagod** *pp.*, *(n.s.m.)* II.96.
uton, *v. (auxiliary)* let us (w. *inf.*): III.14.
uþwita, *m.*, philosopher: *n.s.*, III.6.
uþwitegung, *f.*, philosophy: ~**e** *d.s.*, I.134–35; III.58.

V

Valerianus, *proper name*, Valerian: *n.*, II.8, 32, etc.; ~**e** *vocative*, II.59.

W

wac, *adj.*, mean, of little value, of low quality: *a.s.nt.*, II.215; ~**ne** *a.s.m.*, II.216; III.26.
wacian, *sv.2*, to stay awake: **wacodon** *pret.ind.3p.*, III.50.
waclic, *adj.*, lowly: ~**um** *d.p.m.*, II.152.
wah, *m.*, wall: *a.s.*, III.231.
wahryft, *nt.*, curtain: ~**um** *d.p.*, III.35.
wand, *see* **windan**
wanian, *wv.2*, to wane: **wanode** *pret.ind.3s.*, II.222.
wæarþ, *see* **weorþan**
gewæcan, *wv.1*, to exhaust, weaken: **gewæht** *pp.*, *(n.s.nt.)* II.106.
wædla, *m.*, a poor person: ~**um** *d.p.*, II.159.
wæfersyn, *f.*, spectacle: ~**e** *d.s.*, I.230.
wæht, *see* **wæcan**
wælhreow *adj.*, cruel, fierce, blood-thirsty: ~**a** *n.s.m.*, I.301; ~**ne** *a.s.m.*, I.83; ~**an** *d.s.m.wk.*, I.63 (**wel~**), 110 (**wel~**), 182; III.94–95; ~**um** *d.p.nt.*, I.148.
wæpen, *nt.*, weapon: **wæpnum** *d.p.*, II.190.
wæran, *see* **beon**
wæstm, *m.*, form: (i) fruit: *a.s.*, I.179; (ii) form, stature: ~**e** *d.s.*, III.58.

wæter, *nt.*, water: *a.s.*, I.246; **~e** *d.s.*, II.248, 251, 254.

we, *see* **ic**

(ge)wealdan, *sv.7*, to govern (w. g. or a.): **geweold** *pret.ind.3s.*, III.95.

weallan, *sv.7*, to boil: **weollon** *pret.ind.3p.*, I.153.

weardmann, *m.*, guard: **~menn** *n.p.*, I.301; **~mannum** *d.p.*, I.158.

gewearþ, see **gewurþan**

wel, *adv.*, thoroughly: II.245.

wela, *m.*, wealth: **~um** *d.p.*, II.106.

welhreowan, *see* **wælhreow**

welwillende, *adj.*, benevolent: **~an** *d.s.m.wk.*, I.298.

geweman, *wv.1*, to entice: *inf.*, I.144; III.29; **gewemde** *pret.subj.3s.*, III.60.

gewemman, *wv.1*, to defile: *inf.*, II.23; **gewemmed** *pp.*, **~e** *(n.p.f.)* I.67.

gewemmednyss, *f.*, defilement: **~e** *a.s.*, II.11.

wenan, *wv.1*, to expect, believe: **wene** *pres.ind.1s.*, I.236; **wendon** *pret.ind.3p.*, III.107, 108.

wendan, *wv.1*, to turn: **went** *pres.ind.3s.*, II.23.

gewendan, *wv.1*, to go, turn: **gewende**, *pret. ind.3s.*, II.48, 70; III.85; **gewendon** *pret.ind.3p.*, I.53; II.200; **gewend** *pp.*, **~e** *(n.p.m.)* II.86.

weorc, *nt.*, work, deed: *a.p.*, II.189; **~um** *d.p.*, III.209.

weorcstan, *m.*, building stone: **~e** *d.s.*, III.159–60; **~um** *d.p.*, III.225.

weorþan, wurþan, *sv.3*, (i) to become, to happen: **wurþaþ** *imp.p.*, II.189; **wearþ**, *pret.ind.3s.*, I.59, 155; I.141 (**wæarþ**); II.27, 203, 247; **wurdon** *pret.ind.3p.*, III.50, 86; **wurþe** *pres.subj.1s.*, III.205; **wurde** *pret.subj.2s.*, III.68; *pret.subj.3s.*, II.38; III.7;

(ii) as auxiliary for passive: **wyrþ** *pres.ind.3s.*, II.98; **wearþ** *pret.ind.3s.*, I.7, 23, etc.; I.174 (**wæarþ**); II.7, 88, 209, 259; III.19, 51, etc.; **wurdon** *pret.ind.3p.*, I.20, 151, etc.; II.20, 184, etc.; III.90, 94, etc.; **wurþe**

pres.subj.3s., III.24; **wurde** *pret.subj.3s.*, II.10, 93, 135; III.171; *pret.subj.3p.*, I.81, 224, 232.

geweorþan, gewurþan, *sv.3*, to happen, to come to pass: **gewearþ** *pret.ind.3s.*, II.13; III.62.

wepan, *sv.7*, to weep: *inf.*, III.190 (**weopan**); **weop** *pret.ind.3s.*, II.135, 165; **weopon** *pret.ind.3p.*, II.210; **weopende** *pres. part.*, **~um** *(d.p.nt.)* II.200.

wer, *m.*, man, husband: *n.s.*, III.30, 169; *a.s.*, III.105; **~es** *g.s.*, II.11; **~e** *d.s.*, I.137; III.61; **~um** *d.p.*, I.225.

werod, *nt.*, host: *a.p.*, I.61; **~e** *d.s.*, I.41, 44.

werodlice, *adv.*, sweetly: II.74; III.176.

wiccecræft, *m.*, witchcraft: *a.s.*, III.123.

widgil, *adj.*, vast: **~lan** *g.s.f.wk.*, III.95.

wif, *nt.*, woman, wife: *n.s.*, I.253; III.148; *a.s.*, I.250; **~e** *d.s.*, I.239, 247, etc.; III.77; **~um** *d.p.*, I.51.

wifian, *wv.2*, to marry: *inf.*, I.4; **wifige** *pres.subj.3s.*, III.30.

wiglere, *m.*, sorcerer, diviner: **~as** *a.p.*, III.123.

willa, wylla, *m.*, will, intent: *n.s.*, I.226; II.124; **~n** *a.s.*, I.6, 238; II.71; III.66, 124; *d.s.*, I.62.

[willan, wyllan], *anom. v.*, to will, desire, wish, be willing: **wille** *pres.ind.1s.*, III.125; *pres.subj.1p.*, III.138; **wylt** *pres.ind.2s.*, II.23, 28, 175; **wile** *pres.ind.3s.*, III.30; **wylle, wille** *pres.subj.2s.*, I.148, 189; II.60; III.28; **wyllaþ** *pres.ind.2p.*, III.197; **wolde** *pret.ind.1s.*, III.71; *pret.ind.3s.*, I.4, 17, etc.; II.93, 208, 211; III.62, 205; *pret.subj.1s.*, II.171; *pret.subj.3s.*, I.5, 6, etc.; III.161, 183 (2x); **woldest** *pret.ind.2s.*, I.143; **woldon** *pret.ind.3p.*, II.7, 154, 165; III.163, 180, 195, 217; **woldan** *pret.ind.3p.*, I.175, 177.

gewilnian, *wv.2*, to desire (w. g.): **gewilnode**, *pret.ind.3s.*, II.135, 142.

wimman, *m.*, woman: *n.s.*, II.211.

wind, *m.*, air, wind: **~es** *g.s.*, II.229.

windan, *sv.3*, to fly: **wand** *pret.ind.3s.*,
I.105.
gewinn, *nt.*, conflict: *a.s.*, I.92; ~e *d.s.*,
II.190; III.140.
winter, *m.*, winter: ~**tres** *g.s.*, II.73.
wintertid, *f.*, winter: *n.s.*, I.25.
wiscan, *wv.1*, to desire: **wiscton**
pret.ind.3p., III.152.
wisdom, *m.*, wisdom: ~e *d.s.*, II.211.
wise, *wk.f.*, way: **wisan** *a.s.*, I.102.
gewislice, *adv.*, certainly, for certain:
II.244.
gewisse, *adj.*, certain: **to gewissan**, for
certain, as a certainty: II.172.
gewissian, *wv.2*, to guide: **gewyssodon**
pret.ind.3p., I.61; **gewissode**,
pret.subj.3s, II.38; **gewyssod** *pp.*,
(n.s.m.) I.16.
wit, *see* **ic**
wita, *m.*, senator, counsellor: ~**n** *n.p.*,
II.256; III.5; *see also* **wite**.
witan, *pret. pres. v.*, to know: *inf.*, II.208,
244; **wite** *imp.p.*, III.236;
pres.subj.2s., II.79; **wyste** *pret.ind.3s.*,
I.118; **wiste** *pret.ind.3s.*, I.93;
pret.subj.1s., II.172.
gewitan, *sv.1*, to depart: **gewitaþ** *imp.*
p., I.115; *pres.ind.3p.*, I.66; **gewat**
pret.ind.3s., I.71, 308; II.204; III.167;
gewytan *pret.ind.3p.*, I.57, 70.
wite, **wyte**, *nt.*, punishment, torment,
torture: *a.s.*, I.192, 289; III.153, 190;
d.s., I.308; III.32; **wita** *n.p.*, II.111;
a.p., I.83; III.138; **witum** *d.p.*, I.86,
132, etc.; II.63, 145, 211; III.97, 171,
213.
gewitendlic, *adj.*, transitory: *a.s.nt.*,
II.216.
(ge)witnian, *wv.2*, to punish: *inf.*, III.97;
(ge)witna *imp.s.*, I.147, 189; **witnast**
pres.ind.2s., II.159; **gewitnod** *pp.*, ~e
(n.p.m.) II.98.
witnung, *f.*, punishment: ~e *g.s.*, III.32.
gewittig, *adj.*, conscious: *n.s.nt.*, II.124.
wiþ, *prep. w. a./d.*, against, from,
towards: I.22, 93; II.10; III.174, 179.
wiþinnan, *adv.*, inwardly: III.69.
wiþsacan, *sv.6*, to renounce (w. *a.* or *d.*):

wiþsace *pres.ind.1s.*, I.146; **wiþsoc**
pret.ind.1s., I.217; **wiþsoce**
pret.subj.3s., I.79, 138.
wiþutan, *prep. w. d.*, outside: III.49.
wiþutan, *adv.*, outwardly: III.69.
wlita, *wk.m.*, beauty: *n.s.*, II.58.
wlitig, *adj.*, beautiful: n.s.nt., III.57;
n.s.f., II.210; III.69; *a.p.f.*, II.198; ~e
a.p.nt., III.36.
wlitu, *m.*, beauty: ~e *d.s.*, III.66.
wod, *adj.*, mad: ~**an** *a.p.m.wk.*, I.67.
wodlic, *adj.*, foolish, mad: ~**an**
d.s.m.wk., III.37, 45.
wop, *m.*, weeping: *a.s.*, III.71; ~e *d.s.*,
II.10.
word, *nt.*, word: *n.p.*, II.42, 172; *a.p.*,
I.49; II.200; III.47; ~e *d.s.*, II.48; ~**um**
d.p., II.28, 232; III.64, 84, 105.
woruld, *f.*, (i) world: ~e *g.s.*, II.171; *d.s.*,
I.70; II.132, 204, 220; III.76, 168, 226;
(ii) the next life: ~e *d.s.*, I.311; **a to**
worulde, *adv.*, for ever: I.33; III.249.
woruldlic, *adj.*, earthly: ~**um** *d.s.m.*,
II.15; ~**re** *d.s.f.*, I.134; ~e *a.p.m.*, I.43.
woruldwisdom, *m.*, earthly wisdom: ~e
d.s., III.6.
wraþe, *adv.*, fiercely: I.115.
wrecan, *sv.5*, to avenge: *inf.*, I.282.
wregan, *wv.1*, to accuse: **gewreht** *pp.*, ~e
(n.p.nt.) III.94.
gewrehte, *see previous entry*
gewrit, *nt.*, letter, piece of writing: *a.s.*,
I.182; ~e *d.s.*, II.40, 42.
wudu, *m.*, wood: **wuda** *d.s.*, I.242.
wuldor, *nt.*, glory: *n.s.*, I.311; III.249;
wuldre *d.s.*, I.46, 298; II.175, 214,
261; III.226; **wuldra** *g.p.*, III.32.
wuldorbeah, *m.*, crown (of glory):
wuldorbeage *d.s.*, II.192.
wuldorful, *adj.*, glorious: *a.s.nt.*, II.215;
~**lan** *d.s.m.wk.*, I.70; *a.p.nt.wk.*,
III.229.
wuldrian, *wv.2*, (i) to glorify: **wuldri-**
gende *pres. part.*, III.151; (ii) (w. **on**)
to glory in: **wuldrodest** *pret.ind.2s.*,
I.276.
gewuna, *m.*, custom: ~**n** *d.s.*, I.20.
wundor, *nt.*, miracle: **wundra** *n.p.*,

II.260; III.228, 242; *a.p.*, II.142;
III.154, 241, 242, 245; *g.p.*, II.131.
wundorlice, *adv.*, miraculously, wonder-
fully: II.54; III.56, 106, 133, 176.
wundrian, *wv.2*, to wonder (at) (w. *g.*):
wundrie *pres.ind.1s.*, I.26; II.73
(**wundrige**); **wundrast** *pres.ind.2s.*,
I.30; **wundrode** *pret.ind.3s.*, I.253.
wunian, *wv.2*, to remain, continue,
dwell, live: **to wunigenne** *infl. inf.*,
III.36, 226; **wunaþ** *pres.ind.3s.*,
II.105; **wunode** *pret.ind.3s.*, III.27;
wunodon *pret.ind.3p.*, III.86, 151;
wunigende *pres. part.*, II.62, 121;
III.18, 58, 89.
wur~ *see* **weor~, wyr~**
wurpan, *sv.3*, to throw: *inf.*, III.159;
wurpon *pret.ind.3p.*, III.116.
wurþful, *adj.*, honourable: **~a** *n.s.m.wk.*,
II.14; **~ne** *a.s.m.*, II.217.
(ge)wurþian, *wv.2*, to honour: **wurþast**
pres.ind.2s., III.192; **wurþiaþ**
pres.ind.1p., I.98*; III.236;
pres.ind.3p., I.100; **gewurþode**
pret.ind.3s., III.229; **wurþodest**
pret.ind.2s., III.209; **wurþodon**
pret.ind.1p., II.86; *pret.ind.3p.*, III.5.
wurþlice, *adv.*, fittingly: III.35.
wurþmynt, *m.*, honour: **~e** *d.s.*, II.15;
III.4.
wydewe, *f.*, widow: *n.s.*, II.209.
gewyldan, *wv.1*, to overpower, subdue,
overcome: *inf.*, III.124; **gewylde**
pret.ind.1s., III.122; *pret.ind.3s.*,
III.138; **gewyld** *pp.*, *(n.s.m.)* III.183.
wyll~, *see* **will~**
wynsum, *adj.*, pleasant: *n.s.m.*, III.176;
~a *n.s.m.wk.*, I.29*; II.78; **~an**
g.s.m.wk., I.253; *g.s.nt.wk.*, II.192;
d.s.nt.wk., I.35; **~ne** *a.s.m.*, II.75;
~mum *d.s.m.*, I.155.
wynsumlice, *adv.*, pleasantly: I.26; II.74.
(ge)wyrcan, *wv.1*, to perform, work:

gewyrcst *pres.ind.2s.*, I.39; **wyrcþ**
pres.ind.3s., III.248; **wyrce**
pres.subj.3s., II.229, III.244; **worhte**
pret.ind.3s., II.131, 142; **worhton**
pret.ind.3p., III.241.
wyrm, *m.*, worm: *n.s.*, I.278; **wurmas**
n.p., I.308.
wyrmgalere, *m.*, snake charmer: **wurm-
galeras** *a.p.*, III.124.
wyrsa, *adj.*, worse: **~an** *d.s.nt.wk.*, II.58.
wyrsta, *adj.*, worst: **~n** *d.s.m.wk.*,
III.246.
wyrtbræþ, *m.*, fragrance, scent of
flowers: *n.s.*, I.26; *a.s.*, II.75.
wyssung, *f.*, instruction: **~a** *a.p.*, I.58.
wyste, see **witan**
gewytan, see **gewitan**
gewytnyss, *f.*, knowledge: **~e** *d.s.*, I.55.
wytum, *see* **wite**

Y

yfel, *adj.*, evil: **~e** *a.p.f.*, I.22.
yfelian, *wv.2*, to harm: *inf.*, III.217.
yfelnyss, *f.*, wickedness: **~e** *d.s.*, I.96.
ylca, *adj.*, same: **~n** *d.s.nt.wk.*, I.87;
II.222; *d.s.f.wk.*, I.135; III.57.
yld, *f.*, old age: **~e** *d.s.*, II.107.
yldest, *adj.* (*superl.* of **eald**), oldest: **~a**
n.s.m.wk., I.177.
yldra, *adj.*, (*comp.* of **eald**), older:
n.s.m.wk., II.167.
ymbe (**embe**), *prep. w. a.*, concerning,
about: I.191; II.5 (2x) (**embe**), 71,
etc.
ymbscrydan, *wv.1*, to clothe: **ymbscryd**
pp., **~de** *(n.p.m.)* II.189.
ymbstandan, *sv.6*, to stand by:
ymbstandende *pres. part.*, **~um**
(d.p.nt.) II.196.
yrnan, *sv.3*, to run: *inf.*, III.144; **arn**
pret.ind.3s., I.137; III.177, 193.
yrsian, *wv.2*, to become angry: **yrsodon**
pret.ind.3p., III.103.

Printed and bound by CPI Group (UK) Ltd, Croydon, CR0 4YY

13/04/2025